STERLING G. CALLAHAN

Brigham Young University

A Guide for Student and In-Service Teachers

SUCCESSFUL TEACHING IN SECONDARY SCHOOLS

SCOTT, FORESMAN AND COMPANY

Library of Congress Catalog Card #65-24449

Printed in the United States of America.
Regional offices of Scott, Foresman and Company are located
in Atlanta, Dallas, Glenview, Palo Alto, and Oakland, N.J.

Preface

Why write another textbook concerned with secondary-school methods? As the author reviews this relevant question, four reasons appear worthy of mention:

1. Educational trends since 1945 have left many teachers without adequate philosophic anchorage. Steeped in pragmatic thinking, they are uneasy about facing the instructional problems of the postwar world. Many of them have felt guilty when confronted with the gap between their actual teaching performance and the performance necessary to help students cope intelligently with mounting world problems, exploding fields of knowledge, and the need for acquiring information at an ever-faster rate.

2. The realistic attitude characteristic of the scientist has not found deserved expression in the form of precise procedures in curriculum development and classroom teaching techniques.

3. Many of the concepts underlying current secondary procedures need verification beyond the level of "action" research.

4. A union of the tenets of pragmatism and realism may prove to add real merit to each.

Secondary education will improve. But it can improve no more rapidly than the procedures employed by teachers will permit. The natural ability of gifted teachers is not sufficient; it must be supplemented by a knowledge of the science of teaching and a thorough understanding of its practical applications. "Teaching by ear" no longer represents quality teaching. Effective teaching must be equated with goal achievement, and goals can be reached most effectively only when instruction moves forward under scientific direction.

This book is written, therefore, to serve the needs of beginning as well as in-service teachers who care enough about the quality of their teaching to spend the necessary hours working out plans and procedures that are sound when evaluated by means of the best scientific instructional criteria. Those who view teaching as predominantly an outpouring of the personality will find limited interest in this book. It is intended, instead, for those who wish to superimpose upon an already desirable teaching personality the precision of scientific teaching methods.

Chapters of this text are designed primarily for use in undergraduate secondary methods courses. Although their most fruitful use may be in courses that immediately precede student teaching, they should serve as a guide and source of suggestions to student-teachers. In-service teachers who wish to re-evaluate their performances may also be challenged by specific sections.

In Part One, problems related to secondary planning and teaching are approached through a brief examination of relevant *Teaching Principles.* This emphasis on principles is maintained throughout the book by consistently relating specific suggestions to high-level generalizations. Part Two is directed toward *Planning for Teaching*, with the focus upon unit planning. *Specific Teaching Procedures* are highlighted in Part Three, and *Special Teaching Problems* of classroom control, readiness, motivation, and individual differences are treated in Part Four. The final section of the book is devoted to *Recent Developments in Teaching* and provides a fresh look at programed instruction, team teaching, television instruction, and school housing as they relate to secondary instruction.

The writer's experience in working with college students has shown him that the perusal of principles frequently does not leave the reader with clear concepts—he needs the assistance of specific examples. So, in an attempt to breathe clarity and interest into the text, repeated illustrations of the points discussed have been provided. These examples, for the most part, have been borrowed from actual teaching situations.

Much of the material contained in specific chapters has been tested on undergraduate students in secondary methods courses during the past ten years. Suggestions from students and recommendations originating with several teaching colleagues have been gratefully received and incorporated into chapter revisions. The continuing interest and suggestions of Dr. Percy E. Burrup and Dr. Lester N. Downing have been particularly appreciated.

Philosophic points of view that seem to be supported by scientific research have been used as a basis for chapter discussions. Within this framework the writer has tried to avoid extremes in philosophical thinking. The preparation of this volume has tended to confirm his belief that no one philosophy has all the answers and that verifiable scientific truth is the basis from which sound teaching practice must emerge.

Contents

Part One
TEACHING PRINCIPLES

Part Two
PLANNING FOR TEACHING

11

Additional Student-Centered Procedures 234

12

Recurring Instructional Concerns 258

Part Four
SPECIAL TEACHING PROBLEMS

13

Serving Instructional Purposes Through Discipline 284

PART ONE

TEACHING PRINCIPLES

1

Essential Principles: The Keys to Successful Planning and Teaching

Effective secondary teaching methods are based upon sound psychology; thus, psychology becomes an essential tool in the basic equipment of any ambitious teacher who is willing to put forth the effort necessary to teach systematically. This chapter deals with some of the principles that have a direct bearing on the teaching-learning process:

Principles useful in explaining adolescent student behavior
Principles useful in helping the teacher plan
Principles useful in forming and using concepts

Chapter 2 will discuss principles useful in helping the teacher meet the most frequent instruction-related problems. Later chapters, devoted to the specific procedures involved in planning and teaching, assume an understanding of the principles discussed in these first two chapters.

EXPLAINING ADOLESCENT STUDENT BEHAVIOR

The adolescent's behavior is affected by his needs, by his environmental influences, by parental, peer-group, and teacher expectations, and by developmental changes resulting from his growth. If the teacher understands the effect of such influences upon the teenager and the learning process, his teaching tends to become systematic and gives him both interest and pleasure.

Needs

All students have basic needs.[1] The teacher's understanding of these needs heightens his ability to establish rapport and hence helps him communicate with his students. A superficial acquaintance with these basic needs, however, is not sufficient. The effective teacher must be able to identify such needs as they are expressed in individual behavior and to take action to help the student satisfy them in socially acceptable ways. Because the needs of the group are an extension of the needs of individuals, the identification of group needs must begin with a personal acquaintance with each pupil in the group.

Approval, Affection, and Security

Approval, affection,[2] and security are needs common to all human beings and are the first needs that must be understood by the thoughtful teacher. They are expressed in the desire to conform to peer-group customs (approval), to maintain close ties with home and family (affection), and to avoid physical harm (security). Because these universal needs exert a marked influence on the degree of receptivity to learning situations, an understanding of their effect on teaching and learning is essential.

Each learner responds readily to stimuli that he recognizes as closely related to his perceived needs. Understanding this fact, the well-trained teacher can provide the stimuli for sound motivation. Ignoring the pupil's basic desires, or teaching in ways that run counter to his desires, may retard learning and inhibit pupil-teacher rapport.

Developmental Tasks

Adolescence, furthermore, is characterized by developmental tasks related to physical changes, emancipation from adult controls, and social adjustments.[3] Developmental tasks are essentially major problems related to growth, personal welfare, and individual adjustment that are common to students of a given age. The changing voice in the boy and the breast development in the girl, occasional dissension between adolescent and adult, and the inability to relate oneself easily to the opposite sex are examples of such problems during adolescence.

The teacher who has a warm, human understanding of these

---

[1]See John E. Horrocks, *The Psychology of Adolescence* (Boston: Houghton Mifflin Company, 1962), pp. 502–519, for a full-chapter treatment of "Psychological Needs During Adolescence."

[2]Lee J. Cronbach, *Educational Psychology*, 2d. ed. (New York: Harcourt, Brace and World, 1963), pp. 113–121, discusses the need for approval and affection.

[3]See Robert J. Havighurst, *Human Development and Education* (New York: Longmans, Green and Co., 1953), pp. 111–158, for a complete discussion of developmental tasks.

development-related processes is in a favorable position to comprehend and deal effectively with adolescent behavior. Such a teacher will recognize the adolescent's need for peer-group acceptance, satisfactory heterosexual adjustment, and relative freedom from failure in accomplishing objectives common to his age group. The teacher should be aware of these typical needs and should help students satisfy them.

Environmental Influences

The effect of the surrounding world on pupil behavior must be recognized and understood in order to plan and teach with insight and effectiveness. Of particular concern to the instructional process are those environmental factors related to the home, the peer group, and the school.[4] Cultural forces act upon the basic biological inheritance of the individual to make him what he is. Environmental conditioning largely shapes his state of educational readiness or reticence, forming habit patterns that encourage or discourage effective study and attitudes that further or impede learning.

The Home

Classroom behavior is often related to circumstances in the home over which the individual student has little control. Extreme parental domination may result in teenage instability or aggression, the cause of which may not be recognized by the teacher. Frequent and heated parent-adolescent arguments feed the fires of domestic tension and may cause in-school behavior that is both baffling and disruptive. In addition, siblings may react differently to the same conditions,[5] thus confusing the teacher who hoped to have ready answers to questions about the behavior of youngsters coming from the same home.

The Peer Group

The effect of the peer group upon in-school and out-of-school behavior is pronounced and should not be underestimated by the instructor. The unwarranted assumption, by some teachers and parents, that teenagers generally are more responsive to adult wishes than to the wishes of their peers often creates problems. The formation of close-knit adolescent groups is both necessary for and typical of secondary-school youth. In an environment of their own creation teenagers are largely free of adult restraints. They behave—or misbehave—in conformity to the wishes of their peers, speaking, thinking, and dressing the way the group does.

---

[4]Frederick J. McDonald, *Educational Psychology* (San Francisco: Wadsworth Publishing Company, 1959), pp. 15–16, presents a useful, brief discussion of the school as a contrived environment.

[5]*Ibid.*, p. 11

The School

At the junior and senior high school levels no less than one fourth of the student's total time is spent in the school or in school-related activities during the academic year. It is here that the teacher's influence is felt most strongly. But this influence must compete with all the other influences connected with the school—with after-school activities, with members of the peer group, with the administration, and even with the custodian.

In-school learning, therefore, can be no more efficient than the environment provided by the school for the promotion of learning. Students must have a feeling of security in an atmosphere where learning is the *dominant* concern, and the efficient teacher must know how to provide this feeling.

Expectations

In addition to the environmental pressures and demands of the home, the peer group, and the school, the adolescent is subject to the expectations of his parents, his teachers, his peer group, and himself. Keeping the pressures of these expectations within control is a challenge to any youngster, and for some it is overwhelming.

Parental Expectations

Parents often transfer their own thwarted ambitions to their children without realizing the negative effect such action may have upon the child's capacities, interests, and maturation. The relative instabilities of adolescence require a larger measure of parental love, understanding, and patience than is frequently given.[6] Thus, where parental desires for their children are unrealistic, the teacher has the responsibility for making appropriate intercession.

Teacher Expectations

Because of this frequent necessity for teacher intervention, teacher expectations of students should be based upon an accurate knowledge of the child's capacity, past achievement, home environment, and personal motivation. The teacher's training and his access to confidential records place him in a position to determine what logically can be, and ought to be, expected of his students. On the basis of essential information in his possession, an effective teacher will realistically adapt assignments, make allowances for limited capacities, and give consideration to home problems that may affect a student's receptivity for learning.

Peer-Group Expectations

Peer-group acceptance is of vital concern to the secondary-

[6]Horrocks, *op. cit.*, p. 75.

school student, and he may cast aside parental and teacher expectations in an attempt to measure up to the expectations of his peers. For example, when a choice must be made between adult standards and the standards of close-knit adolescent groups, the adult standards are often disregarded. The shared concepts of his contemporaries are of more immediate and, therefore, of more pressing concern. A case in point is that of a bright student who may arbitrarily lower his academic achievement in order to maintain popularity with his peer group.

Self-Expectations

What the individual expects of himself is the result of concepts derived from personal experience. The image he holds of himself as an interactive person in an adolescent society will help determine his actual behavior.

The adolescent student's behavior will largely fall within the range of behavior viewed as acceptable by his contemporaries. Within this range he will identify the level at which he feels he can function with success. Viewing himself as an unskilled basketball player, for example, the adolescent will not participate in team play. On the other hand, his experiences in mathematics may lead him to believe that he is among the better students. In this field he will compete with enthusiasm.

The student's appraisal of his own ability, or lack of ability, is not infallible, however. He is often hampered because of his overappraisal or underappraisal of what he can do. Frequently estimations are based upon assumption only, without the benefit of experience. On the other hand, where the student has been fortunate enough to acquire a number of usable skills, his self-esteem will be enhanced, as will his mental picture of what he can do. Thus, the boy who has learned to dance has a definite social advantage. The student who has been taught effective study habits can, and probably will, study; self-expectation moves him in this direction.

Growth and Development

As the adolescent moves along the developmental path, it is important that his instructors be professionally equipped to view him realistically in terms of his mental, physical, social, and emotional stature.[7] The interdependence of these four fundamental concerns is apparent, yet the teacher should be able to appraise them independently as an aid to understanding and improving student behavior.

---

[7]For a complete discussion of adolescent physical development see Horrocks, *op. cit.*, Chapters 10–13. Horrocks' Chapter 14 contains a sound treatment of adolescent intellectual development.

Intellectual Growth

The behavior of the individual is limited by his mental ability, which grows at a rate unique to him and which grows more slowly as he advances in age. Although the teacher should have an accurate indication of mental ability, test scores may be unreliable.[8] Culture-oriented intelligence tests occasionally lack validity,[9] and unless they are interpreted with great care, such tests may harm the student's welfare by presenting a distorted picture. Consider, for instance, a case reported by Wellman and Pegram: Preschool orphanage children were enrolled in the University of Iowa Nursery School in the fall, at which time individual I.Q.'s were determined. By the time I.Q.'s were again measured in the spring, the children had made an average gain of seven points.[10] During the intervening months the teachers may have been able to present more difficult learning tasks yet hesitated for fear the children would be unable to grasp them.

Most psychologists recognize the effect of environment on certain intelligence test *scores*, yet they are somewhat unwilling to concede its effect on basic intellectual *capacity*.

Physical Growth

Like mental development, physical growth follows an orderly sequence during adolescence and gives rise to myriad social and emotional problems. Differences in the rate of physical growth between boys and girls, for example, result in teenage bewilderment and teacher frustration.

There is marked variability in height, weight, and general body structure among members of the same sex of a given age. This is readily observable among eighth- and ninth-graders. In many cases the girls are a full head taller than the boys; heterosexual social adjustments are thus complicated. The inability of students to accept normal physiological changes with poise tends to accentuate the social ineptness of the teenager. Adding to the teenager's worries is the frequent occurrence of acne, poor posture, and other uncomfortable manifestations of growth.

Social Growth

With this rapid physical growth and continuing mental growth, the early teens are often characterized by a groping social insecurity, for it is during this period that the student must make his adjustment to the opposite sex within a framework of existing adult conventions

---

[8]Fillmore H. Sanford, *Psychology: A Scientific Study of Man* (San Francisco: Wadsworth Publishing Company, 1961), p. 107.

[9]Morris L. Bigge and Maurice P. Hunt, *Psychological Foundations of Education* (New York: Harper & Brothers, 1962), pp. 138–139.

[10]Beth L. Wellman and Edna L. Pegram, "Binet IQ Changes of Orphanage Preschool Children: A Reanalysis," *Journal of Genetic Psychology*, 1944, 65: 239–263.

and social taboos. Puberty brings the intensified interest of girl for boy and boy for girl, but without the needed social skills.[11]

The degree of social know-how exhibited by students during this period is highly variable. Sue and Billy, both fifteen, are miles apart in social competence. Sue, frequently dated, has achieved a degree of adult sophistication in dress, manners, and speech, while Billy, not yet "Bill," still seeks the courage to ask for his first date.

Adolescents of either sex who consistently withdraw from social contact with their peers frequently have problems that should be investigated by professional experts. Students with problems of extreme aggressiveness or of aggravated antisocial behavior will also benefit by referral to the school counselor.

Emotional Growth

The emotional behavior of secondary-school students varies from extreme self-consciousness to open rebelliousness. The psychologically oriented teacher understands that such behavior is not willful misconduct. If the teacher shows an understanding of the nature and cause of socially disruptive behavior, youngsters may voluntarily channel their emotions into socially useful pursuits.

The tendency to argue, typically found in adolescent boys, reflects growth toward self-directive adulthood. Recognizing this, the teacher should be prepared to meet the verbal explosions with the calmness and reserve born of understanding.

HELPING THE TEACHER PLAN

The understanding and use of principles to deal effectively with adolescent behavior find their counterparts in selected principles that aid the teacher in effective planning. To plan effectively the teacher should relate (1) his course to the total school curriculum and (2) his unit plans to the course. Furthermore, his unit plans should be so designed that they reveal the relationship of objectives to procedures. They must also reflect a genuine concern for materials and resources as well as for evaluation procedures.

Types of Objectives

Content areas in the school curriculum may be thought of as comprised of concepts, skills, symbols (memorizations), and habits to be learned.[12] Some of the concept-centered subjects are mathe-

[11]Horrocks, *op. cit.*, pp. 133–136. Horrocks' Chapter 4 provides a knowledgeable treatment of adolescent social adjustment.

[12]Asahel D. Woodruff, *Basic Concepts of Teaching; with Brief Readings* (San Francisco: Chandler Publishing Company, 1962), p. 72.

See Chapter 4 in the present text for a discussion of the kinds of objectives and their related procedures.

matics, chemistry, biology, and English grammar. Among skill subjects are found typing, physical education, and orchestra. But the need for memorization and for learning habits is common to all content areas.

An examination of a majority of secondary-school subjects reveals that the *concept* is the dominant type of objective. Through the acquisition of concepts (mental pictures), learners acquire the raw materials from which decisions are made and behavior is improved. Unfortunately the concept is often confused with the *symbol* (usually a word) that refers to the concept. A concept, by its very nature, can exist only in the mind.

Skills and *memorizations* deserve curricular attention to the extent to which they are necessary to implement concepts.[13] For example, the motor manipulation of the typewriter (skill) is but a means of carrying out the pictures (concepts) of key placement that exist in the mind. One memorizes formulas in chemistry, not for the sake of memorization, but as a means of thinking and conveying thoughts systematically.

Concepts, similarly, deserve incorporation into the curriculum if they help meet the general aims of education. The concept *a well-rounded diet helps promote physical health* has justification for being taught to the extent to which it can be related to the general aim of *health.* The concepts related to the successful operation of a power saw have educational justification if they can be related to the general aim of increased *vocational efficiency.*

Inseparables: Objectives and Procedures

After acquiring a clear understanding of the aims of the curriculum, a teacher must develop an effective plan. Sound planning calls for the establishment of a clear relationship between objectives and the procedures selected to achieve the objectives.[14] The first concern must be to determine which objectives are appropriate to the students and to the subject to be taught. Goals suitable for average tenth-grade students are probably not suitable for retarded tenth-graders. Learning of the romance of Ann Hathaway and Shakespeare may be appropriate content for an English literature class, but there may be no justification for treating it in a speech class.

Attention should be focused on the procedures necessary to achieve objectives only after the objectives have been carefully selected. Evaluation must also be planned in terms of relevant stated goals, for evaluation is the process of determining the extent to which goals have been reached.

In formulating an effective plan, the teacher must consider the

---

[13]Woodruff, *op. cit.*, pp. 73–74.

[14]Chapter 4 discusses extensively the relationship of objectives to procedures.

procedures that are psychologically sound in terms of the goals sought.[15] Each type of objective calls for its own unique procedures. A habit, for example, is not efficiently taught in the same way as a concept. For the conscientious planner, relating specific kinds of goals to appropriate procedures will be, in the beginning, a slow, painstaking process. But he will have the assurance that, with each succeeding carefully prepared plan, his ability to plan efficiently and systematically will be enhanced.

The Place of Objectives

Improved behavior is the final goal of teaching and learning. This goal can be achieved only when smaller, intermediate goals that result in changed behavior have been identified and reached. For this reason the end-means relationship between objectives and procedures must never be forgotten.[16] Procedures (methods) should be viewed as the means for achieving desired ends (objectives). Goal achievement, therefore, must be the primary instructional consideration, with activities, materials, aids, and evaluation procedures playing contributory roles. The teacher who permits students to engage in activities merely for the sake of activities is on a directionless treadmill.

The extent to which individual students are willing to accept teacher-formed objectives as worthy of pursuit will depend upon whether the objectives accomplish purposes that are of value to students.[17] For this reason goals not only must *be* attainable, but they must also be *considered* attainable by the learner. A budding junior high school athlete is less likely to be motivated by the distant promise of adult health than by the immediate and impressive need for playing a peer-group-approved game of softball—and playing it well.

Thus, the necessity for division and subdivision of larger objectives into *achievable* subportions is readily apparent. Large encompassing objectives are comprised of smaller, short-range objectives that must be approached in the order of their difficulty. These small goals, once achieved, must be interrelated in such a way as to provide meaning for the whole.

For example, it is demoralizing and frustrating to students for their history teacher to state that acquiring a knowledge of United States history is the basic purpose of an eighth-grade course. The immensity of the task tends to discourage and defeat youngsters at the outset. A better procedure involves dealing with the content in terms of units and related unit divisions.

---

[15] Woodruff, *op. cit.*, p. 121.

[16] See Chapter 4 for an expansion of this idea.

[17] Arden N. Frandsen, *Educational Psychology* (New York: McGraw-Hill Book Company, 1961), pp. 225–226.

The Place of Procedures

Each kind of objective (concept, skill, memorization, or habit) calls for its own specific procedures if it is to be taught with efficiency.[18] The common practice of failing to select the procedures associated with the desired objectives accounts for much unsuccessful instruction.

The teaching of concepts, for example, involves bringing the student into direct contact with the referent of the concept (a smoothly planed board in a woodworking class, for example) or providing a substitute experience that approximates the real contact as nearly as possible (such as showing motion pictures of Europe during a unit on European geography).[19] The teaching of skills, on the other hand, calls for repeated practice under supervision, but only after one has a clear mental image of the skill to be performed.[20]

Although they are frequently treated separately in discussions on unit planning, instructional aids, materials, and resources, as well as activities aimed at evaluation,[21] may well be classified under the general category of *procedures*. Here again the purpose of these procedures is to serve as means to goal achievement, not as ends in their own right.

FORMING AND USING CLEAR CONCEPTS

Before the teacher can make effective use of concepts in his teaching, he must understand in some depth the principles governing their operation. He must comprehend the relationship between experience, concept formation, and behavior; he must understand the varying roles of differentiation and integration; he must visualize the relationship between meaning and conceptualization; and he must be able to identify and use concepts of different levels of complexity—from a simple, concrete concept to the more difficult, abstract concepts of analysis and synthesis.

Experience and Behavior

Learning is based upon experience, and perceptual experience is the beginning point of learning.[22] Such perception occurs when some form of energy (light, heat, sound, etc.) stimulates a sensory

[18]The different kinds of objectives and their related procedures are illustrated in the sample units found in Chapter 7.

[19]Woodruff, *op. cit.*, pp. 157–159. A sound development of how to plan for the teaching of concepts is presented in Woodruff's Chapter 7.

[20]See Chapter 4, pp. 76–77, for examples of specific procedures for teaching skills.

[21]See Chapter 6, "Materials, Resources, and Evaluation in Unit Teaching."

[22]Herbert J. Klausmeier, *Learning and Human Abilities: Educational Psychology* (New York: Harper & Brothers, 1961), p. 159.

organ. Each percept (sensory awareness) thus formed results in an impression recorded in the brain. With the addition of other sensory impressions, meanings begin to form that give direction to the learner's behavior.

Deriving Meaning from Experience

The newborn infant, void of meaningful experience, is bombarded with a range of perceptual experiences—odors, pressures, and sounds. Gradually, as the infant develops and reacts to stimuli, these perceptual fragments are interrelated to form small clusters of meaning. It is this meaning that governs his controllable behavior.

Because of its relationship to meaningful experience, learning is entirely an individual matter. One learns only as he identifies the *meaning* in a given experience. If seventh-grade Sandy is ostracized on his first day at the new junior high school because his mother insists that he wear dress pants instead of the peer-group-approved blue jeans, the meaning he derives from the experience will determine his degree of resistance to wearing dress pants in the future. It is evident that a teacher cannot do a student's learning for him, but *the teacher can manipulate circumstances so that the student will be encouraged to learn.*

Using Experience to Aid Learning

The cause of instruction is furthered when a learning experience can be related to a previous meaningful experience. Margaret has less difficulty than most eleventh-graders in visualizing how far away Moscow is because she has already flown to Athens. The establishment of interrelationships between on-going and past experiences is limited or enhanced by the learner's background of meaning. Margaret superimposed the meaning derived from her plane trip to Athens on her new learning task—"how far is it to Moscow?"

Meaning is closely tied in with the range of experiences. If Margaret had actually flown to Moscow several times, her understanding of the distance involved would be clearer still. An individual can understand only what the meaning derived from his earlier experiences permits him to understand.

Individual behavior is determined by the traces of meaning that result from experience.[23] The mental pictures in the mind of the learner give direction to what he does. Margaret has a feeling of general pleasantness and excitement associated with air transportation. Thus, when her father announced a vacation trip to Europe by air, she was delighted.

Concepts, however, are not the sole controlling factors in what an individual does. One's ability in skill performance and one's hab-

---

[23]William H. Burton, Roland B. Kimball, and Richard L. Wing, *Education for Effective Thinking* (New York: Appleton-Century-Crofts, 1960), pp. 160–161.

its also play their role.[24] The patient confined to a wheel chair cannot play tennis; the student with bad study habits studies poorly. Furthermore, individual desires affect behavior. For example, the teenager who seeks teacher approval will exhibit conforming behavior in the presence of the teacher.

Differentiation and Integration

An essential concern of conceptual learning involves identifying the characteristics of a particular *referent* (the thing for which the concept stands) that set it apart from other referents. This process of *differentiation* enables the young learner to arrive at meaningful conclusions with respect to his environment.[25]

Elementary-school youngsters learn to identify differences in social customs of different countries. More advanced learners make finer differentiations; students in a biology class, for example, learn to identify the fine-line differences that characterize various plants.

Determining how one referent relates to another is basic to the development of a well-rounded concept. Perceiving an object quite apart from other objects is important, but meaning is added when the object is viewed as having a particular function in relationship to other objects—as the relationship of the flower and the bee to pollination, of safe driving to good citizenship, and of a knowledge of parts of speech to effective communication. This functional relationship is called *integration.*[26]

Conceptualization and Meaning

Concepts tend to group themselves into meaningful, interrelated patterns.[27] Considered in isolation, they lose some of their meaning. The extent to which the learner is able to visualize relationships between and among the subdivisions of large concepts will determine the meaning the concepts convey to him. When he is able to visualize the existing relationships, the learner is said to possess *insight.*

This interrelationship of concepts is readily seen in a United States history unit concerned with World War II. Facts and minor concepts must be singled out for instructional attention, while those that bear a relationship to the unit's central purpose tend to cluster around major points—the African Campaign, the Normandy Invasion, and the Battle of the Bulge. Facts may thus be related to meaningful large concepts.

It follows that learning by wholes is superior to the learning of isolated parts because of the importance of interrelationships and the

---

[24]Woodruff, *op. cit.*, p. 247.
[25]Bigge and Hunt, *op. cit.*, p. 359.
[26]Woodruff, *op. cit.*, p. 181.
[27]Burton, Kimball, and Wing, *op. cit.*, pp. 160–162.

understanding that results. Furthermore, recall is enhanced through such understanding.

When concepts are used in practical situations, they tend to become enlarged, modified, and clarified. The acquisition of useful concepts serves as motivation for the learner to acquire further concepts. This is particularly true when such concepts help him achieve his own ends.

Sally Ann's case will serve as an illustration. As a noncollege-bound eleventh-grade student, she elected to take a class in homemaking. Concepts she learned in class were tried at home with varying results. When she found that ideas were not working well in practice, she changed them. With use, Sally Ann improved the practical concepts of cooking and sewing to a point where she enjoyed her homemaking class more than any other and looked forward to the time when she could employ these skills in her own home.

Levels of Conceptual Complexity

It is not equally simple to acquire all different types of mental pictures, but all conceptual learning begins with concrete concepts. Furthermore, generalizations, abstractions, and the involved processes of analysis and synthesis rely on the concrete concept for their basic meaning.

Concrete Concepts

Concrete concepts are related to individual sensory impressions. The sights, sounds, and odors of the surrounding environment impose themselves upon the consciousness of the learner[28] regardless of his desire. When these impressions are meaningfully interrelated, mental pictures form that give direction to behavior.

For example, when the prospective truant feels the warm sunshine of springtime on his back, sees the first flowers, and hears the pleasant singing of birds, he knows that spring is at hand. He will then make a decision about school attendance based upon the total impact of these interrelated concrete concepts.

Concrete concepts, those that result from direct sensory experience, are the most vivid pictures the mind commands. Furthermore, they constitute the basic raw materials of which the more complicated concepts are comprised. Mental pictures (concepts) of chairs, animals, books, houses, plants, streets, and automobiles are easily acquired and are the essential parts in the formation of other mental pictures.

Generalized Concepts

Having at its disposal a large number of mental pictures that are particularly clear because of their closeness to the sensory process,

[28]Woodruff, *op. cit.*, p. 125.

the mind begins to classify. Concepts possessing similarities are placed in a common rubric. *Cans, dogs, desks, lights, men,* and hundreds of other items are subject to this process.

At the unsophisticated level of very early childhood, plants that are tall, have very thick stems, and produce leaves are categorized as *trees.* Similarly, creatures that possess four feet are classified as *animals.* This procedure, known as *generalization*, often takes place at the level of the subconscious. A great many generalized concepts are formed as soon as youngsters are able to identify similarities during their preschool years. (Examples: *Animals have four legs. All people do not dress alike. Birds can fly. Rocks are hard.*)

At all school levels extending from the primary grades through graduate study, generalizations are formed. This is true in all fields, but it is most apparent in the highly organized disciplines of the physical and biological sciences, mathematics, and English grammar.[29] In chemistry, elements may be grouped according to specific gravity; in botany, plants with certain characteristics are placed in the bean family; and in grammar, nouns with particular qualities are classified as common nouns.

Abstract Concepts

The formation of the abstract concept, like that of the generalized concept, is dependent upon the learner's mental pictures of concrete referents. After he has a range of experience with specific objects possessing a definite characteristic (hardness, goodness, carefulness, etc.), he finds that he is able to think of the characteristic quite independently of the object. Thus the learner is able to think meaningfully of *goodness* in the abstract without the necessity for relating it to a *good* person. He has now engaged in abstraction or has abstracted (removed) a particular quality from its concrete setting.

The ease with which the learner is able to engage in abstraction will depend partially upon the clarity of his mental images of the qualities to be abstracted at the time they are still associated with concrete objects. Much of the haziness of abstractions can be traced to the lack of such vivid mental pictures. The learner who has contacted a *pleasant* butcher, a *pleasant* physician, a *pleasant* teacher, and a *pleasant* bricklayer without having strongly sensed the *pleasantness* of each person will suffer to some extent in an attempt to think abstractly about this particular quality. An abstraction can be no clearer than the quality of the referent on which it is based.

Having progressed through the steps of *differentiation* and *integration,* which help in the formation of concrete concepts, learners can undertake the conceptual tasks of *generalization* and *abstraction*

[29]See the unit objectives in the sample units of Chapter 7 for examples of generalizations.

with greater promise of success. The actual use of concepts in real situations increases conceptual meaning and tends to fix mental pictures for subsequent use. As the junior high school student partakes of the privileges and responsibilities of democratic citizenship in a junior high school setting, his concept of democracy takes on expanded meaning. After repeated experiences with democratic school life, he is able to think about democracy in the abstract with some degree of insight. His acquired concept of democracy will serve a useful purpose in the tasks of citizenship that lie ahead.

Analysis and Synthesis

Beyond the levels of generalization and abstraction lie the processes of *analysis* (pulling apart, mental disassembly) and *synthesis* (putting together, restucturing in a new way), which are essential to creative thinking in its more restricted sense.[30] These processes are infrequently used by high-school students because they require a level of experience and maturity that they generally do not possess. It should not be assumed, however, that analysis and synthesis offer too great a challenge to secondary-school students of particular talent. Knowing this, the perceptive teacher should identify capable students and give them special guidance in this type of thinking.

PROBLEMS FOR STUDY AND DISCUSSION

1. What would happen if teachers had to plan and instruct without a knowledge of educational psychology and human growth and development?
2. Define *developmental task* in your own words.
3. How do you account for the fact that truant, delinquent youngsters frequently come from middle-class homes where they have enjoyed untroubled relationships with their parents?
4. What are some of the typical forms of in-school misbehavior in which adolescents engage?
5. Describe the ideal in-school learning environment from the point of view of the psychologist.
6. Is learning really the *dominant* concern in American secondary schools? Should it be? Discuss.
7. If you discovered that the parents of one of your students were constantly urging him to achieve at a level above his capacity, what would you do? Be specific. Justify your action.
8. How do you explain, from a psychological point of view, the lack of regard many teenagers have for adult values?
9. What is meant by the interdependence of mental, physical, social, and emotional growth? Discuss.
10. Relate several instances in which you have observed the marked relationship between social maturity and emotional stability in adolescents.

---

[30]Woodruff, *op. cit.*, pp. 143–144.

11. In your own words, define *concept* as it is used in this chapter.

12. Four types of objectives are listed in this chapter. Are there other types that you feel should be added? Discuss your point of view.

13. List some other concept-centered studies besides mathematics, chemistry, biology, and English grammar.

14. State in your own words the point of view of this chapter with respect to the relationship between objectives and procedures.

15. Do you feel that students should assist teachers in the formation of objectives? Why?

16. What is the relationship between perceptual experiences and concept formation? Explain in detail.

17. Why is learning entirely an individual matter?

18. Discuss in some detail the meaning of *meaning.*

19. State three meaningful generalizations. Tell why they are generalizations.

20. State three abstractions. What makes them abstractions?

RECOMMENDED READINGS

Baller, Warren R., and Don C. Charles, *The Psychology of Human Growth and Development.* New York: Holt, Rinehart, and Winston, 1961, Chapter 6.

Bigge, Morris L., and Maurice P. Hunt, *Psychological Foundations of Education.* New York: Harper & Brothers, 1962, Chapter 5 and pp. 356–361.

Bloom, Benjamin S., *et al., Taxonomy of Educational Objectives; Handbook 1, Cognitive Domain.* New York: Longmans, Green and Co., 1956, Chapters 2 and 3.

Burton, William H., Roland B. Kimball, and Richard L. Wing, *Education for Effective Thinking.* New York: Appleton-Century-Crofts, Inc., 1960, Chapters 4 and 9.

Cronbach, Lee J., *Educational Psychology,* 2d. ed. New York: Harcourt, Brace and World, 1963, pp. 100–107.

Fleming, C. M., *Adolescence: Its Social Psychology.* London: Routledge and Kegan Paul, 1948, Chapter 11.

Frandsen, Arden N., *Educational Psychology.* New York: McGraw-Hill Book Company, 1961, Chapters 6, 10, and 13.

Havighurst, Robert J., *Human Development and Education.* New York: Longmans, Green and Co., 1953, pp. 111–158.

Horrocks, John E., *The Psychology of Adolescence,* 2d. ed. Boston: Houghton Mifflin Company, 1962, Chapters 2, 3, 4, 14, and 16.

Klausmeier, Herbert J., *Learning and Human Abilities: Educational Psychology.* New York: Harper & Brothers, 1961, Chapters 6, 8, 11, and 13.

McDonald, Frederick J., *Educational Psychology.* San Francisco: Wadsworth Publishing Company, 1959, Chapter 3.

Sorenson, Herbert, *Psychology in Education,* 3d. ed. New York: McGraw-Hill Book Company, 1954, Chapter 3.

Woodruff, Asahel D., *Basic Concepts of Teaching; with Brief Readings. San Francisco:* Chandler Publishing Company, 1962, Chapters 4–6.

2

Essential Principles: The Keys to Meeting Instruction-Related Problems

The teacher who aspires to a level of teaching above the commonplace must make advance preparation to insure his instructional competence. Such a teacher must be prepared to identify those difficulties that impede the teaching-learning process. Identification of these problems is, of course, only the first step in a necessary sequence leading to practical solutions. Such difficulties are concerned with motivation, interests, readiness, individual differences, adjustment, classroom control, and transfer of learning. Essential principles related to these problem areas are identified and discussed in this chapter.

MOTIVATION

Because there is a *cause* for all student behavior, the teacher who wishes to understand behavior in order to improve instruction must study causation. With the few exceptions related to the functioning of the autonomic nervous system (nutritive, vascular, and reproductive responses), the individual behaves as he does because he is *moved*, or *motivated*, to do so.[1]

To be motivated means to be impelled to seek a goal that seems to have personal value. Paula is fascinated by English literature; as a result she reads much more extensively than class requirements

[1]See Chapter 14, pp. 325–336, for a more extensive discussion of motivation.

demand. She is motivated. Douglas, whose interest in English literature is almost nonexistent, has just bought an old automobile that runs poorly at best. He is thus motivated to take the course in auto mechanics so that he can repair his car.

Intrinsic versus Extrinsic Motivation

Motivation may be either intrinsic or extrinsic.[2] As the biology teacher dissected the lungs of a dead cat, the members of the class gathered around his desk and observed in rapt attention. "Now," he said, "I believe you will want to read more about the respiratory system of mammals." The students not only *wanted* to read more, but they *did,* for they were *intrinsically motivated* (from within) by what they had seen.

On the other hand, the *extrinsically motivated* student is moved by outside pressures. Pat, for example, hated Algebra I, but she handed in her assignments every day. She knew that Mr. Culver would go over them in great detail and, furthermore, that he lacked compassion for the person who submitted a late assignment. Pat was motivated, but her motivation was extrinsic—that is, her incentive was external to the learning itself.

The student whose main concern is to get a high grade or to live up to his parents' expectations rather than to learn the subject is extrinsically motivated. However, a majority of educators view intrinsic motivation as serving a more useful educational purpose.

Procedures as Motivators

A teacher must understand how to motivate his students, and he must master the use of instructional devices, procedures, and materials in order to do so. He should, however, be aware of their limitations and strengths as motivators. Highly motivated learning results from directing the attention and desires of students toward goals with such force that the students are encouraged to persevere in the pursuit of these goals.

First-hand contact with the referent of a concept often results in positive motivation toward the goals set by teacher and student. The boy in the woodshop class, for example, is asked to examine an expertly finished cedar chest and comes away with a strong desire to produce one just like it.

Such a strong desire cannot be fostered in the student unless he accepts the goal as his own. A teacher-imposed goal often misses the mark, largely because it fails to provide the pupil with intrinsic mo-

---

[2]Morris L. Bigge and Maurice P. Hunt, *Psychological Foundations of Education* (New York: Harper & Brothers, 1962), pp. 374–375, give a brief but clear explanation of extrinsic and intrinsic motivation.

tivation. Each individual sees goal achievement in relationship to its effect upon himself. How strongly the student is motivated will determine his persistence and effort in reaching an objective.

Interests as Motivators

Motivation is closely related to the experiences, abilities, and needs of the individual. He will respond to a given learning situation to the extent that it is compatible with his subjective interests. This is simply another way of saying that meaning is fundamental to motivation—that if a student intensely desires something because he understands he will benefit from it, he will strive to achieve it. Because skill in playing popular music is a doorway to peer-group status, many youngsters are willing to spend hours acquiring this skill.

Immediate Goals as Motivators

Motivation is enhanced when students are able to relate immediate goals to remote, but meaningful, objectives.[3] Because the immediate goal is often viewed as easily attainable, it serves as a greater incentive than the more encompassing or remote goal. A student must be able to regard as attainable any educational objective—immediate or distant—that he is supposed to achieve. Otherwise he will develop a "why bother?" attitude. The production of the school yearbook in a special class, therefore, calls for dividing the varied large tasks into small tasks that students feel can be achieved.

Environment as a Motivator

The environment of every secondary-school student is comprised of a wide range of stimuli, all of which vie for attention. The student selects those stimuli that he perceives to be most closely related to his individual wants. In the chemistry class Derward is aware of the following stimuli: the teacher's voice, the bee crawling on the outside window, and the girl sitting beside him. He may choose to exclude other stimuli and focus his attention on the class lecture. If he does so, it will be at the expense of the two other centers of interest. He must make a choice, and it will be his alone.

Students must learn to recognize the relationship between the desires created by their environment and the achievement of goals that will help fulfill these desires. The teacher has the responsibility of helping students in this frequently difficult task.

---

[3]Asahel D. Woodruff, *Basic Concepts of Teaching; with Brief Readings* (San Francisco: Chandler Publishing Company, 1962), pp. 50–51.

Success as a Motivator

Part of the teacher's role is to help the student achieve maximum motivation by helping him maintain the proper balance between his successes and failures.[4] The experience of success usually provides the highest motivation for gifted, average, or dull students alike. To be sure, circumstances may arise that warrant a temporary reversal of this balance for limited periods, particularly for bright students.

Motivation for the bright as well as for the dull student is also related to the self-concept of the learner. Having undergone specific experiences, students develop mental pictures of what they can and will do. After her first month of swimming lessons, Charlotte swam the length of the pool with some difficulty. She had the strong feeling, however, that she would soon be able to do it with great ease, and she was thus further motivated. A confident learner looks forward to success, and the student who consistently experiences success approaches new tasks with confidence. Successful experiences, therefore, are clearly related to motivation and to goal achievement.

Although psychologists and educators generally recognize the stimulating effect of success,[5] more attention should be paid to the fact that teacher-imposed reproof or blame gives rise to stronger student motivation than does a lack of interest on the part of the instructor. A knowledge of how one is progressing serves to stimulate the desire for improvement. If, therefore, grades satisfy the student's need to know his own progress, they will serve as motivators.

Need for Different Incentives

A teacher should carefully consider the incentives he is offering his students, remembering that specific incentives will not serve equally well in motivating all students. Students who vary individually with respect to intelligence, physical make-up, and emotional constitution will also vary with respect to potential for motivation. The teacher should learn to use different incentives in a variety of ways and to expect different results.

Competition, for example, often stirs the student to move with vigor toward a specific goal. Competition must be kept in proper balance, however, and should never be viewed as the goal itself. When a change in pace would add interest to his seventh-grade class, Mr. Willowby permits his students to play instructional games involving the use of teams. Experience has taught him, however, that youthful exuberance can easily carry such a procedure to excess.

---

[4]See Arden N. Frandsen, *Educational Psychology* (New York: McGraw-Hill Book Company, 1961), pp. 222–223, for a helpful discussion concerning the effects of success and failure on learning.

[5]*Ibid.*, p. 222.

Therefore, all games are instructionally sound and are played under close supervision.

But Mr. Willowby and every good teacher must keep in mind that, in spite of stimulation from many sources, the learning process itself is an individual matter. *No one can learn for the student.* This he must do for himself. The teacher at best can serve as an arranger of circumstances that will stimulate students to move in the desired direction.

Reward or Punishment?

To what extent should the teacher reward or punish the learner's behavior? No one can say with certainty. The cultural background, the personality, and the peer-group relationships of the learner must be examined before an answer to this question can be given. The proper course of action should be determined only in consideration of the specific needs of the individual pupils under given circumstances. Sensing a need for greater socialization on the part of a withdrawn youngster, Mrs. Young seated the shy student where he would be encouraged to converse with surrounding chatterboxes. The class clown, on the other hand, was seated at the rear of the class among well-behaved youngsters.

Avoidance of Frustration

The complete avoidance of frustration (goal blockage) in learning is impossible. For this reason the teacher must recognize frustration when it occurs and help the student cope with it effectively. Realistic goal-setting helps reduce the thwarting and enhances the ease of learning. Such goal-setting is important in encouraging achievement. Thus a short time after Mr. Thane permitted the twelfth-grade physics students to select their own individual class projects, he knew he was in for trouble. The least gifted students tended to choose the most difficult projects. But by helping them analyze specific procedures, the equipment to be used, and the conclusions to be drawn, Mr. Thane encouraged his students to set goals more in keeping with their capacities.

INTERESTS

A student is motivated by what interests him—a fact of fundamental concern to the educator. Knowing this fact, the teacher is responsible for identifying precisely those student interests that lead to the most impelling motivation. A real danger lies in the possibility of confusing superficial interests with deeper motivations.[6]

[6]Woodruff, *op. cit.*, pp. 267–268.

Superficial versus Intense Interests

Certain adolescents, as well as certain adults, have superficial interests that are primarily limited to playing games, eating delicacies, watching television, and making light of others. Although such interests give direction to many student activities, intense, abiding, and worthy interests should be identified and harnessed to serve educational purposes. Continuing interest in good music and drama, effort to relate scientific advancements to international politics, and active participation in student body affairs are examples of student interests worthy of cultivation.

Inasmuch as learning (even that considered desirable by the teacher) does not take place without interest,[7] the teacher must examine the various forms and focuses of student interests. The content of a subject may be of interest to an adolescent, or his interest may be aroused simply because his friends enjoy the same activity. Where his immediate needs are being served, there will his interests lie.

Maturity and Interests

If the student possesses a measure of maturity, he may be interested in those things that relate to his post high-school needs and aspirations. For such a student, those activities classified as entertainment should not be allowed to monopolize the time and attention that ought to be given to his more basic interests.[8]

Unfortunately some teachers encourage shallowness by using sensational procedures to arouse student interest. But the best interest is evoked through direct contact with the referent of a concept when that referent will enable the student to relate what he perceives to his past experience.[9] The vividness of a child's experience when he first sees, hears, and smells an elephant at the circus bears this out. He relates the huge animal's size, motions, sounds, and odors to other farm animals he has observed, and these qualities take on additional meaning and, therefore, interest.

This interest arousal can be observed in the boy who dismantles a car motor (referent) in an auto mechanics class. Although he has heard about the parts of the automobile many times before, it is here that he is first able to perceive to his own satisfaction the interrelationship of spark plugs, carburetor, fuel line, and exhaust. Furthermore, the boy's first-hand contact also helps him avoid errors caused by a misunderstanding of words.

---

[7]*Ibid.*, p. 268.
[8]*Ibid.*, p. 268.
[9]*Ibid.*, p. 266.

READINESS

A psychological state of readiness to act exists when the learner feels a need for new or different behavior.[10] When the need has been satisfied, the related behavior will cease. The student in general music who has learned the structure of a major scale is ready to formulate major chords. When he has learned how to make major chords, his desire for this information will abate.

It is helpful to divide readiness into two basic components: the *conceptual* and the *physical.* Other types frequently mentioned, such as *social* and *emotional* readiness, can be meaningfully related to conceptual readiness.

Conceptual Readiness

The sequential arrangement of concepts in certain disciplines like mathematics makes it impossible for the student to advance to a higher conceptual level without having first acquired the more basic concepts. Effective curriculum planning is based upon the assumption that most students of a given grade level will have this readiness ("reaching out" or "need") for the content to be treated at that particular level. Typical ninth-graders are ready to study algebra. To the extent that students lack this readiness, they will have difficulty in acquiring course-related objectives.

Conceptual Deficiency

Similarly, the course content at given grade levels is frequently beyond the grasp of certain learners in the group not because they lack basic capacity, but because they lack an understanding of supporting concepts. This situation is often found in the close-knit, concept-laden fields of English grammar and physical sciences.

Social promotions in school represent a dramatic violation of the need for conceptual readiness. Knowing this, many curriculum workers have hailed the current emphasis on programed learning,[11] which gives full support to the student's need to acquire one concept before he is permitted to move on to the next, more advanced concept.

Mental Maturity

Mental maturity is quite another matter. A youngster is ready to approach a problem with an excellent chance for successful solution only when his maturational progress has reached the point that will

---

[10]See Bigge and Hunt, *op. cit.*, pp. 377–378, for a brief but practical discussion of the relationship of readiness to learning.

[11]Programed texts are designed to permit a large measure of student self-direction. They call for the student's reaction to progressively more difficult concepts (frames). See the extensive discussion of programed learning in Chapter 18.

permit it. For example, the first-grader, because of limited capacity, cannot cope effectively with the complexities of geometry, and third-grade foreign-language students typically cannot comprehend the subjunctive mood.

Experience

Because mental pictures are the result of the learner's experiences, it is possible to speak of experiential readiness for learning. If students lack the experience essential for the formation of needed concepts (mental images), they must be exposed to it.

The foreign student who has not been exposed to American culture is not prepared to cope with the realities of the supermarket, highway traffic jams, unchaperoned dating during adolescence, and general casualness in personal behavior. The understanding of more complex concepts depends on the learner's acquaintance with a vast number of undifferentiated mental pictures.

Physical Readiness

If the student lacks neuro-muscular coordination, he is not able to undertake a task involving coordination even though he may fully possess the concepts necessary to carry it out. This is often the case with the child who has cerebral palsy: he may conceive of playing basketball, but his disease renders him helpless to do so.

In the majority of school subjects the learning of motor skills is inserted in the curriculum at that point when the physical development of students gives them the necessary coordination.[12] Typewriting, for example, is rarely offered at the elementary-school level. The grade placement of a specific subject is somewhat of a problem because of the differences in physical maturation at any given chronological age. Motor manipulations can never be taught successfully before the student is physically ready.

The teacher's identification of student readiness, both conceptual and physical, will provide him with part of the basic information essential to efficient instruction. If the teacher is unaware of the varying kinds and degrees of student readiness, the teacher as well as the learner is apt to lose time, energy, and patience.

INDIVIDUAL DIFFERENCES

No aspect of teaching calls for greater professional judgment than the necessity for dealing realistically with individual differences in students.[13] Among the most important differences with re-

[12]See Chapter 4, pp. 66–67, for a discussion of the teaching of motor skills.

[13]See Chapter 15, pp. 340–353, for a more detailed coverage of individual differences.

spect to the teaching-learning processes are those of intelligence, skills, habits, emotions, experiences, goals, interests, readiness, and adjustment. To be vaguely aware that differences exist in these areas is insufficient for the true professional. He must, instead, organize his teaching so that it reflects his acquaintance with the high degree of variation found among his students.

Students as Individuals

Because learning is highly individualized, the teacher must be prepared to deal with the needs of specific students. For this reason the teacher must know each student as an individual, not just as a member of the group. Nor should just one factor, such as intelligence, be considered the sole cause of differences in students. Viewing students only as group members, or solely as semiadults with limited experience, may injure the teaching-learning process.

Another caution is in order. The assumption, held by a limited number of instructors, that adolescents proceed through their developmental tasks at the same rate can give rise to serious difficulties.[14] The assignment of students to given grades is, unfortunately, based in part upon this assumption. At seventeen Patty may be emotionally independent of her parents, while Rita, her more physically mature classmate, may exhibit the emotional behavior of a twelve-year-old.

Different Rates for Learning Subjects

The rate of learning of a specific student may vary from subject to subject and from one division of content to another.[15] Furthermore, individual learners covering the same content will vary in their speed of learning and in their degree of retention. This is clearly seen in the case of Margo. She is one of the best students in her English literature class, but she acquires each concept in mathematics only after a struggle. In English grammar she does well, although she is not among the upper 20 per cent. Her memory, however, is the envy of her classmates: whatever she learns she retains.

Generalized versus Specific Teaching

Many teachers employ generalized teaching procedures and devote little attention to the separate needs of specific students. Jessie finds the class most challenging when the teacher lectures, but Merrill finds it boring and gets little from it. Because the teacher is wed

---

[14]Frederick J. McDonald, *Educational Psychology* (San Francisco: Wadsworth Publishing Company, 1959), pp. 435–436.

[15]See Lee J. Cronbach, *Educational Psychology*, 2d. ed. (New York: Harcourt, Brace and World, 1963), pp. 298–304, for a discussion of general and individual learning rates.

to the lecture method, Merrill is placed at a disadvantage. Since methods suitable to a majority of the students may be quite unsuitable for a minority, the teacher must be continuously aware of the value of a variety of generalized as well as specific teaching procedures in trying to meet the needs of his students.

Because each learning experience serves as the basis for a further projection of content, complications arise when students arrive at different end results from an identical learning experience. Jessie, for example, learned from the geography lecture that West Germany is more populous than France, that it is highly industrialized, that it has very limited illiteracy, and that all sections of the country do not speak the same dialect. Merrill, on the other hand, intensified his dislike for the study of Europe and particularly for the lecture method. His learning was meager, and he was not in a position to derive much from the subsequent study of other German-speaking populations of Europe.

Differences Within the Learner

Even within the same learner more than one type of learning may be taking place simultaneously, although the instruction is focused in one direction only. Jessie not only learned about German culture, but she also gleaned a few facts about German topography as well as a few German nouns. Such concomitant learning is the rule rather than the exception, and it tends to intensify the variability of the range of what is learned. With Merrill, on the other hand, such beneficial learning on the side was naturally impossible.

ADJUSTMENT

The thoroughly adjusted student[16] is the one whose attention is free to move in any direction dictated by his interest.[17] It follows that a student cannot be intensely preoccupied and still remain properly adjusted for the purpose of learning.

The student cannot avoid being preoccupied if his basic needs are not properly satisfied. A home characterized by constant domestic strife runs counter to the adolescent's basic need for security. His attention will be focused, in a large measure, on the home situation and its implications for himself. Emotional balance is the key to adjustment and requires the individual to be realistically but appropriately satisfied with himself in relationship to his environment. Such adjustment is crucial for proper learning.

---

[16]John E. Horrocks, *The Psychology of Adolescence* (Boston: Houghton Mifflin Company, 1962), pp. 486–496, presents a sound discussion of "Modes of Adjustment."

[17]Woodruff, *op. cit.*, pp. 255–256.

Learning: The Primary Concern

The promotion of such adjustment, however, is a secondary concern of the school.[18] As an educational agency, the school is primarily concerned with teaching and learning. It should, therefore, undertake whatever measures are necessary to insure that the causes of instruction and learning are served. The teacher who envisions himself essentially as a "promoter of happiness" rather than as a "teacher of content" may deny his class needed instructional time. Time that should be devoted to teaching may instead be spent dealing with the aggravated adjustment concerns of students—ill health, domestic strife, or trouble with the police—for which they might well be referred to other professionals.

Adjustments, however, are enhanced when teachers assist their students in meeting developmental tasks. The search for and achievement of adult approval, peer-group approval, independence, and self-respect are basic to adolescent adjustment. Through "teaching content" the teacher may provide, perhaps unconsciously, a means for such adjustment.

The classroom instructor must realistically appraise his role as a transmitter of concepts, skills, and habits. If he dissipates his energies by spending a disproportionate amount of time helping students solve deep-seated emotional problems, his teaching will suffer. Where possible, students with persistent, recurring problems that inhibit classroom communication and learning should be referred to trained counselors, psychologists, and, at times, psychiatrists. Unfortunately psychologists and psychiatrists are usually available only in large school systems, although the services of competent counselors are frequently provided in most schools.

To insure efficient learning, the school should aim at a satisfactory level of adjustment for all of its students. The student's appraisal of his school performance as successful or unsuccessful will promote or hinder adjustment. His adjustment will partially depend upon the relationship that he has established with his teacher, although conflicts that give rise to tensions are not confined to the school alone.

Teacher-Caused Maladjustment

Unfortunately, many cases of student maladjustment are caused by the teacher. The teenager who is humiliated by the instructor in the presence of his peers is a case in point. Inconsistency in the teacher's classroom behavior is another cause. A reduction in the frustration encountered in school should help promote the cause of learning.

Serious tensions brought to school or created in school serve as a

---

[18] *Ibid.*, pp. 261–262.

bottleneck to free teacher-student communication. Often aggressive student behavior is the result of thwarted needs and is misinterpreted as antisocial or, at times, antiteacher behavior. Since such behavior frequently occurs at home, too, parents need assistance in understanding their offspring during the adolescent years. School counselors and guidance-minded teachers can reduce pupil frustration simply by talking matters over informally but purposefully with parents, students, or both.

The adjustment or maladjustment of a specific student should not be determined on the basis of scanty evidence. Careful, pointed observation over a period of time should reveal whether a student is in need of additional help. The matter of self-acceptance—whether the student feels he measures up to his own standards—provides the clue to many aspects of behavior.

CLASSROOM CONTROL

Like all human beings, the adolescent seeks approval of his behavior. Where there is a conflict between the approval of adults and members of the peer group, however, the teenager customarily responds to the value patterns of his companions. Such peer-group approval is constantly sought in the classroom, causing great concern for the teacher attempting to bring about and maintain an effective instructional environment.[19] The teacher often becomes the butt of an adolescent's prank because the act has great peer-group appeal.

Purpose of Classroom Control

An effective classroom control situation may be defined as one in which *optimum learning takes place.*[20] Here again the means-end relationship of discipline and goal achievement must be kept in mind. The reason for imposing certain behavioral demands on students is to improve the possibility of efficient learning. Discipline for the sake of discipline is nonfunctional and empty.

The Teacher's Responsibility

The teacher, more frequently than the student, is held responsible for the quality of the control that exists in a given classroom. Although student participation may be encouraged, the teacher is basically responsible for the setting of goals. If the goals are too difficult or too easy, class morale and deportment suffer. In selecting

[19] Chapter 13 is devoted to a discussion of classroom control.

[20] Henry C. Lindgren, *Educational Psychology in the Classroom,* 2d. ed. (New York: John Wiley and Sons, 1962), pp. 368–374, gives a sound discussion of the purposeful control of the classroom environment.

such goals the teacher should display an intelligent realism, giving attention to the full range of abilities in his class.

The procedures used to establish objectives often give rise to student confusion that may erupt into aggressive resistance. Such resistance occurs when the teacher's preconceived notion of student achievement is arbitrarily imposed on the class without consulting students or giving careful consideration to what is *possible* for the students to achieve.

Because the teacher feels more comfortable using particular methods, he may use them repeatedly in spite of their negative effect on the general control of the class. Small-group discussions, frequently used by social studies teachers, often degenerate into gossip sessions with little or no academic value. Under such circumstances, students frequently take liberties and horseplay often ensues. The deportment of a group of students will be no better than the instructional procedures permit.

Variation Among Subjects

The desirable degree of study-hall silence will vary from subject to subject. The instructor must determine the noise that can be allowed in a given classroom situation without interfering with the teaching-learning process. For the shop and the art room this amount may be quite different than it is for the mathematics classroom.

Teacher Behavior

Youngsters feel relaxed and happy in those school situations where the teacher's behavior is consistent.[21] When students cannot anticipate with some degree of accuracy what the teacher will do, they feel insecure. This insecurity is sometimes expressed in behavioral outbursts that are interpreted as misbehavior. The teacher may exhibit a cheerful, fun-loving, permissive personality on Tuesday, but on Wednesday the curtain has been drawn and gloom prevails. In the face of such personality vacillation, students may overtly express their displeasure.

Unfortunately, many *disciplinary* actions are taken by the teacher without first determining the cause of the apparent misbehavior. Punishments that are imposed in anger accomplish little in the way of rational analysis of problems and lasting solutions. Emotion-laden situations are further strained when the teacher acts in haste.

---

[21]Herbert J. Klausmeier, *Learning and Human Abilities: Educational Psychology* (New York: Harper & Brothers, 1961), pp. 100–102, presents a list of teacher characteristics that, in the opinion of students, distinguish "high" teachers from "low" teachers.

Clearly Defined Goals

Compatible classroom atmospheres are encouraged when students feel that the goals are clearly defined and understood. If, in addition, they believe that the teacher is sincerely helpful and anxious to promote their success, students tend to accept the teacher in spite of minor dislikes. The youngster who is haunted by the fear of academic failure often displays classroom behavior that runs counter to the teacher's wishes.[22] Frequently such a student finds it easy to slip away to the shadowland of daydreams, where, in fantasy, he finds the success he is otherwise denied.

The adolescent has a range of needs that demand fulfillment but that may lead him onto paths incompatible with the learning environment the teacher hopes to maintain. Exhibitionism, which is so strongly tied in with the need for peer-group acceptance and heterosexual adjustment, is one of these paths. The disturbing need for emancipation from adult control is another. The tendency to repeat need-fulfilling behavior is encouraged each time an act satisfies such needs, regardless of its effect on acceptable classroom behavior.[23]

TRANSFER OF LEARNING

Inasmuch as the avowed purpose of education is to improve behavior,[24] the teacher must use those procedures that will encourage the learner to make a maximum transfer of what he has learned to new and recurring situations. Theories, ideas, and processes that have no functional outlet are of little value in changing behavior. The study of grammar for its own sake has limited value; only when it results in improved communication can it be defended as having basic merit. The improvement of behavior is basic to education.

Application and Transfer

If the teacher wishes his students to make practical application of what he has taught them, he must consider the principles on which the transfer of learning is based. First of all, he must help his students identify facts that can be woven into meaningful generalizations. Students may, for example, discover that housing in colonial America was primitive, that white settlers were frequently in combat with Indians, and that many of these frontiersmen perished. From such facts a generalization may emerge—*Colonization of a frontier region is accompanied by many hardships.*

---

[22]Frandsen, *op. cit.*, p. 222.

[23]Lindgren, *op. cit.*, p. 201.

[24]William H. Burton, Roland B. Kimball, and Richard L. Wing, *Education for Effective Thinking* (New York: Appleton-Century-Crofts, 1960), pp. 74–75.

The teacher must then provide for the application of the generalization in a range of situations. Hardships of frontier life may be related to the westward movement, to the colonization of Alaska, or, with some modification, to space exploration. Finally, the teacher must instill an awareness of and a need for further applications.

Demonstration of Transfer

The student is also helped when the teacher demonstrates in a number of situations precisely how to make the transfer from original theory to practical application. Transfer is further enhanced when the materials or devices used for instructional purposes are similar to those that will be met both inside and outside the school.

Well-equipped mathematics classrooms frequently display a giant slide rule mounted above the chalkboard. This visual aid simplifies the teaching of the functions of the slide rule. Many biology teachers insist that specimens (plants, mammals, and insects) be brought into the classroom to provide examples of topics being discussed. Theory thus becomes meaningful. Teaching emphasis can also markedly help the learner recognize the relationship between the generalized concept and its practical application.

Most of the time the teacher should employ goal-related activities that the students feel have application in nonschool situations. In the shorthand class dictation is confined largely to the type of correspondence that students will have to use on the job. In the sewing class girls are required to work on projects that will have current value as well as serve a useful purpose after graduation. When the teacher uses goal-related procedures, the student is more likely to apply his acquired concepts and skills to situations outside the classroom and to find satisfaction in their use.

PROBLEMS FOR STUDY AND DISCUSSION

1. List and discuss the five instruction-related problems that you feel hinder the teacher the most in discharging his responsibilities.
2. Define *motivation* in your own words. Differentiate between intrinsic and extrinsic motivation.
3. From your past experience identify and discuss two student cases in which the balance between success and failure has not been maintained.
4. Cite an example in which the motivation of a slow learner has suffered because of his self-concept.
5. Write a paragraph explaining why no one can learn for the student.
6. Contrast superficial interests with deeper motivations and give examples of each.
7. How different should interest-arousing procedures be? Discuss.
8. Explain the difference between lack of capacity and lack of mental maturity. Give examples of each.

9. Single out the five most important student differences that affect the instructional process.

10. Describe at least one secondary-school student whose rate of learning is quite different in three different subject areas.

11. What does preoccupation have to do with adjustment? Discuss and give an example.

12. What do you find wrong with the following statement: Every teacher should be a guidance expert? Explain.

13. Explain what you feel is the proper guidance role of the teacher.

14. What is meant by an effective classroom-control situation? Discuss.

15. List at least five ways in which teachers often promote poor classroom control.

16. What are the possible results of hasty disciplinary action on the part of the teacher?

17. Indicate the relationship between goals and possible classroom misbehavior.

18. Cite four examples of adolescent student needs that may lead to undesirable classroom behavior.

19. Assuming that the basic purpose of education is to improve behavior, give examples of how behavior is improved as a result of instruction in biology, English literature, and history.

20. How is the transfer of learning assisted by the acquisition of meaningful generalizations? Explain.

RECOMMENDED READINGS

Bigge, Morris L., and Maurice P. Hunt, *Psychological Foundations of Education.* New York: Harper & Brothers, 1962, Chapters 5 and 15; pp. 85–92.

Burton, William H., *The Guidance of Learning Activities,* 3d. ed. New York: Appleton-Century-Crofts, Inc., 1962, Chapter 23; pp. 106–112 and 233–243.

Cronbach, Lee J., *Educational Psychology,* 2d. ed. New York: Harcourt, Brace and World, 1963, Chapters 5–9; pp. 438–454 and 473–483.

Frandsen, Arden N., *Educational Psychology.* New York: McGraw-Hill Book Company, 1961, Chapters 3 and 6; pp. 488–492.

Horrocks, John E., *The Psychology of Adolescence,* 2d. ed. Boston: Houghton Mifflin Company, 1962, Chapters 4, 17, and 18; pp. 13–16 and 486–496.

Klausmeier, Herbert J., *Learning and Human Abilities: Educational Psychology.* New York: Harper & Brothers, 1961, Chapters 5, 11, 12, and 13.

Lindgren, Henry C., *Educational Psychology in the Classroom,* 2d. ed. New York: John Wiley and Sons, 1962, Chapters 2, 6, and 12.

McDonald, Frederick J., *Educational Psychology.* San Francisco: Wadsworth Publishing Company, 1959, Chapters 4 and 13; pp. 377–381, 438–439, and 475–482.

Morse, William C., and G. Max Wingo, *Psychology and Teaching,* 2d. ed. Chicago: Scott, Foresman and Company, 1962, Chapters 10–12, and 14.

Woodruff, Asahel D., *Basic Concepts of Teaching; with Brief Readings.* San Francisco: Chandler Publishing Company, 1962, Chapters 11–13.

PART TWO

PLANNING FOR TEACHING

3

Planning Before Teaching

Since the need for a systematic approach to instruction became apparent in the first faltering attempts of man to communicate his thoughts, controversy over the nature and the extent of planning has tended to confuse well-meaning teachers. In the attempt to present a consistent point of view for such teachers, this chapter examines the need for planning, the purposes and advantages of long-range planning, and the nature of unit planning.

PLANNING–FORERUNNER OF EFFECTIVE INSTRUCTION

"Planning is a waste of time. Look at all the unexpected things that can happen in a high-school teacher's day. Besides, I happen to know that about half of the in-service teachers don't plan, and they ought to know what's good for them. So why should we spend so much time on planning? Let's get on with the teaching and forget the theory."

Such comments might be overheard in discussions in undergraduate planning and methods courses. There is much truth in such statements, but unfortunately the inexperienced teacher–and occasionally the experienced teacher–may draw untrue and unwise inferences.

Need for Planning

Pre-service and in-service teachers often assume that the following statements concerning planning are true:[1]

1. Good teachers do not need to plan.
2. Unit planning is seldom used by teachers in the field.
3. If a teacher does plan, he need not go into detail.
4. Teaching is largely a personality function and has little to do with structured planning.
5. A teacher need not be the master of his subject in order to teach effectively.
6. If a teacher is the master of his subject, he need not be concerned with procedure.
7. Unit planning has only transient value, for teaching units are not useful for future reference.

The competent teacher knows that these assumptions are faulty. Highly successful teachers, who often give the impression of having done little planning, frequently *have* planned initially with unusual care. In addition, they have had repeated practice in presenting specific material. The degree to which a teacher needs to engage in *detailed* planning will depend upon the effect planning has on his teaching. Student teachers and first-year teachers must realize that, as a general rule, it will be necessary for them to plan in considerable detail. The degree of detail will depend upon the presence or absence of certain teacher qualifications and characteristics:

1. Knowledge of content
2. Practical experience in the use of specific procedures
3. Degree of security
4. Organizational ability
5. Ability to anticipate with accuracy the likely classroom problems
6. Memory

In-service teachers frequently do not write out a plan, or they limit their written plans to only one kind. But this lack of planning encourages inferior teaching. There are teachers who rationalize that their experience in a particular subject has made it unnecessary for them to develop written plans; this argument hints strongly that such

---

[1]See Jean D. Grambs, William J. Iverson, and Franklin K. Patterson, *Modern Methods in Secondary Education*, rev. ed. (New York: The Dryden Press, 1958), pp. 124–126, for a brief but sound explanation of the need for planning.

C. Burleigh Wellington and Jean Wellington, *Teaching for Critical Thinking: with Emphasis on Secondary Education* (New York: McGraw-Hill Book Company, 1960), pp. 241–243, present another sound point of view with respect to planning.

teachers are in an ever deepening rut. Since no two classes are ever identical, even where the same general content is taught at the same grade level for the tenth time, plans must be varied to meet the differing needs of new students.

Because the profession is constantly being upgraded, each group of new teachers should recognize the need to improve on the past. Of course, effective planning takes time. The need for time does not, however, relieve the conscientious professional of his responsibility for doing what will improve his instructional success—developing a written plan.

Consistent planning and replanning of units hold the promise of improved instruction from year to year. The efficient teacher looks to the future by saving units for possible later use. Each specific unit should serve the following year as a resource in the preparation of the unit dealing with the same topic. Resource units,[2] consisting of reservoirs of related objectives, procedures, and materials, can be compiled by the teacher in this manner over a period of years.

Planning versus Personality

In this scientific age the concept of teaching as an *outpouring of personality* is being justifiably assailed from all sides. No one would deny that an interesting personality is an effective lubricant in the instructional process,[3] but one would also recall the many times he had been subjected to the conceptual emptiness of *all personality and no content.*

The teacher who is a sound and effective practitioner possesses a storehouse of well-organized professional knowledge that he employs wisely in planning and teaching. Thus, the one-jump-ahead-of-the-class teacher is doomed to be a vanishing American. During times of teacher shortage, school systems have employed certain individuals whose subject-matter competence was not much ahead of their students. With the gradual disappearance of this shortage—a shortage that is more severe in certain subject-matter areas—will come a demand for beginning teachers who are well qualified in content areas.

The poorly prepared teacher cannot transmit insights that he does not possess. The gifted student, particularly, is hampered by the instructor who is not in command of his subject, for the student's

---

[2]See p. 45 for an explanation of the differences between the resource unit and the teaching unit.

[3]A discussion of personality traits essential to secondary-school teachers is found in William L. Carter, Carl W. Hansen, and Margaret G. McKim, *Learning to Teach in the Secondary School* (New York: Macmillan, 1962), pp. 15–22.

Herbert J. Klausmeier, *Teaching in the Secondary School* (New York: Harper & Brothers, 1958), pp. 190–193, discusses teacher personality as an aspect of classroom environment.

chance to advance commensurate with his capacity is handicapped by his teacher's inability to advance with him.

Content Plus Methods

With the emphasis on content mastery has come a growing criticism of the concern for methods from many unknowing persons. This attack is not without virtue, for it forces professional educators to reappraise the proper role of methods (procedures) in instruction. In the social studies class, for example, the dedicated, experience-unit enthusiast is encouraged to view activities as having value *only* as devices for helping achieve goals.

The frequent confusion of the relationship of means to ends[4] is felt strongly in this connection. Acquisition of lesson content, with few exceptions, must be viewed as the end goal, and methods must serve a subservient role as a means to goal achievement. The failure to define with clarity the relationship of the two has encouraged criticism from knowledgeable and perceptive critics.

Criteria Essential to Planning

All planning must be concerned with practical limitations if it is to help improve instruction. Forcing planning into an impractical academic mold will condemn it to a quick demise. The busy teacher simply will not use a time-consuming device that he feels has only limited practical benefit. Planning must observe the following criteria if it is to be of the greatest value:

1. *It must be practical and usable.* The practicality and usefulness of planning must be determined by the planner, not by a school-system supervisor or by an instructor in a methods class. The young teacher who has spent many hours in preparing written plans because course requirements so state may discard these plans as useless when confronted with the pressures of the real teaching situation. When he is free to chart his own course, the teacher will use those planning procedures *he views* as practical and useful.

2. *It must be economical in terms of time.* After examining the immensity of the teacher's task, one might assume that the competent teacher should spend at least six hours each day in planning. But this is an impossibility in view of the total range of professional responsibilities to be fulfilled. Plans should be as short as is compatible with the purpose of improved instruction.

3. *It should result in better teaching.* If the teacher is not able to teach better after having made careful plans, then his planning has served no useful purpose. Overly complicated plans frequently fall

---

[4]See Chapter 1, pp. 9–11, for a brief discussion of the necessary relationship of means to ends.

short of the mark; unnecessarily wordy plans sometimes inhibit rather than help in transmitting concepts. Planning for the sake of planning is but an academic exercise. Only when the teacher's classroom performance influences the lives of youngsters for the better does planning have practical justification. Planning is the means; goal achievement is the end.

PLANNING FOR THE FULL SCHOOL YEAR

Effective long-range planning calls for a realistic appraisal of what can be accomplished during the school year and what procedures will be most helpful. Furthermore, it involves understanding the relationships among different types of plans and knowing how these plans can be used to accomplish long-range goals.

Accumulated years of experience have led teachers to generally agree on the basic types of plans essential to effective teaching, but the terminology used to describe these plans varies widely. The three basic types of plans[5] that should provide an effective framework for successful instruction are:

1. The Overall Plan (Semester or Year)[6]
2. The Unit Plan
3. The Daily Lesson Plan

In structure, the Overall Plan is, perhaps, the simplest of the three. It has two essential characteristics: (1) it provides an overview of the course for the full year or semester by listing in sequence the units to be covered, and (2) it indicates the content and the time to be devoted to each unit. Certain planners encounter difficulty in developing overall plans by making them too lengthy or too complicated; neither type is appropriate.

Examples of Overall Plans

The following examples of secondary-school overall plans vary slightly, but they possess the same general characteristics.

---

[5]See Orville H. Nordberg, James M. Bradfield, and William C. Odell, *Secondary School Teaching* (New York: Macmillan, 1962), Chapter 5, for an analysis of the three types of teaching plans.

Kenneth H. Hansen, *High School Teaching* (Englewood Cliffs, N.J.: Prentice-Hall, 1957), p. 95, provides a helpful statement on the three types of plans.

[6]Robert C. McKean, *Principles and Methods in Secondary Education* (Columbus, Ohio: Charles E. Merrill Books, Inc., 1962), pp. 126–127, points out the need for long-range planning.

Overall Plan for a High-School Physics Course

Unit	Time	Starting Date
1. What Physics Is About	4 days	Sept. 4
2. Gravitational Force in Fluids	8 weeks	Sept. 9
3. Force and Motion	4 weeks	Nov. 4
4. Basic Machines	2½ weeks	Dec. 2
5. Heat	6 weeks	Jan. 6
6. Power and Energy	4 weeks	Feb. 17
7. Electricity and Magnetism	5 weeks	March 17
8. Sound	2½ weeks	April 28
9. Light and Radiations	2½ weeks	May 16

The preceding Overall Plan for a physics course is comprised of units of varying lengths; the longest is eight weeks and the shortest is four days. No subdivisions within units are mentioned although unit planners often find this is helpful. Beginning dates for each unit are merely approximate, with the exception of the first brief introductory unit, but they provide a time check that usually proves to be of assistance.

Overall Plan for a Two-Semester High-School Biology Course

Semester I

1. Familiar Plants (two weeks)
2. Plants and Their Seasons (two weeks)
3. Useful Plants (two weeks)
4. Where Plants Live (one week)
5. The Structure of Plants (two weeks)
6. How Plants Adapt Themselves (one week)
7. Plants in Relation to Other Living Things (one week)
8. How Long Plants Live (two weeks)
9. Plant Diseases (one week)
10. How Plants Originated and Developed (one week)
11. Kinds of Plants (two weeks)
12. Sciences That Study Broad Aspects of Plant Life (one week)

Semester II

1. Familiar Animals (one week)
2. Useful Animals (one week)
3. Where Animals Live (one week)
4. How Animals Adapt Themselves (one week)
5. The Bodies of Animals (two weeks)
6. Animal Behavior (one week)
7. Community Life Among Animals (one week)
8. Animals in Relation to Other Living Things (two weeks)
9. Animal Diseases and Their Treatment (one week)
10. Animal Injuries to Man (two weeks)
11. How Animals Originated and Developed (two weeks)
12. Zoology (two weeks)

Steps in Developing Overall Plans

If the Overall Plan is to serve most usefully as an aid to unit planning, certain sequential steps should be observed. The teacher should:

1. Without consulting outside sources, attempt to identify the units that he will teach during the full school year. (This step presupposes that the teacher has basic mastery of his content field. In the event this assumption is false, a satisfactory level of content mastery will have to be achieved before he may commence. Avoiding outside sources encourages the teacher to review and organize the concepts he currently commands.)
2. Indicate the sequence in which the units should be placed for most advantageous learning.
3. State the approximate amount of time to be devoted to each unit.
4. After exhausting his own thinking, consult three or four carefully selected secondary-school texts.
5. Compare tables of contents painstakingly with his own tentative outline of units.
6. Compare several textbooks.
7. Finally, consult again his own tentative outline, making appropriate adjustments in content, sequence, and time in the light of his new findings.

These steps are particularly helpful to the new teacher who may tend to place undue reliance on the text. If the individual entering the teaching profession has recently been exposed in some depth to the content of the subject he will be teaching, he should be prepared to think independently of the text. If his preparation has been lacking, however, he would do well to select the best possible text and follow it closely.

The alert, experienced teacher will constantly compare his own Overall Plan with the tables of contents in good textbooks. Minor adjustments should be made from year to year if they will assist in the instructional process.

To attempt to begin a year's work without first carefully identifying the major and minor topics to be covered is to invite misused time and misplaced emphasis. The amount of time devoted to a specific unit is a measure of the teacher's emphasis. In the Overall Plan for a High-School Physics Course presented earlier, "Gravitational Force in Fluids" is emphasized—eight weeks are devoted to this unit. The unit on "Basic Machines," however, receives limited emphasis and is intended to take only two and one-half weeks. Accurate timing is important; it is not uncommon to find teachers who have engaged in poor long-range planning (overall planning) entirely distraught toward the end of March because they have covered only half of the desired content of the course.

Fig. 1. Hierarchical arrangement of unit objectives.

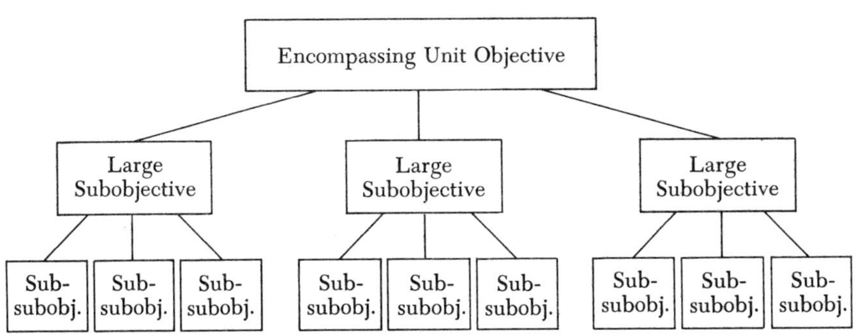

PLANNING FOR THE TEACHING OF UNITS

In order to possess *unity,* any subject or any topic must consist of strongly interrelated parts. This interrelationship is the most essential characteristic of a teaching unit. Not only must the objectives be related to each other, but procedures must be related to objectives.

Unit Defined

It may be helpful to think of the major and minor objectives of a unit as falling into a hierarchical arrangement as seen in Figure 1.[7] The large encompassing unit objective is comprised of smaller objectives. Because of the closeness of their relationship, these objectives can be taught more meaningfully in combination than as separate parts. Concepts, skills, symbols to be memorized, or habits to be acquired may be among the objectives.

A teaching unit may then be defined as *a plan for teaching carefully selected, closely related objectives to specific learners.* Included in the plan will be the appropriate use of learning procedures (activities), materials and resources, and evaluation procedures.

The unit centers attention on one major segment of a course. Below are typical examples of unit titles and their related subjects.

Unit Title	*Subject*
Mathematics in Taxes	General Mathematics
Central America	Geography
Polynomials	Algebra
Arthropods	Biology
Electricity and Magnetism	Physics
Nouns	English Grammar

[7]This hierarchical arrangement of objectives, and their close relationship to each other, can be identified in the sample teaching units in Chapter 7 and in Appendix A.

The unit is comprised of related parts. For example, the unit in English Grammar listed above as *Nouns* will include the following large concepts (parts):

1. Nouns are most easily identified when more than one definition is understood.
2. Nouns may be classified in two groups: common and proper.
3. Nouns have two numbers: singular and plural.
4. Nouns make morphological changes only in the plural and genitive (or possessive) forms.
5. Nouns in English have three recognized genders: masculine, feminine, and neuter.

Each of these concepts in turn could be subdivided into meaningful smaller ideas for the purpose of teaching them more effectively.

Subject-Matter Units and Experience Units

An examination of the development of teaching plans reveals a wide range of attempts to organize and clarify teachable units.[8] Writings of recent years have focused attention primarily on two types—the *subject-matter unit* and the *experience unit*.[9] Variations of these basic types are frequently used.

Subject-Matter Unit

In the subject-matter unit attention is directed toward teaching a major segment (unit) of the content. The objectives and learning experiences are most often predetermined by the unit planner. For example, a subject-matter unit might seek to teach students to solve mathematical problems that call for specific understandings; in literature courses the subject-matter unit might try to teach students to analyze a literary selection by applying certain concepts related to structure and form.

Experience Unit

The experience unit, on the other hand, directs attention toward pupil interests, needs, and problems. Learning procedures are selected on the basis of their social usefulness in solving student prob-

---

[8]Hubert H. Mills and Harl R. Douglass, *Teaching in High School*, 2d. ed. (New York: Ronald Press, 1957), pp. 231–232, present a brief but illuminating discussion concerning unit classifications.

William H. Burton, *The Guidance of Learning Activities*, 3d. ed. (New York: Appleton-Century-Crofts, 1962), pp. 326–328, provides a short historical review of changes in unit development.

See M. L. Goetting, *Teaching in the Secondary School* (New York: Prentice-Hall, 1942), pp. 310–314, for an earlier classification of units.

[9]Grambs, Iverson, and Patterson, *op. cit.*, p. 127.

Burton, *op. cit.*, pp. 327–328.

lems and meeting student needs. In this type of unit students are strongly involved in determining objectives and in selecting procedures.[10] Students might decide, under the direction of their civics teacher, that they want to "establish better relationships between the high school and the community." Learning activities and the assembly of information would be directed toward achieving this goal.

Some educators feel that the purposes of sound psychology are best served where unit emphasis is placed upon the acquisition of clearly identified content. They would, however, be quite unwilling to sanction the blind pursuit of subject-matter content at the expense of student interests and needs. This position argues for intelligent consideration of content as well as of procedures. In view of the emerging realism of the current educational scene, many teachers must give more thought to the serious tasks of planning and teaching. They cannot afford to identify themselves mostly with content or mostly with procedures, largely forgetting other essential instructional concerns.

The Teaching Unit and the Resource Unit

The *teaching unit* is essentially a plan to assist the classroom instructor in teaching a body of related ideas to *specific* students under *known* circumstances. The actual objectives and the implementing activities can be realistically determined only after the planner has an accurate indication of the composition of the group he will teach.

A *resource unit*,[11] although having the same general organizational structure as the teaching unit, serves as a reservoir of useful tools, procedures, and materials that the planner may draw on while developing a specific teaching unit. In the resource unit, for example, a great many more objectives are listed than can possibly be used in any one teaching unit. The same is true with respect to activities, materials and resources, and evaluation procedures.

The well-prepared resource unit serves as an excellent aid in the preparation of the teaching unit. A wise beginning teacher will surround himself with carefully selected resource units of known merit. He will find the preparation of units for his actual classroom instruction much less burdensome if he first surveys the range of ideas presented in the best of the available resource units.

Resource units may be developed as the result of group effort in

---

[10]See Grambs, Iverson, and Patterson, *op. cit.*, pp. 127–129, for a simplified discussion and description of an experience unit in operation.

[11]See McKean, *op. cit.*, pp. 129–136, for an extensive discussion of resource unit parts. A useful example is provided.

See Howard T. Batchelder, Maurice McGlasson, and Raleigh Schorling, *Student Teaching in Secondary Schools*, 4th ed. (New York: McGraw-Hill Book Company, 1964), pp. 125–126, for a helpful discussion of the resource unit.

Fig. 2. Diagrammatic representation of the relationship of specific units to a full course in a United States history text for eleventh-grade students.

19 *days*	22 *days*	17 *days*	20 *days*
A New Nation Emerges from the Old	Beginnings of the New Nation	The United States and the Challenges of Domestic and Foreign Affairs	The United States Survives Strife at Home

which teachers of the same subject combine ideas,[12] or they may result from the cumulative planning (yearly additions) of an individual teacher. Frequently urban school systems of considerable size appoint committees of teachers from a given subject-matter area and grade level (tenth-grade English, e.g.) who are assigned the responsibility for developing resource units. Large city school systems throughout the United States have consistently engaged in the preparation of resource units through this process. Smaller school systems, where the development of such units is impractical, would do well to assemble a current file of these units.

Steps in Developing a Unit

In order to avoid the haphazard development of a unit, a certain sequence of steps should be followed systematically. Only when the first step is satisfactorily completed is the planner ready for the second. The proper order is reflected in the following topics:[13]

I. Basic Information
II. Objectives
III. Procedures
IV. Materials and Resources
V. Evaluation Procedures

Before one can intelligently select the *objectives* for a given unit, he must have an accurate picture of the group to be taught. This is provided through *basic information.* Moreover, before one can de-

---

[12]Klausmeier, *op. cit.*, pp. 148–150, describes how a resource unit may be planned cooperatively by teachers.

[13]Hansen, *op. cit.*, pp. 153–158, provides a useful discussion related to each of the last four topics.

20 days	*18 days*	*16 days*	*15 days*	*15 days*	*13 days*
A Modern Nation Begins to Take Form	Reform in the Nation	The United States As a World Power	National Change Between Two Wars	The United States As a World Leader	Mid-Century Problems and Solutions

termine which *procedures* are appropriate, he must think of them in relationship to the *objectives*. Step IV and Step V involve listing the *materials and resources* and the *evaluation procedures* in organized form after they have been identified among the *procedures*.

When unit planners consider these basic steps in sequence, strong interrelationships and the essential cohesion of the unit will result. Chapter 7 and Appendix A are devoted to the presentation of examples of units structured in conformity to the five-step outline of unit divisions listed above.

The Teaching Unit and the Overall Plan

The relationship of the unit to the course is comparable to the relationship of a single chapter heading to the full table of contents of a book.[14] The major divisions in a typical high-school history text are shown in Figure 2 as units of a school year. Note that the course in United States history is divided into ten units of varying length. Several other facts are also discernible:

1. Although the units are approximately the same length, they vary from thirteen to twenty-two days.
2. Units are based upon a chronological sequence of events, and important incidents that are closely related in time are grouped for instructional purposes.
3. In spite of the fact that each unit title represents a separate area, each one may be subdivided for more specific treatment.
4. The Overall Plan is a composite of the individual units.

---

[14] A short treatment of the relationship between long-range planning and unit planning is found in McKean, *op. cit.*, p. 127.

Klausmeier, *op. cit.*, p. 146, provides a helpful statement on the interrelationship of long-range, unit, and daily lesson plans.

5. The total time encompassed by all units is only thirty-five weeks (175 days), one week short of the typical school year. It is assumed that one week will have to be used in beginning and terminal activities.

It is not surprising that a good textbook can be identified closely with an overall plan and with individual units, such as those in Figure 2. Today's publishers work in close cooperation with experienced teachers throughout the country to achieve this close relationship.

DETERMINING BASIC INFORMATION

In order to develop realistic unit plans, the teacher must have an accurate picture of the nature and composition of the group to be taught[15] and of the length of the unit and its position in the course. Students preparing to become teachers are sometimes required to plan units for hypothetical classes consisting of imaginary individuals, but this does not remove the necessity for having a clear and detailed mental picture of the group.

Specific Information About the Students

Planning for a specific class will require that the teacher have an accurate indication of the following:[16]

1. Individual I.Q.'s as well as the range of I.Q.'s within the group
2. The approximate socioeconomic levels of individual pupils
3. The nature of academic as well as nonacademic difficulties faced by students
4. Potential offenders in terms of classroom control
5. The proportion of girls to boys
6. The range of background experiences of individual class members
7. The past subject-matter achievement of students as measured by course grades and standardized achievement test scores

Armed with this relevant information, the professionally prepared planner can visualize with considerable accuracy the nature of the students he will teach and what will be involved in teaching them most effectively.

If it can be assumed that *planning is preteaching,* the teacher should leave unexplored no avenue that will lead to a better practical

---

[15]Hansen, *op. cit.*, pp. 28–30, makes a telling statement about the importance of understanding the student as a basis for sound methodology.

[16]See Burton, *op. cit.*, Chapter 8, for an authoritative treatment of the effect of the family, the neighborhood, and the social class upon the learner.

understanding of the group. The success of the planning will be in direct proportion to its applicability to the class for which it was intended.

Capacity

In a heterogeneously grouped class where the I.Q. range is extreme, planning based upon inaccurate or incomplete information frequently results in unvarying general assignments, with little attention given to desired differentiation. The knowledgeable teacher realizes that the degree of individual attention that should be focused on particular learners will depend, in some measure, on their capacities. Furthermore, information about the range of capacities of the students will alert the planner to the need for variation in procedures to conform to varying abilities.

Socioeconomic Status

In the planning of activities, a given unit may be entirely inappropriate when considered against the social and economic backgrounds of the pupils. A family living unit on food preparation that emphasizes light, expensive foods customarily served before the main course would have limited practical value for girls living in a slum area. They would benefit, instead, from a unit concerned with preparing substantial but low-cost meals.

Individual Problems

Efficient planning and teaching should give attention to the specific difficulties that confront students. In a class of thirty, these students may be found: a girl of normal intelligence with a cleft palate; a basketball star of average intelligence who has an inflated ego; two boys with marked withdrawal tendencies but high achievement records; a boy and two girls with measured I.Q.'s below 90; a boy who has had repeated encounters with the police; and a cerebral-palsied boy within the range of normal intelligence.

The competent teacher will consistently and consciously be aware of the demands these problems place upon him. Unless they are understood and dealt with at a professional level, such problems can conceivably create serious difficulty for individual students as well as for the class as a whole.

Probable Classroom Behavior

The early identification of students whose behavior is likely to result in poor classroom control is a great aid in planning.[17] More fundamental still is the determination of *why* misbehaving young-

---

[17]See Nordberg, Bradfield, and Odell, *op. cit.*, pp. 217–220. The authors discuss the necessity for giving both immediate as well as long-range attention to behavior problems.

sters behave as they do. If this can be ascertained with accuracy, plans can be laid to entice students away from an undesirable course of action before it ever occurs.

Where it can be determined, for example, that a given boy is an inveterate attention-seeker, the teacher can plan socially acceptable procedures that will provide the desired attention. Gifted students in the class often prove to be troublemakers when they are not constantly challenged. Plans should be drafted for keeping such students meaningfully challenged, thus avoiding trouble.

In addition to these typical problems, adolescence is further fraught with problems related to boy-girl relationships.[18] The classroom provides an arena in which these problems may emerge with considerable force. In early adolescence a certain amount of heterosexual antagonism usually develops, particularly among the boys who have lagged behind in physical development. In late adolescence the problem of dating couples who wish to sit together may prove to be trying.

Varied Backgrounds

Because of the diversity of socioeconomic levels and the increasing mobility of American families, students come to school with widely varying backgrounds. A child of a United States Army officer, for example, might have lived at least two weeks in every one of the fifty states by the time he was in the ninth grade. Contrast the ease of teaching such a student the geography of North America with the difficulties inherent in teaching the same subject to another student of comparable intelligence who had never been more than a hundred miles from his place of birth.

If planning is to be helpful, it must be undertaken with the realization that student experiences have varied considerably.[19] Experiences that are common to all and those that are uniquely individual in nature must be analyzed. The teacher must determine how these unique experiences can serve the purposes of instruction. Furthermore, if students are found to lack essential experiences, the teacher must find ways of providing them.

Subject-Matter Achievement

Somewhat related to the out-of-school experience of students is their subject-matter achievement. Extreme variability is noted among students in virtually all heterogeneously grouped classes. Substantial variation may be found even among students grouped according to some homogeneous measure. This is particularly borne out on the

---

[18]John E. Horrocks, *The Psychology of Adolescence*, 2d. ed. (Boston: Houghton Mifflin Company, 1962), pp. 191–192.

[19]See Morris L. Bigge and Maurice P. Hunt, *Psychological Foundations of Education* (New York: Harper & Brothers, 1962), pp. 115–116, for a short treatment of culturally imposed differences.

upper secondary level, where the range of reading achievement has been found to vary as much as seven years.

The frequently observed fact that *I.Q.* and *achievement* do not invariably bear a close relationship causes a great deal of difficulty for the novice planner. In order to avoid false assumptions, the planner should consider each factor separately before bringing this information together to determine the degree of relationship that actually does exist.

A twelfth-grade student of social problems may achieve at the eighth-grade level in United States history although his I.Q. is 115. Conversely, a ninth-grade pupil with an I.Q. of 98 may achieve at the twelfth-grade level in the area of English grammar. An eighth-grade mathematics teacher reports having given one of three A's to an overachieving girl whose I.Q. was 101, although the average I.Q. for the class was 114. Some students who rank among the upper 25 per cent of their classmates in music and art are sometimes known to have average or below-average intelligence test scores.

Information About the Unit

The basic information about the unit involves accurate recording of the proposed length, together with the time allotted for Introductory, Developmental, and Concluding Activities, and the relationship of the unit to the Overall Plan. Although there may be some error in these approximations, the necessity for recording this information will move the planner in the direction of realistically differentiating between the possible and the impossible, the practical and the impractical.

In terms of class periods required for completion, the unit may last from two days to several weeks. When there is a marked interrelationship of a wide range of concepts, long units are sometimes justified. The typical unit employed in secondary schools varies in length from two to five weeks, but the imposition of rigid time limitations on the units of a course is open to question. Flexibility should help encourage natural relationships among the ideas developed.

The student as well as the teacher should understand the relationship of the specific unit under consideration to other units in the Overall Plan. This should also be recorded as part of the Basic Information to help relate one unit to another in a meaningful way. The planner must constantly remember the need for interrelating the various course concepts in order to move smoothly from the simple to the more difficult.

Although all unit plans should contain this basic information, it is impossible to determine the detail needed in a unit unless one knows teacher needs and is acquainted with the students for whom the unit is planned. Inasmuch as a plan serves as an aid to the teacher, the need for restricted or lengthy plans will vary with the indi-

Fig. 3. Seating chart with a simplified code.

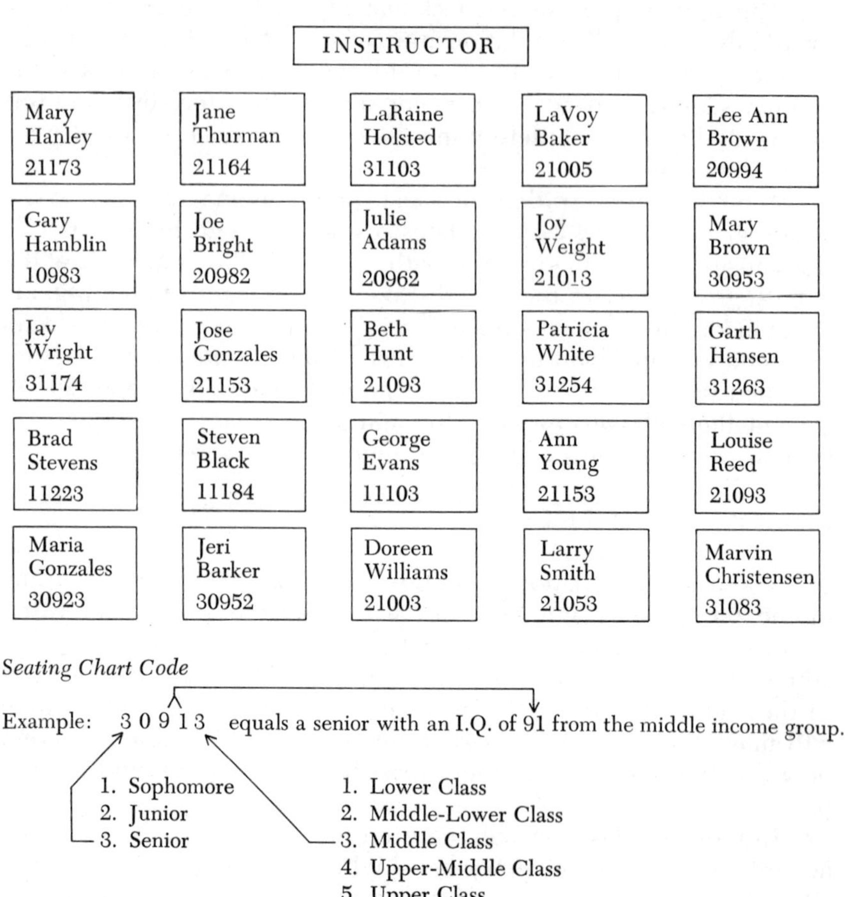

vidual concerned. There is no doubt that the beginning teacher will need more extensive plans than does his seasoned colleague.

Use of a Seating Chart

Teachers have sought a device that would bring many facets of the desired basic information together in a concise, usable form. A coded seating chart,[20] like the one illustrated in Figure 3, is such a device. Since specific facts concerning individual capacities, achievement levels, and socioeconomic status must remain confidential

[20]See Samuel P. Wiggens, *Successful High School Teaching* (Boston: Houghton Mifflin Company, 1958), p. 139. He tells how seating arrangements for the purpose of checking attendance may prove to be helpful.

professional information, such data must be kept in locked files or recorded in code form.

Advantages of a Code

It can be readily determined by examining the code at the bottom of the seating chart in Figure 3 that Mary Hanley is a junior with an I.Q. of 117 who, in the estimation of the instructor, comes from the middle socioeconomic group. Gary Hamblin, who sits directly behind her, is a sophomore. His I.Q. is 98, and he also comes from the middle socioeconomic group.

The key to the code should never appear on the seating chart itself. As soon as it is memorized by the teacher it should be destroyed. Indeed, because of its simplicity, the code need not be written out at all. The key to the code appears here only for purposes of explanation.

The following advantages of this device may be noted:

1. It is simple in make-up and, therefore, usable.
2. It provides much of the essential basic information in a very concise form.
3. It keeps the information confidential.
4. It provides a picture of the exact location of each student together with relevant data pertaining to that student.
5. It encourages realistic planning.

The number of separate bits of information to be coded for individual students will vary with the need and willingness of the teacher to assemble such information. When a teacher is teaching in the same small community in which he was born, it may be sufficient to have a coded indication only of student ages, I.Q.'s, and achievement levels. If his teaching situation, however, is totally new to him, he may need to have other specific items of information available in coded form.

A ninth-grade teacher of algebra found that her coded seating chart (Figure 4) served her purposes very well. She expanded, without sacrificing simplicity and intelligibility, the number of items of information coded.

Note that the "Grade Level Achievement" as it relates to mathematics can be of great assistance to the teacher in planning to meet the needs of students at varying levels. The numerical code defining socioeconomic status, however, may be too narrowly differentiated for practical use. A five-digit code would be sufficiently discreet and would be much easier to handle. The more sophisticated coding involving number reversals and a large number of digits will better protect the confidential nature of the information.

Flexibility Through a Code

The appropriate names and coded information can be written in

Fig. 4. Seating chart with a complex code.

		INSTRUCTOR			
Florence Graff 0992110.5731	Jerri Price 099907.2451	Bill Henlein 095019.0441	Sam Christensen 097908.8561	Elaine Purdy 096908.2451	Rebecca Turf 095019.6414
Ethel Weaver 092119.9541	Lamar White 094019.5451	Robert Gordon 098119.8431	Noel Roach 093019.2341	Blaine Noble 090019.1341	May Devenish 094018.9541
	Abe Silberstein 092018.8441	Lewis Shepherd 098908.2451	Bert Mecham 095019.8541	Helen Anderson 090119.4441	Reed Vincent 0943112.2431
Elsa Zeeman 093017.9541	Merl Vicklund 0911110.3441	Archie Bellows 096219.9541	Marlene Chadwick 094019.4451	Madeline DeHart 097119.8541	Jo Ann Barlow 090018.5451

Key to Seating Chart Code

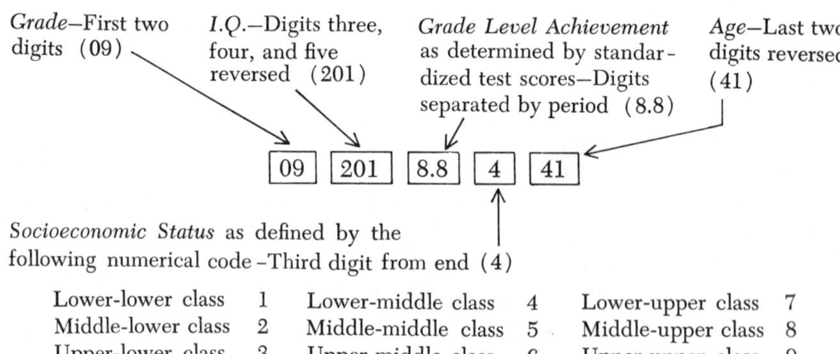

the rectangles representing student seats. If students change seats, names and accompanying data may be erased and inserted in other rectangles. Many teachers who use this device have found it profitable to insert the seating chart in a plastic envelope. The roll may be checked almost instantaneously by placing a grease pencil *X* on the rectangles representing absentees.

Practical use involves keeping the seating chart in the center drawer of the teacher's desk, where it may be consulted frequently to provide information immediately when the teacher is in doubt. Used in this manner, the teacher soon commits to memory the essential data, after which the chart may be filed for further reference throughout the school year.

Realistic Planning Using a Code

Conscientious teachers agree that the planning of objectives and activities for a specific group of students should be undertaken only when the teacher has a clear mental picture of the students in the group. In addition, when the teacher can arrange a planning situation in which freedom from classroom pressures is insured, planning can take place at its best. An accurate seating chart with essential information about the students will thus help the teacher make realistic plans. He will find, for example, that he is less apt to plan procedures that are beyond the comprehension of a given student when the seating chart beside him indicates that the pupil's I.Q. is 94.

Examples of Basic Information

The Basic Information that follows was assembled by a social studies teacher concerned with teaching a unit on "The Low Countries" to a class in world geography.[21]

I. Basic Information
- A. Age and Grade Level
  1. The students are all in the tenth grade.
  2. The age range for the group is from fifteen to seventeen years.
- B. The unit will be approximately six days in length.
- C. This unit will be number twelve in a series of units.
  1. The preceding unit was on France, its history, its relationship to other countries, and its contributions to civilization.
  2. This unit is on the Low Countries (Belgium and the Netherlands), their history, their relationship to other nations, and their contributions to civilization.
  3. The next unit will be on Spain and will include the same general areas as the preceding units.
- D. The Nature of the Class
  1. The I.Q. range is from 86 to 127.
  2. The general social adjustments within the class are good.
  3. There are twenty-four girls and nine boys in the class.
  4. Most of the students come from lower-middle-class families. The majority of their fathers are employed in the local steel plant and maintain small farms on the side.

Although the teacher who assembled this information as a basis for effective planning probably felt that the information was adequate, a beginning teacher might find it advantageous to have addi-

---

[21]Additional examples of how Basic Information is used in the preparation of teaching units are found in Chapter 7 and in Appendix A.

tional information. No mention was made of potential offenders in terms of classroom control, for instance, and there is little information about the students' backgrounds. An indication of general achievement in relationship to the world geography course also would help provide a more realistic picture.

A teacher of first-year Spanish assembled the same general information as that provided for the unit on "The Low Countries" but in a slightly different form and with a somewhat different emphasis. The content of this unit is concerned with vocabulary development; present, past, future, and imperfect tenses; and certain elements of Spanish history.

I. Basic Information
  A. Age: 15-18 years.
  B. Grades: Tenth and eleventh.
  C. I.Q.'s: Average—99.5, high—128, low—87.
  D. Background: Predominantly Protestant in belief. Six are Catholic. The majority of students were born and reared in Sloacum Valley. Two come from Mexican families.
  E. Environment: Semirural.
  F. Socioeconomic Status: With two exceptions, students come from the lower-middle class. The two students come from the upper-lower class.
  G. Student Interests: Several of the boys in the class have considerable interest in farming. All students have expressed considerable interest in travel and languages, although this varies a great deal.
  H. Length of Unit: Four weeks—20 class periods of 50 minutes each.
  I. Number of Students: 25—10 girls and 15 boys.
  J. Purpose of This Unit as Related to the Course: It is expected that the students will have a broad overview of the Spanish language and its place in their lives by the end of this unit. Unit I (this unit) is, therefore, an introduction to the many phases of Spanish and will serve students as a frame of reference as later units are presented.
  K. Specific Information Concerning Certain Students
    1. Mary and Manuel Larra have been in the country for two years, coming from Mexico with their parents. They are in the beginning Spanish class under special arrangements with their counselor. It is felt that helping their fellow students with Spanish will help them learn English more quickly and with less pressure. The class will also benefit. Special assignments will be given Mary and Manuel.
    2. Victor Lee has an extremely high linguistic rating. He

has been placed between Mary and Manuel for maximum benefit.

3. Delbert Tappia is deaf in the left ear. He is seated in the front seat for the best audio range.
4. Richard Newberry is seated directly in front of the teacher's desk because of visual difficulty.
5. John Marks, Barbara Bestwick, and Reid Potter have high learning abilities and should be given outside work both by the instructor and by the Spanish Club.
6. Dee Huff and Alice Newman will need special help because of learning difficulties.
7. Mary Richfield will miss class each Wednesday so that she can visit her mother in Westbrook Hospital. Mary will need additional help in order to keep abreast of the class.

The Basic Information on which the Spanish I unit was based places particular stress on specific information about students. Instructional procedures will clearly have to be altered to meet the needs of these students. Admittedly the identification and recording of relevant, special information about students will take some time, but it should be rewarded with a greater measure of realism in planning and teaching than would be possible otherwise.

PROBLEMS FOR STUDY AND DISCUSSION

1. What leads the uninformed prospective teacher to doubt the necessity for planning?

2. Which of the following types of teachers need to spend the least time planning? Why?

   The fluent one
   The one with ten years of experience
   The one who organizes well
   The one with the pleasing personality
   The one who knows his subject thoroughly
   The one who likes students
   The inexperienced one

3. Why should the beginning teacher today be able to teach better than the beginning teacher of twenty years ago? Discuss.

4. What should be the proper role of teacher *personality* in instruction? Explain in some detail.

5. What should happen to a teaching unit after it has been used? Explain, giving necessary details.

6. What is the *basic* purpose of a teaching unit? Whose purposes are served through unit planning?

7. Why is the Overall Plan often described as the simplest of the three basic types of plans for teaching?

8. Without rereading this chapter, list briefly and in sequence the steps in developing an Overall Plan.

9. From your acquaintance with high-school courses, list at least one unit title not mentioned in this chapter for each of the following subjects:

English Literature	Business Arithmetic
Shorthand	Homemaking
Civics	General Science

10. What is the difference between a *teaching unit* and a *resource unit?* Indicate the two ways in which resource units are assembled.

11. Indicate the sequence of steps that should be employed in the development of a unit. Why is the matter of sequence of basic importance?

12. List, in the order of importance, the most essential information about class members needed by a secondary-school teacher if he wishes to plan effectively.

13. What are the implications for the teacher of the statement *planning is preteaching?* Discuss.

14. List ten difficulties that may arise in teaching when the teacher has planned on the basis of inaccurate or incomplete information about students.

15. Assume that you have in your tenth-grade English class students with the following problems: a girl with very poor vision; twin boys with I.Q.'s in the 90–95 range; an introverted girl with an I.Q. of 138; and a boy of average capacity who lost his right hand, the one with which he wrote, in a hunting accident the preceding summer. Indicate in general the classroom procedures you would employ in meeting the individual needs of these students.

16. Why should the teacher consider the I.Q. and achievement of given students separately?

17. How specific should the planner be in indicating the time to be devoted to introductory, developmental, and concluding activities? Explain.

18. What precautions should the teacher take in using a coded seating chart?

19. What specific advantages are provided when the teacher has an accurate indication of grade-level achievement of individual students in his particular subject and class? List and explain.

20. Exactly what information should be included under the caption *Basic Information* before one can plan a unit realistically? Would this vary from one class to another? Why?

RECOMMENDED READINGS

Batchelder, Howard T., Maurice McGlasson, and Raleigh Schorling, *Student Teaching in Secondary Schools*, 4th ed. New York: McGraw-Hill Book Company, 1964, Chapter 7.

Bigge, Morris L., and Maurice P. Hunt, *Psychological Foundations of Education.* New York: Harper & Brothers, 1962, pp. 115–116.

Burton, William H., *The Guidance of Learning Activities*, 3d. ed. New York: Appleton-Century-Crofts, Inc., 1962, Chapters 8, 13, and 14.

Carter, William L., Carl W. Hansen, and Margaret G. McKim, *Learning to Teach in the Secondary School.* New York: The Macmillan Company, 1962, Chapter 6 and pp. 15–22.

Goetting, M. L., *Teaching in the Secondary School.* New York: Prentice-Hall, Inc., 1942, Chapters 4 and 6.

Grambs, Jean D., William J. Iverson, and Franklin K. Patterson, *Modern Methods in Secondary Education,* rev. ed. New York: The Dryden Press, 1958, Chapter 6 and pp. 124–129.

Horrocks, John E., *The Psychology of Adolescence,* 2d. ed. Boston: Houghton Mifflin Company, 1962, pp. 191–192.

Klausmeier, Herbert J., *Teaching in the Secondary School.* New York: Harper & Brothers, 1958, Chapter 6.

McKean, Robert C., *Principles and Methods in Secondary Education.* Columbus, Ohio: Charles E. Merrill Books, Inc., 1962, Chapter 5.

Mills, Hubert H., and Harl R. Douglass, *Teaching in High School,* 2d. ed. New York: Ronald Press, 1957, Chapter 11.

Nordberg, H. Orville, James M. Bradfield, and William C. Odell, *Secondary School Teaching.* New York: The Macmillan Company, 1962, Chapter 5.

Wellington, C. Burleigh, and Jean Wellington, *Teaching for Critical Thinking: with Emphasis on Secondary Education.* New York: McGraw-Hill Book Company, 1960, Chapter 12.

Wiggens, Samuel P., *Successful High School Teaching.* Boston: Houghton Mifflin Company, 1958, Chapter 9.

4

Objectives and Procedures in a Teaching Unit

Unit activities that are unrelated to unit objectives are unsound.[1] Where activities do assist in the achievement of educational goals, chance has graciously intervened; but thoughtful educators must approach the task of teaching with greater promise for success than can be provided by chance.

With few exceptions, activities are not justified unless they lead rather directly to a desired goal. Activities may appear promising in theory, but unless they prove sound in practice, they should be treated with caution. The responsibility of selecting appropriate objectives for a given unit and determining the most efficient procedures to achieve these objectives is one of the most formidable tasks confronting conscientious teachers. Thus, this chapter focuses on the importance of establishing and maintaining a psychologically sound relationship between objectives and procedures in the unit.

DETERMINING OBJECTIVES FOR A TEACHING UNIT

The meaningful differentiation of the kinds of objectives is basic to any discussion relating procedures to objectives. The teacher must be able to perceive the differences among educational objectives before he can select an appropriate objective and identify the procedures essential to reaching it.

---

[1]H. Orville Nordberg, James M. Bradfield, and William C. Odell, *Secondary School Teaching* (New York: Macmillan, 1962), pp. 39–40, indicate the strong need for relating activities to well-defined goals.

The size of the task involved in the selection and statement of unit objectives is vastly underestimated by the majority of unit planners. The most frequent difficulties encountered in evaluating unit objectives are the following:

1. No differentiation is made between *types* of objectives. It is the *type* of objective, however, that determines the procedure to be employed.
2. Objectives are not stated in their simplest form, with respect to either content or word usage.
3. Objectives are frequently too difficult or too easy for the average student at the particular grade level.
4. Minor objectives are not properly related to major objectives.
5. Concepts are listed in such a way that the development of thinking from the simple to the complex is *not* encouraged.
6. Objectives are not meaningfully interrelated.
7. Concepts to be learned are stated in topic form, thus encouraging vagueness on the part of the planner as well as the learner.
8. Objectives of limited value are often selected.

These problems can be overcome by the average teacher if he is conscientious in his attempt to improve.

The indiscriminate listing of objectives without regard to type can have a far-reaching effect upon the success of a unit. Such a listing betrays the planner's lack of information about how goals are best achieved.

There are several types of objectives with which all planners should be acquainted.[2] In the order of most frequent use they are: concepts, memorization, skills, and habits. The *concept,* the goal sought most frequently in most units and courses, is also involved in the other types of objectives. Proper conceptualization, for example, makes the task of memorization less difficult, and it is the necessary forerunner of the practice involved in learning motor skills.

Concepts

The concept is a mental picture of an object, an event, or a relationship, derived from personal experience with the thing for which the concept stands (the referent). Typical concepts are: two and two are four; heads of state are in danger of assassination; diamonds are chemically comprised of carbon; a verb is often a word of action.

Planning Suggestions

Inasmuch as the large majority of subject areas (English, mathe-

[2]Asahel D. Woodruff, *Basic Concepts of Teaching; with Brief Readings* (San Francisco: Chandler Publishing Company, 1962), pp. 119–120, lists five kinds of behavior that are closely related to the four basic types of objectives considered in this chapter.

matics, science, and social studies) in the curriculum are made up of mental pictures (concepts) to be transmitted to the consciousness of the learner, it is wise to remember some of the problems unit planners encounter in listing concepts as objectives to be learned. Two suggestions should save the planner much time and distress:

1. Concepts are most meaningful to the students as well as to the teacher when they are written in full sentences and stated as simply as possible.

2. An easily identified relationship must be established between major concepts and supporting minor concepts.

Note the effect of these suggestions on a partial list of concepts taken from a unit in biological science:

I. Arthropods are those animals that have segmented appendages and jointed legs.
    A. Each arthropod class has certain distinguishing characteristics.
        1. Class Crustacea
            a. Crustaceans live in water or moist places.
            b. Crustaceans are mostly scavengers.
            c. Many crustaceans have two claws.

Specific Steps

Because of the necessity for frequent revision, conceptual statements must be kept in tentative, rough-draft form until appropriately modified and ready for use. Adherence to these specific steps in strict sequence is helpful:

1. List the concepts in the order they should be taught. For the time being do not focus undue attention on possible error of sequence or wording.

2. Review the list, inserting essential concepts that have been omitted and deleting nonessential details of fact.

3. Check the wording of the concepts. Avoid the use of difficult terms; be certain that concepts are presented in meaningful, complete sentences.

4. Arrange the sentences into a hierarchy of major and minor concepts, as illustrated in the biological science unit.
    a. Place the unit objective that encompasses all minor objectives first.
    b. Place the first important minor objective next.
    c. Then list the subobjectives related to the first minor objective.
    d. Continue to list each succeeding minor objective and its related subobjectives as described in *a* and *b* above.

The teacher who has adequate mastery of his subject matter should be able to complete this task without assistance from other sources. The beginning teacher may wish to seek the assistance of three or four well-chosen textbooks, being careful to avoid the temptation of relying on them too much.

Memorization

Memorization involves the simple process of learning the symbols by which concepts are identified. For this reason it is frequently referred to as *symbolic learning.* There are many degrees of memorization, ranging from bare recognition of symbolic material to total verbatim recall.

Symbolic learning is not confined to the recalling of words and groups of words that are spoken or written. It may involve committing to memory signs, nonverbal symbols, configurations, and pictorializations like the following:

Understanding Concepts

Most symbolic learning (memorization) involves words. In every case the ease and speed with which memorization can take place is enhanced by a clear understanding of the concept for which the word or phrase stands.[3] Note, for example, the difficulties the learner would encounter in memorizing the following terms if he did not have at least a partial understanding of their meaning: *automobile differential, noun clause, Civil War, I.Q., triad,* and *space bar.* Memorization without the comprehension of the underlying concept is a most inefficient, time-consuming, and trying procedure. Unfortunately very few teachers are able to avoid entirely this wasteful process known as *rote memorization.* Conscientious teachers in all subject areas, however, are placing greater emphasis on conceptual clarity and are de-emphasizing memory for its own sake.

Other illustrations of verbal symbols that might be memorized involve more complex combinations of words: *National Socialist German Workers' Party* and *"All the perfumes of Arabia will not sweeten this little hand."* Students will take more interest in committing the first group of words to memory if they understand that this was the official title of the Nazi Party, led by Adolf Hitler, which was responsible for the military build-up in Germany during

[3]Morris L. Bigge and Maurice P. Hunt, *Psychological Foundations of Education* (New York: Harper & Brothers, 1962), pp. 429–433, present a generally accepted discussion of the relationship between understanding and memorization.

the 1930's and 1940's. Furthermore, the task of memorizing the second group of words will seem less burdensome if students know the circumstances that led Lady Macbeth to thus express her anguish.

Specific Steps

The symbol (either spoken or written) takes on meaning only in relationship to the concept for which it stands. This immediately infers the sequence of steps the planner must follow in listing symbols to be memorized:

1. Examine the concepts stated as objectives to be learned. Identify those terms that will have limited meaning for the students.
2. Place these terms in the order in which they are to be memorized once the related concepts are clear.

If a long poem or prose passage is to be learned thoroughly, it will be necessary to single out difficult words, first for conceptual attention and later for memorization.

Efficiency in Memorization

A ninth-grade general science unit on the "Air of the Earth" lists, among others, the following terms to be memorized: *atmosphere, troposphere, stratosphere, ionosphere, exosphere,* and *weather*. Few average students would be able to memorize these words with ease if they had no mental pictures to enhance the meaning of the words. A term such as *weather* may be associated with incomplete, hazy, or faulty concepts. A farm boy in North Dakota, for example, may not associate the tropical typhoon with his general concept of weather, a concept based upon limited experience. The memorization process cannot move along smoothly unless the underlying concepts are clear. On the other hand, it would be a waste of time to have students drill on words such as *hail, sleet, and wind storm,* for which students have well-established mental pictures. Such words, therefore, have been intentionally omitted from the list.

As a general rule, there will be as many terms to memorize in a unit as there are new concepts to comprehend. This is made clear in a partial listing of "Terms, Dates, and People and Places" to be memorized, taken from a twelfth-grade unit on world civilization concerned with "Roman Contributions to Modern Society":

Terms	*Dates*	*People and Places*
Punic Wars	753 B.C. (Rome founded)	Romulus and Remus
Carthage	31 B.C. – 169 A.D. (Pax Romana)	Etruscans
Latin League		Samnites
Practical Science	476 A.D. (Fall of Rome)	Scipio
Pure Science		Hannibal
Julian Calendar		Pliny the Elder
Pax Romana		Galen

The preceding items are listed in the order in which they will be taken up in class.[4] Terms, dates, people, and places of consequence have been singled out for the purpose of memorization; irrelevant and unimportant terms have been omitted. No attempt has been made to state the nature of the concept underlying each symbol, since careful identification of concepts is the function of the section devoted to "Concepts to Be Learned."

Memorization in Foreign Languages

The identification and listing of symbols to be memorized are extremely important in foreign-language study because of the necessary emphasis on vocabulary. Frequently the planner is justified in referring to a well-organized text by page number in his daily lesson plan. Notations in a lesson plan concerned basically with memorization might consist of the following: "Drill students on the vocabulary on page 9; review all idioms listed at the beginning of lesson 3; introduce the pronouns *er, sie,* and *es* on page 10."

Such a procedure leans rather heavily on "textbook" instruction, but this procedure has greater justification in the teaching of foreign languages than in other fields. Foreign-language texts are commonly organized into short two-day and three-day lessons. If such a text is followed rather strictly, planning units becomes difficult. Many teachers today are thus planning foreign-language courses around groups of daily lessons rather than by units. Such daily plans must be closely related to an expanded Overall Plan.

Fields of Limited Memorization

In some units there is often little or no necessity for listing "Symbols to Be Memorized." Where the instruction is primarily concerned with the reorganization, restructuring, or clarification of already existing concepts for which identifying terms are known, little attention needs to be devoted to memorization. This is often true in the fields of family living, physical education, and public speaking; nevertheless, the majority of units in most fields will require some memorization. Look, for example, at the following portion of a unit on junior high school grammar:

Terms or Symbols to Be Memorized After the Proper Concepts Have Been Developed

Subject	Compound	Conjunction
Predicate	Clause	Interjection
Transitive	Phrase	Positive
Intransitive	Adverb	Comparative
Complex	Adjective	Superlative

[4]Chapter 7 and Appendix A contain additional lists of terms to be memorized in specific units.

In most cases the student will learn the essential terms and symbols associated with a particular field as a side effect of acquiring a thorough understanding of the concepts to which they refer. Each subject has its own particular vocabulary that must be learned, but the effort expended in memorization should be determined by one practical consideration—its usefulness to the learner. The usefulness of and, therefore, the need for memorization will vary from one unit to another and from one subject to another.

Skills

The skill, like the concept and memorization, is another of the major types of objectives with which the knowledgeable teacher must be familiar if he is to teach efficiently. If *skills* are defined in a rather limited sense as *motor skills* (involving physical movement), they can be easily identified.[5] With such a definition the so-called *mental skills*—commonly referred to as library skills, social skills, conversational skills, etc.—are properly identified as *minor concepts.* Knowing how to find a book title in the card catalogue, knowing how to ask for a date without embarrassment, and knowing how to engage in pleasant conversation with people of varying ages, all fall basically into the conceptual category. It is necessary to differentiate between *skills* and *concepts*, since the procedures for learning concepts are different from those required for learning skills.

Specific Steps

A skill may be defined as the *coordination of nerves and muscles brought about either through practice or by virtue of natural endowment.* A skill may be developed to any desired level of proficiency, assuming that neural and physical equipment make this possible. The learning of skills requires two processes:[6]

1. Acquiring a clear concept of the motor action involved.
2. Practicing under supervision until the desired level of proficiency has been attained.

Skill Subjects

No subject is solely concerned with learning skills, to the exclusion of concepts, but several subjects are predominantly skill subjects—for example, typing, physical education, instrumental music, vocal music, industrial arts, and art. Certain subjects tend to be skill

---

[5]The definition of *skill* is restricted by Frederick J. McDonald, *Educational Psychology* (San Francisco: Wadsworth Publishing Company, 1959), p. 302.

[6]The essential relationship of concept formation to manipulative behaviors is discussed by McDonald, *op. cit.*, pp. 302–304.

subjects although they are heavily dependent upon concept formation; homemaking and shorthand might be placed in this category.

Major skills, such as typing, playing a trumpet, or broad jumping, may be advantageously divided into minor skills. Classified among the minor skills would be:

1. Operation of the typewriter space bar, tabulator key, back spacer, and capitalization key.
2. Fingering of a trumpet to produce the scale of D minor.
3. Placement of the feet for maximum spring effect prior to the broad jump.

Excellence of performance in the minor skills will add to the general efficiency of the major skill.

Skills obviously play an important part in any physical education class. In a unit on "Basketball" designed for a junior high school physical education class, one teacher felt that the following minor skills should receive attention:

Skills to Be Learned

Guarding and evading an opponent	Jumping
Dribbling	Running (i.e., general maneuverability)
Shooting (set shot, jump shot, hook shot)	Passing
	Screening

Note that each skill is essential to effective total performance on the basketball floor. It is basic, therefore, that a major skill be analyzed in terms of its component minor skills so that specific attention may be properly focused where needed.

A great deal of attention is currently being given to correct pronunciation in foreign-language classes. Inasmuch as physical manipulation of tongue, mouth, and lips is involved, such functional emphasis must be classified as skill learning. This is reflected in the initial unit of a Spanish I class:

Pronunciation Skills to Be Learned

The double *r* (rr)	The double *l* (ll) sound
Each vowel sound	The *n* sound

Skill learning is concerned with the coordination of nerves and muscles. A clear understanding of how this coordination is to take place (conceptualization) should precede the practice of any skill.

Habits

Habit formation—in addition to skill development, memorization, and concept formation—is another essential objective that concerns teachers at all levels. Unfortunately it has been subject to widespread neglect, particularly at the secondary level. A habit has several characteristics:[7]

1. It is learned.
2. It is automatic.
3. It is set off by a cue or triggering stimulus.
4. It takes place without conscious control.
5. It is satisfying to the user.

Typical habits include speech patterns, controllable facial mannerisms, brushing the teeth, motions involved in driving an automobile, and social behavior.

Long-Range Objectives

The nature of the development of habits decrees that they must be thought of as long-range objectives.[8] They actually begin to function at the subconscious level only after a prolonged period of consistent repetition. For this reason it is more practical for the instructor to think of habits as related to the total yearly classroom operation rather than to a single unit that may be of relatively short duration. Once developed, habits can be of great value in helping the instructor and class members achieve certain goals. The positive effect of well-formed habits on general classroom procedures can be observed in the efficient organization of housekeeping details and paper distribution.[9]

If habits are considered in relation to the full school year and consequently in relation to all units, the instructor is responsible for determining which beneficial habits can be developed or encouraged within the limits imposed by classroom contact with students. Selection of habits to serve as long-range objectives (effective study habits or politeness in classroom behavior) is a formidable task requiring considerable planning and thinking. Furthermore, different subjects and different environmental factors in the school call for the formation of distinct, subject-related habits. In the art class, for example, students must be taught to place brushes, paints, and materials in designated drawers and containers.

At the end of the school year teachers may advantageously ask themselves which habits were encouraged that were of benefit to the learning process and which habits were stressed that might well have received less emphasis or might have been removed from consideration entirely.

---

[7]Woodruff, *op. cit.*, p. 227.

[8]See Nordberg, Bradfield, and Odell, *op. cit.*, pp. 21 and 24, for a brief discussion of the effect of repetition on habit formation.

[9]See pp. 79–80 for a discussion of the effect of habits upon classroom control.

Habit Categories

The teacher should consider several general categories of habits, under which specific habits might be listed—for example, routine, classroom control, personal behavior, acceptable speech patterns, and study habits. Admittedly there will be considerable overlap among the specific habits attached to these categories, but they do provide a framework.

The following list shows the five general categories with related specific habits. It will be readily noted that several items could logically be added to each group, but the enumeration is illustrative, not inclusive.

1. Habits Related to Routine:
   a. Abiding by efficient paper distribution procedures.
   b. Exercising personal tidiness around one's desk.
   c. Being in one's seat by the time the bell rings.
   d. Leaving the seats at the close of the class only when dismissed by the teacher.
2. Habits Related to Classroom Control:
   a. Giving consistent attention to the teacher and the instruction.
   b. Sharpening pencils only before and after class.
   c. Abstaining from horseplay during class.
   d. Using the classroom library only at times specified by the teacher.
3. Habits Related to Personal Behavior:
   a. Being consistently polite when addressing the teacher or classmates.
   b. Avoiding running and yelling in the classroom.
   c. Being personally neat at all times.
   d. Avoiding rudeness under all circumstances.
4. Habits Related to Acceptable Speech Patterns:
   a. Using commonly accepted words for effective communication.
   b. Avoiding meaningless clutter words.
   c. Avoiding profanity completely.
   d. Avoiding *ain't* and other illiterate usages.
5. Study Habits:
   a. Getting down to study without unwarranted delay.
   b. Organizing the material to be studied in order to achieve maximum efficiency.
   c. Seeking the help of the teacher only when it is really necessary.
   d. Permitting no interference from classmates when study is expected.

DETERMINING PROCEDURES FOR ACHIEVING OBJECTIVES

Teachers have persistently tried to establish a sound but practical relationship between teaching procedures and objectives. In arriving at a sound relationship, the teacher must place procedures in their proper perspective and identify the procedures suited to the specific objectives.

Unit procedures (methods) are the means for achieving unit goals. If procedures are poorly selected, efficient movement in the direction of the objectives is thwarted.

So great has been the preoccupation of teachers with the necessity for careful selection of teaching procedures that many have come to view methods as ends in their own right. This misplaced emphasis has had a detrimental effect upon the whole of American public education during the last half century. The relationship of *means* to *ends* must be clear to the teacher himself.

The fundamental question that the teacher must, therefore, ask himself in determining procedures is *not:* "Should I use the lecture method, committee work, a field trip, or a resource person?" The basic question *is:* "Of the range of possible procedures that might be employed in achieving a given goal, which procedure will enable learners to achieve the goal most efficiently?" There are, of course, several relevant factors that must be considered:

1. Psychological soundness
2. Time considerations
3. Depth of learning
4. Type of learning
5. Nature of the class being taught
6. Effectiveness of the teacher in using given procedures

What Procedures Are Best?

The poor selection of procedures (means) gives rise to inefficiency in attaining objectives, to negative reaction on the part of learners, and to varying degrees of frustration for both teachers and learners. What procedures *are* best? Any specific response to this question would be shallow and irresponsible. *The best procedure is one that enables students to achieve goals with the greatest efficiency.*

Objective Dictates Procedure

Perhaps the most relevant consideration in selecting procedures involves the determination of the *type of objective,* for the psychology of learning reveals that the kind of objective dictates the most effective learning procedures.[10] Where the desired goal is the devel-

[10]Woodruff, *op. cit.,* pp. 43–45.

opment of proficiency in a given motor skill, procedures known to be effective in motor-skill achievement should be used; procedures appropriate to the achievement of a conceptual objective would be inappropriate. Typing, for example, is basically concerned with drill aimed at the acquisition of skill. It would be inappropriate, therefore, to spend a majority of instructional time teaching students finger position, paper insertion, or carriage return, without letting them practice the theory they had learned. On the other hand, it would be unsound teaching practice to insist that students in an algebra class repeat in rote fashion the steps involved in solving an equation without first clearly understanding the necessity for these steps.

The ineffective, unscientific teacher is often known by his failure to identify correctly the types of objectives sought (whether concepts, skills, memorizations, or habits) and their corresponding procedures.[11] In a history class, which is essentially concerned with the teaching of concepts, such a teacher often requires the memorization of names and dates without first fitting them into a meaningful context. Or, a teacher of high-school chorus, essentially a skill subject, may spend a disproportionate amount of time discussing the various aspects of vocal production. The good teacher, then, needs to have a first-hand acquaintance with a wide range of specific methods. If he has such personal experience, he will be in a much better position to make a meaningful choice of unit procedures.

Desirable Variety

A variety of procedures very often serves instructional purposes better than the use of a limited number of stereotyped methods.[12] The teacher should consider whether it would be desirable to use modifications of any or all of the following approaches to instruction:

- Study periods under the teacher's supervision
- Differentiated assignments
- Modified lectures
- Frequent objective testing
- Committee work under careful teacher supervision
- Frequent bulletin boards prepared by students
- Carefully screened resource people
- Pretests for diagnosis
- Guided self-activity
- Thoroughly planned and supervised field trips
- Application of concepts or skills to a practical situation
- Carefully selected models, diagrams, or charts
- Student-made aids prepared under teacher supervision
- Teaching machines
- Team teaching
- Teaching in very large and/or in very small groups

[11]See William H. Burton, *The Guidance of Learning Activities*, 3d. ed. (New York: Appleton-Century-Crofts, 1962), pp. 365–366, for an excellent treatment of the teacher's responsibility in the use of activities.

[12]Jean D. Grambs, William J. Iverson, and Franklin K. Patterson, *Modern Methods in Secondary Education*, rev. ed. (New York: The Dryden Press, 1958), pp. 146–147.

Obviously there are more procedures or variations of procedures than have ever been tried. The ingenuity of an excellent teacher often gives rise to a teaching procedure or combination of procedures that has unusual promise for accomplishing objectives.

Misused Variety

Of course, a wide variety of procedures is effective only if such procedures are justified in terms of goal achievement. Consider the case of Mrs. Whitney, who thinks of herself as a forward-looking teacher.

MRS. WHITNEY USES A VARIETY OF PROCEDURES

Every Friday students talked about current events in Mrs. Whitney's eighth-grade core class. On this particular Friday, Jane Berner reported on a newspaper article by the Director of the Federal Bureau of Investigation; Jimmy Wilson told about a murder in an adjacent city; and Sally Zimmer read an article about the President's vacation at his summer home. In all, some ten minutes were consumed in the reports. There was no class discussion afterward.

"We'll have to hurry along," the teacher announced. "Now we'll choose sides so that we can play the game of 'State Capitals.' Lowell, you be the captain of one team, and Louise, you be the captain of the other. When you have chosen your teams, line them up on opposite sides of the room."

After considerable commotion and a loss of seven minutes, the teams were chosen and faced each other from opposite sides of the room. The game lasted just eleven minutes, for the teacher had sensed an urgency to move on to another activity. Louise's team won, eliciting groans of dismay from the opposition as the participants took their seats.

"Now we are going to continue the four-minute reports that we started on Wednesday. We'll hear first from Margaret, then Susan, then Bob, and then Mary Jo."

The four-minute reports averaged more nearly two minutes and in one case just thirty seconds. Mrs. Whitney was disturbed, especially in view of her compulsive desire to keep the students active.

"You may select books or magazines from the classroom library and study for the rest of the period," she said. Because only seven minutes were left in the period at this point, there was a great deal more interest in anticipating the end of the period than in getting down to conscientious study. By the end of the period, the class was in a hubbub and the teacher felt frustrated.

Mrs. Whitney's emphasis had been on keeping students busy rather than on having them achieve certain goals. This emphasis had the following results:

1. The students engaged in a much wider range of activities than was desirable.
2. They were moved into another activity just as they were beginning to benefit from the on-going one.

3. They failed to derive the desired satisfaction from their activities.

4. They were subjected to miscellaneous, unrelated activities.

5. The students were unable to relate the activities to a definite goal.

Thoughtful teachers will avoid such problems; effective planning, based upon an acquaintance with student behavior patterns, will enable conscientious teachers to rule out questionable procedures at the planning stage.

In order to achieve success, the teacher must know the precise steps the learner must go through in acquiring specific types of objectives. He must be able to differentiate in a practical teaching situation the steps appropriate to achieving concepts, skills, memorizations, and habits.

The Teaching of Concepts

Concepts may be taught most efficiently when the learner has a *meaningful, vivid* experience or series of experiences with the referent of the concept.[13] Consider what this means in a practical situation.

MR. SCHMIDT TEACHES A BIOLOGY CONCEPT

Mr. Schmidt, the tenth-grade biology teacher, planned that the understanding of the following concept would serve as one of the objectives for the day: *Blood flows into the heart through the veins and out of the heart through the arteries.*

To provide his students with a meaningful, vivid experience with the heart, arteries, and veins, Mr. Schmidt wheeled to the center of the classroom a plastic model exposing the simulated visceral organs of the body. The teacher asked Janice Peters to identify the heart. He made sure that all the students—particularly the less gifted—had a clear picture of the location of the heart in relationship to the other organs of the body.

While making a simplified oral explanation, Mr. Schmidt used a pointer to trace the flow of blood into the heart through the veins and out through the arteries. Students were encouraged to ask questions, which they did. Willy Liston, a boy of average ability, was then asked to restate in his own words what the teacher had said. Willy was able to acquit himself rather well, so Mr. Schmidt assumed that a majority of his class had understood the concept. The model would remain in the room for some time for examination by those students who were still not sure of the concept.

Technical terms related to the phenomenon just observed were placed on the board. A large wall chart on which the heart and its parts were labeled was displayed, discussed, and related to the terms on the board. Part of the assignment for the next day included the memorization of the words on the chart. During the following days the concept of the flow of blood through the

[13] Woodruff, *op. cit.*, pp. 155–156.

heart took on new meaning through discussion and use under varied circumstances, and the associated symbols became fixed in the minds of the students.

Specific Steps

An effective plan for teaching concepts (which incorporates the highly relevant elements of meaningfulness and vividness) involves four steps,[14] each of which was used by Mr. Schmidt in establishing the concept of blood flow in the heart:

1. Showing the referent of the concept.
2. Discussing the concept until it has become clear.
3. Memorizing the symbols related to the concept.
4. Providing for the application of the concept in on-going life situations.

Showing. The first step, *showing the referent,* is fundamental but often neglected or thought unnecessary because it is assumed the students have prior knowledge. Difficulties arise when the referent (the thing itself) cannot be brought into the classroom or is quite some distance from the school. (Note how Mr. Schmidt solved this problem by using a model.) In such instances the instructor must provide substitutes for first-hand experiences.

The showing or presentation of abstract concepts poses real problems that many teachers have not solved satisfactorily. Clothing abstractions with concrete meaning and vividness is a test of teacher ingenuity and a successful way to a rewarding experience for the students.

Discussing. After the referent of the concept has been shown or presented, the major portion of time will be spent on the second step—*discussion.* During this phase unclear and misunderstood aspects of the concept are exposed and made clear; fuzzy edges are brought into sharper focus. When properly conducted, the exchange of ideas among peers can have an illuminating effect upon the mental pictures being developed. Questions in the students' minds can be brought up for class discussion and resolved.

Memorizing. After the concept begins to take form, the symbols identifying the concept itself should be introduced, and the process of *memorization,* the third step, begins. If the concept has been well developed in the two preceding steps, memorization of essential terms will proceed without difficulty. Usually this step occupies little time and takes place simultaneously with the development and expansion of the concept.

Applying. The fourth step, *application,* poses particular problems because in many cases, the classroom does not provide a satisfactory setting for the practical application of the concept. For

[14]*Ibid.*, pp. 209–210.

this reason, the practical effect that comes from functional use will have to take place largely outside the school. This immediately raises a problem, because it is impossible for the teacher to know all that takes place in the out-of-school life of his students.

Steps Applied

Relating the preceding four steps to the development of a concept in auto mechanics will illustrate their usefulness. The concept to be taught: *The gasoline engine carburetor is a mechanical device that mixes gasoline and air in the proper proportions for combustion within the cylinder.*

Showing. In a basic course in high-school auto mechanics, Mr. Dodd, the instructor, asked the boys in his class to gather around him. After he was sure he had their attention, he picked up a carburetor that had been removed from an automobile in the shop and held it in a position so that all could see it without difficulty.

The various parts of the device were explained slowly and painstakingly as the instructor pointed to them. Next, the parts of the carburetor were disassembled, and the interrelationship of the parts to the functioning of the entire device was discussed.

Discussing. Students were asked to take their seats in the classroom adjoining the shop. Mr. Dodd then pulled down a large cross-sectional diagram of a carburetor that graphically displayed its inner workings. He began to question students about the functions of various parts shown on the diagram. As each part was discussed, it was identified by name, and Mr. Dodd wrote each name on the board.

Generally, the students seemed to have the ideas clearly established. When minor errors occurred, other students in the class were asked to make the corrections. Four of the less gifted boys had some difficulty in relating the carburetor to the explosion within the cylinder. One of the more alert boys was asked to clarify this relationship for them.

Students were encouraged to ask questions that were puzzling them. At least ten such questions helped clear up minor details about the carburetor.

Memorizing. Inasmuch as the symbols (names) had been related to each part of the carburetor as it was discussed, the association of concepts and symbols had already been fairly well established in the thinking of class members. The teacher now asked for an oral explanation of each of the terms listed on the board:

Carburetor	Air Cleaner
Float	Auxiliary Air Inlet Valve
Needle Valve	Mixture
Mixing Chamber	Throttle Valve
Spraying Nozzle	Cylinder

A few of the boys had some difficulty in explaining the functions of the engine and carburetor parts, and the teacher promised to give them individual help after class. Mr. Dodd gave a descriptive oral account of the function of each part without mentioning it by name, and each student was asked to write the name of the part on a separate sheet of paper.

No further general class attention was focused on the memorization of terms except when students were having difficulty using the symbols properly.

Applying. The evidence of the students' comprehension of the carburetor and its function was found in the days ahead. Day after day the teacher observed and evaluated the work of students as they tore down and reassembled automobile parts. Determining whether students really understood the carburetor was relatively easy under the practical and controlled conditions of the shop.

When he noted mistakes in the use of the carburetor, Mr. Dodd corrected them, reteaching as he did so. He was also aware from past experience and current student conversation that there was considerable practical use of the carburetor in out-of-class situations.

The Teaching of Skills

Although the teaching of skills has much in common with the teaching of concepts, essential differences in procedures should be noted. The acquiring of motor skills is best accomplished if the instructor makes sure that the learner:

1. Acquires a clear mental picture of the skill involved.
2. Practices the skill under competent supervision until the desired level of proficiency has been achieved.

Examples of motor skills in the process of being learned will illustrate these two processes.

MISS SIMONSEN TEACHES TYPING SKILLS

The beginning typing class was confronted with the task of learning to manipulate the keys of the typewriter with some degree of accuracy. Miss Simonsen, the instructor, properly identified the type of learning involved as that of a motor skill, knowing that the procedures to be used were dictated by the type of learning involved.

Acquiring the Concept. Miss Simonsen first directed the attention of the class to a large colored chart that provided a pictorial representation of the keyboard with the keys identified by letter. An outline of the two hands was superimposed upon the keyboard to indicate that certain fingers were to rest on certain keys.

When each student was seated before a typewriter with blank keys, the instructor said, "Please place your fingers on the second row of keys exactly as seen on the chart." Students attempted to comply, but some of them had minor difficulties that the teacher soon corrected as she circulated among the class members.

"Now, press the key with the little finger of the left hand." Students complied. "Note that this finger controls the letter *a*. Now, press the key with the third finger of the left hand." Again students did as directed. "You will notice that this finger controls the letter *s*."

Each key and its controlling finger were identified in a similar fashion. Students stroked the key and noted the resulting letter. The teacher pointed out by means of the chart that it was not necessary to watch the keyboard if fingers were placed on the proper "home" keys.

Students were now encouraged to press each key, being sure to keep the fingers in the proper position while observing only the chart on the wall. Soon, a mental picture of the home keys and the position of the fingers on these keys began to take shape.

Practice. The development of proficiency in the use of these keys was yet another matter. In the following days Miss Simonsen assigned simple exercises involving the use of the home keys. Whenever she noted improper hand position in relationship to these keys, she was quick to correct it. If a problem proved to be of general concern, she stopped the class and commented on the nature of the difficulty.

SAMMY LEARNS A MUSICAL SKILL

As a first-year band student, Sammy Whipple had no experience in playing the trumpet when the school year began. According to his teacher the first skill he would have to develop would be that of *producing a consistent, sustained tone on his instrument.*

Acquiring the Concept. The first task was to provide Sammy with a clear mental picture of how to produce the desired tone. By way of illustration, the teacher first held the mouthpiece against his own lips, explaining why it was best to hold it in the center of his lips and why it was necessary to have certain lip tension. By means of a wall chart he next showed Sammy the position of the tongue while blowing the note.

Practice. The teacher now asked Sammy to put into practice what he had learned by blowing a clear, sustained tone. His first trial proved to be relatively fruitless, but the instructor gave him certain hints about how to improve the tone. Gradually, with the specific criticism of his instructor and consistent practice for a week, Sammy was able to produce a consistent, sustained tone on his instrument.

The Teaching of Memorization

Memorization takes place most efficiently and is retained longer when consideration is given to these two essential steps:[15]

1. The learner needs to understand the meaning of what is to be memorized.

---

[15]Charles E. Skinner, (ed.), *Educational Psychology*, 4th ed. (Englewood Cliffs, N.J.: Prentice-Hall, 1959), pp. 518–519, stresses the necessity for meaningful memorization but also gives examples of desirable rote memorization.

2. The learner needs to drill on whatever is to be memorized until the desired level of memorization has been achieved.

Specific examples will illustrate the usefulness of these steps.

MR. BUSKIN TEACHES ABOUT A RADIO CONTROL PANEL

While Mr. Buskin's twelfth-grade English class was studying a unit on communication, students were faced with the need for knowing about the various parts of the radio control panel. Because of the nontechnical nature of the course, however, the students did not need to learn the functions of all the knobs on the panel; an acquaintance with six of the key ones would be sufficient.

Acquiring the Concept. During a field trip to the local radio station, the engineer explained in easily understood language the locations, functions, and names of the various control devices on the panel. The instructor then asked that information and names relative to the six key devices be repeated. Afterward students were encouraged to ask any questions about the control panel and the six devices in particular that they felt would be beneficial. Students were asked to make a diagrammatic sketch of the control panel, labeling the six major knobs.

Drill. The next day in class Mr. Buskin discovered that all the students knew the functions of the key control knobs and that all but four students could name the knobs correctly. A special drill on the names was assigned to the four students who were having difficulty. A brief check the following day revealed that two of the students had still not memorized the names of the knobs. Repeated drill was prescribed after the teacher checked again to be sure that these students really understood the functions of the knobs.

A typical violation of correct procedures for teaching memorization is reflected in a social science teacher's class.[16]

MR. PULVER TEACHES ABOUT THE CIVIL WAR

The eleventh-grade class was just beginning a unit on the Civil War. Mr. Pulver wrote twelve terms related to the Civil War on the board as follows:

Manassas	Jefferson Davis
Bull Run	Battle of Franklin
Gettysburg	Harpers Ferry
William T. Sherman	Emancipation Proclamation
Ulysses S. Grant	Robert E. Lee
Federalist	Appomattox

"You will memorize these words for tomorrow," he said. "They will help you a great deal in understanding the Civil War period."

During the class period that followed, a narrative background for the understanding of the period between 1860 and 1864 was laid, but only two of the terms listed on the board were mentioned.

---

[16]See Burton, *op. cit.*, pp. 90–94, for examples and a careful statement about the absurdity of the emphasis on isolated facts and verbalization.

It should have come as no surprise to this instructor that even the most conscientious students found considerable difficulty with the assignment because there was little or no context into which the names might logically fit. Recall would have been enhanced greatly if a series of properly interrelated and meaningful mental pictures had been provided before the memorization assignment was made.

The Teaching of Habits

The theory underlying the teaching of concepts, skills, and memorization is relatively uncomplicated, although the actual use of sound procedures to teach them is often violated. Similarly, the procedures that should be followed in forming a habit are relatively simple but often violated:[17]

1. The learner must perform without variation the specific behavior or act (usually a motor function) that it is hoped will become a habit.
2. He must continue to repeat the behavior time after time, until the performance no longer demands conscious attention.
3. He must find the habit satisfying but not necessarily pleasant.

Conversely, the breaking of an undesirable habit calls for the use of the same general procedure:

1. The learner must consciously avoid performing the habit he wishes to break.
2. He must persist in avoiding the habit until doing so no longer requires his conscious attention.
3. He must find the new form of behavior satisfying but not necessarily pleasant.

Difficulty in Forming Habits

The extreme difficulty encountered in forming or breaking habits is basically associated with the necessity for prolonged, invariable repetition. A majority of lay people and a substantial proportion of teachers are only vaguely aware of the reinforcing effect of repetition. Furthermore, a majority of people are unwilling to exert the effort necessary for desired habit formation.

More often than not, the interested observer in a well-organized classroom takes note of the orderliness with which classroom procedures move forward. What he frequently does not realize is that such orderliness is the result of well-established habits. When the teacher

---

[17]See John E. Horrocks, *The Psychology of Adolescence* (Boston: Houghton Mifflin Company, 1962), pp. 496–499, for a somewhat technical discussion of habit formation and its effect on behavior.

Woodruff, *op. cit.*, pp. 114–115 and 118–119, provides a clear picture of the steps involved in habit formation.

has helped the students form habits of correct classroom behavior that function at the subconscious level, he is then free to concentrate on the main task of promoting learning.

Neglected Classroom Habits

Teachers are often aware that the development of specific habits would be of great advantage to the teaching-learning process. Unfortunately, however, poor teachers as well as average teachers are sometimes characterized by a willingness to do little about habit formation. Although dozens of illustrations might be given, a few accounts will recall other neglected habits.

MISS SNOW NEGLECTS HABITS

When the tardy bell rang, several students were still talking in the hall. Only after Miss Snow went to the door did they move leisurely but noisily toward their seats.

The teacher started to call the roll aloud, but the hubbub in the class made it impossible for her to be heard. She became angry and her cheeks flushed with annoyance. After she had pounded the desk with a book, the noise subsided to a murmur, and she continued calling the roll.

MR. POWELL NEGLECTS HABITS

Mr. Powell announced, "We will now have a study period for the next twenty minutes."

Although the students had generally been orderly, they suddenly grew noisy. Two of the girls began to apply make-up and to comb their hair. Three boys in the back of the room tossed a ball of wadded paper back and forth. The "social hour" had begun, and there was a general exchange of conversational pleasantries.

Several students took advantage of the occasion to sharpen their pencils. They stood in line, waiting unhurriedly for their turns. Each student took ample time for the sharpening process.

Habits that serve the purposes of efficient instruction do not develop spontaneously; they must be encouraged through persistent effort on the part of a teacher who knows their value. Habits that promote poor classroom control can transform an instructionally useful classroom environment into one in which serious work is made difficult, as illustrated by the classes of Miss Snow and Mr. Powell.

The Teaching of Positive Tastes

To teach students how to develop a specific liking—positive taste or feeling—for a particular subject is a problem that confronts all teachers in varying degrees. As a general rule teachers should not attempt to teach positive tastes as such.[18] The reason for this is closely

[18]Inasmuch as the development of taste has to do with emotional reactions, it should not be confused with analysis or conceptual examination.

related to the nature of positive or negative tastes and how they are formed.[19]

As a concept begins to take form in the mind, the learner simultaneously appraises (either consciously or subconsciously) the effect of this concept upon his own welfare. If the effect is thought advantageous, the learner will have a positive feeling toward the concept. If the effect is thought disadvantageous, a negative feeling will result. The key, then, to the development of positive tastes lies in the teaching of clear concepts from which the learner draws his own conclusions about their value to him. A practical example involving the teaching of positive tastes should illuminate the preceding discussion.

MR. DAYHUFF CREATES A LIKING FOR MATHEMATICS

Andrew Dayhuff was greatly concerned that his eighth-grade general mathematics students should really like the subject. Repeated conversations with students, and parents as well, had indicated the distaste that many had for anything connected with mathematics. During the summer he took a course in educational psychology, which was laden with information about how likes and dislikes are formed.

When school began in the autumn, Mr. Dayhuff decided that he would simply avoid the "preachy" sales talks of earlier years. He had repeatedly told his students of the necessity for learning mathematics and how much it would be to their disadvantage if they did not have a thorough mastery of the subject. This year instead, he followed certain steps that he felt were psychologically sound:

1. He made sure that every student understood not only *how* each problem was worked but *why* it was worked a given way.
2. No student was permitted to move to more difficult problems without first satisfying the teacher that he understood the essential concepts on which they were based. Care was exercised to make sure that students who were somewhat slow in developing clear mental pictures did not feel social pressure from either the group or the teacher.
3. No attempt was made to sell students on the subject of mathematics.
4. Practical applications were pointed out repeatedly with respect to virtually every problem assigned or discussed.

The actual carrying out of the proposed steps was no simple task; this was especially true of the first two steps. Mr. Dayhuff discovered after the first six weeks of school that, in spite of concerted efforts, the bright students were far ahead of the less gifted ones, creating serious problems in motivation and classroom control.

During the eighth week an anonymous questionnaire administered to students corroborated what he had assumed—that the less gifted students were *liking* mathematics, many of them for the first time in their lives. Mr. Dayhuff concluded that it was because they were achieving success; they were really understanding *why* certain things took place in mathematics.

---

[19]See Woodruff, *op. cit.*, p. 212, for an enumeration of points with respect to the modification of values.

But what did the questionnaire reveal about the more gifted students? They liked mathematics, yet they wanted to move at a faster pace. Because the class was very large (thirty-eight students) the principal gave the teacher permission to work out a plan for homogeneously grouping the students according to measured mathematical ability and past achievement. The plan was put into effect during the second semester.

Toward the end of the second semester, Mr. Dayhuff again administered an anonymous questionnaire to all students of both classes. The questionnaire was designed to determine to what extent students had developed a *positive taste* (liking) for mathematics. Responses were most revealing. Among slower students, only three of twenty-two students indicated a dislike for mathematics. Students among the more gifted group responded similarly, with only two indicating a mild dislike.

The proportion of students with a positive taste for a given subject is directly related to the clarity of their concepts and their appraisal of these concepts as having particular personal value.

In the main, the teaching of tastes should be approached indirectly through the teaching of concepts, but under particular circumstances there is psychological justification for teaching tastes directly. In so-called appreciation courses, such as Music Appreciation or Art Appreciation, which occur with relative infrequency in the secondary curriculum, the concern of the course and of the teacher is the creation of a liking (a positive feeling) for course content. Although it is impossible to have a feeling independent of a related concept, the emphasis in these courses would be upon the feeling rather than upon the concept itself.

PROBLEMS FOR STUDY AND DISCUSSION

1. What are the most frequent difficulties in selecting and stating unit objectives? Which of these is most closely related to *your* personal weakness?
2. State a concept that might have been taken from a unit in tenth-grade biology. What makes it a concept? Explain.
3. List the types of objectives in the order of the frequency of their occurrence.
4. Which type of objective is found most frequently in your teaching major? Teaching minor?
5. Following the specific steps listed on page 62, list the concepts you hope to include in a brief four-day unit in your teaching major.
6. Do you feel there is justification for using different levels of memorization? Explain your reasoning.
7. Explain the relationship between comprehension and memorization.
8. Contrast the restricted definition of *skill* found in this chapter with the definition commonly assigned to it in everyday usage. Give an example of a skill under each definition. Which definition is more helpful in planning a unit? Why?

9. Divide the large skill of *playing baseball* into its major divisions and subdivisions.

10. Define *habit* in your own words. Now see whether you have incorporated in your definition the characteristics of a habit listed on page 68.

11. List the study habits that you feel are most frequently violated by senior high school students.

12. What is the basic question that a planner should ask himself as he ponders which procedure to use? Why?

13. What is the proper role of variety when considered in relationship to teaching-learning activities? Explain.

14. List in your own words the specific steps through which a learner should be directed to achieve a vivid, meaningful concept. Indicate exactly how this would be done in teaching the following concept to tenth-graders: *Scandinavia and West Germany have a high standard of living.*

15. List the particular problems involved in having students utilize learned concepts.

16. Tell exactly how you would teach the following concept in a class in Social Problems: *Racial strife is a nationwide problem in the urban centers of the United States.*

17. Assumption: As a homemaking teacher you have the responsibility for teaching seventh-grade girls how to hem a dress. Identify the types of learning involved. Tell exactly how you would go about teaching them.

18. Describe from your own experience as a high-school student one or more situations in which a teacher employed incorrect procedures in teaching memorization.

19. According to the discussion in this chapter, how would you break students of the habit of sharpening their pencils unnecessarily? Be specific.

20. What is the best procedure to follow in teaching a positive taste (liking) for history? Explain your point of view.

RECOMMENDED READINGS

Bigge, Morris L., and Maurice P. Hunt, *Psychological Foundations of Education.* New York: Harper & Brothers, 1962, Chapter 17 and pp. 429–433.

Bruner, Jerome S., *The Process of Education.* Cambridge, Mass.: Harvard University Press, 1960, Chapters 1, 2, and 4.

Burton, William H., *The Guidance of Learning Activities*, 3d. ed. New York: Appleton-Century-Crofts, Inc., 1962, Chapter 5 and pp. 65–66.

Burton, William H., Roland B. Kimball, and Richard L. Wing, *Education for Effective Thinking.* New York: Appleton-Century-Crofts, Inc., 1960, Chapters 4, 9, and 10.

Carter, William L., Carl W. Hansen, and Margaret G. McKim, *Learning to Teach in the Secondary School.* New York: The Macmillan Company, 1962, Chapter 6.

Grambs, Jean D., William J. Iverson, and Franklin K. Patterson, *Modern Methods in Secondary Education,* rev. ed. New York: The Dryden Press, 1958, Chapter 6.

Hansen, Kenneth H., *High School Teaching.* Englewood Cliffs, N.J.: Prentice-Hall, Inc., 1957, Chapters 5 and 6.

Horrocks, John E., *The Psychology of Adolescence,* 2d. ed. Boston: Houghton Mifflin Company, 1962, pp. 496–499.

Klausmeier, Herbert J., *Teaching in the Secondary School.* New York: Harper & Brothers, 1958, Chapter 3.

McDonald, Frederick J., *Educational Psychology.* San Francisco: Wadsworth Publishing Company, 1959, Chapters 5–9.

McGuire, Vincent, Robert B. Myers, and Charles L. Durrance, *Your Student Teaching in the Secondary School.* Boston: Allyn and Bacon, Inc., 1959, pp. 134–142 and 219–231.

McKean, Robert C., *Principles and Methods in Secondary Education.* Columbus, Ohio: Charles E. Merrill Books, Inc., 1962, Chapter 5.

Mills, Hubert H., and Harl R. Douglass, *Teaching in High School,* 2d. ed. New York: Ronald Press, 1957, Chapters 7 and 14; pp. 219–224.

Nordberg, H. Orville, James M. Bradfield, and William C. Odell, *Secondary School Training.* New York: The Macmillan Company, 1962, Chapters 3 and 5.

Rivlin, Harry N., *Teaching Adolescents in Secondary Schools,* 2d. ed. New York: Appleton-Century-Crofts, Inc., 1961, Chapters 3 and 4.

Woodruff, Asahel D., *Basic Concepts of Teaching; with Brief Readings.* San Francisco: Chandler Publishing Company, 1962, Chapters 4–9.

5

Organizing Activities for Unit Teaching

The premise "goal achievement is of primary concern and procedures are secondary" should not be construed to mean that procedures are unimportant. They are rather the vehicles that enable the student to reach desired educational goals. Activities (procedures) should be so organized within the unit that they perform this function with maximum efficiency.

Conscientious educators have consistently sought a pattern within which unit activities could be meaningfully grouped, and in recent years they have tended to classify such activities under three headings: introductory activities, developmental activities, and concluding activities.[1] Although all unit activities are basically goal-related, such differentiation encourages planners to consider the essential characteristics of each classification.

INTRODUCTORY ACTIVITIES

Introductory activities are designed to *set the stage* so that the learning of unit objectives can move forward with optimum effectiveness.[2] Their common purpose is *not* to make a direct contribution

[1]Four examples of teaching units in which the three types of unit activities are employed are presented in M. L. Goetting, *Teaching in the Secondary School* (New York: Prentice-Hall, 1942), Chapter 20.

[2]Herbert J. Klausmeier, *Teaching in the Secondary School* (New York: Harper & Brothers, 1958), Chapter 7, discusses introductory activities and gives several practical examples.

to the achievement of unit goals (although this frequently is one of the side effects of well-planned introductory activities); rather, their main purpose is to expose students to the nature and content of the unit in order to awaken an intense and abiding interest.

Sound Activities

Specifically introductory activities follow this sequence:[3]

1. A highly motivating, interest-arousing activity related to the unit is conducted in the classroom.[4]
2. A brief but interesting talk indicating the significance of the unit is given by the teacher.
3. The possible objectives of the unit are examined.
   a. Students are exposed to possible objectives previously identified by the teacher.
   b. Students react to the teacher's suggestions and give some of their own.[5]
   c. Under the teacher's direction, students and teacher modify objectives and determine which are worthy of pursuit.
   d. Students are encouraged to determine how each adopted unit objective is of personal value to themselves.
4. The possible activities suitable for the achievement of stated objectives are discussed.
   a. Students are exposed to possible activities previously identified by the teacher.
   b. Students react to the teacher's suggestions and make additional ones.[6]
   c. Under the teacher's direction, students and teacher determine which activities are best suited to goal achievement.
   d. The role that each student will play in the stated activities is determined.

---

[3]See Harry N. Rivlin, *Teaching Adolescents in Secondary Schools*, 2d. ed. (New York: Appleton-Century-Crofts, 1961), pp. 118–123, for a detailed discussion of how a unit of work is initiated.

Vincent McGuire, Robert B. Myers, and Charles L. Durrance, *Your Student Teaching in the Secondary School* (Boston: Allyn and Bacon, 1959), pp. 134–138, present questions to be considered before completing final introductory plans.

[4]Klausmeier, *op. cit.*, pp. 190–193, views the establishment of a "favorable emotional atmosphere" as an essential concern of introductory activities.

[5]Students should be involved in helping determine unit objectives and procedures. The degree of their involvement should be determined by the teacher on the basis of such factors as maturity of students, history of success or lack of success in similar situations, willingness and desire of students to make useful contributions, and classroom control.

William H. Burton, *The Guidance of Learning Activities*, 3d. ed. (New York: Appleton-Century-Crofts, 1962), pp. 357–362, provides suggestions on student participation in planning.

[6]With respect to the selection of procedures, students may be allowed considerable freedom as long as objectives are matched with psychologically sound activities.

An example will illustrate the use of the above sequence in the introductory activities of a biology unit.

MR. SPEARS INTRODUCES A UNIT ON "FAMILIAR PLANTS"

1. Mr. Spears asked the students to gather around his desk so that they could observe with ease the oversized model of two plants—a sunflower and a rose. "After you have examined these models from all angles for at least five minutes," he said, "I want you to list several characteristics that make the sunflower different from the rose."
   a. Afterward, the teacher asked several students to read their lists aloud. Lists were compared, and the teacher wrote the differentiating characteristics on the board.
   b. Class attention was now directed to the large bulletin board that had been prepared during the past two days by three volunteers. It consisted of a variety of large pictures of roses and sunflowers, taken from various angles. Using a pointer, the teacher related the qualities of the sunflower to the characteristics on the chalkboard.
2. During the next few minutes Mr. Spears explained in very general terms the nature of the total unit, focusing attention on the particular importance of plants to the welfare of man.
3. The understandings and information that the teacher and the students hoped to gain from the unit were discussed.
   a. The teacher wrote on the board the basic concepts he felt should emerge from a careful study of the unit.[7]
   b. Students were encouraged to react openly to the teacher's list. Explanations were made as he sensed student insecurities. Students were now asked to make their own suggestions, and when they differed from those of the teacher, they were listed on the chalkboard.
   c. During a class discussion the essential elements of the student objectives and teacher objectives were combined or resolved. When there were strong differences of opinion, the teacher patiently listened to objections and calmly explained his own point of view. After considerable discussion, the final unit goals, acceptable to all, bore a remarkable similarity to those the teacher had preplanned.
   d. "Now," said Mr. Spears, "will you please list, on a clean sheet of paper to be handed in tomorrow, how the achievement of these goals will be of *personal* value to you."
4. The students and instructor then talked through the possible activities that might be employed in achieving the adopted goals.
   a. The teacher told of several interesting activities that he felt would lead to an understanding of the concepts (goals) sought.[8] These were listed on the chalkboard.
   b. Students were asked how they felt about the teacher's proposed activities; honest objections were solicited. Students were then encouraged to make their own suggestions. These were written on the chalkboard, and the class compared the two lists.

---

[7]These concepts had been very carefully worked out in a preplanned unit after careful consideration of the known composition of the class.

[8]Although he did not mention this to the class, the teacher was careful to relate each objective to correct procedures. Within the framework of sound psychological principles, he allowed students considerable freedom in the selection of activities.

c. After much discussion the students and teacher determined which activities would be followed. These activities were listed on the chalkboard and related to specific objectives.
d. Each student was asked to think through briefly how each activity would personally involve him. There was a general exchange of ideas on this point.

In situations where unit content or procedures are fixed by law or administrative policy, there is little justification for going through the motions of "democratic selection." Furthermore, although a few teachers use democratic classroom procedures extensively, a substantial number of teachers allow students only a limited voice in determining either unit objectives or procedures. The psychological soundness of permitting students a limited voice in such matters has been both questioned and supported by educators holding different philosophical points of view. Many teachers, however, have taught with remarkable effectiveness under circumstances in which content as well as activities have been viewed as the province of the teacher and the school administration.

In the introductory activities of the "sunflower and roses" unit, for instance, one notes a measure of liberality in permitting students a rather strong voice in the determination of objectives and activities. Classroom behavior may be in danger unless the teacher can direct and control this strong student voice.

Where unit objectives and activities have been predetermined, introductory activities may be focused on arousing interest and motivation. This is the case with the introductory activities taken from a unit planned for use in an eighth-grade class in health.

INTRODUCING A UNIT ON "ALCOHOL AND TOBACCO"

1. On the opening day of the unit, students will bring news stories and pictures about alcohol and its use for display on the class bulletin board.
   a. The teacher will read and discuss a few of the more relevant and interesting items for class benefit.
   b. After school a committee of students will arrange the clippings neatly on the bulletin board.
2. The day before the opening of the unit, students will be assigned the responsibility for counting the number of pages of advertising on alcohol and tobacco in several popular magazines and the number of television commercials on alcohol and tobacco seen in one evening during specified hours. Reports of individual surveys will be sampled briefly in class and written on the chalkboard.
3. The Blufftown Chief of Police will give a fifteen-minute talk on "My Experiences with People Who Drink and Drive." Students will be encouraged to ask him questions.
4. A ten-minute Coronet film, "Alcohol and Tobacco: What They Do to Our Bodies," will be shown. Students will be told what to look for before the showing, and afterward they will discuss the film briefly.

5. The teacher will write the predetermined course objectives on the board.
   a. The teacher will discuss the objectives and their relationship to individual student needs.
   b. Related general procedures will also be listed and discussed by the teacher.
   c. Students will be encouraged to ask questions concerning objectives, activities, or any other aspect of the unit.

Variation in Planning

There will, of course, be a high degree of variation in the planning of activities. "Some of the activities will be predetermined by the teacher; some of them determined during the planning stage by teacher-pupil planning; and some determined as the work progresses."[9] This is true for all subject areas and for all teachers.

The introductory activities of the preceding unit on "Alcohol and Tobacco" clearly reflect the work of a conservative planner who feels that his function is to place unit objectives and activities ready-made into the hands of his students. Grambs, Iverson, and Patterson, on the other hand, place considerable emphasis on student participation in unit initiation. Exhibiting their preference for the experience unit, these writers suggest that introductory activities focus on the following key steps:[10]

1. Preliminary realistic diagnosis by the teacher of (a) curriculum requirements and (b) student interests, capacities, needs, and developmental tasks.
2. Tentative selection by the teacher of possible significant problems or areas of learning geared to the preliminary diagnosis.
3. Tentative preplanning by the teacher to clarify for himself the ways in which possible problems and areas may be approached most effectively.
4. Open, direct, and stimulating discussion with the class designed to involve them in further diagnosis and choice of a problem or area for further study in planning.
5. Sufficient preliminary exploration with the class to ensure that all students understand the *why* and *what* of the unit enterprise finally chosen.
6. Use of special materials, films, and activities (such as field trips) that will both clarify understanding of the unit problem and focus interest upon it.
7. Development of teacher-student plans adequate for the effective completion of the unit.

Basic Purposes

The teacher must remember that the basic purposes of activities in introducing a new unit are to:

---

[9]Kenneth H. Hansen, *High School Teaching* (Englewood Cliffs, N.J.: Prentice-Hall, 1957), p. 156.

[10]Jean D. Grambs, William J. Iverson, and Franklin K. Patterson, *Modern Methods in Secondary Education*, rev. ed. (New York: The Dryden Press, 1958), pp. 131–132.

1. Arouse student interest in unit content.
2. Relate unit content to the needs of individual students.
3. Acquaint students with the significance of unit content.
4. Identify and interpret objectives.
5. Select sound procedures for the attainment of objectives.
6. Determine where students stand with respect to the acquisition of unit content.

It is of secondary concern whether the procedures involved in meeting these criteria are largely permissive or largely directive. It is of primary importance, however, that these goals be given careful consideration so that the classroom environment will promote the proper conduct of the developmental activities to follow.

Meeting Interests

In order to accomplish these stage-setting tasks, introductory procedures should take into consideration the general and special interests of the group to be taught. A resource speaker whose vocabulary level far exceeds that of the students being addressed fails to communicate; as a result he does little to further student motivation.

Avoiding Stereotypes

In planning introductory activities, the teacher should attempt to find a fresh, vital approach to the material. The teacher's lecture often fails to elicit interest because it is part of the everyday instructional diet of students. For the same reason, discussions in the social studies class soon become old hat and, consequently, are not useful as introductory activities.

Relating Objectives to Experiences

Students can understand unit objectives only when these objectives are related to their own backgrounds. If the students lack essential experiences, they will fail to catch the excitement the unit affords. If this is generally true of the students, unit goals more in keeping with their backgrounds should be sought, or those experiences must be provided as a part of the unit so that the students will be able to approach the objectives with understanding.

Stressing Vividness

Introductory activities should be so striking and vivid that the students will want to identify themselves with the new unit's major purposes. A boy who has watched a space flight, or a film of it, on television is likely to be interested in rockets, thrust, space capsules, and space travel.

Preparing the Room

The physical preparation of the room plays an important part in beginning the unit because it stimulates student interest. An attractive bulletin board may start the unit on a positive note; different seating arrangements are often helpful.

In addition, special equipment and displays possess the potential for motivating students. Use of individually prepared verb charts for foreign-language classes, oversized slide rules for mathematics classes, and large single-purpose maps of troublesome spots on the globe for a social problems class serve this purpose. Even the commonplace chalkboard may be used in a new way to get the unit off to a good start. In the history or literature class, for example, a neatly printed time line may be placed at the top of or immediately above the chalkboard to lend emphasis to the chronology of important events. The hidden chalkboard method, which calls for keeping the written material covered to enhance the surprise effect, can likewise be used to good advantage.

Relating Units to the Overall Plan

At times students fail to see the relationship between the various units of the overall plan. Thus, at the beginning of each new unit, its place in the total sequence of units must be pointed out to the learner so he will realize that the present unit is closely related to the preceding and following units.

Using Diagnostic Devices

The use of diagnostic devices is viewed by certain writers as an essential initiatory procedure.[11] The diagnostic device may take the form of a formal objective test, an informal written test, a class discussion, or even a game. Many subjects and units, however, would suffer through frequent use of diagnostic procedures. In a mathematics class, for example, if the teacher corrects student papers submitted at two- or three-day intervals, he is, in effect, conducting a continuing diagnosis; no further formalization of the diagnostic process is necessary.

Unsound Activities

The use of second best, unstimulating introductory activities gets many units off to a poor start. As a result students approach the study of such units with apathy, and sometimes they feel such units will be unavoidable drudgery. An examination of the unchallenging beginning activities for two units will illustrate this point. The following introductory activities were taken from a three-week unit on "Reptiles," prepared by the teacher of a tenth-grade biology class.

---

[11]See Hubert H. Mills and Harl R. Douglass, *Teaching in High School,* 2d. ed. (New York: Ronald Press, 1957), p. 235.

1. On the first day of the unit, the teacher will pass out a sheet of paper listing general activities.

2. Students will be asked to examine newspapers to discover articles of current interest concerning reptiles.

These two activities obviously fall far short of fulfilling the requirements of introductory activities as listed on page 90:

1. There is little about either activity that would tend to stimulate interest, although the assignment to examine newspaper articles concerning reptiles points meekly in this direction. If this assignment were made two days before the beginning of the unit, its timing would be much better.
   a. Asking students to bring articles, pictures, or life specimens of the reptile class on the opening day of the unit would create specific interest.
   b. A carefully constructed bulletin board prepared by students under the direction of the teacher would elicit desired attention.
   c. A well-chosen, brief film might serve as a useful interest arouser.
2. No attempt is made to indicate to students the importance of the unit or to relate it to other units in the course.
3. The important consideration of unit objectives is totally neglected.
   a. The students are given no idea of the direction of the unit.
   b. No mention is made as to how these objectives relate to the personal values of students.
4. Activities are mentioned in a rather general way without relating them to unit goals or trying to involve the students.

Many of the same deficiencies can be observed in the proposed activities designed to introduce a ninth-grade unit on "Building Your Vocabulary":

1. A bulletin board will be prepared by the teacher to point out the need for a constantly expanding vocabulary.

2. A vocabulary test will be given to the class.

3. Students will be told that this unit is supposed to (a) increase their vocabularies, (b) clarify the meaning of words already known, and (c) help them use words to their best advantage.

These activities will fail to accomplish what well-organized introductory activities should accomplish. Some of the reasons for this failure are evident:[12]

---

[12]Appendix B provides a series of questions that should be considered in the preparation of introductory activities. See questions 42–50 on page 552.

1. Although the bulletin-board display might well serve as an interest arouser, the description of its proposed content is too meager to serve as a useful guide. The planning is incomplete; it would be necessary to complete the details before the plan would be of practical assistance.
   a. Tape-recorded examples of actual ninth-grade student conversations in which limited vocabularies are obvious might well be interesting and pointed as well as vivid.
   b. A general assignment in which students are asked to listen to the vocabulary strengths and weaknesses of their own peers could serve much the same purpose. Brief reports of their findings might be given in class on the first day of the unit.
2. The teacher makes no attempt to tell students of the importance of vocabulary development or to relate this unit to other units of the course.
3. Objectives of the unit are only vaguely hinted at. Specific goals that are meaningful to students are not identified, and no attempt is made to involve students in the establishment of goals.
4. No mention is made of the important area of goal-related activities; this may well have a negative effect on student motivation.
5. A vocabulary test could serve a very useful purpose in diagnosing current student achievement, but, unfortunately, we are left to wonder what the test is and how it is to be administered.

Specific Suggestions

Any writer who makes definite recommendations without an exact knowledge of the details of the situations to which they might apply invites the possibility of considerable error. For this reason many of the recommendations and cautions throughout the book appear in the form of protective generalizations that have wide application. The specific help that such generalizations may provide for the inexperienced teacher, however, may be open to question, since many teachers find it difficult to apply theory to actual classroom situations.

Planners who wish to make the most effective use of introductory activities will find it helpful to examine the suggestions of competent teachers who have identified their own strengths and weaknesses in the use of such activities. A majority of the proposals listed here are positive recommendations, but several cautions are also included.

Recommendations

1. Gear interest-arousing activities to the specific level of the

group being taught. It is well to remember that what interests one section of a given grade may not interest another.

2. Avoid the commonplace, the usual, the anticipated activity. This is especially important for those introductory activities that are mainly concerned with arousing interest. If a teacher has a tendency to use one particular procedure more frequently than others, he should avoid its use during the introductory phase of the unit.

3. Efficiently conducted and interpreted diagnostic testing will enable the teacher to plan realistically.

4. Be certain that students understand the objectives of the unit in terms of their individual experiences and backgrounds. Remember that when students are permitted to participate, they tend to establish objectives that they feel are attainable. What they assume to be attainable is related, in turn, to their previous experiences.

5. The extent to which students can be and should be involved in the planning of objectives varies greatly with the composition of the class being taught. Intelligent, well-behaved, mature, and largely self-directive students can be permitted a large measure of choice of objectives under the direction of the teacher. Those students, however, who lack maturity, capacity, self-direction, and the essential elements of classroom control may be incapable of making effective contributions to unit planning. In a large number of cases they will feel more comfortable if the teacher directs them in the identification of objectives.

6. Introductory activities should be so interesting and so attractive to students that they will want to identify themselves with the content of the unit. This identification involves a personal as well as a group acceptance of the values to be derived from the study of the unit.

7. Effective bulletin boards frequently add interest to the start of a unit. Timing, of course, is important in using this method, and the teacher must remember that, more frequently than not, his students should prepare bulletin boards under his supervision.

8. The rearrangement of flexible seating often serves a useful purpose in introducing a new unit.

9. Locating and bringing into the classroom reading materials, teaching devices, and special equipment are frequent steps in the initiation of a new unit. The assembly of maps, charts, and graphs is a basic concern, and the chalkboard is often used in a new and different way to get the unit off to an interesting start.

10. Certain activities may extend through the introductory, developmental, and concluding phases of the unit. When this is the case, they must, of course, be started during the introductory activities.

11. Inject enough detail into the written description of the introductory activities to avoid the need for later expansion or rewriting before the activities can be carried out. A sound question the

planner might ask himself is: "Could another equally well-trained teacher read my plans and understand them sufficiently well to be able to carry them out?"

12. By the time the introductory activities are completed, students should sense a strong need for acquiring the content of the unit.

13. By the end of the introductory phase of the unit, students should understand the proposed range and depth of coverage of unit content as well as its significance.

Cautions

1. Don't make the introductory activities too long. Although the proportion of the unit time spent on introductory activities varies a great deal, it generally occupies about one tenth of the total.

2. Don't fail to examine the introductory activities of similar units for ideas that might be incorporated into your own.

3. Don't fail to use variety in your introductory activities.

4. Don't fail to differentiate clearly in your own planning between teacher activities, student activities, and activities that involve both.

5. Don't fail to arrange introductory activities in the most helpful sequence.

DEVELOPMENTAL ACTIVITIES

After the introductory activities have been successfully carried out, the teacher must focus class attention on the developmental activities. The major purpose of *developmental activities*[13] is to achieve the goals established during the preplanning and initiatory stages of the unit.[14] As the name implies, their chief concern is with the *development* of concepts, skills, and habits as well as with the memorization of related terms. So important are these activities that they usually occupy about four fifths of the unit time.

Sound Activities

In well-organized units developmental activities are characterized by the following:[15]

---

[13]Many examples of the use of developmental activities in unit plans are found in Chapter 7 and in Appendix A.

[14]Stressing the necessity for teacher-pupil planning, Grambs, Iverson, and Patterson, *op. cit.*, pp. 134–135, provide specific suggestions about developmental activities.

[15]Klausmeier, *op. cit.*, Chapter 8, focuses attention on developmental activities. Brief weekly descriptions of several units are provided together with a discussion of the essential characteristics of developmental activities.

Two examples of unit objectives and related activities are provided by McGuire, Myers, and Durrance, *op. cit.*, pp. 138–141.

1. The activities reflect the type of objective sought (concept, skill, memorization, or habit). The learning of a concept, for example, requires that the learner proceed through a series of steps quite different from those required for learning a habit.

2. The activities may consist of a wide variety of procedures,[16] but *all* procedures must be appropriate to the type of objective sought.

3. The activities are designed to help the learner achieve objectives through a step-by-step (inductive) progression. Activities, then, are arranged in a sequence that will provide for a gradual unfolding of concepts. Each succeeding experience aimed toward a given goal expands the concept or further develops the skill or habit.

4. Properly organized developmental activities are always directed toward a specific goal. Loosely organized activities reflect the uncertainty of the planner regarding the direction he should take.

5. The activities are planned, for the most part, in considerable detail.[17] This is particularly important for the beginning teacher.

6. The activities continuously motivate the students. Loss of student interest in the middle of a unit can prevent goal achievement.

7. Teacher ingenuity gives rise to a procedure or a combination of procedures that is, in some respects, different from any previously known to the teacher.

8. Flexibility is built into the timing of developmental activities to accommodate unforeseen accelerations or slowdowns.

The foregoing characteristics can be seen in the following examples of developmental activities.[18]

DEVELOPING A UNIT ON WORLD WAR I

In an eleventh-grade history unit on "America and World War I," developmental activities were as follows:

Concepts (Objectives) to Be Developed	*Activities Related to Objectives*[19]
1. Although the United States tried to remain neutral, the country was forced into World War I. a. The United States joined the World Peace Movement.	The instructor will pick a panel of six students to represent the Hague Permanent Court of Arbitration. The instructor and the panel will decide beforehand which students will play

[16]Traditional planners who tend to restrict learning activities to a few types will profit by reading the extensive list prepared by Lois C. Mossman, *The Activity Concept* (New York: Macmillan, 1938), pp. 54–55.

[17]It is the belief of the author that a thoroughly planned unit eliminates the necessity for detail in the daily lesson plan.

[18]See Rivlin, *op. cit.*, pp. 123–139, for other examples of how specific developmental activities are carried out.

[19]The column arrangement is used here to dramatize the necessary one-to-one relationship between objectives and activities. As a general rule, the author prefers that the objectives and related activities of the unit be treated in different sections. See the examples provided in Chapter 7 and in Appendix A.

1) Roosevelt won the Nobel Peace Prize for mediating international disputes.
2) Root and Bryan arbitrated many treaties.

which roles.[20] Four of them will represent nations that have disputes, one will be a justice of the Supreme Court, and the other one will be Roosevelt, Root, or Bryan. The students will act out as best they can how disputes may have been arbitrated by one of the above mentioned Americans. This role playing should take no more than fifteen minutes. The instructor will then discuss the material on the World Peace Movement covered in the text.

b. In 1914 war engulfed Europe.
   1) Imperialism, nationalism, militarism, and alliances were the underlying causes of World War I.
   2) War started when Austria-Hungary declared war on Serbia.

Maps will be employed to show the political boundaries as they were in 1914. The teacher will then explain how the Central Powers and Allied Powers developed their alliances.

c. The United States tried to remain neutral.
   1) Wilson urged Americans to be neutral.
   2) The majority of the Americans sided with the Allies.
   3) The British interfered with our trade to Europe.
   4) German submarine warfare and the sinking of the *Lusitania* angered Americans.
   5) Wilson advocated a build-up of arms.
   6) Wilson tried in vain to negotiate a peaceful settlement of the war.

The instructor will discuss with the students the question of neutrality. He will use the example of thugs beating up an innocent victim while a bystander passively watches. The teacher will ask for student feelings on the subject.

d. The United States declared war on the Central Powers.
   1) Early in 1917 the Germans stepped up their submarine warfare.
   2) The Zimmerman Note and the sinking of American ships forced the Americans to change neutralist policies.
   3) On April 6, 1917, war was declared against the Central Powers.

Students will be asked to tell what they know about submarine warfare. The instructor will then explain why German submarine warfare and the Zimmerman Note changed Wilson's outlook on neutrality.

---

[20]There may be reason for doubting the practicality of this activity in view of its nature and the strong student involvement.

DEVELOPING A UNIT ON HEALTH

The following developmental activities were taken from a unit titled "The Human Body and Digestion" that was intended for a tenth-grade biology class.

Concepts (Objectives) to Be Developed	*Activities Related to Objectives*[21]
3. The body is divided into three cavities. a. The *cranial* cavity is in the head. b. The *thoracic* cavity is under the ribs in the chest region. c. The *abdominal* cavity is under the thoracic cavity; the diaphram separates the abdominal and thoracic cavities.	The teacher will sketch a human figure on the board and ask the class to tell where the three body cavities are located. The students probably will not be able to differentiate between the thoracic and abdominal cavities without help.
4. Humans have an endoskeleton made up of bone and cartilage.	Using a model of a human skeleton, the teacher will explain the term *endoskeleton* and the three uses of the skeleton.[22]
a. There are 206 bones in the body.	The teacher will ask for two or three guesses as to the number of bones in the skeleton model.
b. There are two types of cartilage in a baby's skeleton. 1) *Temporary* cartilage makes up a large part of the skeleton. 2) *Permanent* cartilage makes up the nose, outside ear, larynx, and trachea.	The teacher will point out the model's lack of nose and ears. The students will then be asked to feel their own nose and ears. What they feel is permanent cartilage.
c. The process of the temporary cartilage turning into bone is called *ossification.* 1) Ossification is the depositing of calcium phosphate and calcium carbonate in the cartilage to make it hard.	The teacher will display a large X ray of a baby, pointing out the bone area and the temporary cartilage. He will explain to the class that ossification turns this cartilage into bones and that broken bones grow together in the same way.

[21]These developmental activities were taken from the middle of a unit; thus, other activities both preceded and followed those used here for the purpose of illustration.

[22]Although all activities opposite the major objectives in step 4 tend to illuminate and clarify the basic concept that "humans have an endoskeleton made up of bone and cartilage," they are not necessarily matched with the sequential listing of subconcepts.

2) Ossification will continue throughout life. This is how broken bones heal.	The teacher will demonstrate the strength and hardness of an animal bone, formerly broken but properly healed, by hitting it with a rubber mallet.
d. Bones have several different parts. 1) The outer surface of a bone is the *periosteum.* 2) The main part of the bone has many channels called *Haversian Canals* that carry nourishment to the bone cells.	Using a cross-sectional chart of a human bone, the teacher will point out the periosteum and the Haversian Canals.
3) In the center of the bone are two types of marrow. a) Red marrow produces the red blood cells and also some white ones. b) Yellow marrow is usually inactive.	Animal bone marrow obtained through prior arrangement by a student will be shown to the class. The teacher will discuss the differences between red and yellow marrow.
e. The skeleton has three main purposes. 1) The skeleton supports and forms the body. 2) The skeleton provides for the attachment of muscles. 3) The skeleton protects organs.	The teacher will again use the skeleton model to review the purposes of the skeleton.

Recurring Activities

In order to avoid relisting activities that are repeated throughout the unit, many planners have found that it saves time to identify and list such procedures under a subheading within the general category of developmental activities. The types of activities that lend themselves to this treatment are illustrated in the "Recurring Activities" of a United States history unit:

1. Each week the instructor will give brief quizzes at the beginning of three of the five class periods. They will cover the five most important concepts treated by the textbook material assigned for that day. Students will correct their own papers, and the instructor will discuss any questions that may arise during the correction period. Tests will then be collected so that the instructor can record the grades.

2. Each week three new volunteers will be asked to plan and

assemble, under teacher supervision, a bulletin-board display related to the contents of the material to be covered in class during the week. Basic planning and related work will be done the week before the bulletin board is displayed. The display will be seen by class members on the first day of the unit.

3. On the days when quizzes are not given, students will give short oral reports during the first five minutes of the class. These spontaneous, informal reports will be related to outside reading for the preceding or current day. Students will be encouraged to read articles from periodicals and books other than the text.

4. With one or two exceptions, the last seven minutes of the class period will be devoted to a spirited teacher-led discussion related to the assignment for the following day.

5. During the course of the school year each student will have a chance to give a fifteen-minute report during one of the class periods. One such report will be given during this unit.

Also included as "Recurring Activities" may be procedures related to such routine as paper distribution, certain repetitive types of chalkboard work, and housekeeping details.

Unsound Activities

Developmental activities that are not effective frequently have one or more of the following characteristics:

1. They show little imagination on the part of the planner.
2. They lack a description of specific steps to be taken.
3. They are limited to two or three overused procedures.
4. They do not provide for a gradual unfolding of concepts.
5. They do not devote time to an activity in proportion to the benefit to be derived from it.
6. They are not practical for the class and the circumstances in which the activities must take place.
7. They do not maintain an appropriate balance among oral, written, and reading assignments; between first-hand and vicarious experiences; between long-range and short-range projects; between difficult and easy assignments; between teacher-centered and student-centered activities; and between individual and group work.
8. They fail to recognize the differentiation in assignments and teaching techniques needed to accommodate individual differences in students.
9. They bear little or no relationship to unit objectives.

Some of these deficiencies can be observed in the following brief excerpt taken from the developmental activities of a unit on "Speaking in Public":

Concepts (Objectives) to Be Developed	*Activities Related to Objectives*
1. An effective speaker captures his audience and keeps its interest.	Students will go over their speeches and cut out unnecessary sentences. The teacher will impress upon the class the idea that nothing ruins a speech more easily than a weak ending. Students will be encouraged to keep their voices loud and clear.

Several weaknesses in these unacceptable procedures may be pointed out:[23]

1. They are only vaguely related to the objective they are supposed to achieve.
2. They do not contain enough detail to provide a clear picture of what is to be done.
3. A gradual, sequential unfolding of related concepts is not accomplished. The objective might well be divided into subobjectives to which activities might be more easily related.
4. The activities show little evidence of teacher ingenuity.
5. No attention is given to the procedures of showing, telling, memorizing, and applying, which are essential to the teaching of concepts.[24]

Specific Suggestions

A number of specific recommendations may help the planner in selecting developmental activities.[25] These activities should:

1. Be appropriate to the maturity of the class for which they are intended.
2. Keep students aware of what has been accomplished and what remains to be done.
3. Be written out in considerable detail.
4. Be grouped, where practical, so that the approximate number of activities to be completed during a given day can be ascertained.
5. Indicate which activities are to be carried out by the teacher, which are to be the responsibility of the student, and which are to be joint responsibilities.
6. Conform to the steps appropriate to teaching the particular kind of objective—concept, skill, memorization, and habit.[26]

---

[23]Chapter 7 and Appendix A both contain examples of units in need of revision. An examination of the suggested changes in developmental activities in these two sections will prove profitable.

[24]See Chapter 4, pp. 74–76, for a discussion of the steps for teaching concepts.

[25]Hansen, *op. cit.*, Chapter 7, discusses a range of teaching procedures and their effect upon learning.

[26]See Chapter 4 for a complete discussion about relating correct procedures to a specific type of objective.

7. Be timed realistically in consideration of the total time available to the unit and of the value to be derived from a given activity.

8. Be described in terms of specific things to be done.

9. Keep the relationship between unit activities and unit objectives clearly established in the minds of students.

10. Be educationally sound as well as interesting.

11. Describe the preparation of the students or teacher essential to insuring the success of the activity.

12. Be flexible enough to accommodate unforeseen accelerations or slowdowns.

Certain suggestions with respect to the use of developmental activities apply to only a restricted number of units. A wide range of suggestions and possible activities should be considered, however, before the final selection is made. The unit planner might well ask himself these questions:

1. Have I provided for lengthy study periods where desirable?

2. Have I provided for appropriate use of group work?

3. After examining the results of the pretest, are students given a study guide to help them overcome deficiencies discovered through the test?

4. How desirable is it to use a wide range of procedures in this particular unit?

5. Does the unit provide for an appropriate amount of pupil activity?

6. Have I employed first-hand experiences where desirable?

7. When films, resource speakers, and special presentations are to be used in class, have I accurately indicated the time involved?

8. Have I made appropriate use of activities involving physical movement?

9. Have I planned unusual activities where they serve the best psychological and educational purposes?

10. Have I provided for guided self-activity?[27]

CONCLUDING ACTIVITIES

Concluding activities[28] are primarily designed to clinch basic unit concepts and skills. More frequently than not this is accomplished through procedures involving practical applications of what has been learned. Concluding activities occupy roughly one tenth of the time devoted to the unit. However, the proportion of time devoted to specific kinds of activities will vary greatly depending on the nature of the particular unit.

---

[27]Examples of the use of developmental activities in well-organized unit plans are found in Chapter 7 and in Appendix A.

[28]Mills and Douglass, *op. cit.*, pp. 250–251, briefly state the purposes of culminating activities and give several examples.

Sound Activities

Some commonly used concluding activities are:

1. Papers, themes, or articles
2. Exhibits of items made by students
3. Practical problems that call for the application of several unit concepts
4. Application of newly acquired unit generalizations to new situations
5. Written or oral summaries of the unit by the students or the teacher
6. A teacher-conducted review of basic concepts and important relationships developed during the unit
7. A class project extending throughout the total unit[29]
8. Field trips
9. Unit examinations
10. Movies
11. Resource speakers

These basic concluding activities may, of course, be modified, expanded, or combined for most effective use.

During the concluding (culminating) stage of the unit, activities should compel the students to interrelate the specific concepts they have acquired. As a result, concepts should be expanded, their meanings enlarged and stabilized. This, in turn, necessitates the use of procedures that will encourage this expansion of meaning. Concluding activities should effect a pulling-together of loose ends. Only a limited number of activities are suited to this task.

A ninth-grade general science unit proposes the use of a limited number of concluding activities over a three-day period.[30]

CONCLUDING A UNIT ON "THE AIR OF THE EARTH"

1. The students will make a field trip to the local weather bureau.
   a. The trip will be scheduled for the third period and will extend into a portion of the lunch period.
   b. Students will be asked to list questions and also to be on the lookout for examples or evidence of material already studied.
   c. Prior arrangements will be made so that students can observe a weather map being constructed.

[29]Occasionally an instructor selects a learning activity that extends throughout the introductory, developmental, and concluding phases of the unit. Such an activity may, therefore, be classified as belonging to any one or all three of the categories.

[30]Concluding activities, like developmental activities, must be directed toward goal achievement. Because of their nature, however, they are frequently concerned with an expansion and reinforcement of the overall unit concept. For this reason no attempt has been made to establish a one-to-one relationship between each activity and its related goal.

   d. Students will hear a weather report broadcast through the local radio station by Civil Aeronautics Administration personnel. Students have been listening to this daily broadcast for the past month.
   e. Before entering the bus for the fifteen-minute return trip, students will be handed a short list of questions designed to encourage a synthesis of what they have just seen and to encourage a review for the unit test.
2. Blank weather maps will be distributed to the members of the class.
   a. Students will be asked to place on the map information taken from previously monitored weather broadcasts and from information obtained from the local weather station.
   b. After plotting this information in code symbols, the students will draw the isobars and thermobars as best they can.
   c. They will be asked to study the maps they have drawn. On the basis of their drawings and their experience with local weather, they will be asked to make a forecast for the next day and to predict what the weather instruments will indicate.
3. A final unit examination consisting of objective questions will be given.
   a. When the examination papers have been turned in, the teacher will distribute fresh copies of the same examination.
   b. Using this test as a guide, the teacher will give the correct responses and will answer any student questions concerning the test.

Assuming that these activities are well conducted, one can easily visualize their clinching effect on unit concepts. Furthermore, such activities encourage the students to interrelate concepts and apply them in a meaningful situation.

During the concluding activities of a four-week unit in a twelfth-grade homemaking class, the teacher emphasized the clinching of concepts through practical application. Four days were devoted to this phase of the unit.

CONCLUDING A CHILD-CARE UNIT

1. Students will take an eighty-minute field trip to the children's ward of the general hospital.
   a. Arrangements will be made to make the visit immediately following school. The girls can walk the two blocks to the hospital.
   b. The head nurse will conduct a tour of the ward, explaining the problems of child care and illustrating with specific children.
   c. Each student will prepare ahead of time three practical and relevant questions that she hopes to ask the nurse if time permits.
2. Students will observe for two hours in a day nursery where the children of working mothers are cared for.
   a. Class members will identify prior to the visit twelve specific points to look for.
   b. A short paper on their observations will be prepared for the next day.
3. Under the direction of the teacher, class members will organize and conduct a nursery class for two hours at the close of one school day.
   a. Children of various ages (including siblings) will be brought in.

   b. Girls will be responsible for conducting appropriate play activities for a child who is not of their own family.
   c. Experiences will be discussed in class on the following day.
4. At the beginning of the unit, each girl will be assigned to make a case study of one child.
   a. Specific information will be assembled and recorded on forms prescribed by the teacher.
   b. The case study will be culminated and handed in during the concluding phase of the unit.

Unsound Activities

Students are generally unaware that they have moved from the developmental to the concluding phase of the unit. There is little reason for concern with this lack of pupil sophistication, but when the teacher is unaware of the need for culminating, clinching activities, students may be denied a desirable summarizing experience. This is what happened during the final two days of a unit on the "Biology of Heredity."

MR. BLOCKER CONDUCTS A UNIT ON BIOLOGY

Mr. Blocker's class proceeded as usual. For the first fifteen minutes he lectured on the assignment the students were supposed to have read the previous evening, and for the next fifteen minutes he discussed certain facts that he said were contained in the assignment for tomorrow. The last twenty minutes of the period were devoted to a study period.

During the last two days of the unit the teacher talked about (a) the discovery of fossils that trace genetic lineage to present-day species, (b) how to trace genetic lineage by various means, (c) evidence that supports the doctrine of evolution, and (d) how present-day embryos are related to ancient embryonic stages. Believing in rigid conformity to a time schedule, he terminated the unit on Friday, March 14, with another short lecture and an equally brief test on the assignments of the past three days.

Mr. Blocker was quite unaware that the identification and use of appropriate concluding activities would have added interest, motivation, and sound learning to his well-entrenched routine. He might have considered any of the following possibilities: a carefully selected motion picture, a resource person—probably the geneticist from the local college, a series of study questions aimed at integrating unit content, brief summarizing reports by students, or a carefully prepared unit examination quite different from his typical quiz.

Equally uninspiring were the concluding activities selected by an eleventh-grade English teacher for the final fifty minutes of a unit on "The Values of Correct Theme Writing":

1. The teacher will review the grammar encountered in theme writing.

2. Previously corrected themes will be returned, and students will be permitted to read the teacher's criticisms during the class period.

Specific Suggestions

Careful consideration of these recommendations should reward the planner with improved teaching techniques and provide the student with more interesting experiences.[31]

1. Concluding activities, like introductory activities, should be of great interest to students.
2. They should consist of procedures that are markedly different from those to which the students have been exposed during the body of the unit.
3. Where possible, the students should in some way be brought into direct contact with the referent of the concept.
4. Students should be given the opportunity to make practical applications of the concepts learned.
5. Frequently students should be strongly involved in concluding activities through the use of brief reports, panel discussions, teacher-led discussions, and written exercises.
6. Important relationships between the basic concepts of the unit should be emphasized through new procedures.
7. As a general rule, concluding activities should consist of a range of activities, rather than merely one or two. Time limitations, however, may serve as a restriction.
8. Concluding activities that have been preplanned should be re-evaluated, with student assistance, during the introductory phase of the unit.

PROBLEMS FOR STUDY AND DISCUSSION

1. What is the basic reason for dividing unit activities into three categories?
2. Just how important to the success of the unit is the planning of activities? Explain your point of view.
3. List six specific purposes of introductory activities.
4. What is meant by the *preplanning* of a unit? Are there ever situations that do not involve preplanning? Explain.
5. In which phase of unit planning would you permit the most student participation: in the planning of objectives or in the planning of activities? Why?
6. Which types of introductory activities (field trip, resource speaker,

[31]Additional suggestions related to concluding activities may be derived from an examination of questions 62–73 of Appendix B, pp. 553–554.

movie, etc.) do you consider best suited to initiating a unit? List four activities in the order of their appropriateness to your teaching major. Why do you consider them particularly well suited?

7. Assumption: As an experienced teacher you have been assigned the responsibility of working with a new teacher in your subject-matter major. Because her greatest weakness lies in unit planning, you have decided to list several specific cautions about the planning of introductory activities. Which eight cautions would you list?

8. Should the developmental activity selected reflect the type of objective sought more accurately than the introductory activity? Explain your point of view.

9. Explain inductive progression and give one example taken from your minor field.

10. Give an example of developmental activities taken from your teaching major in which essential detail is lacking.

11. How far should the teacher go in attempting to provide varied activities? Discuss this within a psychological framework.

12. Give five examples of radically different but educationally sound procedures that you could use as developmental activities in teaching a unit in your minor field.

13. What is the purpose of listing recurring developmental activities separately? Give two examples of recurring activities not mentioned in this chapter.

14. Which unsound developmental activities are most likely to be used in your teaching field? Name three.

15. List five developmental activities that you would consider impractical for teaching students of a given grade in your subject-matter specialty.

16. According to this chapter, what is the fundamental purpose of concluding activities? Do you agree or disagree? Why?

17. List at least ten concluding activities that you might use successfully in teaching students of a specified grade in your teaching major.

18. List five concluding activities that would be appropriate in some other subject-matter areas but not in your teaching major or minor.

19. How would you go about selecting a concluding activity quite different from the activities you employed during the earlier sections of the unit? Explain.

20. Why is it better to involve students strongly in concluding activities rather than in developmental activities?

RECOMMENDED READINGS

Batchelder, Howard T., Maurice McGlasson, and Raleigh Schorling, *Student Teaching in Secondary Schools,* 4th ed. New York: McGraw-Hill Book Company, 1964, Chapter 7.

Burton, William H., *The Guidance of Learning Activities,* 3d. ed. New York: Appleton-Century-Crofts, Inc., 1962, Chapters 14 and 15.

Carter, William L., Carl W. Hansen, and Margaret G. McKim, *Learning to Teach in the Secondary School.* New York: The Macmillan Company, 1962, Chapter 6.

Goetting, M. L., *Teaching in the Secondary School.* New York: Prentice-Hall, Inc., 1942, Chapters 11, 16, 17, 18, and 20.

Grambs, Jean D., William J. Iverson, and Franklin K. Patterson, *Modern Methods in Secondary Education,* rev. ed. New York: The Dryden Press, 1958, Chapter 6.

Hansen, Kenneth H., *High School Teaching.* Englewood Cliffs, N.J.: Prentice-Hall, Inc., 1957, Chapters 6 and 7.

Klausmeier, Herbert J., *Teaching in the Secondary School.* New York: Harper & Brothers, 1958, Chapter 7.

McGuire, Vincent, Robert B. Myers, and Charles L. Durrance, *Your Student Teaching in the Secondary School.* Boston: Allyn and Bacon, Inc., 1959, Chapters 6 and 9.

McKean, Robert C., *Principles and Methods in Secondary Education.* Columbus, Ohio: Charles E. Merrill Books, Inc., 1962, Chapters 4 and 5.

Mills, Hubert H., and Harl R. Douglass, *Teaching in High School,* 2d. ed. New York: Ronald Press, 1957, Chapters 10, 11, and 14.

Nordberg, H. Orville, James M. Bradfield, and William C. Odell, *Secondary School Teaching.* New York: The Macmillan Company, 1962, Chapters 5 and 7.

Rivlin, Harry N., *Teaching Adolescents in Secondary Schools,* 2d. ed. New York: Appleton-Century-Crofts, Inc., 1961, Chapters 3 and 4.

Wiggins, Samuel P., *Successful High School Teaching.* Boston: Houghton Mifflin Company, 1958, Chapter 9.

Wiles, Kimball, *Teaching for Better Schools,* 2d. ed. Englewood Cliffs, N.J.: Prentice-Hall, Inc., 1959, Chapter 7.

6

Materials, Resources, and Evaluation in Unit Teaching

In the preparation of the unit the planner focuses his initial attention on unit goals. Only then can he realistically begin to single out the procedures that will help students reach these goals. But if there are only two fundamental concerns in unit planning—objectives and implementing procedures—where do teaching materials and evaluation fit into the planned program?

The function of teaching materials and evaluation is the same as that of general procedures—assisting in efficient movement toward desired goals. In reality the employment of materials, resources, and evaluation involves specific procedures (activities), and their use should be included in the description of unit activities.[1]

Because of the detail involved in the description of activities, many planners include only a token indication of the use of teaching materials and evaluation devices. When the written plans are translated into actual teaching-learning activities, however, teachers often discover that the teaching materials and resources as well as the evaluation procedures have neither been procured nor adequately accounted for. In order to avoid this, several writers have suggested the use of major unit headings such as "Materials and Resources" and "Evaluation Procedures," under which proper lists can be compiled during the planning stage. In order to relate these two headings to the other unit headings, it is desirable to recall the five basic unit divisions that demand the planner's attention:

---

[1]Chapter 7 and Appendix A contain descriptions of unit activities in which teaching materials and evaluation procedures are combined in sequential order with other activities.

I. Basic Information
II. Objectives
III. Activities
IV. Materials and Resources
V. Evaluation Procedures

This chapter will be concerned with the last two divisions.

MATERIALS AND RESOURCES

In order to make varied, interesting, and sound use of teaching materials and resources, teachers must understand their purposes, how they are classified, how they can be used most advantageously in teaching a specific subject, and how mistakes in their use can be avoided. Furthermore, teachers need to have a working acquaintance with essential principles related to the selection and use of materials and resources.

Purpose of Materials and Resources

MR. WANDLESS SHOWS A MOVIE

When the eighth-grade United States history class saw that the movie projector was in place and that the windows were darkened, they knew from past experience that the time for fun had arrived. The film and the misbehavior began together. Although the students looked at the picture most of the time, their viewing had little educational direction. By the time it was over, Mr. Wandless wondered whether the film had served any useful purpose at all.

MRS. STRANG ENCOURAGES DIFFICULT READING

Mrs. Strang believed that students should read a wide range of difficult materials not required by most teachers of tenth-grade English. She reasoned that the students were living in a highly competitive age in which knowledge of the technical and the difficult was essential to progress. She felt that students should encounter difficult reading in the classroom, and she thus gave little attention to differentiating instruction.

A RESOURCE SPEAKER ENCOUNTERS RUDENESS

Terry Bacon, a forest ranger, was invited to talk to Mrs. Walker's tenth-grade biology class, because he had a state-wide reputation for being able to communicate his vast knowledge about snakes to adolescent groups. Unfortunately his talk had been scheduled for the last twenty minutes of the period, just before the emotion-laden pep assembly that was to herald the football game with rival Southwest High School. Students were disinterested, unruly, and rude, and Mr. Bacon felt that he had lost his audience for the first time in several years.

The preceding examples tend to point up the basic problems of using teaching materials and resource persons in achieving unit goals. It is not sufficient that the materials and devices selected are potentially interesting to students; such materials and devices must move the students in the direction dictated by the established objectives. Furthermore, when such materials are employed, conditions must be controlled in order to encourage optimum learning.

Special teaching materials and resources have the potential of making both teaching and learning more interesting; however, this potential is often unfulfilled. Unless the teacher makes a careful appraisal of how the material or resource is to be used and of its effect upon pupil learning, he courts the danger of selecting an attractive activity for the sake of the activity alone.

Classification of Materials and Resources

The basic reason for the classification of teaching materials and resources is to help the unit planner quickly examine a range of possibilities in any one of several categories. The classification is not intended to be inclusive, but it should provide help in identifying aids most suitable for use in a specific classroom situation.

Audio Aids

Some of the audio aids most frequently used are the human voice, the radio, the record player, and the tape recorder. All of these are subject to frequent abuse as well as to correct usage.

The teacher who uses his voice effectively to serve the purposes of instruction has a marked advantage over his colleague who has never considered the voice an aid to learning. Variations in voice may be used to help create the excitement that results in student motivation, to arrest budding misbehavior, to provide the drama that creates a deep impression, to relieve student tensions, and to improve teacher-student relations.

A second audio aid, the record player, provides recorded music, drama, or speech of high quality. Too often beginning as well as seasoned teachers are unaware of the large number of disks currently available for teaching purposes. There are any number of well-organized catalogs listing current audio-visual materials.[2] In every

---

[2]Catalogs listing materials available in school, district, or regional repositories should prove to be of immediate help. Free and inexpensive teaching-material catalogs that serve a nation-wide range of users can also prove to be most rewarding. For this information see Walter A. Wittich, *Educators' Guide to Free Tapes, Scripts, and Transcriptions* (Randolph, Wis.: Educators' Progress Service, 1964), and John W. Diffor and Mary F. Horkheimer, *Educators' Guide to Free Films* (Randolph, Wis.: Educators' Progress Service, 1964).

The Educational Media Index (New York: McGraw-Hill Book Company, 1964), a fourteen-volume series, provides suggestions for the use of many materials in a wide range of subjects.

secondary school such catalogs should not only be made available but should be located so that their use is encouraged.

Because of extreme flexibility in the ways it can be used, the tape recorder has become one of the most popular teaching aids. It affords student or teacher the opportunity to record any sound that will serve an instructional purpose. This may be the recorded message of a public figure, the roar of an intercontinental missile as it streaks skyward, the talk of the high-school principal, or the first oral efforts of a beginning foreign-language student. Battery-operated recorders now make it unnecessary to have electric current readily available, and recent weight reductions make them easier to transport.

Visual Aids

Because 80 per cent of the learner's readily recalled information is the result of his visual perception,[3] the unit planner must give particular attention to those devices that promote such perception. The student is constantly observing, both inside and outside the classroom. Thus it is the teacher's responsibility to direct this observation so that it best serves the purposes of instruction.

Technically speaking, everything the learner views may be classed as a potential visual aid to learning; however, common usage has restricted the meaning. Visual aids most frequently used in the classroom setting include the following:

The teacher	Projected pictures	Charts
Television	Movies	Maps
Models	Filmstrips	Relics
Chalkboard	Slides	Exhibits
Bulletin board	Microprojections	Specimens
Still pictures	Overhead projections	Collections

The teacher as a visual aid. Of all the visual aids available for student perusal, the teacher is seen more often and under more varied circumstances than any other. For this reason, if for no other, the teacher should be consistently aware of the need for projecting the best possible teacher image to his students. This has strong implications for teaching techniques, teacher-student relationships, personality projection, and personal dress. The teaching unit can and will be no better than the teacher as an organizer of learning activities will permit it to be.

Projections. Assuming that students have the desired readiness, a well-chosen motion picture may provide a good approximation of first-hand contact with the referent. The use of projected

[3] A. J. Foy Cross and Irene F. Cypher, *Audio-Visual Education* (New York: Thomas Y. Crowell, 1961), p. 6.

movies, filmstrips, and slides, however, has become so firmly established in the thinking of the teacher-planner that it may tend to preclude the use of other worth-while aids. Although their use often represents sound and desirable teaching, pictures serve only as substitutes for the real thing.

Models. Accurate models can, in certain situations, prove superior to the actual referent in providing vivid mental pictures. This is true, for example, of take-apart models of the inner ear or of the visceral organs of the body. In many cases teachers are bound, as a matter of necessity, to provide students with substitute experiences, but such experiences should be made as realistic as possible. If the average secondary-school pupil could have the first-hand experience of an astronaut in observing the Florida coastline, the vividness of such an experience would make the examination of a coastal relief map anticlimactic. However, because it is impossible to provide the first-hand experience, the teacher should make the substitute experiences as vivid as possible.

Overhead projector. Recent improvements in the quality of the overhead projector and the reduction in its cost have encouraged use of transparencies. Acetate transparencies can be prepared from the printed or typewritten page and from photographs or drawings. They can then be projected in a room of normal illumination. By means of transparent cell overlays, progressive sequences can be portrayed by superimposing one cell upon another. For example, a series of cells could be mounted for instructional use in a bookkeeping class. The first cell may contain a blank ledger sheet, the second cell a simple entry, and the third cell a more complicated entry. Each cell may be shown separately or in combination with others according to the purpose of instruction.

Television. Television has opened up a ready avenue of meaningful, interesting experiences that can be used to enrich unit teaching.[4] Television has application to virtually every secondary-school subject. Commercial television stations, educational stations with state-wide coverage, and closed-circuit stations with school-district coverage now provide a range of educational viewing from which wise planners may select those programs that best meet their objectives.

For several years experiments have been conducted in which closed-circuit educational programs are produced and simultaneously telecast to several states.[5] Because these programs are produced exclusively for classroom use, they are particularly adapted to the needs of students of a given age level and subject. Commercial sta-

---

[4]H. Orville Nordberg, James M. Bradfield, and William C. Odell, *Secondary School Teaching* (New York: Macmillan, 1962), pp. 118–123, provide a short statement about the current status of educational television.

[5]John E. Ivey, Jr., and Bryghte D. Godbold, "MPATI: Breakthrough in Educational Television," *Phi Delta Kappan*, 1961, *42:* 192–196.

tions, too, are anxious to provide teachers with suggested viewing programs that are correlated with content areas. The development of video tapes has encouraged actual classroom use of recorded programs that originate during out-of-school hours.

Inept use of visual aids. Unit teaching is limited to some extent by the inept or bungling use of certain visual aids. Misuse of the chalkboard is a prime example of such bungling. A substantial number of teachers use the board only when they are forced to; it never becomes a part of their calculated plan for teaching. Another example of unsuitable use of a visual aid involves the motion picture. Often the movie is shown without the necessary preview and identification of major points to be looked for. More often, class time is wasted while the mechanics of machine operation are solved.

Charts used in the classroom at times not only reflect poor workmanship but, worse still, are inaccurate. Occasionally maps are so small that they are not properly visible from the back of the room, or they are so full of detail that they are confusing. Specimens or collections may be so worn and aged that they actually convey incorrect impressions.

Audio-Visual Aids

A large proportion of helpful teaching devices are properly classified as both auditory and visual aids.[6] This is true of television, of the motion picture with sound track, and of the teacher himself. Many visual aids (models, charts, filmstrips, collections, and cell overlays) become excellent audio-visual aids when used by a skilled teacher who provides the sound track that brings the aids to life and illuminates their meaning. Conversely, many ingenious teachers have combined auditory aids with visual materials to effect a superior teaching situation. This is the case where the salient points from a tape-recorded message are mimeographed and placed in the hands of the student to assist him in learning as he listens.

Printed Materials

Printed materials comprise so large a proportion of all teaching aids that selecting written materials for the teaching of a given unit poses specific problems. Not only is there a wide range of textual materials, but supplementary materials are available through periodicals and newspapers. In order to make a wise choice, the teacher must understand these basic materials and their potential for effective teaching and learning and must keep up with the publication of new materials.

The textbook. The most frequently used of all printed educa-

---

[6]Howard T. Batchelder, Maurice McGlasson, and Raleigh Schorling, *Student Teaching in Secondary Schools*, 4th ed. (New York: McGraw-Hill Book Company, 1964), pp. 225–227, discuss the most important reasons for using audio-visual aids.

tional materials is the textbook.[7] In the hands of a knowledgeable practitioner, the textbook becomes *one of many* aids to assist the student in acquiring clear concepts of subject matter. It is, perhaps, the student's best single academic friend, if he is taught how to use it correctly.

The textbook provides security for the unprepared teacher. If he has failed to prepare effective unit plans, he can, and often does, fall back on the text. Textbook teaching has provided an escape hatch for the teacher who is incompetent, overloaded with work, or instructing outside his own field of specialization.

Conscientious teachers must see that the textbook is not abused.[8] Improper use of the textbook involves using a text with a vocabulary level either too high or too low for the students; lack of instruction in how the text may best serve the student's purposes; unrealistic assignments with respect to length and difficulty; common assignments in which slow readers are expected to read as rapidly or with as much comprehension as fast readers; chapter-by-chapter treatment of course content where it is often assumed that all students read thoroughly and moderately well; and making a course so textbook-centered that the text, rather than the teacher, gives major direction to classroom activity.

Nontextbook materials. Other suitable types of course-related reading materials, when combined with the correct use of the text, can provide a richness in learning experiences that can be gained in no other way.[9] Each subject-matter area has its own specific sources of information. However, the general kinds of printed or duplicated materials useful in all areas are specific subject-oriented weekly newspapers designed to encourage student interest; daily newspapers; encyclopedias and special reference books; workbooks; duplicated materials to be handed out; teacher-prepared study guides; pamphlets; and articles in popular and professional magazines. Each properly prepared unit will not only identify accurately the supplementary reading materials to be used but will indicate exactly how such materials fit into the sequence of learning activities.

Special Aids

Often the conscientious teacher discovers that he needs an aid that is simply not available. He is faced with the choice of resorting to other teaching aids, doing without the aid, or making it himself. Unfortunately, relatively few teachers are inclined to undertake the

---

[7]For a more complete discussion of the textbook, see Chapter 10, pp. 216–221.

[8]Robert C. McKean, *Principles and Methods in Secondary Education* (Columbus, Ohio: Charles E. Merrill Books, Inc., 1962), pp. 149–155, provides a useful discussion of the selection and use of the textbook.

[9]Jean D. Grambs, William J. Iverson, and Franklin K. Patterson, *Modern Methods in Secondary Education* (New York: The Dryden Press, 1958), Chapter 7, present a general discussion on providing and using teaching materials. The authors include frequent examples to illustrate their points.

making of necessary aids. On the other hand, many motivated teachers have not permitted effective teaching to be thwarted through the lack of readily available aids.

MRS. OLDS ACQUIRES A SHAKESPEAREAN STAGE

Mrs. Olds, a tenth-grade English teacher, found that it was almost impossible for her to teach Shakespeare properly without establishing a mental image of a Shakespearean stage for her students. Her drawings on the board and her verbal accounts proved relatively fruitless. Seizing the initiative, she asked two boys in the class who were gifted in woodwork but somewhat limited in English literature if they were interested in making a large but portable model of a Shakespearean stage. They were.

After explaining her need to the woodshop teacher, she solicited his advice and help. With Mrs. Olds serving as a consultant and with the help of the shop teacher, the boys produced a lifelike replica of the Globe Theatre, with a detachable roof, during a two-week period. Mrs. Olds no longer found it difficult to give students a meaningful picture of the original settings of Shakespearean plays.

Although such devices must be made (or somehow procured) well in advance of their use, they often provide students with a class-related, after-school activity that is interesting as well as educational. Students who are otherwise difficult to motivate may take an active interest in this type of activity.

Community Resources

Almost every community with a population of a thousand or more has many individuals, industries, or business concerns whose services may be marshaled free of charge in the interest of more effective unit teaching.[10] Teachers of specific subjects would do well to establish a file of resource persons and establishments. Such a file can be refined and expanded with each successive teaching of a given unit. During the first year of his teaching in a city of 15,000 inhabitants, for example, Mr. Stange assembled the following list of resource people and organizations. He felt that the resource people might be invited to talk to his senior shorthand transcription class. Class members could also profit from visits to the businesses toward the end of the course.

Resource People: William Holzinger, President of Farmer's Bank
B. Samuel Stroud, Attorney
Mrs. Winifred Cumbee, President of the local Business and Professional Women's Club
Jay S. McGraw, Principal of Grayson High School

---

[10]Kenneth H. Hansen, *High School Teaching* (Englewood Cliffs, N.J.: Prentice-Hall, 1957), pp. 308–314, discusses the human and physical resources of the community as aids to instruction.

Local Businesses: The secretarial pool of the Branch Office of the United States Bureau of Reclamation
The central offices of the United States Steel Corporation, located in an adjacent city

Each subject area requires a somewhat different use of individuals and establishments within a community. In searching for these community resources, teachers find it profitable to have students make suggestions on standard three-by-five cards that may then be incorporated into a file. The final selection of the resource person or of a field trip should be made by the teacher.

Customarily such files need not be related to a specific unit. If they are set up on a course-wide basis, they tend to be more practical. Although teaching as many as three different courses, some teachers have found it more feasible to include all resource persons in a single file. How this is done is largely a matter of individual teacher preference.

Principles Related to the Selection of Materials and Resources

Effective selection and use of teaching materials and resources are enhanced by a working knowledge of relevant teaching principles.[11]

1. The initial learning of concepts is best accomplished by exposing the learner to the concrete referent, the actual thing for which the concept stands.

2. When a concrete referent cannot be used, the teaching of concepts is best accomplished by employing an aid that most closely approximates the referent of the concept. Exceptions to this statement are microscopic projections, oversized models of objects otherwise difficult to observe, slow-motion movies, and certain kinds of maps.

3. The more nearly an abstract concept can be related to a concrete referent that has established meaning for the learner, the easier it is to teach.

4. The best aids are those that promote taking the steps appropriate to the type of objective sought.

5. Since both efficient memorization and the efficient learning of motor skills require that concepts be acquired before drill or practice is undertaken, the teacher should employ materials and resources that are appropriate to the teaching of the underlying concepts.

6. When a concept of the coordination of movements in a skill is to be taught, a movie in slow motion frequently serves best.

7. In their beginning stages, habits are at the conscious level and thus are conceptual in nature. For this reason, the aids used for

[11]A review of Chapter 1, pp. 8–11, will provide a broad basis for the understanding of principles related to the selection and use of teaching aids.

the teaching of habits should be appropriate for the teaching of concepts.

8. The use of printed material will only be meaningful to the extent that it recalls concepts associated with printed words.

Use of Aids in Teaching Specific Subjects

Although teachers frequently have a verbal acquaintance with the principles underlying the use of materials and resources, many find it difficult to make practical use of such knowledge. For example, better-informed instructors are aware that the type of objective sought will determine the necessary instructional steps, but they still make errors in using the information. An examination of the precise steps needed for teaching a given subject may prove profitable.

Vivid Referents for Concepts

In determining what aids are best suited to the teaching of a biology unit on "Reproductive Organs in Flowers," the planner must first ask himself what kinds of objectives are sought. In this case it can be assumed that the unit is almost totally concerned with the teaching of concepts and related names. The planner must then review the specific steps for teaching concepts. They are learned by (a) showing the referent of the concept or a facsimile, (b) telling about the referent, (c) memorizing related terms, and (d) using the concept in an applied situation.

The best aid in this situation would probably be the one that portrays most vividly the reproductive organs of flowers. This would not be a written account, nor would it be a still picture. A close-up motion picture in color would be very helpful because it provides an accurate approximation of the referent. This provides visual contact only, however, and always as seen by the eye of the camera. Because of size and the possibility of observation from any angle, a large, accurate plant model would serve as the best aid if used in conjunction with actual living flowers.

In general, therefore, when a teacher is concerned with teaching concepts, he should use those aids that represent the referent itself or that are as similar to the referent as possible. In the descending order of their appropriateness, these aids are the referent itself, models, motion pictures, still pictures, and oral or written accounts.

If one can be sure that concepts are sufficiently vivid to elicit an accurate recall when the word (symbol) standing for the concept is seen in printed form, printed materials may then be used effectively as aids to instruction. (Seeing the printed word *statue*, for example, should give rise to a *mental picture* of a statue.) Where new concepts are being presented, however, the showing of the referent or a reasonable facsimile is highly desirable. The more abstract the content, the more difficult it becomes to portray such concepts through the use of concrete referents. This accounts for much of the difficulty involved in teaching abstractions.

Demonstration as an Aid

In teaching a skill subject, such as boys' physical education, efficient learning is promoted when the student acquires a clear concept of how a given skill is performed before he undertakes it. If, for example, he is concerned with learning to broad jump, the boy must first acquire a meaningful picture of the correct running approach and jumping form. The aid best suited for this purpose is a demonstration by someone who uses correct form. A motion picture would also serve as an effective aid, although it may not provide the same sensory impact as an actual demonstration. In some cases, a motion picture in slow motion has definite advantages over a demonstration.

Aids Clarify Concepts

Aids, then, serve the purpose of creating and clarifying concepts. They provide no help in the practice of skills except as they help improve the mental pictures that are basic to performance. This is true of typing, vocal production, sewing, or playing an instrument. Once the basic concepts have been acquired, the symbols (words) that stand for these concepts may be used in printed or spoken form to further clarify the concepts. Meaningful memorization, therefore, must first focus attention on the concept to which the symbol refers.

Need for a Comprehensive List

Unit planners will be able to save considerable time and plan with greater efficiency if they have access to a well-organized, comprehensive listing of materials and resources that are specifically related to the subject being taught.[12] Such a list serves as a pool from which ideas may be taken for incorporation into the unit. Suggested lists may be readily compiled through the examination of a number of successful units in the subject area.

Recommendations

Specific suggestions with respect to the identification, procurement, and use of aids may prove of great help to the beginning teacher. If sound steps can be taken and if errors can be avoided, the chances for effective teaching are much enhanced. The following is a list of recommendations that have proven to be of practical benefit. Teachers should:

---

[12]Batchelder, McGlasson, and Schorling, *op. cit.*, p. 229, list a range of audio-visual aids. Use of extensive lists such as this one should prevent overlooking certain aids that might be particularly useful.

1. Use printed (symbolic) materials only after students have acquired the concepts that will make such materials meaningful; use time-consuming first-hand experiences only when students lack readiness for the use of books and printed materials; use models in preference to pictures or verbal materials where the experience of pupils makes this desirable; bring the concrete referent into the classroom if it is readily available and will serve a useful purpose; use audio or visual materials to help students understand abstract relationships.

2. Scan the range of possible aids before making a selection, and consider the teacher as only one of many possible audio-visual aids.

3. Select for class use an appropriate text in view of educational psychology, average reading level of students, interesting presentation, illustrations, and format; make sound use of encyclopedias and other specific references; provide students with a variety of nontextbook reading materials when such materials will assist in the acquisition of desired concepts; determine the extent to which workbooks and programed textbooks can serve a useful purpose; prepare and distribute useful materials; use a well-prepared study guide to assist students in their study.

4. List in unit plans only those materials that are available or that can be produced; employ students in the production and assembly of materials and in the operation of machines when the experience will prove rewarding and save valuable instructional time for the teacher; use students to gather instructional materials where this is practical; allow a sufficient amount of time for the preparation, procurement, or use of teaching aids.

5. Inject variety into the use of teaching aids; use aids as introductory and summary devices as well as for specific concept and skill development; become thoroughly acquainted with aids such as records, filmstrips, or movies before they are shown to the class.

6. Use maps in developing proper concepts of location, direction, relative size, and topography; but use only well-executed maps, charts, or models that leave accurate impressions.

7. Differentiate between the kinds of materials and aids that will be most helpful in teaching individual students; indicate specifically what class members are to look for in a filmstrip, movie, or field trip.

8. Select materials and resources for their educational rather than their entertainment value; coordinate educational radio and television programs with classroom work.

EVALUATION PROCEDURES

Unit evaluation will move forward with greater ease and efficiency if the teacher clearly understands the purpose of evaluation procedures, the principles related to unit evaluation, and the specific categories of unit evaluation. Furthermore, it is a great advantage to general instruction if the teacher is acquainted with a range of proven evaluation procedures that apply to his particular field of specialization.

Purpose of Unit Evaluation

The basic purpose of unit evaluation is improved learning,[13] and improved learning, in turn, should be directed toward unit goals. Unit evaluation procedures, therefore, should aim at determining to what extent the objectives of the unit have been achieved. This type of broad definition dispels many of the older assumptions about testing, recitation, and written assignments.

Evaluation should help students learn more efficiently. Its prime concern, therefore, is not with defeating students but with identifying their learning difficulties so that appropriate help can be given. It is not a scare technique for frightening students into more conscientious study patterns; it should assist them in analyzing their weaknesses. It should set the stage for ready acceptance of teacher help based upon student self-understandings.[14]

Such frequently used evaluation techniques as personality appraisal, evaluation of oral and written English, or the analysis of study habits have little or nothing to do with unit goals. Such techniques are justified only if the teacher recognizes this lack of relationship and if they serve a long-range or nonunit-related purpose.

Principles Related to Unit Evaluation

Years of experimentation on the part of students, teachers, psychologists, and researchers have furnished helpful guidelines for those educators concerned with appraisal techniques. Before choosing specific devices for use in a unit, the teacher should consider the following general guidelines.[15]

1. The teaching-learning process consists of three basic facets: establishing objectives, engaging in goal-related activities, and evaluating to what extent goals have been achieved.

2. Evaluation, including marking procedures, should encourage the student to progress at his own level of capability and in relationship to his past achievement.

3. Diagnosis is one of the chief concerns of evaluation. This

---

[13]William H. Burton, *The Guidance of Learning Activities,* 3d. ed. (New York: Appleton-Century-Crofts, 1962), pp. 480–485, presents a very useful list and discussion of frequently used evaluation devices.

[14]See Chapter 15, pp. 359–371, for a discussion of sound marking and reporting procedures.

[15]William T. Gruhn and Harl R. Douglass, *The Modern Junior High School,* 2d. ed. (New York: Ronald Press, 1956), pp. 316–318, provide a helpful statement of principles that should give direction to evaluation procedures.

process should help the students direct their efforts toward academic areas needing improvement. Self-evaluation, an important adjunct of diagnosis, can be encouraged through various types of tests.

4. Diagnostic statements can be helpful, but a simple indication of grade without additional explanation may do little to encourage self-improvement. The student should always be informed about evaluation procedures and their purposes.

5. After the student clearly understands the standards on which appraisal should be based, he should be encouraged to continuously appraise his own performance. Unit evaluation, in particular, should be organized to promote this type of self-appraisal.

6. When an evaluation procedure does not measure what it is supposed to measure, it is invalid.

7. The accuracy with which evaluation is carried out will help determine its usefulness.

8. Evaluation should be regarded as a continuous program in which attention is focused on balance between testing and nontesting, oral and written, and formal and informal procedures.

9. Emphasis should be on the appraisal of individual improvement rather than on comparison with members of the group.

10. Tests involving performance have greater validity than typical written tests.

11. Evaluation procedures should be arranged so that students do not feel that the learning or use of unit content is at an end when the test paper has been submitted.

12. Not all the objectives of a given unit need to be covered by test items.

13. Students tend to place too much emphasis on the written examination.

14. The types of evaluation procedures employed in a given unit may vary considerably depending upon the needs of that unit. A range of different types of tests should also be employed to serve different purposes.

15. Both essay and objective tests have certain advantages.

16. It is false to assume that all students will exert maximum energy to achieve a high grade, although this is true of a substantial proportion.[16]

Specific Kinds of Evaluation Procedures

The range of evaluation procedures available for use in unit planning is broad.[17] Unfortunately this breadth is frequently not re-

---

[16]Useful suggestions with respect to evaluating pupil learning are presented in narrative form by Samuel P. Wiggens, *Successful High School Teaching* (Boston: Houghton Mifflin Company, 1958), pp. 182–183.

[17]See Nordberg, Bradfield, and Odell, *op. cit.*, pp. 180–186, for a sophisticated brief discussion of measuring procedures.

flected in actual units. Written tests are too often used to the exclusion of other devices.

Among the specific kinds of evaluation devices, the following are most frequently used:

Written Work:
- Unit papers
- Short reports
- Chalkboard work
- Daily assignments

Oral Work:
- Committee reports
- Class discussions
- Debates
- Brief individual oral reports
- Teacher-student conferences

Tests and Examinations:
- Unit examinations
- Mid-unit tests
- Short quizzes
- Oral examinations
  - Class discussions
  - Individual tests
- Written tests
  - Essay tests
  - Objective tests

Miscellaneous:
- Projects
- Case studies

An examination of the evaluation procedures used in specific units should prove helpful at this point.[18] It should be remembered, however, that one cannot fully appraise evaluation procedures without considering unit objectives. The following evaluation procedures were taken from a tenth-grade unit on "Menu Planning." Note that in the absence of unit objectives, evaluation procedures appear somewhat vague.

EVALUATION IN A HOMEMAKING UNIT

1. Plan unit objectives cooperatively with students at the beginning of the unit. At the end of the unit have students indicate in written form how well they feel each of the objectives was achieved.
2. Keep brief anecdotal records of the attitudes that students express informally to note any changes or new attitudes that may have developed.
3. Maintain records of student progress through evaluating:
   a. Oral class responses
   b. Special assignments
   c. Tests, journals, and daily assignments
   d. Class interest, behavior, and attitude
4. Have each student evaluate herself through:
   a. Progress charts
   b. Daily check lists
   c. Her ability to put into practical use what has been taught in class
5. Have each student anonymously evaluate the unit and the teacher by responding on a five-point scale to a series of questions.

---

[18]See Appendix B, questions 162–186. Questions listed in this appendix should suggest other evaluation possibilities that might be of help in unit planning.

Note that these procedures do not include any major written examination on the content of the unit, but in view of the nature of the unit this may well be justified. Emphasis is placed on student self-evaluation as well as unsigned written evaluation of the teacher.

In the following tenth-grade English unit on "Modifiers Make Our Speech Live," evaluation procedures emphasize testing to the exclusion of other procedures. Other class activities that might well serve as appraisal devices have not been listed.

EVALUATION IN AN ENGLISH UNIT

1. A diagnostic test will be given during the introductory activities.
2. Frequent quizzes will be given when they will serve a useful purpose.
3. All tests and quizzes will be reviewed orally in class.
4. A comprehensive unit test will be given as a concluding activity, together with a thorough test on adjectives.
5. Fifty per cent of the student's grade will be based on his formal tests and quizzes, 10 per cent on his theme, 25 per cent on his participation in class, and 15 per cent on cooperation, promptness (in class and with assignments), courtesy, and effort.

Informing students of the weighting of each general area of activity can serve as a helpful motivator and encourage self-direction on the part of students.

A twelfth-grade physics teacher included the following evaluation procedures in a unit on "Heat."[19]

EVALUATION IN A PHYSICS UNIT

1. Related to student self-evaluation:
   a. All student work will be graded and returned as soon as possible.
   b. The overall standing of each pupil will be indicated on returned work about four times during the unit.
2. Related to the teacher's evaluation of students:
   a. Oral reviews will be conducted at frequent intervals.
   b. Problems will be placed on the blackboard once each week for teacher and class criticism.
   c. A short time each day will be devoted to drill on new and old terms.
   d. Quizzes will be given as described in the developmental and culminating activities.
   e. Homework problems will be handed in every other day for correction and evaluation.
   f. The teacher will consistently observe the progress of class members.
   g. Written laboratory reports will be submitted at frequent intervals for teacher criticism.

---

[19]Evaluation procedures typically vary a great deal from one unit to another depending upon the characteristics of the unit and the teacher's preference.

h. Two major tests will be given during the unit. In each case they will consist of (a) problems and (b) theory and definition.
i. On a test related to another unit, questions from this unit will be included to determine pupil retention of basic concepts.

In each unit the planners must include in the introductory, developmental, and concluding activities a description of the exact evaluation procedures and the sequence in which they will take place.[20]

Much time can be saved in the selection of evaluation procedures to be incorporated into the unit if the planner will identify those procedures that have proved most successful in the past. Over a period of a year a resource list of suggestions may be compiled that will eliminate the necessity for careful re-identification of the range of possibilities. Consultation with teaching colleagues in the same subject-matter field may also prove highly profitable.

Categories of Unit Evaluation

Some unit planners prefer to group the types of evaluation procedures into specific categories. Such grouping serves to insure the planner against the omission of essential activities.

Evaluation of Student Knowledge

The category on evaluation of student knowledge includes those activities designed to determine to what extent unit goals have been achieved. Common activities are:

Tests	Board work
Themes	Projects
Reports	Homework
Discussions	Guided self-activity

Student Self-Evaluation

Recent emphasis on student self-direction has pointed up the necessity for student self-evaluation. Thoughtful teachers have devised specific procedures that encourage students to appraise their own progress.[21] They often consist of:

1. Sequential lists of tasks that may be checked off by students when completed.
2. Special self-evaluation report cards on which are recorded the grades of work submitted to the teacher for correction and grading.

---

[20]How evaluation procedures are incorporated into the developmental and concluding activities of the unit can be readily seen by examining the complete units in Chapter 7 and in Appendix A.

[21]Helpful suggestions for involving students in the evaluation of unit objectives and procedures are provided by Hubert H. Mills and Harl R. Douglass, *Teaching in High School*, 2d. ed. (New York: Ronald Press, 1957), p. 196.

3. Descriptive statements of A, B, C, D, and E (or F) students.
4. Questionnaires that force the student to react to his classroom performances.

Evaluation of the Unit and the Teacher

Student appraisal of instructor competence has long been employed by teachers as a device for helping improve instruction as well as teacher-student relationships.[22] The most common device for this purpose has been the use of an anonymous student questionnaire or written response submitted at the end of a long unit or at the end of a semester or school year. Since the identity of the respondent is not known to the teacher, students feel free to air their grievances or praise. Such devices are admittedly highly subjective, but they do afford teachers the opportunity to know how students feel—information that is essential to continuous effective classroom operation. Any number of variations to this procedure can be found; some surveys ask for student reaction to the content and activities of the unit as well.[23]

Recommendations

The conscientious as well as the less painstaking teacher should benefit from some specific suggestions about evaluation procedures. The use of such recommendations should not only save the teacher time and effort but also help him achieve success in unit evaluation.[24] Teachers should:

1. View evaluation as a series of related instructional procedures used by the teacher in helping the student improve academic achievement, not as an arrangement for pitting the teacher against the student by exposing student weaknesses; view evaluation as a continuing activity that may well be a part of introductory, developmental, or concluding activities; extend evaluation procedures to several kinds of activities, avoiding unwarranted emphasis on the written test; attempt to determine through evaluation procedures whether students can apply what they are supposed to have learned; emphasize comprehension rather than memory in most evaluation procedures; include diagnostic procedures in the introductory activities where such procedures will serve a useful purpose.

---

[22]*Ibid.*, pp. 34–38, provides examples of teacher self-evaluation scales.

[23]Kimball Wiles, *Teaching for Better Schools,* 2d. ed. (Englewood Cliffs, N.J.: Prentice-Hall, 1959), pp. 288–289, discusses evaluation as a device for promoting self-improvement.

[24]William L. Carter, Carl W. Hansen, and Margaret G. McKim, *Learning to Teach in the Secondary School* (New York: Macmillan, 1962), pp. 308–315, present several principles that should be considered in selecting and implementing unit evaluation procedures.

2. Avoid an overriding preference for either subjective (essay) tests or objective tests, for each type serves a useful purpose; avoid the consistent use of a specific type of test if it is strongly disliked by a majority of students; recognize the strengths and weakness of each of the four types of objective tests—multiple choice, true and false, matching, and completion; give quizzes as often as they will serve a useful instructional purpose, but try not to antagonize students by giving quizzes with excessive frequency; review each test with class members after it has been corrected; prepare a well-organized examination that tests unit content and serves as an effective summary; include difficult as well as easy test items to accommodate differing achievement levels.

3. Differentiate between formal and informal evaluation devices.

4. Include specific as well as general observations among evaluation procedures; give deserved attention to themes and written work in unit evaluation; view improvement of students' study habits as a part of evaluation; observe the undirected and out-of-class behavior of students as an indication of subject-matter acquisition and retention; make use of individual conferences with students as a part of the evaluation procedure.

5. Give consideration to the need for the student to keep accurate check on his own progress at all times; furthermore, make provision for the student to evaluate the instructor as well as the unit presentation.

Nonunit-Related Evaluation

Although this chapter has focused upon procedures designed to determine the extent to which unit goals have been achieved, not all evaluation procedures bear a close relationship to unit goals. Most of the nonunit-related evaluation procedures are aimed at appraising long-range objectives. For example, measuring the extent of habit formation that serves the purposes of effective study and classroom control is important in the teaching of all units. Determining the needed and actual improvement in teacher-student relationships is a continuing process that extends throughout the school year. This type of appraisal lends itself best to informal evaluation procedures such as teacher observation and student-teacher conferences, although more formalized techniques may be employed. Speed and comprehension in reading are important to all subjects and should be carefully appraised at specified times during the school year.

The administration and interpretation of standardized tests of mental maturity and subject-matter achievement are accepted procedures in accredited secondary schools. These examinations call for the use of specifically prescribed procedures and are usually administered to large groups of students by school personnel who have had special training. Such tests permit interested teachers to compare meaningfully individual student scores with national or regional averages. Standardized examinations may be classified as evaluation procedures but have little direct bearing on the teaching of units.

PROBLEMS FOR STUDY AND DISCUSSION

1. What is the fundamental purpose of teaching materials? Explain.
2. Give three examples of the use of aids that do *not* move in the direction dictated by the established objectives.
3. Give five examples of poor usage of visual aids likely to be found in your subject-matter major.
4. List the advantages of the human voice over other auditory aids.
5. Under what circumstances does a model serve as a better aid than the referent itself? Explain.
6. Assumption: You are determined to make the best possible use of television in your teaching major. Describe the steps you would follow.
7. What is meant by *textbook teaching?* What does it mean in your particular field? Explain.
8. Identify the nontextbook printed materials that are of greatest use in teaching a particular course in your teaching minor. Be specific.
9. List the following aids in order of desirability for teaching concepts in your teaching minor: still pictures, narration, resource speakers, written accounts, and specimens.
10. When is the use of printed material as an aid to learning *not* justified? Explain.
11. What is the role of aids in teaching abstractions? Give two examples.
12. What is the basic purpose of evaluation? Explain.
13. How can one engage in a rigorous evaluation program without defeating students? Explain.
14. How would you use diagnostic procedures in teaching a unit? Explain specifically.
15. Make several suggestions for helping the teacher avoid undue emphasis on written tests.
16. Which type of written work is most often neglected in your teaching major? Do you neglect it? Analyze your reasons.
17. Which type of test is best suited to student evaluation in your teaching minor? Defend your response.
18. What is the value of student self-evaluation? Explain.
19. Precisely how would you obtain an accurate indication of how much knowledge students had acquired in your subject-matter major?
20. Why should the teacher review the test with students once it has been corrected?

RECOMMENDED READINGS

Batchelder, Howard T., Maurice McGlasson, and Raleigh Schorling, *Student Teaching in Secondary Schools*, 4th ed. New York: McGraw-Hill Book Company, 1964, Chapters 12 and 14.

Burton, William H., *The Guidance of Learning Activities*, 3d. ed. New York: Appleton-Century-Crofts, Inc., 1962, Chapters 17, 20, and 21.

Carter, William L., Carl W. Hansen, and Margaret G. McKim, *Learning to Teach in the Secondary School*. New York: The Macmillan Company, 1962, Chapter 11 and pp. 197–199.

Cross, A. J. Foy, and Irene F. Cypher, *Audio-Visual Education*. New York: Thomas Y. Crowell Company, 1961, Chapters 2–13.

Grambs, Jean D., William J. Iverson, and Franklin K. Patterson, *Modern Methods in Secondary Education*, rev. ed. New York: The Dryden Press, 1958, Chapters 7, 8, and 17.

Hansen, Kenneth H., *High School Teaching*. Englewood Cliffs, N.J.: Prentice-Hall, Inc., 1957, Chapters 8 and 9.

Klausmeier, Herbert J., *Teaching in the Secondary School*. New York: Harper & Brothers, 1958, Chapters 8 and 9.

McGuire, Vincent, Robert B. Myers, and Charles L. Durrance, *Your Student Teaching in the Secondary School*. Boston: Allyn and Bacon, Inc., 1959, Chapters 7, 10, and 11.

McKean, Robert C., *Principles and Methods in Secondary Education*. Columbus, Ohio: Charles E. Merrill Books, Inc., 1962, Chapters 6 and 7.

Mills, Hubert H., and Harl R. Douglass, *Teaching in High School*, 2d. ed. New York: Ronald Press, 1957, Chapters 17–21.

Nordberg, H. Orville, James M. Bradfield, and William C. Odell, *Secondary School Teaching*. New York: The Macmillan Company, 1962, Chapters 6 and 8.

Rivlin, Harry N., *Teaching Adolescents in Secondary Schools*, 2d. ed. New York: Appleton-Century-Crofts, Inc., 1961, Chapters 8 and 11.

Wiggins, Samuel P., *Successful High School Teaching*. Boston: Houghton Mifflin Company, 1958, Chapter 8 and pp. 245–256.

Wiles, Kimball, *Teaching for Better Schools*, 2d. ed. Englewood Cliffs, N.J.: Prentice-Hall, Inc., 1959, Chapter 12.

Woodruff, Asahel D., *Basic Concepts of Teaching; with Brief Readings*. San Francisco: Chandler Publishing Company, 1962, Chapter 7.

7

Successful Teaching Units

Although a few teachers proclaim, with some justification, that principles leading to effective teaching can never be captured on paper, the majority of successful teachers believe that no teaching of any consequence should be undertaken before the teaching objectives have been properly related to teaching procedures, and that this relationship can best be accomplished through the careful development of a written unit plan. Indeed, there is almost universal agreement among educators that the best instruction currently being carried on by quality teachers is that based upon sound unit planning.

There are, of course, many processes, functions, details, and routines that do not conform nicely to a unit plan. Every teacher must face the dilemma of relating the Junior Red Cross drive, the championship football game, and class elections to the teaching of high-school chorus, physics, or English. And every teacher must also ponder what bearing roll call, temperature control, and seating have on unit planning and teaching. Such details may be viewed as unavoidable but necessary minutiae in classroom operation, but to ignore them completely is to invite difficulty. Although they typically do not comprise a part of the subject-matter content or objective-related activities in the unit, such details must be dealt with and, therefore, must be considered an integral part of unit planning.

Occasionally one encounters an excellent teacher who apparently has made no written preparation. Usually, however, this teacher has, through the years, evolved a firm command of the subject matter and effective teaching procedures, and successful repetition of these methods has made a written plan superfluous. To assume that such a teacher has not done any careful planning is absurd. In reality years of planning have gone into the course, although it might be difficult for a substitute teacher to teach effectively the same unit in the manner carefully outlined in the experienced teacher's mind.

The real danger in failing to follow a written plan lies in the fact that many student teachers, beginning teachers, and teachers with a limited mastery of their subject matter assume that they can do likewise—and with equal success. Unfortunately poor quality teaching often follows such limited or hit-and-miss unit planning.[1]

Unit planning proceeds with greatest ease when the subject matter is developed along conceptual lines, as in units of mathematics, biological sciences, English grammar, and chemistry. In such subjects as the social sciences, English literature, and music, which are not as definitely structured, it is more difficult to make clear, interrelated statements of unit objectives.

Teachers who deny the value of unit planning often resort to unit plan substitutes, such as extensive daily lesson plans, expanded or modified yearly plans, poorly organized and hastily written notes, or, in some cases, no written plans of any sort. Because there are some logical reasons for *not* strictly following an organized unit plan, a few teachers have tried to rationalize their lack of preparation. The inexperienced teacher, in particular, should avoid such easy rationale.

In some subjects, however, substitutes for unit plans are successful. In the teaching of modern foreign languages, for example, careful and detailed organization of overall (yearly) plans from which daily lesson plans may be developed have proved effective. Most current foreign-language texts, therefore, are organized in short, daily lessons. The range of objectives that must be dealt with in foreign-language teaching (concepts, skills, memorization, and habits) complicates the organization necessary for effective instruction. Many successful teachers still insist on planned teaching units in teaching foreign languages, but the majority of teachers in this field are leaning toward the use of daily lesson plans based upon overall plans.[2]

CHARACTERISTICS OF SUCCESSFUL UNIT PLANS

All successful units must give attention to (a) *what* is to be taught and (b) *how* it is to be taught. This statement is obviously an

---

[1]Howard T. Batchelder, Maurice McGlasson, and Raleigh Schorling, *Student Teaching in Secondary Schools,* 4th ed. (New York: McGraw-Hill Book Company, 1964), pp. 126–129, provide suggestions for unit preparation.

[2]See the examples of foreign-language overall plans and related daily lesson plans in Appendix A.

oversimplification of all that is involved in unit planning, but these two concerns are fundamental to every unit.[3]

Most educators express a preference for five basic steps in unit planning:

1. Information basic to understanding the nature of the group to be taught must be assembled, organized, and recorded.
2. Appropriate major and minor objectives must be determined, carefully worded, organized, and written down.
3. Procedures appropriate for the achievement of each objective must be determined and adequately described.
4. Teaching materials, resources, and devices necessary for the conduct of teaching procedures must be selected and listed.
5. Evaluation procedures that bear a direct relationship to unit objectives must be determined and listed.

Although the core of the unit consists of the *objectives* and their related *procedures,* it is difficult to conceive of any well-planned and teachable unit that does not concern itself with all five of these steps. However, because each unit is devised by a particular teacher to assist him in teaching a specific group of students, one unit plan may not provide adequate help for another teacher in teaching a different group. By its very nature unit planning is subjective. For this reason each of the units presented in this chapter might have been different if it had been prepared by a different teacher for use in another section of the same subject. A variety of detail is to be expected, but *all well-prepared units*[4] *should follow the same general outline.*

Basic Information

Encompassed in the Basic Information[5] of the unit plan will be the grade level and age range of students, the duration of the unit, and the relationship of the particular unit to other units in the Overall Plan. This section will also contain information about the nature of the class—individual I.Q.'s of students and the range of I.Q.'s, the socioeconomic status of the class members, students with particular problems, potential offenders in terms of classroom control, proportion of boys to girls, and the range of backgrounds represented by different students in the class. As much of this information as possible will be frequently recorded in code form on a seating chart that

---

[3]Hubert H. Mills and Harl R. Douglass, *Teaching in High School,* 2d. ed. (New York: Ronald Press, 1957), Chapter 14, present a clarifying discussion of the different types of teaching units.

[4]William H. Burton, *The Guidance of Learning Activities,* 3d. ed. (New York: Appleton-Century-Crofts, 1962), Chapter 15, gives an analysis of a fifth-grade unit. His relevant comments apply to unit plans at all levels.

[5]See Chapter 3, pp. 48–57, for an extensive treatment of Basic Information.

indicates diagrammatically the exact location of each student and relevant information pertaining to him.

Objectives

The unit objectives[6] will:

1. Identify all relevant unit objectives that can and should be treated during the unit.
2. Differentiate and group objectives according to kind—concepts, memorizations, skills, and habits.
3. List major objectives in proper relationship to minor objectives.
4. State objectives in the simplest form compatible with clarity and meaning.

Procedures

Activities (procedures)[7] that are carefully considered along with Basic Information and Objectives will possess certain characteristics. They will be:

1. Frequently grouped according to introductory activities, developmental activities, and concluding activities.
2. Practical, in the sense that they can be carried out with a reasonable expenditure of time and energy.
3. Psychologically sound for the achievement of the specific objective involved.
4. Specifically related to the objectives to be achieved.
5. Selected only after a range of other possibilities has been considered.
6. Of general interest to students in the class.
7. Varied in consideration of student capacity, achievement, and maturity.
8. Described in sufficient detail to enable another teacher to obtain a clear picture of what is to be done.
9. Arranged in sequential order.
10. Flexible enough to permit unforeseen modifications.

Materials and Resources

In planning for the use of audio-visual aids, teaching materials, special devices, and resource persons,[8] the planner will:

1. Select and list the most effective teaching aids.
2. Avoid excess use of any one device.

---

[6]See Chapter 4, pp. 60–69, for an extensive treatment of Objectives.
[7]See Chapter 4, pp. 70–82, and Chapter 5 for an extensive treatment of Procedures.
[8]See Chapter 6, pp. 110–120, for a detailed discussion of Materials and Resources.

3. Examine a wide range of possibilities before making a selection.
4. List only those aids that are available.
5. Make certain aids when it is practical.

Evaluation Procedures

The procedures related to unit evaluation[9] should reflect the planner's effort to:

1. Insure that evaluation serves an instructional purpose.
2. Use a variety of evaluation procedures.
3. Not overemphasize testing.
4. Relate all evaluation activities to unit objectives.
5. Examine a wide range of possible procedures and their effect upon learning before making final selections.

Other General Characteristics

A number of general characteristics do not lend themselves to the preceding categorization. Good unit plans will:

1. Be practical and usable.
2. Be made up only after the examination of a wide range of usable resource materials.
3. Avoid the danger of undesirable brevity or unnecessary length.
4. Be planned in consideration of the teaching experience and subject-matter competence of the teacher who will use them.
5. Be consistent in form and make-up.
6. Possess a strong interrelationship of parts within the unit.

SAMPLE TEACHING UNITS

The unit plans presented in this chapter were prepared by first- and second-year teachers and taught in actual classroom situations. Because the units served the needs of specific teachers under particular circumstances, variation in specific detail is justified. The basic structure of each unit—Basic Information, Objectives, Procedures, Materials and Resources, and Evaluation Procedures—is the same. However, considerable leeway should be allowed each teacher within the framework of this structure in order to meet the needs of the specific students and teacher.[10]

---

[9]See Chapter 6, pp. 120–128, for a discussion of Evaluation Procedures.

[10]Jean D. Grambs, William J. Iverson, and Franklin K. Patterson, *Modern Methods in Secondary Education*, rev. ed. (New York: The Dryden Press, 1958), pp. 129–134, divide unit construction into three stages, providing illustrations of each.

The first two unit plans are soundly developed and illustrate the characteristics of successful teaching units previously discussed. The third unit plan is less well developed and is criticized by means of a "Self-Scoring Instrument for Teaching Units," which makes use of a scheme of numbered scores.

A Teaching Unit in Biological Science

An experienced biology teacher who knows his subject matter and effective teaching methods should be able to teach the following unit with success. If he were without basic experience beyond the student-teaching level, he would probably need additional details before he could teach the unit.

Tenth-Grade Biology: "Root Systems"

I. Basic Information
   A. Age and Grade Level of Class
      1. The students are primarily sophomores but there are a few juniors.
      2. Their ages range from fourteen to seventeen.
   B. Length of Time for Unit
      1. The unit will be taught for three weeks (fifteen school days).
      2. Five days will be spent on the anatomy of roots and the types of roots.
      3. Two days will be spent sketching the anatomy of roots as part of laboratory work.
      4. Five days will be spent discussing the way a root absorbs minerals and water.
      5. One day will be spent in initiating the unit and two days in concluding it.
   C. The Position of This Unit in the Overall Plan
      1. This is the fourth unit taught in the year.
      2. The unit preceding this was "Introducing the Plant Kingdom."
      3. The unit following this is "The Use of the Stem."
   D. Nature of the Class
      1. There are seventeen boys and eight girls in this class.
      2. About half of the students were reared in a rural area, giving them a fair background for the subject.
      3. During the first unit on botany it was learned that four girls and five boys were not very interested in the subject. The girls are Sandra, Glenda, Lorna, and Margaret, and the boys are Wallace, Lewis, Gerald, Eldon, and Clarence. (For I.Q.'s and seating, see the seating chart.)

4. Several of the class members have demonstrated a great deal of ability and interest in the subject.

E. Seating Chart (see p. 137.)

F. This unit is designed to help the students understand the way a plant gets food from the soil and also how the roots help hold the soil and moisture.

II. Objectives[11]

A. Concepts to Be Learned[12]

1. Unit Concept: Two common types of root systems, possessing different characteristics, enable plants to live under many different conditions.

2. Supporting Concepts

a. There are two common types of root systems.

1) A *fibrous* root system has many slender roots of equal size.

2) A *taproot* system has a large primary root and many secondary roots attached to it. It acts as a storehouse for the plant.

b. Plants are able to live under many different conditions because of these two systems.

1) Fibrous roots cover a lot of area and bind the soil.

2) Fibrous roots draw in available water very quickly.

3) Taproots go down to deep water supplies.

4) Taproots are very good anchors.

c. Root hairs are important for absorption.

1) They are one-celled outgrowths of the epidermis of the root.

2) They grow only in the area behind the root tip, pushing out into new territory as the root grows.

d. The root tip is the very end of the root and is made up of four regions.

1) The *root cap* protects the root end and makes it possible for the root to push through the soil. CO_2 (carbon dioxide) is given off by the cap and mixes with H_2O (water) to form carbonic acid, which dissolves minerals and makes it easier for the root to push through the soil.

2) The *embryonic* region is the growing point in the root. The cells are small and in a constant state of division.

3) The *elongation* region is just back of the embryonic region.

---

[11] H. Orville Nordberg, James M. Bradfield, and William C. Odell, *Secondary School Teaching* (New York: Macmillan, 1962), pp. 87–102, give several examples of the body of a unit.

[12] These conceptual statements (objectives) have been carefully prepared and stated.

SEATING CHART

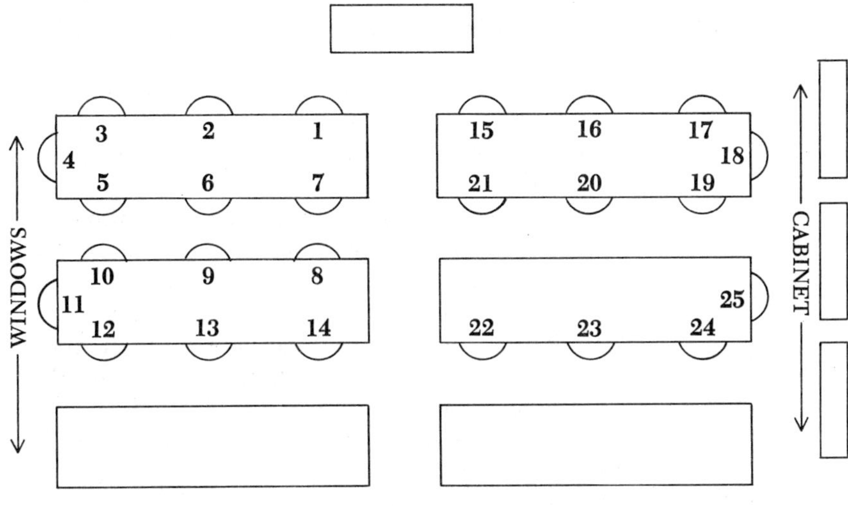

1. Sandra Bing, 0411239
2. Sally Peters, 5321517
3. William Oliphant, 7211426
4. Boyd Franks, 8921418
5. Melissa Williams, 3711421
6. Dean Patrick, 2911422
7. Robert Hill, 6131514
8. Wallace Rhone, 4190147
9. Lewis Grundig, 0590242
10. Herman Allred, 2201338
11. Charles Evans, 7001337
12. Willard Foss, 9980153
13. Gerald Jackman, 3990244
14. Ralph Clayson, 4301230
15. Eldon Ives, 1601337
16. Dale Seymour, 6121429
17. Milton James, 2101234
18. Clarence Holt, 5701346
19. Walter Jones, 3990332
20. Sammy Hinson, 0311431
21. Glade Healey, 7501438
22. Glenda Lee, 2290154
23. Lorna Brown, 0401246
24. Margaret Christen, 7701246
25. Aleen Markwell, 8790242

Key to Seating Chart Code

First number—*meaningless*
Next three numbers—*I.Q. reversed*
Next number—*General academic achievement:* High (5), Low (1)
Next number—*Socioeconomic status:* High (5), Low (1)
Last number—*meaningless*

a) In this region cells grow in length to their full size.
b) This growth pushes the root further out into the soil.

4) In the *maturation* region the cells change to make special tissues.

e. Under the microscope the five parts of the root can be seen.

1) The *epidermis* is a single layer of brick-shaped cells on the outside of the root.

2) The *cortex* is a large area of loosely packed cells under the epidermis and is the chief storage area for the root.
3) The *endodermis* is a single layer of thick-walled cells.
4) The *pericycle* is just inside the endodermis and consists of thin-walled cells one layer deep.
5) The *central cylinder* is the chief conducting and strengthening region.
   a) Here is found the *xylem*, or water-conducting tissues, which take water from the root to the leaves and stems.
   b) The *phloem*, or food-conducting tissues, take food produced in the leaves down to the root.
   c) *Cambium* is the tissue that lies between the phloem and the xylem.
   d) *Pith* is the strengthening tissue in the center.

f. Fleshy taproots become larger through the growth of the cambium. The cambium adds secondary phloem to the outside and secondary xylem to the inside. In the older taproots this growth can be seen in rings.

g. The automatic responses of a plant toward or away from a stimulus is called a *tropism*.
   1) Two types of tropisms influence roots the most.
      a) *Geotropism* is the growth of the root toward gravity.
      b) *Hydrotropism* is the growth of a root towards water.
   2) *Phototropism* (response to light) and *thermotropism* (response to heat) have a greater effect on the stem of the plant than on the root.

h. Roots grow in many different environments.
   1) Soil roots are the most common.
      a) Decaying plants add organic matter to the soil.
      b) Organic matter holds water and makes the soil loose.
      c) Manure, leaf mold, and peat moss are soil conditioners, or *mulches*.
   2) Aquatic roots are found in water.
      a) They have no root hairs for absorption.
      b) They get minerals from the water in which they grow.
   3) Aerial roots are found only in very humid atmospheres.
      a) They get water from the atmosphere.

   b) They obtain minerals from debris that collects around them.

i. Some plants have *adventitious* roots, which develop from the stem or leaves. These roots are helpful to the plants in several ways.
   1) Prop roots help support the plant.
   2) Tip layering roots are for propagation.
   3) Climbing roots cling to the wall and allow the plant to grow upward.

j. There are many commercial uses for roots.
   1) Certain roots, such as carrots and radishes, are crops.
   2) Some roots contain valuable drugs.
   3) Some roots are used for seasonings.
   4) Other roots are used to make dyes.

k. Molecules are always in motion and tend to move into areas of lesser concentration.
   1) The spreading of molecules is called *diffusion.* Diffusion involves the movement of molecules from a more dense to a less dense area.
   2) When molecules are evenly distributed, they are in a state of equilibrium.

l. A thin material that allows molecules to pass through it is called a *membrane.*
   1) When a substance passes through a membrane, the membrane is permeable to the substance.
   2) When one substance goes through and another cannot, the membrane is semipermeable.

m. The passage of water through a semipermeable membrane is called *osmosis.* Water goes from a greater concentration to a lesser concentration of water.

n. The root hairs in the soil take in water by the process of osmosis.
   1) The cell of the root hair contains protoplasm, which is 70 per cent water, and also contains solutions of minerals.
   2) The water in the soil contains minerals in solution.
   3) The concentration of water is greater outside the cell than inside; thus osmosis occurs.

o. Osmosis occurs from cell to cell in the root, moving the water to the upper parts of the plants. The cell-to-cell diffusion of water is called *successive osmosis.*

p. When water enters a cell, it builds up a pressure inside the cell. This is called *osmotic pressure.*

1) This pressure causes the cell to become firm.
2) The firm cells cause the plant to be stiff.
   a) This stiffness is called *turgor.*
   b) Turgor allows the plant to push through the hard ground.

q. Turgor in root cells creates root pressure.
   1) Root pressure can be so great that water is forced out of the leaves of plants.
   2) A loss of this excess water in plants is called *guttation.*

r. When osmosis works in reversal, water is taken from the cells.
   1) The loss of turgor in this way is called *plasmolysis.*
   2) Plasmolysis can occur when the concentration of water is greater on the inside of the cell than on the outside.

s. Absorption of water by a solid, resulting in swelling, is called *imbibition.* Imbibition is necessary to break open seed coats.

B. Terms to Be Memorized

1. Fleshy root
2. Taproot
3. Fibrous root
4. Root system
5. Root cap
6. Root hair
7. Secondary root
8. Primary root
9. Embryonic region
10. Elongation region
11. Maturation region
12. Epidermis
13. Cortex
14. Endodermis
15. Pericycle
16. Phloem
17. Cambium
18. Xylem
19. Pith
20. Geotropism
21. Hydrotropism
22. Phototropism
23. Thermotropism
24. Tropism
25. Aerial roots
26. Aquatic roots
27. Adventitious roots
28. Prop roots
29. Tip layering roots
30. Climbing roots
31. Membrane
32. Osmosis
33. Osmotic pressure
34. Permeable
35. Semipermeable
36. Successive osmosis
37. Plasmolysis
38. Turgor
39. Diffusion
40. Equilibrium
41. Guttation
42. Imbibition

C. Skills to Be Learned

Note: There are no skills to be learned in this unit.

III. Activities Related to Unit Objectives
   A. Introductory Activities[13] (One class period)[14]
      1. The teacher will display several actual plant roots: fleshy taproot (carrot), long taproot (dandelion), fibrous root (grass), prop root (corn), climbing root (ivy), and tip-layering root (raspberry).
      2. The teacher will identify and tell a bit about each type of root.
      3. The teacher will ask the students which root would be best under certain conditions. *Example:* Which plant would grow best in a hardpan soil under shallow topsoil where rain is frequent but gentle? (*Answer:* fibrous roots.) This will demonstrate to the teacher how much knowledge of roots the students already have.
      4. The teacher will outline what is to be covered[15] in the unit.[16]
      5. The teacher will inform the students of the evaluation procedures to be followed in this unit. The students will make and label several drawings of roots.
      6. Under the teacher's direction, each student will set up two bean seeds on a wet nutrient agar. The seeds will be placed between two pieces of blotter paper or moss moistened with nutrient agar. The roots that grow will be studied during the developmental activities.
   B. Developmental Activities[17] (Twelve class periods)
      1. Recurring Activities
         a. Where it is practical and useful, students will study twenty minutes of each class period under teacher supervision. This study period will be arranged so that it does not include the first or the last ten minutes of the period.
         b. Students will assist the teacher in making demonstrations.
         c. Each teacher demonstration will be accompanied

---

[13]Because these activities are largely introductory and motivational in nature, it is difficult to relate them to specific objectives of the unit. The experimental activities, however, can be easily related to the overall unit concept.

[14]The careful approximation and noting of time to be spent on each type of activity encourages more realistic planning.

[15]It might be well to indicate more specifically *what* is to be covered and *how.*

[16]The illustrative units in this chapter were planned without any student participation in determining the objectives. If the teacher wishes to involve the students to some extent, he may have them help modify the objectives and activities during the introductory phase of the unit.

[17]Lack of detail in describing what specifically is to be done may result in teacher frustration when the unit is taught.

by an oral explanation. Colored wall charts will be used to supplement this explanation.

d. At the time of each demonstration, students will be encouraged to ask questions.

e. With student help, large numbers of plant specimens will be obtained for classroom examination.

f. Assignments for each day will be written in the upper right-hand corner of the chalkboard.

g. Brief quizzes will be given at four-day intervals when appropriate.

2. Sequential Listing of Activities[18]

The daily breakdown of activities is as follows:

First Day[19]

1. The teacher will take the roots that were on display the previous day and use them as the starting point in the discussion on the taproot. [II-A-2-a-(2)][20]
2. He will show the class that the taproot is long and will hold up a large plant. [II-A-2-b-(4)]
3. He will draw on the board a deep water supply and show how a taproot reaches it. [II-A-2-b-(3)]

Second Day

4. Using the fibrous root, the teacher will show how it covers a lot of area and binds the soil. [II-A-2-b-(1)]
5. He will explain with the aid of a chart how the many secondary roots draw in a great deal of water when it is available. [II-A-2-b-(2)]
6. He will illustrate at the chalkboard that the hair is one celled and is an outgrowth of the epidermis, or outer layer of the root. [II-A-2-c]
7. Using plant specimens he will explain that the hairs are located right back of the root tip and that as the root grows, the hairs are moved into new territory. [II-A-2-c-(2)]

---

[18]Note that many of the details essential to successful teaching have been omitted under the daily description of activities. For the beginning teacher this would be unwise. To assume that the spelling out of details should be left to the daily lesson plan is somewhat risky. In this plan, assignments, specific student involvement in activities, study period activities, and evaluation procedures have been given little or no attention, although they were mentioned in a general way under Recurring Activities.

[19]Indicating the precise developmental activities to be conducted on each day poses the risk of inflexibility. Adjustments can be made, however, through daily lesson planning. For the individual whose planning tends to be somewhat loose and inexact, this procedure has merit.

[20]The use of letters and numbers in brackets to refer to the objectives stated earlier is an efficient method for relating procedures to objectives.

Third Day

8. The teacher will use a modified lecture method to help the students understand the parts of a root tip. A chalkboard drawing will be used to explain the four different regions. [II-A-2-d]
9. A twelve-minute movie will be shown: "Roots of Plants." It will be previewed by the teacher, and its most important parts will be pointed out before it is shown. The movie shows examples of tap and fibrous roots, their structure and function. It also shows the four regions of the root cap and introduces osmosis. [II-A-2]

Fourth Day

10. The teacher will explain how to make a drawing and what format to use.
11. Ten demonstration microscopes will be set up with root caps under view. Ten students will draw root caps while the rest of the class members draw natural habitat pictures of taproots. When the first ten students are finished with the microscopes, the students will trade projects. [II-A-2-d]

Fifth Day

12. Radish seeds will be examined both with the naked eye and under the microscope. The students will draw a sprouted radish seed as seen with the naked eye and then a detailed view of a root hair as seen with the microscope. [II-A-2-c]

Sixth Day

13. Demonstration microscopes will be set up as on the fourth day, and students will follow the same procedures. Under the microscopes will be a cross section of a root. The different layers will be identified in a short lecture accompanied by a chalkboard drawing. Then the class will be asked to locate those layers on the microscope slide and make a labeled drawing of what they see. [II-A-2-e]

Seventh Day

14. Using examples of plants in the room, the teacher and students will explain and demonstrate the different tropisms. [II-A-2-g]
15. The students will be asked to indicate all the commercial uses of roots that they know of.

A scribe (Sally will act as scribe) will record them on the board. To assure that all the uses are listed, the teacher will help where he feels it necessary. [II-A-2-j]

Eighth Day

16. A teacher-led discussion of the different types of root environments will be held. Examples of all the different types mentioned will be called for. The teacher will see that all the important forms are mentioned and given adequate attention. [II-A-2-h]
17. Using the roots that were brought into the class the first day, the teacher will lead a discussion of adventitious roots. [II-A-2-i]

Ninth Day

18. A drawing of a root cap and a cross section of a root will be given to each student. They will be asked to label all parts shown. This will be used as a short test. [II-A-2-d and e][21]
19. A can of peppermint oil will be opened in the front of the room. As the students begin to smell it, the teacher will explain diffusion and equilibrium. [II-A-2-k-(1) and (2)]
20. A glass of water and several cubes of sugar will be placed at the front of the class. One cube will be dropped into the water. As the sugar dissolves, the water will be tasted by students. They will then explain why the water is sweet. More cubes will be added until the sugar will not dissolve. The students will be asked to explain this. [II-A-2-k-(1) and (2)]

Tenth Day

21. With a thistle tube, muslin, and a beaker of water, the teacher will set up a demonstration to show what a membrane is. (The muslin will represent a membrane.) The result will be explained by the teacher. [II-A-2-l]
22. An animal bladder will be filled with syrup and placed in water. The water will permeate the bladder and fill it. This action will be explained by the teacher. [II-A-2-m]
23. Using the full bladder as an illustration, the teacher will explain turgor. [II-A-2-p and q]

[21]Frequently a given activity moves in the direction of two or more subobjectives. Occasionally one activity seems to focus attention on the overall unit concept.

Eleventh Day

24. A twenty-one minute movie entitled "Osmosis" will be shown. This movie illustrates the operation of osmosis in familiar forms. [II-A-2-m and o]
25. With water in the bladder and syrup in the beaker, the teacher will demonstrate reverse osmosis, or plasmolysis. [II-A-2-r]

Twelfth Day

26. A cutting of a plant will be placed in a concentrated salt solution. As plasmolysis takes place, the students will be asked to explain orally what is happening and why. [II-A-2-r]
27. With the use of a water-logged stick, the teacher will explain imbibition and its uses. [II-A-2-s]

C. Culminating Activities[22] (Two class periods)

1. All the drawings that were made during the laboratory periods will have been corrected and graded by the teacher and will be returned to the students.
2. With the help of the corrected drawings, the students will review the anatomy of a root. Such parts as the xylem and phloem will be stressed to make sure that the students understand their functions.
3. The teacher, using the hidden chalkboard method, will review such terms as: diffusion, equilibrium, membrane, permeable, semipermeable membrane, osmosis, osmotic pressure, successive osmosis, turgor, guttation, plasmolysis, and imbibition. The teacher will selectively sample members of the class to find out whether or not the students understand the meaning of these words. If a student does not understand, one of the brighter students will be given a chance to answer. If none of the students know the answer, the teacher will explain and ask the question later.
4. A unit test will be given. It will take about forty minutes for the slowest students to complete. (For details of this test, see the section on Evaluation.)
5. Students who finish early will be given a mimeographed study help for the next unit on "Stems." They will be allowed to start studying.
6. When all of the tests are in, the teacher will quickly go over the test, giving the answers and clearing up any questions.

---

[22]Burton, *op. cit.*, p. 368, discusses briefly the history and purposes of culminating activities. Specific errors to avoid are pointed out.

IV. Materials and Resources[23]

1. Textbook: *Biology* by Elsbeth Kroeber, Walter H. Wolff, and Richard L. Weaver[24]
2. Display of six types of roots made up of carrot, dandelion, grass, corn, ivy, and raspberry
3. Twelve plates of nutrient agar
4. Bean seeds
5. Radish seeds
6. Fifty pieces of blotter paper
7. Peat moss
8. Ten compound microscopes
9. Slides and cover slips for everyone in the class
10. Razor blades
11. Students' own drawing paper and hard lead pencils
12. Movie "Roots of Plants," 12 minutes, $1.50 rental from T.M.U., A.V.A.
13. Movie "Osmosis," 21 minutes, $3.00 rental from T.M.U., A.V.A.
14. Movie projector
15. A semipermeable membrane (animal bladder)
16. A membrane (muslin)
17. A glass of water and several sugar cubes
18. A thistle tube and stand with clamp
19. Syrup
20. Large beaker of water
21. Cutting from a plant
22. Salt water in glass
23. College text: *The Plant World* by Harry J. Fuller (for the teacher's use)
24. A water-logged stick

V. Evaluation Procedures[25]

A. Tests and Examinations (The weight given each item is shown.)

1. After the anatomy of the root has been studied, a ten-minute test will be given in which a drawing of a root will be labeled by the students. (2/10)
2. A comprehensive examination covering the completed unit will be given. This examination will contain completion, matching, and multiple-choice questions. There will be two essay questions of equal magnitude; students may choose one of the two questions to answer.

---

[23]The essential materials and resources seem to have been identified and listed.

[24]It is important to include the authors of the text if this unit is to be filed as resource material for a later unit.

[25]It is desirable to describe all evaluation procedures in the Developmental Activities.

They will also be asked to identify different parts of a drawing. (5/10)

B. General Evaluation Procedures (The weight given each item is shown.)
   1. The drawings that are made in the laboratory will be graded on completeness and neatness. (1/10)
   2. During the laboratory periods, the teacher will observe the students' work with the microscopes and make notes on their activities. (1/20)
   3. Personal teacher-student talks will indicate strengths and weaknesses. (1/20)
   4. The quality and extent of class participation will be recorded. (1/20)
   5. Teacher's evaluation of the students' abilities and the learning actually taking place will be noted. (1/20)
C. Evaluation of Teaching
   1. After every class the teacher will evaluate the teaching done that day in class.[26] He will note weaknesses and strengths.
   2. After the unit is completed and the students have been evaluated, the teacher will examine the unit objectives to see whether they were reached.[27]
   3. The unit plan will be adjusted as necessary on the basis of the information gathered.

A Teaching Unit in English

The following English unit has the potential for considerable success if taught to the class described under Basic Information. Certain of the activities hold promise of making the dry bones of grammar take on new life.

Good Grammar Is an Aid to Communication[28]

I. Basic Information
   A. Statistics
      1. This is an eighth-grade class of thirty pupils.
      2. Ages range from twelve to fourteen. There are fourteen girls and sixteen boys.
      3. The I.Q. range is from 60 to 126.
   B. This unit will take about three and one-half weeks.

[26]The teacher's concern for continuous improvement is commendable.

[27]Since the achievement of objectives is the most relevant concern of teaching, the instructor must determine whether this has been done.

[28]Harry N. Rivlin, *Teaching Adolescents in Secondary Schools*, 2d. ed. (New York: Appleton-Century-Crofts, 1961), Chapter 4, presents a sound treatment of the essential characteristics of teaching units.

C. Relationship of This Unit to Other Units
   1. The year's work on improving communication is divided into four sections.[29]
      a. Development of abilities to speak well.
      b. Development of abilities to write well.
      c. Development of abilities to read well.
      d. Development of abilities to listen.
   2. This unit is the fourth in a series on improving communication by developing abilities to write well.
   3. This unit is preceded by a unit on "Aids to Better Spelling" and will be followed by a unit on "Punctuation."

D. Nature of the Class
   1. The class contains two nonreaders and three very slow readers who read at about the third-grade level.
   2. One student is on probation from the Juvenile Court. He lives in a foster home but needs special attention. He is inattentive and cannot concentrate on one thing for long.
   3. Among the group are four bright students who have previously led in every class situation. Their behavior presents a problem since a large proportion of the class sits by and lets them lead in almost everything. Eighty per cent of the students are quite passive.
   4. The degree of needed motivation will vary greatly because of the wide range of abilities.
   5. Students have all lived in the same area, and their experiences and backgrounds are about the same.
   6. With four exceptions, students belong to the same religious faith.

II. Objectives

A. Concepts to Be Learned[30]
   1. Unit Concept: An understanding of sentence construction and all of the parts of speech that make up sentences will aid students in better communication.
   2. Supporting Concepts
      a. All sentences have a subject and a predicate and convey a complete thought.[31]
         1) The subject names the person, place, thing, or idea the sentence is about.

---

[29]The relationship of this unit to the other segments of the total year's work is clear.

[30]Because of the formalized approach to English grammar in this unit (with respect to conceptual objectives as well as procedures), one should ask how much value it will have for students somewhat below average in intelligence.

[31]Simplicity and clarity in the full-sentence statements of concepts assist markedly in teaching them to eighth-graders. A question about the advisability of teaching a unit on formal grammar to eighth-grade students is in order, however. Currently there is division in the ranks of English teachers over this point.

2) The subject is a noun or another word or group of words used as a noun.
3) Pronouns take the place of nouns.
4) The complete predicate tells something about the subject.
5) The simple predicate is the verb.
6) The verb makes statements, asks questions, or gives commands.
    a) There are linking auxiliary verbs.
    b) There are transitive verbs, which transfer action from subject to object.
    c) Intransitive verbs may show action but do not transfer action to an object.
    d) There are verb phrases consisting of a main verb and auxiliary verbs.
7) Verbs have three principal parts:
    a) The first part shows *present* time.
    b) The second shows *past* time.
    c) The third shows *past* time with an *auxiliary verb* helper.
    d) Some verbs are more troublesome than others. They are *lie, lay, sit, set, rise,* and *raise.*
8) Verbs have six tenses, showing present, past, future, present perfect, past perfect, and future perfect time.
9) To conjugate a verb is to give in order the form of its several voices, tenses, numbers, and persons.
10) Transitive verbs have voice.
    a) *Active* voice shows the subject as the actor.
    b) *Passive* voice shows the subject as receiver.

b. A simple sentence conveys a complete thought and has a subject and verb, either or both of which may be compound.
    1) *Compound* means more than one.
    2) Compounds help improve choppy sentences.

c. A compound sentence is composed of two complete sentences conveying two closely related complete thoughts.
    1) Compound sentences are connected by a coordinate conjunction: *and, but, or, nor.*
    2) Compound sentences may be connected by a semicolon.

d. A complex sentence conveys one complete thought and is composed of one independent clause and two or more dependent clauses.
    1) A clause has a subject and a verb.
    2) A dependent clause relies on another clause to complete its meaning.

3) An independent clause conveys a complete thought.

e. Descriptive modifiers add meaning to words.

1) Adjectives modify nouns and pronouns by telling kinds, colors, sizes, shapes, which one, and how many.
2) Adverbs modify verbs, adjectives, and other adverbs by telling how, where, and when.
3) A group of related words is called a phrase and may be used as a single adjective or a single adverb.
4) Adjectives and adverbs have three forms of comparison—positive, comparative, and superlative.

B. Terms to Be Memorized[32]

1. Subject
2. Predicate
3. Simple sentence
4. Complex sentence
5. Compound sentence
6. Transitive verb
7. Intransitive verb
8. Active verb
9. Passive verb
10. Linking verb
11. Auxiliary verb
12. Independent clause
13. Dependent clause
14. Phrase
15. Adverb
16. Adjective
17. Conjunction
18. Positive
19. Comparative
20. Superlative

C. Skills to be Learned

Note: Nothing classed as a skill is to be presented during this unit.

III. Activities Related to Unit Objectives

A. Introductory Activities[33] (Two class periods)

1. Reference will be made to the chart outlining the course for the year, which was developed by students and teacher during the first week of school.
2. The need for the units in the second section of the year's work, "Improving Skills in Written Language," will be identified, written on the chalkboard, and discussed for a few moments. The list will be left on the board. After the film, students will add more reasons to the list.
3. The film "How's Your English?" will be shown and followed by a discussion.[34] The film emphasizes the necessity for good word usage and explains how misunderstandings arise because of poor choice of words. The machine

---

[32]Attention has been given to the proper sequence of steps in memorization. Obtaining a clear concept must precede drill.

[33]M. L. Goetting, *Teaching in the Secondary School* (New York: Prentice-Hall, 1942), Chapter 16, points out the essential procedures in initiating a unit.

[34]Failure to indicate the length and source of a film means that this information will have to be determined later.

will be set up and run by the teacher with the aid of two boys, Kent and Roger.

4. The students will be free to suggest desired activities concerning the unit. These will be listed and used if appropriate.
5. The teacher will display two neat student notebooks and discuss their qualities. This will help establish a standard for neat notebooks and written work to be handed in.[35]
6. The teacher will explain why a vocabulary notebook is necessary and how it should be indexed and used. Each student will make one to be used for the rest of the year.[36]

B. Recurring Activities[37]

1. Oral reviews will be presented by the teacher each day. This will last for not more than five or six minutes. Different methods and approaches will be used to keep interest alive.
2. Students will frequently use the chalkboard.
3. There will be supervised fifteen-minute work periods as often as possible. Some weeks they will occur about every day, and at other times less frequently.
4. Short quizzes to determine assimilation and understanding of material will be given each five or six days.
5. Work sheets will be distributed. All students will have a chance to air problems, get help, actually finish an exercise, and get the correct answers. This method will prove beneficial when the material and problems are rather difficult to understand.
6. The students will index a notebook for vocabulary building. As they meet and learn new words, the students will list these words alphabetically in the notebook. These lists will later furnish material for vocabulary tests and spelling lists.
7. Charts and flash cards will be used periodically.
8. Students will often refer to an eighth-grade literature book to find, in context, sentences for analysis and words for spelling lists and vocabulary building.

C. Sequential Listing of Activities[38]

1. The teacher will read several sentences and phrases,

---

[35]It is entirely proper to establish high standards at the beginning of the unit.

[36]There may be some doubt as to whether the students will have a clear idea of the nature of the unit by the time the Introductory Activities are completed.

[37]Goetting, *op. cit.*, Chapter 17, discusses developmental activities as devices for achieving unit goals.

Differentiating between recurring activities and nonrepetitive, sequential activities indicates efficiency in planning.

[38]Activities have generally been carefully selected in consideration of the types of youngsters in this eighth-grade group. Occasionally, however, the planner wishes to use the textbook without specifically stating which exercise he is referring to. These

calling attention to the absence of complete thought and the lack of a subject or verb in the phrases. [II-A-2-a]
2. The students will determine that some groups of words are not sentences because there is no subject or verb; all sentences must have a subject and a verb. [II-A-2-a]
3. The students will eliminate all phrases from a list in the textbook. They will identify all the sentences by finding the subjects and verbs. They will classify them in two columns in their English notebooks, all verbs in one column and all subjects in the other. [II-A-2-a]
4. Students will find and compile lists of nouns classified as people, places, ideas, animals, and things. They will get this information from books, observations, and experiences. [II-A-2-a-(1)]
5. One student will read his list of classified nouns. If others in the room have new ones, they will be added to the list. The students will make sentences with a few of the nouns to be sure they see the relationship of the noun to the sentence. [II-A-2-a-(1) and (2)]
6. A written exercise from the text will be assigned on finding, selecting, and classifying nouns in the four categories. [II-A-2-a-(1)]
7. From examples of simple sentences on the board, students will detect that verbs are not always single words but may be two-, three-, or four-word verbs called *verb phrases*. They will clarify the word *phrase* if its meaning has been forgotten. This will be added to their vocabulary notebooks. [II-A-2-a-(6)-(d)]
8. Students will work an exercise from their books on finding verb phrases. [II-A-2-a-(6)-(d)]
9. The students will find sentences in their readers that contain action verbs. In order to save time, some of the verbs will be quickly written on the board. They will observe that some action verbs transfer action to an object and are called *transitive*. The prefix *trans* will be defined, discussed, and written in the vocabulary notebook. Students will observe that some action verbs and auxiliary (helper) verbs do not transfer action to an object; they are called *intransitive*. The prefix *in* (not) will be defined, discussed, and put in the notebook. The two new words with their meanings will also be listed. [II-A-2-a-(6)-(a), (b), and (c)]
10. The students will work exercises from the textbook on

---

activities have been consistently related to stated objectives. Furthermore, activities have been described well enough to permit a second teacher to get an accurate picture of what is to be done.

finding verbs and classifying them as transitive or intransitive. [II-A-2-b-(6)-(a), (b), and (c)]

11. The students will complete work sheets on transitive and intransitive verbs, also finding subjects in the same sentences. This is to be an informal review. [II-A-2-a-(1) and (6)-(a), (b), and (c)]
12. The students will look at diagrams of sentences in the text containing transitive and intransitive verbs. They will try to diagram four or five sentences containing such verbs from the informal work sheet. They will then correct their own work, using the correct form the teacher puts on the board. [II-A-2-a-(6)-(b) and (c)]
13. The teacher will give a short quiz on finding subjects and verbs (transitive and intransitive) and on diagraming a few simple sentences. [II-A-2-a-(1) through (6)]
14. The students will refer to their texts for charts on the principal parts of verbs. *Principal* will be defined and added to vocabulary notes. Students will observe that many mistakes in usage can be eliminated if they know and understand when to use each of the three parts of verbs: the present part is for what happens now, the past part is for past time, and the third part also shows past time but always has a helper. [II-A-2-a-(7)]
15. The students will review all three parts of the long list of verbs, saying them aloud in a sentence. They will discuss those parts that seem out of the ordinary or strange. [II-A-2-a-(7)]
16. More work will be done on the troublesome verbs—*lie-lay, sit-set, rise-raise*—after it has been determined that students comprehend their principal parts. [II-A-2-a-(7)]
17. The students will be given a dittoed chart with two verbs categorized in their six tenses. [II-A-2-a-(8)]
18. The word *conjugate* will be defined and made meaningful as the teacher points out that the two words in the verb chart have been conjugated, or put in all of the different voices and tenses, using all of the persons and numbers. [II-A-2-a-(9)]
19. Students will each select two verbs and, with the teacher's help, will conjugate them on their charts. [II-A-2-a-(9)]
20. The students will do exercises on the three parts and six tenses of verbs. Work sheets will be completed in class. [II-A-2-b-(7), (8), and (9)]
21. The teacher will make assignments in the text on the parts of verbs and choosing the right verb. [II-A-2-a-(6) through (9)]
22. A game called "Answer Me" will vary the "choose-the-

right-verb" study. Fifteen troublesome verbs will be passed to half the class, fifteen members. Each student will ask a question using the past part of the verb he has been given. He holds the verb up while he is talking. Then the person next to him, without a verb, uses the same verb and answers back with the past participle and a helper. *Question:* I *saw* the circus last night. Did you? *Answer:* No, but I *have seen* one before. [II-A-2-a-(7), (8), and (9)]

23. A written test on the use of fifty verbs will be given. [II-A-2-a-(6) through (10)]
24. The students will be asked to find some interesting descriptive sentences. These will be written on the board for analysis. [II-A-2-a, b, and c]
25. Students will observe that the most vivid words describe the nouns by telling the colors, kinds, sizes, shapes, how many, and which one. These words are called adjectives. The students will then be given a work sheet containing twenty sentences full of vivid adjectives. They will clarify all the adjectives in columns according to what they tell. [II-A-2-e-(1)]
26. The teacher will diagram a couple of sentences on the board and then help the students diagram about six in order to see the relationship of adjectives to nouns. [II-A-2-e-(1)]
27. The students will do some assignments on adjectives from the text, naming what they modify and what they tell about the word. [II-A-2-e-(1)]
28. Students will be shown by the use of objects how to properly compare adjectives (for instance, *big, bigger,* when comparing two items; *big, bigger, biggest,* when comparing more than two items). [II-A-2-e-(4)]
29. They will do an oral exercise on comparison. Each student will think of one adjective that can be compared and then by use of proper sentences will state it in the three degrees. Any mistakes will be corrected. New words will be added to the vocabulary notebook. [II-A-2-e-(4)]
30. A short completion test will be given. The student will select the proper degree of comparison to fill in the space. There will be 25 sentences. *Example:* 1. Of the two boys, John is the _____ (thinner, thinnest). [II-A-2-e-(4)]
31. A set of sentences from the text will be analyzed to find that how, when, and where words are called *adverbs.* [II-A-2-e-(2)]
32. Students will classify adverbs from twelve to fifteen sentences into the three categories. They will determine what kinds of words they modify. [II-A-2-e-(2)]

33. Work sheets will be given to the class. They will find all the adjectives and adverbs and draw arrows pointing to the words they modify. On the arrow they will write what the adjective or adverb tells about the word modified. [II-A-2-e-(1) and (2)]
34. Some examples of simple sentences with compound parts will be analyzed from the book. The students will observe that the compound parts are connected by a conjunction and that conjunctions help relate the parts to each other. [II-A-2-c and d]
35. The students will diagram several simple sentences with compound parts following examples given in the text. New words will be added to the vocabulary notebook. [II-A-2-c]
36. Students will follow the text in analyzing compound sentences, noting that two closely related complete thoughts are connected by a conjunction or semicolon. Any new words will be defined and added to their notebooks. [II-A-2-c]
37. Work sheets will be given to the class. They will find compound parts (subject and verb) and compound sentences, labeling each. Those who wish may try diagraming a sentence of their choice on the chalkboard. The class will criticize. [II-A-2-b and c]
38. An assignment on simple and compound sentences will be given from the text. New words will be added to the vocabulary list. [II-A-2-b and c]
39. An examination will be given on work covered this far. [II-A-2-a, b, c, and d] *Sample examination questions:*
    1. Tell if the sentence is simple or compound by putting *S* or *C* in the margin.
    2. Underline all subjects once, verbs twice.
    3. Write *1* above all adjectives, *2* above all adverbs.
    4. Write (*trans.*) or (*intrans.*) above all verbs.
40. After a short oral review, a test will be given on all terms and words in the vocabulary list. (Flash cards will be used to review words.) The test will be concerned with defining and filling in the blanks. [II-A-2-a, b, c, d and e]
41. Before class, the teacher will write on the board two or three sentences that have complicated parts. By analysis the students will observe that there are phrases and clauses that depend on the rest of the sentence for their meaning. [II-A-2-d and e-(3)]
42. The meaning of and differences between the words *clause* and *phrase* will be clarified and added to vocabulary notes. [II-A-2-d-(1) and e-(3)]
43. From exercises in the text, the students will find clauses

and phrases that act as adjectives, modifying nouns or pronouns. They will find clauses and phrases that act as adverbs, modifying adjectives, adverbs, or verbs and telling how, when, and where. [II-A-2-d and e]

44. They will be encouraged to find clauses that act as nouns and may be used as subjects, predicate nominatives, or objects. [II-A-2-a through e]
45. The students will be shown on the chalkboard how the clauses and phrases are diagramed. They will not diagram these yet. [II-A-2-d and e]
46. Work sheets will be given to the students. They will place parentheses around the clauses and phrases and draw an arrow to the words they modify. They will name the kinds of clauses and phrases. [II-A-2-e]
47. Several exercises from the book on clauses and phrases will follow. There will also be chalkboard work. [II-A-2-d and e]
48. An examination on complex sentences will be given. [II-A-2-d] *Example:* Put parentheses around the dependent clause. Underline the complete independent clause. Circle the connecting link, and draw an arrow to the word to which the dependent clause refers; also tell what kind of clause it is.

D. Culminating Activities (Three or four class periods)

1. A review in the form of an open-book test will precede an overall examination. Sheets of questions (underlining, matching, completion, or short essay) will be handed out. Questions on all material covered so far in the unit will be included in the questions. (The students won't know that this isn't a final.) Under a reasonable time limit the students will answer the problems. When the time is up, the students will be free to open their books and answer all questions that they omitted. Special help will be given to those students with problems. Those who finish early and need no recheck may go to the library. [II-A-2-a through e]
2. Each student will choose from a list of topics a subject upon which to speak for one or two minutes.[39] He will prepare the talk in school and record it on tape. This will be recorded before school and from 3:30 to 4:00 after school. These recordings will be played in the next class period. The students will criticize them on the following:
   a. Proper usage of words
   b. Content

[39]Note the culminating nature of this activity. It calls for the practical use of much of the content of the unit in a real situation.

c. Correctness of subject matter
d. Enunciation and voice

Examples of topics: [II-A-2-a through e]

a. How to use (1) in, into; (2) sit, set; (3) lie, lay.
b. What do adjectives do?
c. How do we use adverbs?
d. What is a compound sentence?
e. What is a verb tense?

3. The students will make a pen or pencil sketch to show some particular outstanding problem in the usage of words that they have overcome in studying this unit.[40] Or they may graphically portray some concept that has been especially interesting. These problems and concepts will be discussed very briefly by each student as he displays his visual object or sketch. These materials will be mounted on the bulletin board. [II-A-2-a through e]
4. The students will take a final examination on all phases covered in this unit. [II-A-2-a through e]

IV. Materials and Resources

A. The following materials and teaching aids will be used during the teaching of the unit:[41]
   1. Work sheets
   2. Extensive use of the chalkboard
   3. Charts
   4. Pictures for bulletin boards
   5. Colored pencils
   6. Drawing paper
   7. Indexed vocabulary notebooks
   8. Tests
   9. English notebooks
   10. Tape recorder
   11. Film projector

B. The following texts will be used during the unit:
   1. *Our English Language* by Matilda Bailey and Lalla Walker.
   2. Eighth Grade Literature Series.[42]

V. Evaluation Procedures

A. Tests and Examinations[43]
   1. Both formal and informal tests will be given to measure the accuracy and extent of the students' learning.

---

[40]Note the teacher's attempt to make the instruction personally meaningful for the student.

[41]The list of teaching materials and aids to be used is concise and complete.

[42]Inexact designation of the literature series tends toward haziness in planning.

[43]Evaluation procedures give evidence of the need for breadth and variation.

SEATING CHART

TEACHER

Clifford X605	Lynn X705	Kathryn X801	James X961	Francis X904	Bill 01102
Susan X852	Bayle X1041	Todd 01053	Beth X1014	Sammy X891	Earl X965
Jay X993	Bonnie 01264	Kent 0854	Kay X1013	Jean 01185	Joan 01073
Linda X1205	Larry 01174	Laurel 01004	Vaughn 01095	Raylene X1022	Jimmy X974
John X913	Laura 01055	Roger 0904	Betty 01074	Wayne 0975	Claudette 0983

Seating Chart Code[44]

X = *Inattentive*
O = *No problem*
101 = *I.Q.*
1-5 = *Discipline*

2. Short quizzes and a final examination will be given.
3. Results of the exams and quizzes will be reviewed and evaluated.
4. Open-book tests will be given periodically to teach the techniques of searching for certain facts, developing abilities in the use of the index, locating and recording important facts, combing out details, and reviewing important concepts.

B. General Evaluation Procedures
1. Informative discussions, in which all of the students participate, will clear up hazy concepts in daily work.
2. The teacher will keep individual records of all the work done by the students and will periodically review their status with them in private conferences. Group relations and adjustment problems may also be discussed at this time.
3. Students will evaluate their own work while listening to tape recordings of their own compositions. They will check

[44]The seating chart might have been more appropriately included as a part of the Basic Information. Questions might be raised about the simplicity of the code and, therefore, the protection it offers in safeguarding confidential information.

for incorrect usage, poor sentences, repetition, unnecessary words, a good speaking voice, and general accuracy of information.

4. Students will rate their own written work according to a chart set up for this purpose. They will check their own notebooks for general appearance, margins, title, proper spacing for paragraphs, completeness, and accuracy.
5. Any stories, sketches, objective material, or observations that students bring in will be rated by the teacher and used for instructional purposes where desirable.
6. Filmstrips will be used to reveal the art of communication and how general principles must be employed to achieve desirable social relations.
7. Teacher-made aids such as posters, pictures, sketches, bulletin boards, and flash cards will be used to motivate and provoke thinking.
8. Students will write questions for quiz games that will serve as good motivation for an overall review.
9. The final grades will give attention to the student's progress as well as his scholarship.

A Teaching Unit Needing Revision

The following unit on United States History has been criticized by means of a "Self-Scoring Instrument for Teaching Units," developed by the author and explained in detail in Appendix B. Consideration is given to the five basic divisions of the unit—Basic Information, Objectives, Procedures, Materials and Resources, and Evaluation Procedures—as well as to the general concerns of unit planning. Questions related to these divisions are numbered and grouped under subheadings within these divisions.

The numbers of individual evaluation questions, together with a numerical evaluation ranging from 0 through 5, are written as close to the evaluated section as possible. A marginal notation of *12–0*, for example, means that the unit planner forgot to include whatever was mentioned in question twelve. The notation *12–3* means that whatever was mentioned in question twelve was present to a moderate extent. A score of *12–5* means that the concern expressed in question twelve was cared for as well as possible. A general evaluation for a given unit division or subdivision is occasionally employed without the mention of specific numbers. *I, D–5* means that all conditions mentioned in questions related to *I, D,* the "Nature of the Class" as listed under "Basic Information," were met as well as possible.

This instrument has the advantage of enabling the user to evaluate a unit according to a structured pattern and with a minimum of writing.

Eleventh-Grade United States History: "Civil War and Reconstruction"

I. Basic Information I-4

- A. Age and Grade level
    - 1. The ages will range from sixteen to eighteen. 1-5
    - 2. All students are seniors except one. 2-5
- B. Length of Time for the unit 3-5
    - 1. This unit will cover a period of five weeks (25 classroom days).
    - 2. This unit will be divided into ten sections.
- C. Relationship of Unit to other units in the Overall Plan
    - 1. This unit is fifth in a series of twelve units of United States History.
    - 4-5 2. It will come after a unit called "Growth of a Nation" and will be followed by a unit called "A World Power."
- D. Nature of the Class
    - 1. Economic and Social Status of Students: Middle class except for four students. One of these is from the lower-upper class and three are from the lower-lower class 7-5
    - 2. Sex: There are sixteen boys and sixteen girls in the class.
    - 3. Problems of the Class 8-5
        - a. Groups
            - 1) Ward, Wayne, Bill S., James, and Edward need to be encouraged to work.
            - 2) Linda and Minnie talk.
        - b. Single
            - 1) Bobby is a slow reader.
            - 2) Randy has a high I.Q. and needs extra work.
            - 3) Bonnie has a speech problem.
            - 4) Lillie has a background problem.
    - 4. Religion
        - a. Twenty are Protestants.
        - b. Eight are Catholics.
        - c. One is Jewish.
    - IE-0 5. Discipline: There is no problem in this class as long as the teacher can hold the interest of the students in the subject matter. 10-4
    - 6. I.Q. Ranges: The I.Q.'s have been received from testing and have been noted in the grade book but <u>not</u> on the seating chart. 5-3
- E. Roll call will be by a system of numbers.

II. Objectives--Concepts II A-3

187-3

Unit Concept

A. The period of the Civil War and Reconstruction in the United States had a grave effect on the political, social, economic, and religious institutions in this country. 19-2

B. Pre-secession activities were a matter of grave concern to both Northern and Southern leaders. 20-5

20-0

1. Statehood privileges in pre-secession era.
2. Commerce rules and regulations were unjust.
3. Man's freedom was in the path of State's Rights.

C. Causes of secession can be traced back to the First Continental Congress in 1774.

Avoid topics - they are less meaningful

1. First Continental Congress and its role in the era
2. Second Continental Congress
3. Mount Vernon Conference
4. Constitutional Convention at Philadelphia
5. Constitution
   a. "Southern Block"
   b. The Ordinance of 1787
6. The Tariff
7. Clay's Compromise
8. Kansas-Nebraska Bill
9. Dred Scott Decision
10. Lincoln's Election
11. Slavery and Sectionalism
12. The south seceded to prevent the subversion of the rights of the state.

20-0

21-0

D. The Civil War in the United States could have been avoided; however, radical abolitionists, revisionists, Southerners, and Northerners saw to it that war, the worst possible solution, occurred.

Avoid topics

1. The secessionists and their role in the war
2. Lincoln's policies force the hand of the secessionists
3. The business of war
   a. Taxes
   b. Borrowing of both the North and the South
4. Political dissensions with North and South administrations
5. Military aspects of the Civil War
   a. Eastern and Western theaters of war
   b. Battles of the Civil War
   c. Outcome of battles
      1) Political
      2) Economic
   d. Dates
   e. Leaders of both sides

20-0

6. The surrenders of Lee, Johnson, and, last, Dick Taylor closed an era of United States History that can never be forgotten.

E. The Reconstruction Era was even more dramatic than the Civil War.

1. Lincoln's policies of reconstruction
2. The death of Lincoln and its grave consequences for the South
3. The organization of the Ku Klux Klan
4. The harsh policies of Andrew Johnson

F. The dramatic reconstruction has long received due attention, but not so the dreary, discouraging years that followed. An entire generation had to struggle under conditions of poverty that inevitably involved cultural as well as economic decline.

II. Objectives--Skills IIC-3 27-0 187-3

Largely conceptual

A. The student may be able to talk on the general Civil War period of United States history with some degree of knowledge.

B. The student has learned the use of certain Civil War reference materials. 27-4 17-0

II. Objectives--Memorization IIB-4

The following is a list of items with which the student <u>should</u> be familiar to the point of memorization.

A. Terms

Ordinance of Secession
25-5 Fort Moultrie
Fort Sumter
26-3 Star of the West
Richmond, Va.
Harper's Ferry
Romney
West Virginia
Manassas (Bull Run)
Department of the Potomac
Port Royal Bay
Fort Pickens
Department of Kentucky
Army of Northern Virginia
Pea Ridge
Big Sandy
Chattanooga
Morgan's Raid
Manassas Gap
Stoneman's Gap
Monitor and Merrimac
Copperheads
Thirteenth Amendment
Emancipation Proclamation
Murfreesboro
Vicksburg
Gainesville
Antietam Campaign
Chancellorsville
Gettysburg
Knights of the Golden Circle
Appomattox Court House

B. Dates

December 20, 1860
January 9, 1861
January 10, 1861
January 11, 1861
January 19, 1861
January 26, 1861
February 1, 1861
February 7, 1861
April 12, 1861
March 9, 1862
November 24, 25, 1863
May 29, 1865
April 3, 1865
April 9, 1865
April 26, 1865
May 26, 1865

C. Names

Major Robert Anderson
Jefferson Davis
Alexander H. Stephens
General P. G. T. Beauregard
Abraham Lincoln
General Nathaniel Lyon
General B. F. Butler
General Robert E. Lee
General G. B. McClellan
General Irvin McDowell
General Ulysses S. Grant
General William T. Sherman
William H. Seward
Judah P. Benjamin

II. Objectives--Tastes: The teacher hopes to inform as well as instill within each individual the important facts and events 34-0 of the Civil War in the United States and the effect they had on the lives of the people. 187-2 33-1

III. Activities

82-5

A. Introductory Activities (1/2 period on Friday)

1. The teacher will introduce the Civil War unit by one
43-4 of the following means: Be specific!
44-3 a. The teacher's ancestors and the Civil War
45-4 b. A short fifteen-minute film on Civil War highlights
46-3 c. Several interesting stories (Humor)
48-0 d. Southern and Northern life during the Civil War

2. A general reading assignment from the textbook will be made for Monday.

B. Developmental Activities (where needed) ? 105-2

54-0 1. Class notes will be taken in the usual manner. The
56-4 teacher will write a general outline on the board as he
58-2 discusses each period.
60-3 2. A Reading List will be handed out, and each student will
75-4 be required to read and make a written report on two
76-4 books.
77-3
82-4 3. Bulletin Boards: Five bulletin boards will be put up by
84-3 members of the class. Detail lacking!

86-3 a. Battles 93-5 115-0
87-3 b. Leaders 112-? 117-2
89-3 c. Presidents 108-2
91-3 109-2
113-0 d. Books

e. OPEN

Be sure concepts are clear first

4. All items in "Objectives--Memorization" will be written down and explained in the class notes. These will be handed in on the last Friday for evaluation by the teacher.

5. One-question (6 min.) quizzes will be given as the teacher thinks they are needed. III H-2

C. Concluding Activities (Two days, Wednesday and Thursday) 82-5

62-3 1. Open-book assignment will be given in class on Tuesday
65-4 and will be due in class on Friday. (See Example 1.)

66-4 2. Wednesday will be given over to a study period for
67-4 finishing up papers, notes, book reports, etc.

69-4 3. Thursday will be a general summary day with the teacher going over high points of the Civil War period and discussing the evaluation that will be given on Friday.

IV. Materials and Resources IV-4

A. Texts to be used as reference materials: 157-5

Which is the basic text? For teachers or students?

1. United States to 1865. John A. Krout. College Outline Series, 1955.
2. The Causes of the Civil War. Kenneth M. Stampp (ed). Prentice-Hall, 1959.
3. A Short History of the Civil War. Fletcher Pratt. William Sloane Associates, Inc., 1952.
4. America's Tragedy. James T. Adams. C. Scribner's Sons, 1934.

How used?

B. Special methods texts to be used: 156-3

1. Teaching the Social Studies in Secondary School. (3rd ed., 1952)
2. Handbook of Social Studies Teaching. Republic. 153-5

C. One fifteen-minute film: "Civil War Highlights" (Cornet) 155-5

D. Maps: 47 individual maps on the battles of the Civil War

E. Reading List: Prepared by the teacher with the cooperation of the librarian 152-5 160-2

F. Bulletin-board material

G. List of library materials for the Civil War period Be specific

V. Evaluation V-3

A. Student evaluation will cover the following items:

1. Work on memorization items
2. Book report
3. Class notes
4. Open-book assignment (See Example 1.)
5. Quizzes
6. Evaluation (See Example 2.)

B. Teacher evaluation

1. The use of all items in student evaluation
2. Continuous check on daily lesson plans and unit concepts

EXAMPLE 1

Open-Book Assignment

1. List all the names and positions of the men who served in the cabinets of Lincoln and Davis.
2. List all the men in Lincoln's 1865 cabinet not yet listed.
3. List all the states that left the union and the dates of secession.
4. List the causes of the Civil War that were discussed in class.
5. Give the Northern and Southern views of slavery.
6. What is egocentric sectionalism?
7. What were the following items?
   a. Kansas-Nebraska Act
   b. Dred Scott Decision
   c. Lecompton Constitution
   d. Ordinance of 1787
   e. Nat Turner Rebellion
   f. Missouri Compromise
   g. Compromise of 1850
   h. Wilmot Proviso
   i. Lincoln-Douglas Debates
   j. John Brown's Raid
   k. Emancipation Proclamation
   l. Ku Klux Klan
8. Pick 10 men we have discussed and tell what role each played in the drama of the Civil War.
9. Give 10 dates in Civil War history and describe the battle or event that took place on each date.
10. List the phase of Civil War history that you liked best.

EXAMPLE 2

Evaluation

A. From the following questions select the correct answer. In the blank space place the letter (a, b, or c) that corresponds to this correct answer.

1. By the middle of the _____ century slavery had become universal in English America.
    - a. 16th
    - b. 17th
    - c. 18th

Interesting. Appears to be sound.

2. The Ordinance of 1787 organized the _____.
    - a. Utah territory
    - b. Northwest territory
    - c. Southeast territory
3. The Northerners charged that the whole country was ruled by a ruthless _____.
    - a. Cotton industry
    - b. Slave power
    - c. Black republicans
4. By the spring of _____ the Southern people felt it both abhorrent and dangerous to continue to live under the same government with the people of the North.
    - a. 1859
    - b. 1860
    - c. 1861
    - d. 1862
5. Jefferson Davis was _____.
    - a. President of the Mississippi delegation
    - b. President of the Confederate States of America
    - c. President of the Confederacy of the South
6. Abraham Lincoln was inaugurated as President of the United States on _____.
    - a. March 3, 1865
    - b. March 4, 1861
    - c. March 8, 1861

Questionable emphasis on exact days

7. General Lee surrendered to General Grant at _____.
    - a. Appomattox, April 9, 1865
    - b. Appomattox, April 6, 1865
    - c. Mrs. McLean's, April 9, 1865
8. One of the major naval engagements of the war involved the sinking of the _____.

a. New York City

b. Alabama

c. Vicksburg

9. The first Confederate victory was at _____.

   a. Manassas

   b. Manassas Gap

   c. Manassas Ferry

B. Identify

1. Ordinance of Secession
2. December 20, 1860
3. Judah P. Benjamin
4. Copperheads
5. Thirteenth Amendment
6. General George B. McClellan
7. May 26, 1865
8. Morgan's Raid
9. General William T. Sherman
10. Ku Klux Klan

C. In each of the following groups, only <u>one</u> statement is correct. In the blank space insert the letter that corresponds to the correct statement.

1. ______________

   a. The Civil War affected only the political and social way of life in the United States.

   b. The Civil War affected the entire process of life in the United States.

   c. The Civil War affected only the Southern way of life.

2. ______________

   a. The causes of the Civil War were slavery and sectionalism.

   b. The causes of the Civil War were political and economic.

   c. The causes of the Civil War can be traced back as far as the Continental Congress.

3. ______________

   a. The Reconstruction Period was like that of any other postwar period in history.

   b. The Reconstruction Period is a blot on the history of the United States.

   c. The Reconstruction Period of the United States was conducted in an orderly, military fashion.

4. ______________

   a. The Civil War could have been avoided.

   b. The Civil War could not have been avoided after Fort Sumter.

   c. The Civil War could have been avoided if England had entered the war.

D. List the information called for

1. Position and names of the members of Lincoln's cabinet
2. Position and names of the members of Davis' cabinet
3. The major battles of the Civil War, including the dates and names of commanders
4. The important dates and events in foreign affairs during the Civil War period

SUCCESSFUL TEACHING UNITS IN REVIEW

The earlier discussion on unit planning and the illustrative units suggest several summary generalizations that explain the need for and the problems related to unit planning.

1. The best classroom instruction is based upon sound unit planning.
2. Unit planning developed from the need for teachers to group related objectives in meaningful ways.
3. Unit planning encourages the establishment of close relationships between objectives and the procedures (including the use of aids) necessary to achieve these objectives.
4. Although unit plans may vary in detail depending upon the needs of students and teachers, all plans must give consideration to basic information about students, objectives, procedures, materials and resources, and evaluation procedures.
5. Units of quality must be practical and usable, avoiding the danger of undesirable brevity or unnecessary length.
6. Activities may be advantageously grouped under three headings—introductory, developmental, and concluding—to meet the purposes of the unit.
7. Subject areas organized along conceptual lines lend themselves particularly well to unit planning. Teachers in skill areas have often elected to employ modified unit and daily lesson plans to fit their particular needs.
8. Unit planners may helpfully evaluate their own units through the use of special self-scoring devices.

PROBLEMS FOR STUDY AND DISCUSSION

1. Aside from the reasons teachers often give for not wanting to make written unit plans, what are their unstated reasons? Discuss.

2. Do you believe that no teaching of any sort should be undertaken without written plans? Explain.

3. List ten activities that are not related to unit content but that must be planned for.

4. Describe an individual who, as a first-year teacher, would not find it necessary to engage in writing unit plans. How closely do *you* approximate this individual?

5. Explain the following statement: Unit planning proceeds with greatest ease where the subject matter is well organized along conceptual lines.

6. What difficulties would you encounter in organizing a unit for teaching a foreign language when the major emphasis is on pronunciation and memorization? Explain.

7. If you were to limit your basic concerns with respect to unit planning to two areas only, what would they be? Why?

8. List the five basic steps that should be considered in unit planning. Of these, which steps are the most important? Why?

9. Describe the characteristics of students in a typical class to which you might teach your subject-matter minor. Give consideration to I.Q.'s, socioeconomic status, student problems, potential troublemakers, and experiential backgrounds.

10. Do you believe that the objectives listed under "Concepts to Be Learned," pages 136–140, are too detailed? Explain.

11. What are the values to be derived from grouping activities under three categories? Explain.

12. What are the advantages and disadvantages of grouping activities according to the day on which they occur, as shown on pages 142–145?

13. On pages 152–156 the use of letters and numbers in brackets following activities referred to specific related objectives. How valuable is this device? Explain. Can you suggest another procedure that would accomplish the same purpose? Explain.

14. Is there value in listing materials and resources if their availability is questionable? Explain.

15. List five aids that are not commercially available for purchase but that you would like to make for teaching your subject-matter major.

16. What are the advantages of dividing developmental activities into *recurring* and *sequential* groups? Would this serve a useful purpose in teaching your subject-matter major?

17. How much detail is necessary in listing the objectives and activities of a unit? Explain.

18. Under what circumstances is it feasible to use a commercially produced film? Explain.

19. In the preparation of a teaching unit, what are the specific advantages to the use of a self-scoring instrument such as the one used for evaluating the "Civil War and Reconstruction" unit?

20. Assuming you have no other professional person to help you, name at least two practical ways for evaluating your unit other than by a self-scoring instrument.

RECOMMENDED READINGS

Batchelder, Howard T., Maurice McGlasson, and Raleigh Schorling, *Student Teaching in Secondary Schools*, 4th ed. New York: McGraw-Hill Book Company, 1964, pp. 126–129.

Burton, William H., *The Guidance of Learning Activities*, 3d. ed. New York: Appleton-Century-Crofts, Inc., 1962, pp. 334–336 and Chapter 15.

Goetting, M. L., *Teaching in the Secondary School*. New York: Prentice-Hall, Inc., 1942, Chapters 16, 17, and 20.

Grambs, Jean D., William J. Iverson, and Franklin K. Patterson, *Modern Methods in Secondary Education*, rev. ed. New York: The Dryden Press, 1958, Chapter 6.

Hansen, Kenneth H., *High School Teaching*. Englewood Cliffs, N.J.: Prentice-Hall, Inc., 1957, pp. 148–163.

Klausmeier, Herbert J., *Teaching in the Secondary School*. New York: Harper & Brothers, 1958, Chapters 6–9.

McKean, Robert C., *Principles and Methods in Secondary Education*. Columbus, Ohio: Charles E. Merrill Books, Inc., 1962, pp. 126–138.

Mills, Hubert H., and Harl R. Douglass, *Teaching in High School*, 2d. ed. New York: Ronald Press, 1957, Chapter 14.

Nordberg, H. Orville, James M. Bradfield, and William C. Odell, *Secondary School Teaching*. New York: The Macmillan Company, 1962, pp. 87–102.

Rivlin, Harry N., *Teaching Adolescents in Secondary Schools*, 2d. ed. New York: Appleton-Century-Crofts, Inc., 1961, Chapter 4.

8

Making a Daily Lesson Plan Effective

The daily lesson plan[1] is a device for keeping the teacher on the track of a carefully planned unit.[2] It is prepared on a day-to-day basis in order to allow for necessary but unforeseen adjustments that cannot be considered in the unit plan. For this reason, it should be prepared after class in anticipation of the needs of the class on the next day. The daily lesson plan is useful because:[3]

1. It encourages the planner to relate the objectives and procedures singled out for daily presentation to the overall objectives and procedures of the unit.
2. It permits making the daily adjustments necessary for effective teaching.
3. It encourages a vivid and up-to-the-minute recall of the content of the unit.
4. It encourages specific planning needed to meet problems related to classroom control, motivation, and differentiated instruction.

---

[1]William H. Burton, *The Guidance of Learning Activities,* 3d. ed. (New York: Appleton-Century-Crofts, 1962), pp. 322–324, provides a brief but stimulating discussion of the history and general nature of daily lesson plans.

Jean D. Grambs, William J. Iverson, and Franklin K. Patterson, *Modern Methods in Secondary Education,* rev. ed. (New York: The Dryden Press, 1958), pp. 145–147, place emphasis on flexibility in daily lesson planning.

[2]A helpful discussion on how the daily lesson plan implements the unit is provided by Herbert J. Klausmeier, *Teaching in the Secondary School* (New York: Harper & Brothers, 1958), pp. 162–169.

[3]Kenneth H. Hansen, *High School Teaching* (Englewood Cliffs, N.J.: Prentice-Hall, 1957), pp. 163–167, speaks out on the need for daily lesson plans and identifies the characteristics of good plans.

ESSENTIAL PARTS OF THE PLAN

It would be misleading to infer that all daily lesson plans have identical organization; they are as varied as the teachers who use them. A number of educators feel that each teacher should be allowed a large measure of freedom in developing daily lesson plan forms and in using such forms to prepare daily lesson plans. It is imperative, however, that the teacher give attention to the following:

1. Specific objectives (including the type of objective)
2. Specific procedures
3. Use of time
4. Materials and resources
5. Assignments[4]
6. Evaluation
7. Relationship of a particular daily lesson plan to its parent unit

During the first year or two of teaching, the beginning teacher should experiment with different forms and plans to determine how these seven areas can best be covered.

Examination of a range of daily lesson plans prepared by a number of different teachers for their specific needs discloses that these areas of concern are common to most planners. Such plans indicate (a) *what* is to be taught (the objectives) and (b) *how* it is to be taught (the procedures). In addition the time to be devoted to each activity is often indicated. More complete lesson plans mention the type of objective being taught (concept, skill, memorization, or habit) and the assignment for the day. In certain cases the objective for the day is related to a larger objective or to the encompassing unit objective.

The "Suggested Format for the Daily Lesson Plan"[5] on page 173 illustrates needed essentials. Designed to assist student teachers, this form contains brief explanatory statements about the type of information to be inserted under the various headings.

Most planners express a preference for the form that is confined to one side of one page. This limitation provides the advantage of a quick overview of the lesson, a clear indication of the relationships between parts of the plan, and an easy means for reproducing and storing the form.

Some teachers have found it advantageous to use two or more different daily lesson plan forms, depending on the needs of a particular day. For example, when students must be reminded of a large number of details, ample space should be provided under *prelim-*

---

[4]See Robert C. McKean, *Principles and Methods in Secondary Education* (Columbus, Ohio: Charles E. Merrill Books, Inc., 1962), pp. 142–144, for a discussion of the importance of the assignment in the daily lesson plan.

[5]Ray T. Wilcox, *Handbook for Student Teachers*, rev. ed. (Provo, Utah: Brigham Young University, 1963), p. 21.

SUGGESTED FORMAT FOR THE DAILY LESSON PLAN

Specific Objective: (Preferably one or a few concepts, symbols, skills, feelings, or habits from the unit plan that can be taught in one lesson.)

What to Teach	How to Teach	What Is Needed	Time
A statement of the few basic concepts to be taught and the related sub-concepts and/or the specific skills to be practiced and/or the symbols to be learned and/or the feelings to be devel-oped and/or the habits to be fostered. (These should be related to the objectives in the unit plan.)	Procedures, methods, experiences, and questions designed to get the students to perceive this subject as clearly as possible and to organize and interpret the stu-dents' perception of the objects and events involved.	Needed instructional resources to portray the subject to stu-dents. This portray-al may include use of maps, books, papers, teaching aids, laboratory equipment, and so forth.	Rough estimate of the time involved for each phase of the lesson.

Assignment: (The assignment should be clear, definite, and stimulating. It should be within the pupils' ability to perform and varied to challenge all shades of ability in the class.)

Evaluation: (What is your reaction to the lesson after it has been taught? Are there points to be remembered that will help to avoid making the same errors when the lesson is taught again? What parts are good enough to repeat?)

inaries on the form. On the other hand, it is often unnecessary for the teacher to give reminders, make announcements, and discuss long-range assignments. On such days the teacher may use a form that focuses full attention on objectives and related activities. Furthermore, the beginning teacher may find it helpful to use a form different from that which the experienced teacher would use. Two forms used with great frequency are represented in Example A and in Example H (pages 176 and 183).

DAILY LESSON PLAN FORMS

The four examples of daily lesson plan forms on pages 176–179 illustrate similarities as well as minor differences that may reasonably exist.[6] Look over the individual forms carefully before reading the discussion of each type.

Comments on Example A (See p. 176.)

There may be some confusion about the difference between "Objectives Stated as Concepts to Be Learned" and "What to Teach." Both headings hint at objectives. Actually, under the first heading the teacher is concerned with general unit objectives as opposed to specific daily objectives. "Other Objectives" refers to other *types* of objectives and should have been so indicated. "Preliminaries" usually consist of announcements, reminders, and other noncontent-related details that often must be dealt with in a class. "Assignments" have been given a deservedly prominent position.

The column arrangement of "What to Teach," "How to Teach," "Time Used," and "Materials" encourages the establishment of a close relationship among these essential concerns. At the bottom of the page provision has been made for "Evaluation Procedures," which in this case refers to the teacher's evaluation of the preceding lesson in order to discover a basis for improvement.

Comments on Example B (See p. 177.)

Information relating to subject, grade, date, and time may be helpful when a teacher has as many as three subject-matter assignments. The identification of the "Types of Learning" is useful in selecting procedures best suited to a given kind of objective. The "Objective" and "What to Teach" must be clearly established. The column concerned with "Time Use" would be more functional if

[6]Harry N. Rivlin, *Teaching Adolescents in Secondary Schools*, 2d. ed. (New York: Appleton-Century-Crofts, 1961), p. 165, provides another suggested form for a daily lesson plan.

placed next to the "How to Teach" column. A differentiation is made between the "Evaluation of Student Learning" and the "Evaluation of the Lesson." Since those two evaluations seem to have a close relationship, this division may be questionable when one is attempting to confine the total lesson plan to one page.

Comments on Example C (See p. 178.)

Use of a unit title or number may serve a useful purpose when individual lesson plans are to be filed away for later reference. The checking of the "Method" to be employed serves no useful purpose because this becomes obvious upon reading the "How to Teach" column. "What to Teach" seems to usurp the function of the "Lesson Objective" when the objective is confined to only the one lesson. The indication of time use is missing, making the plan less specific and useful. As in Example B, the "Evaluation" has been pointed toward the student and the lesson itself. However, these divisions and the small amount of space encourage a brief and general evaluation.

Comments on Example D (See p. 179.)

Inclusion of the teacher's name takes needed space and does not contribute to the lesson plan. The listing of the "General Objective" followed by "Specific Objectives" has the advantage of establishing a clear relationship between the two. It is to be noted that because "Specific Objectives" are listed above, no attention is given to objectives among the column headings. "Teacher Activities" and "Student Activities" might well be combined into one column with an economy of space.[7]

PRACTICAL USE OF SPECIFIC FORMS

The four examples of daily lesson plans on pages 180–183 were designed to give direction to actual classroom presentations. They might have been quite different if they had been made out by different teachers. Note that they are brief, practical, and can be inserted on a prepared form of one typewritten page.[8] Look over the individual forms carefully before reading the discussion of each type.

Comments on Example E (See p. 180.)

The simplicity of the minor concepts in the "What to Teach" column is apparent, and they all bear a close relationship to the

---

[7]Klausmeier, *op. cit.*, p. 163, presents a similar framework for daily lesson planning.

[8]Hubert H. Mills and Harl R. Douglass, *Teaching in High School*, 2d. ed. (New York: Ronald Press, 1957), pp. 184–186, provide another example of a detailed daily lesson plan.

EXAMPLE A

Daily Lesson Plan for________________________________Date__________

Objectives Stated as Concepts to Be Learned:

Other Objectives:

Preliminaries:

Assignments:

What to Teach	How to Teach	Time Used	Materials

Evaluation Procedures:

EXAMPLE B

Subject__________________________________ Date__________

Grade____________________ Time__________

Types of Learning______________________________

Objective__________________________________

Time Use	What to Teach	How to Teach	Materials

Assignment

Evaluation of Student Learning

Evaluation of Lesson

EXAMPLE C

Class________________________________ Unit (Title) (No.)__________

Method:

Discussion___ Illustration___ Demonstration___ Conference___ Lecture___

Type of Learning:

Concept___ Skill___ Memorization___ Tastes and Preferences___

Lesson Objective:________________________________

What to Teach	How to Teach	Materials

Assignment:

Evaluation: Student Lesson

EXAMPLE D

Class____________________Name____________________

Hour____________________Date____________________

General Objective____________________

Specific Objectives____________________

____

Type of Learning____________________

Time	Teacher Activity	Student Activity	Materials

Assignment:

Evaluation:

1.
2.
3.
4.

EXAMPLE E

Objective: The sharpening of a cabinet scraper involves several steps that must be followed in a given order.

Method: Discussion X Illustration___ Demonstration X

Conference___ Lecture X

Type of Learning: Concept X Skill X Memorization X

Tastes and Preferences___

What to Teach	How to Teach	Min.	Materials
1. Check for squareness.	1. Show with T-square how light comes through where uneven.	2	1. Chart of steps to be used: scraper blade, T-square, saw vice
2. Remove old burr.	2. Demonstrate how file is held to remove burr.	1	2. Single cut mill file
3. File beveled edge.	3. Impress upon students that the file is to be used at a 45° angle to the blade.	3	
4. Hone filed blade.	4. Show the students how to hone on the flat side, then on the beveled side.	3	3. Oil stone
5. Burnish the edge.	5. Demonstrate how to properly hold and use burnisher. Stress the importance of burnishing at three angles: 45°, 67°, and 90°.	1	4. Burnishing tool.

Assignment: Have each student sharpen his own scraper, and have it checked by the instructor before the student resumes work on his project. (15 minutes)

Evaluation:

1. Student Learning

2. Lesson Presentation

EXAMPLE F

Subject: U.S. History Time: 2:00 P.M.

Reminders: No school Friday; P.T.A. meets tonight; buy lunch tickets

Lesson Objective: The rapid growth of cities after the Civil War caused many problems.

Supporting Objectives	Time	Procedures
		Briefly review yesterday's class. Quickly outline on the chalkboard questions to be answered in today's lesson. Remind students to look for important questions they would like to have answered or to learn more about.
A. Cities grew rapidly after the Civil War. Examples: New York City, Chicago, Los Angeles, Salt Lake City, Provo.	10	A. Show pictures of large cities. Discuss: world metropolis, largest city in the Midwest, largest city in the West, largest city in Utah, largest city in Utah county. 1. How large does a community have to be to become a city? (Use the chalkboard to show different kinds of people coming to cities.) Make graphs to show the increase in the size of cities between 1790 and 1950: Row 2--New York; Row 3--Chicago; Row 4--Los Angeles; Row 5--Salt Lake City; Everyone--Provo. 2. Are some Western cities growing at a faster rate today than some Eastern cities?
B. The growth of cities brought many problems. 1. Much construction was needed: sewers, water purification plants, firehouses.	10	B. Discuss: 1. Does Provo City have sewers? Does Provo City have water purification plants? Does Provo City have firehouses? Why? (Assign special reports on the above three topics.)
2. Graft and corruption became problems all through the nation. (Boss Tweed & Tammany Hall; Thomas Nast; U. S. Grant)	15	2. Cite an example: School's student-body president elected by a small group asking special favors. School's principal helps man become Superintendent who gives the principal free reign. Ask pupils for examples--Look in newspapers, etc. Tell story of Boss Tweed, Thomas Nast, and U. S. Grant.
3. City slums grew.	10	3. Relate the report of the Board of Health. Do we have slums today? Show picture.

Assignments: 1. Special reports on sewers (John & Sam); Provo Water Department (Jack & Bill); Provo Fire Department (Mary & Betty).
2. Graphs as assigned in A above.
3. Collect news articles about graft. (Did crime pay?)

Unfinished Business: 1. We did not get a chance to discuss whether cities today have solved their problems or what kind of problems they still have.
2. Should cities be abolished?
3. Questions the students still want answered:
a. What is the difference between a city, a town, and a village?
b. Are city children smarter than those who live in small towns?
c. Does it cost more to live in a city?

EXAMPLE G

Subject: Music Fundamentals (Grades 7 through 9)

Kind of Objective: Concept___, Memorization___, Skill___, or Habit___

Objective: The great staff is made up of the treble and the bass clefs, and the line between them is known as Middle C. Notes placed on a specific line or space can be read and played and have the same meaning to all musicians.

What to Teach	How to Teach	Materials
II, A, 4	Teacher will lecture, using the permanent staff on the chalkboard.	Chalkboard
II, A, 5	Students at board will insert notes on staff at request of teacher. Students at seats will check board work.	
	Students will draw treble and bass clefs at seats and fill in notes at the request of the teacher. Students will locate and fill in notes for each of the following sequences in the treble as well as the bass clef: B-C; F-A-C; D-F-A; G-B-D. The class will be organized into pairs. They will check each other's paper.	Paper
	The teacher will then insert the proper notes on the permanent staff at the chalkboard.	
II, A, 6	The teacher will play the notes on the piano. The students will hum them lightly.	
II, A, 4, 5, and 6	Again students will be asked to insert specific notes on the clefs drawn at their seats: C-E-G; D-G-B; A-C-F; A-C-E; A-D-F; B-D-F. Student pairs will again check each other's paper. The teacher will insert the proper notes on the permanent staff and play the notes on the piano.	

Assignment: For tomorrow, students will write the correct letters (A, C, E, etc.) beside the notes on the dittoed copy of "Silent Night," in the key of C.

Evaluation:

Special Concerns: Have a private chat with Martha; see Douglas about his missing assignment; praise Wilma for her excellent board work yesterday.

EXAMPLE H

Subject: French I   Date: November 21st

Routine and Preliminaries:

1. Call roll. Students respond in French.
2. Collect assignments.
3. Reassign seats for Jean, Paul, Terry, and Millie.
4. Ask for three volunteers to work on the bulletin board for next week.

Subject-Matter Treatment:

1. Introduce the verb etre. Conjugate the verb on the board. Give one or two examples of the verb used in sentences.
2. Give examples of the verb in its various conjugations (present tense only). Have students work at the chalkboard for this exercise. Help the students having difficulty. Make constructive criticism as students put examples on the board.
3. Review the French vocabulary by having the students participate in a spelling match. Students are to spell in French as the words are dictated by the teacher from page 37 of the text.

Assignment:

1. Students will complete the exercises related to etre on page 39 of the text.

Miscellaneous Concerns:

1. Promote the French Club meeting to be held on Tuesday.
2. Stimulate Tonya Wilkes' desire to learn French.
3. Send Harry and Hilda to the library to work on special reports during the study period.

larger objective for the day at the top of the form. A primary concern is the teaching of these minor concepts at the start of the lesson. Concepts in the "What to Teach" column are stated as briefly as possible in the interest of saving space. "Check for squareness," concept 1, gives the false impression that it is an activity. If it were stated in its full conceptual form, however, it would be "The first step in sharpening a cabinet scraper is to check for squareness." This is clearly a concept. The development of the needed skill will come through the practice provided for in the assignment. Although little or no direct attention is focused on memorizing the chart of steps, recall is encouraged through proper conceptualization and use. Note that the teaching demonstration involves only ten minutes, with fifteen minutes devoted to the students' use of the concepts already learned. The majority of the class period will be devoted to supervised work on a project.

Comments on Example F (See p. 181.)

Note that to facilitate teaching the larger goal has been broken down into two divisions. Several activities related to each of these two divisions tend to fix the concept in the students' minds. The space for "Reminders" at the top of the form and for "Unfinished Business" at the bottom gives evidence of practical concerns. Column arrangements of "Supporting Objectives," "Time," and "Procedures" clearly indicate the interrelationships.

Comments on Example G (See p. 182.)

Numbers in the "What to Teach" column refer to the objectives in the unit plan. Use of this procedure would necessitate having the unit plan on the teacher's desk so that it could be easily correlated with the daily lesson plan. It would also be possible for the planner to write out the supporting objectives, listing in the adjacent column the number of the activity in the unit plan that corresponds to the given objective. In the main, the procedures used in the form in Example G should be used with extreme caution.

Comments on Example H (See p. 183.)

This form may well serve the purposes of a thoroughly experienced teacher who has taught the same unit a number of times. It would *not* serve the needs of the beginner. Note, for example, that this planner does not explicitly designate objectives and activities. Emphasis in this case is placed on activities.[9] If a teacher does not have a clear picture of the objectives he hopes to teach, he will encounter difficulties.

---

[9]See Vincent McGuire, Robert B. Myers, and Charles L. Durrance, *Your Student Teaching in the Secondary School* (Boston: Allyn and Bacon, 1959), pp. 145–146, for examples of daily lesson plans in which emphasis is placed on procedures.

This lesson plan does have these advantages, however. It is very simple, consisting of four basic headings—"Routine and Preliminaries," "Subject-Matter Treatment," "Assignment," and "Miscellaneous Concerns." Ample space is provided for listing routine and preliminary procedures, but a minimum of space is devoted to subject-matter treatment because of the limited need of the seasoned teacher. At the bottom of the page the planner may insert notes to help him conduct a better lesson.

SPECIFIC SUGGESTIONS

Specific suggestions for the preparation and use of daily lesson plans can be of great practical benefit, particularly to the beginning teacher or to the teacher who wishes to improve the efficiency of his planning. The following recommendations and cautions are aimed at providing such teachers with positive direction and with suggestions for avoiding the errors that often beset the novice.[10]

Recommendations

1. Be sure that the daily lesson plan will enable you to teach the content of the unit.[11]
2. Experiment with several different forms until you have found the forms that best serve your purposes as a planner and teacher.
3. After deciding which forms best serve your purposes and individual tastes, have a supply duplicated for consistent daily use.
4. Organize the daily lesson plan form so that desired attention can be given to major objectives, supporting objectives, procedures, materials and resources, evaluation of the lesson and pupil learning, assignment, and routine.
5. The basic concerns of objectives, procedures, time devoted to procedures, and materials may advantageously serve as headings for adjacent vertical columns. With this organization, corresponding items can be placed in parallel columns.
6. Keep the lesson plan as simple as is compatible with usefulness, clarity, and completeness.
7. With very few exceptions, confine the lesson plan to one page. This suggestion assumes that the basic planning has already been completed during the preparation of the unit.

---

[10]Rivlin, *op. cit.*, Chapter 5, devotes a full chapter to the problems related to preparing and teaching a class lesson.

[11]William L. Carter, Carl W. Hansen, and Margaret G. McKim, *Learning to Teach in the Secondary School* (New York: Macmillan, 1962), pp. 169–174, indicate the importance of planning a single lesson, because a unit will not serve the needs of instruction. The authors describe what they feel a lesson plan for a single class should contain.

8. Remember that the indication of anticipated time use is an approximation but that it is, nonetheless, essential.

9. Establish the relationship between activities occurring on successive days.

10. Establish the relationship of small concepts to large concepts through daily planning.

11. Use the daily lesson plan to make day-to-day adjustments that cannot be anticipated in advance.

12. Single out for treatment on any given day only those objectives (usually supporting objectives) that can be taught effectively. The attempt to cover ground encourages superficiality.

Cautions[12]

1. Don't use another teacher's lesson plan forms unless you have determined that they will serve your specific purposes.

2. Don't assume that only one form or type of form will bring acceptable results.

3. Don't plan a lesson without first establishing its relationship to the unit.

4. Don't make the lesson plan more detailed than will serve a useful purpose.

5. Don't fail to plan for the often neglected concerns of classroom routine and control.

6. Don't forget that the type of goal selected will determine the nature and sequence of procedures.

INFREQUENT USE OF DAILY LESSON PLANS

Even a casual appraisal of the use of daily lesson plans among in-service teachers leaves the impression that the plans are not used as often as they should be. Several reasons for this should be noted.

False Assumptions

Many teachers object to the daily lesson plan because they erroneously assume that it is a lengthy written statement, laden with detail, that is not justified in terms of the time spent on its preparation. Most educators are quite willing to reject such lengthy, wordy, time-consuming plans as impractical. These objections can be overcome, however, when essential but limited information related to the proposed instruction is inserted in a carefully prepared, duplicated

---

[12]Howard T. Batchelder, Maurice McGlasson, and Raleigh Schorling, *Student Teaching in Secondary Schools*, 4th ed. (New York: McGraw-Hill Book Company, 1964), pp. 129–130, provide a list of common errors made in planning.

form. If such a procedure is used in conjunction with a well-prepared unit, the preparation of the daily lesson plan ought not to exceed five or ten minutes.

Impractical Forms

Some individual teachers reject the use of the daily lesson plan because they frequently have not worked out practical forms for their specific personal use. A general form will not be equally helpful in all planning situations. Ideas must be obtained from many sources and combined in a usable form that will best serve the purposes of instruction as seen by the individual teacher.

Limited Experimentation

A substantial number of teachers have not experimented sufficiently with the use of well-organized unit plans to permit them to see that such plans have practical value. They reject lesson plans summarily on the basis of hearsay without taking the opportunity for an unbiased trial appraisal.

The lack of true professional quality in a small minority of in-service teachers leads them to believe that minimum preparation is sufficient. At times this minimum preparation is viewed as a hasty three-minute review of what might be done in the class that begins in three minutes. At other times it is interpreted as no out-of-class preparation at all but simply as "opening the windows of the personality when standing before the class." But this has little to do with the preparation of carefully written plans.

Unwarranted School Requirements

Certain school districts have been known to require written daily plans for each class that is taught. Furthermore, they have prescribed the form and procedures to be employed in making out these plans. Such requirements may be viewed as unwarranted by the older, experienced, and competent teacher, and, in fact, plans produced under such circumstances may prove to be of less practical value than those prepared to serve the experienced teacher's personal needs. The beginning teacher, however, often benefits by having to conform to specific planning procedures until he has developed the competence that will enable him to teach effectively without such restrictions.

Unit Plans Believed Sufficient

Uninformed planners may at times view the daily lesson plan as usurping the function of the unit plan and, therefore, unnecessary.

Such planners misunderstand the function of the daily lesson plan as a device whose main purpose is to keep instructional procedures firmly on the track of the unit plan. There should be no unnecessary duplication between these plans. Each has its particular function.

Some uninformed teachers feel that they can teach directly from the unit plan without going through the essential step of daily lesson planning. Such a procedure is superior to no planning, but it provides little opportunity for relating one day's lesson to another, for planning for unforeseen difficulties, for giving attention to individual differences, and for maintaining an appropriate study climate.

"Others Don't! Why Should I?"

Superficial observation and analysis lead work-evading teachers to jump to the hasty conclusion that because certain colleagues do not use a daily lesson plan, it is not necessary for them to do so. Where such teaching is successful, it is most probably the result of careful planning whether the evidence of the paper work involved is present or not. Furthermore, it would be bold to assume that the same degree of planning is desirable for instructors of varying competence, experience, and professional drive.

Planning Only for the Inexperienced

Experienced teachers at times voice the belief that daily lesson planning is for the neophyte, not for the established teacher. There can be little quarrel with the assumption that the quantity and even the kind of planning should take a somewhat altered form as the inservice instructor advances in knowledge of content and in his ability to present the content to the class. The *quality* of planning, however, must always be at a high level if one is truly professional. This means that planning must be functional—it must help the instructor teach better.

PROBLEMS FOR STUDY AND DISCUSSION

1. What are the essential differences between the unit plan and the daily lesson plan? Discuss each briefly.
2. What are the essential parts of a daily lesson plan? Discuss each.
3. List and discuss three basic justifications for using a daily lesson plan.
4. Are daily lesson plans unnecessary in some subject-matter areas? Explain your thinking.
5. Which daily lesson plan form would be most helpful in teaching your subject-matter major? Why?
6. What is the advantage of placing objectives and related activities in adjacent columns?

7. Is it always advisable to indicate the approximate time to be devoted to each activity? Why?

8. Under what heading would you group such concerns as calling the roll, adjusting the light and temperature, and passing out papers? Should they be considered in the daily lesson plan or in the unit plan? Why?

9. Indicate a subject in which the listing of materials would be of limited value. Indicate one in which it would be of great value. Where does your subject-matter major lie with respect to the need for listing materials?

10. If a teacher states the daily objective at the top of his plan, is it really necessary to list supporting objectives below? Why?

11. How important is it to have a specific place on your daily lesson plan form for evaluating student learning? Why?

12. Is the inclusion of a time column in the daily lesson plan form essential? Discuss.

13. Which of the following items may be omitted from the daily lesson plan form that you will use for teaching your subject-matter major: date, grade, unit, name of teacher, subject, period, type of objective, and specific method? Explain.

14. What are the arguments for confining the daily lesson plan to only one page? List several.

15. Do you believe that it is practical to list numbers referring to unit objectives in the "What to Teach" column? Explain your reasoning.

16. What values do you see in using two or three different daily lesson plan forms on different days? Explain.

17. List six recommendations that should be helpful to the new teacher in preparing and using daily lesson plans.

18. Give five examples of day-to-day adjustments that cannot be considered in the unit plan but that should be covered in the daily lesson plan.

19. Can you use another teacher's daily lesson plan forms? Why?

20. Indicate six reasons why teachers do not use daily lesson plans with greater frequency. Are any of these reasons defensible? Why?

RECOMMENDED READINGS

Batchelder, Howard T., Maurice McGlasson, and Raleigh Schorling, *Student Teaching in Secondary Schools,* 4th ed. New York: McGraw-Hill Book Company, 1964, pp. 129–130.

Burton, William H., *The Guidance of Learning Activities,* 3d. ed. New York: Appleton-Century-Crofts, Inc., 1962, pp. 322–324.

Carter, William L., Carl W. Hansen, and Margaret G. McKim, *Learning to Teach in the Secondary School.* New York: The Macmillan Company, 1962, pp. 169–174.

Grambs, Jean D., William J. Iverson, and Franklin K. Patterson, *Modern Methods in Secondary Education,* rev. ed. New York: The Dryden Press, 1958, pp. 145–147.

Hansen, Kenneth H., *High School Teaching.* Englewood Cliffs, N.J.: Prentice-Hall, Inc., 1957, pp. 163–167.

Klausmeier, Herbert J., *Teaching in the Secondary School.* New York: Harper & Brothers, 1958, pp. 162–169.

McGuire, Vincent, Robert B. Myers, and Charles L. Durrance, *Your Student Teaching in the Secondary School.* Boston: Allyn and Bacon, Inc., 1959, pp. 142–149.

McKean, Robert C., *Principles and Methods in Secondary Education.* Columbus, Ohio: Charles E. Merrill Books, Inc., 1962, pp. 138–144.

Mills, Hubert H., and Harl R. Douglass, *Teaching in High School,* 2d. ed. New York: Ronald Press, 1957, pp. 179–186.

Nordberg, H. Orville, James M. Bradfield, and William C. Odell, *Secondary School Teaching.* New York: The Macmillan Company, 1962, pp. 103–104.

Rivlin, Harry N., *Teaching Adolescents in Secondary Schools,* 2d. ed. New York: Appleton-Century-Crofts, Inc., 1961, Chapter 5.

Wellington, C. Burleigh, and Jean Wellington, *Teaching for Critical Thinking: with Emphasis on Secondary Education.* New York: McGraw-Hill Book Company, Inc., 1960, pp. 256–258.

Wiggins, Samuel P., *Successful High School Teaching.* Boston: Houghton Mifflin Company, 1958, Chapter 10.

PART THREE

SPECIFIC TEACHING PROCEDURES

Teacher-Centered Procedures

The teacher has the basic responsibility for organizing and conducting goal-related activities in the classroom. Very often he involves students, and occasionally resource persons, to further the cause of learning. If he is conscientious, he marshals all resources, including audio-visual aids and special devices, to assist in the process. But aside from his function as an organizer of activities, the teacher more frequently than any other individual occupies the center of the stage as an active disseminator of information, student motivator, and director of thinking.

Certain procedures are by their very nature teacher-centered. It is the purpose of this chapter to discuss three of these procedures—lectures, questions, and demonstrations—and their effect upon the teaching-learning process. Although other procedures might be identified as teacher-centered, the three mentioned here are particularly important because they are used so frequently.

USE OF THE LECTURE

The varied uses of the term *lecture* are confusing to teachers, students, and readers of professional literature. The lecture is commonly described as a teaching procedure in which there is a one-way channel of communication. Under this definition the instructor makes an oral presentation of information to which the student reacts by silently listening and taking notes. Such a definition, however, im-

Fig. 1. Types of Lectures.

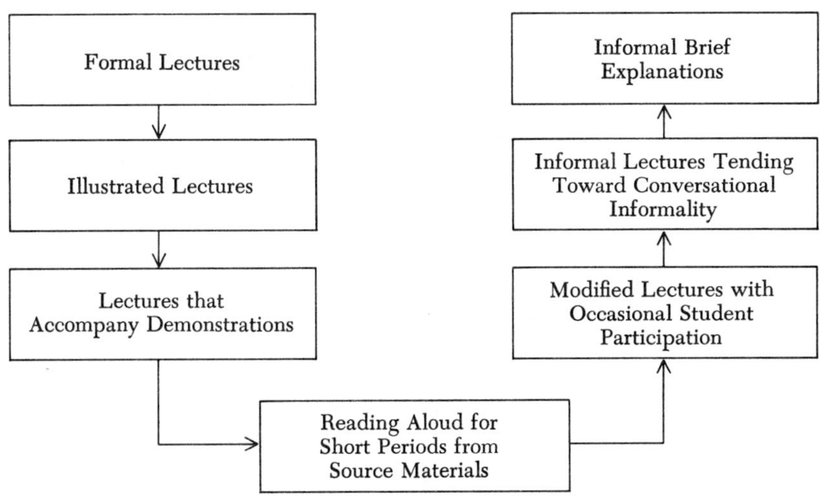

poses certain restrictions on the usefulness and flexibility of the lecture—restrictions that are best avoided.[1]

It is instructionally helpful to think of the lecture as encompassing a range of related procedures in which the one-way flow of ideas is the dominant characteristic. Because of the variation in teacher utterances that are labeled "lecture," it is desirable to think of lectures on a continuum, extending from the highly formal to the highly informal. The diagram in Figure 1 illustrates this continuum and lists the various types of lectures.[2]

Principles Related to Lecturing

Planning for the use of the lecture should rest on a solid platform of relevant psychological principles. Difficulties can be avoided if the planner evaluates lectures by means of the following criteria.

1. The lecture in its pure form is subject to criticism as a classroom procedure. Long formal lectures that present difficult content are unsuited for the average secondary-school classroom.

2. Learning is an active, not a passive, process. For this reason, classroom learning calls for the learner's meaningful reaction to stimuli; if there is no reaction, there is no learning. Passive students

---

[1]C. Burleigh Wellington and Jean Wellington, *Teaching for Critical Thinking: with Emphasis on Secondary Education* (New York: McGraw-Hill Book Company, 1960), Chapter 11, provide a full-chapter treatment of the strengths and limitations of the lecture technique.

[2]*Ibid.*, pp. 220–221, present a brief discussion of the types of lectures.

(those who are not reacting to content) frequently lose interest and become inattentive.

3. Individual instructors should identify the types of procedures best suited to their subject, to their personality, and to their class. These procedures should be modified to meet the instructional needs of a particular group and situation. The lecture, perhaps as much as any teaching procedure, needs this type of modification. The teacher should realize that students have basic needs that must be recognized and reflected in the use of any method. Not all students are equally interested in the same kind of lecture. Similarly, the lecture that is interesting and valuable to the teacher may not be equally interesting and valuable to students in the class. Students are interested in specific methods only to the extent that those methods lead them where they want to go.

4. The lecture, which is comprised of spoken symbols (words), can be only as meaningful as the mental pictures attached to these symbols in the mind of the learner. Thus, students tend to be more interested in the lecture that is specifically related to content already known and liked. Their attention span varies, depending on the individual student's experiences and native capacity, as well as on the communicative ability of the speaker.

5. Language usage (vocabulary level, meaningful examples, fluency, freedom from speech idiosyncrasies, etc.) helps determine how students will react to a lecture.

6. Students may be challenged to work hard to grasp the content of a difficult lecture, but the right kind of humorous comment will ease the strain on them.

7. The teacher who talks too much without really saying anything is recognized as a phony by the class.

8. Certain types of subjects (English literature and history, for example) lend themselves to the use of the lecture more readily than others, and specific variations of the lecture (illustrated lectures, informal brief explanations, etc.) tend to be well suited to certain subjects.

9. The successful lecture is held in a setting where competing stimuli are excluded.

10. The teacher should be realistic in judging how much the class will get out of the lecture.

11. Students tend to accept or reject particular methods in conformity to assumed peer-group standards.

Correct and Incorrect Use

The experienced teacher may identify in the examples below certain reflections of his own use of the lecture. The purpose of these illustrations, however, is (1) to provide a meaningful picture of variations in the use of the lecture and (2) to point out that each variation has strengths as well as limitations, depending on the circumstances surrounding its usage. The marked limitations of the formal lecture, for example, are perhaps most apparent as they relate to secondary-school classroom instruction. Although the merits of the lecture variations illustrated in these examples are not discussed, some of the advantages of each type will be obvious. Furthermore, the specific, practical suggestions for using the lecture (pp. 198 – 199) will be more meaningful against the background of varied examples.

MR. MELLOR PRESENTS A FORMAL LECTURE

William T. Mellor prided himself on his precise use of language. He had undergone an intense and prolonged period of preparation for teaching. As a teacher of eleventh-grade English literature, he felt that he had a thorough grasp of his subject and that when he talked, students should listen.

Many times he felt that it was desirable to lecture for the full period without interruption. As soon as the roll had been called, Mr. Mellor launched into his lecture with genuine enthusiasm. By the end of the first half-hour much of the sparkle of the original presentation had become somewhat dulled. Students became uneasy and gave evidence of lack of interest. The last five minutes of the lecture proved to be a genuine trial for students and teacher alike.[3]

MR. ROBBINS GIVES AN ILLUSTRATED LECTURE

Students are always delighted when Mr. Robbins decides to give another illustrated lecture in their tenth-grade geography class. Because of his long period of military service in the Orient and his very practical hobby of photography, he has acquired several hundred slides of unusual beauty and interest. For each picture, Mr. Robbins has carefully woven together a narrative explanation that capitalizes on the natural interests of teenagers and is factually sound. The only time that Gerald Riding is interested enough to avoid making a disturbance in the class is during these illustrated lectures.[4]

MR. SIMMONS USES A DEMONSTRATION WITH HIS LECTURES

Lloyd Simmons has an enviable reputation among the senior high school chemistry teachers in his school district. This is largely based on the ease with which he explains certain chemical phenomena to his students in the laboratory. His rule for teaching is: *never lecture without showing.* His concern for "showing" apparently works very well, for his students encounter little difficulty in coping with the rigors of college chemistry.

When he gives a demonstration for class benefit, Mr. Simmons asks the students to gather around the teaching area, encircling him and the appara-

---

[3]The unmodified formal lecture is rapidly fading from secondary-school classroom usage, although it is still firmly entrenched in the college classroom.

William H. Burton, *The Guidance of Learning Activities*, 3rd. ed. (New York: Appleton-Century-Crofts, 1962), pp. 264 and 286, indicts the lecture and lists supporting sources of information.

[4]Kenneth H. Hansen, *High School Teaching* (Englewood Cliffs, N.J.: Prentice-Hall, 1957), pp. 180 – 183, provides a brief discussion of the lecture-explanation in which weaknesses and strengths are mentioned.

tus. As chemical reactions begin to take place, he points out what is happening and encourages students to identify the reason for the phenomenon. He is careful to be sure that his oral explanations do not obscure or substitute for perceptive observation on the part of students.[5]

MISS DONAKER READS ALOUD FROM SOURCE MATERIALS

For more than a decade, Miss Donaker, the speech teacher at the Thomas Jefferson Senior High School, has assembled and carefully classified an extensive file of supplementary materials. To illustrate particular points, she often reads aloud short essays, speeches, monologs, and dialogs from her collection. On special holiday occasions she may, to the delight of her class, read certain short poems or readings of particular charm and interest.

PASTOR WOODCOX SUCCEEDS WITH A MODIFIED LECTURE

Pastor Woodcox had learned a great deal about fourteen-year-old ninth-grade boys and girls because his church responsibilities in working with youth groups had brought him into contact with all kinds of youngsters. Of one thing he was certain: Their willingness to listen to long speeches was limited.

Pastor Woodcox was invited to the Woodrow Wilson Junior High School to talk to a ninth-grade civics class about the operation of the local city government. His recently expired term as city commissioner provided him with essential background information. The teacher who contacted him had outlined the basic areas to be covered but left the method of presentation to the discretion of the speaker.

For the first fifteen minutes of his talk, interest remained extremely high. Within five minutes, however, the pastor noted a mild uneasiness among his listeners. It was time, he felt, to involve them actively in the discussion.

"Which one of you," he said, "can tell me the steps that the citizens of this community must go through in order to select the mayor?" After looking around the group and giving each one the impression that he might be called on, the pastor finally selected a student whose hand was raised. Group interest was rekindled, and he continued with his lecture.

Whenever he again felt that interest was beginning to wane, Pastor Woodcox solicited student comments, asked questions, or injected humor into his lecture. At the end of the class one of the students made a statement somewhat representative of the thinking of the group: "Boy, I really believe I know something about city government now. And it was interesting, too."

MR. BRIAN LECTURES INFORMALLY

The thing that students liked most about his class was that Mr. Brian didn't seem to be lecturing to them. It was more as if he were talking to them on their own level. Moreover, students were learning algebra in the bargain.

Although Mr. Brian did most of the talking, students had the impression

---

[5]H. Orville Nordberg, James M. Bradfield, and William C. Odell, *Secondary School Teaching* (New York: Macmillan, 1962), p. 147, stress the value of the lecture-demonstration method while recognizing the weaknesses of the formal lecture.

that they were active participants in the thinking that was taking place. Every now and then he would ask, "Is this reasonable, Bill?" or "Sally, what's wrong with this thinking?"

Even when students posed questions without the formality of raising their hands, the teacher did not seem to object. It was as if his main concern was to keep the path of easy communication open. When students abused their privileges, he had a quiet talk with them after class.[6]

MISS BIGLER GIVES AN INFORMAL BRIEF EXPLANATION

Miss Bigler wants her supervised study periods to get off to a good start. First, she makes sure that motivation is at its peak. Second, she gives the class an exact indication of what is expected of them. At times she writes relevant points on the board. Third, she supervises the initiation of the study with considerable care, answering individual questions quietly as she moves among her students.

The Lecture in Special Situations

Certain modifications of the lecture may be appropriate to the teaching of every subject in the secondary curriculum,[7] but all modifications are not equally appropriate to every subject. Formal lecture, for example, would be out of place in the typing class but may at times be entirely appropriate for English literature. Furthermore, the use of a formal lecture in a class comprised of below-average students would be open to serious question.

Because illustrated lectures closely approximate first-hand contact with the referent, they provide unusual help for students with limited experiences. For this reason illustrated lectures serve well in teaching geography and foreign cultures. If students are concerned with learning new concepts or correcting erroneous concepts, the use of pictures accompanied by an adequate explanation provides a meaningful learning experience.

Demonstrations[8] are frequently combined with an informal lecture to round out student comprehension. As long as the student is acquiring proper concepts through observation, oral explanations may not be necessary. In some cases they actually distract from the more important concern of observing the cause and effect of a given phenomenon. In most situations, however, the teacher will need to accompany a demonstration with an explanation.

Perhaps the most commonly used modification of the lecture involves the encouragement of student questions and reactions as the

---

[6]Harry N. Rivlin, *Teaching Adolescents in Secondary Schools*, 2d. ed. (New York: Appleton-Century-Crofts, 1961), Chapter 6, devotes a full chapter to the treatment of "Discussion as a Way of Learning" but fails to include the term *lecture* in the index of his book.

[7]M. L. Goetting, *Teaching in the Secondary School* (New York: Prentice-Hall, 1942), pp. 166–172, discusses the limitations as well as the strengths of the lecture method.

[8]See pages 207–213 for a discussion of demonstrations.

instructor proceeds with his discussion. This method has the advantage of promoting consistent student attention. Teachers often intersperse relevant questions in their lectures to good advantage. Informality is thus encouraged, and the potential monotony of the straight lecture is frequently averted.

Some teachers achieve pronounced success at times by employing oral presentations that, because of their informality, seem to defy classification as lectures. Informal lecture is best suited for use in a class in which the rapport between student and teacher is wholesome and relaxed. If the inherent informality of the situation encourages misbehavior, the teacher should substitute another procedure more appropriate to the conditions of the class. How much informality may be injected into the teaching situation without harming the teaching-learning process may have to be determined through careful experimentation.

Specific Suggestions

Knowing how to use any teaching method effectively calls for a broad acquaintance with underlying psychological principles. The use of the lecture is no exception. Examination of these principles leads to specific suggestions that give direction to the beginning teacher's—as well as the more experienced teacher's—use of the lecture.

Recommendations

All of the following recommendations are applicable to each variety of lecture method, but some of them have greater applicability to specific types. For example, the encouragement of questions and comments has limited application to the formal lecture, but it may be of great advantage in a modified lecture.[9]

1. Know your subject.
2. Organize your materials thoroughly.
3. Get the attention of the class before you start.
4. Encourage students to take notes.
5. Indicate the relationship of one topic to another.
6. Adapt your lecture to specific listeners; consider their individual differences.
7. Use a vocabulary that is easily understood; be concise but adequate.
8. Speak clearly and fluently; be sure everyone can hear what is said.

---

[9]Hubert H. Mills and Harl R. Douglass, *Teaching in High School*, 2d. ed. (New York: Ronald Press, 1957), pp. 207–219, provide specific hints for the improvement of the modified lecture.

9. Experiment with different modifications of the lecture, carefully analyzing how they can best be employed.

10. Use teaching aids to assist in clarifying meanings.

11. Use meaningful, illustrative stories.

12. Emphasize the important points.

13. Be sure the lecture helps achieve established objectives.

14. When appropriate, plan the lecture to develop critical thinking.[10]

15. When practical, and to avoid monotony, encourage student questions and comments.

Cautions

The above list of positive recommendations does not focus attention on many of the specific errors frequently made in using the lecture. The following cautions should help teachers avoid common pitfalls.

1. Don't use the lecture too frequently or to the exclusion of other methods.
2. Don't assume that students have understood all that was said.
3. Don't introduce irrelevant ideas or materials.
4. Don't extend the lecture beyond the pupils' attention span.
5. Don't use the lecture just to cover the material rapidly.
6. Don't spend unwarranted time on unimportant aspects of the lecture.
7. Don't follow your notes or the textbook verbatim.
8. Don't lecture so rapidly that students cannot follow your thinking.
9. Don't use a monotonous tone in delivering the lecture.
10. Don't use annoying or distracting mannerisms.
11. Don't appear listless and bored.

A careful re-examination of his own lecture habits will reveal to the conscientious teacher many other cautions that should be recorded for further reference.

USE OF QUESTIONS

Questioning can be an aid to instruction—depending upon the skill with which it is employed by the teacher.[11] It has much in com-

---

[10]Wellington and Wellington, *op. cit.*, pp. 222–228, relate the use of the lecture to problem solving.

[11]Burton, *op. cit.*, Chapter 18, presents a full-chapter discussion on improving questioning.

Frank A. Butler, *The Improvement of Teaching in Secondary Schools*, rev. ed. (Chicago: University of Chicago Press, 1946), Chapter 11, provides another sound discussion of questioning techniques, although the book was written during the forties.

Rivlin, *op. cit.*, Chapter 7, discusses thoroughly the use of the question as an aid to learning. Useful examples are provided.

mon with the lecture, for it is essentially a teacher-controlled device for promoting thought, making appraisals, and moving students toward desired goals. Although the teacher is chiefly responsible for questioning related to subject-matter content, he also is responsible for providing the setting in which students will feel free to ask relevant questions.

Purposes of Questions

A range of purposes may be served through the use of questions. Unfortunately, teachers often develop considerable skill with questions that serve only one purpose and ignore other possible uses. Careful examination of these other possibilities reveals that each has unique advantages.

Earlier writers focused attention on the kinds of questions and their specific form, wording, and use. More recent writers, particularly educational psychologists, have directed their attention toward goal achievement and have viewed questioning as a device to assist in this process. A classification of the purposes for which questions are used encourages needed differentiation in the classroom. Questioning is correctly employed to:[12]

1. Stimulate analytical thought.
2. Diagnose student difficulties.
3. Determine progress toward specific goals.
4. Motivate students.
5. Clarify and expand concepts.
6. Encourage new appreciations and attitudes.
7. Give specific direction to thinking.
8. Relate cause to effect.
9. Encourage student self-evaluation.
10. Encourage the application of concepts.

A brief look at each of these purposes will point up the importance of thoroughly understanding the use of the question.

Stimulating Analytical Thought

Getting students to think intensively about subject-matter content and its importance to society is a recurring problem for teachers. The thought-provoking question serves well in this connection if effectively employed; this calls for proper timing and a meaningful statement of the question. Emphasis is not upon a recall of facts but upon thinking about facts in a meaningful, interrelated way. Some

---

[12]See Burton, *op. cit.*, pp. 438–439, for a similar discussion of the purposes of questions.

Illustrations of questioning procedures designed to achieve specific purposes are provided by Butler, *op. cit.*, pp. 214–216.

nonoral questions—such as the essay and, at times, multiple choice and matching—can be used to help stimulate thought.[13] More frequently, however, the thought-provoking question is asked orally as a part of the class discussion.

The thought-provoking question is used by teachers of all subjects, but it is employed with much greater frequency in such concept-centered areas as mathematics, physical sciences, social sciences, and English grammar. The examples below are related to specific subjects:

Tenth-grade English grammar: Why is it important for the college-bound student to understand English grammar?

Ninth-grade civics: What is likely to happen to individual citizens of a city the size of ours if the local government is dishonest?

Twelfth-grade physics: What are the practical applications of the concept that the transmission of sound waves varies with the media through which it is transmitted?

Note that the student is encouraged to provide a response that has been carefully thought out. The quick answer is out of place.

Diagnosing Student Difficulties

All of the various types of questions—objective or subjective, thought-provoking or simple, oral or written—may be helpful in determining the academic trouble spots of students. In fact, to obtain a valid appraisal, it is desirable to use a wide range of question types. The following examples may be directed toward groups or individuals in written or oral form:

Ninth-grade literature: Describe the character of Lady Macbeth.

Tenth-grade biology: Define *taxonomy* in your own words.

Tenth-grade world history: Indicate when Pericles lived and what his major contributions were.

Determining Progress Toward Goals

Various kinds of questions can be used in determining progress toward goals. Objective questions, for example, have the advantage of extensive sampling. Specific weaknesses can thus be discovered, permitting appropriate remedial steps to be taken. Story problems give students the opportunity to exhibit their subject-matter strength in applied situations. The youngster who responds with insight to wisely selected story problems can be assumed to be in command of desired content. Again, it is desirable to use a variety of question types in order to obtain an accurate appraisal.

---

[13]Rivlin, *op. cit.*, p. 214, briefly discusses the need for designing the question to stimulate thinking.

Motivating Students

Student interest can be awakened and perpetuated through the effective use of questions. This is often accomplished during the initiation of the unit, but it may take place at other times as well. For example, the teacher in a twelfth-grade physics unit concerned with motivating the class to study a unit on "Waves and Sounds" may pose this question: "What is the relationship between sound waves and waves caused by dropping a pebble into a tub of water?"

Thought questions are typically viewed as having good potential for motivation. A series of rapid-fire, short-answer questions, however, may also motivate by opening up new possibilities or revealing weaknesses previously unknown to students. Other motivating questions accompany demonstrations during which students are asked to explain the phenomena taking place.

Clarifying and Expanding Concepts

Once a student has formed a partial concept, the teacher may further clarify the concept by posing questions that impel student reactions. This is a case in point: During the study of an eleventh-grade unit on "World War II," students had been highly interested in the details of the conflict, but the teacher wanted them to relate these details to the current world scene. "What is the relationship of the U.S.S.R.'s participation in the defeat of Germany to present world tensions?" he asked.

The use of probing counterquestions in response to student questions may help the student answer his own inquiries—if the counterquestions do not offend or aggravate.

Encouraging Appreciations and Attitudes

To the extent that appreciations and attitudes are comprised of concepts, they are subject to modification. If the teacher wishes to help students think more rationally about race relations, for example, he may wish to modify, clarify, or expand underlying mental pictures. One of the more frequently used techniques for accomplishing this is a thought question, such as, "If you were a member of a racial minority in a small city, how would you approach your fellow citizens with respect to schooling, housing, and social relations?"

Directing Thinking

Class discussions, if permitted to wander, may become quite unrelated to the central theme of a lesson. An inoffensive way to redirect the thinking of class members is to pose an arresting question that will turn their thinking in the direction the teacher wishes it to go. In a tenth-grade biology class, for example, if the discussion has strayed from conservation, a question such as the following might be in order: "What are three conservation practices that help us preserve the wildlife in our own state?"

Relating Cause to Effect

The *why* question is typically used to relate cause to effect. Its prime concern is to avoid the meaningless repetition of facts without a real understanding of their relationships. Examples of sound questions of this type are:

Why was Ulysses S. Grant considered to be a weak President?
Under what circumstances can the atom be split? Why?
Why is the nitrogen cycle essential to the maintenance of life?

Encouraging Self-Evaluation

Students tend to be receptive to criticisms that come from within. Herein lies the value of self-evaluation. If the teacher has had experience and possesses tact, he can pose questions that encourage self-examination. Such questions might include some of the following:

Was your reasoning correct or faulty in this case? Why?
What is the correct answer to the question you missed?
What can you do to make a better score on the next test?
Why did you make a higher score on the last test?

Promoting Application

Questions that call for the application of known ideas are used to good advantage in certain subjects. Story problems, for example, are often helpful in teaching mathematics; concluding activities in mathematics units may be comprised, in part, of such problems. In the typewriting class the question "How do you type a simple business letter?" calls for a specific applied response. In the civics class the question "What specific steps must a foreigner follow in obtaining citizenship?" confronts students with the necessity for recombining facts in a practical way. "How is the carburetor cleaned in a Ford automobile?" calls for application in the auto-mechanics class. Each time students write a paper or theme for any class there is always the implied question "What constitutes a correctly written English composition?"

Principles Related to Questioning

It is helpful to identify how questions can be employed effectively in clarifying concepts, encouraging appreciation, relating cause to effect, and encouraging self-evaluation. Maximum long-range help is provided, however, when minute bits of information derived from the successful use of questions are distilled into sound generalizations.[14] The following are based upon broad principles of education.

[14]"General principles basic to good questioning" are provided by Burton, *op. cit.*, pp. 439–442.

1. Questions provide one means of assisting instruction.
2. Questions are means, not ends.
3. Questioning is only profitable when the student has a background that will enable him to react intelligently.
4. A sequence of questions should lead progressively to specific understandings.
5. There is a close relationship between the teacher's ability to use questions and his knowledge of content.
6. The teacher's ability to use questions effectively is aided by his intelligence and successful experience.[15]
7. Specific types of questions should be used to achieve desired purposes.
8. Teachers should not specialize in one particular type of question to the possible exclusion of other types.
9. Ingenious teachers develop interesting and helpful modifications in the use of the question-answer technique.
10. Questioning should aim at fitting fragments of information into meaningful wholes.
11. The quality of questioning is limited by the teacher's quality of thinking.
12. The form and wording of a question is only secondary to its basic purpose of assisting the teaching-learning process.
13. An essential part of the question-answer technique involves encouraging students to ask questions.

Correct and Incorrect Use

Many common errors are illustrated in this questioning, which took place in a general music class after students had spent portions of two days discussing elementary theory.[16]

Teacher: Do you know what a scale is?

Douglas: No.

Teacher: Tonja, can you tell me?

Tonja: No.

Teacher: Marietta?

Marietta: A scale is a group of notes that are higher than the other notes.

Teacher: That is a poor answer. Only a small part of it is right. William, tell her what it is.

William: A series of tones ascending or descending in pitch that possess certain interval relationships. (Quotes teacher's verbatim statement taken from notes.)

Teacher: Fine, William. That's exactly right.

---

[15]*Ibid.*, p. 437, emphasizes the need for native ability in improving questioning.

[16]Butler, *op. cit.*, pp. 207–208, gives an example of a poor questioning procedure.

Several undesirable procedures are evident in this brief exchange:

1. The first question is irrelevant because it focuses attention not on content, but on whether the student is able to satisfactorily reproduce content. Douglas avoided difficulty by answering "No." Questions that permit one-word responses are typically bad.

2. When Marietta gave a response that contained certain correct elements, she was embarrassed before the class for not having been totally correct.

3. William was forced to come to her rescue.

4. He was praised for repeating a verbatim statement that may or may not have been meaningful to him.

Under the direction of a more skilled teacher, the questioning procedure might have been quite different:

Teacher: Let us all hum a major scale, beginning here. (The tone is sounded and all hum the scale.) Now, why was that a major scale? (After waiting for a minute for all to react, the teacher calls on Douglas.)

Douglas: It just sounds like it.

Teacher: Yes, that's right, but can you think why this is? I believe you're on the right track.

Douglas: If you would play a minor scale after the major scale, I could tell you.

Teacher: All right. (The teacher plays the major scale and then the minor scale.)

Douglas: Now I've got it. We said yesterday that in the major scale the half steps come between the third and fourth steps and between the fifth and sixth steps.

Teacher: Good, but there is something that still needs to be said. (Going to the board, the teacher writes the C major scale on the permanent staff. The half steps between the third and fourth steps and between the seventh and eighth steps are encircled.)

Douglas: Now I see what I missed.

Teacher: Let me play it again for you as Douglas has first suggested. (The incorrect scale is played. Students frown.) Now let me play it the way it appears on the board.

The questioning used by this second teacher leads to several observations:

1. Participation of all students was encouraged, both with respect to singing as well as with respect to the first question.

2. Although Douglas' response was far from satisfactory, the teacher did not say so. Douglas received encouragement. Furthermore, the teacher raised no objection to playing the minor scale for contrast.

3. Although Douglas was only partially correct in his second response, the teacher left him with the feeling of accomplishment.

4. The matter was cleared up through meaningful use of the chalkboard.

5. Playing the scale a second time at the piano tended to clinch the concept.

Specific Suggestions

Specific helps can be drawn from the psychological principles most frequently involved in the use of questions. These suggestions, however, are not intended to serve as a substitute for an understanding of the basic principles, but they should serve as pointed reminders of certain things to remember and certain things to avoid.

Recommendations

1. Use specific kinds of questions to serve specific purposes.[17]
2. Use thought-provoking questions frequently.
3. Use quick, random questions for review.
4. Use related questions that become progressively more difficult if you want students to acquire concepts in depth.
5. Ask questions only when you have a definite purpose for doing so.
6. Ask questions that are within the pupil's own range of experience and knowledge.[18]
7. Ask questions that are free of confusing parenthetical elements.
8. Word questions as simply as possible without distorting meaning.[19]
9. If you wish to have a question answered in a certain way (compare, classify, outline, define, etc.), indicate this clearly.
10. Only accept student replies that are reasonably complete and meaningful.
11. If students do not answer your questions with reasonable completeness and accuracy, make sure the class is not left with false concepts.
12. As a general rule, use some portion of a student's answer if only to encourage him and keep him interested.[20]

---

[17]Howard T. Batchelder, Maurice McGlasson, and Raleigh Schorling, *Student Teaching in Secondary Schools*, 4th ed. (New York: McGraw-Hill Book Company, 1964), pp. 173–175, provide an excellent but brief discussion of the types of questions. Examples are given.

[18]Butler, *op. cit.*, pp. 219–220, lists several practical suggestions that he feels are characteristic of good questioning procedures.

See Rivlin, *op. cit.*, pp. 210–214, for specific hints on how to ask questions in a class. This author also describes three basic characteristics of a good question on pages 208–210.

[19]Burton, *op. cit.*, pp. 442–445, gives several specific hints with respect to the wording and form of questions.

[20]Rivlin, *op. cit.*, pp. 215–219, discusses in some detail how student answers should be treated.

13. Establish a classroom climate in which students will feel free to ask questions.[21]

14. Before asking for a response to a thought question, allow students time to think about it.

Cautions

1. As a general rule, don't ask obvious questions.[22]

2. Don't react emotionally if the student fails to answer a question correctly.

3. Don't ask "Are there any questions?" as a device for determining whether students have understood the lesson. Usually you will get no response even when students do not understand.

4. Don't allow the questioning procedure to lead you and your students away from the planned subject.

5. Don't ask ambiguous questions.

6. Don't direct your questions to a few isolated students. Include as many students as possible in your questioning.

7. Don't attempt to bluff if you are not sure of the answer to a student's question. Say "I don't know" and then find out.

8. Don't discourage student responses to student questions.

9. Don't ask catch questions.

10. Don't ask questions that call for two different and confusing reactions to the same question.

11. Don't ask questions that contain words not understood by students.

12. As a general rule, don't repeat questions. Insist that students listen to what you say.

USE OF DEMONSTRATIONS

By definition a demonstration is concerned with *showing*.[23] Because showing often involves the learner's first-hand contact with the referent of the concept, its sensory impact is extremely vivid. Demonstration, therefore, becomes a very helpful instructional tool in the hands of a knowledgeable teacher. It is properly classified as a

---

[21]*Ibid.*, pp. 219–220, provides suggestions on how the teacher can encourage students to ask questions.

[22]Vincent McGuire, Robert B. Myers, and Charles L. Durrance, *Your Student Teaching in the Secondary School* (Boston: Allyn and Bacon, 1959), p. 158, list a number of specific cautions. Characteristics of good questions and positive suggestions for questioning are presented by the same authors on pages 157 and 159.

[23]Jean D. Grambs, William J. Iverson, and Franklin K. Patterson, *Modern Methods in Secondary Education*, rev. ed. (New York: The Dryden Press, 1958), p. 160, define demonstrations as "visual presentations of things, processes, facts, or ideas to be learned."

See also A. J. Foy Cross and Irene F. Cypher, *Audio-Visual Education* (New York: Thomas Y. Crowell Company, 1961), p. 217.

teacher-centered procedure because the teacher, more often than anyone else, gives the demonstration.

Types of Demonstrations

A majority of current secondary methods texts do not give specific attention to the use of demonstration. Many writers prefer to accord it only token attention as an aid to the lecture method. Demonstration has, however, certain psychological advantages that warrant its separate treatment:

1. It provides sensory impact that the written or spoken word cannot match.
2. It is basically interesting to students.
3. It affords freedom from the boring repetition of lectures.

It is useful to classify types of classroom demonstrations in terms of how closely they approximate the lecture. Note the varied ways in which demonstration may be used:

Pure demonstration with no explanation
Demonstration with a few explanatory comments
Half demonstration—half lecture
Lecture with some demonstration

Pure Demonstration

Occasionally the observation of a given phenomenon requires such attention that any spoken word serves as a distraction. This is the case in an auto-mechanics shop where the instructor is demonstrating the assembly of close-fitting mechanical devices. Comments during a laboratory demonstration in a chemistry class may at times cause the students to miss an important chemical reaction.

Although no comment is made during certain demonstrations, it is desirable for the teacher to indicate in advance what the student is to look for. Similarly, when the sensational portion of a demonstration is finished, a discussion of what has occurred and why is highly desirable. The chemistry teacher, for example, might show students the reaction of sodium in its pure state when exposed to air and water. After the demonstration is over, an explanation would be entirely in order.

Demonstration with Comments

In a typing class the teacher often demonstrates the correct position of the fingers on the keys, using a typewriter mounted on a high stand. He insists that students observe carefully the exact position of his hands as he makes a few explanatory comments. The dominant concern, however, is their observation. In a geometry class the teacher illustrates (shows) various geometric patterns at the chalkboard while he briefly explains them. Here again, the instructor is less concerned with his oral explanation than with the visual impact of his drawings.

Half Demonstration—Half Lecture

In the woodwork shop the teacher tells his students why it is necessary to prepare oak in a given way before finishing it. His explanation accompanies the actual *showing* of how the preparation is done. The homemaking teacher shows students how to use the pinking shears as she explains the reason for their use. The algebra teacher explains how to balance an equation while he demonstrates the process on the chalkboard.[24]

Lecture with Demonstration

A French teacher may explain in some detail about life along the Mediterranean Coast. Later, students are briefly shown a large map and two pictures. Students in a shorthand class take dictation for the major portion of an hour. When the teacher discovers some students using incorrect forms, she stops the class long enough to demonstrate the correct form at the board. Dictation then continues.

A majority of classroom demonstrations take place in the science courses or in skill-related subjects. But many students in other subject areas would benefit from greater emphasis on *showing*. This is particularly true of less gifted students who have limited ability to think abstractly.

Each of the four types of demonstration cited may serve a useful purpose under certain circumstances. More frequently used than the other types is the combination lecture-demonstration.[25] It has the psychological advantage of giving recognition to the most essential steps in teaching concepts—showing and telling.[26] Whether the emphasis should fall on the demonstration or the lecture depends upon several factors: background experiences of students, students' ability to derive meaning from spoken words, the quality of the lecture or demonstration, and student and teacher preferences.

Principles Related to Demonstrations

The principles stated here should give direction to the correct use of the demonstration as a teaching procedure. These guidelines apply to all types of demonstrations.

---

[24]Thomas M. Risk, *Principles and Practices of Teaching in Secondary Schools*, 2d. ed. (New York: American Book Company, 1947), pp. 382–385, discusses the nature, values, and techniques of using the lecture-demonstration procedure.

[25]Wellington and Wellington, *op. cit.*, pp. 224–225, relate the demonstration to the lecture and provide examples.

[26]See Chapter 4, pp. 74–75.

1. Because demonstration often involves first-hand contact with the referent, it provides a vivid learning experience.[27]

2. The kinds of demonstrations vary widely, and each type serves a particular purpose.

3. An oral explanation often adds to the meaning of a demonstration.

4. Concept formation is hindered by an oral explanation if it, rather than the demonstration, becomes the center of focus.

5. Students can derive maximum benefit from a demonstration only when they are physically in a position to perceive the phenomenon or action to be shown.

6. The attention span of students viewing a demonstration varies in proportion to how meaningful it is to them.

7. The slowness and accuracy with which demonstrations are presented determines how well cause-and-effect relationships are seen.

8. Like other methods, the demonstration is a means of helping students achieve goals.

9. Effective demonstration requires practice.

10. A demonstration is most effective when competing stimuli are eliminated.

11. Students gain more from a demonstration when they know what they are looking for.

12. Students will be confused if they do not understand the technical terminology used to explain the phenomena of a given demonstration.

13. A demonstration must serve a specific educational purpose.

Correct and Incorrect Use

MR. JUTSON DEMONSTRATES THE MICROSCOPE

Franklin Jutson, tenth-grade biology teacher, was demonstrating the use of the microscope. While students observed from their seats, he explained briefly the use of the adjustment knobs and turned each one so that all could see. Then he gave a two-minute lecture, emphasizing the necessity for knowing how to operate the microscope.

This teacher violated several principles related to the effective employment of the demonstration as a teaching device:

1. Most of the students were not close enough to the demonstration to observe precisely what was going on.

2. Because the explanation and actual showing of what was to be done were hurried, the slower students missed some of the relevant points.

---

[27]Mills and Douglass, *op. cit.*, p. 224, note the superiority of the demonstration over verbal explanation in teaching concepts.

3. Students were not permitted to try to adjust the microscope. As a result the cause-and-effect relationship was not understood.

4. The teacher did not point out what the students were to look for before the demonstration.

In the room across the hall Mr. Snelsen was conducting the same demonstration, but in quite a different way.[28]

MR. SNELSEN DEMONSTRATES THE MICROSCOPE

After Mr. Snelsen had pulled down the large chart on which the microscope was pictured, he pointed out each important part and explained its function. Then he said to the class, "I want you to leave your seats and gather around my desk so that you can see every move I make as I operate the microscope." As soon as he was sure that all students could observe each detailed movement, he placed a small leaf on the platform and adjusted the focus so that it was properly magnified. "Look through the microscope and tell us what you see, Sue Ann," he said. When she reported the clear magnification, he twisted the focusing screw. "Now what do you see?" he asked. This time she reported a blurring.

One by one each adjustment device was used and explained. Students were encouraged to ask questions. Then a schedule was set up so that each student in turn would have an opportunity to experiment with the operation of the microscope in a practical situation.

Demonstrations in Special Situations

Teachers of skill subjects frequently use the demonstration to good advantage.[29] Demonstration is particulary helpful in foreign-language classes because of the current emphasis on oral use. The teacher says a phrase or sentence, and the students mimic him. In the orchestra or band class, the teacher repeatedly finds it necessary to illustrate how to make the tone he wants his players to reproduce. If he is unable to give a proper demonstration, his chances of getting the right response from the students are limited.

The teacher of home economics often follows a sequence of showing, telling, supervising student practice, and then repeating the sequence as needed. All forms of shop instruction rely heavily on demonstration to give students a correct and vivid impression of a given skill to be performed. Demonstration in combination with other methods is probably the best and most frequently used procedure for providing students with clear mental pictures of skills to be learned in physical education classes.

In addition, demonstrations are often useful when concepts are

---

[28]An example of the use of the demonstration in introducing a unit is provided by Herbert J. Klausmeier, *Teaching in the Secondary School* (New York: Harper & Brothers, 1958), p. 172.

[29]Goetting, *op. cit.*, pp. 245–246, provides a general statement on the nature of the demonstration. The pageant is mentioned as a demonstration device, although it is rarely used at the present time in secondary schools.

being developed. Certain mental processes, such as those involved in algebra, are best explained by example—thus through showing. If the teacher relies solely on the spoken word to teach such processes, he frequently does not get his point across. Analysis of sentence structure may be accomplished in several ways, but many English teachers have employed diagraming for this purpose because it lends itself nicely to demonstration.

Specific Suggestions

Thoughtful teachers rely on a broad acquaintance with educational principles to give direction to their use of specific methods. The following suggestions relate to the use of demonstration as a teaching technique.[30]

Recommendations

1. Re-examine the exact objectives of the lesson before you give a demonstration.
2. Practice the demonstration as many times as necessary to do it effectively.
3. Satisfy yourself that all needed materials are available before starting the demonstration.
4. Be sure that all students can easily observe the demonstration. This may call for reseating students or having them stand in a semicircle around the demonstrator.
5. Exclude all distracting influences before the demonstration is started.
6. Before beginning the demonstration, explain what you are about to demonstrate and the purpose of the demonstration. Tell the students what to look for.
7. Speak clearly and distinctly.
8. Use a vocabulary understood by all.
9. To assure yourself that students are understanding the demonstration, pause at intervals to ask questions or to allow students to ask questions.
10. Face the students as much as possible.
11. Briefly review the key points of the demonstration as soon as it is completed.
12. Employ good safety practices under all circumstances.

Cautions

1. Don't prolong the demonstration. It should usually not exceed twenty-five minutes.
2. Don't present the demonstration so fast that students fail to grasp the key ideas.

---

[30]Nordberg, Bradfield, and Odell, *op. cit.*, pp. 305–306, describe what constitutes a successful demonstration. Specific suggestions are provided.

3. Don't squeeze too many concepts into one demonstration. Make it as simple as possible.

4. Don't draw attention away from the demonstration by a lengthy explanation unless it is justified.

5. Don't use unfamiliar trade or technical terms without explaining their meaning.

6. Never give a demonstration without first having a trial run. There is always the possibility that it may not work.

TEACHER-CENTERED PROCEDURES IN REVIEW

Under specific circumstances, teacher-centered activities achieve unit goals more effectively than do activities requiring maximum student involvement. Three teacher-centered activities—lectures, questions, and demonstrations—have been discussed in this chapter. Each has unique advantages when employed efficiently by a trained teacher.

The several variations of the lecture all serve useful instructional purposes. Of these variations the formal lecture is the least practical for secondary-school instruction. A lecture may be made more or less formal, however, depending upon the nature of the instructional task, the group being taught, and the teacher's preference.

Questions, too, may be used in achieving a range of purposes. They may be used to stimulate thought, diagnose difficulties, determine progress, motivate students, clarify and expand concepts, encourage new appreciations, give direction in thinking, relate cause to effect, encourage self-evaluation, and encourage the application of concepts.

The prime purpose of the demonstration is to *show*, an essential step in the teaching of concepts. Demonstration provides the learner with first-hand contact with the referent, effecting a vivid sensory impact. Among the variations in demonstration are pure demonstration, demonstration with few comments, half demonstration and half lecture, and lecture with demonstration.

PROBLEMS FOR STUDY AND DISCUSSION

1. What are the disadvantages of the formal lecture? List at least five.
2. Give an example in which the use of the formal lecture would be appropriate in teaching your subject-matter major.
3. Describe at least three different situations in which the illustrated lecture would be appropriate in your teaching minor.
4. List several general situations in which reading aloud to the class for a short period is justified.
5. What advantages does the formal lecture have over the modified lecture? Give specific examples.

6. Do you believe that it would be appropriate to permit conversational informality in teaching your minor field? Why?

7. Identify ten situations in which informal brief explanations are warranted.

8. If you were lecturing to a group of students who had widely varying abilities and interests, how would you go about meeting their varied needs? Explain.

9. Explain precisely how thought can be stimulated through asking questions.

10. Give three examples of thought-provoking questions that you might logically ask in teaching your major field.

11. Indicate the advantages of the story problem.

12. What kinds of questions would be most helpful in encouraging students to expand partially formed concepts? Give one example.

13. How can cause be related to effect through questioning? Give two examples of cause-and-effect questions appropriate to your subject-matter minor.

14. Do you tend to use one type of question much more frequently than other types? Is its use justified? Explain.

15. Describe one ingenious and different questioning procedure that you can use in teaching your major field.

16. What are the psychological advantages of demonstration as a method?

17. Which variation of the demonstration do you prefer for teaching your minor field? Give your reasons.

18. Give a description of a teaching situation in your major field in which half demonstration and half lecture would serve a useful instructional purpose.

19. What steps should be taken to eliminate competing stimuli during a demonstration?

20. If a demonstration is carried out well, is it necessary to repeat the main points? Why?

RECOMMENDED READINGS

Lectures

Burton, William H., *The Guidance of Learning Activities,* 3d. ed. New York: Appleton-Century-Crofts, Inc., 1962, pp. 264 and 286.

Goetting, M. L., *Teaching in the Secondary School.* New York: Prentice-Hall, Inc., 1942, pp. 166–172.

Hansen, Kenneth H., *High School Teaching.* Englewood Cliffs, N.J.: Prentice-Hall, Inc., 1957, pp. 180–183.

Klausmeier, Herbert J., *Teaching in the Secondary School.* New York: Harper & Brothers, 1958, pp. 264–265.

Mills, Hubert H., and Harl R. Douglass, *Teaching in High School,* 2d. ed. New York: Ronald Press, 1957, p. 224.

Nordberg, H. Orville, James M. Bradfield, and Willlam C. Odell, *Secondary School Teaching.* New York: The Macmillan Company, 1962, p. 147.

Risk, Thomas M., *Principles and Practices of Teaching in Secondary Schools,* 2d. ed. New York: The American Book Company, 1947, pp. 378–384.

Rivlin, Harry N., *Teaching Adolescents in Secondary Schools,* 2d. ed. New York: Appleton-Century-Crofts, Inc., 1961, Chapter 6.

Wellington, C. Burleigh, and Jean Wellington, *Teaching for Critical Thinking: with Emphasis on Secondary Education.* New York: McGraw-Hill Book Company, 1960, Chapter 11.

Questions

Batchelder, Howard T., Maurice McGlasson, and Raleigh Schorling, *Student Teaching in Secondary Schools,* 4th ed. New York: McGraw-Hill Book Company, 1964, pp. 173–175.

Burton, William H., *The Guidance of Learning Activities,* 3d. ed. New York: Appleton-Century-Crofts, Inc., 1962, Chapter 18.

Butler, Frank A., *The Improvement of Teaching in Secondary Schools,* rev. ed. Chicago: The University of Chicago Press, 1946, Chapter 11.

Hansen, Kenneth H., *High School Teaching.* Englewood Cliffs, N.J.: Prentice-Hall, Inc., 1957, pp. 187–190.

McGuire, Vincent, Robert B. Myers, and Charles L. Durrance, *Your Student Teaching in the Secondary School.* Boston: Allyn and Bacon, Inc., 1959, pp. 157–159.

Rivlin, Harry N., *Teaching Adolescents in Secondary Schools,* 2d. ed. New York: Appleton-Century-Crofts, Inc., 1961, Chapter 7.

Demonstrations

Cross, A. J. Foy, and Irene F. Cypher, *Audio-Visual Education.* New York: Thomas Y. Crowell Company, 1961, pp. 215–224.

Goetting, M. L., *Teaching in the Secondary School.* New York: Prentice-Hall, Inc., 1942, pp. 245–246.

Grambs, Jean D., William J. Iverson, and Franklin K. Patterson, *Modern Methods in Secondary Education,* rev. ed. New York: The Dryden Press, 1958, p. 160.

Klausmeier, Herbert J., *Teaching in the Secondary School.* New York: Harper & Brothers, 1958, pp. 172–175.

Mills, Hubert H., and Harl R. Douglass, *Teaching in High School,* 2d. ed. New York: Ronald Press, 1957, p. 224.

Nordberg, H. Orville, James M. Bradfield, and William C. Odell, *Secondary School Teaching.* New York: The Macmillan Company, 1962, pp. 305–306.

Risk, Thomas M., *Principles and Practices of Teaching in Secondary Schools,* 2d. ed. New York: The American Book Company, 1947, pp. 382–385.

Wellington, C. Burleigh, and Jean Wellington, *Teaching for Critical Thinking: with Emphasis on Secondary Education.* New York: McGraw-Hill Book Company, 1960, pp. 224–225.

10

Student-Centered Procedures

All learning requires the meaningful reaction of the learner, but some procedures demand student participation in order to promote learning. The uses of three such procedures are discussed in this chapter: the textbook, the assignment, and homework; the following chapter will cover additional student-centered procedures.

USE OF THE TEXTBOOK

The textbook is a systematic arrangement of subject material designed to assist the instructor in teaching particular content to students at a specific grade level.[1] In no other one place can the teacher—or the student—find an equivalent concentration of course-related materials.

One of the most commonly used teaching aids, the text may also be one of the most helpful aids to the effective teacher.[2] However, if the teacher selects a poor text or uses a good text poorly, unsatisfactory learning may result. In order to avoid misusing the text, the teacher should first of all know what a textbook is *not*:[3]

[1]See A. J. Foy Cross and Irene F. Cypher, *Audio-Visual Education* (New York: Thomas Y. Crowell Company, 1961), pp. 242–243, for an enumeration of the strengths and weaknesses of textbooks.

[2]Hubert H. Mills and Harl R. Douglass, *Teaching in High School,* 2d. ed. (New York: Ronald Press, 1957), pp. 257–258, provide a useful list of the values of textbooks.

[3]Kenneth H. Hansen, *High School Teaching* (Englewood Cliffs, N.J.: Prentice-Hall, 1957), p. 214, presents a brief discussion of the limitations of the textbook.

1. It is not the teacher.
2. It is not the course.
3. It is not a teaching plan.
4. It is not a device that will enable the incompetent teacher to appear competent.
5. It is not the only book with value for the course.
6. It is not a substitute for all other teaching materials.
7. It is not a device for self-directed learning.[4]
8. It is not equally suitable for all kinds of students.
9. It is not a device for permitting the lazy teacher to escape work.

The well-organized textbook, on the other hand, contains some of the best teaching materials, provides suggestions for specific points worth considering, and suggests a possible range and sequence of units for the course. By carefully examining a good textbook before completing unit and yearly plans, the teacher can often save valuable time.

The reading of a text by all students establishes a common background that is essential to certain teaching procedures. In addition, a well-organized text helps the student understand how various parts of the course content are interrelated and provides him with an easy means of review. The use of high quality photographs, drawings, and charts—many in color—can help clarify difficult content. In the fields of biology, health, and geography, remarkable strides along this line have been made in the past few years.

Principles Related to the Effective Use of the Textbook

Effective use of the textbook is based on the following proven principles.

1. Effective planning is assisted by a sound text that helps identify course objectives.

2. The textbook is only one of many devices to help students achieve educational goals.[5] Furthermore, no one text is suitable for all students. Since they vary in intelligence, background, and subject-matter achievement, different individuals will benefit from the use of different textual as well as nontextual materials. Similarly, the student's liking for a given text will depend upon how well it serves his individual purposes.

3. The vocabulary in a general textbook will help determine its usefulness. The need for variation in vocabulary levels is met by as-

---

[4]Currently available, however, are many so-called programed learning texts of differing quality that assist students toward self-directed learning.

[5]Jean D. Grambs, William J. Iverson, and Franklin K. Patterson, *Modern Methods in Secondary Education,* rev. ed. (New York: The Dryden Press, 1958), pp. 174–175, stress the need for variety in employing the textbook and supplementary materials.

signing carefully selected supplementary textbooks for students with high as well as with low reading abilities.

4. Because students learn concepts through both verbal and graphic symbols, it is essential that textbooks be well illustrated. Illustrations can clarify content that might otherwise be difficult.

5. A student derives meaning from the printed page only to the extent that the printed words (symbols) are related to meaningful concepts. Such concepts can be expanded when the textbook is interesting to the student.

6. A student is ready to use a text if he has (a) general knowledge of its content, (b) mastery of the basic concepts, (c) adequate vocabulary mastery, and (d) proficiency in reading.

7. Use of the textbook to the exclusion of other teaching materials and aids is an unsound teaching practice.[6]

8. Effective textbook use is impossible in classrooms where student behavior is not carefully controlled.

9. Students who are preoccupied with nonschool problems and interests are unable to use the textbook effectively.

Correct and Incorrect Use

Incorrect uses of the textbook are illustrated in the following narrative accounts.

MRS. RYDEN DEMANDS A RIGOROUS PACE

Mrs. Ryden had been given to understand that the educational climate had changed, that students were now expected to accomplish more. So, in her class, The History of California, Mrs. Ryden required students to cover a chapter every three days in spite of the fact that the vocabulary level of the text was roughly one grade beyond them. Students protested, parents complained, and the teacher became disgruntled; but the students were still kept to their rigorous pace.

MR. HULL RELIES ON THE TEXT

W. R. Hull had some traditional ideas about teaching; the text was his Bible. If the students knew the text, they knew the course and, according to him, deserved high grades. Mr. Hull was never known to make assignments outside the text or to use supplementary materials. If students chose to seek additional information, they did it on their own. There were occasional class discussions, but never for very long, and invariably the students were sent back to study their texts.

In Mrs. Ryden's class unrealistic requirements with respect to textbook assignments soon created unfavorable feelings about the

---

[6]Robert C. McKean, *Principles and Methods in Secondary Education* (Columbus, Ohio: Charles E. Merrill Books, Inc., 1962), pp. 156–159, briefly discusses supplementary written materials.

text as well as about the course content. Frustration—from having to cope with a vocabulary that was too difficult—served only to defeat, not to help, the students. Mr. Hull, the second teacher, had fallen into the pattern of textbook teaching and had no intention of being jarred out of this rut.[7]

These difficulties were avoided by Mrs. Willmot, who used the textbook as only one aid among many for teaching a tenth-grade American literature class.

MRS. WILLMOT BUILDS FROM THE BASIC TEXT

At the beginning of the year Mrs. Willmot again ran an inventory of her classroom library. She found books containing selections of varying difficulty, both in content as well as in vocabulary. Gifted and below-average students could all be given reading assignments in keeping with their capabilities.

During the first few days, Mrs. Willmot demonstrated the use of the basic text. Brief assignments were worked out involving the use of footnotes, the table of contents, and the index. After several of these assignments, the students were able to use the text efficiently. The teacher also identified course objectives that required the dominant use of the basic text. However, students were also required to read other sources available in the school library as well as in the classroom library.

Student reading assignments were differentiated to accommodate reading level, interests, and intelligence. While students read during the study period, Mrs. Willmot, seated at the back of the room, held brief diagnostic conferences with students about their own reading problems.

Use in Specific Subjects

The use of the textbook as an aid to instruction varies with course objectives. Skill subjects, for example, call for a somewhat different use of the text than that required in concept-centered subjects. Teachers of typewriting classes employ texts that are predominantly made up of exercises aimed at the improvement of skills, although necessary attention is given to skill-related concepts. In physical education classes, textbooks are used only rarely, since the focus in these classes is on performance ability (skills). The necessary concepts are usually provided orally through lecture and discussion. The school band and orchestra classes typically use no text as such, but they rely extensively on printed music.

In classes where the teaching of concepts is the main concern, textbooks are employed in a variety of ways. Biology teachers often make excellent use of the text's colored plates and cell overlays. In

---

[7]See McKean, *op cit.*, pp. 150–153, for a description of traditional textbook teaching and its implications.

Samuel P. Wiggins, *Successful High School Teaching* (Boston: Houghton Mifflin Company, 1958), pp. 173–179, presents a detailed account of textbook teaching that illustrates points discussed in this chapter.

mathematics classes, teachers often find it profitable to discuss the basic ideas to be covered; these same ideas are then reinforced through reading the text. Literature texts are usually anthologies in which students read widely to fulfill varied assignments.

Specific Suggestions

The following recommendations and cautions are closely related to the principles underlying the sound use of the textbook presented earlier in this chapter. These specific suggestions are based upon the experience of individual teachers.

Recommendations

1. Investigate the various ways in which a textbook may be used.[8]
2. Evaluate the text in terms of course goals.
3. Be sure that the vocabulary and content of the text are appropriate to the class for which they are intended.[9]
4. Use a text that is current.
5. Use the text to help achieve the objectives of the unit and the course.
6. Supplement the textbook with other materials and procedures. Use the reading of the text to stimulate other activities.
7. Discover how other teachers in your subject-matter area have used the textbook advantageously. Adapt the best of their procedures to your own use.
8. Adapt the textbook to the class, not the class to the textbook.
9. Become thoroughly acquainted with the text before giving assignments in it.
10. Teach students how to use the table of contents, the index, headings, topic sentences, marginal notations, and charts.
11. Make allowances for individual differences among the students. Make available three or four supplementary texts that deal with the same content at different vocabulary levels.
12. Identify students with reading difficulties, and provide remedial help for them.
13. Conduct textbook exercises that will enable students to learn how the text can help them understand course content.
14. Explain difficult passages, charts, and illustrations.

---

[8]Specific suggestions for the proper use of the textbook can be found in Howard T. Batchelder, Maurice McGlasson, and Raleigh Schorling, *Student Teaching in Secondary Schools,* 4th ed. (New York: McGraw-Hill Book Company, 1964), pp. 175–177; Herbert J. Klausmeier, *Teaching in the Secondary School* (New York: Harper & Brothers, 1958), pp. 321–324; and Mills and Douglass, *op. cit.*, p. 258.

[9]Batchelder, McGlasson, and Schorling, *op. cit.*, p. 177, list several specific points to consider in selecting a textbook.

Mills and Douglass, *op. cit.*, pp. 259–263, also provide a helpful discussion on textbook selection and evaluation.

15. Encourage intelligent student reaction to textbook discussion.

16. Arrange for appropriate checks to determine that textbook reading has been done consistently and well.

17. Be imaginative, varied, and experimental in the use of the textbook.

18. If some part of a chapter of the text has been unusually well prepared, use this particular portion to advantage.

Cautions

Although many cautions can be inferred from the preceding recommendations, a few pointed admonitions may be helpful.

1. Don't view the text as an end in itself.
2. Don't let the textbook become the course.
3. Don't use the text in a mechanical fashion.
4. Don't rely as strongly on the text once you have gained experience and security in teaching.
5. Don't forego the planning necessary for efficient teaching because textbook teaching appears easier.

USE OF THE ASSIGNMENT

One of the most important procedures requiring strong student participation is the assignment. Like the use of the textbook, the effective use of the assignment poses unique problems for both the teacher and students.

The assignment may be long or short; difficult or easy; general or differentiated; and related to a single lesson, to a unit, or to a full school year.[10] Because of this extreme variety, writers have emerged with a score of different classifications to serve their individual purposes. Assignments are often described in terms of contrast: daily or unit assignments; oral or written assignments; textbook or nontextbook assignments; and individual or group assignments.

More important than the classification of the assignment is the careful understanding of its purpose—to encourage and assist students to reach specified goals. The assignment is one of many instructional devices designed with goal attainment in mind, and it is employed quite frequently—though often inappropriately.

---

[10]Harry N. Rivlin, *Teaching Adolescents in Secondary Schools*, 2d. ed. (New York: Appleton-Century-Crofts, 1961), pp. 169–175, provides a general discussion of the assignment.

William H. Burton, *The Guidance of Learning Activities*, 3d. ed. (New York: Appleton-Century-Crofts, 1962), Chapter 12, discusses the assignment against the background of "The Improvement of Assign-Study-Recite Procedures." His comments are challenging and sound.

Characteristics of Assignments

The assignment may be viewed by students as the teacher's device for imposing school-sanctioned punishment upon learners. In the hands of a wise professional, however, it can be the means of providing students with exciting new opportunities for self-directed learning.[11] Considered independent of the teacher, the assignment is neither good nor bad; the use to which it is put makes it so.

A vague, uninteresting, unmotivated assignment can have a strong negative influence on many students. For some, assignments related to English grammar fall into this category. Yet, grammar assignments can be and are made into exciting challenges when the classroom teacher relates them to individual student needs, provides the necessary background, and arouses student interest.

Heterogeneously grouped classes provide the setting in which students can be frustrated and defeated unless the teacher makes the assignment appropriate, realistic, and stimulating. Students in an Algebra I class may find undifferentiated assignments too difficult for the less gifted student, too easy for the bright student, and appropriate only for those who fall in the middle range.

Principles Related to the Effective Use of Assignments

Because teachers frequently err in their use of the assignment, they need the assistance of principles that will give direction to their planning.[12] The following principles apply to all types of assignments.

1. Assignments are unjustified unless they are related to specific goals.[13]
2. Assignments may serve a range of purposes.
3. The extent to which a student will work hard on an assignment will depend upon the degree of his motivation.
4. The learner will work conscientiously to accomplish an assignment when he realizes that it will serve *his* purposes as *he* sees them.[14]
5. Students study conscientiously to complete assignments that

---

[11]Vincent McGuire, Robert B. Myers, and Charles L. Durrance, *Your Student Teaching in the Secondary School* (Boston: Allyn and Bacon, 1959), pp. 147–149, present seven recommendations that should characterize the good assignment.

Characteristics of a good assignment are also discussed by Rivlin, *op. cit.*, pp. 172–173.

[12]McKean, *op. cit.*, pp. 142–144, presents relevant principles to consider in making assignments.

[13]The necessity for relating assignments to goals is stressed by Mills and Douglass, *op. cit.*, p. 100.

[14]William L. Carter, Carl W. Hansen, and Margaret G. McKim, *Learning to Teach in the Secondary School* (New York: Macmillan, 1962), pp. 219–220, discuss the desirability of having students pursue individual interests.

they have helped plan. Assignments that evolve naturally from unit activities have a good chance of being accepted by students.

6. A student cannot successfully pursue an assignment unless he understands the concepts on which it is based.[15]

7. An assignment can be completed only when students have the readiness essential for its completion. Students must possess adequate reading skills, have a grasp of essential background concepts, and be motivated.

8. Conscientious work on assignments requires a measure of student self-discipline.

9. The assignment is only one of the essential procedures in teaching and should not be used exclusively.

10. Assignments must be differentiated in order to meet the individual needs of students.[16]

11. The assignment is a device to help students learn.

12. The use of special devices (study questions and study guides) gives helpful direction to certain types of assignments.

13. Stereotyped assignments tend to reduce interest in school work.

14. Carefully worded assignments are fundamental to effective planning and teaching.

Correct and Incorrect Use

Perhaps the most ineffective and commonplace assignment is undifferentiated and must be completed by the following day. For such an assignment all students are required to do the same amount of work.[17]

MRS. DAWSON GIVES A HASTY ASSIGNMENT

During the last two minutes of the ninth-grade literature class, Mrs. Dawson became somewhat alarmed. She had not finished her discussion of *Silas Marner* as she had hoped, and the assignment was yet to be given.

Hastily she thumbed through the pages of the text. "You will all read pages 39 through 49 for tomorrow," she said. "I'm sure it will be interesting." Just then the bell rang, and the students filed out of the room.

Mrs. Dawson violated several principles related to giving assignments properly:

---

[15]See Hansen, *op. cit.*, pp. 139–140, for a discussion on making the assignment meaningful.

[16]M. L. Goetting, *Teaching in the Secondary School* (New York: Prentice-Hall, 1942), pp. 78–79, presents a brief treatment of differentiated assignments.

[17]Burton, *op. cit.*, pp. 294–295, identifies several specific difficulties and problems confronting the teacher in making assignments.

Examples of good and poor assignments are described by Grambs, Iverson, and Patterson, *op. cit.*, pp. 140–145. Characteristics of a good assignment are also identified.

1. She made the assignment under pressure without considering its appropriateness.
2. She failed to interest the class in the assignment.
3. She failed to differentiate the assignment by providing for varying abilities among students.
4. She did not permit questions about the assignment.
5. She did not write the assignment on the board.

On the floor above Mrs. Dawson, Sam Crowther, another ninth-grade English teacher, managed to avoid the pitfalls his colleague encountered in giving the assignment.

MR. CROWTHER PLANS CAREFUL ASSIGNMENTS

The first fifteen or twenty minutes of the fifty-minute class were devoted to a lively discussion of *Silas Marner*. Mr. Crowther asked the students to analyze the character of Silas Marner on the basis of their reading. If some students seemed hesitant, the teacher gave hints; and if certain class members seemed to know all the answers, he posed penetrating questions.

After the discussion the teacher read aloud, with insight and meaning, the first three pages of the new chapter. Even the two potential troublemakers in the back row sat in rapt attention. As a result of the class discussion, they could now understand the story better.

Mr. Crowther stopped at the end of the paragraph. "I would like you to read the rest of Chapter 6 during the next twenty minutes. Some of you may find time to read into the next chapter. It's even more interesting than the last one. If you need help, please raise your hand."

The teacher stepped to the board and wrote "Chapter 6 for tomorrow." Then he moved around the room, particularly helping those students who were having difficulty with the vocabulary. Susan finished the chapter in ten minutes, as Mr. Crowther expected, and he asked her to read a discussion on the character of Silas Marner in a college-level text. Before the end of the study period five other fast readers had received supplementary assignments related to their reading. Douglas, a youngster with limited reading ability, was given a simplified version of the story that left the narration intact.

Assignments in Specific Subjects

Assignments can and should be used to aid instruction in every well-organized class. The difficulty, length, type, and circumstances of each assignment should vary, depending on its effectiveness in reaching a desired educational goal.[18]

Large written assignments related to and extending through an entire unit are common in history and English composition classes. Concept-centered courses, such as geography, English literature, history, biology, and the physical sciences, frequently call for assignments involving library work. In these cases gifted students are often

[18]The common assignment and the achievement-level assignment are discussed by Klausmeier, *op. cit.*, pp. 274–276.

sent to the library to engage in self-directed research. Some of the skill subjects are the only areas in which the short reading assignment is not frequently employed.

All subjects in the social sciences have assigned work involving committee deliberations; community contacts are common in civics and social problems classes. In shop and homemaking classes, specific personal projects are typical, but in a journalism class all students may work on a joint project.

To infer that one type of assignment should be associated with a specific subject imposes an unwarranted restriction on teacher ingenuity. Variations in assignments are desirable if they help achieve educational goals and simultaneously maintain student interest.

Specific Suggestions

The conscientious teacher can be sure that he is using the assignment correctly if he is aware of the principles listed on pages 222–223 and observes the related recommendations and cautions enumerated below.

Recommendations

1. Be sure that unit as well as daily assignments bear a close relationship to the unit.
2. Be sure the assignment is understood by all. Permit students to participate in planning certain assignments, and make sure students understand *why* they are undertaking a given assignment. Encourage them to ask questions.
3. When necessary, give students specific help in completing the assignment.
4. Use various kinds of assignments.
5. Gear the assignment to the needs of individual students. Don't make the assignment excessively difficult or so easy that it lacks challenge. By using different aids and teaching materials, make assignments imaginative, varied, and stimulating.
6. Make the assignment meaningful in terms of its perceived value to the student.
7. Be sure that daily assignments fit in logically and consistently with other learning activities.
8. When homework is assigned, allow students time to start it during the supervised study period.
9. Select the best time during the class period for giving the assignments.
10. Write assignments on the chalkboard if this serves a useful purpose.
11. When students lack background information essential to the completion of an assignment, plan experiences that will provide the necessary background.

12. Make certain assignments an opportunity for students to pursue special interests.

13. Use study guides to assist students in fulfilling assignments.

14. Make assignments to promote the continuity of learning. Remember that they are an essential part of a long-range (unit) learning experience.

15. Plan assignments that will make it possible to determine the achievement level of individual students with relative ease.

16. Help students develop adequate study habits through the use of the assignment.

17. Give the assignment when interest has reached a high peak.

Cautions

1. Don't make individual assignments without considering differences among class members.

2. Don't always make the assignment in terms of pages to be read.

3. Don't make the assignment sound as if it were being done for the teacher.

4. Don't threaten students with assignments.[19]

5. Don't use the assignment as a type of punishment.

6. Don't give the assignment after the bell has rung.

7. Don't give day-to-day assignments that tend to fragmentize subject matter.

8. Don't make assignments that interfere with major out-of-school activities.

USE OF HOMEWORK

School assignments to be completed after regular school hours are usually designated as *homework* regardless of where study takes place. It is also common practice to label as homework any class-related preparation that is done outside of class but during school hours. Although homework is a type of assignment, it deserves special consideration because it poses particular problems—for the teacher as well as for the students—that make its effectiveness as a teaching procedure highly variable.

Controversy and Criticism

Because home study is typically undertaken without the benefit of teacher supervision, it is often subject to criticism.[20] The value of

[19]The "threatening assignment" and the "punitive assignment" are criticized by Hansen, *op. cit.*, pp. 138–139.

[20]The value of homework has been questioned by some writers for more than a score of years. See Goetting, *op. cit.*, pp. 502–503.

homework in the total educational program of the adolescent is being seriously questioned on the basis of research evidence. The statement of one authority in the field is worthy of examination:

> The few statistical studies show that home study is not a significant factor in affecting the achievement of pupils. Results are about the same with or without home study.
>
> There is, however, one aspect of this topic which must not be overlooked. Home study of the traditional formal sort may be dispensed with as far as the evidence now shows; however, as we move toward modern teaching which identifies study with learning and which utilizes not one or two but a large number of varied study activities, a different situation emerges.[21]

The increased space-age emphasis on academic rigor in all subjects has encouraged many teachers, administrators, and parents to use any device for increasing academic productivity. As a result, homework has received added impetus in some school districts. In practice the use of home study is being expanded and intensified in certain areas and restricted in others. Unfortunately, controversy among teachers and administrators in the same schools and districts is often in evidence, causing undue student confusion.

Principles Related to the Effective Use of Homework

The following principles suggest a middle-of-the-road approach, designed to assist the teacher in using homework as one device among many for promoting learning.[22]

1. As an educational device, home study is of value only to the extent that it improves learning.
2. Research studies on homework provide a much more reliable basis for homework policies than the anxious admonitions of parents, lay persons, and misinformed educators. The value of homework, however, has not been conclusively proved or disproved through research evidence.
3. A home study program is more likely to be successful if it is related to the total school program. Homework should be viewed as a supplement to the work of the school day.
4. Students can study well only when the environment is conducive to study.
5. The results derived from homework are often directly related to the effectiveness of the teacher's planning for homework assignments.
6. The time required by individual students to complete specific

[21]Burton, *op. cit.*, p. 313.

[22]Mills and Douglass, *op. cit.*, pp. 141–143, provide a helpful general discussion as well as specific suggestions about homework.

assignments will influence the success of the homework program. Well-informed teachers are realistic in what they expect of students.

7. An increase in the amount of work required of students may not improve the quality of their education.

8. Students often react negatively toward home study on the basis of their previous experience.

9. Students become confused if there is controversy among their teachers about the value of homework.

Correct and Incorrect Use

A number of questionable practices can be identified in the homework assignment of the eleventh-grade United States history teacher described below.

MISS COUSINS ASSIGNS WEEKEND HOMEWORK

Miss Cousins was firm in her resolve that there would be homework over the weekend in spite of the basketball game. In addition, she felt that it was only appropriate that the assignment be somewhat heavier than usual because students would have two days free. As a matter of fact, she thought, the class had been particularly unruly that Friday afternoon and needed to be punished.

Several unsound procedures can be observed here:

1. Students were encouraged to develop negative feelings toward homework because it interfered with something they really wanted to do.
2. The assignment was excessive and partially based on retribution.
3. The teacher gave little thought to student motivation.

Note the contrast between Miss Cousins' homework assignment and that of Mr. McGruder.[23]

MR. MCGRUDER PROVIDES INTERESTING HOMEWORK

Fred McGruder, eighth-grade teacher of Iowa History, believed that homework should be limited in quantity as well as in type. By common consent, no teacher in his school made a take-home assignment over the weekend. On Monday, students were assigned the individual responsibility for a brief two-minute oral report to be given the next Monday. As a basis for the reports, the students were to contact any person over seventy years of age who had spent his childhood in Iowa in order to find out what life was like

[23]H. Orville Nordberg, James M. Bradfield, and William C. Odell, *Secondary School Teaching* (New York: Macmillan, 1962), p. 146, provide short examples of good and poor homework assignments.

during their childhood. The reports were to focus attention on transportation, housing, communication, and industry. The teacher motivated the assignment by pointing out the range of interesting facts that might be uncovered.

In this situation the assignment was nonbookish, it was carefully related to the course content, it was reasonable, it was interesting, and it could be carried out without teacher supervision.

Specific Suggestions

Many of the desirable and undesirable practices in the use of the homework assignment are reflected in the recommendations and cautions that follow.

Recommendations

1. Closely relate homework assignments to in-school study.
2. Work with other teachers in the school to establish a homework policy that is educationally sound and understood by all.[24]
3. Differentiate between what can best be accomplished under supervised study and what can best be accomplished through home study.
4. Be careful about assigning homework just because you feel that it is expected.
5. Make certain types of homework optional for students.
6. Use parent conferences to promote better home study conditions.
7. Consider the possibility of group projects during after-school hours.
8. Emphasize homework that does not involve the study of the text.[25]
9. Help students view home study as an added opportunity to learn.
10. Motivate students by saving some of the more interesting assignments for home study.
11. Assign activities that can be effectively carried out without teacher supervision.
12. Be sure that homework assignments are clearly understood.
13. Be sure that students understand the purpose of homework and relate it to their personal needs.

---

[24]Hansen, *op. cit.,* 91–92, stresses the necessity for interrelationship among the various courses of the curriculum.
See also Kimball Wiles, *Teaching for Better Schools,* 2d. ed. (Englewood Cliffs, N.J.: Prentice-Hall, 1959), pp. 250–251.

[25]The desirability of substituting field study for textbook homework is discussed briefly by Grambs, Iverson, and Patterson, *op. cit.,* p. 203.

Cautions

1. Don't assign homework every evening.
2. Don't assume that home circumstances are equally conducive to study for all students.
3. Don't assign homework as punishment.
4. Don't neglect the possibility of group work as desirable out-of-class study.
5. Don't expect the impossible of students.
6. Don't make homework a routine chore.[26]
7. Don't assign busy work for home study.
8. Don't assume that homework will be self-motivating.

STUDENT-CENTERED PROCEDURES IN REVIEW

This chapter has focused attention on three instructional procedures that require a large measure of student participation—the use of the textbook, the assignment, and homework. Each has its own specific contribution to the teacher's storehouse of effective teaching methods, but each may prove to be of limited value if used poorly.

Although subject to frequent abuse, the textbook is one of the basic instructional tools, for in no other place can the student find the same concentration of relevant materials. Furthermore, the well-organized textbook provides the student with a means of effective, self-directed study during the school day and after school hours.

The assignment serves a range of purposes, and if it helps the student achieve his *personal* purposes, he will work hard to complete it. In order to serve most effectively, assignments should be wisely differentiated to meet the needs of individual students and thus provide essential motivation.

Homework has value to the extent that it improves learning, but its efficiency as an instructional device is subject to much criticism. Research evidence does not conclusively support the value of homework, although academic emphasis has increased its use. There is general agreement, however, that a home study program must be closely related to the total school program if it is to be successful.

PROBLEMS FOR STUDY AND DISCUSSION

1. List ten student-centered teaching methods commonly used in your teaching major.
2. List five reasons for the frequent misuse of the textbook.

---

[26]Rivlin, *op. cit.*, p. 169, makes a plea to avoid the unimaginative homework assignment.

3. Write a short paragraph defending the following statement: The well-chosen textbook is the most helpful aid available to the knowledgeable teacher.

4. Describe how a textbook might best be used in your minor field.

5. Describe the role of the textbook in unit planning.

6. If you were responsible for selecting the textbook to be used by all teachers of your subject-matter major in a large school district, what qualities would you look for? List them.

7. How is it possible to meet the needs of students with high reading abilities and the needs of students with low reading abilities through the use of textbooks? Explain.

8. Is there ever justification for the use of the textbook to the exclusion of other teaching materials? Explain.

9. Identify four or more procedures for making a general assignment interesting to students.

10. Give an example of how you propose to differentiate a major unit assignment in your subject-matter specialty in order to meet the needs of heterogeneously grouped students.

11. Discuss the following statement: The assignment is a means, not an end.

12. Describe five errors commonly made in giving assignments.

13. Suggest three or more procedures for motivating assignments in your minor field.

14. How can you make sure that the assignment is understood by all students?

15. Define *homework* in its broad sense.

16. Why is the value of homework being seriously questioned at the present time? Discuss.

17. How do you propose to use homework in your teaching major? Defend your position.

18. How much time can average students be expected to spend on homework in your teaching major? Explain.

19. Identify five practices that you are going to avoid in the use of homework during the school year.

20. Suggest a procedure that will enable teachers in a given school to make homework assignments without interfering with those given by other teachers.

RECOMMENDED READINGS

The Textbook

Batchelder, Howard T., Maurice McGlasson, and Raleigh Schorling, *Student Teaching in Secondary Schools*, 4th ed. New York: McGraw-Hill Book Company, 1964, pp. 175–177.

Cross, A. J. Foy, and Irene F. Cypher, *Audio-Visual Education.* New York: Thomas Y. Crowell Company, 1961, Chapter 11.

Grambs, Jean D., William J. Iverson, and Franklin K. Patterson, *Modern Methods in Secondary Education*, rev. ed. New York: The Dryden Press, 1958, Chapter 7.

Hansen, Kenneth H., *High School Teaching.* Englewood Cliffs, N.J.: Prentice-Hall, Inc., 1957, Chapter 8.

Klausmeier, Herbert J., *Teaching in the Secondary School.* New York: Harper & Brothers, 1958, pp. 321–324.

McKean, Robert C., *Principles and Methods in Secondary Education.* Columbus, Ohio: Charles E. Merrill Books, Inc., 1962, Chapter 6.

Mills, Hubert H., and Harl R. Douglass, *Teaching in High School,* 2d. ed. New York: Ronald Press, 1957, Chapter 15.

Nordberg, H. Orville, James M. Bradfield, and William C. Odell, *Secondary School Teaching.* New York: The Macmillan Company, 1962, pp. 51–52.

Risk, Thomas M., *Principles and Practices of Teaching in Secondary Schools,* 2d. ed. New York: American Book Company, 1947, pp. 532–535.

Wiggins, Samuel P., *Successful High School Teaching.* Boston: Houghton Mifflin Company, 1958, pp. 157–160, 173–179, and 192–198.

The Assignment

Burton, William H., *The Guidance of Learning Activities,* 3d. ed. New York: Appleton-Century-Crofts, Inc., 1962, Chapter 12.

Carter, William L., Carl W. Hansen, and Margaret G. McKim, *Learning to Teach in the Secondary School.* New York: The Macmillan Company, 1962, pp. 203 and 219.

Goetting, M. L., *Teaching in the Secondary School.* New York: Prentice-Hall, Inc., 1942, pp. 78–79, 228–229, and 316.

Grambs, Jean D., William J. Iverson, and Franklin K. Patterson, *Modern Methods in Secondary Education,* rev. ed. New York: The Dryden Press, 1958, pp. 140–145.

Hansen, Kenneth H., *High School Teaching.* Englewood Cliffs, N.J.: Prentice-Hall, Inc., 1957, pp. 136–141.

Klausmeier, Herbert J., *Teaching in the Secondary School.* New York: Harper & Brothers, 1958, pp. 274–279.

McGuire, Vincent, Robert B. Myers, and Charles L. Durrance, *Your Student Teaching in the Secondary School.* Boston: Allyn and Bacon, Inc., 1959, pp. 147–149.

McKean, Robert C., *Principles and Methods in Secondary Education.* Columbus, Ohio: Charles E. Merrill Books, Inc., 1962, pp. 142–144.

Mills, Hubert H., and Harl R. Douglass, *Teaching in High School,* 2d. ed. New York: Ronald Press, 1957, pp. 100–101.

Rivlin, Harry N., *Teaching Adolescents in Secondary Schools,* 2d. ed. New York: Appleton-Century-Crofts, Inc., 1961, pp. 169–175.

Wiggins, Samuel P., *Successful High School Teaching.* Boston: Houghton Mifflin Company, 1958, pp. 142–143.

Wiles, Kimball, *Teaching for Better Schools,* 2d. ed. Englewood Cliffs, N.J.: Prentice-Hall, Inc. 1959, p. 168.

Homework

Burton, William H., *The Guidance of Learning Activities,* 3d. ed. New York: Appleton-Century-Crofts, Inc., 1962, p. 313.

Goetting, M. L., *Teaching in the Secondary School.* New York: Prentice-Hall, Inc., 1942, pp. 502–503.

Grambs, Jean D., William J. Iverson, and Franklin K. Patterson, *Modern*

Methods in Secondary Education, rev. ed. New York: The Dryden Press, 1958, p. 203.

Hansen, Kenneth H., *High School Teaching.* Englewood Cliffs, N.J.: Prentice-Hall, Inc., 1957, pp. 91–92.

Mills, Hubert H., and Harl R. Douglass, *Teaching in High School*, 2d. ed. New York: Ronald Press, 1957, pp. 141–143.

Nordberg, H. Orville, James M. Bradfield, and William C. Odell, *Secondary School Teaching.* New York: The Macmillan Company, 1962, pp. 145–146.

Rivlin, Harry N., *Teaching Adolescents in Secondary Schools*, 2d ed. New York: Appleton-Century-Crofts, Inc., 1961, p. 169.

Wiles, Kimball, *Teaching for Better Schools*, 2d. ed. Englewood Cliffs, N.J.: Prentice-Hall, Inc., 1959, pp. 250–251.

11

Additional Student-Centered Procedures

Four additional teaching methods that demand student participation are group procedures, individualized instruction, supervised study, and the field trip.[1] Each one, by its very nature, is subject to wide variation in classroom use. This chapter focuses on several of these variations and presents the principles and suggestions related to each method.

GROUP PROCEDURES

A large proportion of instructional procedures employed in secondary schools involves some form of social interaction, for any learning activity that is not tutorial in nature or that is not concerned with individualized study involves group effort. Students are often challenged by the variety made possible through the use of groups of differing size. They are also stimulated and motivated by the ideas originating with their peers.

Types of Group Procedures

Different types of group procedures serve specific instructional purposes. The major types are identified here.[2]

[1]A full chapter discussion of the pupil-centered classroom is provided by Hubert H. Mills and Harl R. Douglass, *Teaching in High School*, 2d. ed. (New York: Ronald Press, 1957), Chapter 9.

[2]*Ibid.*, pp. 191–201, discuss several types of group teaching procedures.

The entire class functions as a single unit in a *whole-class discussion.*[3] The teacher informally directs the discussion to achieve understanding of a given topic, and the students make comments and respond to questions posed by their fellow students as well as by the teacher. This large-group discussion is occasionally used as an introductory activity for later and more intensive small-group work within the class.

In a *forum discussion* a small number of students (usually from three to five) present prepared statements on a given topic to a large group or the entire class. After the presentation the speakers may ask questions of each other, and the forum moderator then solicits questions from the audience directed to a given speaker. Classes may also be divided into *panels,* usually four to eight students, that are responsible for obtaining, discussing, and finally presenting findings on a specific topic to the total class. Many variations of the panel have been used effectively.

Informal role playing (unrehearsed dramatization) is employed in social science and literature classes to encourage students to develop greater insight into the characters they are studying. Since they have no script, students must rely on information derived from their reading and from class discussion. *Small study groups*[4] of three or four students are often employed by the classroom teacher for different purposes. Although such groupings are typically based on common interest, they may be developed along various lines.

Debate provides one means of small-group as well as large-group activity in which opposing points of view can be expressed. Usually members of two teams alternate in making five- to eight-minute presentations. After the members are finished, rebuttals are allowed. Other forms of debate call for teacher-directed class discussion following the formal presentation or questions directed to team members.

Values of Group Activities

Group activities naturally tend to encourage socialization. It is the responsibility of the teacher to see that such activities are so structured that they meet the purposes of instruction rather than encourage superficial pleasantries. The exchange of ideas among members of a peer group is often stimulating and, therefore, motivational.

---

[3]See Herbert J. Klausmeier, *Teaching in the Secondary School* (New York: Harper & Brothers, 1958), pp. 258–260, for a useful presentation of whole-class discussion. Vincent McGuire, Robert B. Myers, and Charles L. Durrance, *Your Student Teaching in the Secondary School* (Boston: Allyn and Bacon, 1959), pp. 149–154, examine the role of discussion in teacher-pupil planning. Examples are provided.

[4]Klausmeier, *op. cit.*, pp. 265–273, presents the advantages of different types of small-group activity.

When directed toward an educational goal, this exchange can be a powerful instructional force.[5]

Both small and large groups, if properly organized and conducted, will encourage mental activity on the part of the majority of students. For the student of average intelligence who has difficulty in reading, group discussion may prove to be an academic blessing. The shy individual may find the courage to participate in the small group,[6] while the gifted extrovert may be challenged by the large group.

Social development is encouraged when students work together to accomplish a common task. Teamwork and cooperation are very much in evidence in committee work, especially if the teacher helps students identify the problems to be solved and determine what role each person is to play. In the small group students are called upon to assume responsibilities that, because of the size of the group, cannot be transferred to someone else.

Group participation enhances the individual's power of self-expression and helps him take a more active role in subsequent group work. He also learns the necessity for accepting opposing points of view and for examining all facets of an issue before making a decision. Perhaps his greatest gain is the acquisition of knowledge that he might not have enjoyed without group effort.

Principles Related to Group Procedures

The following principles will give direction to the use of group procedures.[7]

1. A worth-while group activity must have an educational purpose. For this reason, the teacher should select group procedures that will best help the students reach specified goals.

2. Effective group participation is based upon common needs and interests and is focused on the solution of a recognized common problem. Students are eager to discuss topics that they feel are of vital importance to themselves.

3. Basic concepts necessary for effective group work must be developed before the work begins.

4. In group activities calling for student direction, immature stu-

---

[5]C. Burleigh Wellington and Jean Wellington, *Teaching for Critical Thinking: with Emphasis on Secondary Education* (New York: McGraw-Hill Book Company, 1960), pp. 202–218, examine the role of the small group in promoting critical thinking.

[6]Kimball Wiles, *Teaching for Better Schools*, 2d. ed. (Englewood Cliffs, N.J.: Prentice-Hall, 1959), p. 168, tells of the advantages of group activity for the shy youngster.

[7]Jean D. Grambs, William J. Iverson, and Franklin K. Patterson, *Modern Methods in Secondary Education*, rev. ed. (New York: The Dryden Press, 1958), pp. 280–297, devote a full chapter to "Group Techniques in the Classroom."

Principles affecting group procedures are listed and discussed by William H. Burton, *The Guidance of Learning Activities*, 3d. ed. (New York: Appleton-Century-Crofts, 1962), pp. 194–196.

dents are strongly influenced by their immediate interests and by peer-group demands.

5. It is the teacher's responsibility to determine that group work is best suited for achieving the desired objective and to help the students plan group activities effectively.

6. Careful advance identification of appropriate topics gives positive direction to group discussions.

7. Discussion in the absence of relevant information is meaningless.

8. The range of the teacher's experience determines, in part, how meaningfully he can direct discussion.

9. During a well-conducted discussion,[8] all students are mentally alert, even those who do not participate vocally.

10. Effective group work calls for assigning responsibilities to individuals.

11. Students learn to work cooperatively in a group through supervised practice.

12. Cooperative group work calls for the use of democratic procedures in using resources and resolving conflicts.

13. A friendly atmosphere encourages student participation in discussion.

14. At the end of a discussion, the teacher should identify and stress specific conclusions.

Correct and Incorrect Use

Teachers encounter many difficulties in conducting class discussions.[9] Note that the majority of the difficulties in the following narrative could have been avoided through careful consideration of the preceding principles.

MISS LEFTWICH CONDUCTS AN UNPLANNED DISCUSSION

Miss Leftwich was tired on Monday morning and, like her students she had failed to do her homework. The social problems class, however, was one in which class discussion could always serve as a stop-gap method, she reasoned.

"James," she asked, "what was the most significant news item to appear in the newspaper over the weekend?"

"I don't know."

"Mary Lynne, can you tell us?"

"There was a train wreck in New York State."

A note of interest had been touched, and one after another students com-

---

[8]Wellington and Wellington, *op. cit.*, pp. 121 – 139, present a full chapter on "The Discussion Technique."

[9]Samuel P. Wiggens, *Successful High School Teaching* (Boston: Houghton Mifflin Company, 1958), pp. 176 – 178, describes an instructional situation in which socialized recitation (group discussion) is employed.

mented on this particular train wreck, train wrecks they had read about, train wrecks their families had known about, and finally, automobile accidents. Miss Leftwich made no effort to stem the tide, and the discussion ran its course without direction.

If a supervisor had observed her on that particular day, he would have noted that:

1. Miss Leftwich had not noticed the items of real significance in the paper.
2. She had not planned for the discussion.
3. The discussion, once started, received little direction.
4. Students were permitted to talk at length about matters that had little to do with course content.

William Donovan, a social problems teacher in an adjacent town, also made a practice of having a class discussion on Monday covering the most important current event that had taken place over the weekend. His preparation, however, was in marked contrast to that of Miss Leftwich.

MR. DONOVAN LEADS A WORTH-WHILE DISCUSSION

As soon as the bell rang, Mr. Donovan announced that the class would spend the first ten minutes talking about an event of major political significance that had occurred in South America over the weekend.

"What was it?" he inquired. Mr. Donovan paused for a moment to give all students time to react; then he called on Sally Brandt.

"An uprising took place in La Paz, Bolivia," she responded.

"And why is this of concern to the United States?" he probed further. Before Sally could answer four other hands shot up. He gestured to Sally to remain quiet while other students thought about the problem.

Gradually, nearly all of the students gave evidence of mental activity. Only then did he permit student response. First, Jean Bennett gave her opinion, followed by Willis Morgan. Several others spoke up without the formality of the raised hand; the teacher did not object as long as the students observed proper etiquette by not speaking while others were speaking.

During the next five minutes a number of students mentioned three major ideas, but in slightly different ways. Mr. Donovan asked Chris Randle if he could identify these basic points and write them on the board in his own words. He could and did. Making minor modifications, the teacher used these points to summarize the discussion.

Group Procedures in Specific Subjects

Group procedures are used in every class in the secondary curriculum. Modified discussions are frequently used, although they are most typical in those subjects in which concept development is the prime concern. All courses in the social sciences, English, biology, and the physical sciences use the whole-class discussion.

Although employed to only a limited extent in some areas, forum discussion and panels often provide useful variety in both English and the social sciences. Informal role playing is relegated almost entirely to these two areas, while the use of the debate is largely confined to the social sciences.

Tradition has imposed unjustified restrictions on the use of large- and small-group procedures. There is no defensible reason, for example, why the panel discussion could not be used with considerable effectiveness in the mathematics class or why the debate would not serve a useful purpose in homemaking or physical education. Experiment-minded teachers will find new ways of avoiding the stereotype without violating the principles of educational psychology.

Specific Suggestions

The recommendations and cautions below, drawn from the principles stated earlier in this chapter, should provide a basis for effective use of group procedures.

Recommendations

1. Be sure that class discussions are goal-oriented and that they move continuously toward the desired objective.[10]

2. Use the discussion method as a means of identifying, analyzing, and solving problems.[11]

3. Be sure the topic for discussion can be developed through an exchange of ideas.

4. Make sure that students are well enough versed on the discussion topic to participate effectively. If students do not have the information necessary, help them find it.

5. Set up safeguards to prevent the discussion from wandering, but learn to guide without dominating.

6. Conduct the discussion in such a manner that all class members are encouraged to participate; recognize the effect that differences in ability will have upon the students' group participation. Help students develop skill and ease in class discussions.

7. Stimulate thinking by asking thought questions; at the same time, encourage each student to do his own thinking.

8. Before permitting student-directed group activities, make

---

[10]Howard T. Batchelder, Maurice McGlasson, and Raleigh Schorling, *Student Teaching in Secondary Schools*, 4th ed. (New York: McGraw-Hill Book Company, 1964), pp. 154–158, list and discuss specific suggestions related to group discussion.

[11]Harry N. Rivlin, *Teaching Adolescents in Secondary Schools*, 2d. ed. (New York: Appleton-Century-Crofts, 1961), pp. 178–201, provides an extensive treatment of "Discussion as a Way of Learning." A detailed example of a lesson based upon discussion is presented on pp. 199–201.

sure the students understand the purpose of the activity and exactly how it is to be accomplished.[12]

9. See that the class discussion is more than a response to the teacher's questions.

10. Encourage students to evaluate the progress of their group work.

11. Use a different and interesting procedure for stressing conclusions reached in the discussion.

12. Be sure that the physical arrangement of the room is conducive to the type of discussion held.

13. Form small discussion groups when this method will serve a useful purpose.

14. Consider using informal role playing as a classroom procedure.

15. Consider the advisability of concluding a unit with a panel discussion.

Cautions

1. Don't allow group discussions that do not serve the purposes of unit objectives.[13]

2. Don't call for the response of star pupils to the exclusion of the less gifted.

3. Don't be satisfied with the use of one stereotyped discussion or group procedure.

4. Don't allow controversy and resulting emotionalism to bring productive discussion to a standstill.

5. Don't allow ineffective student discussion to continue for a prolonged period.

6. As a teacher, don't dominate the class discussion if its primary purpose is to encourage students to arrive at their own conclusions.

7. Don't lose control of the situation while directing class discussions.

INDIVIDUALIZED INSTRUCTIONAL PROCEDURES

Instructional activities may be classed in terms of the participants as whole-group activities, small-group activities, and individual activities. The last category consists of those procedures that are undertaken without the assistance of other members of the class.

---

[12]William L. Carter, Carl W. Hansen, and Margaret G. McKim, *Learning to Teach in the Secondary School* (New York: Macmillan, 1962), pp. 205–206, stress the necessity for care in allotting certain portions of a problem to small groups for solution.

[13]Grambs, Iverson, and Patterson, *op. cit.*, pp. 234–238, point out the need for careful selection of discussion questions and also criteria for good discussion questions.

Although the teacher may provide help in carrying them out, individual activities are essentially nonsocial in nature.[14] Because of the recent developments in programed learning, educators have become more interested in and concerned about individualized teaching procedures.

Types of Individualized Procedures

Composition—including the writing of themes as well as creative writing—is, obviously, a learning task that lends itself to individual work. *Reading*, the most important and most frequently used learning activity at the secondary and college levels, is essentially done by the individual. Although *laboratory work*[15] and *experimentation* frequently take the form of teacher demonstration or joint student endeavor, they are often carried out by a single learner.

General assignments are given to the entire class with the usual understanding that they are to be completed by individual students. *Individual projects*[16] take the form of a major task to be performed or something to be constructed: making a cedar chest, caring for a farm animal, assembling and preparing an English journal, etc. They call for the use of definite skills in solving specific problems.

Individual contracts, although infrequently used at the present time, are written descriptions of specified unit-related work to be completed by individual students within a certain time. Students are frequently given the option of taking one of three or four contracts, all of which vary in difficulty. In *supervised study*[17] the teacher gives assistance only on request. Although similar to supervised study, *library study*[18] usually calls for a greater measure of self-direction on the part of the student.

Characteristics of Individual Procedures

Man is essentially social. He is stimulated to mental activity through contacts with his fellow human beings, but the actual learning process is entirely individual. No one can learn for him, for

---

[14]Mills and Douglass, *op. cit.*, pp. 190–193, present a brief discussion of the historical Dalton and Winnetka Plans for individualized instruction.

[15]Klausmeier, *op. cit.*, pp. 278–280, discusses laboratory work as a teaching procedure.

[16]Wellington and Wellington, *op. cit.*, pp. 178–179, discuss the values and limitations of individual as well as group projects.

H. Orville Nordberg, James M. Bradfield, and William C. Odell, *Secondary School Teaching* (New York: Macmillan, 1962), pp. 139–140, point out how creativity may be exhibited through the development of individual student projects.

[17]Klausmeier, *op. cit.*, pp. 274–277, describes the use of supervised study and individual projects.

[18]The necessity for training students to use the library effectively is stressed by Nordberg, Bradfield, and Odell, *op. cit.*, pp. 140–141.

learning is the process of reacting meaningfully to incoming stimuli in terms of his own unique experiences.

Individuals for whom the printed page provides adequate stimuli for mental reactions frequently find reading (an individualized learning procedure) the most economical device for learning. It might be a waste of time for such people to depend upon class discussion or small-group interaction to provide information readily available in written form.

Educational experimentation has resulted in the extensive use of both group and individualized instructional procedures. Both are necessary. It is the responsibility of the conscientious teacher to effect a balance between the two that will best serve the purpose of learning.

Under many circumstances the student, in the absence of his peer group, has no choice but to study. Assuming that proper habits have been formed, self-directed study is often the most efficient way to accomplish the learning task, although many adolescent learners find this fact difficult to accept.

Principles Related to Individualized Procedures

The following list of general principles (which are thoroughly treated in textbooks on educational psychology and educational theory) give direction to the sound and effective use of individualized procedures.[19]

1. The most efficient learning is often brought about through individualized procedures since all learning—although it may be stimulated by group activities—is ultimately an individual process.

2. Effective teaching involves knowing whether individualized or group procedures will best serve the needs of specific learners. The choice of group or individual activities should be determined by their efficiency in helping the student achieve desired goals. All learning procedures, regardless of the type, should be related to specific goals.

3. Individualized as well as group learning procedures vary in their motivational effect upon the student. When the learner sees that a learning activity is of personal value, however, he will be strongly motivated.

4. In order for individualized procedures (reading, composition, projects, etc.) to be effective, students must possess specific skills and habits.

5. Individualized learning procedures place major responsibility on the student and promote the development of independent study

[19]Kenneth H. Hansen, *High School Teaching* (Englewood Cliffs, N.J.: Prentice-Hall, 1957), pp. 206–208, briefly examines the theory underlying individual and group work. Specific suggestions are listed.

and work methods. Special skills can be learned only through individual effort.

6. Individualized learning procedures help the teacher meet the varying needs of students.

7. Combinations of individual activities and group activities provide many possibilities from which the teacher can select the methods most appropriate for a certain situation.

Correct and Incorrect Use

Two contrasting examples of the use of individualized instruction in the form of creative writing are provided here. In the first example several of the preceding principles have been violated.

MR. BENTON RESTRICTS STUDENT THEMES

T. H. Benton was an English teacher of the old school. His retirement was imminent, and he looked back with nostalgia on the days when students were told what to do and were expected to do it. A portion of one unit in his tenth-grade class was grudgingly devoted to creative writing.

Students were permitted to select and develop any one of three topics written on the board. Themes were to be two thousand words in length and, according to the teacher, were to reflect good thinking as well as good English usage. Although students were permitted to consult grammar handbooks, little personal assistance was available. Furthermore, compositions were to be completed within a one-week period.

The limitations imposed by Mr. Benton's assignment tended to stifle motivation. Students were restricted not only to certain topics but also to a specific length. Many themes of intense personal interest would, therefore, have to be ruled out. Because creative writing was an area in which the students had very limited experience, they needed the personal attention of the teacher—a need that was not met.

MISS WILTON ENCOURAGES INDIVIDUAL THEMES

Miss Wilton had only three years of teaching experience, but her ideas about ninth-grade English composition were interesting and motivational. Before the creative writing assignment was mentioned, she read the best student theme of the preceding year to a keenly interested class. She then asked students what subjects they would like to write about; several responded with specific topics. Students were requested to list three theme topics of particular interest. During the study period Miss Wilton conferred briefly with individual students, and they jointly decided which of the three topics would be the most appropriate.

Miss Wilton did not believe in imposing a specific theme length on students, but she usually indicated that the longer themes should be between one and two thousand words. During the study periods in which the students worked on their themes, she moved from student to student, providing suggestions and praise as needed.

Miss Wilton recognized that creativity cannot flourish in a highly restricted environment. She also realized that students need help without teacher domination in the selection and development of topics. Part of the help Miss Wilton provided took the form of motivation.

Individualized Instruction in Specific Subjects

Certain subjects lend themselves unusually well to the use of individual projects. This is true of making a cedar chest in the wood shop, making a dress in family living, or caring for farm animals in agriculture. In the biology, chemistry, and physics classes students are frequently required to perform their own experiments under rigidly controlled conditions.

The majority of individualized assignments may be used, with appropriate modifications, for nearly all subjects. This is true of general assignments, compositions, reading, and supervised study, but tends to be less true for such skill subjects as physical education, chorus, and instrumental music. In these latter cases, however, individual practice develops the proficiency in the use of skills essential to group participation.

Specific Suggestions

Specific suggestions relating to individualized procedures are based largely on the assumption that each student is different and, therefore, requires varied instructional treatment.[20]

Recommendations

1. Give the student engaged in an individualized learning activity essential guidance without denying him the desired experience of planning, executing, and evaluating.
2. Provide the types of resources that will encourage individual study.
3. Allow for flexibility in making individual assignments.
4. Recognize that immature students struggling with the problems of self-direction may falter frequently in the pursuit of an educational goal. Help them become efficiently self-directive.
5. Select learning activities that are suitable for meeting the challenge of individual differences in intelligence, achievement, and interests.[21]
6. Encourage students to be self-directive while working on individualized special interest projects.

---

[20]Aspects of individuality usually most significant for secondary schooling are listed by Nordberg, Bradfield, and Odell, *op. cit.*, pp. 26–27.

[21]Burton, *op. cit.*, pp. 239–243, discusses instructional and administrative provisions for individual differences. Specific suggestions are given.

7. Use individualized instructional procedures as supplements to other procedures.

8. Use individual activities in helping students meet vocational interests.

9. Assign certain desirable homework projects to individual students.

Cautions

1. Don't overlook the wide range of individualized instructional procedures and their modifications.

2. Don't use individualized activities to the exclusion of group activities.

3. Don't assign individualized student projects without analyzing whether they are too difficult or too easy for completion.

SUPERVISED STUDY

The urgency of current demands that students work up to capacity has placed renewed emphasis on the teacher's supervision of study. The nature, problems, principles, and practical uses of supervised study must be clearly understood by the teacher.

Characteristics of Supervised Study

In attempting to improve the educational setting in which learning takes place, teachers, for centuries, have viewed the supervision of learning as one of their major responsibilities.[22] When time was set aside during the school day for the specific purpose of individual study, the teacher assumed the responsibility for insuring that an educational purpose was served. A generation ago the *study hall*, where students gathered to study under the teacher's direction, was a scheduled part of every secondary-school student's day.

More often than not, these study halls proved to be inefficient operations, because the supervisor, a regular teacher, had no way of knowing what students should be studying unless they came from his own class. Many students viewed study halls as free periods in which they could do as they wished. Teachers as well as administrators gradually became disenchanted with them.

The study hall has now largely been replaced by a study period incorporated into the regular class period. Because the teacher can thus extend or limit the time devoted to directed study, desired flexibility is provided. Furthermore, the teacher can supervise his own students in a way that serves the best interests of his class.

---

[22] *Ibid.*, pp. 300–301, provides a brief account of the historical development of supervised study.

A current parallel development has been the concept that study (supervised study, home study, or individual study) should be based upon a knowledge of essential techniques and habits that give sound direction to study, regardless of the setting in which it takes place. As a result, writers have increasingly directed their attention to such topics as study skills, guided classroom study, and effective study climates. Emphasis on maximum achievement for gifted students in a space age has focused attention on guided self-activity, and aids to self-direction have appeared in the form of programed learning.

Principles Related to Supervised Study

The many forms in which supervised study is currently taking place call for greater teacher efficiency than ever before. An understanding of the principles on which effective study is based should improve a teacher's efficiency.

1. The purpose of supervised study is to help students reach educational goals efficiently.

2. Because specific study-related habits (note-taking, outlining, efficient reading, comparing, etc.) are essential to effective study, teachers must devote specific attention to helping students acquire these habits.[23] How-to-study courses, if properly organized, conducted, and correlated with class-related materials, provide the best means for teaching study-related habits.

3. Supervised study provides an excellent opportunity to meet the needs of individual students.

4. The desire to study is directly related to the love of learning, and many study problems originate from a lack of interest. A student will study with concentration only when he sees meaning and purpose in doing so.

5. The student must understand a problem before he can work toward its solution. For this reason, teachers need to assist students in making subject-matter analyses in concept-centered courses. The teacher is in a good position to supervise the study of his own students, assuming that he has competence in subject matter as well as in study techniques.

6. Because of the laws of habit formation, the learning of study rules may have little or no effect on changing study habits. However, the teacher should recognize the nature of study problems that affect students in given learning situations and should work with the students in attempting to correct these problems.

7. Skill in reading is essential to most types of study.[24]

---

[23]William G. Brink, *Directing Study Activities in Secondary Schools* (New York: Doubleday, 1937), pp. 41–48, provides a helpful analysis of study aids and habits based upon the examination of sixteen general texts.

[24]Mills and Douglass, *op. cit.*, pp. 153–157, give suggestions about the teaching of reading skills.

8. Poor study often results when students lack knowledge of sources of information and how to use them. Furthermore, many students have difficulty in judging the value of the information they have collected.

9. Although self-directed study can be done at home, the school as a general rule provides the best setting for efficient study.

Correct and Incorrect Use

Teachers' practices in supervising study vary markedly and are often comprised of a mixture of good and poor procedures. The examples given here are focused on extremes in order to point out related strengths and weaknesses.

MR. WENTZ CONDUCTS A STUDY PERIOD

Ten minutes before the final bell, Mr. Wentz made a hurried general assignment[25] to his tenth-grade world geography class. "Now get right to work or you won't have your assignment for tomorrow," he cautioned. Most of the students opened their books, but three or four gave no indication of a desire to study. Instead, they began to talk back and forth, disturbing students who wanted to study.

The teacher sat at his desk correcting the assignment from his preceding class, seemingly unaware of the mounting confusion in the room. Five minutes before the bell, Wally hit Dick on the head with a large book. A loud crack ensued and brought Mr. Wentz to his feet. "Now you listen here," he roared. "I won't stand for that in my class. You boys have disturbed my study period for the last time." His face turned purple, and several of the boys smiled or giggled behind upraised hands. The bawling out gained in momentum until the bell rang.

Mr. Wentz exhibited many of the weaknesses that characterize poor study supervision. He did not allow enough time for students to really become immersed in their study even if they had wanted to, and the study period was so close to the final bell that anxious students just anticipated the end of the period. The teacher made no attempt to supervise study; as a result classroom control problems arose and got out of hand before he became actively aware that they existed. He added further confusion by verbally lashing out at students about conditions for which he had been partially responsible.

In the following example, note the emphasis on creating and maintaining an atmosphere conducive to study.

MRS. ROLLINS RUNS AN ORDERLY STUDY PERIOD

Mrs. Rollins made it a practice to have students study during the middle twenty minutes of the fifty-minute period. This gave her an opportunity to

[25]Klausmeier, *op. cit.*, pp. 274–277, discusses the varied types of assignments and their relationship to supervised study.

motivate the assignment properly after she had discussed new concepts. During the last ten minutes, students were involved in the most interesting activity of the day—a discussion of current events; there was little temptation for them to be distracted and think about the end of the period.

No homework was corrected during the study period in Mrs. Rollins' class. She moved about constantly, stopping to help students when necessary. Occasionally the assignment was modified to meet the needs of specific students. When mild disciplinary infractions arose, the teacher moved to the scene of the trouble and quietly made adjustments without disturbing the class. During her rounds Mrs. Rollins frequently praised hardworking students, particularly the less gifted ones, and gave suggestions for better study procedures.

Supervised Study in Specific Subjects

All subjects in the secondary-school curriculum, including the so-called skill subjects, make use of supervised study, although the form it takes will conform to the nature of the subject. Direction of the high-school band is a type of supervised study aimed at skill improvement. Even the coach's analysis of incorrect form on the basketball floor may properly be termed supervised (directed) study.

Study supervision, however, has usually been equated with quiet, teacher-controlled study. Concept-centered subjects, such as English, social studies, mathematics, and the sciences, especially lend themselves to this type of study.

Specific Suggestions

Both experienced and inexperienced teachers will benefit from specific suggestions related to study supervision,[26] and they should view such suggestions as imperative for continued improvement. The suggestions below are based on broad, proven principles.

Recommendations

1. Identify and teach the most basic study skills.[27] Single out students with reading difficulties and give them appropriate help. Point out ineffective methods of study.
2. Help students apply study procedures with such frequency and consistency that they become habits.
3. Create and maintain a physical environment and a classroom atmosphere that are conducive to study.[28]

---

[26]Hansen, *op. cit.*, pp. 205–206, makes three specific suggestions about study activities.

Specific recommendations for directing classroom study are also provided by Grambs, Iverson, and Patterson, *op. cit.*, pp. 315–317.

[27]Specific hints about the improvement of study habits are provided by Mills and Douglass, *op. cit.*, pp. 145–147.

[28]Klausmeier, *op. cit.*, pp. 318–321, discusses the role of environmental factors and procedures in effective study.

4. Know individual students so well that you can direct their study activities efficiently.[29] Help students plan how they are to accomplish the study tasks with which they are confronted.

5. Vary your approach in encouraging different students to study. Be sure that each student understands what is expected of him in supervised study situations.

6. Arrange the content to be studied in an ascending order of difficulty.

7. Encourage students to start work promptly and to keep at a task until it is completed.

8. Help students devise techniques and procedures for evaluating their study habits and for measuring their progress.

9. Teach students techniques for locating needed information.

10. Be sure that students can relate the specific study tasks to the objectives of the unit.

11. Show students how to summarize the material studied.

12. Help students set realistic goals for a given period.

13. Move around the room in order to observe study procedures more closely.

14. Inquire about the progress students are making.

Cautions

1. Don't do the work for the student in attempting to help him.[30]

2. Don't make the study period so short that students cannot become meaningfully involved in their work.

3. Don't allow the study period to extend to the end of the class unless you are in complete control.

4. Don't display your impatience in attempting to teach students study skills.

5. Don't give students the impression that you are not interested in what they are doing during the study period.

6. Don't spend a disproportionate amount of time supervising either slow or fast learners.

THE FIELD TRIP

A field trip is, in reality, an educational journey, usually designed to supplement and expand concepts already discussed in class. On a field trip the entire class visits a point of instructional interest, such as a museum, art gallery, factory, industrial center, or government installation. The field trip has the following advantages as a teaching procedure:

---

[29]Nordberg, Bradfield, and Odell, *op. cit.*, p. 143, view the role of the teacher during supervised study as aiding students.

[30]Burton, *op. cit.*, p. 314, notes certain cautions to be observed in beginning a program of supervised study.

1. It provides first-hand experience.
2. It is pleasurable because of the vivid learning experience.
3. It is more interesting for a majority of students than many other learning experiences.
4. It provides a common experience upon which meaningful discussions can be based.

Principles Related to the Field Trip

An examination of generalizations related to field trips is profitable for all teachers and provides a type of insurance against mistakes for the beginner.[31] The following principles have developed from the experience of various teachers.

1. The field trip is educationally valuable to the extent that it meaningfully relates phenomena observed outside the school to subject matter taught in school.[32]
2. The student is more likely to understand a concept if he has had direct experience with its referent.
3. Because field trips call for the use of more than one sense organ, they provide an impact that is rarely found in the classroom.
4. Field trips may serve a number of different purposes, including original discovery, verification, and motivation.
5. Field trips should be taken only to fulfill specific goals.
6. Field trips provide the opportunity for students to observe the functional relationships of objects and processes.
7. Field trips encourage students to be aware of their environment.
8. Because of their experience and maturity, secondary-school students derive greater benefit from the field trip than do younger pupils.
9. The planning essential to the efficient conduct of a field trip provides excellent opportunities for cooperative work. For this reason, class members should make advance preparation under the direction of the teacher. Furthermore, definite follow-up procedures should be planned and carried out.
10. If a field trip is desirable, the school administration should be actively concerned with its implementation.

Incorrect Usage

The problems encountered by a first-year English teacher on a field trip to Washington, D.C., are representative of difficulties that

---

[31]Mills and Douglass, *op. cit.*, pp. 332–333, identify procedures that will result in maximum educational benefit from the field trip.

[32]See A. J. Foy Cross and Irene F. Cypher, *Audio-Visual Education* (New York: Thomas Y. Crowell Company, 1961), pp. 228–229, for an enumeration of values to be derived from field trips.

might largely be avoided through detailed planning.[33] Her troubles were unfolded to a sympathetic colleague the day after the trip.

A POORLY PLANNED TRIP

Mrs. Willowby, I didn't know whether we would ever make it back with all students intact. If you have time, I'll tell you the whole story.

We had been studying *Julius Caesar* in my ninth-grade English class. It seemed like a good idea to clinch a number of the points about Shakespeare's life and writings by taking my twenty-nine students on a field trip to the Folger (Shakespearean) Library, just a short distance from the Library of Congress. As you know, it contains an authentic replica of the Shakespearean stage. When I mentioned the possibility to the students, they were wild about the idea.

I suppose everyone has to stumble through the first year of teaching. Next year I'll know better. Well, I found that you have to make special arrangements for transportation by either hiring a bus from the local bus company or waiting two weeks for a time when a school bus would be available. We ended up chartering a bus for a three-hour period and charging each student fifty cents. I finally had to pay the fare for two students who came without their money. I suspect they really couldn't afford it.

You know, I thought that I had remembered everything, but now I wonder whether I remembered anything. For one thing, I forgot to have students obtain written permission to take the trip from their parents. Furthermore, one of the girls ran right in front of a car while we were getting off the bus. I thought for sure that she would be hit—but miraculously she escaped. I wonder if her parents could have sued me if she had been hit?

We waited at the west entrance to the school for ten minutes before the driver showed up. Actually, he had come to the front entrance and waited for us there. I suppose I was at fault by not telling him where to pick us up.

I've never seen my students as rowdy as they were on the bus. You would have thought they had just been released from long prison terms; they acted as if school were out for sure. They yelled back and forth, walked up and down the aisle, and even tossed books around the bus. I tried to get them quieted down, but I couldn't do a thing with them. Finally some of the boys started to rock the bus; I actually thought it might tip over. Just about that time the bus driver pulled over to the curb, stopped the bus, and demanded that everyone get off. He opened the door, and the kids knew he meant business. It took some mighty fast talking to get him to continue the trip without making three of the boys get out. After that they behaved very well.

Most of this teacher's troubles were related to the lack of specific plans. If she had worked out the details of the trip with students two weeks ahead of time, school transportation could have been provided, written permission from the parents could have been obtained and checked, and proper student conduct could have been dis-

[33]McGuire, Myers, and Durrance, *op. cit.*, pp. 182–183, provide a description of the need for detailed planning before the trip is undertaken.

Hansen, *op. cit.*, pp. 231–232, describes a situation involving gross misuse of the field trip.

cussed. She also might have reviewed appropriate control procedures in the event misbehavior did occur.

According to the English teacher's account, little or no time was spent in pinpointing exactly what students were to look for, how they were to make notes and report the evidence of their observations, and what would be expected of them in the way of a follow-up. What took place at the Folger Library itself is not told, but one may assume that the visit was not nearly as profitable as it might have been.

Use of the Field Trip in Specific Subjects

There is no subject in the secondary curriculum that could not be effectively served by some type of field trip.[34] This is true of concept-centered as well as skill areas. Variation in type, length, and purpose is to be expected, but no trip is justified unless it proves to be a more efficient teaching procedure than others that might be chosen.

Bands frequently make trips, not basically for the purpose of observation, but to give students an opportunity to perform. If properly conducted, such trips are often justified. A journey to the state fair by students in a metal shop class in order to observe the work of expert craftsmen can be highly profitable if it is efficiently planned and supervised. A brief trip by shorthand students to a large stenographic pool may provide the motivation necessary for superior classroom performance. The geometry class might well examine and determine reasons for the geometric designs in the skeletal framework of a skyscraper under construction. To limit the use of the field trip to a few subjects is unwarranted; indeed, it is sound practice to consider it as a possibility whenever planning takes place.

Specific Suggestions

Helpful suggestions have been passed from one teacher to another in the attempt to improve class-related field trips. The following suggestions apply to almost every field trip.

Recommendations

1. Be sure all students know the purpose and destination of the field trip. Help them identify what they are supposed to learn from such an experience.[35]

2. Plan essential details with students before the trip.[36] Have

---

[34]*Ibid.*, pp. 311–314, discusses the field trip as one of the educational devices made possible through the use of community resources.

[35]Rivlin, *op. cit.*, pp. 247–250, focuses attention on preparation, the trip itself, and follow-up activities.

[36]Nordberg, Bradfield, and Odell, *op. cit.*, pp. 138–139, lend strong support to the need for detailed planning.

students gather specific advance information about the subject of study and help them prepare a series of questions to be answered while on the field trip.

3. Be sure that students understand the relationship of what is seen on the field trip to what has been discussed in class.

4. As a part of effective planning, with the students' help establish standards of conduct to be observed while on the field trip. Encourage students to think of the trip as a carefully planned learning experience, not as a pleasure excursion.

5. Be aware of legal responsibilities in conducting field trips.

6. Be sure the field trip serves an educational purpose.

7. Solicit the help of the administration and other faculty members in planning and carrying out the field trip. Be sure the trip is adequately supervised, even if it requires the assistance of other teachers or, in some cases, parents.

8. Help students derive maximum benefit from the trip by subsequent pupil appraisals, teacher-led discussions, and class reports.

9. Consider the possibility of short as well as long field trips and of field trips outside of school hours.

10. Permit small groups within the class to take field trips for different reasons if you can be sure that they will serve educational purposes.

Cautions[37]

1. Don't assume that the field trip is essentially a device for teaching elementary-school children.

2. Don't use the field trip to teach concepts that can be taught just as well through less complicated and less time-consuming procedures.

3. Don't overlook the possibility of a short trip that may involve only walking.

4. Don't allow the student's exhilaration to be expressed in misbehavior.

5. Don't allow minor breaches of conduct to grow into major disruptions while on a field trip.

ADDITIONAL STUDENT-CENTERED PROCEDURES IN REVIEW

Four procedures requiring student participation—group procedures, individualized instruction, supervised study, and the field trip—have been discussed in this chapter. Because of their marked differences, these procedures provide the effective teacher with instructional flexibility in helping students achieve desired goals.

---

[37]Grambs, Iverson, and Patterson, *op. cit.*, pp. 204–205, point out needed precautions in working out plans for the field trip.

Group procedures may range from whole-class discussions to small study groups. Capitalizing on student interests, the teacher may utilize such activities to encourage goal-oriented learning. In directing group activities he must develop the concepts on which effective group work is founded and be consistently vigilant in determining that such activities serve the purposes of education.

Individualized instructional procedures include compositions, reading, laboratory experimentation, general assignments, individual projects, and library study. Each of these procedures may have a different motivational effect on the learner, and it is the teacher's responsibility to determine how each method can best be employed.

The purpose of supervised study, like that of other instructional procedures, is to help students reach educational goals more efficiently. By this method, individual differences can be met, study-related habits can be taught, and problems associated with study can be observed and analyzed.

The field trip is an educational journey designed to expand class-related concepts. It provides learners with the advantages of vivid first-hand knowledge, intense interest, and common experience. Although not all field trips are educationally justified, they are valuable to the extent that they meaningfully relate phenomena outside the school to subject matter taught in the school.

PROBLEMS FOR STUDY AND DISCUSSION

1. Define *forum discussion.*
2. List five basic values of group activities. Discuss each briefly.
3. Why must all group discussion procedures be directed toward the achievement of goals? Explain.
4. Describe a large-group discussion in which you participated or observed that accomplished little. Identify the reasons why little was accomplished.
5. List three cautions to be observed in planning and conducting group activities.
6. Describe individual projects in three different subject-matter areas.
7. Expand and clarify the following statement: Learning is entirely an individual matter.
8. Under what circumstances is reading the most economical device for learning? Explain.
9. Discuss the relationship between habit formation and individual study.
10. It has been said that effective study of any sort should be based upon a knowledge of essential techniques and habits. Identify three of each.
11. Name at least two modern aids to self-directed learning.
12. What characterizes efficient teacher supervision of study? Explain.
13. List ten "Do's" designed to serve the purposes of a teacher who wishes to supervise study most efficiently in a secondary-school setting.

14. State in your own words three psychological principles that justify the use of the field trip.

15. Specifically, what kind of planning is necessary to insure the success of a field trip?

16. Describe a field trip in which you participated as a secondary-school student. What problems arose that threatened to nullify the educational value of the trip? Knowing what you know now, how would you have handled these problems?

17. Which of the following group procedures is best suited to effective teaching in your subject-matter major: whole-class discussion, forum discussion, panel discussion, unrehearsed dramatization, small study group activities, or debates? Why?

18. Identify three useful individualized study procedures that are not commonly used in teaching your subject-matter minor.

19. Explain why the old fashioned study hall has lost favor as a device for promoting learning?

20. Assuming that you are teaching your subject-matter major, list five field trips you might promote.

RECOMMENDED READINGS

Group Procedures

Batchelder, Howard T., Maurice McGlasson, and Raleigh Schorling, *Student Teaching in Secondary Schools*, 4th ed. New York: McGraw-Hill Book Company, 1964, pp. 152–158.

Burton, William H., *The Guidance of Learning Activities*, 3d. ed. New York: Appleton-Century-Crofts, Inc., 1962, Chapter 9.

Carter, William L., Carl W. Hansen, and Margaret G. McKim, *Learning to Teach in the Secondary School*. New York: The Macmillan Company, 1962, pp. 174–179 and 203–210.

Grambs, Jean D., William J. Iverson, and Franklin K. Patterson, *Modern Methods in Secondary Education*, rev. ed. New York: The Dryden Press, 1958, Chapters 9 and 10.

Hansen, Kenneth H., *High School Teaching*. Englewood Cliffs, N.J.: Prentice-Hall Inc., 1957, pp. 206–208.

Klausmeier, Herbert J., *Teaching in the Secondary School*. New York: Harper & Brothers, 1958, pp. 256–273.

McGuire, Vincent, Robert B. Myers, and Charles L. Durrance, *Your Student Teaching in the Secondary School*. Boston: Allyn and Bacon, Inc., 1959, pp. 149–154.

McKean, Robert C., *Principles and Methods in Secondary Education*. Columbus, Ohio: Charles E. Merrill Books, Inc., 1962, pp. 101–102.

Mills, Hubert H., and Harl R. Douglass, *Teaching in High School*, 2d. ed. New York: Ronald Press, 1957, Chapter 12.

Rivlin, Harry N., *Teaching Adolescents in Secondary Schools*, 2d. ed. New York: Appleton-Century-Crofts, Inc., 1961, Chapter 6 and pp. 404–405.

Wellington, C. Burleigh, and Jean Wellington, *Teaching for Critical Thinking: with Emphasis on Secondary Education*. New York: McGraw-Hill Book Company, 1960, Chapters 6 and 10.

Wiggins, Samuel P., *Successful High School Teaching.* Boston: Houghton Mifflin Company, 1958, pp. 176–178.

Wiles, Kimball, *Teaching for Better Schools*, 2d. ed. Englewood Cliffs, N.J.: Prentice-Hall, Inc., 1959, p. 168.

Individualized Instructional Procedures

Batchelder, Howard T., Maurice McGlasson, and Raleigh Schorling, *Student Teaching in Secondary Schools*, 4th ed. New York: McGraw-Hill Book Company, 1964, pp. 150–151.

Burton, William H., *The Guidance of Learning Activities*, 3d. ed. New York: Appleton-Century-Crofts, Inc., 1962, pp. 239–243.

Hansen, Kenneth H., *High School Teaching.* Englewood Cliffs N.J.: Prentice-Hall, Inc., 1957, pp. 206–208.

Klausmeier, Herbert J., *Teaching in the Secondary School.* New York: Harper & Brothers, 1958, pp. 273–281.

Mills, Hubert H., and Harl R. Douglass, *Teaching in High School*, 2d. ed. New York: Ronald Press, 1957, Chapter 9.

Nordberg, H. Orville, James M. Bradfield, and William C. Odell, *Secondary School Teaching.* New York: The Macmillan Company, 1962, pp. 26–27, 130–134, 139–141, and 143–144.

Wellingron, C. Burleigh, and Jean Wellington, *Teaching for Critical Thinking: with Emphasis on Secondary Education.* New York: McGraw-Hill Book Company, 1960, pp. 178–179.

Supervised Study

Batchelder, Howard T., Maurice McGlasson, and Raleigh Schorling, *Student Teaching in Secondary Schools*, 4th ed. New York: McGraw-Hill Book Company, 1964, pp. 171–172.

Burton, William H., *The Guidance of Learning Activities*, 3d. ed. New York: Appleton-Century-Crofts, Inc., 1962, pp. 298–315.

Grambs, Jean D., William J. Iverson, and Franklin K. Patterson, *Modern Methods in Secondary Education*, rev. ed. New York: The Dryden Press, 1958, pp. 315–317.

Hansen, Kenneth H., *High School Teaching.* Englewood Cliffs, N.J.: Prentice-Hall, Inc., 1957, pp. 205–207.

Klausmeier, Herbert J., *Teaching in the Secondary School.* New York: Harper & Brothers, 1958, pp. 274–280 and 318–320.

Mills, Hubert H., and Harl R. Douglass, *Teaching in High School*, 2d. ed. New York: Ronald Press, 1957, Chapter 9.

Nordberg, H. Orville, James M. Bradfield, and William C. Odell, *Secondary School Teaching.* New York: The Macmillan Company, 1962, p. 143.

Rivlin, Harry N., *Teaching Adolescents in Secondary Schools*, 2d. ed. New York: Appleton-Century-Crofts, Inc., 1961, Chapter 9.

The Field Trip

Cross, A. J. Foy, and Irene F. Cypher, *Audio-Visual Education.* New York: Thomas Y. Crowell Company, 1961, pp. 226–230.

Grambs, Jean D., William J. Iverson, and Franklin K. Patterson, *Modern Methods in Secondary Education*, rev. ed. New York: The Dryden Press, 1958, pp. 201–205.

Hansen, Kenneth H., *High School Teaching.* Englewood Cliffs, N.J.: Prentice-Hall, Inc., 1957, pp. 231–232, 311, and 314.

Klausmeier, Herbert J., *Teaching in the Secondary School.* New York: Harper & Brothers, 1958, pp. 261–263.

McGuire, Vincent, Robert B. Myers, and Charles L. Durrance, *Your Student Teaching in the Secondary School.* Boston: Allyn and Bacon, Inc., 1959, pp. 182–183.

Mills, Hubert H., and Harl R. Douglass, *Teaching in High School,* 2d. ed. New York: Ronald Press, 1957, pp. 332–333.

Nordberg, H. Orville, James M. Bradfield, and William C. Odell, *Secondary School Teaching.* New York: The Macmillan Company, 1962, pp. 138–139.

Rivlin, Harry N., *Teaching Adolescents in Secondary Schools,* 2d. ed. New York: Appleton-Century-Crofts, Inc., 1961, pp. 247–250.

Wellington, C. Burleigh, and Jean Wellington, *Teaching for Critical Thinking: with Emphasis on Secondary Education.* New York: McGraw-Hill Book Company, 1960, p. 155.

12

Recurring Instructional Concerns

Many instructional problems arise almost every school day, while others occur with varying degrees of frequency. Although some of these concerns are relatively trivial in nature, others are basic to effective instruction. This chapter is addressed to three of these basic concerns—continuous study of the student, the use of resource persons, and the use of teacher-prepared materials.

CONTINUOUS STUDY OF THE STUDENT

Knowledge of the student provides the teacher with a basis for the effective and realistic use of content and methods. The conscientious teacher must discover ways of acquiring such knowledge and keeping it current. All factors that tend to influence the teaching-learning process must be examined to determine how they can best be used to improve the academic as well as the nonacademic behavior of students. A continuous study of students helps provide teachers with the essential information.

The study of students, so important to efficient, scientific teaching, is something much more fundamental than "being nice" to students, giving and correcting assignments, or maintaining an atmosphere conducive to study. It is the procedure whereby the teacher uses scientifically proven as well as less sophisticated devices to determine the mental, physical, social, and emotional status of his students.[1] Because the individual's status in all of these areas is subject to variation, the study must be a continuing one if it is to provide current information. Furthermore, the acquisition of this information must precede planning and teaching if it is to serve most helpfully in improving instruction.[2]

Special Information About Students

In acquiring up-to-date knowledge of the student, the teacher needs to be particularly aware of certain important areas.[3]

Capacity

Although some research evidence shows that I.Q.'s have been influenced through environment, most psychologists support the assumption that one's basic capacity remains relatively stable. A real problem arises, however, when a teacher draws false conclusions about the student's capacity, regardless of what it may be. For this reason, it is important that the teacher corroborate his subjective evaluation of a student's intelligence by examining the results of standardized tests of mental maturity. When the teacher has reason to doubt the reliability of a student's score on a group test, he may wish to recommend that the student be given an individually administered examination.

Subject-Matter Achievement

Because it largely depends on student effort and teaching skill, student achievement in content areas is subject to considerable variation. The teacher, therefore, should be aware of the academic standing of individual class members in most subject areas. This need requires the use of specific evaluation procedures to inform the teacher as well as the student and calls for the establishment of accurate, flexible, and practical record-keeping procedures.

Experiences

During a few short months a student may be exposed to a number of major experiences that have a marked influence on his aca-

---

[1]Hubert H. Mills and Harl R. Douglass, *Teaching in High School,* 2d. ed. (New York: Ronald Press, 1957), p. 67, list the types of information needed about students and the means of obtaining it.

[2]See Chapter 3, pp. 48–57, for a discussion of the basic information necessary for effective planning.

[3]The need for individual information about students is pointed up through brief descriptions of students given by C. Burleigh Wellington and Jean Wellington, *Teaching for Critical Thinking: with Emphasis on Secondary Education* (New York: McGraw-Hill Book Company, 1960), pp. 66–67.

See also Chapter 1 in the present text for keys to understanding adolescent student behavior.

demic performance and his attitude toward school.[4] It is possible, for example, that one student may take a trip across the country and into Canada, suffer the loss of a parent, and receive his first failing grade in school. If the teacher neglects keeping pace with such events, his planning and teaching may result in academic injury for that particular student.

Family Status

The student may have a very pleasant relationship with his parents during the early years of adolescence;[5] then, a sudden eruption into overt rebelliousness during middle adolescence leaves parents, teacher—and student—stunned. If this happens, academic performance, classroom behavior, and general attitude toward teachers and school may be affected. The teacher who looks for a consistently tranquil student personality during the turbulence of adolescence is often disappointed and finds it difficult to adjust to the unexpected new personality. Because there is marked variability in personality development, a teacher's best insurance against the unexpected is to maintain consistent contact with those factors in a student's life that affect his personality.

Peer-Group Status

Conformity or lack of conformity to the values of peers can have an overnight effect on the popularity of a student. Since the teacher is rarely invited into the intimate council of the peer group, he may be entirely unaware of the status of its members. As a result, he must be particularly observant to determine the current degree of peer-group acceptance of the members of his class, for acceptance or non-acceptance can have a marked effect on a student's behavior and classroom activity.[6]

Self-Concept

How a student views himself will, to some degree, affect his peer-group relationships, his behavior at home, and his performance in the classroom. Major events in his life may dramatically alter his self-concept and give rise to rejection or approval. In attempting to help the student acquire and maintain the mental health essential to effective study and learning, the teacher should keep abreast of stu-

---

[4]Harry N. Rivlin, *Teaching Adolescents in Secondary Schools*, 2d. ed. (New York: Appleton-Century-Crofts, 1961), pp. 399–403, discusses the family, the society, the individual, and the school as sources of adolescent problems.

[5]The family and friendship groups are covered by Robert C. McKean, *Principles and Methods in Secondary Education* (Columbus, Ohio: Charles E. Merrill Books, Inc. 1962), pp. 49–50.

[6]John E. Horrocks, *The Psychology of Adolescence*, 2d. ed. (Boston: Houghton Mifflin Company, 1962), Chapter 4, discusses widening social contacts, changing roles as a result of development, the importance of contemporaries' opinions, and the adolescent's concept of his own role.

dent successes and failures in academic, nonacademic, and peer-group settings and of their effect upon student behavior. Because of their changing nature, interests may also give new direction to student desires and activities, and the teacher must be aware of such changes.

Devices Used in the Study of Students

Effective continuous study of individual learners must be so organized that it proceeds systematically and purposefully, using devices known to have merit.[7] Several of these devices will be of interest to the new teacher.

Cumulative Records

A majority of well-administered schools currently maintain permanent records on which essential information relating to individual students is recorded from year to year.[8] Such records customarily contain standardized I.Q. and achievement test scores and the student's final marks in different subjects. Frequently, major disciplinary infractions as well as police records are also noted. Although there is considerable variation in the types of cumulative records kept, they always provide confidential information to help the teacher understand his students as individuals.

Teacher-Student Conferences

The informal conference is one of the better devices for helping the teacher become more fully acquainted with his students. Often these conferences take the form of a private conversation at the teacher's desk or at the pupil's work station. A somewhat more formal situation is the private before-school or after-school chat. If the teacher has an office, private conferences are also possible during the school day. Because of the frequency with which they may take place, teacher-student conferences afford advantages not found in other procedures.

Teacher Conferences

Information about students obtained from other responsible teachers may save a great deal of time. In certain circumstances a meeting of several teachers who have relevant information about a

---

[7]Wellington and Wellington, *op. cit.*, pp. 68–72, discuss the cumulative record folder, observation, written reports, checklists, and sociograms as devices for helping the teacher know his students.

William L. Carter, Carl W. Hansen, and Margaret G. McKim, *Learning to Teach in the Secondary School* (New York: Macmillan, 1962), pp. 109–120, describe various procedures and devices that provide daily opportunities for the study of students.

[8]See Mills and Douglass, *op. cit.*, p. 68, for a list of the helpful information contained on the cumulative record.

specific student or situation may be desirable.[9] The subjective nature of this type of information should be recognized, however; in some cases it will be necessary to discount certain information because of the teacher's emotional involvement.

Parent-Teacher Conferences

Much light can be shed on classroom behavior through a parent-teacher discussion. Domestic tensions may be aired, evidence of parental domination may come to light, or problems of concern to parents may be reviewed. Occasionally, when it will serve a useful purpose, the student is included in such conferences.

Sociometric Devices

Specific techniques have been devised for measuring the feelings that group members have for each other.[10] One of the most common and useful devices is the *sociogram,* which attempts to measure the pattern of friendships in a class.[11] Because sociograms can assist the teacher in identifying friendless students (isolates), popular students (stars), and students with specific social problems, they, too, can serve a useful purpose—if they are employed with care.

Purposeful Observation

A good share of the teacher's classroom time is spent observing students under varying circumstances. This observation, if not directed toward particular ends, may be of limited value in providing or confirming information about students. If, however, the teacher observes student behavior to determine changes in social adjustment, such observation becomes specific and can be of great help. Observation may be undertaken for a wide range of reasons, such as discovering poor study habits, determining teacher-pupil rapport, identifying potential disciplinary trouble spots, or locating students with poor peer-group adjustments.

Autobiographies

Themes and autobiographies in which students are given freedom to write of their experiences, successes and failure, likes and dislikes, personal points of view, and self-concepts often reveal heretofore unknown aspects of their personality that can be valuable

---

[9]The necessity for maintaining communications among teachers and counselors as a means of becoming acquainted with students is stressed by H. Orville Nordberg, James M. Bradfield, and William C. Odell, *Secondary School Teaching* (New York: Macmillan, 1962), p. 75.

[10]Mills and Douglass, *op. cit.,* pp. 70–73, briefly discuss sociometric techniques, personal interviews, anecdotal records, and autobiographies as means for understanding students.

[11]Herbert J. Klausmeier, *Teaching in the Secondary School* (New York: Harper & Brothers, 1958), pp. 51–58, provides a helpful discussion on the nature of the sociogram and its practical use.

to the teacher. Such information can be utilized in more effectively organizing teaching procedures and materials to meet the individual needs and desires of students.

Procedures for Recording Information

Once relevant information has been obtained, it should be organized and recorded in the manner best suited for future use. Incorporating such coded information as a part of a seating chart enables the teacher to have before him relevant confidential information about students (I.Q., socioeconomic status, subject-matter achievement, etc.) to which he can refer at will.[12] Some teachers write relevant bits of information on five-by-eight cards, which are then filed alphabetically. Remarks concerning rate of progress, student problems, and study habits are sometimes included. A similar procedure involves using an individual folder for each student in which the teacher from time to time inserts notes or anecdotal accounts concerning classroom behavior. As long as subjectivity can be minimized in this type of reporting, the accumulation of such accounts over a period of time may be very helpful in interpreting student behavior.

Principles Related to the Study of Students

Generalizations about student behavior and its causes contribute to the understanding of specific acts that comprise in-school behavior. Several of these principles are identified here.[13]

1. Each student is a composite of the biological and environmental factors that make him what he is. Therefore, student behavior varies depending on the environmental factors that give direction to behavior. Maturation is affected by both heredity and environment.

2. Because of the changing nature of the student's environment, the student is constantly changing. Thus, continuous study of the student is necessary to keep abreast of changes that might influence teaching and learning. Student values, of course, change as the adolescent moves toward maturity; so also does his development-related behavior. Since emotions and social and personal feelings cannot be isolated from the learning process, they are also frequently subject to modification.

3. The range of information needed about students as a basis for effective instruction is so extensive that repeated and continuing student contacts are required. Of great assistance to the teacher in furthering the cause of planning and teaching is information about student intelligence, achievement, home environment, peer-group

[12]See Chapter 7, pp. 137 and 158, for examples of this device.

[13]William H. Burton, *The Guidance of Learning Activities*, 3d. ed. (New York: Appleton-Century-Crofts, 1962), pp. 150–151, presents a useful set of principles concerned with the growth processes of the learner.

status, and interests. Although the various facets of the whole person may be examined individually, the fluctuating interdependence of the mental, physical, social, and emotional nature of the individual should be considered as a possible explanation for his behavior.

4. Better teacher-student rapport is established when the teacher gives evidence of consistent interest in all aspects of the student's welfare. However, the teacher should not become so preoccupied with the study of the student that he forgets to teach subject matter. Conversely, he should not become so concerned with transmitting content that he forgets the person he is teaching and how the changing nature of the student affects learning.

5. The choice of teaching methods should be directly related to the characteristics of the students to be taught;[14] similarly, the changing composition of a student group may make it necessary to modify teaching procedures.

6. The day-to-day behavior of a given student may be inconsistent, and students of the same chronological age may exhibit markedly different behavioral variations. Errors are minimized if the study of students is conducted on a continuing basis.

7. Society may erroneously regard the adolescent as a delinquent, an adult, a child, or a threat to adult authority without considering the possible range of behavioral variations.

8. Student attitudes toward academic achievement will vary, depending on peer-group and home influences and on student maturity.

9. The student reacts to learning stimuli as a unified whole, not as a physical, social, or emotional entity only.

Correct and Incorrect Procedures

Errors frequently made by teachers in assembling and using information about their students are reflected in the description of Mrs. Widdison's procedures.

MRS. WIDDISON HAS A LIMITED KNOWLEDGE OF HER CLASS

Mrs. Widdison was aware that many other teachers spent a good deal of time gathering and analyzing information about students. But, after all, why should she? She was, she reasoned, teaching as well as the average teacher. If she went to the front office to obtain I.Q. and achievement test scores, it would have to be done after school and would consume additional hours.

After the first three weeks she felt that she knew the students; in any event, what she didn't know she could discover by asking the teacher across the hall. During the supervised study period she could observe students generally and fill in any missing information.

---

[14]Kenneth H. Hansen, *High School Teaching* (Englewood Cliffs, N.J.: Prentice-Hall, 1957), pp. 28–29, stresses the necessary relationship between student characteristics and the teaching methods employed.

Because she had a good memory, Mrs. Widdison didn't find it necessary to make any notes on student behavior. Moreover, she felt that if she had a couple of chats with a student at the beginning of the school year, she had him analyzed fairly well, and there was little need for further exploration.

This teacher's behavior revealed several weaknesses:

1. She viewed the teaching profession as having little to do with a close and continuing personal acquaintance with students.
2. She did not want to spend the energy necessary to gather and organize relevant information about each student.
3. She gave no attention to the possibility of using parent-teacher conferences, sociometric devices, autobiographies, and pointed observation.
4. The small amount of information that she obtained was not recorded or processed for further use.

Lewis Whitney had a different concept of his responsibility for obtaining information about individual students.

MR. WHITNEY GATHERS IMPORTANT INFORMATION

Preregistration procedures enabled Mr. Whitney to know in advance approximately 80 per cent of the students who would be in his classes. During the week prior to the opening of school, he spent many hours examining cumulative records. The students' subject-matter achievement test scores, I.Q.'s, and socioeconomic status were usually available. Much of this information was recorded in code form for later transfer to seating charts.

During the first three weeks of the new school year, Mr. Whitney tried to have a brief, exploratory, personal chat with every student. As a general rule, these early talks tended to corroborate the information contained on the cumulative records. Relevant bits of information were written down and inserted in individual student folders.

During the study periods the teacher often moved from one student to another—helping, probing, teaching, and supporting. He conferred most frequently with students known to have particular difficulties, and when he discovered students with problems of deep concern, he often referred them to the school counselor.

Mr. Whitney viewed all of his information about students as tentative and, therefore, subject to verification. For this reason, his study of students was a continuous one. Believing in careful record keeping, he recorded all test scores in a way that would permit comparison. His observation of students was frequent and pointed. He viewed parent-teacher conferences as an essential part of effective teaching, and he often talked about specific student-related matters with teachers in possession of needed information.

Specific Suggestions

Some of the practices carried out by Mr. Whitney in his attempt to keep abreast of student problems, behavior, and work habits are reflected in the following suggestions.

Recommendations

1. Study students systematically. Set aside a specific time for studying a particular student or students.

2. Record essential information in permanent form so that it will be useful in the future. Devise a practical procedure for making anecdotal records of relevant student behavior, and use the cumulative records in the front office to supplement basic information.

3. Be continuously aware of the factors that tend to affect personality development in students, and establish organized procedures for discovering additional information.

4. Become familiar with standardized tests that provide pertinent specific information. Compare students in terms of one characteristic at a time, such as I.Q. Later compare them in terms of another trait, such as subject-matter achievement.

5. Recognize your own limitations in analyzing student behavior and prescribing treatment for students with deep-seated problems. Seek the assistance of guidance experts, administrators, psychologists, and, at times, psychiatrists in your work with disturbed students.

6. Have teacher-parent conferences at least once each year and more often if needed.

7. Make periodic checks on the academic standing of all students in the class.

8. Recognize the subjective nature of observations.

Cautions

1. Don't jump to hasty conclusions about the cause of student behavior.

2. Don't assume you know all about students after a limited number of personal contacts.

3. Don't forget that the physical health of individual students is not always obvious.

4. Don't use lack of time as an excuse for not knowing your students better.

5. Don't allow your emotions to sway your appraisal of student behavior.

USE OF RESOURCE PERSONS

The use of resource persons, like the continuous study of students, is a basic instructional concern. Nearly all communities afford many resources on which the alert teacher can call to enrich his teaching. Among community-related learning activities are visits to museums, concerts, lectures, industrial and government installations, newspapers, television and radio programs, legislative assemblies, and special exhibits. One of the most frequently used resources of the community, however, is the individual specialist who is brought into the classroom to supplement the teacher's instruction.[15]

Advantages of Using Resource Persons

Conscientious teachers are aware of the instructional advantages to be gained by using carefully selected resource persons.[16] They provide students with a vivid and realistic contact with life outside the school that could not otherwise be achieved. The traveler who has just returned from residence abroad, for example, is able to give students an enthusiastic account of what he has seen and heard. Such an account can be surpassed only by first-hand experience on the part of the learner himself.

Resource individuals often expose students to the activities and functions of the community in a meaningful and helpful way. The police chief who is invited to talk to students about the incidence of crime in their own city will probably leave a lasting impression. Not an infrequent advantage is the impression of the school that the resource person takes back to the community. If the impression is a negative one, however, it can prove to be a great disadvantage.

If the teacher has taken the trouble to assemble a file of carefully selected resource persons,[17] he may be in a position to identify and invite to his class the most useful individual from a range of possibilities. Furthermore, the teacher is in a position to exercise selectivity in terms of established criteria: degree of specialization, current experience, and the ability to communicate effectively. In larger communities people of national prominence have been known to give of their services willingly if it can be demonstrated that students will benefit from their presentations.[18]

Contact with a person who is immersed in an important enterprise related to the course content is a real and exciting experience for students. For example, a local FBI agent may be invited to talk to an American problems class or combination of classes about the dangers of foreign espionage in our missile industry. Class members tend to look with considerable respect upon such an individual; as a result, they listen attentively.

---

[15] A few of the outstanding people in the community on whom the teacher can call are listed by Howard T. Batchelder, Maurice McGlasson, and Raleigh Schorling, *Student Teaching in Secondary Schools,* 4th ed. (New York: McGraw-Hill Book Company, 1964), p. 183.

[16] A. J. Foy Cross and Irene F. Cypher, *Audio-Visual Education* (New York: Thomas Y. Crowell Company, 1961), p. 218, list some of the reasons for calling on a resource person.

[17] See pp. 116–117 for a more detailed discussion of the preparation of a file of resource persons.

[18] Samuel P. Wiggins, *Successful High School Teaching* (Boston: Houghton Mifflin Company, 1958), p. 165, cautions against the assumption that citizens are always too busy to help in the classroom.

The change of pace afforded by the appearance of a new status figure in the classroom often has a rejuvinating effect on students. Those who have been bored may suddenly awaken to new interest if the resource person is chosen with care. If students are involved in contacting the resource person and serving as official hosts during his stay in the school building, they have the added advantage of a new and interesting learning experience.

Principles Related to the Use of Resource Persons

An understanding of the role of resource people in the total range of possible teaching procedures will help the teacher use such individuals most effectively. The general principles below are applicable to many specific teaching situations.

1. The classroom teacher often lacks the degree of specialization that enables him to teach a particular portion of his subject with insight and enthusiasm; resource persons, on the other hand, frequently possess the desired specialized knowledge. Individuals with a particular competence are frequently glad to share their knowledge with student groups, and there are few communities that do not contain at least a few prominent specialists who might profitably be used to enrich instruction.

2. All possible procedures, including the use of the resource person, should be examined to determine which one will be most helpful in moving students efficiently toward a particular goal. The resource individual represents only one of many community resources that can be utilized for instructional purposes.[19]

3. Student motivation is often enhanced through the use of carefully selected resource persons. The students benefit from hearing a subject explained by a person who has an intimate acquaintance with it and thus can be expected to provide authentic information.

4. Poorly selected resource people may prove to be instructionally undesirable. For example, if the vocabulary used by a resource speaker is over the heads of students, the authority's speech will serve a no more useful purpose than an overly difficult reading assignment.

5. Resource persons may be used to demonstrate certain complicated processes as well as to lecture.

6. Students often know persons in the community (frequently relatives) who may advantageously be used to supplement instruction. An invitation to such specialists gives students the opportunity to make proper arrangements, under the direction of the teacher, for the person's appearance in school.

---

[19]Hansen, *op. cit.*, pp. 309–311, writes of the desirability of using resource groups as well as resource persons.

Correct and Incorrect Use

Some teachers have good intentions with respect to teaching but make errors in implementing certain procedures. The case of Mr. Adkins, the senior high school foreign-language teacher who wished to use Mr. Fritz Neumann as a resource person in the first-year German class, is a good illustration.

POOR PREPARATION FOR A RESOURCE PERSON

Mr. Adkins, the instructor, asked Sally Venable to invite Mr. Fritz Neumann, an immigrant who had been in the country for three years, to come to the German class on Tuesday, November 12. Arriving at the school at the designated hour, the visitor reported to the front office. After some delay, it was decided that he was to go to the German class. When he finally found the room, he was embarrassed because he was late. Not knowing what he was expected to say or do, Mr. Neumann launched into a discussion of German agriculture, and the students soon became bored.

The use of this resource person was a failure because inadequate advance preparation had been made to insure the best use of his special knowledge. Mr. Adkins had wanted Mr. Neumann to illustrate the native pronunciation of the German *l, r, sch,* and vowel sounds. The guest, unfortunately, had not been informed of the purpose of his visit. Sally, who made the original contact, had not been given specific instructions. Furthermore, students should have met the guest at the main entrance and taken him to the classroom. Gracious behavior as hosts also called for appropriate introduction of the subject and the speaker as well as expressions of appreciation following the presentation.

A marked contrast is seen in the procedures followed in Mr. Hillman's visit to a high-school chemistry class.

MR. BING CAREFULLY PREPARES FOR AN OUTSIDE SPEAKER

During a casual encounter on the street, Mr. Bing, the chemistry teacher, had an opportunity to renew his acquaintance with Mr. Hillman, a well-known chemical specialist employed in the local steel industry. Mr. Bing was singularly pleased when the chemist indicated his willingness to serve as a resource person for Mr. Bing's high-school chemistry class.

A short time later the teacher asked two student volunteers to contact the proposed guest about the details of his presentation. They were given specific instructions that they were to relay tactfully to Mr. Hillman: (1) He was to come on Tuesday morning, March 14, at 10:35 A.M. (2) He would be met at the main door of the school and shown to the classroom by Dave Small, one of the volunteers making the original contact. (3) He would occupy the last twenty minutes of the period, from 10:40 to 11:00 A.M. (4) His demonstration and discussion were to be concerned with "Acids and Their Effect on Different Metals."

Mr. Hillman was asked by the student volunteers precisely what materials and equipment he desired for the purpose of his demonstration; these materials were provided and placed in usable order before his visit. Billy Southall, one of the volunteers, assumed responsibility for introducing the guest and extending appreciation when the presentation was completed.

Use in Specific Subjects

Among the resource people frequently brought into the school are those who are able to demonstrate efficiently a process, activity, device, or manufactured item.[20] In the band class, for example, the use of woodwind specialists to illustrate specific techniques can be very helpful. Typing classes occasionally have the opportunity to view a demonstration by a champion typist at speeds in excess of one hundred words per minute.

In the attempt to motivate students to consider scientific fields as career possibilities, industry has in recent years encouraged cooperation on the part of schools and industry to improve secondary-school science instruction. As a result, specialists actively engaged in scientific pursuits are frequently invited into the schools to give demonstrations and lectures in physics and chemistry classes.

Foreign-language classes lend themselves very well to the use of the native who can illustrate exact pronunciation and conversational fluency. Skill subjects—including vocal and instrumental music, typing and shorthand, physical education, homemaking, and shop courses—are particularly adapted to the use of demonstration and, therefore, to the use of specialists from both inside as well as outside the school.

The majority of resource people who are invited into the school give talks on their specialty; this is typical in such classes as English, history, and mathematics. Unfortunately, qualified speakers are not used as frequently as warranted by their abilities and their effect upon pupil learning. The individual who has something to say about a subject, who communicates with ease and at the level of the learners involved, and who views his talk to students as a community service can be an interesting and helpful aid to the teacher. The use of a carefully selected outside person has the advantage of novelty and, furthermore, often provides a desirable change of pace for the teacher and the students. All subjects in the secondary curriculum would benefit from the occasional use of such resource specialists.

Specific Suggestions

Many practical suggestions may be gained by examining the preceding examples of the use of resource people. Teachers will find

---

[20]Cross and Cypher, *op. cit.*, pp. 225–226, provide a useful discussion on when to use resource persons.

it helpful, however, to review this list of specific recommendations and cautions before they schedule the visit of a resource person.[21]

Recommendations

1. Keep a current file of the resource persons in your community who can and will contribute effectively to your teaching.

2. Select only the individual whose work, knowledge, skill, or experience enables him to make a contribution of high quality. Select a person who is able to express himself with fluency and ease and who will not talk over the heads of students. (It is possible for an individual to be so highly specialized that students cannot understand his particular message.)

3. Contact the resource person in time for him to prepare his contribution.[22] Let him know exactly what is expected of him in terms of subject-matter treatment and the timing of his presentation. Encourage the resource person to contribute his own ideas for improving the presentation. (Given an opportunity, he may offer a service not previously considered or suggest an improvement that has merit.)

4. Show consideration and courtesy to the resource person from the time of the original contact until he leaves the school building.

5. Allow students the opportunity to express their appreciation to the resource person for his visit to the class. Personally thank him for his assistance. (This may take the form of an oral expression of thanks as well as a written "thank you.")

Cautions

1. Don't ignore the possibility of using parents and recent graduates as resource persons.[23]

2. Don't forget to provide the resource person with all essential information necessary to make his presentation successful.

3. Don't stifle the originality of the resource person by insisting on rigid conformity to established procedures.

4. Don't fail to establish procedures for limiting the time spent by a given resource person and for keeping him on the subject.

5. Don't forget to prepare students for the visit of a resource person.

6. Don't fail to publicize the resource person's visit if students from other classes, or the public, are to be invited.

---

[21]Mills and Douglass, *op. cit.*, p. 334, list certain essential class activities related to the visit of a resource person.

[22]Jean D. Grambs, William J. Iverson, and Franklin K. Patterson, *Modern Methods in Secondary Education*, rev. ed. (New York: The Dryden Press, 1958), pp. 207–209, enumerate specific suggestions to aid in preparing for the resource visitor.

[23]*Ibid.*, pp. 209–210, stress the desirability of using parents and graduates as resource visitors.

Kimball Wiles, *Teaching for Better Schools*, 2d. ed. (Englewood Cliffs, N.J.: Prentice-Hall, 1959), pp. 267–269, points out the need for inviting parents into the classroom.

7. Don't fail to enlist the cooperation of other teachers in making a resource visitor's presentation successful if students from their classes are to be in the audience.

USE OF TEACHER-PREPARED MATERIALS

The use of teacher-prepared materials, like the continuous study of students and the effective use of resource persons, is a basic concern of sound instruction. However, teachers often tend to limit themselves to teaching materials found in the text and to other readily available supplementary materials. They sometimes feel they are incapable of producing materials that will assist in the instructional process better than materials already available.

Although the need for teacher-prepared instructional materials depends greatly upon the subject involved, it is common for teachers to rationalize that they have more materials now than they can use or that they cannot possibly afford the time to work out more themselves.[24] Among superior teachers in both large and small school systems, however, one finds individuals who consistently exercise ingenuity in producing materials that will serve the purposes of student learning better than any materials available.

The range of usable ideas is limited only by the teacher's ingenuity. Virtually all teachers, regardless of the quality of their instruction, make many of their own tests, and teachers of average ability often produce course outlines, study guides, and reading lists. Superior teachers, however, are known for their use of wide varieties of teaching materials to accomplish course objectives and for their inventiveness in producing their own materials and devices to serve the needs of specific students.

Classification of Materials

In order to survey the types of materials commonly produced by secondary-school teachers, it is necessary to assign these materials to certain arbitrary categories.[25]

Duplicated Materials

The most frequently used teacher-made instructional aids fall into the category of duplicated materials. Because of the large number of efficient duplicating machines currently available for the school, the teacher is able to produce cheaply, and with a minimum expenditure of time, written materials that serve as desirable supple-

---

[24]Unfortunately, few current general methods texts devote more than token attention to the important topic of preparation and use of teacher-made materials.

[25]See Chapter 6, pp. 110–120, for a discussion of the general use of materials and resources in unit instruction.

ments to textual materials. The following guides, aids, and supplements are some of the materials commonly duplicated:

- Course or unit objectives
- Course or unit outlines
- Sequential list of unit activities
- Unit assignment sheets
- Study questions
- Reading lists
- Examples of correct or incorrect student work
- Drawings, charts, or graphs
- Subjective and objective tests
- Evaluation checklists
- Self-appraisal devices
- Supplementary materials not found in the text or library
- Important announcements
- Messages to parents
- Study hints

Collected Materials

Many teachers have made effective use of certain types of materials that have been assembled over a period of time. Although such materials are seldom teacher made, they are collected and compiled by the teacher. Often they help meet the needs of students whose ability varies markedly from the class average. Such collections include:

- Relevant newspaper and magazine articles
- Course-related stories
- Course-related pamphlets
- Textbooks of differing interest and reading levels
- Student work of good and poor quality[26]

Materials for Meeting Individual Differences

Many teachers produce special materials in order to provide adequately for individual differences in their students. Unit contracts, typically calling for a three-step differentiation in work required of students—*difficult*, *average*, or *easy*—and many modifications of the basic contract idea are currently being used. Often years of experience have taught the teacher the value of using specific written help to assist less gifted students with their more difficult study problems. Study guides, reading lists, and self-evaluation checklists serve helpfully in this connection.

Materials to Aid in Student Self-Direction

Although quality teachers have consistently encouraged students to be self-directive, the recent emphasis on the importance of student self-direction has led inventive teachers to develop several different devices. They have developed self-evaluation report cards that encourage students to maintain an accurate record of their grades and progress in a given course; they have worked out checklists to be

[26]Student anonymity must be maintained whenever such collections are used.

employed by students in the self-correction of themes, grammar usage, and subject-matter content; and they have adapted or developed study guides that give direction to efficient study.

Miscellaneous Materials

Much of the teacher's time and ingenuity are devoted to producing materials and aids that, because of their diversity, are best grouped under the miscellaneous heading:

- Displays (Dioramas, woodwork exhibits, etc.)[27]
- Collections (Rocks, artifacts, best student themes, etc.)
- Specimens (Pressed flowers, stuffed animals, etc.)[28]
- Scale models (House, Shakespearean stage, etc.)
- Simple maps[29]
- Relief maps
- Charts
- Graphs
- Flat pictures[30]
- Personal photographs
- Color slides[31]
- Transparencies
- Filmstrips
- Microscopic slides
- Teaching machines
- Programed learning materials

Even a casual examination of the above list conveys the impression that teachers who wish to prepare their own teaching materials and devices must devote scores of hours to the task. Some teachers are willing to pay this price because they are convinced of the instructional value of teacher-made materials. A few teachers have been successful in making very simplified teaching machines for classroom use, and a small number have adapted certain segments of the course content to programed learning. The latter undertaking, however, calls for time expenditures, professional understanding, and facilities that the typical classroom teacher does not have.

Special Advantages

When the teacher goes to the trouble of preparing his own materials, it is usually because he feels strongly that they will serve the needs of the teaching-learning situation better than conventional materials. One of the basic advantages of teacher-made devices is

[27]See Cross and Cypher, *op. cit.*, Chapter 7, for a full treatment of displays and exhibits.

[28]Objects, models, and specimens are discussed by Mills and Douglass, *op. cit.*, pp. 302–304.

[29]Cross and Cypher, *op. cit.*, Chapter 6, provide an extensive treatment of the advantages and uses of maps, charts, and graphs.

[30]Rivlin, *op. cit.*, pp. 233–235, discusses the purposes and uses of flat pictures, charts, and diagrams.

[31]Mills and Douglass, *op. cit.*, pp. 289–290, list the factors to be considered in the selection of visual instructional materials.

Four important suggestions about the intelligent use of audio-visual materials are listed by Klausmeier, *op. cit.*, pp. 305–307.

that they are prepared with specific students in mind and are intended to serve particular purposes. The "Study Hints" sheet prepared for distribution to students who find it difficult to study effectively is a good illustration of the individualized use of a teacher-prepared device. If the teacher prepares such an aid for specific students, he usually considers their unique interests. When interest is present, students are motivated, and motivation encourages learning.

The teacher has the chance to exercise individual ingenuity whenever he makes or prepares his own materials and devices. He also has the opportunity to involve students in the production. This participation can have a positive effect on student learning as well as on interest arousal.

Because students—and teachers—are often bored by the commonplace, the uninspiring, and the expected, the teacher should welcome the opportunity to be different. If he can inject appropriate cleverness into the production of his own teaching materials and aids, the teacher may be effective as well as different. To be different just for the sake of being different is of little value, but to be different because it serves an instructional purpose is justified.

Principles Related to the Use of Teacher-Prepared Materials

An examination of the following principles, which apply to all teacher-made instructional materials, should help provide a foundation on which the teacher can base the production and use of his own teaching aids.

1. The production and use of teacher-prepared materials may take any form that serves the needs of instruction. How effective such materials will be as teaching devices depends upon their significance to the students, which, in turn, depends upon the extent to which they are related to the student's past experiences.

2. Teacher-prepared materials and devices can expand and strengthen course-related concepts, skills, memorizations, and attitudes.[32] At the same time, these materials may be used to meet the individual needs of students.

3. Teacher-prepared materials should be designed to help students achieve unit objectives. Unless other procedures better serve the educational purpose, teacher-prepared materials should be used frequently.

4. The duplication of written materials provides one device for supplementing basic oral or written materials. When duplicated materials are employed, their relationship to unit objectives must be clear to the learner. Although duplicated materials serve most frequently as supplements, they may also be used to present basic information to the class.

---

[32]A short discussion on enrichment materials is provided by Hansen, *op. cit.*, p. 222.

5. The extent to which duplicated materials are used will be determined, in some measure, by the availability of clerical help and duplicating machines.

6. The occasional use of well-prepared hand-out materials can add interest to routine instruction.

7. The effectiveness of teacher-made materials should be appraised each time they are used.

Correct and Incorrect Use

The brief examples below illustrate ways in which teacher-prepared materials are misused.

MRS. KAYE TEACHES BY THE TEXT

Mrs. Kaye taught tenth-grade English. Her supervisor had indicated on his rating sheet that her classroom performance was slightly below that of the average teacher in the school district. But Mrs. Kaye felt that keeping abreast of the task of teaching was about all she could manage without being concerned with producing additional hand-outs, reading guides, and differentiated assignment sheets. She taught by the text. When she gave a test (an infrequent occurrence), she either read the test items aloud or wrote them on the chalkboard before class and covered them with the movie screen.

MR. MENLO USES EXCESSIVE MATERIALS

L. M. Menlo was determined to make a good showing during his first year of teaching. Although his ninth-grade algebra class was using a sound text, he felt that supplemental hand-outs should be distributed about every third day. For the first month he was able to prepare and duplicate the hand-outs—but at the expense of time needed for other more pressing instructional duties. The students soon began to react negatively to each new distribution, and Mr. Menlo received complaints from the front office regarding the excessive use of ditto paper.

Proper use of a number of teacher-prepared materials as aids to goal achievement is the objective of many well-rounded teachers. They recognize the necessity for avoiding the excessive use of particular aids while neglecting other potentially helpful devices. The errors of Mrs. Kaye and Mr. Menlo are avoided in the case described below.

MR. SUTTON EMPLOYS TEACHING MATERIALS EFFECTIVELY

Steven Sutton was in his fifth year of teaching, and he loved his job. As a teacher of eleventh-grade United States history, he realized the necessity for providing students with a number of aids that would make their learning concrete, interesting, and meaningful.

At the first of the school year he laid out his master plan for the use of teacher- and student-made aids. New bulletin boards that were correlated with unit content would be displayed every Monday morning; they would be planned and worked out by students under teacher supervision. Hand-out materials would be distributed about once every six or seven days, whenever they seemed to serve a useful purpose. Students would be given exact instructions on how these materials were to be used and would be cautioned to keep them for further reference. Tentative plans called for giving students an outline of each new unit and for using study questions and occasional duplicated objective tests.

Mr. Sutton also planned for the extensive use of individual blank maps that students were to fill in according to instructions. Judy Seiter and Marilinn Bean, gifted art students, would occasionally be asked to draw maps on the board. Tom Wahl, who had considerable interest in woodwork, would be approached about making a scale model of a pioneer log cabin for display when the class was discussing the westward movement. Because of the teacher's intense interest in American history, he had traveled to many areas of historical significance and had taken numerous thirty-five-millimeter slides. These slides would be shown at the appropriate time.

Use in Specific Subjects

Certain subjects lend themselves well to the use of specific aids. The teaching of Spanish, for example, calls for the use of teacher-collected items that reflect Spanish culture as well as provide effective motivation for vocabulary drill. In the interest of effective instruction, the teacher might develop flash cards with words on one side and equivalent drawings on the other, assemble pictures portraying different aspects of the culture, or record native speech on tapes.

The mathematics teacher should continuously seek to develop means for simplifying difficult concepts. An ambitious teacher of geometry might build various shapes (spheres, cubes, triangles, circles, parabolas, cones, etc.) that he could employ in class with a high degree of success. The teacher of physics can find a helpful supply of teaching materials in radio and television repair shops. Such items are often available at no cost to the teacher if their purpose is explained.

Duplicated music is used effectively in vocal and instrumental classes. Choral groups at times are asked to learn a certain selection when only a single copy of the music is available. The needed music can be reproduced from a single copy with a minimum expenditure of time and effort if the necessary equipment and facilities are available.

In social studies classes, teachers make excellent use of acetate pockets in which a map can be inserted, leaving it visible to the class. By means of a grease pencil the teacher may then trace out a certain route, encircle an area of particular importance, or pinpoint a given spot without injury to the map itself.

The teaching of all secondary-school subjects can be made more effective through the use of aids and devices that have been carefully constructed by teachers to serve a particular purpose. Mathematics is one area in which much more could and should be done through the use of special teaching devices to make difficult abstract concepts more concrete. This calls for ingenuity and experimentation on the part of dedicated, capable mathematics teachers.

Specific Suggestions

The following suggestions may be usefully adapted by the individual who has had experience in the use of teacher-prepared materials.

Recommendations

1. Be sure that each teacher-made device serves a specific instructional purpose, and give careful consideration to the *type* of objective it is designed to help achieve. Furthermore, make sure that students understand the relationship of teacher-developed materials to the unit and to the course.

2. Use teacher-devised materials to help meet the individual needs of students by providing motivation for students with special problems, helping gifted students work to their capacities, and encouraging student self-direction.

3. Organize duplicated materials attractively and simply so that their purpose is clear, and be sure that the vocabulary in such materials is readily understood by a majority of students. Give an easily understood oral or written explanation of how these hand-out materials should be used.

4. Use teacher-prepared materials to serve a range of instructional purposes. Think of different ways of using such materials to promote learning.

5. Prepare materials to meet student interest as long as a useful instructional purpose is served. If humor is introduced through the use of these materials, take steps to see that it, too, serves an instructional purpose.

6. Encourage school administrators to provide physical facilities, equipment, and clerical help so that all teachers will be able to produce their own instructional materials.

7. Reproduce the best materials and aids made by your colleagues if such devices will help you teach better. Duplicate noncopyrighted materials of particular value to instruction if they are not easily accessible to students.

Cautions

1. Don't overlook the possible value of student-prepared materials.

2. Don't view duplicated materials as the only teacher-prepared aid to instruction.

3. Distribute hand-out materials *only* when this is the best instructional procedure.

RECURRING INSTRUCTIONAL CONCERNS IN REVIEW

Three recurring instructional concerns—continuous study of the student, the use of resource persons, and the use of teacher-prepared materials—have been examined in this chapter. Employed effectively by a well-organized teacher, each has a unique contribution to make to the teaching-learning process.

A continuous study of the student provides the teacher with a basis for the effective use of content and methods. The information gained involves an acquaintance with the mental, physical, social, and emotional status of students, all of which are subject to variation. Several devices are used in acquiring and keeping this information current—cumulative records, teacher-student conferences, parent-teacher conferences, sociometric devices, and purposeful observation.

The resource person may be used by the alert teacher to enrich his instruction. With the aid of a carefully assembled file of resource persons, such a teacher can invite to his class the most helpful individual from a range of possibilities. Thus, specialists within the community can be employed to add variety and to serve particular instructional needs.

Superior teachers consistently exercise ingenuity in planning, assembling, and producing materials that serve the purposes of student learning. Among these materials are duplicated items, collections of various types, and a wide range of miscellaneous devices—displays, specimens, models, maps, charts, pictures, slides, and simple teaching machines. The production and use of such teacher-prepared materials may take any form that serves the needs of instruction.

PROBLEMS FOR STUDY AND DISCUSSION

1. Explain fully the following statement: Improved student behavior is the basic concern of education.
2. Why is the *continuous* study of students repeatedly emphasized in this chapter?
3. If you found that students in your teaching major were achieving in a range extending over three grade levels, how would you alter procedures to meet the students' needs? Be specific.
4. Suggest three procedures that the teacher can follow to keep up-to-date on the changing relationship of students to their peers. Be specific.
5. How does the cumulative record aid in the continuous study of students? Explain.

6. What is the difference between general observation and specific observation of students? Does each have a definite purpose? Explain.

7. Assumption: You have discovered there are three social isolates in your class of thirty students. Would this affect your teaching procedures? How?

8. Give an example taken from your own experience as a high-school student or from your friends' experiences in which your teacher used incorrect procedures in the continuous study of his students.

9. List the main resources in your community that can be employed to help you teach your subject-matter major more efficiently. Of these, which is the most helpful? Why?

10. In the order of their importance, list the traits that should characterize the effective resource person.

11. Explain the specific steps you would take in assembling a file of resource persons.

12. In what specific area of your teaching minor do you have weaknesses that might be partially compensated for by the use of a resource person? List two or more weaknesses.

13. Why are interest and motivation said to be aroused by the use of well-chosen resource persons? Be specific.

14. Assumption: As an experienced teacher you have been approached by a new teacher for suggestions relating to the use of the resource person. List the cautions you would propose.

15. List seven types of duplicated materials that are frequently produced and used by teachers in your teaching major.

16. Indicate the types of teacher-made collections that serve the most useful educational purpose. Which one will be most helpful to you in teaching your subject-matter major?

17. Identify at least three practical devices the teacher might use to help students become self-directive.

18. Which three of the following teacher-made or student-made devices will be of greatest help in teaching your subject-matter minor: specimens, displays, models, relief maps, charts, personal photographs, flat pictures, and transparencies? Why?

19. Identify a teacher you currently know who has been singularly successful in the production and use of self-made aids. Why is he successful in this particular area? Could you be equally successful? Why?

20. Which specific subjects lend themselves best to the use of teacher-made materials? Why?

RECOMMENDED READINGS

Continuous Study of the Student

Burton, William H., *The Guidance of Learning Activities*, 3d. ed. New York: Appleton-Century-Crofts, Inc., 1962, pp. 150–151 and Chapters 8–10.

Carter, William L., Carl W. Hansen, and Margaret G. McKim, *Learning to Teach in the Secondary School.* New York: The Macmillan Company, 1962, Chapter 4.

Grambs, Jean D., William J. Iverson, and Franklin K. Patterson, *Modern Methods in Secondary Education*, rev. ed. New York: The Dryden Press, 1958, pp. 47–49 and Chapter 3.

Hansen, Kenneth H., *High School Teaching.* Englewood Cliffs, N.J.: Prentice-Hall, Inc., 1957, Chapter 2.

Horrocks, John E., *The Psychology of Adolescence,* 2d. ed. Boston: Houghton Mifflin Company, 1962, Chapters 2–7.

Klausmeier, Herbert J., *Teaching in the Secondary School.* New York: Harper & Brothers, 1958, Chapter 2.

McKean, Robert C., *Principles and Methods in Secondary Education.* Columbus, Ohio: Charles E. Merrill Books, Inc., 1962, Chapter 2.

Mills, Hubert H., and Harl R. Douglass, *Teaching in High School,* 2d. ed. New York: Ronald Press, 1957, Chapters 4 and 5.

Nordberg, H. Orville, James M. Bradfield, and William C. Odell, *Secondary School Teaching.* New York: The Macmillan Company, 1962, Chapter 4.

Rivlin, Harry N., *Teaching Adolescents in Secondary Schools,* 2d. ed. New York: Appleton-Century-Crofts, Inc., 1961, Chapter 14.

Wellington, C. Burleigh, and Jean Wellington, *Teaching for Critical Thinking: with Emphasis on Secondary Education.* New York: McGraw-Hill Book Company, 1960, Chapter 3.

Use of Resource Persons

Batchelder, Howard T., Maurice McGlasson, and Raleigh Schorling, *Student Teaching in Secondary Schools,* 4th ed. New York: McGraw-Hill Book Company, 1964, pp. 182–183.

Cross, A. J. Foy, and Irene F. Cypher, *Audio-Visual Education.* New York: Thomas Y. Crowell Company, 1961, pp. 218 and 225–226.

Grambs, Jean D., William J. Iverson, and Franklin K. Patterson, *Modern Methods in Secondary Education,* rev. ed. New York: The Dryden Press, 1958, pp. 205–210.

Hansen, Kenneth H., *High School Teaching.* Englewood Cliffs, N.J.: Prentice-Hall, Inc., 1957, pp. 308–311.

McKean, Robert C., *Principles and Methods in Secondary Education.* Columbus, Ohio: Charles E. Merrill Books, Inc., 1962, pp. 167–168.

Mills, Hubert H., and Harl R. Douglass, *Teaching in High School,* 2d. ed. New York: Ronald Press, 1957, pp. 333–334.
pp. 209–210.

Wiggins, Samuel P., *Successful High School Teaching.* Boston: Houghton Mifflin Company, 1958, pp. 164–165.

Wiles, Kimball, *Teaching for Better Schools,* 2d. ed. Englewood Cliffs, N.J.: Prentice-Hall, Inc., 1959, pp. 267–269.

Use of Teacher-Prepared Materials

Cross, A. J. Foy, and Irene F. Cypher, *Audio-Visual Education.* New York: Thomas Y. Crowell Company, 1961, Chapters 4–9.

Hansen, Kenneth H., *High School Teaching.* Englewood Cliffs, N.J.: Prentice-Hall, Inc., 1957, pp. 220–237.

Klausmeier, Herbert J., *Teaching in the Secondary School.* New York: Harper & Brothers, 1958, Chapter 11.

Mills, Hubert H., and Harl R. Douglass, *Teaching in High School,* 2d. ed. New York: Ronald Press, 1957, pp. 294–304.

Rivlin, Harry N., *Teaching Adolescents in Secondary Schools,* 2d. ed. New York: Appleton-Century-Crofts, Inc., 1961, Chapter 8.

PART FOUR

SPECIAL TEACHING PROBLEMS

13

Serving Instructional Purposes Through Discipline

The best classroom environment is one that results in efficient learning,[1] and any controls imposed upon a group of students should promote instruction. Burdening students with authoritarian edicts simply to assert the right of command is not only educationally unsound but also unjustifiable in terms of human relationships.[2] Sound classroom control may be defined as *the intelligent manipulation of all circumstances and factors in the schoolroom to serve the purposes of instruction.*

Effective discipline is closely related to classroom control. Discipline involves the use of guidance techniques to encourage students to become self-directive; it is not basically coercive in nature.[3] The end result of successful discipline, then, is *intelligent self-direction.*[4] Teachers who help students toward meaningful, `conscious self-direction also achieve sound classroom control.

---

[1]Lee J. Cronbach, *Educational Psychology,* 2d. ed. (New York: Harcourt, Brace and World, 1963), p. 498, views additional learning as one of the benefits of effective classroom management.

[2]George J. Mouly, *Psychology for Effective Teaching* (New York: Henry Holt, 1960), p. 461, indicates that constructive "discipline embodies the principles of mental hygiene and hence can be an important force in promoting mental health on the part of the child."

[3]The limitations of punishment as a means of achieving changed behavior are discussed by Frederick J. McDonald, *Educational Psychology* (San Francisco: Wadsworth Publishing Company, 1959), pp. 505–508.

[4]Arden N. Frandsen, *Educational Psychology* (New York: McGraw-Hill Book Company, 1961), pp. 489–490, states that the teacher's basic concern in assisting students toward social development is to encourage rational self-discipline as an end result.

George V. Sheviakov and Fritz Redl, *Discipline for Today's Children and Youth,*

The negative implications of the term *discipline* worry the future teacher, and the in-service teacher is frequently concerned because his attempts to maintain discipline have been unsuccessful. Anxiety is justifiably felt by a large proportion of teachers, for several studies have reported that the inability to control the classroom behavior of students is the number one cause of teacher failure.[5]

Many administrators think that the best way to evaluate a potentially successful teacher is to ask: "Can he (or she) control the class?" If the prospective teacher fails to give the impression that he can effectively control the class, he is not hired.

The experienced teacher knows that if he is unable to create and maintain an effective but tension-free classroom environment, the efficiency of his teaching will be markedly diminished.[6] Reducing the role of the teacher to that of a policeman is a humbling experience to which many instructors have been subjected. When it is necessary to maintain order through the exercise of brute force, learning suffers and teaching, if such it be, lacks satisfaction.

Educators have repeatedly attempted to classify classroom control problems according to kind and cause.[7] This type of grouping is useful and provides a framework within which the details of classroom control can be intelligently considered.

Batchelder, McGlasson, and Schorling propose a useful breakdown for considering the many facets of classroom control: (1) constructive discipline, (2) preventive discipline, and (3) remedial discipline.[8] Other writers have viewed constructive discipline as an aspect of preventive discipline and have combined these two general categories.

Others view discipline from four somewhat varying philosophical points of view. These differences are apparent in the following statements:[9]

---

rev. ed. (Washington, D.C.: National Education Association, [ASCD], 1956), pp. 17–22, speak out strongly on the need for educating for self-discipline.

Edwin J. Brown and Arthur T. Phelps, *Managing the Classroom*, 2d. ed. (New York: Ronald Press, 1961), pp. 118–119, list three progressive steps leading toward self-control.

[5]W. R. Flesher, "The Beginning Teacher," *Educational Research Bulletin*, 1945 (Jan.), *24*: 14–18+.

[6]Cronbach, *op. cit.*, p. 502, speaks out for a middle-of-the-road approach between teacher domination and total lack of teacher control.

[7]Brown and Phelps, *op. cit.*, p. 119, identify several of the general causes of pupil offenses.

William H. Burton, *The Guidance of Learning Activities*, 3d. ed. (New York: Appleton-Century-Crofts, 1962), pp. 551–552, classifies specific acts of assumed misbehavior under several headings.

Causes of disciplinary infractions are discussed by Gail M. Inlow, *Maturity in High School Teaching* (Englewood Cliffs, N.J.: Prentice-Hall, 1963), pp. 346–349.

[8]Howard T. Batchelder, Maurice McGlasson, and Raleigh Schorling, *Student Teaching in Secondary Schools*, 4th ed. (New York: McGraw-Hill Book Company, 1964), p. 81.

[9]Adapted from Norma E. Cutts and Nicholas Moseley, "Four Schools of School Discipline; a synthesis," *School and Society*, 1959 (Feb.), 87:87.

School One: The term *discipline* is not recognized as a problem of classroom operation. The teacher who is teaching effectively and well will have the full cooperation of his students.

School Two: A traditional approach to discipline is a sound one. All infractions result in punishment, sometimes severe.

School Three: Although students occasionally engage in disruptive behavior, this is understandable and normal. It will be necessary to exercise a measure of control at times to protect the rights of other students, but severe punishment in the traditional sense of the word is not sanctioned.

School Four: Misbehavior in the classroom is symptomatic of some problem. Proper classroom control consists of identifying the causes and taking whatever steps are necessary to remove the causes.

Classroom control can also be analyzed by categorizing problems according to the principles involved. This procedure is used in the following section, where the principles related to various aspects of teaching are discussed.

PRINCIPLES BASIC TO EFFECTIVE CLASSROOM CONTROL

Although it is possible to cite numerous examples of disciplinary situations that were effectively or ineffectively handled, it will serve a more useful purpose if the principles that underlie sound solutions to classroom behavior problems are first identified and discussed.[10] It is quite impossible to memorize a solution for each situation that can arise, but if one is guided by a sound knowledge of relevant principles,[11] he can be considered well equipped to cope with discipline problems.

A discussion of all the principles related to classroom control is impractical, for there is hardly a principle in the field of educational psychology that does not have some bearing on student classroom behavior. Those that have particular relevance are singled out here for brief mention.

The Effect of the Curriculum

Classroom control becomes easier when the curriculum is geared to the students' achievement and interests. Youngsters who

---

[10]Principles for governing student behavior together with procedures to be used in the development of self-control are listed and discussed by Burton, *op. cit.*, pp. 557–559.

Four basic democratic principles and related subprinciples essential to effective classroom discipline are presented by Sheviakov and Redl, *op. cit.*, pp. 10–16.

[11]Mouly, *op. cit.*, pp. 159–160, expresses a sound point of view on the use of generalizations as a guide to the solution of classroom discipline problems.

find the course too difficult are frequently uninterested, discouraged, and, therefore, disruptive. Those who find the course too easy are similarly affected, so that both groups have the potential for creating situations that adversely affect discipline.

The student who feels that the curriculum will further his personal interests is likely to engage in goal-oriented activities and, therefore, is not inclined to misbehave.[12] Young would-be mechanics usually have tremendous interest in the auto-mechanics shop and in class-related activities, while girls who know that they must seek employment as soon as they graduate listen to every hint the teacher gives for improving their shorthand speed.

The Effect of Planning

The selection of second-best procedures for achieving instructional goals invites classroom disturbances. Continuation of a classroom lecture long beyond the attention span of average members of the class will result in inattention and restlessness. Classroom attention *is* encouraged, however, when effective planning precedes the attempt to teach. Teaching by ear not only leads students haltingly toward poorly defined goals, but it also sets the stage for student misbehavior.

Planning should meet the varied needs of all students in the group.[13] A knowledge of the range of ability, background, achievement, and desire to learn will help the teacher plan realistically and, therefore, achieve sound classroom control. Individual differences among students include variation in intelligence, aptitude, achievement, training, and motivation. Failure to deal intelligently with these factors means that poor teaching and, hence, poor discipline will probably result.[14] Efficient planning must be based upon a thorough acquaintance with individual class members, for each student can pose a control problem if the instructional approach is inappropriate for him.

The knowledgeable teacher plans from day to day to meet specific classroom control problems he knows will arise. In tension-free preparation after school, he can plan sound solutions to the problems he feels will have to be met the next day. For example, he knows that the procedures he uses in the class held just before the football game must be particularly interesting.

---

[12]*Ibid.*, pp. 494–495.

[13]Three different methods of planning and control—undirected activities, teacher-controlled activities, and group-controlled activities—are illustrated and discussed by Cronbach, *op. cit.*, pp. 499–502.

A helpful treatment of essential teacher preparation for the first day of school is provided by Burton, *op. cit.*, pp. 542–544.

[14]Sheviakov and Redl, *op. cit.*, pp. 46–47, relate problems of discipline to dissatisfactions in the work process.

Inefficient use of aids in a classroom often sets off a flurry of irrelevant comments and results in wasted time. Such inefficiency can be avoided by careful advance planning. Planning is particularly necessary when using motion pictures, slide projections, tape recorders, and other devices that require some skill in operation.

The Effect of Objectives and Procedures

Goals that seem unachievable to the learner may cause behavior difficulties.[15] Large objectives should be approached step by step, and the student should advance to the next step only after he has understood the preceding ones.[16] Before a student attempts the study of calculus, for example, he must first acquire the progressively more difficult concepts in algebra.

When the teacher selects an inappropriate procedure for achieving a specific goal, he is hindering the child's desire to be attentive. For instance, when the homemaking teacher permits students to go through the trial and error of making a special dessert without explaining how it is to be done, attention and interest are soon lost. Carefully chosen procedures, on the other hand, promote desired classroom attention.

The Effect of Activity and Experience

The student must learn for himself, even though the teacher may set the stage for effective stimulation through group participation. The danger lies in the assumption that group activities naturally result in efficient learning. Frequently they are quite inefficient, as when immature youngsters are allowed to discuss problems of national importance without adequate teacher direction.

Students who come from culturally deprived environments will usually reflect that environment, even though their behavior runs counter to the teacher's desire. Occasionally unknowing and uninformed teachers punish students for supposed infractions that they could not avoid because of their environmental conditioning.[17] Poor speech habits, the lack of common courtesies, and the lack of personal cleanliness are all weaknesses arising from poor environmental conditions.

---

[15]A brief but helpful examination of the relationship of classroom goals and motivation for learning is provided by Cronbach, *op. cit.*, pp. 525–526.

The danger of imposing adult goals upon immature learners is pointed out by Mouly, *op. cit.*, p. 493.

[16]See the discussion of the hierarchical nature of objectives by Asahel D. Woodruff, *Basic Concepts of Teaching; with Brief Readings* (San Francisco: Chandler Publishing Company, 1962), pp. 71–73.

[17]Helpful criteria for determining whether punishment should be employed are provided by Herbert J. Klausmeier, *Teaching in the Secondary School* (New York: Harper & Brothers, 1958), p. 398.

The Effect of Meaning

When meaning is emphasized in preference to rote memorization, students tend to be less resistant to learning. Sound study patterns and desirable classroom behavior are by-products of situations in which comprehension is a dominant concern.[18] A case in point is the enthusiasm of a class whose English teacher is able to read Shakespeare and make it meaningful to the students at their own level of understanding.

Learners who are able to relate parts to the whole meaningfully tend to be interested in details as well as in the overall picture. Denied the insights made possible through such relationships, they tend to lose interest. A student in shop, for example, will generally be interested in learning how to sharpen a plane if he can see that it will help him produce a desired end table.

The Effect of Habits

Habits of misbehavior can result in poor classroom conduct.[19] For this reason, the teacher who is concerned with creating and maintaining effective classroom control should devote considerable attention to helping students develop habits that will facilitate learning. Among such worth-while habits are politeness in personal relationships, listening thoughtfully to classroom discussions, and studying effectively alone when it is expected.

Habits, both good and bad, resist change and can be perpetuated through only occasional repetition. The habit of rudeness within the classroom will be reinforced by an occasional outburst, even if the student does not exhibit rudeness all the time in dealing with his classmates.

The breaking of habits harmful to effective classroom behavior calls for repeated avoidance of the habit. Each time the students show a desire to follow a wrong habit pattern, they must meet the teacher's firm insistence that they behave otherwise. No variation, no compromise should be allowed until a new habit is well established.

The Effect of Growth and Development

Changes that occur in students during the adolescent years underlie many of the so-called disciplinary difficulties in the classroom. A teacher who does not understand the nature and cause of these changes is severely handicapped in dealing intelligently with related classroom behavior problems. For example, a teacher who is not

---

[18]Woodruff, *op. cit.*, p. 247, reviews the role of concepts in the control of behavior.

[19]*Ibid.*, pp. 114–121, provides a useful treatment of the nature and formation of habits.

aware of the reason for the lack of emotional control in a pubescent girl may jump to faulty conclusions, such as the assumption that she is basically unstable.

Mental Ability

One, but only one, of the factors that determine the individual student's behavior in the classroom is intellectual capacity. A student can achieve no more than his natural ability will permit. When teachers consistently pressure students to overachieve, emotional reactions may arise that, in turn, create an unfavorable bias toward study and a continuing aversion to learning. Both dull and bright students may become discouraged or bored and may turn to pursuits that are not in the interest of effective learning. The wise teacher knows his students and gears his teaching to individual capacities.

Because students vary a great deal in the rate at which mental ability grows, unseasoned and uninformed teachers often make unjustified comparisons of student capacities, effort, or achievement. Normal students of the same chronological age may differ markedly in their ability to be attentive to classroom procedures because of the rate of growth of their mental abilities. Misbehaving Walter, slow in maturing, may find it quite impossible to become interested in the teacher's lecture on city government.

If subnormal capacities are indicated by recently administered intelligence tests and are corroborated by personal observation, the teacher may find it desirable and in the interest of the entire class to refer students with such marked intellectual limitations to special agencies within the school district or community. Often these agencies can provide better educational opportunities for these youngsters than can the school. Such youngsters with subnormal capacities can be a consistent distraction to other students and may retard general class progress.

Since studies during the past few years have revealed that intelligence test scores are influenced by environmental factors,[20] it is wise for a teacher to withhold judgment about the capacity of a misbehaving youngster (or any youngster) until he has had an opportunity to observe the child's behavior under a range of circumstances. Certain teachers tend to equate misbehavior with lack of capacity. For example, the history teacher was quite sure that Tammy was somewhat limited in capacity because she was always seeking attention in ways that disturbed the class. When he had the opportunity to examine her score on the standardized mental maturity test, he was surprised to discover that her I.Q. was 112.

Physical and Social Maturation

Because girls achieve physical maturity more rapidly than boys,

---

[20]See Mouly, *op. cit.*, pp. 211–214.

social problems frequently develop during adolescence. These problems can affect the study climate of the classroom and give rise to misbehavior. Certain socially aggressive girls, for example, are known for their constant classroom chattering, a practice pursued without regard for its effect on the class.[21]

The change in attitude toward the opposite sex that comes with the onset of puberty is reflected in classroom behavior. The teacher must see that the newly intensified interest does not interfere with the main function of the school. He must realize, however, that this interest is a normal outgrowth of biological development and will play an increasingly important role in personality development.

Adolescents find it difficult to accept fully some of their classmates because of obvious variations in body structure, height, and weight. Self-acceptance of these physical changes is equally difficult. Poor social adjustments are aggravated by a lack of acceptance, and withdrawal tendencies are not uncommon at this age. JoAnn, for example, is a head taller than most of the girls in the room, while Dave, who is the same age, is the shortest person in the class. Both students are having problems making adequate social adjustments.

A physical problem may be the source of a student's academic failure. Such problems as poor vision, poor hearing, limited muscular coordination, heart disease, or lung ailments may result in extensive or limited academic failure, which, in turn, may lead to misbehavior.

Well-nourished, healthy students are more likely to exhibit acceptable classroom behavior than hungry students, who are often uncooperative, grouchy, and disruptive. Furthermore, students who are at a physical disadvantage because of inadequate nourishment, also often suffer social and cultural disadvantages because they come from economically marginal or submarginal homes.

The explosive physical energy of the teenager may give rise to horseplay within the classroom in the form of scuffling, throwing books, or running. When provision is made for extensive and vigorous exercise during the school day, the tendency for horseplay is diminished.

The student who consistently withdraws from activity with his peers poses a problem to himself and a challenge to the teacher. To the extent that this withdrawal hampers the student in developing effective social behavior patterns, it should be of concern to the teacher.

The Effect of Environmental Influences

The conditioning influences of the home, the peer group, and the teacher help determine the classroom behavior of each student.

[21]Typical examples of disciplinary situations resulting from student interaction are described by Jean D. Grambs, William J. Iverson, and Franklin K. Patterson, *Modern Methods in Secondary Education*, rev. ed. (New York: The Dryden Press, 1958), pp. 424–426.

Each of these factors plays a unique and varied role in furthering or inhibiting individual adjustment, personal attitudes, and academic success.

The Home

Students who come from democratically oriented homes tend to be more disobedient, although they are more self-directive and inquisitive than youngsters from autocratic homes. The autocratic teacher may find that the child from the democratic home will have difficulty adjusting to teacher expectations.

Certain forms of adolescent instability may be related to earlier rigid controls in the home.[22] The tendency to be argumentative, a habit often characteristic of certain adolescent periods, is encouraged in an authoritarian home environment and may be transplanted to the school setting. Paul, for example, viewed his father as a tyrant with whom he was always in conflict. When he discovered that his teacher also insisted on having his own way, Paul exhibited his argumentative nature in the classroom.

The youngster whose home life has encouraged emotional stability will tend to exhibit mature behavior in the classroom. Conversely, emotional outbursts, such as aggressive behavior, excessive argumentation, displays of temper, and frequent crying, may be related to unstable home environments.

Culturally deprived environments impose restrictions that may be reflected in certain types of classroom misbehavior. Barney not only misused the English language through gross violations of standard grammar, but he also abused it through a constant torrent of profanity. Knowing Barney's family background, his teacher could see that it was difficult for the boy to speak otherwise.

Furthermore, unhappy home environments can cause in-school behavior problems for which the teacher has no solution or even an explanation. The teacher is often placed in the position of having few facts about the out-of-school life of a student to help him deal effectively with that student. This is the case with Kurt, a troubled, surly youngster who brings his domestic tensions to school without the teacher's knowing the origin of his behavior.

Students often come to school after mistreatment and abuse at home. Winifred found it impossible to focus on her studies at school because her thoughts were on the beating her father had given her the night before. In some instances when restraining home influences are discarded in the more permissive atmosphere of the school, students tend to misbehave.[23] Janet was reared in a lower-

---

[22]Inlow, *op. cit.*, p. 347, describes three home situations that make it difficult for an adolescent to adjust to a properly conducted classroom situation.

[23]Mouly, *op. cit.*, p. 33, suggests that children from autocratic homes may feel insecure in the permissive atmosphere of certain classrooms. He feels that, in such cases, behavioral limits are necessary.

class home where she was dominated by her father, four older brothers and sisters, and an unmarried aunt. As a result, Janet used every opportunity to exert her own authority in the classroom with domineering, ungracious behavior toward her peers and her teacher.

The students' habits and outlook on life are also strongly influenced by television. A taste for a certain type of entertainment, some patterns of speech, and certain behavioral characteristics are encouraged by this medium and are reflected in the classroom.

Another factor to remember is that siblings subjected to the same home influences may exhibit quite different traits in the classroom. Because Lorna has been classified by her teachers as a discipline problem, these teachers will be inclined to think of her brother Arthur as posing the same sort of problem. Judgment, however, should be withheld, pending first-hand experience, since Arthur may be a different type of individual altogether.

The Peer Group

A student's acceptability to a peer-group clique may be related to the social status of his family. Many classrooms contain students who are ostracized because of poverty, poor dress, or socially unacceptable manners or speech resulting from cultural impoverishment. When such a situation exists, the teacher must shape the classroom environment so that the needs of the class as well as those of the individual may be met.

Social adjustments essential to adolescent development are encouraged in the informality of play situations involving other members of the peer group. Denied opportunities for such desirable activities under school sponsorship, students tend to compensate through horseplay and social exchanges in the classroom. A well-organized school activities program will benefit classroom control.

Language usage among adolescents, freed of conformity to adult standards, may be evidence of the existence of a new culture—a subculture—unique to them. The slang, the tendency for vulgar speech and profanity, and the disregard for correct grammar all point in this direction. Even a determined effort on the part of the teacher may not stem the tide, but it may exert a moderating influence.

The Teacher

The teacher should try to establish a personal relationship with each student in his class, a relationship that will aid the cause of instruction. Ideally, the teacher will attempt to create an environment in which the student feels confident and secure but in which he views the classroom as a place where learning is promoted.[24]

---

[24]McDonald, *op. cit.*, pp. 514–518, provides a useful explanation of the influence of classroom environment on student behavior.

Objectives that the teacher views as worthy of achievement may have little relationship to the individual goals that the students will work hard to achieve. Consider, for example, the learning of difficult grammatical structure. The teacher views this objective as worth while; the student often does not. Interestingly enough, many specialists in the field are now supporting the student's point of view. Student-teacher antagonisms, which impede instruction, often arise from the lack of common goals.

The learner who is intellectually stimulated tends to acquire a range of usable concepts (mental pictures). If the necessary stimulation is not provided either in the home or in the classroom, the student's progress may be retarded and classroom control problems may result. Youngsters of all capacities need intellectual stimulation.

The Effect of Adolescent Needs

The fulfillment or lack of fulfillment of adolescent needs will strongly influence the type of behavior that is exhibited in the classroom.[25] Adolescents need to be understood by a teacher who strives to help them meet their unsatisfied needs in socially acceptable ways; they need freedom from absorbing preoccupations; and they need affection, both at home and at school.

Teacher Understanding

Teachers who basically understand why students behave as they do are in a position to give positive direction to student behavior. Youngsters who engage in loud, boisterous, and sometimes coarse talk may be appraised by such teachers as adolescents who are ineptly and unskillfully reaching out for adult independence. Knowing that such behavior is transitional, these teachers can inoffensively guide student behavior to less extreme forms.

It is essential that the teacher understand each student as a person as well as a member of a group.[26] Within a group of thirty students, the wise teacher will identify many students whose actions are far from the class average. For instance, if Mary Jane is superior in English composition but below the mean in the physical sciences, the teacher will seek the reasons for this discrepancy as a basis for sound action. He must be prepared to deal intelligently with all students in terms of their individual differences.

Pressures from Unsatisfied Needs

When an adolescent's basic needs are not satisfied, pressures build up that may erupt into nonconforming or socially undesirable

[25]*Ibid.*, p. 504, points out that the means employed by students in satisfying needs are not always compatible with the goals of a learning situation.

[26]The desirability of understanding the students as individuals is stressed by Klausmeier, *op. cit.*, pp. 381–383.

behavior. Denied peer-group approval, for example, teenagers will brave adult wrath to gain such approval. Students often ride roughshod over the values of their teachers if they can thus win the praise of other students. Making light of the teacher's methods or personal mannerisms is a common device for winning the praise of adolescent peers.

If a student is missing something that he views as essential to the preservation of his personal, social, or biological life, he is ready to respond to any stimulus that he feels will help make up that deficiency.[27] A fifteen-year-old girl may be highly sensitive to the attention shown her by boys two years older. She is socially receptive to this stimulus, although it may prove to be a distraction to many of her teachers.

Age-related developmental tasks are of such absorbing concern to most teenagers that such tasks frequently overshadow academic concerns. When the teenage boy is confronted with a situation in which he must choose whether he will attend a basketball game or go unprepared to his English class the following day, the decision is most often in favor of going to the game with his peer group. Teenagers know that peer-group approval comes through participation in common endeavors.

Freedom from Preoccupations

Optimum adjustment presupposes a balanced satisfaction of basic needs. The well-adjusted student is one who is free of persistent absorbing preoccupations, who is accepted by his peers and by members of the opposite sex, and who has sound and rewarding associations with adults. As a result, he is secure and self-confident. Optimum adjustment, however, does not mean that a student's classroom behavior will conform to what an autocratic teacher assumes to be the ideal.

The secondary-school student's needs, as he sees them, are often in conflict with his needs as viewed by adults in authority over him. Mark's desire to play baseball after school was only enhanced by the teacher's insistence that he stay in to make amends for rude and unbecoming behavior toward two girls in the class. Anita's resolve to be the top student in her shorthand class led her to practice during the history lecture. This behavior, however, was in sharp contrast to her history teacher's concept of what her behavior should be.

Need for Affection

All adolescents need affection, although the behavioral manifes-

---

[27]Woodruff, *op. cit.*, p. 274.

McDonald, *op. cit.*, p. 505, tells of the case of a boy who obtained satisfaction by provoking his peers to laughter and of how the teacher met the situation through motivational techniques.

tations of this need often take strange forms.[28] This was the case with Evan. At sixteen his relationship with his stern, inflexible father had reached the point where Evan felt that the easiest solution was to leave home. Evan's reactions to his father's demands were violent, profane, and abusive. He needed the approval of understanding parents who were willing to give tangible evidence of their affection during the unstable adolescent years. Furthermore, Evan would have benefited from the patient understanding of his teachers, who instead tended to view him as a discipline problem.

The need for approval by the peer group—an extension of the need for affection—is particularly strong during adolescence,[29] but adolescents also need the approval of adults with whom they have repeated contact.[30] This becomes apparent when a young person is alone with his teacher; gone is the necessity for misbehavior geared to win the approval of his peers. Now he has only himself to please, and the real need for teacher approval is often discernible.

Ridicule and loss of prestige are extremely distasteful to the teenager, especially when they take place in the presence of his peers. Repeated studies of why students dislike certain teachers have revealed that ridicule is one of their most objectionable traits. In most cases, the wise teacher avoids punishing a student in the presence of his friends.

The Effect of Expectations

Realistic expectations on the part of parents, teachers, the peer group, and the student himself encourage consistent student effort that, in turn, promotes sound classroom behavior.

Parental Expectations

Parents at times impose upon their children unrealistic ambitions that run counter to the aptitudes, interests, and wishes of the children. The thwarted desire of a parent to complete medical school, for example, may cause the parent to select medicine as a desired professional goal for a son without considering his son's ability and desire. The teacher who finds a youngster bearing the burden of someone else's ambitions often finds a rebellious and frustrated youngster who presents a difficult behavior problem.

Teacher Expectations

The teacher's expectations should reflect a realistic acquaintance with student capacities, academic achievement, and personal de-

---

[28]According to Frandsen, *op. cit.*, p. 488, the rejected child may behave uncooperatively or destructively in the classroom.

[29]Cronbach, *op. cit.*, pp. 116–121, provides a helpful statement about the need for peer-group approval.

[30]See the discussion of "Need for Approval by Authority" by Cronbach, *op. cit.*, pp. 115–116.

sires. Teachers, like other adults, may err by expecting too much or too little of students.[31] To err either way is to invite the possibility of overt or covert rebellion.

Peer-Group Expectations

An adolescent who wishes to join or who is a member of a particular peer group will usually exert great effort to conform to the expectations of the group. If the peer group expects a member to be a troublemaker, he will try to conform in spite of the teacher's wish to the contrary.

Teenagers learn that there is a range of academic and social behavior acceptable to their peers, and they attempt to adjust their own behavior within this range. When the teacher expects behavior that goes beyond this range, he will probably encounter varying degrees of resistance. The student is frequently supported in this resistance by members of his peer group.

Self-Expectations

What a student expects of himself will be the result of his past experience and the concepts he has learned from these experiences. If he has found that he has mechanical aptitude, a student is likely to develop an interest in mechanics and acquire some competence in this area. If he suffers one social defeat after another, his self-image as a social person will suffer, and he may exhibit withdrawal tendencies. When his teachers have given him the impression that he is a troublemaker, he may conform to their picture of him.

The possession of a range of skills promotes self-confidence and heightens one's self-expectations. A student who has a limited number of skills to aid him in academic or social situations is severely handicapped. He often meets with failure and turns to the simpler task of gaining attention through unacceptable classroom behavior.

Desirable behavior is more often exhibited when the student feels he is a person of merit. The teacher can be of great assistance in helping the adolescent create a healthy and psychologically sound self-image. Each youngster, regardless of capacity, should encounter some measure of success to build his self-image, and it is the teacher's responsibility to help him succeed. The student will not, as a general rule, violate his belief that he is a person of worth and that he deserves respect.

The Effect of Readiness

Teachers often overlook how certain types of readiness affect the individual student's willingness and ability to engage in goal-oriented

[31]Problems caused by unrealistic teacher expectations are discussed by Klausmeier, *op. cit.*, pp. 387–389.

behavior.[32] Careful analysis of readiness factors can be useful to teachers in promoting an effective classroom study climate.

Readiness for a Voluntary Change

When the student feels a need for a change in behavior, he is ready for change. This need, however, must be a very personal one. The intensity with which the teacher feels the need for change in a given student's behavior may have no effect on the student. The mathematics teacher would have paid almost any price if Dean would stop making those semiaudible, depreciating remarks in the back of the room. They served Dean's ego needs, and he was not ready to give them up.

Gaining a clear mental picture of the need for behavioral change underlies the actual change. Before misbehaving students are willing to change their own disruptive behavior, they must understand that it is in their interest to do so. Voluntary change comes after proper insights have been acquired.

Mental Maturity and Conceptual Readiness

Immaturity is the cause of a lack of conceptual readiness in many students. Mental maturity is related to the process of maturation and should not be confused with slow learning.[33] Students not sufficiently mature to grasp specific concepts will feel great frustration if pressed for impossible achievement. Although the placement of course content at a given grade level presupposes that students are ready to learn it, this supposition is frequently false—as the failure of students at all grade levels attests.

The teacher should try to recognize the moment of optimum readiness for the introduction of a new concept, because premature exposure to difficult concepts may result in negative reactions and student inattention.[34] When the physics teacher introduced concepts that a large majority of the class could not understand, the students concentrated for a while, but their minds soon began to wander. Some students began to converse.

Physical Readiness

Physical readiness, related to neuro-muscular coordination, can impose restrictions on learning that are just as severe as those imposed by conceptual readiness.[35] The would-be typist who has poor muscular coordination will never be able to type at a high rate of

---

[32]Woodruff's discussion of "Readiness for Learning," *op. cit.*, Chapter 13, contains several implications for classroom discipline.

Chapter 14 in the present text contains a more detailed treatment of the effect of readiness on learning.

[33]See the discussion of the growth of mental ability on page 290.

[34]Lack of readiness as a possible cause of disinterest is discussed by Frandsen, *op. cit.*, p. 64.

[35]See Woodruff, *op. cit.*, p. 285.

speed unless, through the process of maturation, better coordination is achieved. Similarly, if the physically immature seventh-grade boy is thrust into athletic competition where he consistently fails, strong disruptive antagonisms may assert themselves. Motor skills can never be taught successfully before the student is physically ready to learn them.

The Effect of Motivation

How well a student responds to classroom procedures will depend partly on his motivation.[36] If his motivation is weak, he will probably seek more interesting pursuits. Frequently this takes the form of misbehavior. Norma was so highly interested in biological science that the teacher found it difficult to provide her with challenging reading materials. Yielding to his responsibility to the total group, the instructor left Norma to her own devices. Because her teacher neglected to help her and because she was not sufficiently motivated to find materials on her own, she became a troublemaker in the class.

The assumption that learners are equally motivated by the same set of circumstances is false. A teaching procedure that proves particularly interesting for one student may be quite boring for other students. And bored students tend to cause behavior problems.

If the teacher exercises appropriate controls, the need for approval and belonging as well as the desire for aggressive behavior may be made to serve as motivators. Competition in the classroom[37] is a form of aggression, while committee and small-group work may help satisfy the need for affiliation.

Motivation Through Self-Interest

Each individual relates all perceived occurrences to his own person and evaluates them in terms of their assumed effect on him and his environment. Reactions to classroom situations are, similarly, related to their assumed effect upon the student. If he feels that it will be advantageous for him to misbehave, he will misbehave. Thus Donna cut class and went to a movie with a girl friend because she knew that Mr. Bogg's lecture would be uninteresting.

When the learner places great value on certain goals, he will expend tremendous energy to achieve them. If the valued goal is to make an impression on a certain member of the opposite sex, motivation may be strong, and the adolescent may expend a great deal of

[36]*Ibid.*, Chapter 12, presents several basic concepts related to motivation that are of particular value to the student of classroom control.

Chapter 14 in the present text includes a more detailed treatment of the effect of motivation on learning.

[37]The advantages and disadvantages of competition are discussed and illustrated by Frandsen, *op. cit.*, pp. 218–220.

effort to achieve this goal. Classroom convention and teacher-imposed rules standing in his way may simply intensify his effort.

Motivation Through Successful Experiences

Motivation may be held at a desirable level by providing the learner with a proper balance between successes and failures. Unwise use of either praise or blame may also affect motivation and, consequently, classroom control.

Successful experiences tend to strengthen the student's self-concept and his desire to achieve higher goals. The person whose attention is centered on unit goals is seldom troublesome. Stella had been an excellent student in English grammar. Because she was successful, the more she learned, the more she wanted to learn. When the class began to study difficult noun clauses, her interest continued.

The desirable amount of praise or blame given by an instructor will vary with the student and the circumstances in which it is given. Lavish praise from a teacher, for example, can prove humiliating to a fifteen-year-old boy if given in the presence of his peer group. Teacher-student rapport may thus be disturbed. Mrs. Jex, another teacher, makes a policy of discovering the strong points of below-average students so that she can legitimately praise their work. On the other hand, she limits the praise given to gifted students—success is often its own reward.

When the teacher quickly rewards desired behavior with praise that results in satisfaction, there is a good chance that this behavior will recur. Therefore, teachers who wish to perpetuate certain behavior should praise it. Mr. Parris took advantage of the P.T.A. meeting to tell Mr. and Mrs. McIntyre how much improvement their son Blaine had shown in his last English theme. The teacher was aware that Blaine had received considerable pressure from home to improve and anticipated that this praise would free Blaine from undue parental pressure as well as stimulate him to further improvement.

Motivation Through Realistic Goal Setting

If goals are not carefully selected in consideration of student abilities, it is quite probable that students will meet with great frustration, and the stage will be set for disruptive behavior. Hoping that it might have a helpful influence, the physical education instructor placed Lindsey on a basketball team consisting of boys who played much better than he did. Because he could not measure up to team expectations, Lindsey became antagonistic and abusive.

Motivation Through Attention and Interest

Learning cannot take place if the learner is inattentive. Whether inattention leads to disruptive behavior or to daydreaming (overt and covert expressions of inattention), the net instructional result is negative. Leslie was preoccupied with thoughts of going away to college next year, and for her the Latin II class might just as well have been omitted.

Students focus attention on what interests them. A basic aspect of effective teaching involves identifying individual student interests and using them to achieve a high degree of motivation. The interested person is the attentive person, and the attentive individual usually does not create discipline problems.

Many student interests are lacking in depth and are, therefore, of limited help in promoting learning. The conscientious teacher is concerned about tapping the deeper motivations of immature students. Virtually all adolescents are interested in play activities, but the secondary-school instructor whose teaching procedures are largely composed of play-related activities will soon find himself in difficulty. Such was the case with Mr. Averett, who had difficulty keeping his general mathematics class interested. When students became extremely noisy and troublesome, he often announced that the class would play a game, although at times the game had little to do with unit goals. Frequent bending to superficial student interests may quickly subvert the real purpose of instruction, and the teacher must be aware of this possibility.

Motivation Through Contacting the Referent

The extent to which the student makes first-hand contact with the referent of the concept or a realistic facsimile will largely determine his interest in the concept. Vivid, real experiences promote interest and thus promote good behavior. Students in the civics class were enthusiastic about their visit to the city hall, where they had an opportunity to meet the city manager personally and hear him tell about the problems of city government.

CLASSROOM CONTROL IN PRACTICE

There can be no substitute for a knowledge of the principles underlying so-called discipline problems, but knowledge alone is not enough. One must have sufficient practice in the application of principles so that fumbling, trial-and-error attempts are replaced by a degree of sophistication in maintaining classroom discipline. Specific examples of discipline practices will help the beginning and experienced teacher alike to relate the preceding principles to actual practice.[38]

---

[38]Grambs, Iverson, and Patterson, *op. cit.*, pp. 459–461, present a number of descriptive classroom control situations aimed at giving prospective teachers and in-service teachers the opportunity to test their theories of discipline.

H. Orville Nordberg, James M. Bradfield, and William C. Odell, *Secondary School Teaching* (New York: Macmillan, 1962), pp. 219–220, provide similar test situations.

Unsound Procedures

Questionable classroom control practices are a matter of great concern to conscientious educators. The following examples point out different manifestations of unsound behavior.

MR. FOLKNER REACTED EMOTIONALLY

J. J. Folkner was a nervous teacher. Minor student infractions that should not have upset him gave rise to extreme reactions. When he observed that students were chewing gum, he stopped the class for a five-minute lecture on the social evils of gum chewing. If he discovered that students were whispering during the study period, he lost his temper. Occasionally, when students submitted late papers, he reacted violently before the entire class, although only a small minority of the class was at fault. His tenth-grade biology class was tense and lacking in warmth.

MISS INGRAM ACTED ON IMPULSE

Sally Ingram was a first-year teacher, fresh from a secondary methods class in which she had become acquainted with the necessity for maintaining discipline at all costs. On her first day in the new job she was put to the test by Bill Whitley, age fifteen. Seated in the rear of the class and being somewhat bored with the classroom procedures, Bill tossed his ninth-grade geography book to his friend two aisles to his right. Miss Ingram decided that this type of behavior must be stopped at once.

"Bill Whitley, leave the room and go to the principal's office immediately," she called loudly.

The boy hastily complied, confused and thunderstruck at the abruptness of his new teacher. Miss Ingram wondered what procedures she should follow from this point.

MR. BRINKS MADE AN ABRUPT CHANGE

Throughout the school year, the eleventh-grade United States history class had been permitted a measure of freedom customarily denied students in many other classes. They were allowed to talk freely at their seats. Even during the study period the instructor made no attempt to stifle this informal exchange of ideas, unless the noise reached unusual proportions.

It was only when Mr. Brinks made an exchange visit to the history class of a teacher of excellent reputation in another city that he realized his class was too noisy for study purposes. Shortly afterwards, Mr. Brinks was informed of his supervisor's imminent visit to his classroom. Panicked by the news, Mr. Brinks tried to impose a decree of total silence on his boisterous students. Overt rebellion was the result, since the students had become used to his laxity.

MRS. RUSKIN SHOWED INCONSISTENCY

Besides teaching a full six-period load, Mrs. Ruskin had been working hard to complete her master's degree. Sometimes she came to school fatigued before the day began. On such days her irritability was reflected in her relationships with students; virtually nothing went well. Student behavior was poor, and her teaching was correspondingly poor. At other times, when she had the opportunity for a weekend of rest, student behavior seemed to improve tremendously, and she exuded warmth and good humor. Students found it hard to interpret her inconsistency, however; they were never quite sure whether they could expect acceptance or rejection, praise or blame, warmth or coldness.

Variations of the unsound classroom control practices illustrated in the preceding examples occur in many classrooms. Mr. Folkner was unable to control his emotions when confronted with tension-producing classroom situations. Miss Ingram decided to act quickly but without fully considering the effect of her action on class members. Faced with the need for immediate general improvement in classroom control, Mr. Brinks sought to change student habits that had been fixed through prolonged repetition. Mrs. Ruskin's inconsistencies caused confusion in teacher-student relationships, which inevitably resulted in misbehavior.

Sound Procedures

Certain teachers in every secondary school are known for their ability to deal effectively and inoffensively with classroom control problems by using preventive as well as remedial discipline. Specific practices of such teachers are described in the following narrative accounts.[39]

MR. MOON COLLECTED INFORMATION ABOUT STUDENTS

From the first day of school Mr. Moon seemed to be entirely in command of his students, even his troublesome eighth-grade general mathematics class. The students liked him, and he was fond of them. When a new teacher asked him to explain his success in promoting desirable classroom behavior, he replied that he felt it was related to his study of each student as an individual.

"As soon as I can," he said, "I begin to collect information about each student. I talk to them about their interests; I determine what their likes and dislikes are. It is a wise practice, I feel, to form an opinion about the student's capacity based upon careful observation and first-hand experience before looking at the test-determined I.Q. They're not always in agreement, you know.

"As soon as I have a substantial amount of information, I try to put it to good use in my teaching. If a student has a limited capacity, he may not be able to acquire certain concepts, and his limitation has to be taken into account. This approach is realism in teaching. Students with specific interests should be encouraged to relate these interests to the classwork as much as possible. Youngsters with culturally impoverished backgrounds are not re-

[39]Several examples of disciplinary problems that were handled adequately by teachers are described by Grambs, Iverson, and Patterson, *op. cit.*, pp. 429–430.

sponsible for many of their academic difficulties, and it should not be inferred that they are. They need, of course, consistent, step-by-step assistance to bring them up to the desired level of competence."

MR. HONE EMPLOYED QUIET FIRMNESS

Two minutes before the final bell was to ring, the smoldering quarrel between Homer and Lynn erupted into a bona-fide fist fight. There were several exchanges of blows before Mr. Hone could separate the boys. The teacher spoke quietly and firmly.

"I will not tolerate this in my room. Homer, you sit on this side of the room, and, Lynn, you sit on the opposite side until the bell rings."

After the bell rang, Mr. Hone called both boys to his desk.

"I want to talk to you individually about this before I decide what is to be done."

In separate talks with the boys the cause of the difficulty came to light. Then, in joint discussion, Mr. Hone and the two boys reached an agreement and determined appropriate classroom behavior. Nothing was said to the class about the outcome of the incident. Inasmuch as the instructor assumed that no useful purpose would be served through punishment, none was given.

MISS KNELL KEPT UP-TO-DATE IN HER SUBJECT

Two girls were conversing as they left Miss Knell's eleventh-grade English literature class.

"She keeps things moving all the time, doesn't she?" said Jennie. Mary said, "It's more fun to listen to her lessons than it is to talk to the other kids. I don't know how she does it. She's the first teacher I ever had who kept me so interested I didn't want to cut up."

The principal, who had overheard the conversation, could have told them the answer. It was the basic subject-matter preparation of the teacher. She knew her subject thoroughly—keeping up with the journals, attending workshops, and taking advanced courses at the university.

Although vigorous disciplinary action may be warranted under extreme circumstances, knowing one's students, being relaxed in one's control of them, and keeping current in one's own subject all help maintain an atmosphere in which optimum learning can take place. The practices of Mr. Moon, Mr. Hone, and Miss Knell lend support to this conclusion.

THE ROLE OF THE TEACHER

Teachers whose classrooms are characterized by poor discipline often blame the students rather than themselves.[40] Reasons frequently cited by teachers are:

---

[40]A range of teacher-caused discipline problems is listed by Grambs, Iverson, and Patterson, *op. cit.*, pp. 418–421.

See Brown and Phelps, *op. cit.*, pp. 121–122, for a useful presentation of the impact of teaching skill on classroom control.

1. "This class is the worst one I have."
2. "There are more troublemakers in this class than I have ever had before."
3. "Today's adolescents are totally without respect for adults. It wasn't that way when I went to school."
4. "I have three or four poor readers in this second period who are always making trouble."
5. "The majority of students are just not interested in schoolwork if it involves paying attention and working."
6. "During the last period of the day most of the students are inattentive and little can be accomplished."

Few teachers will admit that most disciplinary problems are caused by the teacher. It is quite true that directionless teenagers will frequently take over a classroom situation where teacher leadership is lacking.[41] However, it is the teacher's responsibility to give positive direction and control to the goal-oriented behavior of students. It is not his role to stand idly by, assuming that the native goodness of adolescents will somehow induce them to want to conform to the teacher's desire.[42]

Teacher-Caused Student Misbehavior

A substantial share of teacher-caused student misbehavior originates with a *lack of planning*.[43] Effective planning for classroom control begins with an analysis of the individual students that compose the group to be taught. At the level of thought—not at the level of action—the teacher must examine the causes of behavior in the unemotional light of reason. Then he can plan intelligently how to forestall disciplinary infractions before they occur.[44] When infractions do happen, as they inevitably will, appropriate steps can be taken so that as little injury as possible is done to the learning process.[45]

Several different behavior patterns of the instructor are harmful to teacher-student relationships and tend to encourage student mis-

---

[41]Cronbach, *op. cit.*, pp. 534–535, views "disciplinary problems as a failure of leadership."

[42]Brown and Phelps, *op. cit.*, pp. 125–129, discuss (1) increasing pupil activity, (2) improving school morale, and (3) improving personal attitudes as procedures for helping achieve effective classroom control.

[43]Many of the advantages of group planning are identified in a case study presented by Cronbach, *op. cit.*, pp. 506–510.

[44]The prevention of disciplinary infractions is examined under several different headings by Inlow, *op. cit.*, pp. 349–356.

[45]E. G. Williamson and J. D. Foley, *Counseling and Discipline* (New York: McGraw-Hill Book Company, 1949), Chapter 2, provide a sound treatment of "Misbehavior Viewed as Behavior."

Inlow, *op. cit.*, pp. 367–369, discusses common errors to be avoided in correcting misbehavior.

conduct.[46] *Inconsistency* in the teacher's dealings with the class leaves students somewhat frustrated and without a basis for predicting the teacher's reactions. The resulting insecurity is expressed in an unwillingness to follow the teacher's suggestions, in general tension, and in attempts to anticipate the teacher's next move.

Another form of teacher behavior that promotes student misconduct is the *failure to communicate* to class members the desirable standards of classroom conduct and the *failure to insist that such standards be maintained.* Students and teachers should come to a working agreement about desirable standards of classroom behavior, such as consistent politeness, not interrupting the teacher, and listening when others are speaking. The teacher must, of course, be responsible for determining that the desired behavior is consistently carried out until proper habits are formed.

The teacher who consistently *threatens students* with punishment[47] for infractions is encouraging misbehavior—unless the threat is carried out. Because each unfulfilled promise of disciplinary action creates an impression that the teacher will never carry through with a threat, the student's subsequent behavior is geared to what he believes will or will not happen, not to what the teacher *says* will happen.[48]

Maintenance of Specific Routines

The establishment and maintenance of specific routine procedures is one of the neglected areas of classroom control. The teacher must, of necessity, assume responsibility for initiating these procedures and for seeing that they are continued or modified as necessary. Failure to give adequate attention to these routines can spell disciplinary defeat in classrooms that are otherwise well conducted.[49] Problems related to routine include:

1. Temperature control
2. Ventilation
3. Being seated when the bell rings
4. Paper distribution
5. Handing in the papers

---

[46]According to McDonald, *op. cit.*, p. 525, "a teacher may be predisposed to attend to certain kinds of pupil behavior and to ignore other kinds. In this way the teacher's perceptions of a pupil's characteristics are limited to the kinds of behaviors that the teacher sees as desirable or undesirable in the classroom setting."

[47]See Fritz Redl and William W. Wattenberg, *Mental Hygiene in Teaching* (New York: Harcourt, Brace and Co., 1959), pp. 365–367, for a helpful treatment of threats.

[48]McDonald, *op. cit.*, p. 526, finds that "teacher control of pupil behavior is related to the kinds of expectations pupils have about the patterns of control."

[49]Aspects of the physical environment that affect classroom behavior are listed by Brown and Phelps, *op. cit.*, p. 125.

Burton, *op. cit.*, p. 537, identifies several elements of classroom management that can become routine.

6. Cleaning the chalkboard
7. Cleaning desks and areas around desks at a prescribed time
8. Time for pencil sharpening
9. Time for talking to the teacher (not gathering around desk)
10. Class dismissal
11. Roll call procedure
12. Movement from one procedure to another without undue commotion

A classroom situation in which many aspects of effective routine are violated will illustrate the harm possible.

MR. SCHILLING NEGLECTS ROUTINE

When Mr. Johnson, the supervisor, paid an unexpected call on Sam Schilling, he found a most revealing situation. Seated in the back of the room at an empty desk, he was able to observe the entire operation of the class.

After the bell rang, students were still conversing in the hall. When all except two students were finally in their seats, the teacher began to call the roll. A murmur ran through the class as he spoke each name and received in return the unfailing "Here" or "Present."

"Now, pass in your homework for today," said Mr. Schilling. Everyone began to talk, and somehow one fourth of the papers did not arrive at the front of the class. In desperation the teacher moved swiftly along each row of seats, picking up the missing assignments from the desks.

Toward the middle of the period, Mr. Johnson noticed that the room was unusually warm. The wall thermometer beside him registered 80 degrees. Several students were obviously drowsy, and three of them had their heads down on their desks. Finally the boy nearest the windows threw open two of them, letting in a chilling blast of sub-zero February air.

"Close those windows right now," snapped Mr. Schilling. Reluctantly the offender did so.

After a prolonged lecture and discussion period, the teacher declared that the remaining ten minutes would be a study period. As soon as the teacher had made his announcement, three boys went to the pencil sharpener, where they stood in line, waiting their turn. They were soon joined by four other students who playfully sauntered over.

During the so-called study period, one student came to Mr. Schilling's desk to ask a question. Before the student could get the answer, another student stood at the desk waiting for her question to be answered. Within five minutes several more students crowded around the teacher's desk, seeking help and obscuring the teacher's view of the class. Just when it appeared that the class might get completely out of control, the bell rang and the class members filed out without a final word from their teacher.

Mr. Schilling failed to control several aspects of classroom routine: Students were not ready to start work when the bell rang; papers were not handed in systematically; temperature control was neglected; students were not required to study during the study period; and the procedures employed in responding to student questions aggravated the already existing confusion.

CLASSROOM CONTROL PRACTICES IN DIFFERENT SUBJECTS

Must the art class be as quiet as the mathematics class? Should students in a shop class avoid loud conversations just as their friends in an English class are expected to do? A generalization will be useful: *Classroom control is sound if it promotes efficient instruction.* In this statement nothing is said about the intensity of noise. Instead, attention is focused upon learning and sound instruction, not upon discipline-oriented teaching procedures.

Most teachers today realize that there need not be absolute silence in order for learning to take place. Instead, students learn best in a tension-free atmosphere where they are highly motivated to achieve goals known to be educationally sound. Effective education, however, does require a sensible and serious attitude.

Skill Subjects

Some teachers conduct a classroom in which there is little semblance of order and in which learning moves forward at a reduced pace. Teachers often justify their lack of control by rationalizing that stricter discipline would stifle creativity and represent unwarranted rigidity. The tendency for this laxity is sometimes found in classes involving motor manipulations and physical skills.

Music classes concerned with instrumental or vocal work can get out of hand very easily, unless students are required to behave in a way that promotes instruction and learning. In physical education classes, students may view games and exercises as pure play. Although composing a substantial proportion of the activities in such a course, play must be so directed or restricted that it serves the specific purposes of instruction. Because of the noise occasioned by the nature of the activity, typing classes encourage loud talking among students unless the teacher takes appropriate steps to avoid it. Classes concerned with painting and drawing serve as ready-made temptations to the less self-directive students,[50] because free movement of students about the room is normally essential to the conduct of the class. When students are permitted to abuse this necessary privilege, however, disorder soon prevails. Shop classes involving auto mechanics, woodwork, and metalwork pose many of the same control problems. If the nature of the class leads students to misbehave, the teacher must plan in advance to counter this tendency.

Concept-Centered Subjects

Concept-centered classes, which are basically concerned with mental rather than physical activities, present a different type of

---

[50]An interesting case study in which an art teacher discovers the strengths and limitations of undirected class activities is told by Cronbach, *op. cit.*, pp. 503–506.

classroom control challenge. In the algebra class, for example, even a moderate amount of noise may interfere markedly with the students' concentration during a study period. In an English class, the teacher's reading of a particular literary selection may require the undivided attention of every member of the class if maximum benefit is to be derived. For less gifted students, the mastery of some of the concepts of English grammar may require a great deal of uninterrupted concentration. Each instructor must determine for himself the extent to which given elements in the classroom environment interfere with, or promote, the cause of learning.

Social-Centered Procedures

A wide range of social activities are employed in teaching. Among them are committee work, working in pairs, and large-group discussions. Because of the students' tendency to use these class projects for promoting their own social life rather than the teacher's proposed goal, some teachers feel that such activities are not sufficiently productive to warrant more than occasional use.

SPECIFIC SUGGESTIONS

Listed here are a number of specific hints that should be of pointed assistance to the beginning teacher as well as the seasoned instructor who is still encountering difficulties in the general area of discipline.[51]

Recommendations

1. Set up desirable standards of classroom behavior and insist that the students maintain these standards.[52] Be firm in your dealings with students, especially during the period when habits are being formed for the school year.[53]

2. Indicate to the misbehaving student that although you dislike the infraction you do not dislike him.

---

[51]Herbert J. Klausmeier, *Learning and Human Abilities: Educational Psychology* (New York: Harper & Brothers, 1961), pp. 143–145, views the sound teacher as a helpful person regardless of the type of leadership he exercises.

Sheviakov and Redl, *op. cit.*, pp. 62–64, make eight basic recommendations that provide help to teachers who encounter classroom behavior problems.

Nordberg, Bradfield, and Odell, *op. cit.*, pp. 216–271, also provide "specific guidelines for developing desirable control."

[52]According to Redl and Wattenberg, *op. cit.*, pp. 361–362, instructional needs are served when the teacher defines, reasonably and unemotionally, the limits of classroom behavior.

[53]Klausmeier, *Teaching in the Secondary School,* pp. 383–385, discusses the necessity for the teacher to establish himself as the figure of authority in the classroom.

3. Put classroom suggestions on a positive rather than a negative basis.

4. Encourage your students to respect other students and adults; insist that students treat you with respect at all times.

5. Identify as quickly as possible the students whose behavior might give rise to classroom control problems. Learn how to use group leaders in solving such problems, and use social pressure to encourage misbehaving students to conform to group standards.[54]

6. Always be fair in your dealings with the entire class as well as with individual students.

7. Be appropriately friendly with students, especially with those who have adjustment problems.[55]

8. When students have deep-seated problems with which you are not qualified to cope, refer them to appropriate professionals within the school or community.

9. Create an atmosphere of general pleasantness and scholarship in which students will not want to disturb others. Smile frequently, particularly when it is necessary to establish an atmosphere of general warmth.

10. Develop a sincere sense of humor that has student appeal, but make it serve the cause of instruction.

11. Make a practice of carefully reviewing and appraising your classroom control problems at the end of the school day. Incorporate into your daily lesson plan appropriate action for the next day.[56]

12. Free yourself of personal idiosyncrasies and annoying mannerisms.

13. Use correct and appropriate English.

14. Take a keen interest in student activities and in current events, relating them to your classwork where possible.

15. Plan interesting, informative, and varied activities for your students, but be sure these procedures are psychologically sound. Know when and when not to involve students in planning; but if student ideas are sound, use them.

16. Know each student's name, his friends, and his interests; then consider the effect of differences in age, maturity, interests, and intelligence upon classroom control. Furthermore, recognize the effect that adverse home environments may have upon an individual's classroom behavior.

17. Use the seating plan to help maintain order by separating students who would create a disturbance if they were seated together.

---

[54]Redl and Wattenberg, *op. cit.*, pp. 348–353, suggest several devices for providing supporting self-control for the child with tendencies for misbehavior.

[55]Personality traits of teachers who have many or few classroom control problems are identified in a comparison chart provided by Brown and Phelps, *op. cit.*, p. 123.

[56]Redl and Wattenberg, *op. cit.*, pp. 354–358, suggest restructuring the learning situation as a means of assisting learners to cope more effectively with specific problems.

18. Establish and maintain well-understood, definite procedures for distributing and collecting papers and materials.

19. Be sure that each student feels that he is important and that he has accomplished something worth while. Moreover, help him feel that he is accepted by the teacher as well as by other students.

20. Try to make each student aware that it is possible for him to improve and that it is important for him to do so.

21. Indicate that you have confidence in what students can and will do.

22. Be sure that classwork is not too difficult or too easy for individual students.

23. Talk privately with students about severe infractions. Once remedial disciplinary action is started, follow through with it, but keep the nature of any such action confidential.[57]

24. Under certain circumstances, conferences with teaching colleagues and administrators may prove to be helpful.

25. In cases of marked misbehavior, it may be helpful to encourage the offending student to compose and sign an agreement whereby he promises to improve. The signatures of parents and counselors may also be warranted in certain cases. At times, a telephone call to interested parents may prove to be the most helpful and efficient way to improve student behavior. Teacher-parent conferences may be most informative and rewarding in attacking specific discipline-related problems.

26. Students change their behavior voluntarily when they see it is in their interest to do so.

27. During teacher presentations, learn to make eye contact with students, particularly with those tending toward misbehavior. When the attention of particular students begins to waver, call on them.

28. In handling disciplinary infractions be calm and dignified as well as firm.

29. When misbehavior begins to assume large proportions, it may be wise to isolate the offender from the group until the situation has been resolved.

30. Allow a student time for meditation before discussing his misbehavior with him.

31. When property is damaged or destroyed, restitution is essential. This may be sufficient punishment in many cases.

Cautions

1. Don't raise your voice as a means of maintaining order.
2. Don't become belligerent in attempting to be firm.
3. Don't resort to force as a solution to a discipline problem.

---

[57]The limitations of punishment as a classroom control procedure are examined by Cronbach, *op. cit.*, pp. 492–494.

4. Don't display your emotions in the presence of the class.

5. Don't allow small infractions to grow to a point where they become generally disruptive.

6. Don't threaten students, but take action, if necessary, after thinking through the situation.

7. Don't expect more of students than their capacities, interests, and motivation will permit.

8. Don't convey the idea that you are functioning only as a policeman to keep everybody in line.

9. Don't send students to the principal's office for minor infractions.[58] Unless a problem is particularly severe, solve it yourself.

10. Don't allow students to move around the room unless it serves the purpose of teaching and learning.

11. Don't discuss personal matters of great concern to students in the presence of other students.

12. Don't place yourself in the position of arguing with the class or individuals within the class.

13. Don't hesitate to change the seats of students if this will serve a useful purpose.

14. Don't willfully antagonize students.

15. Don't be pointlessly autocratic.

16. Don't use a laissez-faire approach to classroom control.[59]

17. Don't be tactless in your dealings with students.

18. Don't waste time unnecessarily in changing from one activity to another.

19. Don't make snap judgments with respect to what remedial action is best.

20. Don't hold a grudge against a student.

21. Don't "allow yourself to be fooled by the surface appearance of a discipline problem."[60]

CLASSROOM CONTROL IN REVIEW

The best classroom environment is one that results in efficient learning. Discipline involves employing guidance and teaching techniques to encourage students to become self-directive and thus to create an atmosphere conducive to learning.

Sound classroom control is achieved most efficiently if the teacher is equipped with a theoretical and working knowledge of relevant principles that underlie classroom behavior—principles related to curriculum, planning, objectives and procedures, activity and ex-

---

[58]A helpful list of principles related to the punishment of disciplinary offenses is provided by Brown and Phelps, *op. cit.*, pp. 131–132.

[59]Klausmeier, *Learning and Human Abilities*, pp. 133–137, discusses research related to authoritarian, democratic, and laissez-faire leadership and points out implications for classroom behavior.

[60]Sheviakov and Redl, *op. cit.*, p. 57.

perience, meaning and behavior, habits, growth and development, environmental influences, adolescent needs, expectations, readiness, and motivation. Only when the teacher has acquired genuine skill in relating such principles to the classroom behavior of students is he free to focus his attention on the other concerns of instruction.

PROBLEMS FOR STUDY AND DISCUSSION

1. Why is the ultimate goal of discipline often described as self-discipline? Discuss.
2. Define discipline as the traditionalists of fifty years ago would have defined it. Why is it defined differently today? Explain.
3. Identify at least ten reasons why more teachers fail because of poor class discipline than for any other reason.
4. Are superintendents justified in placing so much emphasis on the teacher's ability to control the class? Explain your reasons.
5. What is the advantage of a knowledge of basic principles of classroom behavior as opposed to an acquaintance with very specific suggestions?
6. List ten common classroom disciplinary problems that might be avoided through effective planning.
7. Should the teacher plan for meeting disciplinary problems in his daily lesson plan, in his unit plan, or in his yearly plan? Why?
8. Describe three typical classroom situations in which the inefficient use of audio-visual aids tends to promote misbehavior.
9. Example: Ninth-grade Florence (I.Q. 103) had gradually ceased to try in her English I class. In addition, her classroom behavior during the past month had been very disturbing to the teacher. She held frequent loud peer-group chats during class and was prone to show off. On the basis of this scanty evidence, indicate (1) possible causes for her misbehavior and (2) the desired action on the part of the teacher for each possible cause. List the most likely cause first, the next most likely cause second, etc.
10. Assumption: An eleventh-grade boy has a tendency to swear occasionally in your classroom. Describe the steps you would take to meet this situation.
11. Is the teacher ever justified in employing punitive discipline? Discuss, giving examples.
12. If you wanted the students in your class to form five basic habits that would encourage effective classroom control, what would they be?
13. What is the effect of peer-group acceptance on classroom behavior?
14. Discuss the relationship of heterosexual adjustment to classroom behavior.
15. Give several examples taken from your teaching major in which objectives assumed to be of particular value by teachers are rejected as personal goals by the students.
16. It is generally held that all adolescents need affection. How is this need expressed in classroom peer-group relationships?
17. In what ways may students attempt to adjust their academic and social behavior to make it acceptable to their peers? Discuss, giving examples.
18. Give several examples taken from your teaching minor in which lack of readiness promotes classroom misbehavior.

19. A substantial share of teacher-caused misbehavior originates with lack of planning. Give several examples that lend support to this statement.

20. How quiet should a class in art be? In social science? In orchestra? Explain.

RECOMMENDED READINGS

Batchelder, Howard T., Maurice McGlasson, and Raleigh Schorling, *Student Teaching in Secondary Schools*, 4th ed. New York: McGraw-Hill Book Company, 1964, Chapter 5.

Brown, Edwin J., and Arthur T. Phelps, *Managing the Classroom*, 2d. ed. New York: Ronald Press, 1961, Chapters 4 and 6.

Burton, William H., *The Guidance of Learning Activities*, 3d. ed. New York: Appleton-Century-Crofts, Inc., 1962, Chapter 23.

Cronbach, Lee J., *Educational Psychology*, 2d. ed. New York: Harcourt, Brace and World, 1963, Chapter 15.

Flesher, W. R., "The Beginning Teacher," *Educational Research Bulletin*, 1945 (January), *24*:14–18+.

Frandsen, Arden N., *Educational Psychology*. New York: McGraw-Hill Book Company, 1961, pp. 488–492.

Grambs, Jean D., William J. Iverson, and Franklin K. Patterson, *Modern Methods in Secondary Education*, rev. ed. New York: The Dryden Press, 1958, Chapters 15 and 16.

Inlow, Gail M., *Maturity in High School Teaching*. Englewood Cliffs, N.J.: Prentice-Hall, Inc., 1963, Chapters 15–17.

Klausmeier, Herbert J., *Learning and Human Abilities: Educational Psychology*. New York: Harper & Brothers, 1961, Chapter 5.

Klausmeier, Herbert J., *Teaching in the Secondary School*. New York: Harper & Brothers, 1958, Chapter 14.

McDonald, Frederick J., *Educational Psychology*. San Francisco: Wadsworth Publishing Company, 1959, Chapter 13.

McKean, Robert C., *Principles and Methods in Secondary Education*. Columbus, Ohio: Charles E. Merrill Books, Inc., 1962, Chapter 9.

Mouly, George J., *Psychology for Effective Teaching*. New York: Henry Holt and Co., 1960, Chapter 6, and pp. 461–462 and 493–501.

Nordberg, H. Orville, James M. Bradfield, and William C. Odell, *Secondary School Teaching*. New York: The Macmillan Company, 1962, Chapter 10.

Redl, Fritz, and William W. Wattenberg, *Mental Hygiene in Teaching*. New York: Harcourt, Brace and Co., 1959, pp. 56–57 and Chapter 13.

Rivlin, Harry N., *Teaching Adolescents in Secondary Schools*, 2d. ed. New York: Appleton-Century-Crofts, Inc., 1961, Chapter 14.

Sheviakov, George V., and Fritz Redl, *Discipline for Today's Children and Youth*, rev. ed. Washington, D.C.: National Education Association (ASCD), 1956, pp. 1–64.

Williamson, E. G., and J. D. Foley, *Counseling and Discipline*. New York: McGraw-Hill Book Company, 1949, Chapters 4 and 7.

Woodruff, Asahel D., *Basic Concepts of Teaching; with Brief Readings*. San Francisco: Chandler Publishing Company, 1962, Chapters 4, 5, 11, 12, and 13.

14

Readiness and Motivation

Beginning teachers soon learn what experienced teachers have consistently observed—that readiness and motivation profoundly influence the learning process. This chapter is devoted to a discussion of principles, practices, and specific suggestions aimed at enabling the teacher to make more effective use of readiness and motivation in classroom situations.

EFFECT OF READINESS ON LEARNING

The absence of readiness affects the learning process in one clear-cut manner: the student simply cannot learn.[1] Fortunately, readiness is neither totally present nor totally lacking. Students at any grade level usually possess some degree of readiness for the study of that year's curriculum content, although students with limited achievement, ability, and motivation may be far below the desired level for optimum learning. The eleventh-grade boy of average intelligence who reads with the comprehension and speed of an eighth-grader is only partially ready to read the eleventh-grade United States history text. He is not, however, totally lacking in readiness.

The learner is said to be *ready* to undertake a given learning task when he has reached the point in his mental, physical, social, and

[1]Asahel D. Woodruff, *Basic Concepts of Teaching; with Brief Readings* (San Francisco: Chandler Publishing Company, 1962), p. 278.

emotional development where the accomplishment of that task is possible as well as desirable. Unfortunately, uninformed laymen and teachers often view physical readiness as the sole determiner of the readiness to learn.[2] The same error is committed when the student's readiness is determined solely on the basis of his social, mental, and emotional maturity. This oversimplification is responsible for many basic errors that impede the learning process.[3]

Types of Readiness

Because physical, mental, social, and emotional development are all essential to readiness, and because a student can arrive at varying stages of readiness in these categories, each area should be examined individually to discover its general nature and to determine its effect under specific circumstances.[4]

Physical Readiness

The learning of skill subjects, such as typing, instrumental music, or physical education, requires neuro-muscular coordination. Students excelling in these areas are customarily those who are physically ready to learn the basic techniques and who are willing to practice to achieve the necessary coordination.

In a typing class one occasionally finds a bright and apparently physically normal senior high school student whose coordination does not enable him to achieve beyond a bare minimum in typing skills. If he is not ready, no amount of effort on his part will result in his typing at a high rate of speed. Similarly, the physical education teacher is often aware of the clumsiness of certain students in his class, a clumsiness that cannot be overcome through practice. If this lack of coordination is related to slow maturation, there is little that the teacher can do except wait for physical growth to provide the desired readiness.

Intellectual Readiness

Three factors contribute to intellectual readiness—neural growth, native capacity, and experience. For example, the preschool child, regardless of native capacity, cannot hope to cope with the complexities of nuclear physics, because the physical development of his

---

[2]William H. Burton, *The Guidance of Learning Activities*, 3d. ed. (New York: Appleton-Century-Crofts, 1962), p. 160, points out that there are many forms of readiness.

[3]Henry C. Lindgren, *Educational Psychology in the Classroom*, 2d. ed. (New York: John Wiley and Sons, 1962), p. 274, indicates that psychologists view readiness as a complex phenomenon.

[4]Herbert J. Klausmeier, *Teaching in the Secondary School* (New York: Harper & Brothers, 1958), pp. 312–318, discusses physical condition, social and emotional adjustment, previous achievement, established study habits, and intellectual capacity as aspects of student readiness.

brain and nervous system is not sufficiently advanced to permit his understanding. Similarly, the possibility that a twelve-year-old can function as a business executive is restricted by neural growth, in spite of his I.Q. or experience.

Students with limited mental capacities will never be ready to undertake certain intellectual tasks. The dull youngster, for example, may flounder in second-year algebra and in the physical sciences. Because his inability to think abstractly restricts his mental activity, he is able to solve only relatively simple problems. The above-average student, on the other hand, can learn progressively more difficult and complex ideas because he is able to grasp the basic concepts necessary to his understanding.

Experience also affects a student's intellectual, or conceptual, readiness,[5] since concepts can be acquired only through meaningful experiences.[6] The individual who has had the opportunity for extensive travel has a great advantage over the nontraveler in a geography course. Similarly, the readiness of any given student to understand national and world problems comes as a direct result of wide reading and experience gathered from talking to many people.

Conceptual readiness to learn a certain task or a more complex concept also relies on the knowledge of the necessary basic concepts. The beginning clarinet player who aspires to play in the school band must learn tone production and fingering, as well as how to play in a small group, before he is ready to participate in the full band. If a typical seventh-grade student were suddenly confronted with the task of learning quantum physics, a subject for which he had no prerequisite training, he would lack essential readiness. Although he might have the study skills, emotional stability, coordination of hand and eye, and essential social skills, he would still lack the basic concepts necessary for an understanding of the new subject. He could progress no more rapidly than the acquisition of the supporting concepts would permit.

Social Readiness

Forced participation in a large class is a frightening experience for students who tend to be introverted. The wise teacher, however, may induce the timid youngster to participate to some extent by asking carefully selected questions. Such questions should enable the student to experience success and should build up his image as a competent class participant in his own mind as well as in the minds of his peers. Once his confidence is built up, the student may be able to answer more difficult questions and to share his ideas more freely.

---

[5]Woodruff, *op. cit.*, pp. 279–281, provides a brief discussion of the hierarchical arrangement of concepts derived from experience.

[6]Hubert H. Mills and Harl R. Douglass, *Teaching in High School*, 2d. ed. (New York: Ronald Press, 1957), p. 91, tell of the relocation of curriculum based upon the re-examination of the students' experiences.

Later he may participate with enthusiasm in discussions that are of real interest to him.

Emotional Readiness

Emotional adjustments have a close relationship to the social readiness of a student. Few problems are of more pressing and real concern to the teenager than peer-group acceptance. An eleventh-grade girl who is excluded from membership in a cliquish group to which she very much wants to belong is preoccupied with her rejection and its assumed impact on her personal welfare. During this period she may lack emotional readiness for serious study.

Another serious form of emotional unreadiness is found in the junior high school student who comes from an overprotective home. Having been denied contact with a realistic world and the toughening effect of occasional failure, the student finds it difficult to get along with his peers and is unequipped to meet the rigorous competition without severe emotional discomfort. When he receives a grade lower than he had anticipated, he responds emotionally; if he is then deservedly scolded by the teacher, he sulks and feels unjustly treated.

Other Types of Readiness

Although many other classifications of readiness are to be found in professional writings, they usually represent variations or divisions of mental, physical, social, or emotional readiness. Among these other types are experiential readiness, reading readiness, motivational readiness, maturational readiness, attitudinal readiness, and achievement readiness. More fundamental for the teacher than any system of classification, however, is the need for a careful consideration of all readiness factors and their effect upon the teaching-learning process.

A Range of Readiness

A ninth-grade social dancing class presents a picture of varying degrees of readiness. Because the girls have matured physically more rapidly than the boys, their movements are well coordinated and, in many cases, skilled; with few exceptions they are physically ready to participate in social dancing. Among the boys, however, only those who are considerably above average in physical development have the neural and muscular control necessary to dance with ease and grace.

Inasmuch as dancing is a social as well as a physical activity, varied heterosexual social adjustments complicate the already great problem of differences in physical readiness among the boys and girls. At this age girls often express a strong, overt interest in boys. They are socially *ready* for this type of activity. Boys, on the other hand, possess a covert interest in girls, which is infrequently expressed in actual social contact. Given their choice, boys of this age often avoid heterosexual social contact altogether. It should be noted, however, that there is wide variation in the degree of readiness of members of the same sex.

Still another aspect of readiness is observable in the dancing class. Girls generally have acquired a conceptual readiness for dancing, have learned the latest steps, and have gained a measure of proficiency in performance that is matched by few boys.

Readiness for a Specific Learning Task

If the teacher understands the student's readiness for undertaking given learning tasks, he can plan much more realistically for instruction. He must realize that just as students vary in their physical, mental, social, and emotional make-up, so they vary in their readiness in these areas. Determining differences in readiness among students, then, should be one of the teacher's major concerns.[7]

Determining Physical Readiness

It is advisable for students to have a physical examination by a competent physician at regular intervals throughout their school years. If physical difficulties are discovered that may influence in-school behavior, the teacher should be informed so that he can help the student either overcome his difficulty or achieve within the framework of his limitations. Unfortunately, youngsters do not have physical checkups very frequently after early childhood.

Specialists in the field of physical education have played a key role in developing instruments that measure the various elements of motor ability—agility, sensory and motor coordination, and steadiness.[8] Specific tests have also been designed to measure the degree of athletic skill as well as the muscular strength and organic fitness of individual students.[9] However, in skill areas other than physical education—band, orchestra, typing, shorthand, and shop—means of appraising needed readiness, as represented by muscular coordination, are not so fully developed.

Determining Intellectual Readiness

Nearly all secondary schools throughout the United States have organized programs of standardized testing in which intelligence

---

[7]William C. Morse and G. Max Wingo, *Psychology and Teaching*, 2d. ed. (Chicago: Scott, Foresman and Company, 1962), pp. 268–270, provide an excellent brief treatment of the general sources of information and psychological tests used in evaluating readiness for learning.

[8]See Georgia Sachs Adams and Theodore L. Torgerson, *Measurement and Evaluation for the Secondary-School Teacher* (New York: The Dryden Press, 1956), p. 473.

[9]*Ibid.*, Chapter 23, provide a detailed discussion of "Measurement and Evaluation in Physical Education."

testing is the dominant concern. Currently available are numerous group tests that have demonstrated both a high degree of validity and reliability.[10] Although intelligence tests are administered to groups as a general rule, many school systems have the personnel and facilities to administer individual intelligence tests as well.

The teacher who, through careful observation, has developed skill in verifying or disproving intelligence test results is in a favorable position to appraise students' intellectual readiness. In many cases, however, teacher observation is so loosely carried out that it is of little worth in evaluating student readiness.

Standardized achievement tests in each of the content areas have received a great deal of attention in recent years. In the social studies field, for example, several standardized tests are available for measuring recall and understanding, and a few tests have been produced that evaluate the skills needed for studying social studies.[11] Similar tests have been developed for appraising mastery of subject matter in other basic areas of the secondary curriculum. Of greater flexibility, however, is the teacher-made test designed to measure achievement. If valid, reliable, complete, and well administered, such a test provides a useful indication of whether the student is ready to take the next academic step.

Determining Social Readiness

The many facets of social readiness make any measurement in this area very difficult. Sociometric techniques (procedures for measuring the social structure of a given group)[12] have been of considerable help to teachers in assaying social readiness for learning, but the validity and reliability of these tests may be seriously challenged. When the evidence they provide has been corroborated by careful observation, however, the teacher has a basis for planning classroom social situations that will promote learning.

Determining Emotional Readiness

Emotional readiness for learning must be largely inferred from the results of tests designed to measure academic adjustment, personal social adjustment, and social status. Although such tests are being improved, their validity and reliability still leave much to be desired.

As in other areas, thoughtful classroom observation by the teacher reveals many individual emotional problems. Occasionally the help of other specialists in the school system (counselors, psycholo-

---

[10]*Ibid.*, pp. 41–52, discuss the determiners of and the need for validity and reliability.

[11]*Ibid.*, pp. 379–397.

[12]Frederick J. McDonald, *Educational Psychology* (San Francisco: Wadsworth Publishing Company, 1959), pp. 598–603, presents a brief discussion of the measurement of the social structure of a class.

gists, and psychiatrists) is needed to determine the emotional status of such students, and it may be desirable to refer students to such specialists for individual help.

Principles Related to Readiness

The psychological principles that have a close relationship to readiness are so numerous that this chapter can list only those that seem to have the greatest relevance.

1. Many kinds of readiness are essential to efficient learning. Furthermore, "each subject has its own unique set of readiness factors,"[13] and each student possesses varying degrees of readiness.

2. Readiness factors for an individual student can change rapidly. Bearing this in mind, the teacher should continuously check to determine the student's readiness for schoolwork.

3. Readiness for learning should be one of the criteria for grouping students. The content for a particular grade level is selected on the assumption that students are ready to learn that content. Effective classroom teaching, however, involves identifying *if* and *when* each learner is ready for a given learning task.

4. An individual's readiness for learning is partially dependent upon his physical, mental, social, and emotional status. A student is not in an optimum state of readiness when he is physically ill, when he lacks essential concepts, or when he is preoccupied with pressing problems. On the other hand, a student is ready for a learning task when he has the mental maturity to cope with the task, and he is ready to engage in a motor skill when he has the required coordination of nerves and muscles.

5. The student is conceptually ready to take the next learning step when he understands the prerequisite concepts, and he cannot succeed in learning tasks for which he is not conceptually ready. Thus the learner is ready to memorize when he understands the meaning of the symbols to be memorized, and he is ready to undertake difficult social tasks when he has mastered the basic tasks on which the more difficult ones rely.

6. Postponing the introduction of concepts beyond the point of optimum readiness may be as harmful as premature introduction. The teacher, however, can determine whether readiness has been achieved by assigning students a learning task and by observing the results.[14] The alert teacher should quickly identify the state of readiness and adjust the learners' task to meet this condition.

7. If the learner wants something that he feels has great value, he is ready to behave in ways that he feels will meet this desire.

---

[13]H. Orville Nordberg, James M. Bradfield, and William C. Odell, *Secondary School Teaching* (New York: Macmillan, 1962), p. 72.

[14]Burton, *op. cit.*, p. 161.

Therefore, readiness to study (not to be confused with readiness to be curious) depends upon how useful the study appears to the individual learner.[15]

8. Effective study habits help develop readiness for learning. When students are known to have study problems, readiness factors should be considered as possible causes.

9. Although readiness factors are typically given greater attention in the elementary school than in the high school, they are equally applicable to learning situations at both levels.

10. Interests, needs, and motivation may be considered aspects of readiness.

11. Opportunity and encouragement are important in promoting readiness for learning.

Correct and Incorrect Use

The violation of the need for conceptual readiness is apparent in all school systems that automatically promote poor achievers and dull students with the rest of the age group without regard for subject-matter comprehension. This factor alone accounts for much of the distaste for arithmetic and mathematics that students feel during their elementary- and high-school days and that they carry over into their adult life. The same factors are at play in the English grammar course when students are required to keep in step with the class, although they may understand very little of what has been taught. As a result, there are senior high school students who make errors in punctuation and spelling in every line they write, and English teachers are faced with reteaching, year after year, those elements of grammar that students have only partially learned. The unfortunate payoff for the student who has been consistently but undeservedly promoted may come when he undertakes his first paid position. In the harsh competition of the nonschool world, such a student is forced to face reality.

Although curriculum planners attempt to place specific educational activities at grade levels where a majority of students will be ready for them, problems still exist.[16] One such problem is described below.

NORMAN'S READINESS TO LEARN IS INCONSISTENT

Norman Dudley was a bright boy, a fact that his teachers, the administration, and his parents readily admitted. At the insistence of his parents he moved through the three years of an ungraded primary unit in two years and at the age of twelve found himself in the eighth grade. Academically, Nor-

---

[15]Woodruff, *op. cit.*, p. 9.

[16]Robert C. McKean, *Principles and Methods in Secondary Education* (Columbus, Ohio: Charles E. Merrill Books, Inc., 1962), p. 110, describes three procedures often employed by teachers in attempting to deal with the problems of readiness.

man was maintaining pace with his peers very well, but in the physical education class and in social contacts with schoolmates of both sexes he was left far behind.

Because his physical development was slow, because he came from a family of physically small persons, and because he was advanced by one year, Norman's performance in the gym class was among the poorest in the group. He simply did not have the neuro-muscular development that would enable him to compete effectively with his peers. The physical education instructor realized that in another two years Norman's physical development would probably enable him to keep pace with the class. Unfortunately, there was no provision for holding Norman back for this desired period.

The case of Norman illustrates the impossibility of providing optimum educational opportunities for all youngsters under an inflexible grade placement. Even if a student is socially ready for a learning experience, he may not be physically and mentally ready. Such cases point to the desirability of reorganizing the secondary curriculum in a way that will more effectively serve the varying needs of individual students.[17] There is reason to doubt whether this can be done without disrupting the present graded arrangement.

Recent experimental developments, however, have given a bright new outlook for certain secondary schools that have been searching for a means of more effectively meeting the individual needs of students.[18]

SAMMY USES A PROGRAMED TEXT

At the beginning of the school year, tests showed that Sammy Pitkin was a full year ahead of his classmates in mathematics aptitude and achievement. Mr. Waltham was determined to find some way to develop Sammy's potential. After he had examined several available programed texts for first-year algebra, he chose the one that seemed to be most carefully worked out in detail, sequential placement of concepts, and ease of usage. He also made sure that programed texts in the same series were available for second-year algebra, trigonometry, and elementary calculus.

The teacher, the student, and his parents jointly decided that Sammy would work independently of the class. Under Mr. Waltham's supervision Sammy began work on the first-year algebra book, moving as rapidly as he felt he could.

The use of the special text forced Sammy to react immediately and meaningfully to the concepts presented. Furthermore, it was structured so that he could not proceed to the next concept until he had a satisfactory comprehension of the preceding ones. Troublesome concepts that remained unre-

---

[17]Herbert J. Klausmeier, *Learning and Human Abilities: Educational Psychology* (New York: Harper & Brothers, 1961), p. 88, describes the violation of readiness principles in which individual differences in students are not given the desired consideration.

[18]The Brigham Young University Laboratory School is currently involved in experimental efforts in which mathematics instruction and special materials are used to meet the individual needs of students. Learners move rapidly along a path of sequentially arranged mathematical concepts, but at their own pace.

solved after careful reading and reacting to the frames of the programed text were discussed with the teacher. When Sammy was ready for the more difficult concept, he was able to move along at his own speed. He was intensely interested.

Around the first of December, Sammy announced that he had completed the first-year algebra book. When Mr. Waltham administered a comprehensive examination covering the content of first-year algebra, he discovered that Sammy scored among the upper 25 per cent of the students who had taken a full year to complete the course. Together they re-examined the errors made on the test and decided that Sammy was ready to begin studying second-year algebra. Although he did not progress as rapidly as he had in the first course, by the end of May Sammy had completed second-year algebra.

In this next case, Mrs. Smythe, a tenth-grade homemaking teacher, displays real insight by considering the individual needs of a student and guiding her toward social readiness.[19]

MRS. SMYTHE AIDS SOCIAL GROWTH

Mildred Knowles was of average height and appearance, but she seemed to be without friends. Thus Mrs. Smythe, her teacher, set about determining why. Mildred, she discovered, was in the lowest one third of the class in terms of socioeconomic status. Because Mildred lived on a farm, she had limited out-of-school contact with children outside her own family. Slow physical maturation left her with the figure of a child and the height of an adult. In addition, her social skills were poorly developed; she appeared awkward in any social situation.

Mrs. Smythe planned to help Mildred achieve social readiness through several steps. Since there was nothing that could be done about physical development except wait for the growth process to continue, Mrs. Smythe identified the girl's academic strong points and assigned her certain tasks requiring in-class participation and placing her in a favorable light. She gave Mildred deserved praise both before the class and in private talks. The teacher also changed the seats of several girls so that Mildred found herself in a compatible classroom atmosphere where she was encouraged to be friendly with other girls.

By the end of the school year, Mrs. Smythe was gratified to notice several changes. Mildred now conversed freely with her classmates, and her defensive look had disappeared. She seemed to enjoy limited popularity among members of her own sex, and her class participation had become more uninhibited and useful. As a result, she was gradually developing social skills and a degree of self-confidence.

Specific Suggestions

Because readiness is composed of so many facets, teachers often tend to focus attention upon only a few of these facets to the exclusion of others. A helpful device for avoiding this omission is for the

[19]Lindgren, *op. cit.*, p. 275, points out that skill and sensitivity are essential teacher traits in determining whether students are ready to undertake certain learning tasks.

individual teacher to prescribe for himself a series of specific recommendations and cautions that take into consideration the major facets of readiness. The starting point for such a list is presented here.

Recommendations

1. Help students develop the readiness essential to effective study.
2. Continuously check on the students' mental, physical, social, and emotional readiness for learning.
3. Be sure that standardized tests of mental maturity (I.Q. tests) are given at regular intervals, and use the results of these tests as a source of information about the intellectual readiness of the students.
4. Be aware of in-school and out-of-school factors that may influence the students' emotional readiness to learn.
5. Assemble and maintain continuous information about a student's achievement to assist in evaluating his scholastic readiness.
6. Use standardized tests as well as teacher-constructed tests to determine achievement levels in various subject areas.
7. Carefully observe the students to determine their readiness for specific school-related tasks.
8. Remember that even under ideal teaching-learning situations readiness factors impose limits to accomplishment.

Cautions

1. Don't forget that readiness consists of many facets.
2. Don't oversimplify your thinking about any type of mental, physical, emotional, or social readiness.
3. Don't forget that readiness comes as a result of a long series of related preliminary developments.
4. Don't assume that readiness for undertaking a given task is present without investigating.
5. Don't assume that a student is ready for specific learning tasks just because he has reached a given chronological age.
6. Don't require students to become involved in learning tasks for which they are not ready.[20]
7. Don't ignore the influence of study habits on readiness.
8. Don't overlook the value of stimulation, opportunity, and experimentation as means for encouraging certain types of readiness.[21]

EFFECT OF MOTIVATION ON LEARNING

Readiness and motivation are closely related concerns of the instructional process, and both must be present if serious, goal-

---

[20]Mills and Douglass, *op. cit.*, p. 91.
[21]Burton, *op. cit.*, p. 160.

oriented learning is to take place. Because motivation plays such an important role in the teaching-learning process, writers of responsible methods textbooks devote considerable attention to it, and educational psychologists feel that an understanding of its principles is basic to sound teaching. The use of motivational devices has become so much a part of the instructional process that many teachers go about this aspect of their teaching somewhat mechanically. A good case, however, can be made for careful, conscious, frequent re-evaluation of motivational teaching procedures.

When a learner identifies a goal that has personal value for him, he tries to reach that goal.[22] *Motivation* may thus be described as the personal, internal process that determines the strength and direction of a person's behavior or line of action. Motivation may also involve a second person (for example, the teacher) trying to arouse the first to greater effort.

According to McDonald,[23] motivation consists of three elements: (1) an energy change takes place in the neurophysiological system of the learner; (2) feelings (psychological tensions) about the goal are aroused; and (3) the learner makes those responses that will lead him to the desired goal. Stated somewhat differently, motivation is a combination of forces that (1) begin the movement toward a desired goal; (2) determine the direction this movement will take; and (3) sustain goal-directed behavior.[24] For example, the college-bound tenth-grade student of English grammar may (1) begin his course with a general desire to learn grammar; (2) discover that he is particularly weak in subject-verb agreement, an area of major emphasis in the college entrance examination he hopes to pass; and (3) concentrate his attention for a prolonged period on meeting this deficiency. The wise teacher should be aware of such a need and help the student accomplish his goal.

It is often useful to differentiate between extrinsic and intrinsic motivation.[25] *Extrinsic* (external) forces exist outside of the learner and tend to press him into a given course of action. Among these external forces are rewards, punishments, physical circumstances, and the desires of others. The teacher's praise, the teacher's rebuke, a fire alarm in the school building, and parental ambitions may thus be viewed as extrinsic motivators.

Intrinsic (internal)[26] forces, on the other hand, originate within

---

[22]Kimball Wiles, *Teaching for Better Schools*, 2d. ed. (Englewood Cliffs, N.J.: Prentice-Hall, 1959), pp. 201–220, devotes a full chapter to "Guidance in the Formation of Goals."

[23]McDonald, *op. cit.*, pp. 77–78.

[24]Morse and Wingo, *op. cit.*, p. 287.

[25]Lindgren, *op. cit.*, pp. 23–24, provides a clarifying discussion of internal and external forces.

[26]McKean, *op. cit.*, pp. 107–108, stresses the superiority of intrinsic motivation. Burton, *op. cit.*, p. 55, also believes that intrinsic motivation serves the purposes of education better than extrinsic motivation.

the individual and impel him to seek a given goal. Such forces include attitudes, needs, and anxieties. An interest in music, an attitude toward a racial minority, the need for food, and the fear of failing the chemistry test are all expressions that motivate certain behavior.

No Learning Without Motivation

Try to visualize a secondary school in which there is a total absence of student motivation. What would it be like? Naturally, such a situation could not possibly exist—and certainly if it did, learning would be at a standstill, for all segments of the school curriculum are made up of goals that can be achieved only through motivation.[27] No book would be opened; no social conversation would be held. In fact, students would not come to school—they would have no motive for doing so. To visualize such a school is not only difficult but ridiculous.

Not so ridiculous, however, are the many classroom situations in which student motivation is at a minimum and in which learning is correspondingly slow and labored. Few students have escaped the boredom of an unmotivated class. Such a class is characterized by the teacher who leaves his students with half-formed and hazy concepts; by the teacher who makes no attempt to select procedures that will be interesting to students; by the teacher who criticizes students negatively rather than constructively; and by strained personal relationships between students and teacher. In such a classroom, student desires are not considered, and the teacher assumes total responsibility for establishing instructional goals. No attempt is made to surround students with new and different teaching devices to arouse their interests. Furthermore, the teacher is not sufficiently well acquainted with individual members of his class to employ motivational techniques to best advantage.

Student motivation is often at a minimum in required courses, as teachers of English, history, and general mathematics are well aware. As a result, such courses pose difficult problems of motivation. The instructor is faced with the necessity for encouraging learners to see personal value in course objectives even when the students' personal inclinations run in the opposite direction.[28] How, for example, does one motivate a youngster from a lower-class rural family to study United States history?

To achieve motivation, the teacher can make the course content as meaningful as possible by (1) carefully selecting and using textbooks and supplementary reading materials, (2) including interesting narrative accounts in class lectures, (3) relating certain aspects of

[27]Nordberg, Bradfield, and Odell, *op. cit.*, p. 19.

[28]Woodruff, *op. cit.*, pp. 268–269, discusses the necessity for training the learner to accept the value of study and development.

the course content to the life of the student, and (4) using course-related projects geared to the student's interests. Furthermore, the teacher can permit a degree of student participation in establishing unit goals, in devising and using interesting aids to convey concepts, and in providing experiences in which the student can succeed.

Motivational Influences

The successful teacher must be aware of the various factors that influence motivation, and he must manipulate these factors as best he can in order to arouse the student's motivation to learn.[29]

Student Interests and Desires

What interests a student will motivate him;[30] conversely, what does not interest a student will not motivate him. Marvin, the son of an electrical engineer, developed a sizable technical vocabulary and an abiding interest in the field of engineering. By the time he reached high school, Marvin was reading most of the popular and some of the technical articles related to his special interest. He was motivated to choose any subject that seemed related to engineering.

Although teachers have always known that student interests and desires play an important role in motivation, they frequently fail to make practical use of this truth. The mathematics teacher knows of Darrell's interest in farming; yet, though Darrell is failing, the teacher refuses to adapt the story problems in mathematics to the boy's interest. On the other hand, Darrell's English teacher permits her students to write on any topic that interests them, as long as she feels it serves an educational purpose.

If a student perceives a subject or a unit as having particular value for him, he will study to achieve its goals; if he finds little relationship between subject-matter goals and his personal desires, he will respond apathetically or negatively. Kathy has always viewed her role in life as a domestic one; thus she loved her homemaking course and worked hard in it. When she became engaged during her senior year, she had an additional incentive to learn as much as possible about sewing, cooking, child care, and general household management. Her teacher said she had never seen a girl work so hard.

A somewhat similar case is that of Warren Sutter. Since he had previously been a C student in English, Warren realized that his

---

[29]Samuel P. Wiggins, *Successful High School Teaching* (Boston: Houghton Mifflin Company, 1958), pp. 214–217, provides a brief general discussion of the "Ways of Motivation."

See Chapter 2, pp. 18–22, in the present text for a general discussion of motivation and its influencing factors.

[30]Woodruff, *op. cit.*, p. 267, points out the need to differentiate between transitory interests and deeper motivation and stresses the desirability of having the learner acquire a "vision of high life goals for himself" as a basis for the most effective kind of learning.

chance for making a respectable score on the freshman English examination at the state university next year would depend largely upon how much information he could acquire during the current year. To enter the university was the most important goal in his life right now. As a result Warren studied English as he had never studied before. After school he often sought the help of the teacher, and he spent between one and two hours every evening on English. But his supreme sacrifice came when he decided that going out for the basketball team would consume too much of his time. His desired goal determined his motivation and effort to learn English.

Environment

Every individual views all environmental factors in terms of their effect on his personal welfare. This applies to all curriculum- and instructional-related situations as well as to the actual physical environment.

The biology laboratory equipped with numerous specimens, individual study stations, and an adequate number of microscopes; the English classroom with displays of effective student themes, a well-equipped classroom library, and adjoining small rooms for special study projects; the social studies classroom with a large moveable globe, a plentiful supply of retractable maps mounted above the chalkboard, and an extensive file of photographs of historical events—all are representative of a desirable physical environment to motivate learning.

Some students view certain subjects as threats to their personal well-being. The poor achiever in mathematics who is suddenly thrust into a class situation in which he cannot hope for even a small measure of success is subject to frustration. Similarly, the physically underdeveloped youngster who is expected to compete effectively with his peers on the gym floor may feel that his inability is detrimental to his personal status. Before these two students can be adequately motivated, the impediments to their achievement—mathematics background and physical development—will have to be resolved.

Success

Students are motivated if a proper balance between successful and unsuccessful experiences can be maintained. A major responsibility of the teacher is to assist the student in achieving success, for success often serves as an effective motivator. The student who has a past record of achievement develops the confidence necessary for undertaking more difficult tasks.

Below-average and retarded youngsters in classes composed largely of average students are continually confronted with defeats. Instruction geared to the average student does not and cannot meet the needs of the slower students. As a result, few of them achieve even what their limited capacities would permit. For this reason, a homogeneous grouping of students helps provide a setting in which youngsters can achieve success most of the time. However, it is neither necessary nor desirable for students to achieve success under *all* circumstances. The bright student who finds himself in an average group may gain success with limited effort. His motivation becomes dulled, his interest wanes, and poor habits are formed. He is, therefore, denied the challenge he deserves.

Any student's level of aspiration[31] is related to the experiences he has had and the concepts he has derived from those experiences. In other words, the learner wants to achieve what his past achievement has taught him he probably can achieve. If his achievement has been low, his aspiration for future achievement will be correspondingly low. The student who scored above 90 per cent on the history tests he took during the first semester has reason to believe that his test scores will be high during the second semester. His aspirations are high. It is important to realize, however, that this belief does not always guarantee optimum motivation.

Goals

If a student sees that an established instructional goal lies in the same direction as his personal desires, he will be motivated.[32] The course goals for a class in auto mechanics, for example, may aim to give students a detailed acquaintance with engine parts and enable them to diagnose and, finally, to repair mechanical difficulties. Students often register for this elective course because their personal goals and the course goals are identical.

Any goal that students view as unattainable hinders motivation. This is often true for below-average students, but it may be true for above-average and bright students as well. A teacher who requires students to complete a full week of assignments in two days stifles motivation, for students react to assignments in terms of what they believe can or cannot be done. In such a situation, defeat is probable from the start.

Incentives

No one incentive will motivate all students equally.[33] Beginning teachers often assume that a threat of low grades will stimulate all students to greater effort. Experienced teachers, however, readily agree that one can expect highly variable reactions to such a threat. Similarly, the promise of higher pay and better job opportunities in

---

[31]See McDonald, *op. cit.*, pp. 107–109, for a discussion of levels of aspiration and how they are affected by success and failure.

[32]Klausmeier, *Teaching in the Secondary School*, pp. 74–75, provides a useful discussion of the relationship between goals and student motivation.

See also Mills and Douglass, *op. cit.*, pp. 100–101.

Burton, *op. cit.*, p. 54, makes a strong plea for student involvement in goal indentification.

[33]The classroom use of incentives is covered by McDonald, *op. cit.*, pp. 119–120.

the future for students who consistently work hard will motivate only a portion of the class members.

Principles Related to Motivation

The proper use of motivation to promote learning calls for a knowledge of readiness, individual differences, adjustment, and learning theory, as well as for an acquaintance with other related areas. Hence, principles directly related to motivation are numerous,[34] but only those that provide the greatest help to the teacher are listed below.

1. All behavior (except that governed by the autonomic nervous system) is motivated.
2. The mind may be stimulated by an external force, but it is the learner's reaction to the stimulus that results in learning.
3. Motivation is best viewed as a tool to assist instruction, not as an end in itself.
4. Each individual views environmental factors in terms of their assumed effect on his personal welfare. If the individual is lacking something he views as essential to the maintenance of his way of life, he is ready to take whatever action he believes will supply that lack.[35]
5. Since each learner sees only what his experience and ability enable him to see, his motivation will result partly from what he sees in a particular situation.
6. Interests motivate students, and, in the absence of interest, learning does not take place. It is easy, however, to confuse superficial interests with deeper motivation.
7. When a student recognizes a goal to be of personal importance to him, he is motivated.[36] Conversely, if he believes that what he is learning will not help him achieve his desired goals, his responsiveness will be limited. A student who is strongly committed to a goal will exert great effort to achieve that goal.
8. Learning that brings reward and satisfaction to the student acts as a motivator for further learning.
9. The student's level of aspiration is the result of experience from which he develops a concept of what he will be able to do.

---

[34]Klausmeier, *Teaching in the Secondary School*, pp. 340–348, lists and discusses eight useful principles of motivation.

Morse and Wingo, *op. cit.*, p. 304, enumerate eighteen very helpful generalizations related to motivation for learning.

[35]Nordberg, Bradfield, and Odell, *op. cit.*, p. 70, list several factors that should be considered in determining the motivational state of individual students.

See also Harry N. Rivlin, *Teaching Adolescents in Secondary Schools*, 2d. ed. (New York: Appleton-Century-Crofts, 1961), pp. 78–85.

[36]Morse and Wingo, *op. cit.*, pp. 294–298, examine the implications of one set of goals for the teacher and another set for the learner.

See also the discussion by Wiles, *op. cit.*, pp. 201–203.

Success tends to raise his level of aspiration, and failure tends to depress it. Motivation is thus enhanced by maintaining a proper balance between success and failure. Subject-matter content that has been thoroughly learned gives a feeling of success to each student. Such success is motivational.

Correct and Incorrect Use

Many teachers achieve a degree of student motivation by chance. Although they teach in traditional ways and without any specific intention to motivate, their instruction still results in some movement toward goals. The pronounced inefficiency with which this movement takes place, however, often differentiates the unskilled teacher from the skilled. The examples below point out this difference.

MR. GREENWOOD'S UNMOTIVATED MIXED CHORUS

Mr. Greenwood's senior high school mixed chorus class was unmotivated. As he indicated to his students at the beginning of the semester, the class was not organized to prepare numbers for public presentation. Its purpose was to teach students to sing in a mixed group. Sometimes the roll call, the distribution of music, and the settling of the class at the beginning of the period consumed as much as seven minutes. Usually students exerted pressure to sing the old and familiar songs, including some that lacked quality. Seasonal favorites were sung at Christmas time, but little attention was paid to learning songs related to other holidays. Often the class was disturbed by horseplay that made it impossible for the teacher to proceed.

Several factors in Mr. Greenwood's class show his lack of knowledge about motivation. The purpose of the course was described in such a general way that it had little motivating effect. Objectives were vague and students had difficulty determining exactly what was expected of them. Inefficiency in the conduct of classroom routine left students with the impression that course content, actual participation in singing, was of limited value. The teacher's standards of vocal quality were unjustifiably low, and, sensing this, students geared their own aspirations to those of the teacher. Because they were bored, students turned to misbehavior. In a highly motivated class neither the teacher nor the strongly motivated students would have tolerated this action.

MR. BOWDEN HAMPERS MOTIVATION

The eleventh-grade United States history class was known to all the students because Mr. Bowden, the teacher, was unrelenting in his demand for strict discipline. Since he was an authoritarian, he placed ready-made course and unit objectives into the hands of students. The daily procedure consisted of a class lecture for the first twenty minutes, followed by a half-hour study period in which students studied from their texts and answered study questions prepared by the teacher. There was no variation from this procedure. Mr. Bowden paid no direct attention to individual differences among his students; however, he did tell them that they could read supplemental materials outside of class if they wished.

This teaching situation emphasizes the fact that there is much more to motivation than stern classroom control. Because students were given no voice in determining objectives or were not encouraged to ask questions about them, they found it difficult to accept the course objectives as their own. A lecture procedure in which student participation is severely restricted is not conducive to learning. Although this procedure may serve the needs of a limited number of students, it is quite unsuited to a majority. Furthermore, the inflexibility of any set procedure is open to challenge on the grounds that it fails to motivate.

There are, happily, many teachers whose professional knowledge enables them to use motivational techniques effectively. Look, for example, at Mrs. Kapp.

MRS. KAPP ACHIEVES MOTIVATION

Mrs. Kapp was determined to get her tenth-grade world geography unit on the Middle East off to a good start. Although she devoted a good deal of time to preplanning class objectives, she discussed them in detail with members of her class and asked for their suggestions. The teacher insisted that students not only understand the objectives, but that they personally accept them as being important.

A diagnostic test given at the beginning of the unit revealed approximately what each student knew about the Middle East. Mrs. Kapp could plan realistically from this point on, giving consideration to individual differences in achievement and ability. Assignments were often differentiated to take this into consideration, and students were thus kept interested.

Mrs. Kapp frequently showed and explained colored slides during this unit. Two attractive bulletin boards were prepared by students under the teacher's direction, and special oral reports, which supplemented textbook study, were given by student volunteers.

During the supervised study periods, which were held when Mrs. Kapp felt they would serve a useful purpose, the teacher moved among the members of her class, helping, suggesting, and, in many cases, praising. Students were encouraged to be realistic in what they expected of themselves.

Mrs. Kapp knew how to motivate students. She was aware of the basic motivational need for students to personally accept course objectives as their own. Furthermore, she planned realistically for the teaching of content on the basis of an up-to-date knowledge of student achievement.[37] Desirable stimuli were provided through inter-

[37]Jean D. Grambs, William J. Iverson, and Franklin K. Patterson, *Modern Methods in Secondary Education*, rev. ed. (New York: The Dryden Press, 1958), pp. 137–145, provide a range of specific suggestions for planning and motivation.

esting teaching aids, and she helped establish and maintain effective rapport with her students through assistance given during the supervised study period.

MR. HAYMOND'S ENTHUSIASM MOTIVATES

Students were not quite sure why they liked Mr. Haymond so much, but his supervisor could have identified the reason very quickly: Mr. Haymond knew how to motivate students. There were several significant factors that the supervisor noticed when he visited Mr. Haymond's ninth-grade English class.

Mr. Haymond was enthusiastic whenever he talked about English literature; it was as if he were discussing the most important thing in the world. But he didn't stop there. When he assigned a literary selection, he carefully identified, with student help, the most difficult words; he then explained and wrote them on the board. Students were told to look for specific subtle meanings. With interest, dramatic flourish, and meaning, Mr. Haymond read aloud the first page of the selection. The students soon began reading enthusiastically on the strength of their own motivation and interest.

When general student interest began to diminish, Mr. Haymond held a brief discussion in which he asked specific questions designed to reveal the real reasons for this lack of interest. The students were then willing to get back to their reading. During the study period Mr. Haymond talked briefly and informally with individual students about what they were reading and its meaning to them. In order to make the material meaningful, he related his explanations to the students' background. He also used the information he had gained during the question-and-answer period to reawaken their interest and help meet individual needs.

Through his observation of the class, the supervisor singled out the reasons for Mr. Haymond's unusual skill in motivating students. The teacher was intensely interested in the content he was teaching and was well prepared to teach it. This interest was, in turn, communicated to his students.[38] He was realistic in understanding that all students would not be equally interested, and he made a conscious effort to keep alive the interest of the less gifted students. The identification and explanation of difficult terms and subtle meanings helped solve difficulties in comprehension before they could arise and aided in sustaining interest.

Specific Suggestions

For both beginning and experienced teachers, the following recommendations and cautions should serve as helpful guidelines for the effective use of motivational procedures.

Recommendations

1. Identify, through experimentation, the incentives that moti-

[38] *Ibid.*, p. 138, include a brief discussion on conveying enthusiasm for learning.

vate different students in your class. Use direct contact with natural phenomena as a means of motivation.[39] Employ teaching procedures that are interesting to students.

2. Help students identify the personal value that specific academic goals will have for them, and also help them establish realistic and educationally sound goals for themselves.[40]

3. Be aware of the motivational effect of grades; then use them sparingly for this purpose. However, as a basis for motivation, keep students informed about their academic progress.[41]

4. Provide students with a sound balance between successful and unsuccessful experiences. Arrange for successful experiences that will build their self-expectations, and help students achieve good grades where possible.

5. Maintain a desirable balance between approval and disapproval while helping bring about optimum student motivation. Constructive criticism is preferable to negative criticism in dealing with students, but occasional negative criticism is better than no criticism at all.

6. Find means for establishing and maintaining rapport with students. Help the individual student manage his tensions and his emotions.

7. Make your lessons meaningful so that students will be stimulated. Help the student interpret what is desirable performance for himself in consideration of his unique characteristics.

8. Learn to identify the physiological, social, and emotional deficiencies in the lives of students. Their attempts to meet these problems may explain certain kinds of student behavior.

9. Surround students with stimuli that will help make course content more interesting and desirable.

10. Teach your subject so well that students will develop a liking for it and for all that is related to it.

11. Minimize student frustrations through effective teaching.

Cautions

1. Don't forget that all behavior is motivated.

2. Don't assume that each student will accept the stated goal of the class as his own personal goal.

3. Don't assume that one incentive or one kind of incentive will motivate all youngsters.

---

[39]Woodruff, *op. cit.*, p. 266.

[40]Howard T. Batchelder, Maurice McGlasson, and Raleigh Schorling, *Student Teaching in Secondary Schools*, 4th ed, (New York: McGraw-Hill Book Company, 1964), p. 146, stress the importance of relating academic goals to the needs and interests of students.

Klausmeier, *Teaching in the Secondary School*, pp. 328–333, provides a useful discussion of goals and goal setting.

[41]See Mills and Douglass, *op. cit.*, p. 101.

4. Don't use competition as an end in itself, but only as a supplementary form of motivation.[42]

5. Don't use rewards and punishments unless you are sure that they will serve as desirable motivators.

6. Don't emphasize the failing aspects of a student's performance even though he is academically weak or limited in capacity.

7. Don't confuse educationally justified, interesting activities with entertainment.

8. Don't assume that all students will be equally interested in the same activity.

READINESS AND MOTIVATION IN REVIEW

This chapter has been concerned with the examination of two fundamental instructional concerns—readiness and motivation. Efficient learning would be impossible if either one were absent.

Several kinds of readiness may simultaneously influence the effectiveness of learning; however, each kind of readiness can exert its own effect. Physical readiness, for example, is essential for learning skill subjects, such as typing, instrumental music, and physical education. Neural growth, native capacity, and experience—the three aspects of intellectual readiness—determine whether a student can undertake complex mental tasks. Similarly, social experience provides essential knowledge and self-assurance that result in social readiness.

Motivation may be described as a state of arousal in which an individual wishes to achieve a specific goal and exerts effort to do so. Therefore, motivation is of fundamental concern to all teachers in helping promote efficient learning. How responsive a learner is to an instructional situation and how hard he will work to achieve a goal will depend upon his motivation. If a student sees that instructional objectives parallel the direction of his personal values, he will be strongly motivated.

PROBLEMS FOR STUDY AND DISCUSSION

1. Describe in some detail the characteristics of the student who would be ready to study effectively in the area of your teaching major.

2. How does I.Q. affect readiness? Discuss. Give examples that support your discussion.

3. Assumption: Two boys of the same chronological age (15) live in the

---

[42]The contradiction of urging students to be cooperative as well as competitive is discussed by Klausmeier, *Teaching in the Secondary School*, pp. 335–337.

same neighborhood. One is a slow learner (I.Q. 89), and the other boy is bright (I.Q. 132). In what respects and under what circumstances may the slow learner be more nearly ready than the bright boy to undertake learning tasks in a ninth-grade English class?

4. Discuss the relationship of concept formation to intellectual readiness.

5. Assumption: You have a girl in your tenth-grade class who is academically above average but who is excessively shy and lacking in social confidence. Describe the specific steps you would take in helping her achieve social readiness.

6. Describe three classroom situations in which students exhibit lack of emotional readiness for learning.

7. Explain the following statement: In the absence of readiness the student cannot learn.

8. Discuss the effect of unearned promotion on the student's readiness to learn.

9. Is the intelligence test an accurate measure of the student's intellectual readiness to undertake a given learning task? Explain.

10. Describe the unique set of readiness factors that relate to your teaching minor.

11. Describe a classroom situation related to your teaching major in which motivation is at a minimum. How closely does your teaching approximate this situation?

12. Differentiate between teacher goals and student goals. Why should the teacher be concerned with student goals?

13. Indicate how you would motivate a group of slow learners to learn general mathematics. Be specific.

14. Give three examples, from your own experience, in which strong motivation has caused students to work unusually hard.

15. What is the relationship between failure and motivation? Discuss and provide illustrations.

16. Explain this statement: Retarded youngsters seldom achieve what they could achieve.

17. Assumption: The teacher views the unit goals as attainable, but students in the class believe the goals cannot be attained. Whose will should prevail? Discuss.

18. Discuss the relationship between the student's level of aspiration and his past experiences. What does this relationship have to do with motivation?

19. Give five examples of intrinsic motivation that can be used to good advantage in your teaching major.

20. Explain the following statement: All behavior (except that governed by the autonomic nervous system) is motivated.

RECOMMENDED READINGS

Readiness

Adams, Georgia Sachs, and Theodore L. Torgerson, *Measurement and Evaluation for the Secondary-School Teacher.* New York: The Dryden Press, 1956, Chapters 4–10.

Burton, William H., *The Guidance of Learning Activities,* 3d. ed. New York: Appleton-Century-Crofts, Inc., 1962, pp. 160–161.

Klausmeier, Herbert J., *Learning and Human Abilities: Educational Psychology.* New York: Harper & Brothers, 1961, Chapter 3.

Klausmeier, Herbert J., *Teaching in the Secondary School.* New York: Harper & Brothers, 1958, pp. 312–318.

Lindgren, Henry C., *Educational Psychology in the Classroom,* 2d. ed. New York: John Wiley and Sons, 1962, pp. 274–275.

McDonald, Frederick J., *Educational Psychology.* San Francisco: Wadsworth Publishing Company, 1959, pp. 598–603.

McKean, Robert C., *Principles and Methods in Secondary Education.* Columbus, Ohio: Charles E. Merrill Books, Inc., 1962, p. 110.

Mills, Hubert H., and Harl R. Douglass, *Teaching in High School,* 2d. ed. New York: Ronald Press, 1957, pp. 90–91.

Morse, William C., and G. Max Wingo, *Psychology and Teaching,* 2d. ed. Chicago: Scott, Foresman and Company, 1962, Chapter 11.

Nordberg, H. Orville, James M. Bradfield, and William C. Odell, *Secondary School Teaching.* New York: The Macmillan Company, 1962, pp. 71–73.

Wiggins, Samuel P., *Successful High School Teaching.* Boston: Houghton Mifflin Company, 1958, p. 208.

Woodruff, Asahel D., *Basic Concepts of Teaching; with Brief Readings.* San Francisco: Chandler Publishing Company, 1962, Chapter 13.

Motivation

Batchelder, Howard T., Maurice McGlasson, and Raleigh Schorling, *Student Teaching in Secondary Schools,* 4th ed. New York: McGraw-Hill Book Company, 1964, pp. 142–162.

Burton, William H., *The Guidance of Learning Activities,* 3d. ed. New York: Appleton-Century-Crofts, Inc., 1962, pp. 54–69.

Grambs, Jean D., William J. Iverson, and Franklin K. Patterson, *Modern Methods in Secondary Education,* rev. ed. New York: The Dryden Press, 1958, pp. 137–145.

Hansen, Kenneth H., *High School Teaching.* Englewood Cliffs, N.J.: Prentice-Hall, Inc., 1957, pp. 129–136 and 301–302.

Klausmeier, Herbert J., *Learning and Human Abilities: Educational Psychology.* New York: Harper & Brothers, 1961, Chapter 11.

Klausmeier, Herbert J., *Teaching in the Secondary School.* New York: Harper & Brothers, 1958, pp. 70–75.

Lindgren, Henry C., *Educational Psychology in the Classroom,* 2d. ed. New York: John Wiley and Sons, 1962, Chapter 2.

McDonald, Frederick J., *Educational Psychology.* San Francisco: Wadsworth Publishing Company, Inc., 1959, Chapter 4.

McKean, Robert C., *Principles and Methods in Secondary Education.* Columbus, Ohio: Charles E. Merrill Books, Inc., 1962, pp. 107–109.

Mills, Hubert H., and Harl R. Douglass, *Teaching in High School,* 2d. ed. New York: Ronald Press, 1957, Chapter 12.

Morse, William C., and G. Max Wingo, *Psychology and Teaching,* 2d. ed. Chicago: Scott, Foresman and Company, 1962, Chapter 12.

Nordberg, H. Orville, James M. Bradfield, and William C. Odell, *Sec-*

ondary School Teaching. New York: The Macmillan Company, 1962, pp. 19, 28–30, 69–70, and 185.

Rivlin, Harry N., *Teaching Adolescents in Secondary Schools,* 2d. ed. New York: Appleton-Century-Crofts, Inc., 1961, pp. 78–85.

Wellington, C. Burleigh, and Jean Wellington, *Teaching for Critical Thinking: with Emphasis on Secondary Education.* New York: McGraw-Hill Book Company, 1960, Chapter 5.

Wiggins, Samuel P., *Successful High School Teaching.* Boston: Houghton Mifflin Company, 1958, pp. 212–217.

Wiles, Kimball, *Teaching for Better Schools,* 2d. ed. Englewood Cliffs, N.J.: Prentice-Hall, Inc., 1959, Chapter 11.

Woodruff, Asahel D., *Basic Concepts of Teaching; with Brief Readings.* San Francisco: Chandler Publishing Company, 1962, Chapter 12.

15

Individual Differences, Remedial Teaching, and the Reporting of Pupil Progress

This chapter presents a discussion of three of the basic instructional responsibilities that are of continuing concern to the conscientious teacher: meeting the individual differences of students, providing remedial instruction, and reporting the progress of the students.

MEETING INDIVIDUAL DIFFERENCES

Because learning is an individual matter, the consideration of individual differences among students heightens learning efficiency.[1] Each person must learn for himself at his own speed. When the selection of methods, rate of content coverage, teacher expectations, and so forth are geared to the individual student's level, the student can achieve success. Learning procedures selected because they suit an individual student make the subject more interesting to that student and encourage motivation. This is often the case when slow learners in a heterogeneously grouped class are regrouped according to ability

[1]Asahel D. Woodruff, *Basic Concepts of Teaching; with Brief Readings* (San Francisco: Chandler Publishing Company, 1962), p. 48, points out that the learning process is the same for all learners but that there are individual differences in the readiness to learn.

and procedures and expectations are modified to meet the needs of the new group.[2]

Teachers are aware of the wide range of differences among secondary-school students.[3] Students vary not only in physical characteristics—such as height, skin texture, and color of hair—but also in the size of the family and the student's position in it; in cultural and experiential background; in general intelligence; in verbal, numerical, manual, or athletic ability; in personality; and in personal tastes, such as in the choice of clothing. It is the responsibility of the conscientious teacher to identify which of these innumerable differences have the most direct bearing on the teaching-learning process.[4]

Fortunately, psychologists and educators largely agree about the characteristics that are most significant to education. Those most frequently mentioned are intelligence,[5] emotional stability, physical health, social adjustment, experiential background, aspirations, interests, school achievement, attitudes, temperament and disposition, readiness, and specific skills, including reading skills. The sensitive teacher will be aware of these and other factors in the classroom situation when he attempts to improve instruction.

Advantages of Knowing Individual Differences

Instruction geared to the individual pupil has many advantages that are missing in group instruction. The very nature of our current school organization, however, rules out the possibility of large-scale tutorial instruction, so that the teacher must find some practical means of differentiating instruction for individuals in his class. An accurate appraisal of the characteristics that make the individual different from his classmates is necessary to establish a basis for careful, individualized teaching.

When the teacher has this basic information, he can employ a range of activities geared to the interest and comprehension levels of different students, or groups of students, instead of using one learning activity suitable for only a small portion of the class. His instructional plans are more apt to succeed because they will be geared to meet the specific needs of individuals. Because he knows that Carolyn is gifted in art work but socially insecure, the teacher can ask her to help dec-

---

[2]Kimball Wiles, *Teaching for Better Schools*, 2d. ed. (Englewood Cliffs, N.J.: Prentice-Hall, 1959), pp. 161–163, presents useful descriptions of the underachieving pupil, the aggressive child, the withdrawing child, etc.

[3]Frederick J. McDonald, *Educational Psychology* (San Francisco: Wadsworth Publishing Company, 1959), pp. 419–430, discusses the "range of individual differences."

[4]Vincent McGuire, Robert B. Myers, and Charles L. Durrance, *Your Student Teaching in the Secondary School* (Boston: Allyn and Bacon, 1959), pp. 240–245, provide descriptions of differences among students that affect teaching and learning.

[5]William H. Burton, *The Guidance of Learning Activities*, 3d. ed. (New York: Appleton-Century-Crofts, 1962), pp. 234–235, discusses the differences in student intelligence.

orate the bulletin boards rather than give an oral report before the class—an assignment doomed to defeat. If Carolyn's work on the bulletin board is good, the teacher will have an opportunity to give her deserved praise, which will help Carolyn develop self-confidence.

Using Materials Effectively

Effective use of materials and equipment requires specific as well as general knowledge of the students in a class. The teacher is aware, for example, that gifted Lynn Wesley will be bored if he is required to read the text used by a majority of students in eleventh-grade United States history. As a result, Lynn is assigned a college-level text and given freedom to study in the library. Similarly, the shop teacher has discovered through experience that Theron Heaps does not exhibit the same degree of responsibility in the use of power tools as do other students. As a result, the teacher plans to allow Theron to use the power saw only under teacher supervision. Furthermore, the teacher insists that Theron rigidly observe all safety precautions when using any power tool.

Improving Socialization

The teacher may plan to group students in order to improve socialization. Ethel Hill, for example, a girl with high social aspirations and marked cliquish tendencies, never associates with students below the upper-middle class from which she comes. Mr. Angus changed her seat so that Ethel was surrounded by lower-middle class students who were quite socially acceptable to the others in the class.

Planning Assignments

More realistic assignments can be planned if the teacher knows the academic strengths and weaknesses of his students. The biology teacher knows that Dean Cook is limited in interest and intelligence. As a result, the specific assignment planned for Dean is less demanding than that required of the average student, although it provides the essential concepts. In the same tenth-grade class is a student of average capacity who is intensely interested in biology but who reads at the sixth-grade level. Assignments planned for this boy involve the use of special materials and the exchange of course-related ideas with a group of interested and bright youngsters.

Increasing Motivation

The steps taken to motivate students often bear a direct relationship to what the teacher knows about his students.[6] He may know, for

[6]C. Burleigh Wellington and Jean Wellington, *Teaching for Critical Thinking; with Emphasis on Secondary Education* (New York: McGraw-Hill Book Company, 1960), pp. 106–108, point out the need for a broad understanding of the diversity among learners as an aid to motivation.

example, that although Ralph hopes to become an attorney, his oral English is hardly what one would expect to find in the courtroom and must be improved if he is to achieve his goal. At appropriate times and under the desired circumstances, this fact is called to Ralph's attention. Eleanor Van Leuven, a student in the same class, hopes to become a newspaper reporter. At the suggestion of the teacher, Eleanor makes several contributions to the local paper as well as the school paper, but only after the articles have been examined by her instructor. She is also given the assignment of clipping out class-related newspaper articles to display on the bulletin board.

Developing Rapport

The development of rapport between student and teacher, so essential to effective instruction, is enhanced through the teacher's personal acquaintance with each student. Max Underwood, the band director, made it a policy to find out about the musical as well as the nonmusical, out-of-school activities of his students. Before and after school, before and after class, and whenever he met students in the hall, he would make such friendly comments as "I heard that you played very well in the young people's meeting last night, Glen" or "Lucy tells me that you have decided to form a string ensemble." To convey through teaching procedures the unmistakable attitude that students are nothing more than members of the crowd inhibits rapport and promotes antagonism. Students should be regarded as individuals at all times and dealt with on an individual basis whenever possible.

Gearing Methods to Learners

Learning efficiency is enhanced by the selection of those methods that are best suited to the specific characteristics of the students. Slow learners, for example, respond poorly to a straight lecture method. They may, however, learn effectively from a carefully planned informal discussion geared to their own interest and vocabulary level. Gifted students, on the other hand, often profit from procedures involving intensive self-directed reading. Furthermore, the learner who is preoccupied with a serious personal problem will require a different instructional procedure than the student who can focus his conscious attention in any direction.

Procedures for Differentiating Instruction

Literally dozens of techniques are currently employed in the attempt to meet the individual needs of students effectively.[7] These

---

[7]Harry N. Rivlin, *Teaching Adolescents in Secondary Schools*, 2d. ed. (New York: Appleton-Century-Crofts, 1961), pp. 350–351, discusses cocurricular activities as a means of meeting the individual interests of students.

techniques may be helpfully categorized as (1) administrative provisions and (2) instructional provisions. Those listed and discussed below represent procedures that have received varying degrees of emphasis from teachers and specific school systems.

Administrative Provisions

Administrative provisions for differentiating instruction are under the direct control of the school superintendent or principal.[8] Teachers are also, of necessity, strongly involved in helping implement these procedures. Some of the most frequently used administrative provisions are:

- Grouping by sections according to ability
- Variation in number of subjects a student may take
- Exploratory courses aimed at vocational guidance
- Special classes for slow learners and retarded pupils
- Special classes for the gifted
- Team teaching
- Provision for individual progress in a subject without regard to grade level
- Mid-year promotions
- Accelerations
- Nonpromotion or elimination
- Special guidance services

Grouping according to ability. One frequently used administrative procedure is that of grouping students in sections according to ability. Although there has been considerable fluctuation of educators' willingness to group students homogeneously, the postwar emphasis on science and international competition has exerted force in this direction. A large majority of secondary schools, however, currently group their students heterogeneously in spite of widespread experimentation and pressures.

Academic load related to ability. Some schools restrict the number of subjects a student may take on the basis of his past performance. On the other hand, a student with high academic ability and high achievement is often permitted or even encouraged to take a heavier load.

Exploratory courses and special classes. Secondary schools offer a number of exploratory courses aimed at vocational guidance. Among these are shop courses of various types, homemaking, and business courses.

Large school systems frequently provide special classes for slow learners and retarded pupils. Such classes, however, pose very real difficulties for small school districts in terms of staff, housing, and financial support. Although special classes for the gifted have long

[8]See Burton, *op. cit.*, pp. 240–241, for a useful examination of administrative provisions for meeting individual differences.

existed in large metropolitan areas, they are now being developed with increasing frequency in smaller cities. National pressures and resulting public support have encouraged this movement.

Team teaching. Team teaching, which involves the use of two or more professionals or para-professionals in an instructional situation, has received considerable attention during the past few years.[9] Varieties of teaching teams have been assembled and used with varying degrees of success at all levels of the secondary school. The classes taught range from very large groups to small and homogeneous groups.

Specially prepared materials. Many secondary schools throughout the United States are experimenting with programed learning. Specially prepared materials permit step-by-step and largely self-directed progress in learning a particular subject. Students may move slowly if limited by academic ability or poor past achievement, or they may move rapidly from one step to another if their comprehension permits.

In order to encourage differentiation in instruction, administrators in forward-looking school systems often encourage the collection of a range of specially prepared units gathered from many sources. This material can thus be readily available to all the teachers in the system. When necessary materials are not available, administrators—particularly in large, well-financed districts—sometimes activate committees to undertake the production of such materials on an extra-pay or released-time basis.

Promotions. Mid-year promotions serve a useful purpose by permitting slow students who are one semester behind their age group to advance in grade without waiting a full year. Similarly, bright students who have taken extra courses may in a few years earn sufficient credits to warrant a promotion at the mid-year mark. Neither practice is typical, however.

Accelerations and nonpromotions, so frequent in the 1930's, are now largely a matter of history, because they violated the need for gradual step-by-step advancement. Although the desirability of having students proceed at rates suitable to their capacities and achievement is well recognized, other provisions serve these needs much more effectively. One such provision is a special guidance service that provides specific help in the areas of vocational, social, academic, and personal adjustment.[10]

Instructional Provisions

The procedures employed by teachers to differentiate instruction for students are numerous and varied. Differentiation frequently

---

[9]See Chapter 19, pp. 472–483, for a more detailed discussion of team teaching.

[10]Henry C. Lindgren, *Educational Psychology in the Classroom*, 2d. ed. (New York: John Wiley and Sons, 1962), Chapter 17, discusses guidance services as a means of providing individualized help for the learner.

takes place at the level of unit planning when three kinds of activities are listed—those suitable for slow, average, and fast learners. Objectives may be similarly differentiated. The daily lesson plan may pinpoint specific procedures for students with special problems. Some of the most frequently used instructional provisions are:

- Differentiation in unit planning
- Supervised study
- Differentiated assignments[11]
- Informal grouping
- Subject-matter enrichment
- Differentiated questions
- Consideration of interests
- Modification of content
- Use of varied texts and other teaching materials
- Tutorial help
- Remedial teaching
- Out-of-school projects
- Differing student contracts[12]
- Use of practical problems
- Nonacademic guidance as needed
- Referral as needed[13]
- Laboratory instruction
- Special marking and reporting procedures

Supervised study and assignments. Supervised study permits the teacher to identify students with academic problems and to give them appropriate help. During a full study period, a range of students may receive such assistance. Frequently this help is focused on in-class assignments that have been designed to meet the needs of individual students. Although many teachers yield to the work-saving approach of making one assignment to all members of the class, more knowledgeable instructors recognize the need for differentiating assignments realistically in terms of student achievement and ability.

Grouping. Within the individual classroom, informal groups may be established to serve many useful purposes—committee work, review, demonstrations, and work on projects. Although in-class grouping is more common at the elementary-school level, it deserves much wider experimentation and use at the secondary levels.

Enrichment. A widely used means of differentiating academic work for the high achiever is the enrichment of subject-matter content through additional reading tasks that expand the student's knowledge. Because such enrichment frequently calls for "more of the same" without desired penetration of more difficult concepts, such procedures have been subject to repeated criticism. Some teachers view enrichment as a type of pin counting that has little academic value;

---

[11]Hubert H. Mills and Harl R. Douglass, *Teaching in High School,* 2d. ed. (New York: Ronald Press, 1957), pp. 395–398, discuss and give examples of differentiated assignments.

[12]*Ibid.*, pp. 397–398, present examples of differing contracts.

[13]Robert C. McKean, *Principles and Methods in Secondary Education* (Columbus, Ohio: Charles E. Merrill Books, Inc., 1962), p. 272, provides a brief but helpful discussion of the need for student referral and indicates the people to whom referral is most frequently made.

yet, this instructional provision can effectively meet the needs of certain individuals.

Questioning. Skillful use of the question is another effective way of meeting student differences in ability and achievement and of relating subject matter to student interests. Because of its extreme flexibility, the question may be used in connection with many instructional procedures and provides one of the most effective means for bringing student, subject matter, and teacher together.

Modification of content. Modification of course content through deletion or addition of material is often desirable. For slow learners, one possibility is to delete one or two difficult units during the school year. For rapid as well as slow learners, the use of textbooks of varying difficulty is common practice among better teachers. This practice may be extended by providing students with a wide range of non-textbook materials of varying difficulty. Newspapers and magazines serve well in this connection.

Tutorial help. If rapport between student and teacher is solidly established, tutorial help may be effectively given during study periods and before and after school. The limitation of this procedure is the time the teacher can devote to the task. Remedial teaching often involves tutorial help that may be provided by the teacher or by another student under teacher supervision.

Projects. In serving the educational needs of high-achievers and bright students, individual projects and special contracts can be employed. Often individual projects can be geared to particular high-level interests and abilities of bright students. Advanced students may also be encouraged to assume leadership roles in small groups.

Principles Related to Differentiation

It is important for the teacher to be able to determine the value of specific instructional procedures designed to meet the individual needs of his students. If he is to do this consistently and effectively, he must be able to relate specific procedures to generalizations that have wide application.[14] An acquaintance with the following principles is therefore basic.

1. Students vary in many ways that influence teaching and learning. For this reason the teacher must consider the individual differences of each student if teaching and learning are to be realistic. There is little value in recognizing individual differences unless the teacher uses this information to promote effective learning.[15]

---

[14]Herbert J. Klausmeier, *Learning and Human Abilities: Educational Psychology* (New York: Harper & Brothers, 1961), pp. 378–387, lists and discusses eight principles of particular relevance in providing for individual instruction.

[15]Kenneth H. Hansen, *High School Teaching* (Englewood Cliffs, N.J.: Prentice-Hall, 1957), p. 51, points out that teachers often fail to consider individual differences because they falsely assume that there is little they can do to meet these differences.

2. Differences among students that have the greatest effect on the teaching-learning process are related to intelligence, achievement, goals, interests, skills, habits, emotions, abilities, readiness, adjustment, socioeconomic status, personal health, and past experiences. Although intelligence is frequently singled out as the most important, it is only one of many factors.

3. Certain kinds of differences affect specific types of learning.

4. Because both heredity and environment play a marked role in determining individual differences, teacher expectations should be based on the careful appraisal of the abilities and backgrounds of the students.[16]

5. Adolescents do not go through the developmental tasks in the same sequence and at the same rate.

6. A student's academic behavior is not consistently the same under all circumstances, and his behavior may vary within a generally consistent pattern of development.

7. More than one type of learning can go on at the same time in a given individual. In addition, the student's rate of learning may vary from subject to subject.

8. The gifted child may be generally bright or bright in one area primarily. Exceptional talent and severe retardation are easily discernible, but the variations between these two extremes are less obvious and thus often receive limited attention. The fact that students may be handicapped in one area but gifted in another further complicates effective instruction.

9. Students must first be understood as individuals *apart* from the group and later as individuals functioning *within* the group.

10. A highly trained school staff is needed to insure that maximum learning takes place in spite of individual differences among students.[17]

11. Meeting individual differences effectively requires that helpful facilities and teaching materials be available. Differentiation of instruction also requires the use of many procedures, devices, and techniques; one or two procedures are insufficient.

12. A general teaching approach suitable to a majority of students in a given class may be quite ineffective for a minority of students in the same class. In addition, exposure to the same teaching procedures and environment may not produce the same results in all learners.

13. Students grouped homogeneously according to one measure will exhibit differences with respect to other measures.

---

[16]William L. Carter, Carl W. Hansen, and Margaret G. McKim, *Learning to Teach in the Secondary School* (New York: Macmillan, 1962), pp. 314–317, provide suggestions to teachers for adjusting standards to student abilities and backgrounds.

[17]See Klausmeier, *op. cit.*, pp. 381–382, for a brief discussion of the need for a competent school staff in providing for individual differences.

14. Individual guidance should be used as a device for helping the student achieve the most he possibly can.[18]

Correct and Incorrect Procedures

Differentiation of instruction to serve the needs of specific learners is universally recognized by teachers as imperative, but many of them do not exhibit adequate techniques of differentiation in the actual classroom.

Incorrect Procedures

The following examples point out certain teacher weaknesses in differentiating instruction.

MR. PICKETT HAS DIFFICULTY MEETING STUDENT DIFFERENCES

Arlo Pickett believed in heterogeneous grouping, but he admitted that he had a serious problem keeping all members of his mathematics class together because the I.Q.'s in the group ranged from 87 to 129. Instruction was geared to the middle one half of the class; as a result the brighter students were often bored during discussions and finished their assignments in half the time required by below-average students. In order to keep these brighter students occupied, Mr. Pickett required that they work on enrichment materials. If they finished this assigned work early, they performed clerical tasks for the teacher or prepared bulletin boards instead of working on additional challenging problems.

MRS. McCOARD WORKS WITH A SLOW SECTION

Mrs. McCoard had taught eleventh-grade English for six years without ever teaching one of the slow sections. When she was inevitably assigned a slow group, she was crushed. She had high academic standards and was determined to see that these students measured up to her expectations. Assignments were difficult and long. Even when students failed to comprehend an idea after what she assumed was an appropriate explanation, Mrs. McCoard felt justified in moving to the next point. Gradually students became apathetic and began to misbehave; Mrs. McCoard declared that it was impossible for these students to cope with the course.

MR. SPENCER RESTRICTS STUDENT CHOICE

Mr. J. W. Spencer decided to introduce theme writing to his ninth-grade English class. Students exhibited some interest in this new work until they discovered that they could write only on one of three topics selected by the teacher. Three of the students entered a vigorous protest, but Mr. Spencer held firm: They would write on one of the three topics. Peggy Rollins, a shy and retiring student, would have given anything to be able to write on her current interest—James Joyce's novels—but she said nothing.

---

[18]McKean, *op. cit.*, p. 272, makes a plea for a guidance approach to teaching in which the errors of mass education may be avoided.

Serious errors or omissions in differentiating instruction can be identified in each of the preceding examples. Mr. Pickett attempted to assist the bright students through the use of enrichment materials, but additional work on more difficult content was denied them. Lack of realism is reflected in the teaching of Mrs. McCoard, who tried to force students to learn beyond what their capacities and past achievement would permit. The effect of inflexibility and an unwillingness to consider student interest is illustrated by Mr. Spencer's action.

Correct Procedures

Effective use of teaching techniques, devices, and a school staff is illustrated in the cases below.

MISS MANSFIELD PLANS FOR DIFFERENTIATION

Hillsdale Consolidated Senior High School was made up of students from a range of social and economic circumstances. The administration and faculty members, however, had cast their lot in favor of heterogeneous grouping, realizing that teachers would have to exhibit considerable skill in meeting the individual differences of their students.

Miss Mansfield viewed her two classes of active and highly varied tenth-graders as an instructional challenge. Knowing there was a wide range of differences among her students, she assembled specific information on each student with respect to I.Q. and achievement in world history, the subject she was teaching. As the class progressed, she experimented with in-class grouping in order to (1) aid social adjustment, (2) assist with classroom control, and (3) serve the academic needs of students.

In her unit plans the teacher described assignments with three levels of difficulty. Further adjustments were often made during the study periods after the basic assignments had been given. No one was allowed to loaf in Miss Mansfield's classes, but she made sure that the less gifted students were not asked to do work that was beyond their capacities and their level of conceptual readiness. Gifted students, on the other hand, were directed to more difficult reading and were encouraged to work on individual projects that provided genuine challenge.

MR. WALTMAN MEETS THE NEEDS OF SLOW LEARNERS

Many of his colleagues were amazed when Mr. Waltman asked to be assigned one slow-learning group each semester. His experience over a period of ten years, however, had taught him that gearing the level of instruction to the individuals within the group resulted in effective learning for the students and deep personal satisfaction for the teacher.

Realizing that there are marked differences even among twenty-five homogeneously grouped slow learners in ninth-grade general mathematics, Mr. Waltman collected and analyzed basic information for each student. No student was allowed to move to the next concept until the teacher was satisfied that the student understood the requisite concepts. Movement in the class was slow, but students were finally able to comprehend what had been glossed over in earlier years.

Groups within the class were established to enable students to discuss problems of common concern; the teacher was frequently involved in these discussions. No student was given the impression that he was failing as long as he exerted effort commensurate with his capacity. Whenever possible the teacher gave liberal praise, particularly to those students who lacked confidence or were below the class average in achievement.

Math problems were related to the lives of the students as much as possible, and the teacher exhibited a personal interest in each student, regardless of any established reputation for misbehavior. Considerable flexibility was exhibited in gearing assignments and methods to student interests.

The basic text was carefully selected because of simplicity in content and vocabulary. Even simpler texts were used for poor readers and for those having difficulty with content. Mr. Waltman focused special attention on concrete teaching devices. On several occasions students with particular problems were referred to the school counselor for assistance.

Use in Specific Subjects

Certain types of differences have a marked effect on learning in specific content areas. For example, students who have marked numerical ability can be expected to perform more effectively in a mathematics class than students of comparable intelligence who are less gifted in numerical ability. On the other hand, students who have above-average verbal ability can be expected to be more successful in the English class than their classmates of average ability. It is quite possible, of course, for a given student to be above average with respect to one factor and below average with respect to another. This fact may cause special problems for the teacher.

Concept-Centered Subjects

Learners who have limited general intelligence will have academic difficulties, particularly in areas demanding abstract thinking—such as mathematics, chemistry, physics, biology, English grammar, and certain areas in the social sciences. Confusion often arises, however, because of the failure to differentiate between the lack of capacity and a record of poor achievement. It is possible for a bright student to do poorly in mathematics for many reasons, including poor teaching, lack of motivation, limited reading ability, or conceptual gaps in his learning. To conclude that the poor achiever is necessarily a dull student is an unwarranted and shallow assumption.

Skill Subjects

Poor neuro-muscular coordination can inhibit performance in any skill subject, such as typing, band, orchestra, shorthand, and physical education. Difficulties may arise when this lack of coordination is not immediately recognized or when poor performance is attributed to a lack of effort or a lack of motivation. No amount of instructional effort can bring about efficient muscle coordination if the student is not physically ready.

Subjects Requiring Some Prior Experience

Work experiences and incidental experiences related to the student's environment often provide the background essential to success in specific subjects. A student's interest in farm mechanics, for example, is often related to his farm background. It is unrealistic to assume that the occasional city-bred youngster who gets into a farm-mechanics class will have the same experience-related concepts as a farm youth, although his interest may be as high. Similarly, the youngster of low socioeconomic status who has been brought up in an impoverished language environment can hardly be expected to show the same interest in correct speech as the student from more favored circumstances.

Specific Suggestions

Specific suggestions for meeting the teaching-learning needs of differing students serve a useful purpose in the hands of the beginning as well as the experienced teacher, for they present various directions that instruction may take[19] and may also trigger the recall of other useful ideas.

Recommendations

1. Create learning situations in which students are encouraged to work to their capacity, learning situations that are not too difficult but that provide challenge for all.
2. Explore the possibility of grouping students according to academic ability and achievement.[20] Students may also be grouped informally in the classroom to serve social, instructional, or classroom control purposes.
3. Provide special groups for students whose differences are extreme. Make case studies of students with special problems.
4. Use a variety of procedures to differentiate instruction in view of student interests. Use the best programed materials available to implement this instruction.
5. Teach the same content in a shorter period than usual as one means of keeping the bright youngster challenged. Encourage carefully selected bright students to enter college early.

---

[19]See Herbert J. Klausmeier, *Teaching in the Secondary School* (New York: Harper & Brothers, 1958), pp. 370–371, for a few specific recommendations for teachers about meeting the individual needs of students.

[20]William C. Morse and G. Max Wingo, *Psychology and Teaching*, 2d. ed. (Chicago: Scott, Foresman and Company, 1962), pp. 324–329, provide a thorough discussion of grouping for individual differences.

6. Do not deny promotion to slow-learning students.[21] Modify the curriculum to meet their needs;[22] involve them in class activities; and develop an atmosphere of understanding to help these students achieve their potential.

7. Make assignments flexible in consideration of differing interests and abilities. Individualize instruction through the use of special assignments and contracts.

8. Experiment with different means of meeting individual needs.

9. Encourage students to make continuous vertical advancement even if it is at the expense of horizontal enrichment.[23]

10. Plan units and daily lessons carefully for the differentiation of instruction.

11. Use the supervised study period to evaluate student effort and achievement and to redirect student efforts as needed. Give students individual help to the extent that time will permit.

12. Rephrase or reword questions to serve the needs of individual students.

13. Use a range of textbooks and other materials of varying difficulty.

14. Remember that students seek different personal goals and that their goals may be different from those the teacher has in mind.

15. Explore the possibility of using team teaching.

Cautions

1. Don't overemphasize the individual I.Q. as a measure of ability.

2. Don't expect all students to learn at the same rate.

3. Don't permit double promotions unless the school system has no better means of providing for the educationally gifted child.

IDENTIFYING A SOUND REMEDIAL TEACHING PROGRAM

Remedial teaching is a special type of instruction aimed at helping students overcome academic difficulties not caused by a marked limitation in general capacity.[24] The teaching of the mentally retarded is not included under remedial teaching, although slow-

---

[21]Homogeneous grouping, multi-track curriculums, and several types of individualized instruction may be employed to insure consistent, earned promotion for students without violating conceptual readiness.

[22]Suggestions for teaching slow-learning students are provided by Jean D. Grambs, William J. Iverson, and Franklin K. Patterson, *Modern Methods in Secondary Education,* rev. ed. (New York: The Dryden Press, 1958), pp. 357–362.

Mills and Douglass, *op. cit.,* p. 396, present an extensive list of provisions for less capable students in English.

[23]Burton, *op. cit.,* p. 242, voices strong opposition to "busy work" as a means of providing for individual differences.

[24]Wiles, *op. cit.,* pp. 151–162, discusses the characteristics of several types of learners who would benefit from remedial help.

learning youngsters often need remedial teaching and are frequently found in such programs.[25]

Most remedial teaching is currently being carried on in heterogeneous classes in which extremes of student ability and achievement are pronounced. Less common are homogeneously grouped classes in which attention can be focused on the individual learning problems of the students. Perhaps a majority of the attempts to provide special help are made through individual contacts with students during the study period or before and after school.

If several students in a class display the same difficulty, a special in-class group, small or large, may be formed to economize the time and effort spent on reteaching. If the teacher discovers that a particular concept simply has not been comprehended by his students, the entire class may require special help.

In large secondary schools standardized examinations may reveal common marked deficiencies among a substantial portion of the student body. In this case, remedial classes may be established as part of the curriculum. Some large schools have classes that are comprised of students who have previously failed a particular course; such classes essentially provide remedial instruction geared to the level of the class.

One recognized impediment to effective learning is poor reading ability, a problem that affects a substantial portion of the total secondary-school population. Classes in remedial reading are, therefore, common in large schools and are frequently found as noncredit courses in college curriculums.

Goals of Remedial Teaching

Because academic problems are often unique to the learner, their diagnosis and treatment will have to be geared to the individual. If effectively carried out, remedial teaching helps students identify the specific academic problems that are causing difficulty. It is, therefore, diagnostic in nature. Once the difficulty is pinpointed, a definite course of action must be charted to improve learning. Remedial teaching thus has the advantage of permitting a direct attack on the individual problems of students.

Mistaken concepts are a frequent source of difficulty. A budding typist, for example, may wrongly assume that a rhythmic pattern is basic to the acquisition of high speed. Remedial teaching can correct such false concepts. Remedial teaching also seeks to supply missing concepts essential to academic progress. An understanding of the Civil War depends upon a comprehension of events prior to the war;

---

[25]Grambs, Iverson, and Patterson, *op. cit.*, pp. 357–362, provide specific suggestions for helping the slow learner in homogeneously and heterogeneously grouped classes. See Burton, *op. cit.*, p. 235, for a description of the characteristics of the dull pupil.

in a program of remedial teaching, such events can be identified and taught.

If the interrelationship of concepts is not clear to the learner, remedial teaching can again correct the difficulty. A student in a grammar course, for instance, may not see the connection between dependent clauses and effective written composition. Such relationships must be grasped before the student can make satisfactory progress in the course.

If the teacher can assist the student in overcoming persistent academic problems before they result in general disappointment, defeat, and decreased motivation, he is teaching effectively. Unfortunately, it is not uncommon to find even conscientious students who have been left to flounder for prolonged periods because teachers could not or did not help. A remedial teaching program aims at early diagnosis of the individual learner's problems and at teaching him what specifically can and should be done to overcome his difficulties.

Principles Related to Remedial Teaching

The teacher concerned with remedial teaching needs to identify guidelines that give direction to his instruction. Several of these guidelines are listed below.

1. Academic difficulties requiring remedial teaching may stem from culturally impoverished environments, poor teaching, poor study habits, lack of interest, and limited capacities. Students may also need special help with a range of problems not directly related to academic performance. The sympathetic, helpful teacher exerts a positive influence on the student who is encountering multiple difficulties.

2. Emotional difficulties, like academic difficulties, can be helped through remedial teaching.[26] Indeed, self-concepts may be enhanced if remedial teaching enables students to achieve success often.

3. Many kinds of remedial groups may be established—for example, groups of high-achieving students whose performance and achievement are below their potential, groups of average students who are deficient in one specific area, and groups of slow learners. Although many average and some brilliant children need remedial help, they need help less frequently and with a smaller range of problems than do below-average students.[27]

4. Published standardized tests provide a sound means of helping diagnose student problems preparatory to undertaking a remedial program. Remedial teaching itself often requires other special instructional materials and facilities.

---

[26]Lee J. Cronbach, *Educational Psychology*, 2d. ed. (New York: Harcourt, Brace and World, 1963), pp. 646–651, discusses the need for and effect of remedial effort on learners with emotional difficulties.

[27]Provisions for dealing with slow-learning children are discussed by Klausmeier, *Learning and Human Abilities*, pp. 404–406.

5. Remedial teaching should only follow an accurate diagnosis of learning difficulties.

6. Teaching procedures effective for most students may be ineffective for students in a remedial program. In such a program, standards need to be adjusted realistically to meet student capacities, interests, and personal goals.

7. If a student is lacking basic skills, it may be necessary to call in a remedial teaching specialist. Special training is highly desirable for any teacher who has a major responsibility for remedial teaching.

8. Inability to read at the desired level has an adverse effect on academic achievement in nearly all subjects. Special work in this area may be needed by students at all levels of achievement and capacity.

9. Students often need remedial work to improve study habits.

10. Professional attention to physical difficulties can help improve learning.

11. Remedial assistance should continue until the recipient has reached the desired level of achievement.

Correct and Incorrect Procedures

Teachers with limited experience often provide inadequate remedial instruction or neglect such instruction entirely. This is borne out in the two illustrations that follow.

MISS SYMONS NEGLECTS LOW ACHIEVERS

Bessie Symons enjoyed her first year of teaching Algebra I to ninth-graders. Her students—twenty-seven in all, with I.Q.'s ranging from 97 to 136—were grouped heterogeneously, and she was finding it difficult to keep them all progressing at the same rate.

By the end of November the teacher realized that students were separating themselves largely into two groups—the high achievers and the low achievers. Division of the class into two sections would have helped her teaching, but the administration was opposed to it. Miss Symons chose an easy solution to her problem: Her teaching was directed to the high achievers, and the low achievers were left to flounder. Occasional help was given to slower students during the study period, but Miss Symons reasoned that the brighter students had just as much claim to her help as the less gifted. By the end of the semester the low achievers were thoroughly discouraged and near the point of open rebellion.

MR. PYPER'S SEVERITY REPELS STUDENTS

E. S. Pyper was strong on discipline. He permitted no monkey business, as all students were well aware. In his eighth-grade core class he had students whose abilities and achievement ranged from quite low to above average. Because of the severity of the classroom climate, however, the students who were having difficulties felt they could not approach their teacher. The examination of test scores would have provided some indication of the students' difficulties, but once the scores were recorded, they were put to no further use. Mr. Pyper was entirely unaware that five of his students were reading below the level of the average sixth-grader. He had long since labeled them dull and written them off as poor educational risks.

Miss Symons exhibited neglect of her students; her few efforts to institute remedial teaching procedures were half-hearted at best. Mr. Pyper confused stern classroom control with effective teaching. He employed no diagnostic procedures to assist him in determining student strengths and weaknesses; even essential information concerning their achievement in important areas, including reading, had gone unchecked. Furthermore, he found it impossible to maintain effective rapport with students.

Successful use of remedial teaching procedures is reflected in the work of the teacher described below.

MR. TATE USES EFFECTIVE REMEDIAL PROCEDURES

As soon as the principal informed Frank Tate that he would have the responsibility for the 10B's, the slow group that two teachers had already declared unteachable, he knew that his ingenuity would be challenged. There was one thing in his favor, however: Students were more or less homogeneously grouped—their I.Q.'s extended only from 86 to 103.

Mr. Tate began by readministering the history achievement test that had been given at the end of the previous school year. Scores were recorded in code form on a seating chart that also contained a coded I.Q. He gained permission from the administration to move as slowly as he thought advisable for the group being taught. The first week was devoted largely to corroborating what achievement test scores had revealed and to establishing rapport with the group.

Mr. Tate found that students hated a straight lecture but that they were most responsive in an informal situation. The teacher used this knowledge to great advantage. As the school year advanced, a range of diagnostic procedures was used to determine the nature of learning difficulties. A reading test, for example, revealed what the teacher had assumed—that only a very small proportion of his group was reading at the tenth-grade level. He therefore used a range of simplified texts geared to the individual reading abilities.

Once rapport had been established, Mr. Tate concentrated on having students acquire effective study habits, and he spent time looking into the home backgrounds of specific students. Praise was used effectively in motivating students. If a student completed a learning task that had been simplified to provide him with a successful experience, he was praised. No one was made to feel that he was failing.

The teacher employed methods that were known to make subject matter meaningful to students. Narration accompanied by dramatics proved successful. Carefully selected resource persons were well received, and field trips provided meaningful learning experiences. Several students indicated that they were enjoying school for the first time in their lives.

Examination of Mr. Tate's teaching procedures reveals that he was realistic in his expectations. Furthermore, these expectations were based upon careful assembly and weighing of the facts. He established rapport with his students, creating the impression that he was their ally. Methods and materials were adjusted to what the students could and would accept. Because he realized that the students did not possess effective study habits, the teacher directed attention to establishing such habits.

Use in Specific Subjects

All courses demanding student achievement may result in partial failure and academic problems. Students frequently encounter their greatest academic frustrations in highly organized, concept-centered subjects. For this reason, the need for remedial teaching is greatest in such subjects as mathematics, English grammar, biology, bookkeeping, chemistry, and physics. The study of other, more loosely structured subjects, such as history, geography, and homemaking, may give rise to difficulties, but they are usually less pronounced and less frequent. Usually the skill subjects are less dependent on conceptual content; therefore, student frustrations are minimized. The study of a subject like shorthand, however, in which a high degree of motor skill is required in addition to a thorough knowledge of the meaning and use of symbols, may cause severe academic distress and necessitate remedial teaching.

Specific Suggestions

The following specific suggestions for conducting programs of remedial teaching bear a close relationship to the principles presented earlier.[28]

Recommendations

1. Use a range of procedures to diagnose learning difficulties.
2. Determine the reading level of students in your classes at least once each year.[29]
3. Maintain close personal contact with the academic achievement of each student.
4. Establish rapport with students and encourage them to seek your help when they need it. Make the student feel that you are always sympathetic to his problems, regardless of their cause.
5. Remember that students can achieve only what their capacities permit them to achieve. Determine what these capacities are.
6. Experiment with the use of different procedures in providing remedial help for students.

---

[28]Hansen, *op. cit.*, p. 290, offers several suggestions for setting up a remedial program.

[29]Mills and Douglass, *op. cit.*, pp. 156–157, discuss the functions and purposes of a remedial reading class.

7. Devise means for improving the poor study habits of students.

8. While seeking the possible causes of poor learning, determine the relationship of physical, social, and emotional factors to the need for remedial work. Ascertain whether environmental influences have been responsible for problems that affect learning.

9. Identify questionable teaching procedures that make it necessary to reteach content.

10. Procure and use the facilities and materials necessary for conducting an efficient remedial teaching program.

11. Call in remedial teaching specialists as needed to solve particular problems.

12. Help students achieve success.

Cautions

1. Don't assume that the student in need of remedial work is necessarily dull.

2. Don't assume that bright students never need remedial help.[30]

3. Don't attempt to engage in remedial teaching without first having diagnosed a student's difficulties.

4. Don't make a public point of the fact that certain students are engaged in remedial work.

USING SOUND MARKING AND REPORTING PROCEDURES

Broadly conceived, the fundamental purpose of assigning grades and reporting these grades to parents is to help students achieve desirable educational goals. More specifically, however, marking and reporting help:

1. Determine student progress toward specific objectives.
2. Stimulate students to continued effort or to greater effort.
3. Keep students informed of their individual progress.
4. Acquaint students with their deficiencies.
5. Indicate students' standing in a given class or with respect to national norms.
6. Provide an administrative record of student achievement.
7. Inform parents of pupil progress.
8. Maintain contact with the home.[31]

Several writers have noted that the purpose of marking has been in a state of transformation, moving away from merely assigning and

[30]Specific suggestions for assisting the fast learner in homogeneous and heterogeneous classes are offered by Grambs, Iverson, and Patterson, *op. cit.*, pp. 365–367.

[31]Relationships between home and school are improved through the effective use of a carefully prepared report form. See Klausmeier, *Teaching in the Secondary School*, pp. 473–478.

reporting marks to improving pupil learning.[32] In spite of this change, current practice still emphasizes the reporting of marks.

Controversy with respect to marking on a competitive basis is strong. Vredevoe[33] and Fine[34] indicated that although elementary schools tend to discount competitive marking, high schools are reluctant to give it up because grades are useful in gaining admission to colleges. A general trend toward rigor in assigning grades for secondary-school students has received strong support from the current emphasis on international competition in the sciences and on education in general.

That marks are considered lacking in validity and reliability is borne out by several research findings. One writer[35] concluded that marks are based in part upon intelligence as well as upon achievement and that girls receive higher grades than boys. Another discovered a positive relationship between marks received and most-liked and least-liked students.[36] Still a third writer found that most teachers differ in their interpretations of achievement and that the value assigned to a given mark differed from school to school and even from teacher to teacher in the same school.[37] In spite of these problems, the marking and reporting of pupil progress serve an important purpose in education and deserve serious attention.

Differences in Marking and Reporting

During the past half century many different types of grading systems have made their appearance. Some of these have been modified; a few have been discarded. At the present time three basic systems are being used: numerical grades, letter grades, and descriptions of progress.[38]

Numerical Grades

The numerical grade may take the form of a percentage score, a percentile rank, or numbers ranging from one to five or one to ten.

---

[32]Edward C. Bolmeier, "Principles Pertaining to Marking and Reporting Pupil Progress," *School Review*, 1951, *59:* 15–24.

Dan F. Cagle, "How May We Make the Evaluation and Reporting of Student Achievement More Meaningful?" *National Association of Secondary-School Principals Bulletin*, 1955 (April), *39:* 24–27.

[33]Lawrence E. Vredvoe, "How May We Make the Recording and Reporting of Pupil Achievement More Meaningful?" *National Association of Secondary-School Principals Bulletin*, 1953 (April), *37:* 179–182.

[34]Benjamin Fine, "A, B, C of Grading Puzzles Parents," *New York Times*, November 18, 1957, p. 33.

[35]Robert S. Carter, "How Invalid Are Marks Assigned by Teachers?" *Journal of Educational Psychology*, 1952, *43:* 218–228.

[36]S. Trevor Hadley, "School Mark—Fact or Fancy?" *Educational Administration and Supervision*, 1954, *40:* 305–312.

[37]Vredvoe, *loc. cit.*

[38]Burton, *op. cit.*, pp. 509–513, elaborates on these three systems of marking.

Because of its flexibility, the percentage score is frequently employed by teachers. A given percentage score on a test, however, may be relatively meaningless to parents in the absence of information about test difficulty, the group tested, and instructions that preceded testing. The percentage system is, nevertheless, traditionally entrenched, and many parents prefer it because of its assumed ease of interpretation.

Percentile rank is a statistical measure that indicates the percentage of the class above and below a particular student. In a class of one hundred, for example, a student with a percentile rank of sixty-four would have achieved a higher mark than sixty-four (or 64 per cent) of his classmates. A percentile rank mark is infrequently employed because it requires an involved explanation and extensive computation by the teacher.

Simple number scores are also seldom used in secondary schools, although they permit a quick computation of grade-point averages. A grade-point average of *3.0*, for example, means that all grades received by a given student have averaged 3.0, or the equivalent of *B* on the following five-point scale: E = 0, D = 1, C = 2, B = 3, and A = 4. Often this scoring procedure is modified to encompass numbers one through ten.

Letter Grades

Letter grades have been and still are the most popular means of reporting student progress.[39] A system of five letter grades, usually A, B, C, D, and E, is most frequently employed. (Occasionally the letter F is substituted for E as the lowest mark.)

Descriptive words such as *Excellent, Good,* and *Poor,* together with their letter equivalents—*E, G,* and *P*—are still to be found, but the use of this system is diminishing. *S (Satisfactory)* and *U (Unsatisfactory)* probably represent the most simplified use of letters for grading purposes. The words *Pass* and *Fail (P* and *F)* also serve the same purpose. The two-letter systems, however, have been severely criticized by parents.

Because parents are acquainted with the use of a four- or five-letter procedure in grading, they often prefer it to other schemes involving the use of letters. Although letter grades are inherently no more meaningful than a percentage system, many parents are accustomed to them and feel that letters can be interpreted more accurately.

Descriptive Statements

During the past two decades, descriptive statements have been employed with increasing frequency in secondary schools as a means of reporting student progress to parents. Originating in the elementary schools, descriptive statements were slow to be adopted at the more conservative secondary levels. Although such statements have many

[39]See McKean, *op. cit.*, p. 214.

different forms, the following examples, taken from report cards of students in an eleventh-grade United States history class, indicate the general nature of the descriptive method:

> Although Jim's capacity is good, he seems to be more interested in sports than in history. His present achievement is below the class average.
>
> Tanya is a consistently good student. Her study habits are excellent, and she works hard. Improvement in her reading speed and comprehension would be of great help to her.
>
> Sammy did an outstanding job of helping prepare his committee's bulletin board, but his test scores have placed him in the lower 25 per cent of the class. He finds it hard to pay attention and has a tendency to show off. I believe that a parent-teacher conference may be helpful.

The descriptive statement has many advantages: It usually conveys a more meaningful message to the parent than the letter or number grade; it enables the teacher to mention specifically those strengths or weaknesses about which parents should be informed; and it can be used as an explanatory supplement to a letter or number grade.

Descriptive statements of A, B, C, D, and E students can be worked out by the teacher or jointly developed by students and the teacher. Such statements tend to make the percentage or letter grade more meaningful for students as well as parents. The following paragraph describes the *A* pupil in a junior high school:[40]

> "A" Pupil (95-100 Per Cent, Superior Work): One (1) whose work consistently shows an intelligent comprehension of the subject matter through his ability to retain facts and principles learned; (2) who is able to apply subject matter learned to new problems; (3) who organizes his work well; (4) who speaks clearly and forcibly in discussions; (5) who presents neat, well-arranged, accurate, complete work on time; (6) who performs required skills with a high degree of techniques; (7) who completes both the average and the enriched assignment; (8) who has good study habits; (9) who has the power of analyzing his own work to discover his strong and weak points; (10) who shows marked initiative, industry, and attention.

The marking procedures described above do not cover the many possible combinations that are used widely and successfully by school systems. In some systems, for example, a letter grade is rarely given without a descriptive word or statement intended to clarify its meaning, and a descriptive statement of student progress is often accompanied by a letter grade.

---

[40]Burton, *op. cit.*, p. 512.

Principles Related to Marking and Reporting

General principles giving sound direction to marking and reporting practices of both beginning and experienced teachers are presented here.[41]

1. The judgment-making process involved in marking and reporting student progress calls for the understanding and help of students, parents, and teachers. The home and school must work cooperatively in furthering the cause of learning, and meaningful reporting of pupil progress helps serve this purpose. Parents want to know about the strengths and weaknesses of their children, and, as a basis for understanding student grades, parents should understand the objectives students are trying to achieve.[42]

2. Symbols used to report student progress may be interpreted differently by students, teachers, and parents. Because parents are generally not professionally trained in the field of education, reporting devices should be easily understood and reasonably complete. Parent-teacher conferences and descriptive reports to parents are more helpful devices for reporting student progress than the traditional report card.

3. Report-card grades and comments should be recorded only after a careful examination of the quality of student performance on all class-related activities. A single report-card grade is a relatively meaningless and subjective composite of several grading factors. Meaningful evaluation and reporting require differentiation in grading for achievement, effort, and citizenship.

4. Each marking system has specific advantages and disadvantages. All grades, however, are relative.[43] A mark given for specific academic performance may vary from teacher to teacher, from subject to subject, from circumstance to circumstance, and from school to school. In addition, grades frequently lack reliability and validity.

5. The students, as well as their parents, need to know how they are doing in school. Thus, a basic purpose of marking is to provide students with a definite indication of their performance. A corollary purpose is to provide them with an incentive for improving that performance. Unfortunately, grade-conscious students work for high grades rather than for the mastery of content.

6. An overemphasis on marks can seriously interfere with specific aspects of the learning process. The teacher's development of a wholesome attitude toward marks is a primary step in establishing a worth-while grading system.

---

[41]*Ibid.*, pp. 513–515, discusses several principles that should be considered in developing a sound marking system.

[42]An example of a report card in which attention is focused on academic as well as nonacademic objectives is presented by Klausmeier, *Teaching in the Secondary School*, p. 470.

[43]Hansen, *op. cit.*, p. 255, discusses the relativity of grades.

7. "The procedures for evaluating, marking, reporting, and recording pupil progress should be developed as a whole."[44] A policy with respect to marking and reporting student progress should be extended to all teachers in a given school and under certain circumstances to all teachers in a school district.

8. Differences in student abilities should be reflected in the evaluation, marking, and reporting of student achievement.

9. Student self-evaluation is highly desirable and should be encouraged.

10. Teachers have the responsibility for devising procedures to accurately measure and appraise the extent to which students have attained desired school goals.

11. Teachers tend to discriminate against certain types of students in determining grades.[45]

12. The use of curves in assigning a given letter grade to a definite proportion of students is indefensible in many cases and should be used with extreme caution.

Current Practices in Reporting Pupil Progress

If report-card grades are to provide an accurate indication of achievement, the quality of student performance must be determined and recorded quite frequently. Ideally, marks should be assigned on a daily basis, but, in view of the clerical work required by such a procedure, this is usually impossible. For a marking procedure to be acceptable, however, marks must be assigned as frequently as possible in view of the teacher's work load and the psychological effects on the student.

Knowing Areas to Be Evaluated

The teacher must know in advance the areas to be evaluated, and he must plan his teaching so that he will have a number of marks in each of these relevant areas by the time the report-card period is at an end. Although his main concern will be academic achievement, he should also note progress with respect to citizenship and effort.[46] When several scores are accumulated in each area, the task of computing averages is relatively simple. Unfortunately, teachers often rationalize that they do not have the time to properly systematize their marking and grading procedures. The result is an incomplete and perhaps unreliable grading system.

---

[44]Mills and Douglass, *op. cit.*, p. 381.

[45]Hansen, *op. cit.*, pp. 256–257, identifies the students whom teachers tend to discriminate against.

[46]A sound discussion of the need for excluding certain extraneous factors in assigning academic grades is presented by Burton, *op. cit.*, p. 515.

Using Grades as a Threat

Students—and frequently teachers, too—are conditioned to think of marks as the primary educational goal. Few teachers avoid using the threat of low grades to spur students to greater effort, in spite of the fact that there is general professional agreement that this represents a second-best type of motivation.

Misusing the Normal Curve

Poorly informed teachers are sometimes led to believe that they must assign grades according to a normal curve of distribution.[47] This misunderstanding gives rise to guilt feelings on the part of the teacher, antagonism on the part of students, and general lack of classroom rapport. The assumption that a given percentage of a class should receive a certain letter grade presupposes a very large number of students, approximately a thousand, selected randomly from a general population. These necessary conditions cannot be met in the typical classroom. Used with caution, however, distribution curves may be modified to serve a useful purpose in grading a specific group.

Misusing the Inclusive Grade

A practice that is deservedly losing ground involves assigning only one grade on the basis of several dissimilar factors, such as ability, subject-matter achievement, effort, and classroom behavior. This procedure has the great disadvantage of confusing the parent as well as the student, for they can only guess at the meaning of the grade.[48] Furthermore, such a procedure encourages a lack of precise thinking in arriving at the grades.

Well-administered schools and school districts assign different marks for academic achievement, effort, citizenship, and other relevant factors. The interpretation of grades is thus enhanced, and students who rank low in one area may be above average in another. In the past there has been a particular temptation on the part of well-meaning teachers to allow consistent strong effort and excellent classroom behavior to overcompensate for low academic achievement. In the composite one-letter grade, true academic achievement can be disguised or hidden. Differentiated grading helps overcome this.

"Shall I mark the group of low ability on the same basis as the group of high ability?" This troublesome question has not been adequately answered.[49] When evaluated in relationship to a fixed stand-

---

[47]Improper use of distribution curves is discussed by Burton, *op. cit.*, p. 518. Mills and Douglass, *op. cit.*, pp. 375–377, also call attention to errors made in using the normal curve of distribution.

[48]The students' and parents' basic lack of understanding of some report-card grades is indicated by Grambs, Iverson, and Patterson, *op. cit.*, pp. 512–513.

[49]McKean, *op. cit.*, pp. 211–212, provides a helpful discussion on grading in ability groups.

A sound approach to assigning marks in differing homogeneous groups is presented by Burton, *op. cit.*, p. 516.

ard in a large school, low-achieving students, although grouped together, would receive consistently low grades. Conversely, high-achieving students would receive high grades. In developing a marking procedure, the teacher should consider its effect on such factors as student motivation, teacher-student rapport, and student learning. Of these factors, student learning is the most important.

Marking on a Relative Basis

Some schools have adopted a policy of marking students in relationship to other students in the same homogeneously grouped class. In order to provide an honest picture of student achievement with respect to a fixed standard, however, coded symbols on the school transcript may indicate the nature of the homogeneous group in which the mark was received. Such a procedure provides help for the college admissions officer faced with the decision of whether to admit a student on the basis of his academic achievement.

Some teachers assign students relative numerical ranks according to academic performance. The student who receives the highest average is designated as student number one, while the student with the lowest average is identified as number twenty-nine in a class of that size. Letter grades may then be assigned according to numerical rank: The top four students may receive A grades, the next six B's, etc.

Rank-order grading and competitive marking are viewed by most educators and psychologists as running counter to known facts about learning.[50] Under such a system differences in rate of learning, ability, interests, and background are not considered. As a result, motivation suffers. Undue attention is focused on achievement for the sake of achievement. Furthermore, the slow but conscientious learner feels defeated and discouraged.

Reporting to Parents

Many different procedures are followed in reporting grades to parents. Report cards are now usually issued on a quarterly (nine weeks) basis, although some school districts issue them only at the end of the semester. The more frequent approach is much more desirable because it tends to maintain a more constant contact with the home. A six-week report-card period is still employed by some school systems.

Simplicity essential. The development of simplified procedures for reporting grades to parents has come to be a basic concern of school administrators. Parents who do not understand grades cannot react to them. Unfortunately, they seldom bother to inquire even if they do not understand, and parent-teacher relations on behalf of the student suffer. Frequently, a committee comprised of teachers

---

[50] *Ibid.*, p. 519.

and administrators is set up to review the report form and the procedures used in conveying information to parents. In such cases the opinions of parents may be sought to insure simplicity, practicality, and usefulness.

A simplified but meaningful reporting procedure is to indicate on the report card whether the student is above grade level, at grade level, or below grade level in academic achievement. Because it avoids many of the dangers implicit in the rank-order system, this procedure enables students and parents to make broad comparisons with other learners in the class.[51] As the student approaches the final years of his secondary schooling, he needs to be realistically aware of his general standing in the class. Parents need this same information as a means of guiding their children through difficult decisions concerning their future.

Multiple reports. Although the single report card is feasible and practical in the elementary school, the involvement of many teachers per student at the secondary level makes this somewhat impractical. When employed in secondary schools, the single report card necessitates the transfer of grades submitted by different teachers to a single card – a clerical burden for the teacher charged with compiling grades. An attempt to reduce this clerical load has led to experimentation with new punch-card systems that may provide an easier means of sorting, compiling, and mailing report cards.[52]

Supplementary reports. Many teachers have found it helpful to send home an informal report from time to time as a supplement to the regularly issued report card. But teacher commitments restrict rather markedly the time that can be devoted to this extra reporting. A more frequent practice is to send home with the report card duplicated or printed letters that provide a general explanation of the nature and meaning of the report card and its contents.

Parent-teacher conferences. The need for parents to understand report-card grades has been so pronounced that many secondary schools have adopted the elementary-school procedure of setting aside a specific block of time for parent-teacher conferences. Because of the much larger number of students per teacher in the secondary schools (150 as opposed to 30, for instance), the parent-teacher conference has severe limitations. It is often used, however, in the attempt to solve aggravated student problems.

Although a few secondary schools use the parent-teacher conference as the major means of reporting student progress, this practice is not widespread. As progress is made in reducing the clerical tasks

[51]Klausmeier, *Teaching in the Secondary School*, pp. 464 – 469, stresses the importance of indicating comparative achievement to parents.

[52]Howard Dalman, "What Are Some New Trends in Reporting Student Growth and Achievement to Parents?" *National Association of Secondary-School Principals Bulletin*, 1960 (April), *44:* 146 – 147.

of the secondary-school teacher, more of the teacher's time can be spent in essential conferences of this sort.[53]

Descriptive statements. Perhaps the reporting method least susceptible to misunderstanding is the descriptive statement. Although it is admittedly subjective, there is little chance that parents will misinterpret a statement such as "Polly needs help with her reading." Many schools are using this procedure in combination with other grades, but the practice is not as widespread as it might be. If the teacher's work load could be reduced, many schools and teachers who are not using this system of descriptive statements would find it possible and desirable to do so.

Information provided by parents. Parents may play a vital role in providing teachers with essential information about their adolescent children. Although such information is seldom sought or provided with the regularity of a report card, printed or duplicated forms occasionally are used to obtain needed information. Habits, health status, out-of-school activities, personality traits, and emotional concerns are typical of the kinds of information that parents can and should provide in helping the school help the child.

Sample report card. The "Report to Students and Parents" of the Monona Grove High School, Madison, Wisconsin (Figure 1), incorporates many of the features that educators feel are desirable in a report form.[54] It calls for assigning letter grades (A to F) for student performance with respect to three basic areas: Individual Performance, School Citizenship, and Knowledge and Skills in Subject. Subheadings under each basic heading (Works up to ability, Has a positive attitude, etc.) are assigned a mark of plus, minus, or no mark. A composite mark for Total Growth and Performance is given at the bottom of the page. The three major divisions are given equal weight in determining this summary grade.

On the reverse side of the report form (Figure 2) provision is made for dated comments by either parents or the teacher.[55] Space limitations on this particular form, however, may encourage brief comments or, in some cases, no comments at all. Parents find it easy to make arrangements for a parent-teacher conference by placing a check mark in the appropriate square or by calling a specific telephone number.

---

[53]Klausmeier, *Teaching in the Secondary School,* pp. 478–484, discusses the need for and the conduct of parent-teacher conferences.

McGuire, Myers, and Durrance, *op. cit.*, p. 264, describe the advantages of teacher-student conferences at the time report cards are issued.

[54]This report form is taken from Klausmeier, *Learning and Human Abilities,* pp. 485–486.

Burton, *op. cit.*, pp. 525–530, includes a variety of report forms that illustrate the need for different emphases.

[55]Mills and Douglass, *op. cit.*, pp. 379–380, present a report card with descriptive statements that may be crossed out if they do not apply.

Fig. 1. Sample report card (front).

REPORT TO STUDENTS AND PARENTS

MONONA GROVE HIGH SCHOOL

MADISON, WISCONSIN

Fr. ☐ Jr. ☐

Name -- So. ☐ Sr. ☐

Subject ---------------------- Teacher Mr. / Mrs. / Miss --------------------

Term beginning September 10, 1956—ending June 12, 1957

GRADING SYSTEM

A=Excellent	D=Poor	+ **Mark** indicates very satisfactory progress
B=Good	F=Failure	**No Mark** indicates reasonable progress
C=Average	Inc=Incomplete	— **Mark** indicates need for improvement

	First Quarter	Second Quarter	Third Quarter	Fourth Quarter	Final Grade
INDIVIDUAL PERFORMANCE					
Works up to ability					
Has a positive attitude					
Shows self-direction					
Plans work wisely					
SCHOOL CITIZENSHIP					
Cooperates with group					
Respects the rights and feelings of others					
Contributes his share					
Is a good leader or follower					
Takes care of school and personal property					
KNOWLEDGE AND SKILLS IN SUBJECT					
Develops skills					
Completes assignments					
Scores satisfactorily on tests and exams					
TOTAL GROWTH AND PERFORMANCE					
Days Absent					
Times Tardy					

OVER

Specific Suggestions

The specific suggestions listed below are derived from general principles and may be of particular help to the beginning teacher or the teacher with limited experience.[56]

[56]McKean, *op. cit.*, pp. 216–217, lists several suggestions for improving the reporting of student grades to parents.

Howard T. Batchelder, Maurice McGlasson, and Raleigh Schorling, *Student Teaching in Secondary Schools*, 4th ed. (New York: McGraw-Hill Book Company, 1964), pp. 284–288, cover some of the newer appraisal techniques.

Hansen, *op. cit.*, pp. 259–260, lists and discusses the features that should be incorporated into the modified report card.

Fig. 2. Sample report card (**back**).

TO PARENTS—

We share with you a mutual interest in helping your son or daughter become a well adjusted and socially competent person. We encourage your understanding and ask for your cooperation.

THE FACULTY
Monona Grove High School

DATE	PARENT OR TEACHER COMMENTS

SIGNATURE OF PARENT OR GUARDIAN

FIRST QUARTER -- ☐

SECOND QUARTER --- ☐

THIRD QUARTER -- ☐

If a conference with the teacher is desired, please check space above or telephone CH 4-6268

Recommendations

1. Help develop a marking system that will be understood and supported by parents, teachers, administrators, and students alike.
2. Review marking procedures at regular intervals and make appropriate modifications where desirable.
3. Base the report-card grade on a range of relevant grades.
4. Make simplified, meaningful, descriptive statements of student progress to supplement number or letter grades.
5. Use a marking system that enables students to see their standing in relationship to other students in the class.
6. Establish a procedure for frequently recording a mark for daily classroom performance.

7. Mark on other relevant factors in addition to academic achievement.

8. Solicit parents' opinions with respect to the form and use of the report card.

9. Keep parents aware of what the school is trying to achieve.

10. Be sure that parents and students know what each mark means.

11. Arrange for parent-teacher conferences at least once each year and more often as occasion demands.

12. Encourage students to work for the acquisition of subject-matter content rather than for high grades.

13. Keep students informed of their own progress.

14. Encourage students to practice self-evaluation.

Cautions

1. Don't wait until the report card is issued to contact parents about problems of unusual concern.

2. Don't stifle student motivation through marking procedures.

3. Don't permit the report card to be the only teacher contact with the home.

4. Don't overemphasize marks.[57]

5. Don't use a marking system to force students to bend to your will.

6. Don't use the same standard for marking groups of students with different abilities.

7. Don't use the unmodified normal curve as a basis for apportioning marks.

8. Don't combine several grading factors (achievement, effort, etc.) into one composite grade.

INDIVIDUAL DIFFERENCES, REMEDIAL TEACHING, AND REPORTING PUPIL PROGRESS IN REVIEW

This chapter has focused attention on the role of teaching to meet individual differences, on remedial teaching, and on reporting pupil progress.

Although students differ in literally hundreds of ways, educators have devoted their attention to those differences that exert the greatest influence on teaching and learning: intelligence, emotional stability, physical health, social adjustment, experiential background, aspirations, interests, school achievement, attitudes, temperament and disposition, readiness, and skills. Techniques currently employed in the attempt to meet the individual needs of students may be classified as administrative provisions and instructional provisions.

---

[57]Rivlin, *op. cit.*, p. 340, expands on the need for not overemphasizing marks.

Remedial teaching is a special type of instruction aimed at helping students overcome academic difficulties. Academic problems requiring such teaching may stem from limited cultural environments, inefficient teaching, poor study habits, or lack of interest.

Although the basic purpose of grading and reporting is to help students achieve desirable educational goals, a range of more immediate goals are also served. Three types of grading systems are currently being used: numerical grades, letter grades, and descriptions of progress.

PROBLEMS FOR STUDY AND DISCUSSION

1. List the ten individual differences among students that you feel have the greatest effect on the teaching-learning process.
2. Assumption: In your tenth-grade world history class you have the following students: Sandra, who is socially withdrawn; William, who is very bright; Sara, who is totally disinterested; James, who is thoroughly conceited; and Tina, who is culturally impoverished. Describe how you would plan to teach world history and still meet these students' individual differences.
3. Describe how you would realistically differentiate unit assignments in your subject-matter major to meet the individual differences likely to be found in a typical class.
4. List five procedures that should be avoided in teaching slow learners. Explain your reasoning.
5. List five important administrative provisions for meeting individual differences among students.
6. Do you believe that students in your subject-matter minor should be grouped homogeneously? Defend your position.
7. Describe five different ways in which you could use in-class groupings to differentiate instruction.
8. Assumption: Patty has an I.Q. of 125 but poor muscular coordination. In which subjects is she most likely to be successful? In which will she be likely to encounter difficulty? Why?
9. Is remedial teaching necessary in a homogeneously grouped class of bright students? Explain.
10. In your teaching major, which concepts are most likely to require remedial teaching?
11. What is the relationship between a culturally impoverished environment and the need for remedial teaching?
12. Describe the special materials you would need in conducting an effective program of remedial teaching in your subject-matter major.
13. Assumption: You are teaching a student whose reading level is three grades below that of the average student in the class. How would this probably affect his achievement? What steps would you take to help this student?
14. What is the fundamental purpose in grading students? Explain.
15. Why are letter grades the most popular means of reporting student progress? Explain.

16. List five advantages of using descriptive statements in reporting student progress.

17. Write a brief paragraph that summarizes your philosophy about marks and marking.

18. Explain each of the following statements: (1) All grades are relative. (2) Teachers tend to discriminate against certain types of students in grading. (3) Different ability groupings within the same school complicate marking.

19. What grading factors in addition to academic achievement should be considered in reporting progress to parents? Defend your position.

20. Assumption: You have the responsibility for teaching two homogeneously grouped classes, one of low ability and one of high ability. Should students in these classes be marked in relationship to a fixed standard or in relationship to other students in their individual groups? Explain.

RECOMMENDED READINGS

Individual Differences

Batchelder, Howard T., Maurice McGlasson, and Raleigh Schorling, *Student Teaching in Secondary Schools*, 4th ed. New York: McGraw-Hill Book Company, 1964, pp. 161–162.

Burton, William H., *The Guidance of Learning Activities*, 3d. ed. New York: Appleton-Century-Crofts, Inc., 1962, pp. 233–243.

Carter, William L., Carl W. Hansen, and Margaret G. McKim, *Learning to Teach in the Secondary School*. New York: The Macmillan Company, 1962, pp. 190–191 and 314–317.

Grambs, Jean D., William J. Iverson, and Franklin K. Patterson, *Modern Methods in Secondary Education*, rev. ed. New York: The Dryden Press, 1958, Chapter 13.

Hansen, Kenneth H., *High School Teaching*. Englewood Cliffs, N.J.: Prentice-Hall, Inc., 1957, pp. 50–54 and 271–274.

Klausmeier, Herbert J., *Learning and Human Abilities: Educational Psychology*. New York: Harper & Brothers, 1961, Chapter 13.

Lindgren, Henry C., *Educational Psychology in the Classroom*, 2d. ed. New York: John Wiley and Sons, 1962, Chapter 17.

McDonald, Frederick J., *Educational Psychology*. San Francisco: Wadsworth Publishing Company, 1959, pp. 419–430.

McGuire, Vincent, Robert B. Myers, and Charles L. Durrance, *Your Student Teaching in the Secondary School*. Boston: Allyn and Bacon, Inc., 1959, pp. 240–245.

McKean, Robert C., *Principles and Methods in Secondary Education*. Columbus, Ohio: Charles E. Merrill Books, Inc., 1962, pp. 272–275 and 286–287.

Mills, Hubert H., and Harl R. Douglass, *Teaching in High School*, 2d. ed. New York: Ronald Press, 1957, Chapter 23.

Morse, William C., and G. Max Wingo, *Psychology and Teaching*, 2d. ed. Chicago: Scott, Foresman and Company, 1962, pp. 325–329.

Nordberg, H. Orville, James M. Bradfield, and William C. Odell, *Sec-*

ondary School Teaching. New York: The Macmillan Company, 1962, pp. 25–26.

Rivlin, Harry N., *Teaching Adolescents in Secondary Schools,* 2d. ed. New York: Appleton-Century-Crofts, Inc., 1961, pp. 97–103, 110–112, 168, 307–308, and 350–351.

Wellington, C. Burleigh, and Jean Wellington, *Teaching for Critical Thinking; with Emphasis on Secondary Education.* New York: McGraw-Hill Book Company, 1960, pp. 106–107.

Wiggins, Samuel P., *Successful High School Teaching.* Boston: Houghton Mifflin Company, 1958, Chapter 12.

Wiles, Kimball, *Teaching for Better Schools,* 2d. ed. Englewood Cliffs, N.J.: Prentice-Hall, Inc., 1959, Chapter 8.

Remedial Teaching

Burton, William H., *The Guidance of Learning Activities,* 3d. ed. New York: Appleton-Century-Crofts, Inc., 1962, pp. 234–236.

Carter, William L., Carl W. Hansen, and Margaret G. McKim, *Learning to Teach in the Secondary School.* New York: The Macmillan Company, 1962, pp. 314–317.

Cronbach, Lee J., *Educational Psychology,* 2d. ed. New York: Harcourt, Brace and World, 1963, pp. 646–652.

Grambs, Jean D., William J. Iverson, and Franklin K. Patterson, *Modern Methods in Secondary Education,* rev. ed. New York: The Dryden Press, 1958, pp. 350–367.

Hansen, Kenneth H., *High School Teaching.* Englewood Cliffs, N.J.: Prentice-Hall, Inc., 1957, pp. 290–292.

Klausmeier, Herbert J., *Learning and Human Abilities: Educational Psychology.* New York: Harper & Brothers, 1961, pp. 404–406.

Klausmeier, Herbert J., *Teaching in the Secondary School.* New York: Harper & Brothers, 1958, pp. 401–406.

Mills, Hubert H., and Harl R. Douglass, *Teaching in High School,* 2d. ed. New York: Ronald Press, 1957, pp. 156–157.

Morse, William C., and G. Max Wingo, *Psychology and Teaching,* 2d. ed. Chicago: Scott, Foresman and Company, 1962, pp. 378–379.

Nordberg, H. Orville, James M. Bradfield, and William C. Odell, *Secondary School Teaching.* New York: The Macmillan Company, 1962, pp. 148 and 178–179.

Rivlin, Harry N., *Teaching Adolescents in Secondary Schools,* 2d. ed. New York: Appleton-Century-Crofts, Inc., 1961, pp. 285–286.

Wellington, C. Burleigh, and Jean Wellington, *Teaching for Critical Thinking; with Emphasis on Secondary Education.* New York: McGraw-Hill Book Company, 1960, pp. 285–287.

Wiggins, Samuel P., *Successful High School Teaching.* Boston: Houghton Mifflin Company, 1958, pp. 233–234.

Wiles, Kimball, *Teaching for Better Schools,* 2d. ed. Englewood Cliffs, N.J.: Prentice-Hall, Inc., 1959, pp. 151–162.

Marking and Reporting

Batchelder, Howard T., Maurice McGlasson, and Raleigh Schorling, *Student Teaching in Secondary Schools,* 4th ed. New York: McGraw-Hill Book Company, 1964, pp. 286–288.

Burton, William H., *The Guidance of Learning Activities*, 3d. ed. New York: Appleton-Century-Crofts, Inc., 1962, Chapter 22.

Carter, William L., Carl W. Hansen, and Margaret G. McKim, *Learning to Teach in the Secondary School.* New York: The Macmillan Company, 1962, pp. 125–127.

Cronbach, Lee J., *Educational Psychology,* 2d. ed. New York: Harcourt, Brace and World, 1963, pp. 531–534.

Grambs, Jean D., William J. Iverson, and Franklin K. Patterson, *Modern Methods in Secondary Education,* rev. ed. New York: The Dryden Press, 1958, Chapter 18.

Hansen, Kenneth H., *High School Teaching.* Englewood Cliffs, N.J.: Prentice-Hall, Inc., 1957, pp. 255–264.

Klausmeier, Herbert J., *Learning and Human Abilities: Educational Psychology.* New York: Harper & Brothers, 1961, pp. 483–486.

McGuire, Vincent, Robert B. Myers, and Charles L. Durrance, *Your Student Teaching in the Secondary School.* Boston: Allyn and Bacon, Inc., 1959, pp. 261–266.

McKean, Robert C., *Principles and Methods in Secondary Education.* Columbus, Ohio: Charles E. Merrill Books, Inc., 1962, Chapter 8.

Mills, Hubert H., and Harl R. Douglass, *Teaching in High School,* 2d. ed. New York: Ronald Press, 1957, Chapter 22.

Morse, William C., and G. Max Wingo, *Psychology and Teaching,* 2d. ed. Chicago: Scott, Foresman and Company, 1962, pp. 392–398.

Nordberg, H. Orville, James M. Bradfield, and William C. Odell, *Secondary School Teaching.* New York: The Macmillan Company, 1962, Chapter 8.

Rivlin, Harry N., *Teaching Adolescents in Secondary Schools.* New York: Appleton-Century-Crofts, Inc., Chapter 11.

Wellington, C. Burleigh, and Jean Wellington, *Teaching for Critical Thinking; with Emphasis on Secondary Education.* New York: McGraw-Hill Book Company, 1960, pp. 287–304.

Wiggins, Samuel P., *Successful High School Teaching.* Boston: Houghton Mifflin Company, 1958, pp. 256–258.

Wiles, Kimball, *Teaching for Better Schools,* 2d. ed. Englewood Cliffs, N.J.: Prentice-Hall, Inc., 1959, Chapter 12.

16

Consistent Improvement in Instruction

The knowledgeable instructor is aware of the need for consistently and specifically improving instruction as a means of upgrading student achievement. The beginning teacher generally has a particular need for bettering himself, and the conscientious experienced teacher is often plagued by a vivid awareness of his own deficiencies. However, the type of improvement occasioned by intermittent guilt feelings at not having done a better job or characterized by sporadic attempts to improve is not the kind of improvement that produces the true professional.

Attaining instructional excellence is a complicated process. The teacher must have a basic command of his subject matter. He must keep abreast of his field and be able to communicate his knowledge effectively to others at their level of comprehension. He must have a thorough acquaintance with psychological principles and be able to make practical use of them in teaching. Above all, the teacher must desire to improve. He would do well to devise, then follow, a carefully constructed plan for improvement. In a quest for betterment, consistency is a key concern. Without consistency, the teacher will soon find that the cumulative effect of his efforts is diminished, continuity is thwarted, and improvement moves forward at an unsteady pace.

The individual instructor can develop his own program for self-improvement by:

Identifying what comprises effective teaching[1]

Identifying personal weaknesses in teaching

Establishing a systematic program of self-appraisal

Devising and identifying procedures that will lead to improvement

Using the suggestions of other professionals—teachers, supervisors, and administrators

Making effective use of student opinions

Identifying and using rating scales and other devices in self-appraisal

Appraising his subject-matter competence

Carefully analyzing his personality[2]

Appraising the effectiveness of his methods

Evaluating student-teacher relationships

Analyzing the effect of membership and participation in professional organizations

Recognizing the benefits of additional graduate work

Recognizing the benefits of specific types of in-service training

SPECIFIC PRACTICES FOR IMPROVING INSTRUCTION

Although most sincere teachers are interested in improving their instructional competence, only a minority of them, unfortunately, are willing to pay the price of *planned* improvement that calls for systematic evaluation by others; honest, structured self-appraisal; and consistent effort. This minority, however, has developed a wide range of successful improvement practices. An examination of several of these will be useful.

Identifying Effective Teaching

The attempt to discover with scientific exactness what comprises effective teaching is a never ending quest.[3] In the past decade, for example, there have been repeated attempts to analyze teaching in order to establish a justifiable basis for merit pay. None of these efforts has resulted in a conclusive scientific statement concerning the precise nature of effective teaching. There is, however, general agree-

---

[1]William L. Carter, Carl W. Hansen, and Margaret G. McKim, *Learning to Teach in the Secondary School* (New York: Macmillan, 1962), pp. 364–368, stress the necessity for the teacher's being able to analyze effective teaching.

[2]Robert W. Richey, *Planning for Teaching*, 3d. ed. (New York: McGraw-Hill Book Company, 1963), pp. 73–76, describes the characteristics of the well-adjusted teacher.

[3]Renato Mazzei, "Desirable Traits of Successful Teachers," *Journal of Teacher Education*, 1951 (Dec.), *2:* 291–294, provides a well-documented review of attempts to identify desirable teacher traits.

ment among teachers and people concerned with teacher appraisal that certain characteristics are indispensable for an effective teacher:[4]

He is intelligent.
He is in command of his subject.
He knows how to communicate his subject to students.
He is able to establish and reach objectives.
He uses methods effectively.
He varies instruction to hold student interest and to allow for individual differences.
He understands and likes students.
He is able to motivate students.
He can accurately appraise student readiness for learning.
He plans effectively.
He has an effective teaching personality.

The relative importance of these traits poses a dilemma for those wishing to make an objective appraisal of instruction. Is it more important, for example, that a teacher be highly intelligent or that he be in command of his subject matter? Does a teacher's outgoing personality have a greater effect on student learning than does his careful planning? Although the relative importance of such characteristics is still to be discovered, *all* are important for effective teaching.

Realizing that evidence about specific teacher traits is inconclusive, what can the improvement-minded teacher do? If he waits for educational research to arrive at incontrovertible conclusions before he begins his program of planned improvement, he may wait a long time indeed. He must therefore select, as the basis for his action, conclusions that reflect the best in scientific, educational thinking.

Gaining Command of Content

Knowing that he can do relatively little to improve his basic capacity, the improvement-minded teacher turns to specific areas in which he can progress. A United States history teacher, for example, may discover that he is only partially in command of his subject. Identifying areas of weakness (the westward movement, for instance) will enable him to set up a specific program designed to round out his knowledge.

Occasionally teachers are confronted with the necessity for teaching subjects for which they have had limited preparation. In such cases, taking the necessary college courses is highly recommended.

---

[4]William C. Morse and G. Max Wingo, *Psychology and Teaching*, 2d. ed. (Chicago: Scott, Foresman and Company, 1962), pp. 398–399, report on an earlier study by Kelly and Perkins and list thirty-three test items that were used in their study to discriminate between good and poor teachers.

If this is impossible, a rigorous schedule of reading and self-instruction is indispensable.

Evaluating Methods

In order to determine whether he is communicating subject matter effectively to his students, the teacher is forced to examine his methods. He may find it helpful to ask himself the following questions:[5]

Do I use methods that move students directly toward desired educational goals?

Do I use procedures that are varied to meet the needs of individual students?

Do I plan effectively for the use of specific methods?

Are the methods used appropriate to the type of goal sought?

Are too many or too few activities used?

Is there an appropriate balance between individual and group activities?

Are activities conducted in the most productive sequence?

Are the methods interesting to the majority of students?

When specific weaknesses in methodology are discovered, equally specific countermeasures should be taken. Reminders can be helpful in meeting these weaknesses. For example, a talk with his supervisor made a teacher of junior high school English aware that a majority of his questions were directed to the upper 10 per cent of his class. Acting in good faith, the teacher wrote a note to himself on a three-by-five card in large block letters: EQUAL TIME FOR ALL. This was kept on his desk for the next month as an ever present reminder of his deficiency.

Methods that are used most frequently should be subject to searching reappraisal. Because the teacher becomes subjectively attached to certain procedures, he may need the help of his colleagues in making an accurate appraisal. Five mathematics teachers in a large high school on the east coast worked out, with the approval of the school administration, a reciprocal arrangement in which they observed the instruction of one other colleague for a full period at least once each month. Following each observation, the observer and the observed teacher met for a helpful exchange of ideas, many of which were directed toward improving methods.

---

[5]Kenneth H. Hansen, *High School Teaching* (Englewood Cliffs, N.J.: Prentice-Hall, 1957), p. 387, points out that classroom activities are "amenable to constant improvement."

See Appendix B in the present text (pp. 552–556) for an extensive list of questions to evaluate the adequacy of specific procedures.

Improving the Voice

The teacher's voice is often less effective than it could be.[6] Unattractive voices and speech patterns can result from speaking too loud or too soft, using a monotonous tone, displaying speech idiosyncracies, and using faltering speech.

Frequently the teacher has a high-pitched voice or a voice with a nasal quality that proves annoying to students and sets the stage for student mimicry. Occasionally a voice-conscious teacher speaks so softly or uses such deep tones that students think his speech affected, and communication is inhibited. The tone of some teachers' voices consistently implies criticism of the students and reveals unwarranted defensiveness. Student-teacher relationships cannot help but be negatively affected under such circumstances. Moreover, the teacher who raises his voice so that he can be heard in an unruly classroom is encouraging continued student misbehavior.

The ideal teacher's voice is one that serves as a useful aid in the instructional process. It is a voice that generally exudes warmth, friendliness, and enthusiasm but can, when occasion demands, project force and firmness that evoke student respect. It is a voice that is varied—sometimes soft, sometimes loud; sometimes high, sometimes low; sometimes gentle, sometimes firm. But more than anything else, it is a voice that communicates enthusiasm for the subject and a general liking of and respect for students.

Many teachers have benefited from the analytical review of tape recordings of their class presentations, a device that can be both revealing and helpful. Others have learned to use their voices more effectively by taking speech classes in which they are encouraged to inject variety and color into their speech. Still others have solicited the criticism of an interested and competent fellow professional—usually another teacher or the supervisor—to make constructive comments after observing a class presentation. A combination of all three procedures has many advantages.

Making Use of Personality

Personality may be viewed as the dynamic organization of those traits and characteristic patterns of behavior that are unique to the individual. The effective use of a teacher's personality is essential in conducting most classroom activities. Personality projection aids teaching, for communication takes place between persons—even in the absence of the spoken word.

---

[6]Richey, *op. cit.*, pp. 79–80, makes specific recommendations for the improvement of the voice.

The teacher whose personality helps create and maintain a classroom environment in which students feel comfortable and in which they want to learn is said to have a desirable teaching personality. Scientific examination of the teacher's personality, however, does not warrant the statement that the effective teacher possesses specific personality traits to a definite, known degree.[7] There is often a marked variation in personal characteristics among the many teachers rated as excellent. The teacher's adjustment to individual circumstances, the school, and the community may further modify his personality.[8]

Numerous attempts have been made to provide personality checklists, rating scales, and other devices to assist the teacher in improving his personality.[9] Wellington and Wellington,[10] for example, provide a series of ten basic questions and subquestions aimed at helping the teacher discover the type of person he is. The authors assume that if the teacher is aware of the type of person he is, he can then employ his unique characteristics to the best advantage in teaching.

Many devices have been developed to enable the teacher to rate himself on such personality characteristics as helpfulness, approachableness, friendliness, fairness, sincerity, etc. Batchelder, McGlasson, and Schorling[11] provide a checklist of ten basic questions, each with accompanying descriptive statements, that may be checked by the teacher. Other checklists might consist of several basic divisions of traits on which teachers can grade themselves.

In spite of limited progress made in attempting to relate teacher personality to effective teaching,[12] few educators would deny that such a relationship exists. Consideration of others, ability to react quickly in emergencies, creativeness, intelligence, and willingness to defer judgment are qualities that should be periodically reappraised by the conscientious teacher. Admittedly, current research evidence may not enable the teacher to know the precise traits he should concentrate on, but those characteristics generally accepted

---

[7]Myron Lieberman, *Education as a Profession* (Englewood Cliffs, N.J.: Prentice-Hall, 1956), p. 255, criticizes the assumption that there is only one effective type of teaching personality.

[8]See Hubert H. Mills and Harl R. Douglass, *Teaching in High School,* 2d. ed. (New York: Ronald Press, 1957), p. 39.

[9]The desirability of using prepared aids in a program of systematic self-appraisal is stressed by Carter, Hansen, and McKim, *op. cit.*, pp. 367–371.

[10]C. Burleigh Wellington and Jean Wellington, *Teaching for Critical Thinking; with Emphasis on Secondary Education* (New York: McGraw-Hill Book Company, 1960), pp. 311–312.

[11]Howard T. Batchelder, Maurice McGlasson, and Raleigh Schorling, *Student Teaching in Secondary Schools*, 4th ed. (New York: McGraw-Hill Book Company, 1964), pp. 289–291.

[12]Lieberman, *op. cit.*, p. 239, properly indicates that "the scientific study of personality is still in its infancy."

as influencing teaching effectiveness will justifiably serve as the objects of attention until such evidence is presented.

Using Supervisory Help

The supervisor's role is a difficult one, because it involves both giving positive suggestions and encouragement and supplying essential criticism.[13] Many times, because of the delicate nature of his relationship to in-service teachers, the supervisor visits only at the teacher's request. Unfortunately, some conscientious teachers find it difficult or embarrassing to invite the supervisor in for a visit, even if they stand to derive considerable benefit. Supervisors as well as principals, who often engage in supervisory functions, respect the teacher who asks for assistance when it is needed. It is highly desirable to establish rapport that will enable such visits to be made without undue strain.

Another possible source of help is informal teacher discussions directed toward matters of common instructional concern. If rapport that permits an uninhibited exchange of ideas can be established, much practical benefit can be derived from frequent, frank discussions about methods, classroom control, teacher personality, and general classroom operation. New teachers, in particular, stand to benefit from the exchange of ideas with a helpful, experienced, and competent teacher.

Using Student Opinion

Secondary-school students are generally willing to comment uninhibitedly on the quality of the teacher's classroom performance if anonymity can be assured.[14] In six related minor studies in the Washington, D.C., area, students were asked to identify the characteristics of their most disliked secondary-school teachers.[15] Participants in the six studies seemed to feel that a weak personality is the most typical characteristic of the poor teacher. The following negative traits, listed in order of frequency, were mentioned by students as characteristic of their most disliked teachers:[16]

---

[13]Carter, Hansen, and McKim, *op. cit.*, pp. 365–367, discuss the advantages of the supervisory conference as an aid to instructional improvement.

[14]Harry N. Rivlin, *Teaching Adolescents in Secondary Schools*, 2d. ed. (New York: Appleton-Century-Crofts, 1961), pp. 437–438, discusses different ways of using student opinion to help improve instruction.

[15]Sterling G. Callahan, "A Comparative Study of Student Dislikes Found in Teachers with Special Reference to the Secondary Level" (unpublished master's thesis, George Washington University, 1947).

[16]*Ibid.*, pp. 208–209.

Ridiculed, was sarcastic
Was partial to certain students
Was unsympathetic toward students
Had disagreeable personality
Unreasonable
Narrow-minded
Threatened and frightened students
Unkind
Impatient, always wanted to hurry students
Did not understand the problems of students
Did not make students want to do more
Old-fashioned in appearance and thought
Was domineering
Had no sense of humor
Rude

Student likes or dislikes may have little relationship to teaching effectiveness. And, because teaching effectiveness has not been scientifically defined, the establishment of such a relationship would, at best, rest on an unstable foundation. However, teachers generally find that classroom procedures move forward with ease when care has been taken to establish rapport between teacher and students. Since it is difficult to establish rapport in an atmosphere in which teacher traits are viewed as negative and harmful to the interests of students, the teacher finds it advisable to find out how his students feel about him.

Useful Procedures

Many different procedures are used to obtain students' opinions about the teacher's strengths and weaknesses. Checklists covering a range of possible teacher traits (fairness, scholarship, ability to put subject over, likableness, effectiveness in use of methods, and interest in students) are often provided students at the end of a semester or long unit of work. The students are asked to rate the teacher's traits as outstanding, very good, satisfactory, poor, or very poor. Some checklists also have a number of blank spaces in which students may insert additional teacher traits or make specific comments.

Another appraisal device is less elaborate.[17] Students are asked to list on a blank sheet of paper what they liked most about the teacher and the class instruction. On a separate sheet they are asked to enumerate the teacher characteristics and instructional procedures most disliked. Because of the extreme diversity of responses, however, this procedure does not lend itself easily to tabulation. The combination of a checklist and free response appears to have the greatest advantage, especially if responses are tabulated and processed so that they can be of maximum use to the teacher.

---

[17]A form used for pupil rating of student teachers at DePauw University is reproduced by Vincent McGuire, Robert B. Myers, and Charles L. Durrance, *Your Student Teaching in the Secondary School* (Boston: Allyn and Bacon, 1959), pp. 290–292. This form provides for two possible responses—"especially strong" or "rather weak"—to twenty-three traits.

Because anonymity must be assured to encourage honest responses, students are told not to sign their names and are encouraged to disguise their handwriting so that individuals cannot be identified. Some teachers have found it advisable to ask for responses only after report cards have been made out as a guarantee that responses will not reflect the students' hopes for higher grades.

Advantages of Tabulation

When tabulation of student responses is possible, a helpful picture of major likes and dislikes emerges that may be used advantageously by the teacher to improve his personality and his classroom instruction. Because they have similar values, students tend to think alike about teacher traits. For example, when a teacher has asked students in his five sections of English (approximately 150 students) to give him the benefit of their reactions to his teaching and personality, he may discover that over one hundred of them feel that he is *unfair.* What *he* may personally feel about his being unfair is of secondary importance in establishing student-teacher rapport, for a large majority of his students honestly feel that he is unfair. The teacher could help establish better rapport by taking steps to improve his image in the eyes of his students.

When student anonymity is assured, it is not uncommon to find a few irresponsible statements among a large group of students. But if fewer than ten of the 150 students indicated that the teacher was unfair, it would be quite evident that the feeling was not general. Although the teacher might wish to identify the reasons that would cause any students to view him as unfair, it should not be the basis for grave concern. If a large minority of students responded by singling out a procedure, such as *assignments are too hard,* the teacher should re-examine this procedure to determine whether the students' complaint is justified.

Making the Improvement Program Systematic

The pious desire to improve is a far cry from the fulfillment of that wish. Although the wish itself is a beginning, it must be followed by a period of conscientious planning and implementation of plans. Of basic concern is a systematic program. The following questions related to improvement should be answered specifically:

Exactly what self-appraisal can I and should I undertake? How often should I evaluate specific procedures?

Which of my fellow professionals are best suited to provide the type of criticism I need? Can I establish specific times to avail myself of their help?

How can I employ student opinions in a practical way to help me improve? How often and under what circumstances should student opinions be sought? What devices should be used in obtaining their opinions?

Which professional organizations afford the greatest promise of helping me improve?

What type of in-service help is offered by my school district? How and when can I obtain this help?

What graduate courses do I need to round out my professional and subject-matter competence?

When these inquiries have been answered through careful study, the teacher is in a position to outline the precise steps he should take in his improvement program.

Affiliating with Professional Organizations

Joining an organization for no better purpose than to be able to say that one is a member reflects shallowness. Many organizations in professional education, however, were established for the prime purpose of helping teachers improve,[18] and they often cater to special needs and interests. Every subject-matter area in the secondary-school curriculum is at present represented by one or more national organizations. With few exceptions these organizations function as departments within the National Education Association. Among these are the Music Educators National Conference, National Council for the Social Studies, National Council of Teachers of Mathematics, National Science Teachers Association, and the Speech Association of America.

Each of these organizations publishes its own periodical, usually at monthly intervals throughout the school year, and many of them also publish a yearbook that reflects current findings in their own particular field. Professional growth is encouraged through consistent reading of such national publications.

At the national conventions held by these professional groups, members have the opportunity to hear from leaders in their respective fields and to exchange ideas in small groups. The state and local organizations often afford the opportunity for active participation in stimulating projects. Many teachers hold membership in professional organizations at the national, state, and local levels and maintain a degree of activity at all levels.

Pursuing Graduate Work

Any honest self-appraisal reveals some teacher weaknesses in methodology, personal behavior, and subject-matter competence.

---

[18]Hansen, *op. cit.*, pp. 394–396, points out the relationship between membership in professional organizations and teaching success.

Fortunately, these deficiencies may be overcome through effective study in carefully selected graduate courses.[19] So great has been the faith of state boards of education in the value of additional graduate work that the renewal of teaching certificates is generally granted only upon completion of a specified number of graduate hours.[20]

A desirable procedure in selecting graduate work involves first identifying the areas of greatest deficiency and then selecting those courses that provide the needed help.[21] Although course work can help the teacher keep informed of current developments in his subject matter and methodology, certain teachers have unfortunately rejected this opportunity and have selected classes that afforded easy credit.

PRINCIPLES RELATED TO INSTRUCTIONAL IMPROVEMENT

Because the principles related to the improvement of instruction are so numerous, only the most relevant ones are singled out for discussion here.

1. A well-planned program of self-appraisal, which calls for the systematic examination of instructional practices at specified intervals, is superior to general, haphazard self-evaluation. The competent teacher views himself as a learner who must identify his own weaknesses and take positive action to correct them. He employs various devices, such as carefully constructed scales, in his self-evaluation.[22] Furthermore, the teacher makes use of frank student appraisal of his instruction and personality as clues to self-improvement.

2. Development of skill in the evaluation of learning is essential in improving teaching. By improving his instruction the teacher improves his ability to help students reach educational goals.[23]

3. The generally accepted minimum level of instructional competence is far from the ideal,[24] and the conscientious teacher continuously seeks to surpass this minimum level.

---

[19]The value of graduate work for professional improvement is stressed by Mills and Douglass, *op. cit.*, pp. 485–486.

[20]Certain state boards of education will accept undergraduate credit toward certificate renewal but usually with the stipulation that the undergraduate hours exceed the graduate hours otherwise required.

[21]Carter, Hansen, and McKim, *op. cit.*, pp. 375–377, stress the need for the careful planning of additional graduate work as a means of furthering professional growth.

McGuire, Myers, and Durrance, *op. cit.*, p. 327, suggest several questions to be considered in planning a program of graduate study.

[22]Ina Corinne Brown, "Twenty Questions—A Personal Rating Scale," *The Peabody Journal of Education*, 1950 (Sept.), 28: 89–91, provides a series of questions that, if answered affirmatively, tend to indicate teacher growth.

[23]Herbert J. Klausmeier, *Teaching in the Secondary School* (New York: Harper & Brothers, 1958), pp. 224–225, discusses the need for relating teacher evaluation to the students' goal achievement.

[24]Kimball Wiles, *Teaching for Better Schools*, 2d. ed. (Englewood Cliffs, N.J.: Prentice-Hall, 1959), pp. 10–13, describes the teacher who meets minimum requirements only.

4. The conscientious study of how other teachers have improved their teaching serves as a great aid to an improvement-minded instructor. Because he is professionally oriented, he learns how to make the most effective professional use of his supervisors, administrators, and fellow teachers. Such a teacher is also aware that the basic concern of in-service training is the improvement of instruction. He knows how to take advantage of well-organized and well-conducted faculty meetings, and he attends workshops that enable him to investigate specific instructional problems under the supervision of specialists. Informal study groups composed of teachers often provide practical assistance. Similarly, demonstrations by other teachers evoke interest and encourage professional growth.

5. Teachers cannot teach effectively unless they possess a thorough knowledge of their subject matter. Reading carefully selected books and periodicals helps them keep abreast of developments in their fields and related methods. Active membership in professional organizations can provide encouragement for improved teaching, while graduate study serves as a helpful aid to professional growth, especially if it follows or accompanies teaching experience. Professional writing based upon experience or research promotes individual growth.

6. Skill in the use of teaching procedures is fundamental to teaching success. Continuous improvement in the selection, production, and use of materials thus contributes to better instruction.

7. Efficient teacher growth is related to intellectual alertness; a constantly improving teacher maintains good mental health.

8. The teacher can evaluate progress toward instructional efficiency only if he is well informed about the qualities that compose such efficiency.

9. Desired improvement in teaching does not necessarily come as a result of experience.

10. Employing superintendents tend to stress the prospective teacher's personality.[25] Thus it is important to be aware of certain traits that need improvement.

11. The effective teacher is interested in and expresses concern for individual students.

12. Carefully organized classroom experimentation designed to improve instruction may motivate students as well as the teacher.

CORRECT AND INCORRECT PRACTICES

Practices aimed at instructional improvement range from the practical to the impossible, from the difficult to the relatively simple,

[25]Charles W. Hardaway, "Factors Considered by School Superintendents in the Selection of Beginning Teachers," *Teachers' College Journal*, 1950, (Jan.) *21*: 80–81, reports the preferences of certain superintendents.

from the obvious to the ingenious, and from those involving the help of others to those involving self-appraisal only.[26] Because improvement procedures must be geared to the individual needs and circumstances of a specific teacher, they will be highly varied.

Incorrect Practices

The following examples describe a range of ineffective practices aimed at instructional improvement.

MISS NATHAN ESTABLISHES UNREALISTIC GOALS

Afton Nathan was a perfectionist. When she completed college and took a position in a large urban junior high school, she vowed that she would be the best teacher in the school before the year was over. After she had had an opportunity to survey the qualities of the fifty-five teachers in the school, she realized that she had established a formidable goal for herself.

Miss Nathan planned her program for self-improvement with great care and carried it out as effectively as she could. She selected and used self-evaluation devices, solicited student opinions, and sought the help of her professional colleagues.

By the end of the school year, she was quite a different person from the neophyte teacher who had undertaken her first paid teaching position just nine months before. She had made substantial gains in self-confidence and in her ability to teach; but, as she evaluated the classroom performances of the four or five teachers with reputations for outstanding teaching, she realized that she fell far short of their achievement.

MR. STORRS FAILS TO PLAN FOR IMPROVEMENT

For the third time in seven years of teaching, Arthur Storrs found himself in a new teaching situation. He was aware that he had many deficiencies as a teacher, for his infrequent contacts with supervisors and supervising principals had left him with the definite impression that his classroom performance was below average. Furthermore, many students made no attempt to hide their dislike for Mr. Storrs and his teaching procedures.

But Mr. Storrs was a stubborn individual; he refused to be driven out of teaching. After all, he had his pride, and no principal or supervisor was going to tell him how to run his class. He knew that it was absolutely essential that he improve his classes and he wanted to improve, but what could he do?

MR. SEARLE VIOLATES STUDENT ANONYMITY

Shortly before grades were issued at the close of each semester, John C. Searle asked his students to evaluate him and his teaching. Students were simply told to write a paragraph about the teacher and a paragraph about his

---

[26]Hansen, *op. cit.*, pp. 384–385, provides contrasting examples of how two teachers approached the matter of professional growth.

Wiles, *op. cit.*, pp. 3–10, describes several teachers with varying degrees of competence.

teaching techniques, indicating what they liked or disliked. All statements were signed.

Mr. Searle was most gratified with student responses. Only a few widely dispersed statements hinted at deficiencies. He was particularly pleased that the four boys in the third-period class who were consistent troublemakers had so many fine things to say about him.

Although Miss Nathan's desire to make rapid improvement was commendable, her perfectionism was unrealistic. The process of ripening into a mature, thoroughly efficient teacher is not accomplished in one or two years; it requires continuing effort over a long period of time. Mr. Storrs accomplished little by his defensive approach to his problems. With the active help of well-meaning supervisors, he could have charted a gradual, yet practical approach to the improvement of his teaching. Desire alone was not sufficient. Mr. Searle could not hope for honest responses from his students without insuring anonymity, and because of the varied nature of student comments, it was impossible to tabulate them effectively for more efficient use. Furthermore, students were asked to evaluate the teacher at a time when they might feel that their responses could have a bearing on their forthcoming grades.

Correct Practices

Some more promising procedures used by teachers in attempting to improve their teaching are illustrated in the following examples.

MR. MELVIN PLANS EFFECTIVELY

At the close of his second year as a mathematics teacher at Richards High School, Mr. Melvin made several disconcerting observations with respect to his professional achievement. His growth was at a standstill, and he wondered for some time whether he should remain in teaching. His grasp of subject matter was entirely inadequate. Furthermore, he felt lost when other teachers began to talk about the values of programed learning, team teaching, and the newer developments in education.

After considerable introspection, Mr. Melvin decided that he would stay in teaching but that, in order to make it interesting for himself and beneficial to his students, he would have to make some marked improvements. Over a period of several weeks, he thought through and spelled out a specific program that he felt would lead to continued betterment:

1. He would go to the state university during the summer term, and he knew precisely which three courses he would take: Programed Learning, Behavior Problems in the Secondary School, and a rigorous undergraduate course in mathematics.

2. For the next school year he would plan his units and daily lessons with particular care. At the completion of each lesson and unit he would write an informal appraisal, pointing out strengths and weaknesses.

3. He would join the National Council of Teachers of Mathematics and read *The Mathematics Teacher* regularly for useful hints. Furthermore, he

would take an active part in the work of his own local professional organization.

4. He would ask the district supervisor, Mr. Burnham, to visit his classes approximately once each month and to set aside time to discuss various problems that arose in the classroom.

5. He would ask Mr. Long, the principal, to make an occasional visit to his class and to then react privately to his teaching methods and effectiveness.

6. He would attempt to get the three other mathematics teachers to set aside one hour each week to discuss common problems related to the teaching of mathematics.

7. Toward the end of September he would use an extensive checklist to rate himself with respect to characteristics essential to successful teachers. This process would be repeated again in April as a basis for comparison.

8. He would administer a standardized mathematics achievement test to all students during the first two weeks of the school year. During the final week of the school year he would administer another form of the same test. Grade level gains—or losses—in mathematics would be evidence of his competence or lack of competence as a teacher.

9. As a continuing check on his teaching efficiency, Mr. Melvin would use a range of evaluation devices to determine the progress made by students during the development of each unit.

10. At the end of each nine-week report-card period, he would ask students to rate him anonymously on twenty-three teacher characteristics. Each successive student rating would be compared with earlier ratings. He would rate himself and compare his evaluation with those of his students.

11. At the end of each day, he would analyze his teaching performance by means of a duplicated checklist and assign himself a letter grade.

Mr. Melvin charted a rigorous program of improvement for himself, but he realized that if his carefully laid plans were not carried out, his professional advancement might be thwarted.

THE WILLIAMS FACULTY USES STUDENT OPINION

After two faculty meetings had been devoted to the discussion of the merits of using student opinions in helping instructors evaluate their own teaching competence, the teachers at Williams Senior High School voted to construct and use a special student evaluation form. After an additional planning session, the following major points were proposed:

1. No one would see the students' evaluation except the teacher being appraised.

2. Student opinions are subjective and should be viewed as one of many aids for improving instruction.

3. The evaluation device should consist of a range of specific, relevant traits to which students could respond plus blank spaces for the insertion of other comments.

4. Student anonymity would be insured in every case.

5. Student responses would be solicited at the close of each semester.

6. Teachers could use student responses in any way they might choose to improve their teaching.

7. During the first faculty meeting of the following year teachers would determine whether they wanted to continue student evaluation.

MR. OSTLER'S TEACHERS VISIT A LARGE SCHOOL

Over a period of three years Alton Ostler, a rural secondary-school supervisor, had established a rapport with his teachers that was the envy of surrounding school districts. Through joint discussion, he and his teachers decided that a visit to a large high school located in a city thirty miles away would be both interesting and rewarding. As a result, arrangements were made to observe the instruction of competent teachers in the large school.

Scheduled visits were made during seven months of the school year. English teachers observed English teachers, mathematics teachers observed mathematics teachers, etc. Provision was also made for the visiting teacher to have an opportunity to discuss classroom procedures with the observed teacher. By the end of the school year, every teacher in the rural school had at least one opportunity to observe excellent teaching by his subject-matter counterpart in the large school. A rich accumulation of ideas was taken back to the school to share with other teachers.

SPECIFIC SUGGESTIONS

Although the conscientious teacher may be equipped with a storehouse of principles related to instructional evaluation, he is still confronted with this question: "What specific steps can I take to improve my teaching?" The suggestions below are designed to help answer this question.

Recommendations

1. Find out how respected educational psychologists define effective teaching; then evaluate yourself according to their standards.
2. Start improving your instruction as soon as you begin to teach, and continue to improve throughout your teaching career.[27]
3. List in specific, written form the steps you will take to improve your teaching; then carry them out.
4. Identify your most pronounced instructional weaknesses and work on overcoming them.[28] Make use of carefully constructed rating scales in identifying your weaknesses.
5. Recognize your strengths as well as your weaknesses. Using a personality inventory of known validity and reliability, analyze your own personality. Determine the frequency with which you should use such a device.
6. Identify the people who can be of greatest assistance to you in improving your instruction; then seek their help. Have frequent and frank chats with your supervisor and principal about your instructional competence. Establish a friendly relationship with col-

[27]Robert C. McKean, *Principles and Methods in Secondary Education* (Columbus, Ohio: Charles E. Merrill Books, Inc., 1962), pp. 82–84, describes conditions that should prevail if teachers are to work individually on the improvement of instruction.

[28]Wellington and Wellington, *op. cit.*, pp. 323–327, identify and discuss many of the common mistakes of the beginning teacher.

leagues who teach the same subject, and discuss professional problems with them often.[29]

7. Promote and support in-service training that will lead to professional improvement. Help organize and participate in informal study groups within your school, and arrange to see demonstrations of superior teaching.[30]

8. Devise specific procedures for making the most effective use of student opinions about your personality and teaching competence. If written opinions are solicited, student anonymity must be assured.

9. Examine carefully your own subject-matter competence in your teaching major and minor. Take a graduate course aimed at professional improvement at least once every other year.

10. Evaluate the methods you use in terms of their helpfulness in moving students toward desired educational goals. Use a carefully planned checklist to measure the effectiveness of your teaching procedures. In the attempt to improve, experiment with assignments, grouping, testing techniques, and programed learning.[31]

11. At least once every six months read a challenging new professional book.[32] Become active in the national and local professional organizations most closely related to your teaching major.

12. Write a brief evaluation of each unit taught. Determine the effectiveness of your use of teaching aids as a part of this evaluation. Provide a space on your daily lesson plan form for evaluating how well the lesson was taught and how improvements could be made.

13. Appraise your enthusiasm for teaching, particularly for units in areas of limited preparation. Be aware of how the learner will be affected by your attitude toward the unit.

14. At the close of each day ask yourself: "How well did I teach today? What did I do wrong that I can improve tomorrow?"

15. Evaluate your personal relationship with each student at least once during each report-card period.

16. Make a systematic evaluation of your mental health yearly.[33]

17. Compare the picture of the teacher you are with the picture of the teacher you feel you should be.

Cautions

1. Don't postpone establishing and following a personal, well-planned program of instructional evaluation and improvement.

---

[29]Group work as a means of improving instruction is discussed by McKean, *op. cit.*, pp. 84–85.

[30]Mills and Douglass, *op. cit.*, p. 472, stress the value of observing a well-planned demonstration.

[31]Hansen, *op. cit.*, pp. 388–390, urges experimentation as a means of instructional improvement.

[32]Specific suggestions for improving one's professional reading are provided by Mills and Douglass, *op. cit.*, pp. 483–484.

[33]Liberman, *op. cit.*, pp. 234–238, provides a well-documented discussion of the mental health of teachers.

2. Don't view a single aspect of instructional evaluation as comprising a program.

3. Don't make plans that cannot be carried through.

4. Don't seek the help of incompetent teachers.

5. Don't spend an unjustified amount of time in worrying about your instructional deficiencies.

PROBLEMS FOR STUDY AND DISCUSSION

1. Why has it been impossible to ascertain with scientific precision the characteristics of the ideal teacher? Explain.

2. Describe the difference between a carefully constructed plan for the improvement of instruction and a general desire to improve. Give examples.

3. How important is consistency in improving instruction? Give two examples of teachers who were inconsistent in attempting to improve.

4. Suggest five ways to identify personal weaknesses in your teaching.

5. In fifteen to twenty brief statements, describe the qualities that you feel are characteristic of the effective teacher.

6. Describe in some detail a systematic and practical program for instructional improvement that would extend throughout a full school year.

7. Assumption: You are teaching in a consolidated high school in which there are fifteen teachers. Indicate exactly how you would make use of your school principal in attempting to improve your instruction during your first year of teaching.

8. If you had to choose between excellence in subject-matter knowledge and excellence in the use of instructional procedures, which would you choose? Why? Explain in detail.

9. List six practical procedures for helping you gain better command of your subject.

10. Without consulting the text, list ten relevant questions to use in appraising your teaching methods.

11. Assumption: You teach in a school district that has a general secondary-school supervisor. Although you have not encountered particular difficulty in your teaching, you are anxious to accelerate your rate of improvement. Tell exactly how you would use the supervisor to accomplish this end.

12. Describe in a brief paragraph the ideal voice for teaching. Now rate your own voice, using the descriptive paragraph as a measuring device.

13. Appraise your teaching personality by means of one of the checklists or devices mentioned in this chapter. What are your chief personality weaknesses? What steps can you take to overcome them?

14. What are the advantages of teacher self-evaluation as opposed to evaluation by others? Explain.

15. Name ten cautions to be observed in the use of student evaluation of the teacher.

16. Describe at least three different devices that could be used for student evaluation of teachers. Which do you find most helpful? Why?

17. What is the advantage of being able to tabulate student reactions to the teacher?

18. List the three professional organizations at the local, state, or national levels that would be of greatest help in furthering your professional growth.

19. Identify five professional and subject-matter courses that you can and should take in order to insure growth and overcome deficiencies.

20. Outline a specific program of professional reading aimed at your instructional improvement.

RECOMMENDED READINGS

Batchelder, Howard T., Maurice McGlasson, and Raleigh Schorling, *Student Teaching in Secondary Schools,* 4th ed. New York: McGraw-Hill Book Company, 1964, Chapter 15.

Carter, William L., Carl W. Hansen, and Margaret G. McKim, *Learning to Teach in the Secondary School.* New York: The Macmillan Company, 1962, Chapter 13.

Grambs, Jean D., William J. Iverson, and Franklin K. Patterson, *Modern Methods in Secondary Education,* rev. ed. New York: The Dryden Press, 1958, Chapter 23.

Hansen, Kenneth H., *High School Teaching.* Englewood Cliffs, N.J.: Prentice-Hall, Inc., 1957, Chapter 14.

Klausmeier, Herbert J., *Teaching in the Secondary School.* New York: Harper & Brothers, 1958, pp. 224–228.

Lieberman, Myron, *Education As a Profession.* Englewood Cliffs, N.J.: Prentice-Hall, Inc., 1956, Chapters 8 and 9, and pp. 393–402.

McGuire, Vincent, Robert B. Myers, and Charles L. Durrance, *Your Student Teaching in the Secondary School.* Boston: Allyn and Bacon, Inc., 1959, pp. 290–292 and 326–327.

McKean, Robert C., *Principles and Methods in Secondary Education.* Columbus, Ohio: Charles E. Merrill Books, Inc., 1962, pp. 82–85 and 302–308

Mills, Hubert H., and Harl R. Douglass, *Teaching in High School,* 2d. ed. New York: Ronald Press, 1957, Chapter 28.

Morse, William C., and G. Max Wingo, *Psychology and Teaching,* 2d. ed. Chicago: Scott, Foresman and Company, 1962, pp. 398–400.

Nordberg, H. Orville, James M. Bradfield, and William C. Odell, *Secondary School Teaching.* New York: The Macmillan Company, 1962, pp. 44–45, 104, and 380–381.

Riccio, Anthony C., and Frederick R. Cyphert (eds.), *Teaching in America.* Columbus, Ohio: Charles E. Merrill Books, Inc., 1962, pp. 347–442.

Richey, Robert W., *Planning for Teaching,* 3d. ed. New York: McGraw-Hill Book Company, 1963, Chapter 3.

Rivlin, Harry N., *Teaching Adolescents in Secondary Schools,* 2d. ed. New York: Appleton-Century-Crofts, Inc., 1961, Chapter 15.

Wellington, C. Burleigh, and Jean Wellington, *Teaching for Critical Thinking; with Emphasis on Secondary Education.* New York: McGraw-Hill Book Company, 1960, Chapter 15.

Wiggins, Samuel P., *Successful High School Teaching.* Boston: Houghton Mifflin Company, 1958, pp. 328 and 344–352.

Wiles, Kimball, *Teaching for Better Schools,* 2d. ed. Englewood Cliffs, N.J.: Prentice-Hall, Inc., 1959, Chapters 1 and 3.

17

Directing Cocurricular Activities

Cocurricular activities play an important role in the total curriculum of every secondary school and can contribute to the learning experiences of every student. For these reasons, the teacher must be familiar with the nature of these activities and know how to use them most effectively.

EVOLUTION OF COCURRICULAR ACTIVITIES

The historical development of school-related, extraclass activities can be divided into three readily identifiable periods.[1] During the first period cocurricular activities were virtually ignored by school faculties. In the second period strong teacher opposition predominated—opposition based on the assumption that such activities detracted student attention from scholarship. It was not until 1920 that the third phase was ushered in with widespread recognition that activities could serve a useful educational purpose.

Although the controversy over the value of incorporating activities into the school program has been revived since the end of World War II, teachers generally believe that activities are educationally justified. At the present time it would be difficult to find a junior or senior high school in which athletic contests, student government, and social events are not woven into the fabric of school operation.

---

[1]Harry C. McKown, *Extracurricular Activities*, 3d. ed. (New York: Macmillan, 1952), pp. 2–3.

Reacting to the cry for a more rigorous academic program, however, many schools have de-emphasized nonclass-related activities and have instituted reforms in curriculum and methods designed to strengthen student achievement.

A study of nonacademic school activities reveals a gradual change in their relationship to the academic curriculum. In its early years American secondary education did not give official recognition to activities that were not specifically academic, although sports enthusiasts in the cities hired coaches to work with boys during after-school hours, and one or more leading citizens of the community provided instruction on a private basis.[2] Later, activities were organized by the students themselves, but without administrative authorization or teacher sponsorship. Teachers next began sponsoring activities (frequently athletics) without official recognition. Finally, with the administrative recognition of school activities came the use of the term *extracurricular*, designed to insure that activities would not be confused with the curriculum itself. With the growth of extracurricular activities and the weakening of official objection, the range of activities spread, and activity periods were gradually incorporated into many school schedules; the term *extra*, however, still persisted.

Several areas, such as music and athletics, were admitted to the curriculum only after they had served an apprenticeship as activities *external* to subjects that already had the academic blessing. In the relatively recent past driver training, ballroom dancing, journalism, and auto mechanics made their entrance into the curriculum in this back-door fashion. Several activities—photography, debate, and certain clubs—still occupy a position that is difficult to classify strictly as either a part of the curriculum or external to it.

In the mid-thirties a movement developed that recognized all learning experiences under the supervision of teaching personnel as a part of the curriculum. This movement quickly gained momentum, and writers and educators began to discard the term *extracurricular* in favor of terms that indicated the close relationship between activities and the curriculum: *cocurricular, extraclass, auxiliary,* and *class-related.*[3] Of these, the term *cocurricular* is currently used most frequently.

Some of the more optimistic writers of the past few years have willfully rejected such terms, because they prefer to think of any school-related activity as part of the curriculum itself. This preference, however, is not widespread among teachers and administrators whose practical school experiences have led them to the realistic conclusion that the terms *cocurriculum* and even *extracurriculum* are

---

[2]W. L. Wrinkle and R. S. Gilchrist, *Secondary Education for American Democracy* (New York: Farrar and Rinehart, 1942), p. 339.

[3]Harl R. Douglass (ed.), *The High School Curriculum*, 3d. ed. (New York: Ronald Press, 1964), pp. 517–518, identifies the problems faced in the attempt to integrate the cocurriculum with the curriculum.

still very much in evidence.[4] Current school practices warrant the use of these terms and will for some years to come.[5]

THE TEACHER AND COCURRICULAR ACTIVITIES

Because cocurricular activities constitute an aspect of the educational program of every junior and senior high school, teachers are expected to assist in the direction and sponsorship of these activities. The conscientious administrator who seeks to insure the best possible cocurricular program is confronted with a number of problems related to sponsorship: How can special teacher abilities be best employed in activity sponsorship? Who are to be sponsors? What are the duties of specific sponsors? What are the specific problems of sponsorship?

Special Abilities and Employment

It is not uncommon for a superintendent to choose between two prospective teachers of comparable professional and academic background on the basis of their assumed ability to participate effectively in a cocurricular program. Rural superintendents, particularly, express great interest in the special talents of applicants for teaching positions. These special abilities often make the teacher a highly useful sponsor of school activities and assist in raising the cultural level of the community.

Principals are often provided with advance information about the special interests and talents of new teachers. If such information has not been furnished, many principals obtain it through personal interviews or from a detailed survey form. Barring unanticipated difficulties, administrators usually ask teachers to sponsor those activities in which they have greatest interest and for which they have some preparation.

Selection of Sponsors

In small schools the entire faculty, as well as the principal, is often involved in assisting, directing, or sponsoring some activity, and teachers whose talents lie in several areas may even be asked to assist in more than one activity. This practice can result in a very heavy burden for the teacher if he does not receive the necessary administrative protection. The primary concern of teachers should be

---

[4]Kenneth H. Hansen, *High School Teaching* (Englewood Cliffs, N.J.: Prentice-Hall, 1957), p. 329, indicates that there are practical reasons for differentiating between curricular and cocurricular activities.

[5]As late as 1952 one of the most widely used texts concerned with secondary activities (*Extracurricular Activities*, by Harry McKown) bore the term *extracurricular.*

in-class instruction. If an extraclass activities program absorbs so much of the teacher's time that his classroom performance suffers, he should be relieved of some of his extra load.

In large schools as well, relatively few teachers are free from club and activity sponsorship.[6] Certain school districts provide additional pay for those teachers who are overloaded with activity sponsorship. Usually this additional salary is only a token payment for the actual expenditure of time and energy. In certain cases where school boards have not provided a pay differential for teachers who render additional professional services, special teacher groups (coaches, band directors, etc.) have been organized to present a convincing argument to the school board.

Duties of the Sponsor

Because the nature of school activities varies, the responsibilities of the faculty sponsor also vary greatly.[7] The specific duties of the director of the senior play are quite different from the advisory tasks of the chess club sponsor. Furthermore, what is expected of a sponsor may partially depend upon the grade level of the students with whom he is working.

One author's suggestions to new faculty advisors include several responsibilities:[8]

1. The activity sponsor should attend all meetings of the organization.
2. He should meet with activity officers and committees, encouraging the exercise of student initiative.
3. He should attend all meetings of the Steering Committee and encourage the presence of the student president of the organization.
4. He should confer with the director of student activities about the progress of the organization and determine the scheduling of specific events.

Student Views on Sponsorship

Secondary-school students have preconceived ideas about the responsibilities of their activity sponsors. They expect the ideal sponsor to permit students to assume the major responsibility for the operation of their own affairs. Where faculty direction is needed, they feel that it should be dispensed with appropriate tact and without domi-

[6]W. S. Sterner, "Preparing Teachers to Sponsor Activities," *National Association of Secondary-School Principals Bulletin*, 1952 (Feb.), *36*: 33, reported that 96 per cent of 323 beginning public-school teachers sponsored school activities.

[7]Jean D. Grambs, William J. Iverson, and Franklin K. Patterson, *Modern Methods in Secondary Education*, rev. ed. (New York: The Dryden Press, 1958), pp. 620–624, identify several of the general cocurricular responsibilities of the teacher.

[8]Adapted from Fred A. Bennett, "A Letter to New Faculty Advisers," *School Activities*, 1954 (Sept.), *26*: 13.

nation. They prize the ability of the sponsor who can establish and maintain friendly relationships outside of the classroom, and the teacher-adviser who reflects a sympathetic understanding of student problems is well liked. Students place considerable importance on the sponsor's degree of specialization in the activity under his direction. They also esteem a pleasant personality in the sponsor, and an important part of this personality is a sense of humor.

Educational, Moral, and Legal Duties

One specialist chooses to discuss the sponsor's duties in terms of his educational, moral, and legal responsibilities.[9] Of these, the educational responsibility is the dominant one. In trying to help students achieve the educational goals of the school, the sponsor is concerned with developing effective citizenship, guiding social, moral, and intellectual growth, and encouraging recognition of the value of group effort directed toward common objectives.

Activity sponsorship affords a rich opportunity for encouraging the development of high morality among students. Honesty, personal integrity, and proper relationships with members of the peer group, regardless of sex, are of prime concern. In order to function effectively in promoting student morality, the sponsor himself must exhibit desirable moral traits.

The sponsor must determine his legal responsibilities if he is to perform efficiently and avoid difficulty. Although most sponsors will serve for years without encountering legal involvements, the chance situation that does arise points to the need for caution. Lack of knowledge about contracts, for instance, has been known to cause real problems. Because oral agreements are legally enforceable under certain circumstances, the teacher-sponsor would do well to avoid them. In addition, the student, as a minor, cannot generally be held responsible for contractual arrangements made with parties outside the school. Poor community relations are often incurred, however, when students are allowed unwarranted and unsupervised freedom in conducting club affairs.

The possibility of injury to students engaging in school activities is ever present. Although most sponsors are conscientious in their attempts to prevent physical harm to students, accidents do occur. Whether injury comes as the result of accident or negligence, legal action is always a possibility. In some cases the activity sponsor may become the sole defendant.

Specific Problems of Sponsorship

The adviser of any secondary-school activity can save himself trouble and help make the activity a success if he identifies in advance

[9]Robert W. Frederick, *The Third Curriculum* (New York: Appleton-Century-Crofts, 1959), pp. 229–232.

the problems of greatest concern.[10] Some of the sponsor's major concerns are:

1. Determining that the sponsored activity is educationally defensible.
2. Developing and maintaining student, as well as teacher, enthusiasm for the activity.
3. Determining that the activity is scheduled at a time that permits its success.
4. Encouraging careful organization of the activity.
5. Encouraging students to elect responsible activity officers.
6. Determining that alumni involvement (if any) serves the purposes of education.
7. Securing adequate financing of the activity.
8. Maintaining a realistic teacher work load so that adequate time can be devoted to activity sponsorship.
9. Encouraging continuity in the activity from year to year.
10. Providing for adequate bookkeeping and record keeping.
11. Seeing that eligibility requirements serve the purposes of education.
12. Keeping activity-related status considerations (peer-group worship of the varsity team member, for example) under control.
13. Evaluating the activity program at desired intervals.

Educational Value

Of the scores of activities currently being carried on in the secondary schools in the United States, many have little educational value. The postwar emphasis on a hard-core curriculum and academic rigor has influenced administrators to restrict—and in some cases to drop entirely—certain traditional school activities. Among those subject to critical re-examination are the weekly school-sponsored dance, competitive athletics, the pep rally, the long senior trip at the end of the school year, the all-night graduation party, and the frequent out-of-school performances of musical groups.

Since the primary concern of the school is to provide and give direction to activities that are educational in nature, the conscientious sponsor will align himself with those cocurricular activities that will accomplish this end. He may well pose some of the following questions: "How can I make the activity that I am sponsoring educationally more beneficial without sacrificing student interest?" "Is the club activity I sponsor being given adequate attention by agencies outside the school?" "Would the existence of the activity I sponsor be justified if the element of pure fun were eliminated?"

---

[10]Samuel P. Wiggins, *Successful High School Teaching* (Boston: Houghton Mifflin Company, 1958), pp. 300–302, identifies the role of the teacher-sponsor as that of a "constructive critic" rather than a "naïve do-gooder."

Although teachers readily espouse, in theory at least, the doctrine that every school activity must have an underlying educational purpose, many of them become so engrossed in the pleasurable aspects of their sponsorship that they resist any change in the direction of more learning. Students, especially, have come to view the out-of-class activity as something that is primarily fun; it is viewed as having little to do with learning as such.

Occasionally student activities get so far out of hand that they appear to be totally without sponsorship. This unwarranted student freedom is rationalized by saying that the activity is, after all, a *student* activity and that whatever benefit is derived from it will be the result of individual student participation. The term *sponsorship*, however, implies that adult, mature direction is being given consistently although the teacher-sponsor may hold the reigns somewhat less firmly than he customarily does in the classroom.

Getting students to realize that cocurricular activities are not really extracurricular is one of the basic tasks of the sponsor. He must accomplish this, of course, without subduing the natural enthusiasm that helps make the activity a success. If students, parents, teachers, and the administration are of the opinion that activities for the sake of activities alone are justified, little will be done to make these activities educational experiences.

Enthusiasm

Creating and maintaining enthusiasm for cocurricular activities is, with few exceptions, one of the basic concerns of the activity sponsor. This task is made more difficult by the fact that educationally worth-while activities are often not as interesting as more sensational and frequently less demanding activities. For example, encouraging journalism club members to improve their writing to the point where their articles deserve publication in the school newspaper calls for ingenuity and work on the part of the sponsor. On the other hand, students have a built-in enthusiasm for participation in after-school sports, and little promotion is required on the part of the sponsor. Whether the student will elect to play softball or to work on the school newspaper is often determined by teacher-engendered enthusiasm.

Of more critical concern to the long-range operation of an activity is the sponsor's personal enthusiasm for the activity. The teacher who approaches an activity or club with apathy seals its doom at the very outset. A teacher who is but mildly enthusiastic about a particular activity assignment at the beginning of the school year may quickly develop a deep, contagious enthusiasm for the activity through study, sympathetic work with his students, and a desire to succeed. In order to insure enthusiasm, teachers are frequently allowed to indicate their preference for activity sponsorship.

Often, after the novelty of participation has worn away, students lose some of their interest in an activity. It is at this point that the teacher should call on his reserve enthusiasm to rekindle student interest. Closely related to student disinterest is minimum or limited student participation. Whether disinterested students continue to take part in the activity as a matter of duty or completely refuse to participate any further, their lack of interest hinders learning. The teacher is responsible for quickly identifying these trouble signs and providing the stimulus that will result in genuine enthusiasm.

Scheduling

Activities take time, and if they are to attract students, they must be scheduled at a time when they do not conflict with more glamorous activities and with sufficient frequency to encourage success. The debating club that is limited to a thirty-minute period once a week, for example, has little chance to permit extensive student participation in debates and the necessary teacher criticism. The scheduling of the activity period as a part of the regular school day (such as the third period on Monday, Wednesday, and Friday) does much to insure that there will be enough time to make specific activities successful.

Many kinds of activities are scheduled to meet before school or after school in order to guarantee a lengthy period. This is typical for many musical and athletic groups. Where students depend upon bus transportation, however, activities scheduled for nonschool hours have definite limitations. The youngster who must be transported to school should have just as much opportunity to participate in the activity of his choice as does the student who lives within walking distance.

Organization

Once an activity has been identified as worthy of a place in the cocurricular program,[11] it should be organized to encourage its success. Frequently this calls for the election of student officers who will serve responsibly to further the cause of the organization. Such officers are usually elected by the members of the organization. If the organization elects officers, the sponsor should try to (1) encourage members to make sound judgments of the candidates' qualifications for office so that they will be able to vote for the most capable individuals and (2) insure that elected officers discharge their responsibilities conscientiously. Sponsors should devote a substantial share of their time and energy to encouraging immature students to assume the responsibilities of effective citizenship.

When a new organization is formed, it is important that its official name, membership requirements, purposes, general organization, and officers be known to all its members. In many cases the sponsor will

---

[11]*Ibid.*, pp. 299–300, poses questions aimed at helping the sponsor and administrator determine whether a new activity should be introduced or whether an old one should be discontinued.

need to exert consistent but gentle persuasion to insure student participation in acquiring and presenting this important information. The sponsor must be sure, however, that his concern for the organization does not overshadow his concern for student participation in the organization's activities—the major purpose of cocurricular organizations. Under certain circumstances it may be advisable for the members to write, with the guidance of the sponsor, a simplified, short, understandable constitution and bylaws.

Alumni Involvement

In many schools alumni interest in interscholastic sports activities has reached the point where it severely hampers the conduct of an educationally sound physical education program. In this situation the coach must offer appropriate resistance to undesirable nonschool pressures without alienating interested parents and former students. It is well to remember that the school often relies on parents and townspeople for the support of certain activities that attract paying audiences.

Recent graduates occasionally attend school dances. When these graduates interfere with the participation of younger students, this practice should be curbed, and some schools have found it advisable to exclude all recent graduates in the interest of proper conduct. School patrons and parents, on the other hand, are frequently invited to attend dances as guests of the sponsoring organization.

Financing

Because cocurricular activities frequently cost money, the sponsor is confronted with the task of assuring that his club or activity is adequately financed. Clubs are often financed through modest weekly or monthly dues. The adviser, however, must be constantly aware of the possibility of imposing undesirable financial burdens upon poor youngsters, and he must keep dues at a workable minimum. In planning activities, students from wealthier homes may give little consideration to the financial limitations of others; in this case, the adviser must exercise mature judgment on behalf of his less affluent students. If a student honestly is unable to afford certain activities, arrangements should be made to allow his full participation without any embarrassment to him.

In some schools students are admitted to major school events upon presentation of a student activity card. This simple, easily administered procedure not only encourages student participation but also solves many of the financial problems of needy students.

Continuity

In order to insure continuity in those activities that recur annually, the school administrator often appoints a sponsor whose teaching responsibilities are most closely related to the activity. For example, the dramatic arts teacher sponsors the senior play, the music teacher sponsors the spring music festival, and the physical education instructor assumes responsibility for the intramural sports program. Many such sponsors have been known to serve the same club for years, improving the activity each year as a result of their experience.[12]

Club leadership, too frequently lacking stability, needs the same type of continuity. A measure of stability may be secured by having the president, vice-president, and secretary-treasurer come from the senior, junior, and sophomore classes, respectively. Continuity is further helped when the vice-president automatically becomes the president of the organization the following year. Under these provisions new club members may be oriented by club officers who were active the preceding year.

Keeping Records

Inadequate bookkeeping and improper maintenance of records weaken activities and contribute to a lack of continuity. In large, well-organized schools a member of the faculty is usually designated as the custodian of the funds for all activities. In such cases, he frequently requires that all clubs deposit their money with him, keep accurate records of their expenditures, and obtain his countersignature on all checks. Such procedures are usually carried out by the club treasurer under the supervision of the sponsor.

In far too many cases, club finances are handled very unsystematically—to the disadvantage of club operation. The sponsor who does not insist on careful bookkeeping operations may find himself involved in operational as well as financial difficulties.

Written records of activities within an organization are essential to subsequent smooth operation. The secretary should keep minutes of club meetings and record major organizational activities. In addition, membership rolls should be kept accurate and up-to-date. Such records enable club members and sponsors of later years to obtain an accurate picture of club operation.

Eligibility

The matter of eligibility for school organizations eventually becomes the concern of all teacher-sponsors. The most common requirement relates to scholarship. In many schools students must achieve a certain minimum grade-point average in order to serve as officers, and students whose grades fall below a given level may not play on school teams. The value of this type of restriction is still being debated in educational circles, particularly as it relates to participation in interscholastic sports. The current trend is to require high marks for those who are to represent the school in competitive activities.

---

[12]Frederick, *op. cit.*, pp. 233–235, discusses some of the administrative problems related to change in activity sponsorship.

Because of the controversial nature of this eligibility problem, teachers should understand the issues involved.[13] There is a real question about the advisability of applying a common standard for eligibility in all school activities. Certainly all students, low as well as high achievers, have the right to participate in some activities. In fact, many low achievers achieve their greatest success in cocurricular activities. Since it is the responsibility of the school to lead the individual student as far along the path of learning as possible, eligibility requirements should be geared to serve the needs of varying groups and individuals.

Prestige

The status of an activity is of great importance to students as well as to adults. To be a member of the winning basketball team provides its own reward; participation in a well-presented school play inflates a young actor's ego; singing with the a cappella choir before a packed house is a tremendous thrill for the choir member. The majority of school activities, however, do not lend themselves to the praise of spectators and to audience-pleasing star performances.

In most cases teacher-sponsors have the responsibility of making and keeping their cocurricular activities so worth while, educational, and interesting that students will seek membership in the organization. The club that does little of value, has no planned program, and lacks enthusiastic membership often suffers a slow death.

External evidence of status is often found in the form of organization sweaters, badges, and insignias. The desirability of these symbols should be examined rather closely, however, because they tend to promote exclusiveness—and they are also expensive.

Evaluation

A key concern of the sponsor is continuous improvement in the activity. In order to achieve improvement the teacher may find it advisable to plan a specific program of evaluation. Several devices lend themselves to this purpose:[14]

1. Questionnaires concerning several aspects of organization activities.
2. Checklists in which students may quickly rate various facets of the organization's operations.
3. Evaluation conferences in which the members of the organization discuss its strengths and weaknesses and suggest improvements.
4. Free responses to specific questions in which students are

---

[13]The issues involved in eligibility requirements are examined by Frederick, *op. cit.*, pp. 276–281.

[14]*Ibid.*, pp. 131–133, provides a brief discussion and examples of instruments used to evaluate student activities.

asked to indicate, in their own words, how they feel about the activity involved.

The need for systematizing the evaluation of cocurricular activities is stressed by Frederick.[15] He indicates that these evaluation judgments should be guided, focused on specific points, adjusted to the size and impact of the activity, and recorded. These judgments should then lead to suggested action. Frederick also makes a plea for the careful selection of personnel to help evaluate the activities.

Evaluation is one area in which the sponsor must assume the initiative. If evaluation is neglected or poorly planned and executed, the responsibility for any lack of success of the organization will largely fall on the sponsor.

CATEGORIES OF COCURRICULAR ACTIVITIES

Each teacher-sponsor must be aware that the activity for which he is responsible is only one of many in the typical secondary school.[16] In order to gain proper perspective, he must see how his cocurricular activity relates to the subject-matter curriculum, to all other aspects of the cocurriculum, and to the total educational offering of the school. To live in instructional isolation within the framework of one's own activity or subject is unprofessional. It is also harmful to students who are attempting to achieve a well-rounded education.

It is possible to classify extraclass activities in a number of ways.[17] Often such activities are classed as social, musical, dramatic, athletic, publication, and club activities. Certain schools differentiate between major and minor activities, basing this division on the average amount of time students devote to them. In some schools varying numbers of points are assigned for participation in specific activities. This procedure makes it possible to identify students who tend to be hyperactive and, if assumed desirable, to restrict their activities.

Semi-Curricular Activities

The term *semi-curricular* designates those activities that are part of the traditional cocurricular offering but have little direct relationship to subject-matter content. Among these are the assembly, the homeroom, the student council, and the school commencement.

The Assembly

No school escapes the need or the desire for holding an occa-

---

[15]*Ibid.*, pp. 128–130.

[16]Wiggins, *op. cit.*, pp. 289–296, briefly discusses the types of activities.

[17]Frederick, *op. cit.*, pp. 429–433, provides a helpful classification of student activities that is used as the basis for the discussion here.

sional assembly.[18] Assembly programs designed to highlight specific occasions or special aspects of national life appear in a new format each year. Columbus Day, Thanksgiving, Christmas, and Easter frequently inspire assembly programs, and other programs focus attention on specifically designated occasions such as American Education Week. Standard assemblies may also include the annual dramatic presentations, programs prepared by the music department, and pep assemblies. Some special types are the exchange programs from other schools, the talent assembly, faculty programs, and audience-participation programs. Forums, panels, and addresses by prominent individuals are sometimes featured.

Although they take many different forms, school assemblies should be educational.[19] It must be readily admitted, however, that many of them fall short of the mark. Each proposed assembly should be evaluated in terms of its educational value for the student body as a whole. The worth of the speaker who talks over the head of his teenage audience and the benefit of the rowdy pep assembly may be open to question. Talks on safe driving, first aid, and world cultures, however, are received with less suspicion.

Although the role of the assembly sponsor may vary greatly from school to school, he has the basic responsibility for determining that assembly programs are educational and stimulating. By working with responsible students, he must see that high standards are established and maintained. Assembly programs should:[20]

1. Be flexible and appropriately varied.
2. Allow a wide range of student participation.
3. Be interesting.
4. Reflect careful planning and practice.
5. Be in good taste.
6. Be inoffensive but not without spirit; controversial programs are not necessarily offensive.
7. Be accurately timed.
8. Reflect efficient handling of mechanics.

The Homeroom

The homeroom serves its function best if students are allowed a measure of freedom under careful teacher supervision. Because the freedom essential to effective homeroom operation may be in marked contrast to the rigid standards required in certain classes, the role of

---

[18] *Ibid.*, pp. 312–315, includes a comprehensive list of the best assembly programs named by 280 secondary schools, a list adapted from a study conducted by the Association of Secondary-School Principals.

[19] Specific objectives and principles that should give direction to the preparation and presentation of school assemblies are discussed by Franklin A. Miller, James H. Moyer, and Robert B. Patrick, *Planning Student Activities* (Englewood Cliffs, N.J.: Prentice-Hall, 1956), pp. 499–513.

[20] Frederick, *op. cit.*, pp. 316–319.

the teacher-sponsor is doubly difficult.[21] In the classroom his focus of attention is the subject and its mastery by students, but in the homeroom his interest is centered on the student as a person. Here, some of the most effective guidance may take place.[22]

Many schools require that each teacher supervise a homeroom as well as teach. This dual role calls for added effort and responsibility, particularly if the teacher has had no professional guidance training. The need for counseling skill is indicated in the general purposes of the homeroom:[23]

1. To establish a base of operations in the school where the student can feel comfortable and accepted.
2. To enable the teacher to become thoroughly acquainted with the student and to enable the student to come to know his homeroom teacher as a friend.
3. To provide a situation in which the teacher can and will help students make sound decisions with respect to educational, social, personal, and vocational choices.
4. To provide a setting in which essential administrative matters can be cared for.

Because there is a high degree of variability in the homeroom operation within different schools, the teacher who transfers from one school district to another or from one state to another must be prepared to adjust to a new situation.

The Student Council

Widespread attempts to democratize the administrative functions of secondary schools by involving students resulted in the organization of student or school councils.[24] The objectives of such groups are listed by the National Association of Student Councils as:[25]

1. Selection of student representatives.
2. Student involvement in the real problems of the school.
3. Communication of ideas to students and among students.
4. Development of desired student skills.
5. Development of desired student attitudes and behavior.

---

[21]Hubert H. Mills and Harl R. Douglass, *Teaching in High School*, 2d. ed. (New York: Ronald Press, 1957), pp. 421–433, provide a detailed discussion of homeroom sponsorship.

[22]Hansen, *op. cit.*, pp. 332–334, stresses the need for having a vital and important program of activities in the homeroom.

[23]Douglass, *op. cit.*, pp. 522–523, identifies the chief objectives of the homeroom and lists specific subject-related topics that may be discussed in the homeroom.

[24]See Miller, Moyer, and Patrick, *op. cit.*, Chapter 8, for a well-organized discussion of the student council.

[25]National Association of Student Councils, *Student Council in the Secondary School: A Handbook for Student Councils and Their Advisers* (Washington, D.C.: National Association of Secondary-School Principals, 1950), pp. 11–13.

To meet these objectives, student representatives must be effectively directed by an advisor who is fully aware of the implications of irresponsible student council conduct. Because student council representatives are allowed decision-making privileges denied the average student, the teacher-sponsor must encourage action that will be in the interest of education and of the other students.[26] Frequently this highly responsible sponsorship is assigned to the principal, the assistant principal, or a respected teacher who has demonstrated ability to work with students. The first-year teacher is rarely given the opportunity of working with the student council.

The nature of the decisions assigned to the jurisdiction of the student council are usually restricted by administrative decree or school regulations. Professional decisions are best left to professionals. The kinds of action that student representatives can logically be expected to take must be constantly reviewed by the student council sponsor and the school administration.

Commencement

As with all school activities, the graduation exercises or school commencement should be an educational experience.[27] The current trend is to have a much larger proportion of the graduating class take part in the program than was the case ten or fifteen years ago.[28] An outside speaker is less frequently brought in to give the graduation address. Instead, several students, usually those with the highest academic standing, are asked to give short inspirational talks. Musical organizations within the school are also asked to participate.

The task of coordinating the commencement activities often falls on the shoulders of the senior class sponsor. In large schools this responsibility may be shared by teacher-sponsors whose homerooms will be graduating. Very often, however, one certain teacher may assume the annual task of coordinating the many details related to the graduation ceremony in order to maintain continuity from one commencement to the next.

Large Technical Activities

Among the cocurricular activities that fall into the technical category are athletics, musical activities, dramatics, speech activities,

---

[26]Douglass, *op. cit.*, p. 524, presents a sound approach to student participation in school administration.

J. Cecil Parker, T. Bentley Edwards, and William H. Stegeman, *Curriculum in America* (New York: Thomas Y. Crowell Company, 1962), pp. 461–462, express a liberal point of view on student involvement in school operation. These authors believe that although students need the counsel and support of the administrator, they also need the freedom to make many of their own decisions.

[27]See Miller, Moyer, and Patrick, *op. cit.*, Chapter 19, for a thorough discussion of senior class and graduation activities.

[28]McKown, *op. cit.*, pp. 491–496, voices objections to the typical secondary-school commencement.

and publications.[29] Each one has its own unique sponsorship requirements and may give rise to special problems.[30]

Athletics

Competitive sports are the chief target for many critics of school activities. More numerous and vocal, however, are the supporters of competitive sports, both inside and outside the school. For this reason the sponsor of such activities, usually the physical education instructor, must identify a rational position and be prepared to defend it zealously.[31] He must guard against an unwarranted emphasis on the glorification of the team, on winning at all costs, on team proficiency at the expense of the academic program, and on furthering the interests of a few participants while neglecting the majority. The secondary-school coach must always keep before him this essential principle: School activities should, by virtue of their setting, be educational in nature. The matter of spectator interest should be of secondary concern.[32]

Major competitive sports that require the direction of a coach include football, basketball, baseball, and track, and sometimes soccer and swimming. In the typical high school the physical education instructor is usually expected to serve as the coach of one or more of the school teams. If the school is small, he will probably coach all the teams. In large schools that employ more than one physical education instructor, the major sports are often assigned to different coaches. Because of his frequent and close contacts with team members, the coach is in a good position to establish rapport with students and provide helpful counsel.

Competitive intramural sports afford a much wider range of student participation[33] and thus come closer to fulfilling the requirements of a sound educational activity than do interscholastic sports. Intramural programs may include nearly all sports associated with the competition between schools, although some sports may assume a slightly modified form—touch football instead of tackle football, softball instead of baseball, etc.

An intramural sports program also affords students the opportunity to participate in sports and games that usually do not attract competing school teams. Ping-pong, badminton, tumbling, volleyball, roller skating, horseshoes, archery, trampoline, and fencing are but a few of the wide range of sports that have great appeal to secondary-school youngsters and that can be effectively sponsored within the

[29]See Frederick, *op. cit.*, pp. 430–431.

[30]Hansen, *op. cit.*, pp. 342–343, points out the possible dangers involved in cocurricular activities in music, dramatics, and athletics.

[31]Douglass, *op. cit.*, pp. 527–528, presents a sound point of view concerning school teams.

[32]Miller, Moyer, and Patrick, *op. cit.*, pp. 351–352, list criteria for evaluating a high-school athletic program.

[33]Frederick, *op. cit.*, p. 107, stresses the need for mass participation in sports.

framework of a cocurricular activities program. Although they may lack the glamour of the traditional spectator sports, they provide excellent learning opportunities as well as sound physical exercise.

Musical Activities

The dividing line between the curricular and cocurricular activities of many school musical organizations is difficult to establish.[34] The mixed chorus, for example, often practices in class for the traditional Christmas concert to which all students and parents are invited. During the basketball game the school band adds to the spirit of the occasion by playing selections learned in the classroom.

Sponsorship of musical organizations usually falls to the instrumental or vocal music teacher. In small schools both responsibilities are often vested in one person. Because of the informality of many extraclass musical activities, professional competence as a musician is no guarantee that the teacher will function effectively as a sponsor. He must be prepared to exercise control over student groups without stifling enthusiasm.

Among the vocal activities are choirs, choruses, and glee clubs, all of which function as extensions of regularly offered music classes. Very large schools may have several such organizations in addition to numerous small groups, trios, quartets, and double quartets. Recent years have found the once popular high-school operetta losing ground.

Instrumental music is usually represented by two typical musical organizations—the band and the orchestra. The types of bands include the marching band, the dance band, and the concert band. The school orchestra may give rise to chamber music groups, ensembles, and special instrumental groups, all of which may perform outside the classroom.

Dramatics

Because dramatic organizations in a school of some size are numerous, their sponsorship may be assigned to interested teachers in addition to the instructor of dramatic arts. The dramatic arts club; the senior, junior, and school plays; and the stagecraft, make-up, and theater-lighting clubs all vie for the attention of the trained sponsor.[35] Usually, however, one person will sponsor several such activities during the course of a school year.

Speech Activities

Speech and dramatic activities are frequently sponsored by the same teacher, particularly in small schools. Speech activities include

---

[34]The purposes and use of musical activities in the high school are discussed by Miller, Moyer, and Patrick, *op. cit.*, Chapter 13.

[35]*Ibid.*, Chapter 14, provide a discussion of the problems involved in promotion and sponsorship of dramatics as well as speech activities.

debating, public speaking, choral speech, extemporaneous speaking, and interpretive reading, some of which call for presentations outside the classroom and, in a few cases, outside the school. Speech activities are often viewed as a desirable supplement to the English program, and in some schools they are incorporated with the other English activities.

Publications

Of great importance to cohesiveness and communication within the school community is the successful publication of a school newspaper.[36] The sponsor of the paper is largely responsible for establishing the standards that make a quality publication possible. He must not only have professional training, but he must also be able to communicate his knowledge to untrained adolescents so that they can consistently make worth-while contributions to the paper.[37]

The production of the school yearbook[38] is expensive and, therefore, often subject to criticism. It is the sponsor's responsibility to determine that yearbook expenditures are reasonable. Often the yearbook sponsor is a teacher of art, English, or journalism. The recent trend is to incorporate the yearbook, as well as the school newspaper, into the school curriculum, granting participating students academic credits. Although the literary magazine generally lacks popularity, it is often undertaken as a project related to an English class.

Other Types of Cocurricular Activities

Other cocurricular activities cannot be classified under general headings and are thus discussed separately below.

Subject-Related Activities

There is hardly a subject in the secondary-school curriculum that has not at one time or another given rise to the formation of a related club or group.[39] In agriculture alone, stock-judging groups, garden clubs, and the Future Farmers of America function as outgrowths of specific classes. In the area of English, poetry groups, book clubs, library clubs, and literary societies flourish. Foreign-language clubs are frequently associated with each foreign language taught in the school. Similarly, there are mathematics clubs, science clubs, and

---

[36]*Ibid.*, Chapter 16, present an extensive discussion of the publication of the school newspaper.

[37]Wiggins, *op. cit.*, pp. 292–294, has a sound point of view about school publications.

[38]See McKown, *op. cit.*, Chapter 18, for a review of the types and purposes of yearbooks and their content and organization.

[39]Miller, Moyer, and Patrick, *op. cit.*, p. 315, point out the desired emphasis on the relationship between cocurricular club activities and classroom activities.

Herbert J. Klausmeier, *Teaching in the Secondary School* (New York: Harper & Brothers, 1958), p. 442, briefly discusses subject-affiliated clubs.

automotive repair clubs related to the established curriculum. The sponsor of such groups must have basic subject-matter competence if he is to provide essential guidance.

Special Interest Clubs

A wide range of school groups can be classified as special interest clubs, for they are held together by the bond of common interest.[40] With few exceptions they are recreational or avocational in nature. The law club, the chess club, the art club, the Shakespeare club, and the style club are all born of special interests. Although all subjects in the curriculum at one time or another give rise to one or more related special-interest clubs, many other such clubs have little or no relationship to the school program.

Social Activities

The most prominent school-sponsored social activity is the school dance. Because it possesses the potential for much good or much harm in the lives of students, the dance deserves the most able sponsorship the school affords. Special dances, such as the Junior Prom, often have one major teacher-sponsor, as well as several invited guests who simultaneously function as chaperones. If a dance is to enjoy singular success, it must be thoroughly planned, adequately financed, and attended by a large proportion of the students. It is largely the responsibility of the sponsor to see that all this is achieved.

All school-sponsored social activities—parties, picnics, and sleigh rides, as well as school dances—should be carried out with the assistance of qualified sponsors who are aware of the needs, behavior patterns, and tendencies of adolescents in social situations. Wise sponsors should know how to manipulate social situations to achieve needed social ends without offense to the participating students and in many cases without their knowledge. The natural development of acceptable social behavior in the presence of the opposite sex can be enhanced through the careful manipulation of social groups.[41]

Scholarship Activities

Schools have recently focused renewed attention on organizations concerned basically with promoting scholarship.[42] Among these groups are the National Honor Society and local service and honor

---

[40]Harl R. Douglass, *Education for Life Adjustment* (New York: Ronald Press, 1950), pp. 343–344, lists several objectives that he feels are frequently sought by clubs. Since the publication of this text, however, it may be assumed that club activity has become more closely related to course work and has taken on some of the rigor of the academic program.

[41]Douglass, *The High School Curriculum*, p. 531, suggests the need for school-sponsored social activities that encourage the participation of larger numbers of students.

[42]See McKown, *op. cit.*, Chapter 20, for an extensive discussion of honor societies and awards.

groups requiring high academic standing for membership. Emphasis has also been placed on establishing honor rolls and dean's lists in many secondary schools.

Cooperatively Sponsored Activities

A substantial number of school organizations, which may or may not be closely related to subjects in the school curriculum, are sponsored with the cooperation and assistance of agencies external to the school. Among these organizations are the National Honor Society, the Boy Scouts of America, 4-H Clubs, Future Teachers of America, American Junior Red Cross, and Distributive Education Clubs. The activities of such groups are largely predetermined and call for continuing sponsorship from one year to the next.

Fairs, Pageants, and Carnivals

Some schools sponsor seasonal displays, festivals, and celebrations that may be historical, educational, or purely recreational in nature. Among such activities are historical displays of local significance, seasonal agricultural fairs, and winter carnivals. It is the responsibility of the sponsor to determine that the planning, preparation, and execution of such activities provide the students with an educational experience.

Camping and Outdoor Activities

The World War II emphasis on physical fitness led many schools to introduce camping and outdoor living activities combined with structured learning experiences.[43] Some school districts purchased camps with this in mind and employed qualified teacher-sponsors to make sure that the camps were educational. Hiking, skiing, and a variety of water sports (sailing, canoeing, and skin diving) have also been conducted under school sponsorship to add variety and interest to cocurricular programs.

Trips and Excursions

Field trips are common class-related activities. Musical organizations, dramatic groups, and school teams often present programs at some distant location. The senior class trip has come to be a traditional part of the graduation activities of some schools. Without thorough planning and careful supervision, many such excursions prove to be lacking in educational value and, in some cases, highly undesirable.

Fraternities and Sororities

Because they tend to be cliquish, fraternities and sororities run

---

[43]Miller, Moyer, and Patrick, *op. cit.*, pp. 342–344, describe effective practices in outdoor education.

counter to the purposes of democratic education.[44] They exist, in many cases, without school sanction; and if officially banned, they frequently go underground. This only adds to their allure. Educators generally agree that fraternities and sororities find it difficult to gain a foothold for any prolonged period in a school that has a thoroughly organized, effectively sponsored, interesting, and varied activities program.

Special Senior Activities

An ever expanding cluster of activities related to the senior class has evolved since the turn of the century. Many of them are directly related to graduation and take place at the end of the school year —the commencement exercises, the post-graduation party, and the senior breakfast. Others—the senior ball, senior day, class night, and alumni day—occur at various times throughout the senior year. Although the senior class sponsor will find it necessary to assume responsibility for many of these class-related activities, he would do well to seek the assistance of competent colleagues, particularly if the school is large enough to make the task a heavy burden.

PRINCIPLES RELATED TO COCURRICULAR ACTIVITIES

Cocurricular activities are most likely to be successful when responsible teachers and administrators are thoroughly acquainted with the operation of basic educational principles. Listed below are principles that may help the teacher avoid the many possible difficulties inherent in sponsoring student activities.[45]

1. The purpose of all school activities, including cocurricular activities, is to educate students. Learning a given process leading to a desired educational goal—frequently essential to participation in cocurricular activities—may be as important as reaching the goal itself.

2. Classroom instruction and cocurricular activities should be organized so that they complement and motivate each other. Cocurricular activities that are carefully selected, planned, and supervised can provide a valuable educational experience and can encourage the necessary relationship between the curriculum and the cocurriculum.

3. Concepts are learned through real-life experiences as well as through organized classroom experiences. Cocurricular activities

---

[44]McKown, *op. cit.*, Chapter 9, presents the arguments for and against secret societies and provides specific suggestions on how to deal with them.

Wiggins, *op. cit.*, pp. 294–296, presents an unbiased position concerning school sororities and fraternities.

[45]Miller, Moyer, and Patrick, *op. cit.*, pp. 21–25, list and discuss several principles essential to the conduct of a sound cocurricular program.

provide first-hand experiences that are helpful in the formation of clear concepts and often provide for the application of concepts learned in the classroom.

4. As a citizen of the school community, the student has the privilege and responsibility of assisting in the selection and conduct of cocurricular activities.[46] Such activities help educate students to civic responsibilities and encourage responsible decision-making.

5. Students can participate effectively in cocurricular activities to the extent that their maturity, knowledge, interest, and desires permit. Slow learners, for example, often learn through the meaningful repetition that is provided by activities. Such students may find success in cocurricular activities that they cannot achieve in the classroom.

6. Activities provide an opportunity for student growth in leadership and, if effectively supervised, promote character development.

7. Cocurricular activities provide a situation in which complex social interactions may take place and in which social growth may be enhanced through participation.

8. A school activities program should be well-balanced and broad enough to enable all students to participate in an activity of particular interest. Therefore, a range of cocurricular activities should be provided to meet the varying needs and interests of the students.

9. A school activity should be viewed as a joint endeavor, calling for the support of students, faculty, and administration. Cooperative teacher-student planning is encouraged through well-organized school activities.

10. The quality of leadership exhibited by the sponsor will largely determine the effectiveness of a cocurricular activity.[47] The primary role of a sponsor is to advise and counsel, services that can be provided best in the informality of out-of-class activities.[48] The informal activity provides an excellent opportunity for the teacher to observe and discover specific information about the student that may be used to aid his growth. Desirable rapport in teacher-student relationships may also be encouraged.

11. Participation in organized recreation under the supervision of the school helps some students maintain sound mental health.

12. Concepts are best learned through personal experience. Such learning helps the student avoid meaningless verbalization of concepts.

13. Teachers are usually happy to sponsor those school activities that are closely related to their personal interests.

---

[46]*Ibid.*, p. 21, briefly discuss the student as a citizen of the school.

[47]Klausmeier, *op. cit.*, pp. 452–458, presents several ideas to support his basic assumption that cocurricular activities require responsible leadership.

[48]William L. Carter, Carl W. Hansen, and Margaret G. McKim, *Learning to Teach in the Secondary School* (New York: Macmillan, 1962), pp. 293–294, stress the necessity for capitalizing on the guidance possibilities of cocurricular activities.

14. In an activities program, an excellent performance should be secondary to a desirable learning experience.[49]

15. The success of certain activities relies heavily on the availability of essential facilities and equipment.[50]

CORRECT AND INCORRECT PROCEDURES

The success of a cocurricular activity largely depends upon the wisdom and enthusiasm of its sponsor. If the sponsor is ineffective, the activity is all too often characterized by a failure to achieve desirable educational goals and by a decrease in student participation and membership.[51] This is borne out in the examples below.

MISS WENTZ' DEBATING CLUB LOSES INTEREST

When students approached Miss Wentz, the speech teacher, about sponsoring a debating club, she was very much in favor of the idea. After she had received proper clearance from the principal, she and the interested students went ahead with the organization of the club.

But Miss Wentz soon discovered that there was more to sponsoring a debating club than appeared on the surface. Although she had ample enthusiasm for teaching her major subject, she had never once been involved in a formal debate—and it had been years since she had even heard one. Students relied on her for suggestions she could not provide.

Since she was also busy preparing for a class that she had never taught before, Miss Wentz simply felt that she could not spare the time to read up on affirmative and negative speeches, rebuttals, and debating protocol. In the absence of needed leadership, students became discouraged, and before the year was over student enthusiasm was gone. Club members decided there was no point in trying the debating club for a second year.

MR. WHEATLY RUNS THE STUDENT COUNCIL

Springdale Senior High School, with an enrollment of 500, was in need of a student council adviser. Although the principal had assumed this responsibility the preceding year, it had taken a great deal of his time, and he welcomed the opportunity to assign it to John Wheatly, an efficient-looking newcomer to his staff.

Mr. Wheatly had some fixed opinions about the functions of a student coun-

---

[49]Frederick, *op. cit.*, pp. 144–145, makes a plea for differentiating between the need for perfection and the need for a passable performance.

[50]The need for facilities and equipment is stressed by McKown, *op. cit.*, p. 23.

[51]Vernon E. Anderson and William T. Gruhn, *Principles and Practices of Secondary Education,* 2d. ed. (New York: Ronald Press, 1962), pp. 285–291, identify practices in several different kinds of activities.

Robert C. McKean, *Principles and Methods in Secondary Education* (Columbus, Ohio: Charles E. Merrill Books, Inc., 1962), pp. 254–260, provides a description of an interscholastic athletic program that has gotten out of hand, discusses its effects on the educational program, proposes constructive measures, and identifies some of the positive values of a well-conducted program.

cil. All of the responsible decisions of the school, he felt, should be made by the school administrators. In his opinion, then, the student council could function only to carry out desired administrative action or deal with matters that were of little or no importance.

Under the direction of the new sponsor, the student council met irregularly; its duties were not clearly defined; and when students proposed to consider matters that they felt were important, Mr. Wheatly quickly indicated that such matters were beyond the jurisdiction of the council. The status formerly associated with student council membership began to lose its luster, and several students questioned the value of coming to meetings at all.

MISS CLUFF IS A PERFECTIONIST

Marian Cluff, girls' physical education instructor, was asked to sponsor the Junior Prom. She was delighted with the assignment, but she had a basic fault—she was a perfectionist. She soon decided that the students' ideas were second best and that their ability to carry out good ideas was very limited indeed.

Miss Cluff insisted that her ideas prevail. Because students found it impossible to measure up to her standards of perfection, she found herself redoing much of their work. Gradually, the responsibilities that had been delegated to students were assumed by the sponsor, and she found herself spending every night for the month before the Prom making intricate decorations.

By the time the heralded occasion finally arrived, Miss Cluff was ready to quit teaching. Although she felt that the decorations were beautiful, student praise was relatively mild, and the sale of tickets was far below expectations.

In the preceding examples it becomes clear that a basic requirement of effective sponsorship is knowledge about the activity. Miss Wentz did not possess the knowledge or the time to acquire it. Mr. Wheatly did not bother to inquire about the official jurisdiction of the student council because of a stubborn fixation carried from the school where he was previously employed. Miss Cluff suffered from problems born of strenuous demands and an unwillingness to delegate responsibility when student involvement was vital to the success of the project.

The following examples portray more effective sponsorship of activities.

MR. STOKER ORGANIZES JUNIOR HIGH SCHOOL SPORTS

As a physical education teacher in the junior high school, Ned Stoker attempted to carry out many of his ideas on athletic competition. He firmly believed that athletic competition among schools should be de-emphasized, that vigorous participation in sports should extend to all students, and that sports activities should be varied enough to meet the needs and interests of the students.

At the beginning of the school year he made a careful analysis of the athletic interests, capabilities, and needs of the boys in his physical education classes. Mr. Stoker varied the games played according to season in order to accommodate the specific interests of most of his students. Although a large portion of each class was devoted to developing necessary skills, much time was spent actually playing the game. Students of comparable ability were grouped together as much as possible and given appropriate hints on how to improve.[52]

Shortly after the school year began, each homeroom was asked to organize a touch football team to represent them in competition against other homerooms at the same grade level within the school. Games would be held both before and after school. Throughout the year all sports were highlighted, and teams were organized in turn for basketball and softball. Students were encouraged to attend if their homeroom team was playing, but the main emphasis was on large-scale participation. Mr. Stoker estimated that more than one third of the boys in the school were involved in intramural competition of this sort. Even though the intramural program did not include some of the boys who most needed it, Mr. Stoker felt that these less skilled boys received adequate exposure to vigorous physical activity in regular gym classes. Teams were similarly organized for the girls.

To serve the varying interests of students, Mr. Stoker, with the help of other teachers, organized and found proper sponsorship for a ping-pong club, a horseshoe club, a trampoline club, and a badminton club. Each club was organized to insure maximum participation of its members.

MR. BEACH ENCOURAGES EXTENSIVE PARTICIPATION

When C. S. Beach undertook the sponsorship of the school newspaper, a four-page weekly, he decided that the paper would have to be largely a student product. Furthermore, he decided that it would be inadvisable to permit four or five students with aptitudes for writing to be the primary contributors. Thus each homeroom was invited to elect a reporter who would write up matters of importance.

Whenever a reporter failed to submit anything for the period of one month, Mr. Beach had a staff member contact the reporter to determine why. Responsibility for rewriting articles and determining their newsworthiness was left almost entirely to the editor and assistant editor. Newspaper policy was discussed thoroughly at the beginning of the school year with the full staff, and Mr. Beach made it clear that staff members were to insure that newspaper policy was not violated. Mr. Beach was always aware of what was going on, and students knew that he was thoroughly informed. An occasional check was sufficient to keep the newspaper machinery operating efficiently. Since the majority of the newspaper staff members were in his journalism class, Mr. Beach was able to combine effective teaching with practical newspaper production.

USE OF COCURRICULAR ACTIVITIES IN SPECIFIC SUBJECTS

Cocurricular organizations, both small and large, have been used effectively by instructors to further the cause of their specific subject.

---

[52] Miller, Moyer, and Patrick, *op. cit.*, pp. 352–373, discuss the operation of an intramural athletic program and provide examples of acceptable programs.

The secretaries' club, for example, offers its members status as well as practical experience in assisting the principal and work-laden teachers by typing, transcribing letters, and performing miscellaneous clerical tasks. Typing and shorthand teachers are, of course, delighted with such an arrangement, but they have the responsibility for seeing that involvement in cocurricular activities does not detract from efficient learning.

Ideally, students are encouraged to apply classroom-developed concepts and skills through participation in cocurricular activities. This concern for practical application of classroom learning is found in most areas of the secondary school curriculum. Members of a dramatic arts class, for instance, might form an ushers club to render a needed service while other members of the class are performing on the stage. Members of the homemaking club in a small school welcome the opportunity to prepare and serve a special luncheon to the principal and members of the faculty. Students in the science club assume major responsibility, under teacher direction, for the preparation of interesting displays for the annual science fair.

Although cocurricular activities should not be emphasized at the expense of curricular goals, it is understandable that the desire to be at one's best in a public appearance is a great motivator. Thus high-school choral and instrumental groups have been known to practice the selections to be used in the spring concert or the music festival to the exclusion of many other worth-while selections.

Practical application of classroom learning in cocurricular activities can benefit the entire school as well as the individual student. Students can produce a respectable school paper by applying what they have learned about effective written communication in the English or journalism class. The knowledge of effective color combinations encourages students to seek more harmonious color tones for the Junior Prom decorations. The social dancing that many girls learn in physical education classes helps them meet the challenge of the school dance with confidence and ease. Having learned the key points that characterize the animal of quality, individual students are able to compete successfully in stock judging contests. They may also utilize their skills and knowledge to further their own financial interests through careful selection of animals for purchase.

SPECIFIC SUGGESTIONS

A number of suggestions should be of particular value to the teacher who is approaching the responsibilities of activity sponsorship for the first time.[53]

---

[53]Several helpful suggestions on club sponsorship are made by Parker, Edwards, and Stegeman, *op. cit.*, pp. 455–456.

Recommendations

1. Seek the sponsorship of an activity that particularly interests you; if this is impossible, try to become interested in the activity you are asked to sponsor. However, if you cannot develop an interest, ask to be changed as soon as possible without disrupting the cocurricular program. In the event that you lack basic competence in the area you have been asked to sponsor, acquire this competence as rapidly as you can.

2. Encourage students to be intelligently self-directive in the conduct of cocurricular affairs. Help them see the implications of their own decisions, but also help them feel that they are a part of the team in planning and carrying out activities. Show them the essential steps in careful, long-range planning.

3. Utilize the close student-teacher relationship made possible through informal activities to help students with their specific problems. Carefully observe students engaged in such activities to discover facts that may be used to help them. Make effective use of the informal situation to promote social growth and character development.

4. Identify the reasons why certain students are not active in cocurricular activities, and make an effort to arouse the interest of apathetic students.[54]

5. Where practical, encourage the application of concepts learned in the classroom to cocurricular activities. Be sure that the activity you sponsor is educationally sound.

6. Make a periodical analysis of your role as a sponsor and of the general operation and value of your activity.[55]

7. As a new sponsor, seek the counsel of teachers who have previously sponsored the same activity.

8. Help students who are academically weak achieve genuine success in cocurricular activities.

9. Arrange the schedule and organization of an activity so that nonparticipating students will find it possible to become active members.

10. Help direct students into those activities that will be of greatest interest and benefit to them.

11. Help students achieve a feeling of pride in belonging to the organization you sponsor.

---

[54]Harry N. Rivlin, *Teaching Adolescents in Secondary Schools*, 2d. ed. (New York: Appleton-Century-Crofts, 1961), pp. 360–361, provides practical suggestions for discovering and treating the causes of inadequate student participation.

[55]The Texas Junior High School Criteria Study, *Criteria for Evaluating Junior High Schools*, Research Study No. 15 (Austin, Texas: The Texas Study of Secondary Education, 1954), pp. 128–131, provides a helpful set of criteria for evaluating junior high school activities.

Cautions

1. Don't assume that all interesting activities are necessarily educational.[56]

2. Don't permit a small number of students to dominate the activities of a cocurricular organization.[57]

3. Don't allow students unlimited freedom in conducting cocurricular activities.

PROBLEMS FOR STUDY AND DISCUSSION

1. Identify five activities currently found in secondary-school cocurricular programs that you would like to sponsor. What qualifications do you possess for sponsoring each?

2. Write a brief paragraph describing the change in attitude toward extraclass activities in the secondary school.

3. What are the chances that the beginning teacher will be asked to sponsor a cocurricular organization? Explain.

4. List five basic responsibilities of every cocurricular activity sponsor.

5. Give an example of a legal responsibility that arises out of club sponsorship.

6. Defend this statement: The basic responsibility of the sponsor is to see that the activity serves an educational purpose.

7. Can student enthusiasm in a club compensate for sponsor apathy? Explain your position.

8. Give an example of unwarranted and undesirable alumni involvement in student activities. Explain why this is undesirable.

9. Describe the steps that should be followed either by club members or by the club sponsor to insure continuity from one year to another.

10. Should students who have low grades be permitted to play on school teams? Justify your answer in a two-paragraph statement, and identify the issues involved.

11. Name at least four different devices that may be used in evaluating student activities.

12. What special characteristics should the student council sponsor possess?

13. Describe an educationally sound position that the coach of a football team in a large high school should take and be willing to defend.

14. Why is it difficult to differentiate between curricular and cocurricular musical activities?

15. Should the dramatic arts teacher be entitled to additional pay for sponsoring a school play? Explain your position.

16. Name at least four school activities that are sponsored with the assistance of agencies outside the school.

---

[56]Several dangers to be avoided in conducting cocurricular activities are identified and listed by Mills and Douglass, *op. cit.*, pp. 420–421.

[57]Rivlin, *op. cit.*, pp. 363–365, describes how one club sponsor helped encourage democratic action within the organization he sponsored.

17. Why does the school dance have so much potential for good or harm?

18. What is the best procedure for removing fraternities and sororities from the high school? Explain.

19. Give three examples to illustrate the point that academically weak students may find success in cocurricular activities.

20. State five educational principles that give direction to cocurricular activities.

RECOMMENDED READINGS

Alberty, Harold B., and Elsie J. Alberty, *Reorganizing the High-School Curriculum*, 3d. ed. New York: The Macmillan Company, 1962, pp. 344–362.

Anderson, Vernon E., and William T. Gruhn, *Principles and Practices of Secondary Education*, 2d. ed. New York: Ronald Press, 1962, Chapter 12.

Carter, William L., Carl W. Hansen, and Margaret G. McKim, *Learning to Teach in the Secondary School*. New York: The Macmillan Company, 1962, pp. 282–295.

Douglass, Harl R. (ed.), *The High School Curriculum*, 3d. ed. New York: Ronald Press, 1964, Chapter 26.

Frederick, Robert W., *The Third Curriculum*. New York: Appleton-Century-Crofts, Inc., 1959, Chapters 2, 3, 5, 9, 12–14, 19, 28–34, 39, 41, and Appendix B.

Grambs, Jean D., William J. Iverson, and Franklin K. Patterson, *Modern Methods in Secondary Education*, rev. ed. New York: The Dryden Press, 1958, pp. 620–624.

Hansen, Kenneth H., *High School Teaching*. Englewood Cliffs, N.J.: Prentice-Hall, Inc., 1957, Chapter 12.

Klausmeier, Herbert J., *Teaching in the Secondary School*. New York: Harper & Brothers, 1958, Chapter 16.

McKean, Robert C., *Principles and Methods in Secondary Education*. Columbus, Ohio: Charles E. Merrill Books, Inc., 1962, Chapter 10.

McKown, Harry C., *Extracurricular Activities*, 3d. ed. New York: The Macmillan Company, 1952, Chapters 1, 3–9, 11–16, 18, 20, 21, and 25.

Miller, Franklin A., James H. Moyer, and Robert B. Patrick, *Planning Student Activities*. Englewood Cliffs, N.J.: Prentice-Hall, Inc., 1956, Chapters 1, 4, 6–19, and 21.

Mills, Hubert H., and Harl R. Douglass, *Teaching in High School*, 2d. ed. New York: Ronald Press, 1957, Chapter 25.

Nordberg, H. Orville, James M. Bradfield, and William C. Odell, *Secondary School Teaching*. New York: The Macmillan Company, 1962, Chapter 16.

Parker, J. Cecil, T. Bentley Edwards, and William H. Stegeman, *Curriculum in America*. New York: Thomas Y. Crowell Company, 1962, Chapter 14.

Rivlin, Harry N., *Teaching Adolescents in Secondary Schools*, 2d. ed. New York: Appleton-Century-Crofts, Inc., 1961, Chapter 12.

Wiggins, Samuel P., *Successful High School Teaching*. Boston: Houghton Mifflin Company, 1958, Chapter 15.

PART FIVE

RECENT DEVELOPMENTS IN TEACHING

18

Programed Instruction

Few educational developments throughout history have captured the fancy of professional educators and the general public as has programed instruction. Its promise of accelerating learning, its relationship to mechanization, its fascinating novelty—all have invested programed learning with an allure that makes an objective appraisal especially difficult.

DEFINITION OF PROGRAMED INSTRUCTION

In programed instruction, concepts are presented to the student by means of specific sequentially placed statements, called *frames*. This *program*, presented on a machine or in book form, leads the student through a body of material in small steps. The learner sees a stimulus (frame), responds to it, and receives an immediate indication of whether his answer is correct or incorrect. Thus the psychological principles of *stimulus, response,* and *reinforcement* are an integral part of programed instruction.

During the past few years programs have been adopted with increasing frequency in schools concerned with individualizing instruction, and the term *programed instruction* has become generally accepted and widely used in the educational community. *Automated teaching, auto-instruction,* and *machine teaching* are variant terms, all referring to instruction that requires the use of programed (systematically organized and presented) materials. The tendency to use the phrase *machine teaching* as synonymous with programed learning is misleading because presentation by machine is by no means essential to programed instruction. Machine teaching is one type of programed instruction.[1]

Programed learning that follows the procedures introduced by B. F. Skinner has several characteristics:[2]

1. The content to be learned is organized in a sequence designed to promote optimum learning.
2. The learner is required to respond actively to the content presented.
3. He is given an immediate indication of whether his responses are correct or incorrect.
4. He advances by small steps through the content.
5. The content is organized to provide a preponderance of correct responses.
6. The learner starts at his own level of comprehension and moves gradually and systematically toward the desired objectives.

Psychologists generally restrict the definition of programed instruction to include those materials and devices that (a) provide a stimulus, (b) call for the learner's response, and (c) provide for reinforcement of the response. This definition has been helpful in establishing precise and meaningful communication among educators. According to this definition certain mechanical devices and printed materials—for example, the reading pacer and the workbook—cannot be categorized as programed instructional materials, since, while they possess some, they do not have all of these characteristics.

HISTORY OF PROGRAMED INSTRUCTION

The assumption that experimentation in programed learning originated during the 1950's belies the facts. Teaching by machine—one aspect of programed learning—began prior to the Depression.[3]

Early Experiments

Sydney L. Pressey, a noted psychologist, is credited with having focused attention on the possibility of teaching through the use of

[1]The nature, operation, and use of teaching machines are covered in a simplified yet sound discussion by Samuel and Beryl Epstein, *The First Book of Teaching Machines* (New York: Franklin Watts, 1961).

[2]Although non-Skinnerian programs are being developed and used (see pages 435–436), Skinner-type programs account for well over 90 per cent of those currently in use.

[3]A list of patents for educational devices issued by the U.S. Patent Office from the turn of the century until 1930 is provided by I. Mellan, "Teaching and Educational Inventions," *Journal of Experimental Education,* 1936 (March), *4:* 291–300. Although patent numbers are listed, the devices are not described.

machines during the late 1920's. He produced a machine that called for student responses to multiple-choice items. The student was required to press answer buttons numbered to correspond to multiple-choice test items. If the correct response was selected, the machine automatically moved to the next question; if an incorrect response was selected, the error was mechanically noted, and the student had to make additional responses until he selected the correct one.

Pressey noted that devices such as this could actually teach, since the student was provided with an immediate knowledge of correct and incorrect responses. In addition, students of varying abilities and achievement could move at their own pace. Although Pressey's early enthusiasm did not result in an immediate move toward the mechanization of instruction, it helped point the way. In 1932, after suffering several defeats in his attempts to obtain adequate financing and engineering assistance, Pressey announced that he was abandoning further work on his project.[4]

Mid-Century Interest

In 1954 B. F. Skinner redirected attention to the possibilities inherent in the use of teaching machines.[5] His ideas circulated widely among psychologists and educators, reawakening interest in systematic self-instruction. From that time on, programed instruction received widespread publicity, both in professional journals and in popular magazines, and inspired experimental effort directed toward basic research as well as the production and use of teaching materials.

The initial favorable reaction led to many rash claims, including statements that:

1. The use of programed material would greatly reduce or do away with the need for teachers.
2. Conventional textbooks would be replaced by programed textbooks.
3. Students would be able to learn several times faster than the normal rate through the use of programed material.

Entranced with the possibility of relief from the drudgery of classroom drill, teachers grasped hopefully at the idea of mechanized instruction; and the military and private industry at home and abroad were quick to anticipate the possibility of accelerating training programs through the use of teaching machines. Various companies fed these hopes by hurrying unproven and improperly tested programs and devices into production. Even those who were sincerely inter-

---

[4]B. F. Skinner, "Teaching Machines," *Science*, 1958 (Oct. 24), *128:* 969–977, provides an interesting account of Pressey's early contributions and the reasons for their limited acceptance.

[5]*Ibid.*, pp. 970–977, discusses in some detail the principles involved in bringing about behavioral changes in experimental subjects and their implications for classroom learning.

ested in serving the cause of education through the new medium lost some of their objectivity in their zeal. "Ironically," as Schramm points out,[6]

it might have been better for programed instruction if, at times during the beginning years, it could have been delivered from its friends. Its friends were sometimes too friendly, too full of enthusiasm to be critical, too absorbed in their own work to take a broad look at what was happening to programs, too close to developments to be good guides either for educators or for the public.

Current Trends

The initial flurry of rash claims for programed instruction has given way to more careful examination of the facts. From the first, of course, experiments were carried out to test the validity of assumptions about the new teaching tool. Indeed, Schramm reports that approximately one hundred experiments had been conducted by November 1962.[7] But many of the early claims for programed instruction were based on experiments of short duration and limited coverage. Recent experiments tend to be longer, more solidly based, and more sharply focused.

The amount of repetition employed in programs is a matter of considerable controversy, and several studies have been set up to establish guidelines. Concern with the size of the learning step from one frame to the next has also led to extensive research, though conclusive answers have not yet been obtained. Another area of experimentation has centered on the question of whether overt responses produce results demonstrably superior to those achieved through covert responses. Of equal concern is the question of whether the *constructed* response, in which the student fills in a blank, or the *selected* response, in which he marks a multiple-choice item, is preferable as a learning method. Although immediate reinforcement is generally accepted as an essential feature of programed instruction, researchers thus far disagree as to what kinds and how much reinforcement are desirable. Educators and psychologists are also currently involved in determining the role that programed instruction will play in relation to existing methods and devices designed to facilitate the learning process.[8]

Because of the public interest, both the Federal government and national foundations have granted substantial sums for research on programed instruction. The military—particularly the Air Force Personnel and Training Center—has also been very active in encouraging

---

[6]Wilbur Schramm, *Programed Instruction Today and Tomorrow* (New York: Fund for the Advancement of Education, 1962), p. 15.

[7]*Ibid.*, p. 11.

[8]An accurate account of the status of programed instruction as of 1962 is provided by Schramm, *op. cit.*

and applying research on self-instructional devices.[9] Unfortunately, however, much of this current effort is reported only in mimeographed form to a selected number of interested persons, and there is often a disturbing lapse of time before the results of such research appear in the professional journals and receive general distribution. Indeed, keeping up-to-date in this area is virtually impossible.

Meanwhile, although the proliferation of "hardware" that accompanied the programing boom of the late 1950's has subsided, the production of programed materials can still be termed exploratory. This fact is evident in the development of several different kinds of programed texts and in the manufacture of a range of devices for presenting programs. Some programs are now available in text form and for use in machines, both with and without branching. In brief, there has been no commercial decision as to the "best" method of programing or of presenting programs.

A wider range of experiments, a careful evaluation of existing studies, and the moderating influence of time have encouraged early supporters of programed learning to speak now with studied caution about its effects on education as a whole. The extreme and hopeful statements of a few years ago have given way to realism based upon careful study and analysis. Professional writing in the field is now typified by specific statements of research findings as opposed to former extravagant and unsupported claims. As Eigen has stated,[10]

> It is fairly clear at this time that programed instruction, in its present form and state of development, is not the panacea that some of its more enthusiastic adherents had predicted it to be; it is equally clear that it is not the tremendous danger to the mental well-being of both student and teacher that some of the more hysterical opponents predicted it would be.

PROFESSIONAL REACTION TO PROGRAMED INSTRUCTION

Because of the recent impact of programed learning on the educational scene, questions are being asked that point up the hopes as well as the anxieties of teachers:

> Will such machines take over much of the science of teaching, as Hilgard predicts? What are the limitations of teaching machines? What effect will programmed instruction have on curriculum development and curriculum structure? Can teaching machines be utilized successfully with all types of students—the bright, the dull, the average? What new and different physical

---

[9]A. A. Lumsdaine and Robert Glaser (eds.), *Teaching Machines and Programmed Learning: A Source Book* (Washington, D.C.: National Education Association, 1960), pp. 257–394, provide a helpful compilation of articles describing the contributions of the military and other groups to programed instruction.

[10]Lewis D. Eigen, "Programing Poses Problems," *Phi Delta Kappan*, 1963, *44:* 242.

facilities are necessary? Can teaching machines be used to provide more effectively for individual differences.[11]

The answers given by those most actively engaged in producing and using programed materials range in tone from extreme caution to unbridled optimism.

Limitations of Programed Instruction

Some of the limitations of automated teaching devices are identified by Morse and Wingo:[12]

> Since the teaching machines are based on the principle of telling the learner at once whether he is right or wrong, their utility will of necessity be limited to material where there is *a right answer.* Structured information, concepts, relationships, associations, differentiations, abstractions, identification of key elements—all of these are of such a nature that they can be put into programs calling for a series of "correct" responses. Much school learning is of this kind. But much of it is not—for example, where value judgments must be made. Sometimes the most important thing for a pupil to learn is that there are *not* any pat answers. . . .
>
> A machine can provide informational background, but beyond this, where intelligent opinion can differ, it can only help identify what the alternatives are. It cannot ask any questions to which original, different answers are equally correct. It cannot ask "what do you think and why" questions. Nor can it ask questions that need more than a few words to answer. . . .
>
> Finally, the kind of learning that can come out of an experience is limited by the quality of that experience. For motor learning, you need motor experience; for emotional and social learning, you need emotional and social experience. The learning possible from teaching machines will be limited to the learning that can come through the experience of reading (or perhaps listening to) a series of items and answering a question after each one. This pretty well limits the content to visual (or auditory) and ideational learning.

Because of its expense, the teaching machine is viewed by certain educators as impractical. According to one article:[13]

> When the cost of teaching machines is considered, and especially the cost of selected response machines, there seems to be at this time little or no justification for their use in schools, whether the programed materials are of the selected or constructed response type.

---

[11]B. J. Chandler, Lindley J. Stiles, and John I. Kitsuse (eds.), *Education in Urban Society* (New York: Dodd, Mead, 1962), pp. 29–30.

[12]William C. Morse and G. Max Wingo, *Psychology and Teaching*, 2d. ed. (Chicago: Scott, Foresman and Company, 1962), pp. 163–164.

[13]John B. Hough and Bernard Revsin, "Programed Instruction at the College Level: A Study of Several Factors Influencing Learning," *Phi Delta Kappan*, 1963, *44:* 290.

Certain psychologists and educators persist in vigorously opposing programed instruction. Says one:[14]

> The logical questions to ask now are these: Is the teaching machine movement a failure? Is programed learning material in any way more effective than simpler narrative presentations by text, teacher, or television? A growing tide of research evidence, classroom experience, and personal sentiment suggests a "yes" to the first question, a "no" to the second.

The writings of several other educators reflect the need for caution before approval is granted to the various facets of programed instruction.[15] Rivlin's statement is typical of those of many conservatives. He feels that

> the devices used in automated teaching are only tools, and tools must be judged by what they accomplish and not by their inherent value. It would be as futile to attempt to evaluate the motion picture projector or the television camera as either good or bad. . . . The key element in the evaluation of automated teaching . . . lies in the quality of the programming and in the appropriateness of programming as a way of helping students to learn.[16]

Advantages of Programed Instruction

Guarded optimism seems to characterize the thinking of many of the specialists working in this field. Stolurow, for instance, feels that programed instruction encourages a scientific approach to the production of teaching materials:

> In my view, programed learning is here to stay. However, the forms it will take are anybody's guess at the moment. Even if no other use is made of it than to develop instructional materials, I think it safe to say that it will eliminate from instructional materials much if not all of the hack writing and the ineffective methods more justified as "artistry." Playing by ear, which is what we have had to do up to now, can produce both effective and ineffective materials without discriminating between them. The method of programed instruction, however, does provide a means by which the effectiveness of the product can be determined.[17]

Komoski's view reflects the opinion held by certain psychologists that under given circumstances all segments of the curriculum

---

[14]John F. Feldhusen, "Taps for Teaching Machines," *Phi Delta Kappan*, 1963, *44:* 265.

[15]A statement reflecting the need for caution in the appraisal and use of programed instruction is provided by Vernon E. Anderson and William T. Gruhn, *Principles and Practices of Secondary Education*, 2d. ed. (New York: Ronald Press, 1962), pp. 188–189.

[16]Harry N. Rivlin, *Teaching Adolescents in Secondary Schools*, 2d. ed. (New York: Appleton-Century-Crofts, 1961), p. 256.

[17]Lawrence M. Stolurow, "Let's Be Informed on Programed Instruction," *Phi Delta Kappan*, 1963, *44:* 257.

might be programed, an assumption that is currently open to considerable debate:

> Six years ago, as a newcomer to the world of programed instruction and teaching machines, this was the question I most frequently asked of the psychologists who were pioneering the field: "What are the things that can and cannot be programed for a teaching machine?" It wasn't long before I learned the stock reply of my psychologist friends: "This is a question that can only be answered experimentally; *experimentation* and time will tell what can and cannot be programed. However," the reply continued, "given a specific statement of what is to be learned in clear, detailed, unambiguous *behavioral* or operational language, there is no reason why anything should be impossible to program."[18]

Many other writers believe that programed instruction will help increase the efficiency of learning. They feel that the mounting complexity of modern education and industrial training requires the use of the most effective instructional procedures and devices to provide thorough education for an ever increasing number of students. The development of auto-instructional materials, based upon proven psychological principles, is an essential step in achieving this goal.

McNeil feels that methodology has assumed a new rigor because of the interest in programed instruction:

> As a chief consequence of programed instruction, experimental methodology will become more characteristic of curriculum research, a field formerly known for its dependence upon the procedures of natural observation, clinical judgment, and the normative survey.[19]

The promise of relief from some of the most tiresome aspects of classroom drudgery encourages the teacher to keep up-to-date on the newest developments in programed learning, for, as McKean points out, "routine, repetitive, factual learning may be mechanized and the time and energies of the skilled teacher saved for more demanding instructional situations."[20]

While still anticipating the possibilities of important changes, other proponents of programed instruction express the need for caution in predicting its effect on the total school operation. Although they are firm in their contention that significant changes in classroom procedures and teacher responsibilities will take place as a result of programed learning, they admit that it is difficult to predict how quickly this method will influence the procedures, staff, and plant facilities of school systems.

---

[18] P. Kenneth Komoski, "Programed Instruction—A Prologue to What?" *Phi Delta Kappan,* 1963, *44:* 293.

[19] John D. McNeil, "The Influence of Programed Instruction upon Curriculum Research," *Phi Delta Kappan,* 1963, *44:* 264.

[20] Robert C. McKean, *Principles and Methods in Secondary Education* (Columbus, Ohio: Charles E. Merrill Books, Inc., 1962), p. 115.

Another group recognizes the revolutionary possibilities of programed learning but finds that, in the main, the potentialities have not been fulfilled. While affirming their confidence in the present and continuing value of programed instruction, these writers cautiously point out that educators are only in the first stages of developing a technology of instruction and that a great deal of experimentation remains to be carried out.

BASIC TYPES OF PROGRAMS

Two basic types of programs, bearing the names of their chief proponents, B. F. Skinner and Norman A. Crowder, have been used most frequently by educational programers. Each type appears to have particular advantages and should be examined separately.

Skinnerian Programing

Roughly nineteen out of twenty programs currently being produced are developed according to the principles identified and used by B. F. Skinner.[21] It is his belief that progress toward specific goals should be made in very small steps in order to reduce the possibility of error and provide for a preponderance of successful responses. This belief is explained by one of Skinner's co-workers:[22]

> It is intended that the student be led through a series of carefully graded steps, none of which is too difficult to answer, yet each of which is slightly more difficult than the preceding one. This procedure, leading an organism to emit a response which is initially at low strength in his repertoire by reinforcing responses which more and more closely approximate the required one, is known in many laboratories as the reinforcement of successive approximations.

The use of small steps is illustrated in the frames in Figure 1, taken from a program based upon the principles employed by Skinner.[23] Notice that each successive correct response moves the student one step forward, in linear fashion, toward the ultimate desired comprehension of arithmetic.

In these arithmetic frames it should be observed that (1) the stimulus appears in the form of sequentially placed, numbered frames; (2) student response is called for in the blank spaces to the right of each frame; and (3) reinforcement is provided by the correct

---

[21]Schramm, *op. cit.*, p. 2.

[22]Lloyd E. Homme, "The Rationale of Teaching by Skinner's Machines," in Lumsdaine and Glaser, *op. cit.*, p. 133.

[23]From *Arithmetic U-3008*, published by Universal Electronics Laboratories Corp. In *Programs '62, A Guide to Programed Instructional Materials* (Washington, D.C.: Center for Programed Instruction, 1962), p. 218.

Fig. 1. Sample page from a programed arithmetic text.

SPECIAL INSTRUCTIONS		
55 This special group has how many dots in it? __ ::::::		10
56 Groups of 10 are very important in our number system. The two figures we use to write the number 10 are 1 and _.		0
57 The 1 in the number 10 means one group of ten things. How many groups of 10 dots are here? _ ::::::		1
58 The 0 in the number 10 means that we do not have any units left. Here we have just enough dots to make one group of __. ::::::		10
59 Here are 13 dots. The figure 1 in the number 13 tells us that we have one group of ____.		10 or ten
60 The 3 in the number 13 tells us that we have 3 units left. The number 13 means we have 1 group of ten with 3 _______ left.		units

answers in the extreme right-hand column, exposed by a sliding shield after response.

Crowderian Programing

Norman A. Crowder has developed certain programed instructional techniques that vary somewhat from those of the Skinnerians. Crowder believed that individual differences in rate of progress and the optimum size of learning steps were not being adequately provided for in Skinnerian programs, and, like Pressey, he rejected the Skinnerian view that multiple-choice items were pedagogically unsound because they exposed the student to error. The following passage is his own description of "automatic tutoring by intrinsic programming":[24]

> The student is given the material to be learned in small logical units (usually a paragraph, or less, in length) and is tested on each unit immediately. The test result is used automatically to conduct the material that the student sees next. If the student passes the test question, he is automatically given the next unit of information and the next question. If he fails the test question, the preceding unit of information is reviewed, the nature of his error is explained to him, and he is retested. The test questions are multiple-choice questions, and there is a separate set of correctional materials for each wrong answer that is included in the multiple-choice alternative. The technique of using a student's choice of an answer to a multiple-choice question to determine the next material to which he will be exposed has been called "intrinsic programming."

The use of Crowder's techniques to individualize instruction according to student response is illustrated in the following passage, designed to acquaint students with certain concepts related to tests:[25]

> Scores on a test are usually referred to as "raw" scores, and each raw score is simply the number of correct answers. A raw score of 34 means that a certain student answered 34 questions correctly. A percentage score is slightly different, since a raw score of 34 could mean 100%, or 50%, or any percentage between 1 and 100. If there were only 34 items on the test, a raw score of 34 would be 100% correct, and if there were 68 items on the test, a raw score of 34 would be 50% correct. A percentage is easily calculated by dividing the raw score by the total number of items on the test. If a raw score of 15 is 25% correct, how many questions were there on the test? 60, of course. If there were 30 items on the test, and the highest score is 27 items correct, and the lowest raw score is 15, the highest raw score is what percentage correct?

If your answer is:	Turn to:
27%	page 2, top half of the page
81%	page 7, bottom half of the page
90%	page 11, bottom half of the page

Programs for Use in Machines

Both the Crowderian and the Skinnerian types of programs may be adapted for use in machines. Devices that make use of the principles adopted by Crowder have certain general characteristics: Subject-matter content to be presented is placed upon microfilm as individual frames or content steps to which the student may react. (As many as 10,000 or more frames may be used in teaching a given pro-

[24]Norman A. Crowder, "Automatic Tutoring by Intrinsic Programming," in Lumsdaine and Glaser, *op. cit.*, p. 286.

[25]From William A. Deterline, *An Introduction to Programed Instruction.* © 1962, by permission of Prentice-Hall, Inc., Englewood Cliffs, New Jersey, p. 84.

gram.) The student using the machine begins with frame one of the sequence. He reacts by pressing a button that is numbered or lettered to correspond to the multiple-choice item he selects. If his answer is correct, a new frame appears that so informs him, and then new material (a frame) is presented to which he is supposed to react by again pressing the correct button. If his answer is incorrect, however, he is instructed to press a button that automatically brings correctional material to the viewing screen. After the student has reacted with the desired response to the correctional material, he is directed to press another button that returns him to the main stream of sequentially placed frames. As long as he responds correctly, he is given progressively more difficult material.[26]

The introduction of correctional materials for students who have responded incorrectly marks one of the essential differences between Crowderian and Skinnerian programing. Skinnerians contend that if steps are kept sufficiently small and related to preceding steps, no correctional teaching is necessary. Crowderians, on the other hand, feel that if remedial or correctional branching is built into a program, large steps may be taken until difficulties are encountered, at which time remedial frames may be logically introduced.

Programed Textbooks

Although a great deal of interest has been focused on the use of teaching machines, the programed textbook has been used more frequently. After the first excitement engendered by the hope for mechanization of instruction, advocates of programed instruction began to examine cost factors and review the available research on the use of machine teaching as opposed to a programed text. Many concluded that the teaching machine provides no basic advantage.

The programed text, which affords the great advantage of economy to a school district, appears in a variety of forms depending upon subject matter and student needs. In the Crowderian text, sometimes referred to as the scrambled text, the student reads and reacts to a single stimulus item that is printed on a given page. Deterline explains the organization of the scrambled text as follows:[27]

> The pages of the book are numbered sequentially, but the material is assigned to pages randomly and the student is directed to turn to a page number which is determined by his choice of an answer to each question. For example, on page one he may read several short paragraphs and then a multiple-choice question that has a different page number printed beside each of the answer choices:

---

[26]A sound, well-illustrated discussion of the development of teaching machines is provided by Lawrence M. Stolurow, *Teaching by Machine* (Washington, D.C.: U.S. Office of Education, 1962).

[27]From William A. Deterline, *An Introduction to Programed Instruction*. © 1962, by permission of Prentice-Hall, Inc., Englewood Cliffs, New Jersey, p. 44.

If your answer is:	Turn to page:
Choice a	5
Choice b	23
Choice c	10
Choice d	19

Suppose that the correct answer is Choice b, and that the student turns to page 23. He is told that his choice is the correct answer, and is then told to continue reading the rest of page 23 and to answer the next multiple-choice question at the bottom of that page. Each of the incorrect alternatives on page 1 sends the student to a different page where he is informed that his choice is not correct, told why it is not correct, and provided with more information designed to help him answer the question correctly. Then the student is told to return to page 1 and to select the correct answer. The correct sequence is from page 1 to page 23, with three alternate routes to handle students who don't select the correct answer. Page 23 contains another multiple-choice question which has only one correct answer and three incorrect answers, each of which leads to its respective correcting branch. An errorless route through the first seven frames might follow this sequence: 1–23–7–25–12–3–18. It is assumed that the student who follows this sequence has adequately learned the material on each page in the series, and it is further assumed that the alternate response-determined branches have adequately corrected any misconceptions or misunderstanding on the part of the students who have made errors, but who have eventually also reached page 18.

English 2600, A Scientific Program in Grammar and Usage,[28] a text that has been used extensively throughout the United States, is classified as a Skinner-type program. Designed as a grammar course for students in grades nine and ten, this book provides 2600 frames that lead the student by very small steps through the intricacies of English grammar. The general structure of the text is revealed in the instructions to the students:[29]

> The first work frame is Frame 2 (on page 3). After you complete Frame 2, turn to Frame 3 *in the same position* on the next *right-hand* page (page 5). In the column to the left of Frame 3, you will find the correct answer to Frame 2. If your answer is not correct, turn back and correct it before doing Frame 3. You will always find the answer to a frame in the column to the left of the frame that you are to do next. Thus you find the answer to Frame 3 to the left of Frame 4, the answer to Frame 4 to the left of Frame 5, and so on.
>
> Go completely through the book, taking only the top gray frame on each *right-hand* page (3, 5, 7, 9, 11, etc.) until you reach the end. When you reach the end of the book, turn back to page 1 and follow the second band – a white one – through the book, still working only on the *right-hand* pages. Then proceed to the third horizontal band . . . .

---

[28]This text is written by Joseph C. Blumenthal and was first published by Harcourt, Brace and World in 1960. *English 3200* is a more sophisticated treatment of the same content designed for students in grades eleven and twelve; *English 2200*, published in 1964, is designed for grades seven and eight.

[29]*English 2600*, pp. iv–v.

A programed text so organized is often designated as a *horizontal* text in order to distinguish it from a *vertical* text in which several frames may appear in sequential order on the same page. The first few frames (1061-1063) of Lesson 26, "Avoiding Sentence Fragments," are shown in Figures 2a-2c.[30]

GENERALIZATIONS ABOUT PROGRAMED INSTRUCTION

Several generalizations that have been widely accepted by psychologists and educators should prove helpful at this point.

1. Although programed instruction is not new, it is still in the experimental stage. Effective teachers have employed and still employ the principles on which programed learning is based, even if they are not always aware of it.
2. Programed instruction may or may not involve the use of teaching machines, and it may appear in a variety of different forms.
3. Teaching machines and programed materials afford the promise of helping the teacher as well as the student make more economical use of his time, but they do not serve as a substitute for the teacher. Programed instruction provides some but not all of the advantages of tutoring. It is essentially concerned with individualizing instruction.
4. Subjects that are highly structured (mathematics and science) lend themselves more readily to programed instruction than do less systematic subjects (history or literature). Programed instruction tends to emphasize the science of teaching. Although the use of programed materials is largely limited to fields in which there is a fixed, correct answer, many concepts are not of this nature and, therefore, cannot be programed with much success.
5. Some programs are worked out to redirect the student's attention to areas in which he has shown a weakness. In such cases the student's response is used to determine the material he will cover next. These branching programs redirect learning once errors have been made.
6. Programed materials, like other teaching materials, should be selected to meet the individual needs of learners as nearly as possible. The same program may not be equally helpful for all students: the better student may need to take fewer steps to reach a goal than the slow or average student. Individual differences among students and variation in content among different subjects necessitate differentiation in spacing of material, speed of presentation, and method of programing. Programed learning provides needed opportunities for individual instruction in schools where advanced courses or courses of limited difficulty are not part of the curriculum.

---

[30]From *English 2600*, Revised edition, by Joseph C. Blumenthal, © 1960, 1962, by Harcourt, Brace & World, Inc., and reprinted with their permission. Pp. 361, 363, and 365.

Fig. 2a. Sample page from a programed English text.

noun verb 180	Is the italicized word a *noun* or a *verb?* **This pencil** ***breaks*** **too easily.** __________ **Some bad** ***breaks*** **in the pavement slowed down traffic.** __________ 181
but, or 400	**We can buy or rent a tent.** This sentence has compound __________. 401
position 620	Some prepositions show **direction.** DIRECTION: *from, to, toward, down, up, at* **We walked toward the corner.** The preposition **toward** shows the __________ in which we **walked.** 621
Yes 840	a. **Our sales increased** *when we lowered our price.* b. *When we lowered our price,* **our sales increased.** A comma is needed when the adverb clause comes (*before, after*) the main statement of the sentence. 841
	A **fragment** means "a broken piece"—like a fragment of glass or wood. A **sentence fragment** is a piece of a sentence that is written as though it were a complete __________. 1061
have 1280	The form of the verb **see** that ends with **–en** or **–n** is ______. 1281

page 361

7. Programed instructional devices should be evaluated in terms of goals achieved and not in terms of inherent or potential value. All the programed device can do is to present the available content in a way that facilitates learning.

8. The use of programed devices and automated teaching ma-

Fig. 2b. Sample page from a programed English text.

Answer	Frame
verb noun 181	**plant forget** Which one of the above words could be used as both a *noun* and a *verb?* (Think of actual sentences before writing your answer.) ________ 182
verbs 401	**Bob and the new boy soon became friends.** This sentence has a compound ____________. 402
direction 621	**The space <u>between</u> the two cars was small.** The preposition **between** shows (*position, direction*) 622
before 841	**A salesman will call** *if you leave your name.* No comma is needed in this sentence because the adverb clause comes (*before, after*) the main statement. 842
sentence 1061	To be a sentence, a group of words must pass two tests: 1. Does it have a subject and verb? 2. Does it make sense by itself? **The large book with the brown cover.** The above word group is a (*fragment, sentence*). 1062
seen 1281	**I have . . . much better movies than this.** What form of the verb **see** is required? ________ 1282

page 363

chines is influencing and will continue to influence curriculums at all levels.

9. Certain units of a course may be taught by conventional materials, while other units are taught with programed materials.

10. Subject-matter content that is carefully programed encour-

Fig. 2c. Sample page from a programed English text.

plant 182	Is the italicized word a *noun* or a *verb?* **The *plant* needs water.** ________ **Many farmers *plant* corn.** ________ 183
subject 402	**Fred stayed in his room and studied.** This sentence has compound ________. 403
position 622	**We flew to Miami.** The preposition **to** shows (*position, direction*). 623
after 842	*If you leave your name,* **a salesman will call.** Now a comma is needed because the adverb clause comes at the (*beginning, end*) of the sentence. 843
fragment 1062	**The large book with the brown cover.** This word group is a fragment because it names something **(book)** but makes no statement about it. In other words, this word group is not a sentence because it lacks a (*subject, verb*). 1063
seen 1282	**see saw have seen** a. **I have saw much better movies than this.** b. **I have seen much better movies than this.** Which sentence is wrong because the simple past form, instead of the helper form, is used after the helper **have?** 1283

page 365

ages the student to see relationships between the segments of content he is learning.

11. Programing is a technical task that requires a thorough acquaintance with the content to be programed as well as an understanding of the techniques of programing.

12. The development and use of programed materials and devices is not sufficiently well advanced to permit a sound prediction of the precise role they will play in education.

AREAS USING PROGRAMED INSTRUCTION

As interest and experimentation in programed learning increase, new studies are being reported for almost every subject in the secondary-school curriculum. In fact, the successful use of programed materials has been extended from the preschool level to postgraduate work.[31] Although the many studies report varying degrees of success, they are evidence of the willingness and effort on the part of experimenters to perfect techniques to a point where a greater measure of success with programing is imminent.

An examination of the subject areas for which programs have been produced reveals the greatest number in mathematics, general science, English grammar, and other structured subjects. These subjects were the first to attract the attention of trained programers. Since than, however, a wide range of programs have been produced for less well-structured subjects such as history and literature. Of a total of 352 programs listed by the United States Office of Education in 1963, 35 per cent were concerned with mathematics, 20 per cent with the sciences, 7 per cent with grammar usage and spelling, 7 per cent with the language arts, and 5 per cent with social studies.[32]

The Sciences

As early as 1948 a modified Pressey punchboard (one of the first teaching machines) was reported being used to teach chemistry at Syracuse University.[33] Results of this study indicated that learning is significantly enhanced if the student is provided with immediate knowledge of examination results—as was the case when using the punchboard device.

Programs '63 identifies sixty-nine programs available in the fields of applied science, general science, biology, chemistry, physics, and psychology.[34] Sample frames from a course on "The Body and How It Works" are presented in Figure 3.[35]

---

[31]Schramm, *op. cit.*, p. 45.

[32]*Programs '63, A Guide to Programed Instructional Materials* (Washington, D.C.: Center for Programed Instruction, 1963), p. vi. This publication is scheduled to appear annually and contains information on all the programed materials available at the time of publication.

[33]George W. Angell and Maurice E. Troyer, "A New Self-Scoring Test Device for Improving Instruction," *School and Society*, 1948 (Jan. 31), 67:84–85.

[34]*Programs '63*, p. vi.

[35]From *Fundamentals of Human Physiology, The Body and How It Works*, by John P. Fullilove, Donald T. Tosti, and Polo C. deBaca. © 1962, Teaching Machines, Inc., Albuquerque, New Mexico. In *Programs '62*, p. 312.

Fig. 3. Sample page from a programed biology text.

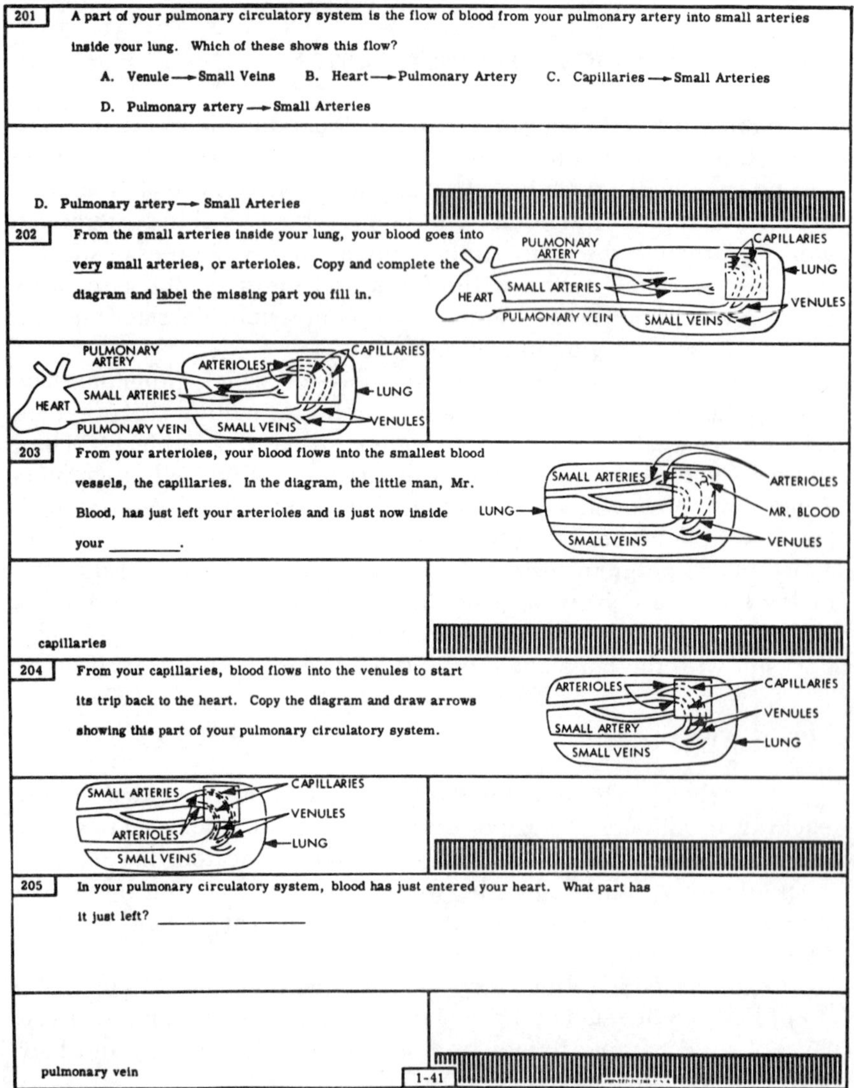

201 A part of your pulmonary circulatory system is the flow of blood from your pulmonary artery into small arteries inside your lung. Which of these shows this flow?

A. Venule → Small Veins B. Heart → Pulmonary Artery C. Capillaries → Small Arteries

D. Pulmonary artery → Small Arteries

D. Pulmonary artery → Small Arteries

202 From the small arteries inside your lung, your blood goes into very small arteries, or arterioles. Copy and complete the diagram and label the missing part you fill in.

arterioles

203 From your arterioles, your blood flows into the smallest blood vessels, the capillaries. In the diagram, the little man, Mr. Blood, has just left your arterioles and is just now inside your ________.

capillaries

204 From your capillaries, blood flows into the venules to start its trip back to the heart. Copy the diagram and draw arrows showing this part of your pulmonary circulatory system.

205 In your pulmonary circulatory system, blood has just entered your heart. What part has it just left? ________ ________

pulmonary vein

1-41

Psychology

Several programs concerned with the presentation of basic psychology are also currently available. Perhaps the best known of these is the Holland and Skinner text, *The Analysis of Behavior*,[36]

[36]This text is written by James G. Holland and B. F. Skinner and was published by McGraw-Hill Book Company in 1961.

Fig. 4. Sample page from a programed unit in a student guide for a psychology text.

rest	1. By *massed* practice we mean putting *trials*, or practice sessions, close together, that is, having a subject continue with one trial right after the other without any ________ periods in between.
massed	2. If we have a subject learning a list of nonsense syllables (a common experiment in learning) and we tell him to continue on the next trial each time he gets to the end of the list, without resting in between, we have instructed him to use ____________ practice.
trials	3. *Distributed* practice, on the other hand, implies *rest* periods in between ____________, or sessions.
distributed	4. If we ask the subject who is learning nonsense syllables to rest for one minute between each trial, we are using ____________________ practice.
distributed	5. It has been found in many experiments that the rest period between trials seems to improve the efficiency of learning. Therefore it is stated that, in general, the ____________________ practice method is the better one to use.
distributed massed	6. In spite of the fact that ____________________ practice is, in general, better than ____________ practice, there are some conditions under which the latter is the better method to use. These exceptions to the general rule are pointed out in the text.
not	7. In memorizing a poem, then, one can use either the distributed practice or the massed practice method. It was pointed out above that the distributed method is usually better, although this rule does ______ always hold true.
whole	8. In memorizing a poem, you would probably also want to decide whether to learn the poem one stanza at a time or to try to learn it as a w________.
together	9. If one learns the poem one stanza at a time he is using the *part* method. The idea here is that once one knows each stanza, he can then put the stanzas ______________ and recite the poem from beginning to end.

a linear program for college students. Roth[37] found varied reactions to the use of this text: A majority of students at both the undergraduate and the graduate level indicated initial interest in the program, but dislike and boredom developed later; only a minority of students enjoyed the program throughout.

An example of the use of programed units to help students acquire the content of a course in psychology appears in Figure 4.[38]

---

[37] Robert H. Roth, "Student Reactions to Programed Instruction," *Phi Delta Kappan*, 1963, *44:* 278–281.

[38] From *Student Guide with Programed Units for Hilgard's Introduction to Psychology*, 3rd edition, copyright, 1953, © 1957, 1962, by Harcourt, Brace & World, Inc. and reprinted with their permission. P. 119.

Fig. 5. Sample page from a programed solid geometry text.

1342. Suppose we are given that two lines *FG* and *GH* are both perpendicular to line *JG* at point *G*. Is it true that the plane determined by the intersecting lines *FG* and *GH* is perpendicular to line *JG*? ________________ . Yes

1343. Theorem 7 states that one and only one perpendicular to a plane can be drawn from an external point.
A point is said to be external to a plane if it does not ________________ in the plane. lie

1344. The distance from a point to a plane is defined to be the length of the ________________ from that point to that plane. perpendicular

1345. It is also true that there is one and only one line perpendicular to a given plane at a point in that plane. Sketch Figure 104, and then draw a line perpendicular to plane p at point *A*. Is there more than one such line? ________________ . No

Figure 104

1346. The statement of the previous frame tells us that there is a single ________________ perpendicular to a given plane at a given point in the plane. line

1347. We remember that a straight line lies *entirely* within a plane if it has at least ________________ point(s) in common with the plane. two

Mathematics

The greatest number of programs currently available in any one field deal with teaching mathematics. Perhaps the basic reason for this fact is that mathematics is a highly structured subject in which there can be definite answers.

One program in solid geometry (see Figure 5)[39] calls for a constructed (written) response in each frame. The correct answer appears in printed form opposite each frame, but it is hidden by a sliding

[39]Reprinted by permission from *Solid Geometry* by David C. Luckham, TEMAC Programmed Learning Materials. © 1962, 1963 by Encyclopædia Brittanica Press, Inc., p. 225.

shield. At any time he wishes, the program user may expose the correct answer, although he is cautioned not to do so until he has made his own response. Teachers who have used this and similar programs report that the tendency to cheat by prematurely exposing the correct answers is minimized when learners become aware of the thorough, teacher-administered testing procedure that is employed as a part of the program.

Foreign Languages

Seeking to accelerate the learning of their students, foreign-language teachers have enthusiastically turned to a wide variety of stimulus-response devices. Introductory programed courses for seven different foreign languages—French, German, Hebrew, Italian, Japanese, Russian, and Spanish—are identified and illustrated in *Programs '63*.[40] The largest number of these have been developed as aids for teaching Spanish.

French

At Hamilton College the content of a French course was programed, with 35 visual units of sixty frames each, 35 corresponding audio units, and 35 units in a workbook. Results showed that students taking the new programed course averaged about 20 per cent higher on standardized tests of written French, grammar, and translation than did students who had taken the old course.[41] Such evidence encourages the use of programed materials for other language courses.

German

One programed device for a German course (see Figure 6)[42] presents printed pairs of sentences, first in English and then in German. By moving a mask upward, the student first exposes an English phrase or sentence and writes the German equivalent on another sheet of paper. Moving the mask up again exposes the correct German equivalent so that the learner may check his translation. If it is correct, he moves on to the next statement.

Spanish

A recent investigation of programed instruction involved teaching first-year Spanish to six thousand elementary-school pupils grouped in experimental and control sections. The researchers concluded that

---

[40]*Programs '63*, pp. 257–306.

[41]Schramm, *op. cit.*, p. 47.

[42]From Charles B. Ferster and Stanley M. Sapon, "An Application of Recent Developments in Psychology to the Teaching of German," in A. A. Lumsdaine and Robert Glaser, *Teaching Machines and Programmed Learning: A Source Book* (Washington, D.C.: National Education Association, 1960), p. 176.

Fig. 6. Sample page from a programed German text.

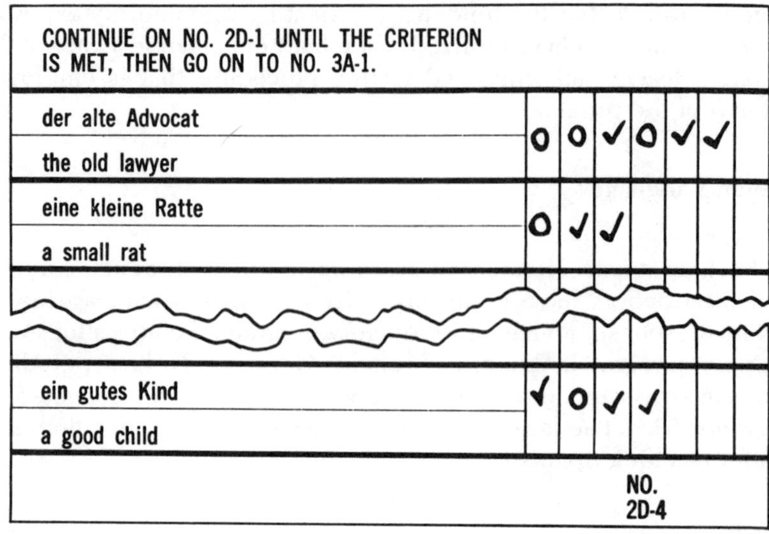

with proper conditions and at least with the rather mechanical, non-creative type learning involved in this study, automated instruction can be as effective as the more traditional teacher-directed method. In fact, the teaching machine results suggest that automated instruction can be superior, though conditions for superiority are uncertain.[43]

PRINCIPLES RELATED TO PROGRAMED INSTRUCTION

The psychological principles that constitute the basis for programed instruction are relatively simple and are generally familiar to the qualified teacher. Stimulus, response, and reinforcement must be understood by all who are concerned with the production and use of programed materials.

Stimulus:

1. Every response is the result of a stimulus. Programed instruction involves providing appropriate stimuli to which the learner can make the desired response.

Response:

2. Programed learning prevents passivity on the part of the learner, since it calls for student response to specific segments of information.

---

[43]Delbert Barcus, John L. Hayman, Jr., and James T. Johnson, Jr., "Programing Instruction in Elementary Spanish," *Phi Delta Kappan,* 1963, *44:* 272.

3. Response to questions or other stimulus items keeps the student in a state of continuing mental activity.

4. Programed materials provide the student with an opportunity for giving correct responses.

Reinforcement:

5. Programed materials keep the student continuously informed of his progress.

6. The student is motivated when he gets an immediate indication of whether his response has been right or wrong.

7. Immediate reinforcement adds to the speed, efficiency, and interest of learning.

8. The learner benefits by being able to move immediately to the next item of content if he has responded correctly or by being immediately referred back to misunderstood or partially understood content for restudy.

9. When learners are immediately apprised of errors, they can make the necessary corrections before repeated use has tended to reinforce their mistakes.

General:

10. Individuals may learn effectively, and without the aid of a teacher, by responding to sequentially placed items.

11. Motivation to learn may in some cases be aided by programed learning because many of the negative elements of interpersonal teacher-student relationships are absent.

12. In programed learning the student may start at his own level and proceed toward the desired goal by acquiring carefully graduated concepts.

13. When using programed materials, the learner may proceed as rapidly or as slowly as he wishes.

CORRECT AND INCORRECT USE

The chance for teacher error in the selection and use of programed instructional materials is great because of their experimental nature. Therefore, the teacher who proposes to use such materials would do well to read a number of relevant current articles, to discuss the nature of programed materials with teachers who are successfully using such material, and—only then—to proceed, with appropriate caution.[44]

Procedures with Limitations

The desire to keep abreast of the new instructional practices has led many teachers and administrators to make hasty and sometimes

[44]Schramm, *op. cit.*, pp. 52–70, presents a sound discussion about the conditions that contribute to effective programed instruction.

unsound decisions. This danger is inherent in the use of programed materials. Look, for example, at the cases of William Addison and Phyllis Vance.

MR. ADDISON'S ENTHUSIASM MEETS WITH DIFFICULTY

After his visit to the ASCD Convention in Chicago, Principal William Addison was an enthusiastic convert to the idea of teaching machines. As he wandered from one display to another in the exhibition hall, he conjured up repeated visions of how the learning process in his own consolidated high school would be mechanized and streamlined through the use of machines.

Upon his return Mr. Addison lost no time in voicing his enthusiasm to his superintendent and the members of the school board. In the face of his persistent eagerness, they finally consented to the purchase of two complicated electronic machines at a cost of $1100 each.

Although the teachers in his school expressed great interest in machine teaching, they had little more than a passing acquaintance with all that was involved. Before the teachers could hope to use the machines efficiently, the principal found it necessary to conduct an in-service training program to acquaint them with literature in the field.

Mr. Addison was somewhat distressed when he discovered that programs for teaching United States history and chemistry were not available for the machines he had purchased. By the time he had trained his teachers and obtained programs that could be used in the machines, many months had elapsed.

MISS VANCE ACQUIRES NEEDED INFORMATION

Miss Phyllis Vance was always determined to be the first one in her school district to try new innovations in education. She was the first of the "life adjustment" advocates—and the first to discard it when the hard-core curriculum bandwagon passed her way. She pushed for the cause of television instruction but shortly thereafter declared it to be impractical and undesirable.

In a similar manner Miss Vance expressed an immediate preference for machine teaching when she heard about it. According to her, machine teaching would soon relieve teachers of their burdensome routine tasks and elevate them to the level of instructional engineers who could flip the switch and watch learning take place. But Miss Vance's principal insisted that much careful thought, study, and cautious experimentation precede the endorsement of a new procedure.

Under his direction Miss Vance was encouraged to read widely about programed instruction, and he made it possible for her to attend a workshop in which the theory underlying the new medium was exposed. Finally, he encouraged her to talk to several teachers in an adjacent school district who had experimented with programed instruction. Only then did he feel that it was time to ask Miss Vance to appraise carefully how their high school could make the most effective use of programed instruction.

Both Mr. Addison and Miss Vance fell prey to the fascinating novelty of machine teaching. Without adequate knowledge of the principles upon which programed instruction is based, they launched into new programs, limiting their chances for success at the outset. Fortunately Miss Vance received the type of guidance she needed; Mr. Addison was not so lucky.

Procedures with Promise

Recognition of the many problems related to the introduction and use of programed instructional materials has led other teachers and administrators to exercise varying degrees of caution. Two such educators are Mary Bacon and Thomas Dalley.

MRS. BACON PREPARES FOR SUCCESSFUL PROGRAMED INSTRUCTION

Mary Bacon, known to her teaching colleagues and administrators as a stable, conscientious, hard-working, and successful teacher, was asked by her principal to investigate the possibility of using programed instruction in teaching ninth-grade English grammar. When she accepted the responsibility, she indicated the need for allowing adequate time for study and examination of programs already in operation.

Taking her job seriously, Mrs. Bacon acquired the latest available bibliography on programed instruction and began to learn about this new field. She found that textbooks were of limited use in providing current information; thus most of her reading was confined to periodical literature. Gradually she identified the major strengths and weaknesses of programed instruction. Early in her reading she became convinced that the quality of professional work that had gone into developing a program greatly determined its potential for success.

Mrs. Bacon had several informative discussions with teachers in other districts who were using programed materials in teaching English grammar. She discovered that programed materials could be used to serve a variety of instructional needs; not only could they be used to provide accelerated learning, but they could also be used to serve the needs of the slow learner. Furthermore, they could serve as remedial aids and as devices for review.

After investigating the cost and value of machines in which English grammar programs could be used, she decided that programed texts would provide essentially the same experience at a fraction of the cost. She reported back to her principal that she would like to experiment on a limited scale with the use of programed materials during the next semester. Further use, she indicated, should be based upon the evaluation of the limited experiment.

MR. DALLEY DISCOVERS PROGRAMED INSTRUCTION THROUGH COURSE WORK

The graduate course in programed instruction that Mr. Dalley took at the state university proved to be an eye opener. He returned to his teaching determined to use programed instruction in his own classes. Armed with his course-acquired knowledge and following the move-with-caution procedure stressed by his professor, Mr. Dalley set up a program for himself.

In March he approached his principal about the possible use of programed instruction in his algebra classes. The principal was much better informed than Mr. Dalley had assumed he would be; he expressed interest in the possibility and promised the necessary administrative backing, providing that this experiment did not disrupt the already existing curriculum.

Mr. Dalley then wrote to the publishers of elementary-algebra programed textbooks, asking them to send him examination copies. From the range of texts he selected the one that he felt most nearly served his purposes. Permission was granted to order ten of these texts for use in his two beginning algebra sections starting in September.

He decided he would experiment by having the top eight students in the two sections move through the programed text as rapidly as possible. Tests would be given at frequent intervals, and Mr. Dalley would have a personal interview with each student at least once every week.

If his early experimental efforts proved to be satisfactory, he would include more students in the program during the second semester. If the efforts proved to be unsatisfactory, however, he would restrict the use of programed materials until he thoroughly analyzed the causes of the poor results.

Programed materials would also be used experimentally to provide a self-directed review of course segments found to be causing students difficulty. Mr. Dalley would obtain the latest bibliography on programed instruction issued by the National Education Association and keep abreast of the latest developments in the field.

If the results of the first year proved to be singularly successful, he would consider using programed texts for teaching all first-year algebra students the following year.

Mrs. Bacon approached the investigation of programed instruction with desirable caution. She read the relevant literature until she had a firm basis for whatever action was to be taken. In addition, she discussed the use of programed materials with other teachers who had employed them successfully. Finally, she suggested that experimentation in her own school be initially conducted on a limited scale. Mr. Dalley, likewise, systematized his movement into programed instruction. Each successive step he took in this direction was carefully identified and analyzed; little was left to chance.

SPECIFIC SUGGESTIONS

Conscientious teachers, with the best of intentions, sometimes meet with limited success in using programed materials to promote the cause of learning. The possibility of effective use of such materials is increased if detailed planning, continued reading, and an alert appraisal of the role of programed learning in the total educational process precede the actual use of the materials. Recommendations and cautions for the use of programed instruction are provided below.

Recommendations

1. Become acquainted with the advantages and disadvantages of programed instruction before you try it out; profit by the experience

of other school districts. Also become acquainted with programed materials and teaching machines that have been used successfully in your area of specialization.

2. Remember that the potential for success of any programed course or unit is directly related to the quality of the professional work that has gone into the program.

3. Select programs that best promote your course objectives.

4. Use programed materials to help meet the individual differences of students.

5. Determine the specific points that characterize an effective programed course before you select the material to use in your teaching.

6. Be willing to experiment with programed materials on a limited scale in your classroom.

Cautions

1. Don't assume that programed material will serve as a substitute for the teacher.

2. Don't assume that machine teaching is necessarily the most efficient all-purpose method of teaching.

3. Don't confuse the commercial zeal exhibited in selling an automated teaching device with the educational value of the product.

PROGRAMED INSTRUCTION IN REVIEW

Programed instruction refers to the use of systematically organized materials and calls for the application of the psychological principles of stimulus, response, and reinforcement. Items (frames) in sequence may be presented in a programed text or prepared for use in a machine. Machine teaching, however, is best described as one type of programed instruction.

Two major types of programs are currently being used—Skinnerian, or linear, programs and Crowderian, or branching, programs. Skinnerian programs call for advancement by very small steps with content structured to provide a preponderance of correct responses. In a Crowderian program the student who makes an incorrect response does not proceed with the program until he has successfully completed a remedial frame or loop. Both types of programs have strong proponents, but approximately 90 per cent of those programs currently in use fall into the Skinnerian category.

Although most of the statements concerning programed instruction made by responsible psychologists reflect cautious optimism, statements may range from sweeping denunciation to unqualified endorsement. For this reason it is highly desirable for the prospective user of programed materials to become fully informed about such materials before attempting to use them. To become knowledgeable the teacher must read current descriptions of programs, discuss the strengths and weaknesses of such programs with teachers who have used the materials, and cautiously experiment with the materials only after careful plans have been made.

PROBLEMS FOR STUDY AND DISCUSSION

1. Define programed learning in your own words.
2. What are the basic psychological principles involved in programed instruction?
3. Differentiate between Crowderian programing and Skinnerian programing.
4. Name five advantages claimed for programed instruction.
5. Define the following terms as they relate to programed instruction:

Reinforcement	Intrinsic programing
Step	Linear programing
Frame	Branching
Scrambled textbook	Loops

6. Differentiate between programed instruction and machine teaching.
7. Is a workbook a teaching machine according to the currently accepted definition of the term? Explain.
8. Describe Pressey's contribution to programed instruction.
9. How do you account for the skepticism of many of the critics of programed instruction? Explain.
10. Write a careful, one-paragraph statement about the future of programed instruction based upon a consideration of its current status.
11. Name three extensively used programed texts suitable for secondary schools.
12. What are the advantages of a programed text as opposed to a teaching machine?
13. What are the advantages of taking large steps in programed materials? What are the disadvantages? Explain.
14. At what grade levels has programed instruction been tried?
15. Identify the areas in the secondary curriculum in which programed materials have been used most frequently up to the present time. How do you account for this?
16. Discuss several different ways in which programed textbooks can be used by the classroom teacher.
17. Identify the title, author, and publisher of a programed text in your teaching major or minor.
18. About how many programs are currently available in the United States at all educational levels?
19. List in order the steps you would take to inaugurate the use of programed materials in your teaching major or minor. Assume that programed materials have not been used in your school before.
20. List in your own words at least five cautions that should be of particular value to the new teacher who wishes to use programed instructional materials.

RECOMMENDED READINGS

Anderson, Vernon E., and William T. Gruhn, *Principles and Practices of Secondary Education,* 2d. ed. New York: Ronald Press, 1962, pp. 188–189.

Angell, George W., and Maurice E. Troyer, "A New Self-Scoring Test Device for Improving Instruction," *School and Society,* 1948 (January 31), *67:* 84–85.

Barcus, Delbert, John L. Hayman, Jr., and James T. Johnson, Jr., "Programing Instruction in Elementary Spanish," *Phi Delta Kappan,* 1963, *44:* 269–272.

Chandler, B. J., Lindley J. Stiles, and John I. Kitsuse (eds.), *Education in Urban Society.* New York: Dodd, Mead and Company, 1962, pp. 29–30.

Cronbach, Lee J., "What Research Says About Programed Instruction," *NEA Journal,* 1962 (December), *51:* 45–47.

Crowder, Norman A., "Automatic Tutoring by Intrinsic Programming," in A. A. Lumsdaine and Robert Glaser (eds.), *Teaching Machines and Programmed Learning.* Washington, D.C.: National Education Association, 1960, pp. 286–298.

Deterline, William A., *An Introduction to Programed Instruction.* Englewood Cliffs, N.J.: Prentice-Hall, Inc., 1962, Chapters 1–6.

Eigen, Lewis D., "Programing Poses Problems," *Phi Delta Kappan,* 1963, *44:* 242.

Epstein, Samuel, and Beryl Epstein, *The First Book of Teaching Machines.* New York: Franklin Watts, Inc., 1961, pp. 1–48.

Feldhusen, John F., "Taps for Teaching Machines," *Phi Delta Kappan,* 1963, *44:* 265–267.

Ferster, Charles B., and Stanley M. Sapon, "An Application of Recent Developments in Psychology to the Teaching of German," in A. A. Lumsdaine and Robert Glaser (eds.), *Teaching Machines and Programmed Learning.* Washington, D.C.: National Education Association, 1960, pp. 173–185.

Filep, Robert T., *Prospectives in Programing.* New York: The Macmillan Company, 1963, Sections 1–5.

Hendershot, Carl H., *Programmed Learning: A Bibliography of Programs and Presentation Devices.* Bay City, Mich.: Carl H. Hendershot, 1964–.

Homme, Lloyd E., "The Rationale of Teaching by Skinner's Machines," in A. A. Lumsdaine and Robert Glaser (eds.), *Teaching Machines and Programmed Learning.* Washington, D.C.: National Education Association, 1960, pp. 133–136.

Hough, John B., and Bernard Revsin, "Programed Instruction at the College Level: A Study of Several Factors Influencing Learning," *Phi Delta Kappan,* 1963, *44:* 286–291.

Keislar, Evan R., "The Development of Understanding in Arithmetic by a Teaching Machine," in A. A. Lumsdaine and Robert Glaser (eds.), *Teaching Machines and Programmed Learning.* Washington, D.C.: National Education Association, 1960, pp. 425–436.

Komoski, P. Kenneth, "Programed Instruction—A Prologue to What?" *Phi Delta Kappan,* 1963, *44:* 292–295.

Lumsdaine, A. A., and Robert Glaser (eds.), *Teaching Machines and Programmed Learning: A Source Book.* Washington, D.C.: National Education Association, 1960.

McKean, Robert C., *Principles and Methods in Secondary Education.* Columbus, Ohio: Charles E. Merrill Books, Inc., 1962, pp. 114–115.

McNeil, John D., "The Influence of Programed Learning upon Curriculum Research," *Phi Delta Kappan,* 1963, *44:* 261–264.

Mellan, I., "Teaching and Educational Inventions," *Journal of Experimental Education.* 1936 (March), *4:* 291–300.

Morse, William C., and G. Max Wingo, *Psychology and Teaching,* 2d. ed. Chicago: Scott, Foresman and Company, 1962, pp. 162–164, 183, and 279.

Nordberg, H. Orville, James M. Bradfield, and William C. Odell, *Secondary School Teaching.* New York: The Macmillan Company, 1962, pp. 124–125.

Porter, Douglas, "A Report on Instructional Devices in Foreign Language Teaching," in A. A. Lumsdaine and Robert Glaser (eds.), *Teaching Machines and Programmed Learning.* Washington, D.C.: National Education Association, 1960, pp. 186–205.

Programs '63, A Guide to Programed Instructional Materials. Washington, D.C.: Center for Programed Instruction, Inc., 1963.

Programs '62, A Guide to Programed Instructional Materials. Center Washington, D.C.: Center for Programed Instruction, Inc., 1962.

Rivlin, Harry N., *Teaching Adolescents in Secondary Schools,* 2d. ed. New York: Appleton-Century-Crofts, Inc., 1961, pp. 253–257.

Roth, Robert H., "Student Reactions to Programed Learning," *Phi Delta Kappan,* 1963, *44:* 278–281.

Schramm, Wilbur, *Programed Instruction Today and Tomorrow.* New York: Fund for the Advancement of Education, 1962.

Skinner, B. F., "Teaching Machines," *Science,* 1958 (October 24), *128:* 969–977.

Stolurow, Lawrence M., "Let's Be Informed on Programed Instruction," *Phi Delta Kappan,* 1963, *44:* 255–257.

Stolurow, Lawrence M., *Teaching by Machine.* Washington, D.C.: U.S. Office of Education, 1962, pp. 1–150.

19

Television and Team Teaching in the Modern Classroom

Television instruction and team teaching have been two of the most influential postwar teaching innovations. Both have been improved, and the widespread experimentation currently being carried on should lead to continued improvement. The conscientious, forward-looking teacher will be a front-line participant in this experimentation.

TELEVISION INSTRUCTION

The problem of how to provide instruction of the highest quality for large groups of students has existed since learners were first grouped for the purpose of instruction. Admittedly, classroom teachers vary greatly in their instructional abilities, and administrators and teachers have long sought a procedure by which more students could have contact with the most competent teachers. Television instruction seems to provide one possible answer to this problem.

As a result of past research, the question of whether television can serve as an effective instructional medium is no longer an issue. Studies indicate that students taught by means of television make gains in achievement comparable to, and in some cases exceeding, gains made by students taught by conventional procedures.[1] Schramm, for instance, reports that

[1]*Teaching by Television,* A Report from the Ford Foundation and the Fund for the Advancement of Education, 2d. ed. (New York: The Ford Foundation, 1961), p. 7.

instructional television is at least as effective as ordinary classroom instruction, when the results are measured by the usual final examinations or by standardized tests made by testing bureaus. . . . we can say with considerable confidence that in 65 percent of a very large number of comparisons [393], between televised and classroom teaching, there is no significant difference.[2]

In spite of these findings, much research must still be done before there can be a definite answer to the question of how television can best be used in education.[3]

History of Teaching by Television

The history of television instruction is relatively brief. Utilizing the technical know-how acquired piecemeal during the thirties[4] and early forties, commercial television made its debut in the years immediately following World War II. It was not until commercial television had reached considerable stature, however, that attention was seriously focused on the new medium's potentials as an instructional device.[5]

Experiments of the Mid-Fifties

In the mid-fifties the schools of Pittsburgh became the first of many educational institutions to become involved in television instruction. Programs were telecast to assist in teaching arithmetic, French, and fifth-grade reading. These programs were so successful that one educational television station was not enough, and a second was started in 1957. At the present time, educational television is being employed in Pittsburgh's elementary and secondary schools and adult education programs.

Hagerstown, Maryland, is the seat of one of the best-known closed-circuit instructional television projects. When the project was started in September 1956, 5300 students received one full lesson each day by television. A year later 12,000 students were being taught by television; by 1959, 16,500 of the 18,000 students enrolled

---

[2]Wilbur Schramm, "What We Know About Learning from Instructional Television," in *Educational Television in the Next Ten Years* (Stanford: Institute for Communication Research, 1962), p. 53.

[3]Alexander Frazier and Harold E. Wigren (eds.), *Opportunities for Learning: Guidelines for Television* (Washington, D.C.: Department of Audio-Visual Instruction, NEA, 1960), pp. 18–57, present fourteen statements by educational specialists concerned with educational television that indicate the direction this teaching medium should be taking.

[4]One of the early sustained efforts at providing educational television is recounted by E. B. Kurtz, *Pioneering in Educational Television, 1932–1939* (Iowa City: State University of Iowa, 1959).

[5]Dave Chapman, *Design for ETV: Planning for Schools with Television* (New York: Educational Facilities Laboratories, 1960), pp. 21–22, provides a brief, readable history of educational television up to 1960.

in the elementary schools in Washington County, Maryland, were being instructed through the new medium.

Use in College and Adult Education

The advantages of television instruction for college and adult education were quickly recognized. In 1954 Pennsylvania State College became the first college-level institution to employ educational television. Other institutions, such as the Chicago City Junior College, have made extensive use of television to reach a large adult audience. Since 1956 this Chicago college has been broadcasting a home educational television program that in 1960 had an estimated viewing audience of between 30,000 and 50,000 adult students with a median age of thirty-five.

By 1960 coast-to-coast educational programs were appearing over commercial networks.[6] *Continental Classroom*, one such program, reportedly had 414,000 viewers for an early morning course in "Modern Chemistry."

According to Chapman,[7] in early 1960, 569 school districts throughout the nation were regularly using televised instruction, 117 colleges and universities were giving credit for televised courses, 144 closed-circuit television systems were in operation in educational institutions, and 45 educational television stations were in use.

Multi-State Cooperative Use

The most extensive single project involving the use of television solely for instructional purposes is currently operating in a six-state area in the Midwest.[8] Known as the Midwest Program on Airborne Television Instruction (MPATI), this project helps serve the instructional needs of 5,000,000 pupils and 200,000 teachers in the area covered.[9] An airplane flying at an altitude of 20,000 feet makes it possible to telecast prerecorded lessons to remote sections that could not otherwise be reached by television.

Three hundred carefully selected teachers prepare, teach, and record lessons for use in the MPATI program. Because of its success, this project has been expanded every year since its inception. Elementary and secondary schools, as well as colleges and universities, are taking advantage of this unusual service. A wide range of courses are transmitted at various times throughout the day, including courses that are difficult to teach as well as conventional courses.

---

[6]An accurate picture of the status of educational television as of August 1961 is presented in *Teaching by Television*, pp. 1–18.

[7]Chapman, *op. cit.*, p. 22.

[8]The six states participating in this project are Indiana, Ohio, Kentucky, Illinois, Michigan, and Wisconsin.

[9]Walter A. Wittich and Charles F. Schuller, *Audiovisual Materials: Their Nature and Use*, 3d. ed. (New York: Harper & Brothers, 1962), pp. 419–420, provide an informative account of the MPATI program.

Approaches to Teaching by Television

Ever since television captured the public fancy during the late forties, educators have expressed keen interest in its possible use in education. There have been repeated attempts to make commercial television more nearly conform to desired educational standards. Profit-minded telecasters, however, have exerted strong opposition to any educational innovations that might reduce the viewing audience, although they have been willing to recognize the need for a general cultural elevation of most commercial programs. Educators, desiring to use television specifically in behalf of education, supported the establishment of television channels used exclusively for educational purposes.

According to Fletcher,[10] four major types of broadcasting can be used within or in conjunction with the schools: educational television stations, commercial educational programing, closed-circuit production, and low-power commercial broadcasting over ultra-high-frequency (UHF) channels.

Educational Television Stations

In order to protect the educational interests of television viewers in the United States, the Federal Communications Commission (FCC) has reserved 309 television channels (more than half of which are in the ultra-high-frequency range) for the exclusive purpose of telecasting educational programs.[11] Commercial television stations are not permitted to use these channels. Most states have one educational television station at the present time, and several states have two or more. As of March 1965, there were 59 VHF (very-high-frequency) and 56 UHF stations in addition to three noncommercial educational television stations, for a total of 118 authorized educational television stations in operation.[12] Because they are under the control of the FCC, these stations are committed to operate on a nonprofit basis, and the programs they present must be educational. Furthermore, they must make their facilities available to a range of nonprofit agencies within the community, such as service clubs and public service agencies.

Because of their singleness of purpose, these stations provide the largest proportion of television viewing that is pointedly educational. Public-school systems frequently present programs at specifically desired times, usually during school hours. During nonschool hours, well-established stations present a range of cultural offerings that compete with commercially sponsored programs. Many of these

---

[10]Leon C. Fletcher, *TV's New Engagement—Showmanship and Scholarship* (San Francisco: Fearon Publishers, 1958), pp. 2–3.

[11]Giraud Chester, Garnet R. Garrison, and Edgar E. Willis, *Television and Radio*, 3d. ed. (New York: Appleton-Century-Crofts, 1963), p. 204.

[12]*Broadcasting: The Business Weekly of Television and Radio*, 1965 (March 22), 68:12.

programs are interesting and entertaining as well as educational, but the proportion of the total viewing audience that they attract is relatively small.

Commercial Educational Programing

Although frequently criticized by educators and interested lay groups for not devoting a larger proportion of their total time to educational programing, all commercial television stations produce a wide variety of programs that have educational value. Movies about historical events that are technically and factually sound or movies about science, such as "Our Mr. Sun" and "Hemo, the Magnificent," have been shown on commercial channels. Many other programs of public interest, such as the launching of the astronauts or the national political conventions, have educational merit. Commercially sponsored news broadcasts are daily events, and on several programs students have the opportunity to see and hear prominent national and international figures.

Many educational television programs originate as commercial network presentations, but a substantial number are produced and telecast by local stations. Limited state-wide telecasts provide students with the opportunity to hear official pronouncements of the governor, to see and hear members of the state legislature discuss critical issues, and to view cultural programs of particular merit presented by universities within the state.

Closed-Circuit Production

Closed-circuit television affords the opportunity of showing phenomena or presentations that are of interest only to a restricted audience.[13] This type of television is not "broadcast" in the conventional sense of the term; it is rather sent out over wires or by means of microwaves to specially equipped receiving sets.

Some of the uses of closed-circuit television include observation of certain processes when immediate contact with the phenomenon could entail danger to the viewer—such as steel production—and observation of group processes and behavior both with and without the knowledge of the group. Because of its unique flexibility and relative economy, closed-circuit television is used more frequently for instructional purposes than are the other telecasting procedures.

Low-Power Television

Much experimentation is currently being conducted on the use of low-power transmission over ultra-high-frequency channels. Because the range of coverage is proportionate to the strength of broad-

---

[13]An illustrated report of the use of closed-circuit television in a college setting is presented in the *Television Project Report from San Jose State College, San Jose, California: Instructional Closed-Circuit Television—Installation, Operation, and Potential* (Pictorial Report Number 1), September 1958.

casting signals, only limited areas can be served effectively by these low-powered open circuits.

By September 1963, the FCC had authorized the use of 31 television channels for educational television in the 2500-2690 megacycle band.[14] The Commission specified that these high-frequency channels were to be used for the transmission of "instructional and cultural material to schools and other selected receiver locations."

Advantages of Television Instruction

A review of the advantages of instructional television reveals several reasons why its proponents have become increasingly enthusiastic about its prospects for improving education.[15] It must be remembered, however, that evidence of its specific advantages awaits repeated trial and evaluation.

Presenting Real Events

Because television makes use of both sight and sound, it can present the natural phenomena of the world in actual form.[16] The noisy excitement of a large steel mill, remote corners of the globe, or even outer space itself may be brought forcibly and realistically to the attention of the learner. Many aspects of the problems of human relations can be effectively portrayed, and incidents of racial unrest in Africa, China, or Washington, D.C., may be shown while still fresh or even while happening. Telestar enables the public to see events on other continents as they happen, and the possibility of additional global television programs specially adapted to educational use is currently being explored.

Revealing Specialized Photographic Views

Microscopic forms of life can be magnified, photographed, and presented on television to unlock secrets hidden from the naked eye. Slow growth processes can be accelerated. Thus stages in the development of a rose, which actually extends over several hours or days, may take on new and vital meaning when seen in a few seconds. Conversely, rapid activity—such as combustion within a cylinder, the performance of a mile runner, or the flight of a hummingbird—can be shown in slow motion with marked educational advantages.

---

[14]*RCA Educational Television News*, Issue 70 (Camden, N.J.: Radio Corporation of America, 1963).

[15]John W. Wentworth, "Television in the Classroom" (mimeographed paper presented at The School Board Institute of the Pennsylvania School Study Council, March 22, 1961), pp. 1–16, outlines and discusses the specific advantages of classroom television.

[16]Jean D. Grambs, William J. Iverson, and Franklin K. Patterson, *Modern Methods in Secondary Education*, rev. ed. (New York: The Dryden Press, 1958), pp. 176–177, point out the need for utilizing the unique advantages of television as well as of the motion picture.

Portraying Past Events

Past events can be brought to life and made meaningful through dramatizations on television. These dramatizations may be live plays or recorded on film. The effect of the Depression on human lives and values, the way of life peculiar to the colonial period, and the major battles of the Civil War have been accurately re-created and recorded on film and made available for television viewers. Carefully selected films and other forms of dramatization provide impact possible through no other medium.

Teaching Large Audiences

Television affords the opportunity for large audiences in the same auditorium or in different locations to view clearly a demonstration or a lecture that may be given in the next city, in another part of the country, or on the other side of the world. Television also provides a ready means for showing students valuable material that may be one of a kind (a specific document, painting, or play) or available in limited supply (rare breeds of animals or exotic plants).

Offering Needed Courses and Programs

Through television students can take courses that are not offered by their school. Both commercial and educational television stations present early morning classes in mathematics, physical sciences, foreign languages, and other subjects, and some courses are given for academic credit.[17]

Television also provides the opportunity for curriculum enrichment that could not possibly be found otherwise. Commercial channels, for example, provide excellent news coverage of significant events throughout the world as well as interpretation of news by nationally known commentators.

Using Educational Facilities More Efficiently

Proponents of educational television believe that this medium is economically advantageous. Very large classes are made possible, space in a building can be better utilized, special teachers and particularly valuable outside lecturers and resources can be used efficiently, and teaching presentations of unusual quality can be filmed for re-use.[18] Shortages of teachers in special subjects (languages, music, and science), inadequate facilities (laboratories and demonstration devices), and space limitations may be partially overcome through the use of television.

---

[17]Vernon E. Anderson and William T. Gruhn, *Principles and Practices of Secondary Education*, 2d. ed. (New York: Ronald Press, 1962), p. 264, identify a current practice in the San Francisco school system whereby selected high-school students may take university television courses in languages, sciences, and other fields for credit by special arrangement with the San Francisco State College.

[18]Wittich and Schuller, *op. cit.*, pp. 421–423, describe the processes used in visually recording instructional presentations.

Encouraging Quality Presentations

Because of the size of the prospective audience, instructors and teams of assistants make a special effort to produce a teaching presentation of unusual quality. The nature of television teaching demands detailed preparation, and a substantial portion of the total preparation time must be devoted to developing audio-visual aids that can be used effectively before the cameras. Because of this extremely detailed preparation, the quality of instruction that appears on television is often superior to that of the typical classroom.

Limitations of Television Instruction

Although television has instructional advantages, it also has limitations, especially when compared with the versatility of a competent classroom teacher.[19] As yet there is no conclusive evidence to indicate that television instruction is superior to well-planned, effective classroom instruction.

Although television can present demonstrations or lectures of high quality, live presentations may not be available at the specific time needed to provide maximum instructional help for the teacher and students. Programs recorded on video tape, however, may be telecast at any time that serves the needs of the school district.

Because televised lessons move at a fixed rate of speed and teach specific content in a predetermined sequence, the individual needs of students cannot be easily met. If a student, although attentive, has failed to comprehend a particular concept, there is no opportunity for the teacher to re-explain. Television instruction does not permit the exchange of ideas between the teacher and his students; generally it provides for one-way communication only.[20] The individualization of instruction must, therefore, be cared for through other procedures.

Television instruction is limited to the showing and discussion aspects of concept and skill teaching. If the student makes an error in his thinking or in the performance of a skill, the television teacher cannot modify his instruction to help the student correct his mistake. The necessary drill under supervision, essential to the perfection of a skill, is impossible in television instruction.

Because the teacher is unaware of any classroom control problems

---

[19]Harry N. Rivlin, *Teaching Adolescents in Secondary Schools*, 2d. ed. (New York: Appleton-Century-Crofts, 1961), pp. 242–246, provides a concise but perceptive discussion of the general nature and limitations of television as an educational medium.

[20]A few educational television experiments involving the oral participation of students located in a different building from the lecturer have been tried with varying degrees of success. Most television instructors, however, teach classes in which there is no possibility for student response.

The desirability of teacher-student interaction to programs viewed on television is emphasized by Finette P. Foshay, *Interaction in Learning: Implications for Television* (Washington, D.C.: Department of Audio-Visual Instruction, NEA, 1959).

during his presentation, he cannot stop his lecture to redirect the attention of the wayward or inattentive student. As a result, the regular classroom teacher must insure that the classroom climate promotes attentive viewing during such presentations.

The use of educational television is limited by the availability of facilities in the schools and by the trained staff needed to present the programs effectively. If programs are telecast from a central studio in a large school system, a great deal of expensive electronic equipment is essential. This equipment must be either controlled or supervised by technicians who usually demand sizeable salaries. Moreover, full or part-time artists are frequently employed to prepare visual materials.

Some school systems have found it necessary to reduce the nature and extent of their educational television offerings because of budgetary considerations. The cost of television instruction for small, isolated school districts precludes the possibility of its use in most cases. In large school districts with a sizeable capital investment in television facilities, even the cost of video tapes can be substantial. Such tapes, however, can be stored for further use or erased and reused at will.

Some highly effective teachers do not want to televise their presentations; others strongly object to the many hours they must spend planning and preparing materials for educational telecasts, because they feel that the time thus spent would have been better invested in conventional teaching. The most frequent complaint of television instructors, however, is that they miss the satisfaction that comes from personal contact with students. The total impersonalization of teaching an unseen audience robs many television teachers of the enthusiasm that is maintained spontaneously in the conventional classroom.

Principles Related to Teaching by Television

A number of principles related to television have found widespread acceptance[21] and are currently giving strong direction to educational practices in this relatively new area. Additional experimentation may lead to some modification of these principles.

1. Although television is a useful instructional tool, its precise role in American education has yet to be defined conclusively.
2. Educational television involves the two senses that most strongly influence the learning process—sight and hearing.
3. The coordinated teamwork of many people goes into the production, transmission, and final classroom consumption of educational television.
4. Educational television is best suited for certain kinds of teach-

[21]Basic principles that have a specific bearing on television instruction are identified and discussed by Frazier and Wigren, *op. cit.*, pp. 7–10.

ing procedures—especially demonstration and lecture—and is subject to the limitations of these procedures. Although a wide range of concept-centered subjects may be taught effectively by television, it does not provide a general solution to all learning problems.

5. All students are not equally receptive to television instruction. Because of its emphasis on showing, television may be particularly helpful to poor readers. In addition, students who find it difficult to learn from lectures may find television demonstrations vivid and stimulating.

6. All teachers are not equally suited to serving as television instructors. Only those individuals who are suited by disposition, preparation, and personal preference should be encouraged to engage in such instruction.

7. Educational television, like other instructional media, has many strengths and limitations, and its instructional effectiveness will depend upon the skill and ingenuity of the teacher who uses it.

8. The quality of television instruction may vary from teacher to teacher, from district to district, and from school to school. In order to use this medium most effectively, the teacher and the administrator should constantly seek to identify the components of quality television instruction wherever they find it. They should also keep abreast of current research on the problems of television viewing and conduct their own research comparing the effectiveness of television instruction with other types of instruction.[22]

9. Television is a means, not an end; it is one of many highly useful devices for improving education. In general, this medium should be employed only in situations where it is superior to other possible teaching procedures. The purpose of educational television is to teach with efficiency; if this goal is not achieved, another method should be sought.

10. Commercial television has a strong impact on the unstructured education of children and youth during their out-of-school hours.[23] Teachers and parents share the responsibility for determining that students make the most effective educational use of this commercial medium, which has great potential for good or harm.

Sound and Unsound Practices

Because television instruction is a relatively new field, teachers are not always acquainted with the most effective ways it can be used. Several common mistakes are reflected in the descriptive accounts below.

---

[22]The basic and continuing need for "plan-trial-evaluation" as it relates to instructional television is emphasized by Rivlin, *op. cit.*, pp. 242–243.

[23]Kimball Wiles, *Teaching for Better Schools*, 2d. ed. (Englewood Cliffs, N.J.: Prentice-Hall, 1959), p. 264, supports the assumption that television has a greater impact on boys and girls than does radio.

SUPERINTENDENT GOULD UNDERESTIMATES TECHNICAL NEEDS

Superintendent A. William Gould had always viewed himself as being in the forefront of educational progress. During the early fifties he read about exciting experiments that were being conducted with the new medium of television in some of the larger cities. Although he administered a school district of only 6000 elementary- and secondary-school students, he felt that it was mandatory that he move into the area of television instruction.

Since there was no educational television station in his state, he decided that the best use of the new medium would be to project closed-circuit programs to schools in his district. Acting on his insistent and enthusiastic requests, the school board finally agreed to provide $75,000 for the initial experiment. Although Superintendent Gould had done a great deal of reading on educational television and had visited two districts in which it was operating, he soon found that there were technical concerns to be resolved that he knew virtually nothing about.

He hired technical personnel to place the closed-circuit station in working order, but as the work progressed, he discovered the need for additional technical help. Plans for extending the coaxial cables from the high school to two elementary schools had to be abandoned in the interest of economy. It was finally decided to confine the original experiment to the high school.

Before the first pictures were projected into the high-school auditorium for student viewing, the original appropriation had been spent, and the superintendent found it necessary to explain his miscalculations to the school board and ask for additional funds.

PRINCIPAL JARMAN FINDS TEAMWORK ESSENTIAL

When Principal J. Willard Jarman disclosed his plans for the use of closed-circuit television in his high school of 2000 students, the teachers were generally enthusiastic. Their enthusiasm waned, however, as they began to encounter the hard realism of television production, even on a small scale.

They soon discovered that although the twenty-five or fifty-minute presentations were not long, each one required many hours of painstaking planning. Charts and aids had to be prepared with particular care because of the larger number of viewers, and possible teacher errors in presentation had to be identified in advance.

The necessity for functioning as a team soon became apparent. Teacher-monitors who were not on camera had to insure that students were giving the program their complete attention and that televised presentations were related to the unit. Answering questions, evaluating and recording progress, and maintaining classroom control were a part of their responsibility.

After two scheduled presentations had to be canceled because of technical difficulties, it was obvious that the engineering personnel played an essential role. Mr. Jarman finally decided that interested students with limited knowledge and backgrounds could not serve as adequate substitutes for individuals with the desired technical training.

MRS. SWINBURNE FAILS TO USE COMMERCIAL TELEVISION

Mrs. Margaret Swinburne taught high-school English in a district that, because of size and economic factors, did not have closed-circuit television.

Furthermore, reception of the one educational television station in the state was impossible. By means of a booster, however, commercial television was very good on two channels.

Although Mrs. Swinburne was an avid television viewer, she never once made an outside viewing assignment related to the course work. Shakespeare's *Macbeth, Hamlet,* and other excellent dramatic presentations were shown on commercial channels at about the same time they were being discussed in class. It was by chance alone that several students saw the shows.

A lack of knowledge about technical matters accounted for many of the initial difficulties Mr. Gould encountered in using professional and technical personnel. Mr. Jarman not only ran into technical difficulties but also faced problems of teacher cooperation. Mrs. Swinburne limited the effectiveness of her instruction because she did not use commercial programs to supplement her classroom work.

Conscientious, alert teachers who wish to keep pace with the latest educational developments have attempted to make the most effective use of television in promoting instruction. Television is most likely to be employed successfully in urban areas where closed-circuit educational programs, educational channels, and commercial telecasts provide a range of possibilities to choose from.

MR. SNARR USES MPATI PROGRAMS

Donald H. Snarr was an eleventh-grade history teacher in a large Cincinnati high school. After reading about some of the research in education, he had become fascinated with the possibilities of using television teaching. It was the opportunity for using television instruction that had made him want to teach in Cincinnati rather than in a rural district. In the city he found that he could make effective use of the lessons being telecast from aircraft flying over the area. Because of the extensive participation of schools in the region, programs of high quality and variety were frequently available. In addition, commercial channels provided a number of history-related programs, many of which were sufficiently authentic to be used as educational supplements.

Mr. Snarr used the MPATI programs frequently. He found that the written instructions prepared to enable classroom teachers to make the best use of these programs were most helpful. From the major commercial television networks he obtained a list of programs for the school year that were reported to have particular value for students of United States history. After carefully examining these lists, he selected those programs that he felt were authentic, interesting, and educational.

The well-coordinated efforts of the large number of teaching and technical personnel involved in preparing and broadcasting MPATI programs often result in productive educational tools that the classroom teacher may use as an integral part of the total classroom learning situation. Close cooperation on the part of all members of the team concerned with the preparation and presentation of television lessons for use in a single school district is also essential if success is to be achieved. This fact is illustrated in the following case.

PRINCIPAL PARKER VIEWS TELEVISION TEACHING AS TEAM EFFORT

Principal Claude W. Parker of McKinley Junior High School decided to make a team endeavor of television teaching. At Christmastime his teachers were informed that during the next school year the school district would be sending its own educational programs over coaxial cables into each of the schools and that McKinley would present programs as well as receive them.

After considerable discussion, the school board decided that for the first year the experiment would focus on ninth-grade English. All six of the ninth-grade English teachers thus became a team to work out the problems of teaching in the new medium. Throughout the second semester Mr. Parker held semiweekly meetings to analyze the content to be stressed, the aids to be employed, and the teaching presentation itself. By March 15 certain conclusions were reached:

1. Each teacher would take his turn before the camera, teaching the content he felt he could present most effectively.
2. During the ten days prior to a presentation, all teachers would serve as a team to help prepare content, make aids, and provide suggestions. The teacher who was to give the presentation would serve as team chairman.
3. Prior to the actual telecast two trial runs would be made. Two members of the team would criticize these trial runs by using a checklist and making appropriate written comments.
4. All team members would observe the actual telecast, and each teacher would rate it on a checklist.
5. All six sections of ninth-grade English (180 students) would receive television instruction at the same time. During the first semester television instruction would occupy no more than one fifth of the total instructional time. Each teacher would be responsible for teaching his particular section when they were not viewing closed-circuit television.
6. It would be highly desirable to hire a part-time employee to do lettering, charts, and other artwork that might be necessary.

At the suggestion of the teaching team, team members would be allowed to return a month early, with salary, to insure that the details of preparation would be adequately cared for.

Use of Television in Specific Subjects

The teaching of all subjects in the secondary-school curriculum can benefit from the use of television.[24] It is misleading, however, to assume that television instruction serves as an equally valuable aid for teaching all subjects.

Skill Subjects

Conceptual aspects and techniques of skill development may be presented visually. For example, it might be helpful to film the hand position and finger mechanics of a world-famous pianist for a television program. Similarly, the slow-motion performance of champion-

---

[24]A number of recent public-school practices involving the use of educational television are described in *Teaching by Television,* pp. 40–46.

ship high jumpers might provide a clear picture of how the skill is performed. The student, however, cannot develop a particular skill without practice. In addition, only through personal contact between teacher and students can the imperative needs of skill development (teaching of concept—student trial—correctional coaching—retrial—and recoaching) be met. Television alone does not permit direct contact or provide actual practice.

Concept-Centered Subjects

Those subjects that are predominantly concerned with acquiring understanding (mental pictures)—such as mathematics, physics, chemistry, biology, English grammar, and the social studies—lend themselves best to television teaching. The social studies class, for example, can learn from exposure to social phenomena, narrative accounts, historical events, and current happenings. Commercial television programs are largely concerned with this type of content. Some producers of such programs yield to the temptation for sensation, with the result that much of the content is not authentic and thus is unsuitable for instructional purposes. Under the persistent goading of educators and an alert press, however, commercial television has produced, and is continuing to produce, some programs of social and historical significance that are factually sound and interest-arousing, sometimes to its own financial disadvantage. The knowledgeable social studies teacher can use television programs effectively by carefully selecting the specific viewing assignments and by following through with related in-class discussions.

Specific Suggestions

A number of specific suggestions will help promote the effective use of television for instructional purposes.[25]

Recommendations

1. Ask commercial television stations to provide you with a list of course-related programs,[26] and make assignments that involve viewing these programs.

2. Remember that television is only one of a range of audio-visual media that can be used to further the cause of instruction.

3. Use television in combination with other needed procedures to help you reach sound educational goals.

---

[25]General recommendations for educational television program planning, for the use of television, and for making the most of television's possibilities to improve learning are discussed by Frazier and Wigren, *op. cit.*, pp. 59–76.

[26]The desirability of correlating in-class instruction with carefully selected commercial telecasts is emphasized by Wittich and Schuller, *op. cit.*, pp. 423–424.

Samuel P. Wiggens, *Successful High School Teaching* (Boston: Houghton Mifflin Company, 1958), p. 163, points out the need for making more effective use of commercial television.

4. Become thoroughly acquainted with the programs being offered by the educational television stations in your area.

5. Determine which areas in your teaching field best lend themselves to television instruction. In addition, while planning your teaching units, give specific attention to the possibility of using television for enrichment.

6. Volunteer to help produce an educational television program related to the subject you are teaching. Make arrangements for recording teaching presentations of unusual merit for future use.

7. Visit a high school in which closed-circuit educational telecasting has been used successfully for some time. Determine the feasibility of closed-circuit telecasting within your own school district if it is not currently available.

8. Identify the most successful teachers in your subject area within the school district. Inquire how they use educational television.

9. Visit the nearest educational television station with some of your professional colleagues.

10. Keep up-to-date on the research findings related to educational television.[27]

11. Make a survey of the television viewing habits of students in your classes. Determine to what extent these habits serve an educational purpose.

12. When the students are to watch a televised program, be sure a classroom teacher is supervising the viewing. Encourage intelligent reaction to what is seen through note-taking, a follow-up discussion, testing, and related problem solving.

Cautions

1. Don't neglect the use of commercial television programs in helping students achieve educational goals.

2. Don't forget that in television instruction concepts must be taught to all viewers at a fixed rate.

3. Don't attempt to appear before the television camera without adequate preparation and rehearsal.

4. Don't forget that many necessary types of instruction do not lend themselves to television presentation.

5. Don't forget that television instruction is relatively expensive when it is transmitted to a limited number of students.

6. Don't be suspicious of educational television; try it out.[28]

7. Don't forget that television instruction is limited to those procedures that can be televised.

---

[27]Harl R. Douglass (ed.), *The High School Curriculum,* 3d. ed. (New York: Ronald Press, 1964), p. 201, reports on a large-scale study involving a comparison of the effectiveness of conventional classroom procedures with television instruction.

[28]According to Chester D. Babcock, "The Teacher, TV, and Teaching Machines," *NEA Journal,* 1960 (May), *49*:30, both the teaching machine and educational television are viewed with suspicion by some teachers.

TEAM TEACHING

Team teaching, like educational television, encourages the use of teachers of particular competence for instructing large numbers of students. Both procedures claim to have effected a general improvement in instruction as well as a more efficient use of the superior teacher. School administrators have also been concerned with the most efficient use of all faculty members. They have expressed particular interest in the possibility of reaching educational goals efficiently through cooperative staff effort. As a result there have been frequent individual school experiments or experiments involving arrangements between two teachers in the pursuit of common objectives.

Development of Team Teaching

In the elementary schools two or more teachers have worked effectively together to improve instruction for several decades; the secondary schools have been much slower to see the merits of combined teacher effort. During the mid-fifties the Commission on the Experimental Study of the Utilization of the Staff in the Secondary School—established by the National Association of Secondary-School Principals and supported by the Ford Foundation—initiated a number of studies concerned with staff utilization in the secondary schools. The most prominent of these investigations involved team teaching.[29]

The concepts underlying this method are not new; one need only examine earlier plans for grouping children and providing an atmosphere for sound instruction to catch glimpses of its inception. The Lancastrian Plan, the Dalton Plan, the Winnetka Plan, Wirt's Platoon System, Hosic's Cooperative Group Plan, and finally the ungraded school contained varying traces of what has come to be known as team teaching.[30] Burton reports that

> the new development probably started in the Franklin School at Lexington, Massachusetts, in 1957, as part of the joint program of research and development sponsored by the Harvard Graduate School of Education and certain public school systems.[31]

Since that time the growth of experimentation in team teaching has attracted national attention. A large number of team teaching projects have been tried in every section of the country, and the results have been reported in professional journals. For example, the January

---

[29]Anderson and Gruhn, *op. cit.*, pp. 163–164, provide a brief history of the development of team teaching.

[30]William H. Burton, *The Guidance of Learning Activities*, 3d. ed. (New York: Appleton-Century-Crofts, 1962), p. 286.

[31]*Ibid.*, p. 286.

issues of the *National Association of Secondary-School Principals Bulletin* from 1958 through 1962 have been devoted to the review of staff utilization practices, primarily team teaching.

Definition of Team Teaching

In team teaching two or more teachers cooperatively formulate a plan, carry it out, and evaluate its effectiveness as it relates to a specific group of students. Although many varieties of teaching teams are being experimented with throughout the United States at this time, most of them have certain common features:[32]

1. Several sections, usually two to four, of a given class (ninth-grade English, for example) meet at the same hour.

2. Teachers of the respective sections usually constitute the teaching team. The librarian or a clerical person may be considered a team member and occasionally an administrator or an audio-visual specialist is also included.[33]

3. Sometimes the team leader is the one who most nearly qualifies as a master teacher. Other times there is no designated chairman, and the team members assume the leadership role depending upon their degree of involvement in large-group presentations.

4. Frequently, perhaps once or twice a week, all sections meet together for a teacher-centered presentation. Most of the time, however, they meet individually under the direction of their particular teacher.

5. When the sections meet in one large group, seating facilities other than the typical classroom are required. Sometimes the students meet in specially constructed facilities, but frequently they meet in the library, the cafeteria, or the auditorium.

6. Specific teaching presentations to the combined sections are usually made by the team member who is best qualified in terms of preparation, personality, and preference. Teachers are thus given the opportunity to capitalize on their strengths and avoid embarrassment in their weak areas.

7. In each individual section teachers are free to use whatever methods they wish, as long as the methods are appropriate to the goals sought. Usually there is a close relationship between the content covered in the large and in the small groups.

---

[32]Gail M. Inlow, *Maturity in High School Teaching* (Englewood Cliffs, N.J.: Prentice-Hall, 1963), pp. 116–117, provides a helpful description of the characteristics of team teaching.

Another helpful discussion of team teaching can be found in J. Lloyd Trump, *Images of the Future: A New Approach to the Secondary School* (Urbana, Illinois: Commission on the Experimental Study of the Utilization of the Staff in the Secondary School, 1959), pp. 5–33.

[33]B. J. Chandler, Lindley J. Stiles, and John I. Kitsuse (eds.) *Education in Urban Society* (New York: Dodd, Mead, 1962), p. 172, prefer the term *instructional team,* since it covers team members who do not actually teach.

8. Planning for team teaching is frequently carried out under the direction of the team leader during a period set aside for this purpose. Such planning may be a joint responsibility, or it may be delegated to a single member of the team, depending upon specific needs.

9. Special materials and audio-visual devices are used extensively, especially during the large-group presentations.

Current Variations in Team Teaching Methods

A look at several current team teaching practices will indicate their similarities as well as their differences.[34]

Team Teachers in the Same Subject

In the Alfred Plant Junior High School in West Hartford, Connecticut, a number of teachers of general science have teamed their efforts to achieve more effective instruction through the joint planning and teaching of specific topics.[35] This arrangement is particularly advantageous in general science, because one teacher usually cannot claim mastery of all the areas of specialization. Classes taught by members of the science team are scheduled for the same period of the day, thus permitting large-group instruction when desired. Movies, demonstrations, and resource speakers of particular value can be presented to the combined groups. Team members plan their work together, and help is frequently obtained from the librarian and the audio-visual director of the school.

Students Grouped by Programs

The Claremont, California, Teaching Team Program involves five distinct groups of individuals – student teams, faculty teams, team leaders, teaching aides, and talented citizens of the community.[36] Student teams consist of 90 – 180 students enrolled in similar programs – college preparatory program, general program, or vocational program. Each student team is assigned to a faculty team made up of three to six competent teachers, each of whom represents a different subject area. Student teams meet in one large group or in several small groups, depending on the instructional plans of the faculty team. Faculty team members have the same conference period each day. An elected or appointed team leader assumes responsibility for the efficient operation of his team and is given an additional free period

---

[34]Several helpful examples of types of teaching teams are provided by Anderson and Gruhn, *op. cit.*, pp. 164 – 167.

The diverse nature of teaching teams is emphasized in descriptive accounts of specific teams presented by J. Lloyd Trump and Dorsey Baynham, *Focus on Change: Guide to Better Schools* (Chicago: Rand McNally, 1961), pp. 83 – 86.

[35]Anderson and Gruhn, *op. cit.*, pp. 164 – 165.

[36]John A. Brownell, *The Claremont Teaching Team Program* (Claremont, Calif.: Claremont Graduate School, 1961), pp. 4 – 31.

as well as additional pay. Each team is assigned a teaching aide[37] who performs clerical duties (typing, filing, duplicating, taking attendance, etc.) and takes care of other routine aspects of teaching, such as correcting tests, supervising study, and marking themes. Talented citizens of the community who are particularly competent in artistic, intellectual, or vocational pursuits are invited to meet with team students to help enliven instruction and provide a clearer understanding of the relationship of school work to everyday life.

Sections Grouped for Instruction

A marked departure from the typical team teaching approach is represented by the experiment of three Corvalis, Oregon, high-school teachers.[38] Outside resource speakers were used to introduce several major areas of a course in "Problems of American Democracy" to large student groups, usually consisting of fifteen combined sections. Student acceptance of the different resource speakers varied. One of the speakers, a professor, took twenty-five of the students to the auditorium platform where they served as participating members of a small class. The student responses as well as the comments of the professor were broadcast to the student audience of 250.

Team Teaching with Flexible Schedules

The Wayland, Massachusetts, High School team teaching project uses several experimental practices.[39] Instructional groups, for example, do not always meet at the same time each day; a flexible weekly schedule is used instead of a daily schedule.

After a thorough self-appraisal, the teachers decide upon their individual roles within the teaching teams. Prior arrangements are made with nearby universities to use teaching and nonteaching interns to carry out instruction-related tasks. Lay individuals are employed to handle clerical tasks and other routine procedures.

The courses are organized in different ways depending upon the nature of the subject. Some, such as typing, are taught only in large-group sessions; others, such as science and language laboratories, meet only in small groups. Large-group lessons form an important segment of the total week's instruction, and small groups allow more personal interaction. Approximately 50 per cent of the teacher's weekly schedule is devoted to teaching small groups, and about 20 per cent of the students' time is spent in small-group sessions.[40]

---

[37]Trump and Baynham, *op. cit.*, pp. 80–83, explain how teaching assistants can be used in several instructional situations.

[38]Burton, *op. cit.*, pp. 286–287.

[39]William M. Griffin, "Some Ideas and New Patterns at Wayland, Massachusetts, High School," *National Association of Secondary-School Principals Bulletin*, 1962 (Jan.), *46*:123–126.

[40]According to Trump, *Images of the Future*, p. 9, about 40 per cent of the student's time should be spent in large-group instruction, about 20 per cent in small-group instruction, and about 40 per cent in individual study.

Team members share the responsibility for teaching the large groups, an arrangement quite different from the master-teacher approach that uses only one instructor to teach the large groups.

The individual teacher's total work time is divided between classroom teaching (about two thirds) and school-related, nonteaching responsibilities (one third). Students, similarly, spend about two thirds of their time in classroom instruction and about one third in school-related supportive roles, such as library study, teacher-student conferences, and projects in the art center.

Rotating Schedule

Use of team teaching with a rotating class schedule is described in an account of the Hurricane, Utah, High School staff utilization project:[41]

> A rotation system was worked out so the teacher could prepare a unit of work in his special field [a previously designated area in language arts] which could be taught in about seven or eight weeks. He could then teach this unit the entire year, seven or eight weeks to each of five groups.
>
> When the teacher had only one eight-week unit to prepare, it made it possible to save a great deal of teacher preparation time and still give the teacher an opportunity to make a more thorough preparation than if he had to prepare five such units during the year.

Advantages of Team Teaching

Advocates of team teaching strongly believe that students taught by this method do as well as, and in some cases better than, students taught by the usual classroom method.[42] These supporters point out that team teaching has several basic advantages over the conventional teaching system using individual classroom teachers.[43]

1. Teaching teams can be organized in a number of different ways to meet the needs of the particular school and the course content.[44] Certain content may best be learned through a teacher-centered approach in a large-group situation;[45] other content may be learned most

---

[41]Matthew F. Noall and Maurice Nuttall, "Hurricane, Utah, High School Ungraded English Project," *National Association of Secondary-School Principals Bulletin,* 1962 (Jan.), *46*:187–188.

[42]Alvin C. Eurich, "Some Expendable Shibboleths," *Improving College and University Teaching,* 1961 (Spring), 9.

[43]Specific advantages of team teaching are discussed by Laurence D. Haskew and Jonathon C. McLendon, *This Is Teaching,* rev. ed. (Chicago: Scott, Foresman and Company, 1962), pp. 189–190.

Basic advantages of team teaching are also identified by Anderson and Gruhn, *op. cit.,* p. 164.

Inlow, *op. cit.,* pp. 119–120, includes eight advantages of team teaching as well as twelve disadvantages.

[44]Luvern L. Cunningham, "Keys to Team Teaching," *Overview,* 1960 (Oct.), *1*:54–55.

[45]The nature and values of large-group instruction are discussed by Trump and Baynham, *op. cit.,* pp. 74–77.

H. L. Slichenmyer, "Summary of the Presentation Made on Team Teaching,"

effectively through interaction among students and teacher[46] or through individual study.

2. Individual students learn differently in groups of varying sizes; and team teaching, which usually provides for instruction in both large and small groups, can meet these individual student differences better than the usual classroom system.

3. The large-group instruction in team teaching gives both students and teachers a welcome break from the monotony of conventional small-group instruction.

4. Large-group sessions enable more students to benefit from instruction by the most skilled teachers.

5. Under team teaching students can beneficially be exposed to teachers with varying backgrounds and different areas of specialization.

6. When noncertified personnel and clerical aides are part of the team, the experienced teachers can be freed of nonprofessional, time-consuming tasks.[47]

7. Because team members must plan carefully and have the time in which to do so, the quality of instruction possible in a team project is often better than that possible in conventional classroom instruction. Team teaching also permits flexibility in organizing the teacher's time.

8. Team teaching provides the setting for more effective student participation in the teaching-learning process by means of small-group instruction. Under this sytem, students usually are given greater opportunity for self-directed study and independent research.

9. The content of different subjects may be coordinated more effectively in a team program than in a system where individual subjects are always taught in separate classes.

10. Team teaching allows for more efficient and economical use of building space and teacher personnel.[48] Seldom-used auditoriums as well as small offices may be used to advantage, and team teachers not involved in actual instruction may spend a larger portion of their time on necessary nonteaching responsibilities.

Limitations of Team Teaching

Although team teaching has grown dramatically since the late fifties, it poses no real threat to the existence of the one-teacher classroom. Proponents of team teaching are quick to point out its strengths,

---

National Association of Secondary-School Principals Bulletin, 1960 (April), *44*:7–8, identifies situations in which large-group instruction can be used advantageously.

[46]Trump and Baynham, *op. cit.*, pp. 78–80, explore the practical advantages of small-group discussion in specific teaching situations.

[47]Rivlin, *op. cit.*, p. 449, cautions that teachers' assistants can improve secondary education only if they are used wisely.

[48]*Ibid.*, p. 449, reminds us that "the most important justification for team teaching is not economy, but the possibilities it offers for improving the quality of education."

but its opponents are just as quick to identify its limitations. Some of these limitations are listed here.

1. Many teachers are not suited by training or disposition to engage in the cooperative planning and varied use of procedures, resources, and personnel that are essential in team teaching. In fact, it is often maintained that if a teacher is thoroughly competent in teaching his particular subject, team teaching is not necessary.

Some administrators—wishing to appear progressive—encourage faculty members to engage in team teaching although they may possess little inclination or aptitude for it. Members of a teaching team must possess special characteristics, and the variety essential to this type of teaching often taxes their ingenuity.

2. Team teaching calls for the use of special physical facilities. If these facilities are not available, they must be provided at considerable expense to the school district. Many older schools simply do not have the large rooms that are necessary for many team teaching situations.

3. Special planning periods must be scheduled at a time when all team members can meet. In order to make such meetings possible, the administrator sometimes must ask for concessions for team members or impose restrictions on nonteam members.

4. The per-student cost of team teaching is sometimes higher than the per-student cost of conventional teaching, because many teams are comprised of nonprofessional aides, para-professionals, and clerical assistants in addition to full-time certified teachers.

5. The necessary impersonality of large-group instruction hampers the emotional, social, and academic progress of certain students who need consistent, individual contact with their teachers. Team teachers seldom become well-enough acquainted with the individual students in the large group to be able to meet their needs effectively.

6. Planning essential to productive team teaching often becomes unduly complicated; the end result may not justify the expenditure of professional time and energy. If individualized instruction and instruction in both the small and large groups is not planned with great care, team teaching may be less effective than traditional classroom instruction.

Principles Related to Team Teaching

Examination of team teaching projects reported in professional literature reveals common principles basic to all projects. A number of these principles are listed below.

1. The chief purpose of team teaching is to improve the quality of instruction and learning by using the school staff as efficiently as possible.

2. The effectiveness of team teaching largely depends upon the

variety of strengths of individual team members[49] and their ability to work together as a group. Team teaching permits teachers to capitalize on their particular strengths and to minimize their weaknesses.

3. Team teaching requires cooperative planning and capitalizes on group thinking.

4. Certain types of information lend themselves to different methods of teaching—independent study, small groups, or large groups.

5. In order to serve the needs of different instructional situations, teaching teams can be organized to teach the same subject to combined groups, to cross subject-matter boundaries, to take advantage of unique facilities and individuals within a community, or to individualize instruction as dictated by student needs.

6. Team teaching has inherent instructional flexibility possessed by no other teaching method. It may employ all types of audio-visual media, including television; a range of different teachers, each presenting the lesson he teaches best; and small or large blocks of time in teaching small or large groups of students.

7. Although team teaching may be used with marked success in one school, it may fail in another for several reasons: inability of teachers to plan effectively as a team, lack of interest on the part of the team members or the administrator, unrealistic expectations about team operation, insufficient time or space for planning, domination of team effort by one or more members of the team, or wrong team membership in view of instructional objectives.

8. Successful team teaching presupposes the team members' willingness to experiment and the availability of classrooms of varied sizes, conference rooms,[50] and a range of audio-visual aids.

Sound and Unsound Practices

Effective team teaching does not happen by chance; it is the result of careful planning. In team teaching the various segments of instruction taught by different participants have to be correlated. What happens when team teaching is not thoroughly planned is illustrated in the following examples.

THREE TEAM TEACHERS UNDERESTIMATE THE JOB

In February, Principal Ewell asked for volunteers to participate in the twelfth-grade English team experiment to begin the following year. Mrs.

---

[49]Robert C. McKean, *Principles and Methods in Secondary Education* (Columbus, Ohio: Charles E. Merrill Books, Inc., 1962), p. 115, stresses the advantages of using the team members' special skills.

[50]Walter L. Cooper, "J. Sterling Morton High School and Junior College, Cicero, Illinois, Uses Tapes, Language Laboratories, and Team Teaching," *National Association of Secondary-School Principals Bulletin,* 1961 (Jan.), *45*:79–84, points out the necessity for using a wide range of school facilities in team teaching.

Bertha Smythe, Miss Bonnie Ruff, and Mr. Bertrand Diamond, three of the ten twelfth-grade English teachers, volunteered. Each teacher had three or more years of successful experience and appeared eager to try out the new procedure.

Mr. Diamond, the senior member of the team, was appointed chairman. Because the teachers assumed it was not necessary to rework units they had taught successfully before, they decided that planning could be deferred until one week before school started, when they would devote full time to the task. When school opened, the team members were still attempting to think through the methodological implications of team teaching. The principal set aside time for a common planning session in which the teachers could meet together three times each week. Large-group instruction for eighty-five students (three sections) was scheduled for twice each week.

The three team teachers soon found themselves planning and teaching on a day-to-day basis, hoping that somehow they would be able to reap some of the benefits of team teaching. In their insecurity they reverted to the traditional procedures in which they had confidence; unit planning geared to team teaching and utilizing the special abilities of team members was largely overlooked. Mr. Diamond, a dominant personality, assigned himself the major responsibility for teaching the large combined group, and the other team members yielded submissively.

TEAM TEACHING SUCCESS IS NOT PROVEN

For three years Wilkins Senior High School boasted of their team teaching program. The principal and team members, as well as the students themselves, seemed to take great pride in this new approach until the new assistant superintendent asked for objective evidence of the advantages of team teaching over traditional teaching. To his great embarrassment, the principal found it necessary to explain that the project had not been structured so that specific, verifiable conclusions could be drawn.

The useful involvement of the administrator, librarian, and school secretary, as well as regular team members, is portrayed in the following account.

NON-TEACHERS ARE MEMBERS OF A TEACHING TEAM

James Underwood, principal of Bryan Junior High School, strongly felt that a team approach might improve the quality of instruction in his eighth-grade English and history classes. After contacting the state Department of Education, he discovered that foundation money might be made available for such a team project if it were structured within certain limits. He consulted with the state representative of the foundation on several occasions before an acceptable project design was evolved. When the project was finally accepted, the foundation provided funds for (a) paying team teachers during workshops before and after the school year, (b) hiring a university curriculum consultant and a statistician, (c) buying certain needed audio-visual materials, and (d) purchasing standardized tests.

Because the school was small (300 students), all four eighth-grade teachers of English and social studies were invited to participate as members of the team. Because of his intense interest, the principal was frequently involved in team planning sessions. The librarian also met regularly with the four teachers, and the front office secretary gave clerical assistance whenever it was requested.

In the pre-school workshop, which began two weeks before the opening of school, the university consultant helped the teachers think through the type of planning most appropriate to the students and the content being taught. Specific ideas gradually took form:

1. Team teaching would consist of large-group instruction in which all sections (103 students) would participate as often as desirable. The auditorium would be available for their use at virtually all times.

2. Four small groups (sections consisting of approximately twenty-five students each) would meet under the direction of individual teachers. Students in individual sections would be grouped homogeneously on the basis of recorded I.Q. and past achievement.

3. Two eighth-grade subjects, English and United States history, would be correlated where possible and practical to lend added meaning to content.

4. Units correlating the two subjects would be worked out in rough form by team members during the daily planning periods. Each unit would be further refined by the librarian and then sent to the university consultant for his criticism. Necessary clerical work would be taken care of by the front office secretary under the direction of the librarian.

5. Audio-visual aids and resource persons in the community would be used extensively. The district superintendent promised to buy an overhead projector and a machine that would produce cell overlays quickly. A special room in the library would serve as a curriculum workroom and an audio-visual repository under the direction of the librarian. The art teacher and certain of his students would be asked to assist in producing special aids.

6. The university consultant would visit the school once each month for a two-hour conference with team teachers. It was decided that the meeting was not to be planned in advance but was to serve the immediate concerns of team members.

7. The two team members with English teaching majors had minors in history and sociology, respectively. The two teachers with history teaching majors had minors in English and journalism, respectively. The team members decided to capitalize on their areas of specialization and particular interest. One of the English teachers loved to make dramatic presentations of literary selections; she was to plan such a presentation for the large-group session. One history teacher had accumulated a number of slides of the battle sites of the Revolutionary War. He would develop, with the English teacher, a unit correlating the literature of this period with its historical content.

8. Evaluation procedures would consist of the following: (a) Students would be given standardized achievement tests in English and United States history at the beginning and end of the school year; both individual and average gains would be recorded. The same achievement tests would be administered to comparable eighth-grade students in two other schools of an adjacent school district; meaningful statistical comparisons could thus be made by a competent statistician. (b) Twice during the school year, once in November and again in May, students would indicate in written form their likes and dislikes of team teaching. (c) Parents would also be asked to react twice. (d) Teachers would be interviewed individually by the university consultant

during late October and again in May to determine their problems as well as their likes and dislikes of the program. (e) At the end of each unit team members would write a brief critique of the unit—and the teachers' criticisms would then be filed away for possible modification and use as a resource for the second year of the project.

At the end of the first year of team teaching, Principal Underwood could point with pride to the objective evidence of substantial student gains in subject-matter achievement in both history and English. Furthermore, his students had made somewhat better achievement scores than the students in the two control schools. Teachers, parents, and students were in general agreement that team teaching was an effective and interesting procedure.

Specific Suggestions

Although the newcomer to team teaching is apt to need particular guidance, both the inexperienced and experienced teacher may receive helpful direction from the following suggestions.

Recommendations

1. Prepare thoroughly before engaging in team teaching; be sure that the other team members also plan carefully.[51]

2. Select team members who possess specific qualities that contribute to team effort as well as to general instructional competence. Team teaching can only be as effective as the quality of the team members permits it to be.

3. Become informed on the current projects involving team teaching that are being tried throughout the nation.

4. During the planning phase of each unit identify the precise role each member of the teaching team is to play.

5. Make sure that the psychological principles of learning are not violated during large-group lectures.

6. Make sure that the necessary personal contact between team teacher and individual student is maintained in spite of large-group instruction.

7. Work for consistent improvement in team teaching even after one or two experimental years have been completed.

8. Be sure that the design for team teaching makes it possible to arrive at verifiable conclusions about its success or lack of success. Work out procedures for evaluating the efficiency of all aspects of team teaching.

Cautions

1. Don't assume that educational achievements are unimportant because they cannot be tested by paper-and-pencil tests. Student interest, teacher-student relationships, and appreciation for the sub-

---

[51]Inlow, *op. cit.*, p. 119, points out that team teaching makes definite demands on teachers.

ject—all of which may be positively affected by team teaching—are important educational gains that do not lend themselves readily to objective measurement.

2. Don't assume that all instructional experts are proponents of team teaching. Remember that the current evaluation of team teaching frequently is based on personal opinion.

3. Don't launch into an extensive program of team teaching unless the first experimental efforts prove to be unusually rewarding.

TELEVISION AND TEAM TEACHING IN REVIEW

Both educational television and team teaching have had a marked impact on instructional procedures and pupil learning since World War II. Educators have engaged in repeated experiments to determine how these tools can best be employed in instruction. Although educational television and team teaching are now established devices, all signs point to a continuation of testing in a search for their most effective use.

Because educational television makes use of both sight and sound, it can present natural phenomena and current events to the learners. Many school systems have employed educational television extensively, while others have used it only on a limited scale. Four major types of television facilities can be employed in education: (1) educational television stations, (2) commercial network educational programing, (3) closed-circuit production, and (4) low-power transmission by local commercial stations over UHF channels.

Team teaching consists of instructional procedures in which two or more teachers cooperatively work out a plan, carry it out, and evaluate its effectiveness as it relates to a specific group of students. Although many varieties of teaching teams are being experimented with, most such projects include large-group instruction under the direction of a team member, frequently a master teacher; small-group discussions in which each team member directs one group; special building and audio-visual facilities; and cooperative planning sessions at a specifically designated hour.

PROBLEMS FOR STUDY AND DISCUSSION

1. Identify and discuss briefly at least five major advantages of television instruction.

2. Identify and discuss at least five disadvantages of television instruction.

3. Give a one-paragraph description of the Hagerstown, Maryland, educational television experiment.

4. How is commercial television currently being employed for educational purposes?

5. What are the unique features of the MPATI program?

6. Discuss the nature of the programing on the educational television stations in your state.

7. What is closed-circuit television? What are its specific advantages?

8. List the specific ways television could best be used in your subject-matter area.

9. Why do some teachers view educational television with suspicion?

10. List the steps an administrator and teachers should take in preparing a presentation for closed-circuit television.

11. What advantages does the classroom teacher have over the television instructor? Explain.

12. Why is it impossible to teach skills effectively by means of television?

13. Make eight key recommendations that would be of particular value to a new teacher anxious to use television effectively.

14. Identify five characteristics typical of all team teaching projects.

15. How do you account for the many types of team teaching programs?

16. What role has the National Association of Secondary-School Principals played in furthering the cause of team teaching?

17. Briefly describe the unique features of the team teaching projects in each of the following schools: Franklin School, Lexington, Massachusetts; Corvalis, Oregon, High School; Hurricane, Utah, High School.

18. List six important principles underlying team teaching.

19. Through reading and inquiry determine what team teaching projects are currently being conducted in your state. Describe one of these projects in detail.

20. List and discuss briefly five reasons why your teaching major would or would not lend itself well to team teaching.

RECOMMENDED READINGS

Television Instruction

Anderson, Vernon E., and William T. Gruhn, *Principles and Practices of Secondary Education*, 2d. ed. New York: Ronald Press, 1962, pp. 187–188.

Babcock, Chester D., "The Teacher, TV, and Teaching Machines," *NEA Journal*, 1960 (May), *49*:30–31.

Burns, John L., "The Promise of Classroom Television," *Reader's Digest*, 1960 (November), *7*:125–129.

Chandler, B. J., Lindley J. Stiles, and John I. Kitsuse (eds.), *Education in Urban Society*. New York: Dodd, Mead and Company, 1962, pp. 174–175.

Chapman, Dave, *Design for ETV: Planning for Schools with Television*. New York: Educational Facilities Laboratories, 1960, pp. 21–46.

Douglass, Harl R. (ed.), *The High School Curriculum*, 3d. ed. New York: Ronald Press, 1964, p. 201.

Frazier, Alexander, and Harold E. Wigren (eds.), *Opportunities for Learning: Guidelines for Television* (A report of a seminar held at NEA headquarters, May 16–18, 1959). Washington, D.C.: Department of Audio-Visual Instruction, NEA, 1960, pp. 7–10.

Grambs, Jean D., William J. Iverson, and Franklin K. Patterson, *Modern Methods in Secondary Education,* rev. ed. New York: The Dryden Press, 1958, pp. 176–178.

Klausmeier, Herbert J., *Teaching in the Secondary School.* New York: Harper & Brothers, 1958, pp. 303–305.

Kurtz, E. B., *Pioneering in Educational Television, 1932–1939.* Iowa City: The State University of Iowa, 1959, pp. 1–164.

McKean, Robert C., *Principles and Methods in Secondary Education.* Columbus, Ohio: Charles E. Merrill Books, Inc., 1962, pp. 113–114.

Rivlin, Harry N., *Teaching Adolescents in Secondary Schools,* 2d. ed. New York: Appleton-Century-Crofts, Inc., 1961, pp. 242–246.

Teaching by Television (A Report from the Ford Foundation and the Fund for the Advancement of Education), 2d. ed. New York: The Ford Foundation, 1961, pp. 1–79.

Television Project Report from San Jose State College, San Jose, California: Instructional Closed Circuit Television—Installation, Operation, and Potential (Pictorial Report Number 1), September 1958, pp. 2–31.

Wentworth, John W., "Television in the Classroom" (mimeographed paper presented at the School Board Institute of the Pennsylvania School Study Council, University Park, Pennsylvania, March 22, 1961), pp. 1–16.

Wiggins, Samuel P., *Successful High School Teaching.* Boston: Houghton Mifflin Company, 1958, pp. 162–163.

Wiles, Kimball, *Teaching for Better Schools,* 2d. ed. Englewood Cliffs, N.J.: Prentice-Hall, Inc., 1959, p. 264.

Wittich, Walter A., and Charles F. Schuller, *Audiovisual Materials: Their Nature and Use,* 3d. ed. New York: Harper & Brothers, 1962, Chapter 14.

Team Teaching

Anderson, Robert H., and Donald P. Mitchell, "Team Teaching, New Learning Concepts Demand Changes in School Plant Design," *Nations Schools,* 1960 (June), 65:75–82.

Anderson, Vernon E., and William T. Gruhn, *Principles and Practices of Secondary Education,* 2d. ed. New York: Ronald Press, 1962, pp. 163–167.

Bloomenshine, Lee L., and T. Malcomb Brown, "San Diego, California, Conducts Two-Year Experiment with Team Teaching," *National Association of Secondary-School Principals Bulletin,* 1961 (January), *45:*146–166.

Brownell, John A., *The Claremont Teaching Team Program,* Claremont, California: Claremont Graduate School, 1961, pp. 4–31.

National Association of Secondary-School Principals Bulletin, Vols. 42–46, 1958–1962, January issues only.

Burton, William H., *The Guidance of Learning Activities,* 3d. ed., New York: Appleton-Century-Crofts, Inc., 1962, pp. 285–287.

Bush, Robert N., "Team Teaching Bandwagon," *California Journal of Secondary Education,* 1960 (April), *35:*207–208.

Chandler, B. J., Lindley J. Stiles, and John I. Kitsuse (eds.), *Education in Urban Society.* New York: Dodd, Mead and Company, 1962, pp. 172–173.

Cooper, Walter L., "J. Sterling Morton High School and Junior College, Cicero, Illinois, Uses Tapes, Language Laboratories, and Team Teaching," *National Association of Secondary-School Principals Bulletin,* 1961 (January), *45:*79–84.

Cunningham, Luvern L., "Keys to Team Teaching," *Overview* 1960 (October), *1*:54 –55.

Eurich, Alvin C., "Some Expendable Shibboleths," *Improving College and University Teaching,* 1961 (Spring), 9.

Haskew, Laurence D., and Jonathon C. McLendon, *This is Teaching,* rev. ed. Chicago: Scott, Foresman and Company, 1962, pp. 189 – 190.

Inlow, Gail M., *Maturity in High School Teaching.* Englewood Cliffs, N.J.: Prentice-Hall, Inc., 1963, pp. 116 – 121.

McKean, Robert C., *Principles and Methods in Secondary Education.* Columbus, Ohio: Charles E. Merrill Books, Inc., 1962, pp. 115 – 116.

Noall, Matthew F., and Gale Rose, "Team Teaching at the Wahlquist Junior High School, Weber County, Utah," *National Association of Secondary-School Principals Bulletin,* 1960 (May), *44*:164 – 171.

Nordberg, H. Orville, James M. Bradfield, and William C. Odell, *Secondary School Teaching.* New York: The Macmillan Company, 1962, pp. 151 – 153.

Rivlin, Harry N., *Teaching Adolescents in Secondary Schools,* 2d. ed. New York: Appleton-Century-Crofts, Inc., 1961, pp. 448 – 449.

Slichenmyer, H. L., "Summary of the Presentation Made on Team Teaching," *National Association of Secondary-School Principals Bulletin,* 1960 (April), *44*:6 – 7.

"Team-Taught Biology Students at Wausau High Measure Up to Control Group in Achievement," *The Wisconsin Improvement Program Reporter,* 1963 (May), *4*:1 – 5.

Trump, J. Lloyd, and Dorsey Baynham, *Focus on Change: Guide to Better Schools.* Chicago: Rand McNally and Company, 1961, pp. 1 – 147.

Trump, J. Lloyd, *Images of the Future: A New Approach to the Secondary School.* Urbana, Illinois: Commission on the Experimental Study of the Utilization of the Staff in the Secondary School, 1959, pp. 5 – 33.

20

Housing a Modern Secondary School

The preceding chapters have been largely devoted to the examination of learning principles, effective planning, and specific techniques in order to provide the teacher with an understanding of the teaching-learning process. But it is also essential that the teacher understand the role of the school plant in aiding instruction. This chapter attempts to clarify the relationship of effective teaching to modern school housing.

The frequent opposition to desirable school housing is a puzzling paradox, since the positive correlation between effective instruction and adequate school buildings is rarely contested by careful observers.[1] Secondary-school students, who typically spend from six to eight hours of each school day in or on school property, are entitled to a physical environment that promotes maximum learning, and it is difficult to divorce the building and classroom facilities from the learning process. Global geography, for example, cannot be taught meaningfully without maps and special arrangements for caring for these and other aids; homemaking concepts cannot be presented effectively in the absence of an environment similar to the modern home; and a physical education program cannot be conducted successfully in cramped quarters with inadequate equipment and facilities.

Responsible educators, teachers, and administrators need to marshal their forces in an intelligent effort to provide the instructional

[1]*Planning America's School Buildings* (Washington, D.C.: American Association of School Administrators, 1960), Chapter 1, presents a forward-looking discussion of the needs for functional school housing.

environment in which students may make optimum progress. To do less is to give evidence of irresponsibility and a lack of understanding of what modern education entails.

PRINCIPLES RELATED TO SCHOOL HOUSING

The administrator or school architect often asks teachers to help in planning or improving the classroom and other plant facilities. Thus the analysis of a number of the principles related to school housing should benefit every teacher.[2]

1. The basic question concerning the school plant is its educational adequacy, for the "school plant exists to facilitate instruction."[3] Planning for a new school building must, therefore, begin with educational specifications.

2. School construction should provide for the most effective instructional practices in each area of the curriculum. Each classroom should thus be planned according to the functions to be performed there.[4]

3. Because effective instruction requires a wide range of procedures, materials, and facilities, the school plant should be designed to encourage needed variety.

4. Those responsible for planning a school plant should be acquainted with recent special teaching techniques that make certain instructional facilities highly desirable.[5] For example, the modern, adequately equipped secondary school will provide the space and electronic equipment necessary for the operation of television sets, teaching machines, and a wide range of other devices.

5. School housing should reflect the attempt to meet the physical, mental, social, and emotional needs of individual students.

6. The equipment and furnishings of a school should be planned with the same care as the building itself.

7. Auxiliary facilities—library, auditorium, gymnasium, cafeteria, health units, multiple-purpose rooms, administration facilities, and storage facilities—should also be carefully designed.[6]

8. Only an informed and understanding public is willing to provide the financial support necessary for the operation of a sound and

---

[2]A simplified, thought-provoking list of principles related to school housing is provided by Jon S. Peters (ed.), *Planning Tomorrow's Secondary Schools* (Stanford, Calif.: Stanford University School Planning Laboratory, 1954), pp. 1–46.

[3]*Ibid.*, pp. 28–30, expands on this point.

[4]Glen F. Ovard, "It's Time to Plan Academic Classrooms," *American School Board Journal*, 1962 (Jan.), *144*: 26, makes a strong plea for academic classrooms.

[5]*Profiles of Significant Schools: Schools for Team Teaching* (New York: Educational Facilities Laboratories, 1961), pp. 32–35, provides drawings and descriptions of a junior high school designed for team teaching.

[6]J. Cecil Parker, T. Bentley Edwards, and William Stegeman, *Curriculum in America* (New York: Thomas Y. Crowell Company, 1962), p. 13, present an optimistic picture of the wide-ranging auxiliary features in the school of the future.

modern instructional program.[7] Moreover, school planning calls for cooperative effort by members of the community and the school personnel.[8]

9. The school plant should be planned to make long-range economies possible without limiting the instructional program. School buildings should thus be designed so that anticipated changes can be made with minimum expenditures. Often economic considerations take precedence over long-range judgment in determining whether to remodel an existing school plant or build a new structure.

10. School planners need the freedom to plan for educational programs instead of for construction schedules.[9]

11. Modern schools should be constructed to provide adequate maintenance and operation at minimum expense.

12. School buildings need to be re-evaluated at frequent intervals to determine how adequately they serve the needs of instruction.

13. Unused, nonfunctioning facilities are of no value in the school plant.

INDIVIDUAL DIFFERENCES AND SCHOOL HOUSING

Because school housing affects instruction, it should be designed to meet the individual needs of the students.

Facilities for Exceptional Students

Intellectual differences in students require various teaching facilities. Bright youngsters who have a marked capacity for self-direction will find it particularly advantageous to have carrels in which they may independently pursue their studies.[10] Less gifted students, however, may find it more helpful to have small rooms in which they may be brought together for discussion and clarification of their common problems.

Gifted students may elect to take difficult, challenging courses such as calculus or quantum physics. Such classes are often considerably smaller than conventional classes and can be taught with success in smaller classrooms. Slow learners and retarded students are often grouped in small classes where the teacher-pupil ratio is low. Be-

---

[7]Walter McQuade (ed.), *Schoolhouse* (New York: Simon and Schuster, 1958), Chapter 6, discusses the problems involved in convincing the community of the need for supporting a school housing program.

[8]*Planning America's School Buildings*, pp. 88–89, includes a discussion of the role of lay individuals in school planning.

[9]The necessity for focusing central attention on the academic program instead of on the construction schedule is emphasized by Peters, *op. cit.*, p. 44.

[10]Progressive ideas on providing the best in learning space for gifted children are put forth in "Classrooms for the Gifted," *Educational Executives' Overview*, 1962 (May), 3: 50–51.

cause these students have a short attention span and require extensive use of special materials and equipment, the classroom should provide space for adequate student movement.

Special Physical Education Facilities

Secondary schools try to provide for as many physical education activities as possible in order to meet the differing needs, interests, and capacities of students. In a large school the range of physical education activities may include wrestling, badminton, tennis, swimming, and dancing in addition to more common sports such as football and basketball. These activities demand various outdoor and indoor facilities as well as a large variety of equipment. Some schools, however, allot a disproportionate share of the school plant budget to the athletic facilities.

Guidance Facilities

Guidance-minded school planners have given deserved attention to facilities specifically for professional counseling. Well-equipped secondary schools frequently have small counseling rooms where professionally trained counselors may discuss problems with students in a friendly and comfortable, yet private, atmosphere. Matters of common concern to an average-size group or to the total student body may call for using a classroom or the school auditorium. A substantial proportion of new schools provide glass-paneled offices for teachers where private conferences may be held as needed. When such offices are a part or an extension of the classroom, the teacher can observe the behavior of class members while holding a private conference.

Recreational Facilities

The differing social needs of students have led to a number of innovations in the school's physical plant. No longer is the gymnasium assumed to meet the recreational needs of all students. The rotunda and foyer of the building, with their terrazzo floors, might provide a central location for lunchtime dancing. Game rooms are sometimes made available to students before and after school for such games as checkers, chess, or table tennis. Picnics may be held in outdoor recreational areas, and concerts and even dramatic productions may be performed outside when weather and climatic conditions permit.

HOUSING NEEDS AND TEACHING TECHNIQUES

The success of each teaching technique depends in some measure upon the physical facilities of classrooms and the school plant. Teachers, therefore, are justified in taking a personal interest in classroom size, shape, and equipment, and they should be consulted about their instructional desires while the building is still in the planning stage. Specific procedures and the physical plant facilities they require are discussed below.

Lecture and Discussion

By its very nature a lecture has certain limitations. The use of proper equipment and housing, however, tends to offset these limitations. Lecturing to a large audience, for example, is made much easier through the use of a loudspeaker, and few auditoriums today are not so equipped. Small-group discussion, on the other hand, is carried out best in a small room, where a relaxed atmosphere facilitates communication. Rooms of varying sizes with different types of desired equipment are often found in modern schools.

The use of aids to add interest and meaning to lectures requires storage space for maps, charts, and projection equipment. When such space is lacking, equipment is frequently injured or lost, and teachers rationalize that, under the circumstances, they are justified in not using aids at all.

Demonstration

Most types of demonstrations require a table on which equipment or display items may be placed. If demonstration is a frequent method, as in physical and biological science courses, it is essential that the table be in front of the class and at such a height that all students can observe easily. Furthermore, chairs must be grouped to facilitate observation, or the students may stand in a semicircle around the demonstrator. Adequate space must be provided for storing display items—perhaps in glass cases in the halls or, in a few instances, in specially constructed classrooms.

Textbook Use

The range of reading abilities within a typical class necessitates the use of textbooks with different vocabulary levels, supplementary printed material, and, frequently, visual aids that clarify the textual content. These materials should, for the most part, be kept in the classroom, where they will be readily available when needed. This can only be done if there are appropriate files and shelves in the room.

The Assignment

School assignments get off to a better start when the teacher is able to move among student desks, providing help and encouragement where needed. In a crowded classroom the teacher is severely hampered. Unfortunately, economy-minded school boards too often exert only limited effort to relieve this lack of necessary space.

Supervised Study

Some of the most rewarding study occurs when students work under teacher supervision in special booths or carrels where they can move at their own pace, usually with the aid of a programed text. Certain schools have gone to considerable expense in providing such study accommodations.

Conventional facilities for supervised study require adequate lighting, heating, ventilation, desk height, and easy access to a range of study materials. The teacher's desk must be placed so that he can exercise a degree of supervision, even when seated. Moreover the teacher may wish to rearrange student desks for the study period.

Individual Projects

Individual projects usually require special space considerations. For example, the boy who decides to make a maple coffee table for his woodshop project must have space in which to saw, scrape, sand, and paint. Similarly, the girl in the homemaking class who is concerned with setting the table for a formal occasion must not only have working space but also essential equipment—a table, tablecloth, silverware, china, and material for a centerpiece. Even a group project, such as preparing a special bulletin board, demands work areas and special equipment if it is to be carried out with efficiency. The lack of working space for students properly engaged in curricular or cocurricular activities inhibits their productivity and dims their enthusiasm.

Duplicated Materials

Although duplicating machines are seldom kept in the conventional classroom, space must be provided for them in the secretarial area of the front office, in the teachers' workroom, or in the typing room. In the classroom itself, the teacher will find it advantageous to have a filing cabinet in which he can store duplicated materials or the masters. The careful storing of master copies can save the teacher a great deal of time later on.

Programed Instruction

If programed instruction involves the use of teaching machines, special provisions should be made for the most advantageous placement of the equipment. Fortunately, conventional outlets serve as a power source for the operation of these machines, but sufficient outlets must be available. Programed texts should be handled and stored with particular care, for not only are these texts used more frequently than the conventional text, but the nature of their use—the constant turning of pages—tends to wear them out.

Television Teaching

No secondary-school plant can be considered up-to-date unless there is provision for the use of television sets in the classrooms.[11] Often the set is suspended from the ceiling to insure maximum eye and body comfort for the viewer.

When schools engage in closed-circuit television broadcasting, essential studio facilities, including a television camera, must be provided. A technical staff with sufficient competence to operate such a station is also essential. Fortunately, both commercial and closed-circuit educational telecasts can be received on the same set.

Team Teaching

Because of the necessity for dealing with student groups of varying sizes, team teaching demands classrooms with different capacities.[12] Large groups consisting of from seventy-five to two hundred students require the use of facilities usually available only in specially constructed schools. Many schools have resorted to using the school auditorium, although it has many limitations not typical of the well-equipped modern classroom.

Team-taught classes of conventional size may use the regular classrooms, which can be modified to serve specific needs. Small student groups of ten to fifteen, however, are frequently asked to meet in large rooms that are incompatible with the size of the group and the nature of the activity.

TRENDS IN SCHOOL HOUSING

Trends in secondary-school housing are, with few exceptions, a result of the desire of teachers and administrators to improve the in-

---

[11]Dave Chapman, *Design for ETV: Planning for Schools with Television* (New York: Educational Facilities Laboratories, 1960), pp. 28–40, provides a helpful series of suggestions on planning for the use of educational television. Many sketches and drawings are also included.

[12]The desirability of classrooms of differing sizes is pointed out by J. Lloyd Trump and Dorsey Baynham, *Focus on Change: Guide to Better Schools* (Chicago: Rand McNally, 1961), pp. 24–32.

structional environment.[13] Specific trends concern flexibility in the use of space, illumination and temperature control, classroom furnishings, and library and special study facilities.

Practices Providing Flexibility

MacConnell and Ovard identify four procedures for achieving flexibility in the use of classroom space: extension, conversion, expansion, and versatility.[14]

Extension

Areas within the school building that are designed for other instructional or noninstructional purposes may be used to extend the available classroom space. Among such areas are storage rooms, projection rooms, teacher work centers, and the library. The flexibility that can be achieved by extension depends upon the current utilization of existing plant facilities and upon teacher ingenuity.

Conversion

Physical changes within the classroom itself may serve a specific instructional purpose. For example, a change in teaching units may warrant not only a new bulletin board but also a rearrangement of flexible seating. In addition, limited enrollments and higher temperatures may make the arrangement of the classroom for summer school different from the arrangement for the regular school year. Frequent changes in chalkboard decoration and use, movement of auxiliary bulletin boards, furniture rearrangement, or the introduction of new and unusual aids add interest and appeal to the classroom environment.

Expansion

Movable, nonweight-bearing partitions provide essential flexibility in school building construction. If partitions can be moved with relative ease, rooms may be adjusted in size to meet the needs of varied student enrollments from year to year. If such partitions are not available, however, remodeling may be called for to provide the means for expansion.

Versatility

Effective use of modern teaching techniques—ranging from large-group instruction to independent, self-directed study—calls for ver-

---

[13]Wallace H. Strevell and Arvid J. Burke, *Administration of the School Building Program* (New York: McGraw-Hill Book Company, 1959), pp. 383–390, discuss basic trends in school plant design.

Trends in school planning are reviewed briefly by H. Orville Nordberg, James M. Bradfield, and William C. Odell, *Secondary School Teaching* (New York: Macmillan, 1962), pp. 191–194.

[14]James D. MacConnell and Glen F. Ovard, "On Planning Academic Classrooms," *American School Board Journal*, 1962 (Feb.), *144*: 36.

satility in the use of classroom space, and the degree of versatility that can be exercised depends largely upon the availability of space.[15] For this reason informed school planners recommend classrooms with spacious floor areas, a need long recognized by competent teachers. Effective instructional grouping in the same classroom cannot take place easily unless there is room for the free movement of student desks. Adequate classroom space also encourages the proper and varied use of teaching aids.

Illumination and Temperature Control

Of the many factors of the physical environment that influence the teaching-learning process, none are more important than classroom illumination and temperature control. The conscientious teacher must, therefore, be sensitive to maintaining optimum illumination and temperatures throughout the school day.

Lighting

The visual environment of the student strongly influences the effectiveness of his learning. For this reason, the teacher must be aware of the need for both artificial and natural lighting, a range of lighting levels, glare-free illumination, and contrast.

Need for both artificial and natural lighting. Consideration must be given to both natural lighting and artificial illumination in the classroom:

> In other words, daylight should no longer be regarded as the prime source, with electric light as supplementary to it. It is now possible to consider a choice of either source or, as usually happens, a combination of both. Daylight and electric light are equally important sources of illumination in the classroom. Both should be considered; both need to be controlled; and savings made in favor of one at the expense of the other will adversely affect the total visual environment.[16]

Earlier preoccupation with the source of light has given way to a concern for its quality, and light meters have been developed that enable the nonspecialist to take objective readings of the illumination in the classroom—whether artificial or natural.

Range of lighting levels. Based upon a careful analysis of the Blackwell report[17] and their own study, representatives of the National Council on Schoolhouse Construction concluded that the large number of visual tasks at every grade level calls for a wide range of

---

[15] Strevell and Burke, *op. cit.*, pp. 172–176, discuss the multiple use of spaces in a school plant.

[16] *Planning America's School Buildings*, p. 118.

[17] H. Richard Blackwell, "Development and Use of a Quantitative Method for Specification of Interior Illumination Levels on the Basis of Performance Data," *Illuminating Engineering*, 1959 (June), *54*: 317.

lighting levels. They also indicated that "there was no one dominant task falling within a limited range of foot-candle levels on any grade level."[18]

Glare-free illumination. Another discovery emphasized by the Blackwell research was that glare-free illumination permits a very substantial reduction in the number of foot-candles required for satisfactory illumination.[19] As a result of this finding, school officials, lighting engineers, and architects have sought to reduce classroom glare through the use of overhangs, louvers, trees, reflective screening, special blinds, fluorescent lighting, and special diffusion devices. The teacher should be aware of these devices and should be skilled in using them.

Brightness contrast. Closely related to the need for glare-free illumination is the desirability of brightness contrast in visual tasks. Several suggestions are provided by McQuade:[20]

1. The page to be read or viewed should be at least as bright as the immediate surroundings. It is better if it is slightly brighter.
2. When the student glances away from his reading, he should not have to look at anything more than ten times the brightness of his task.
3. Surfaces seen by students when they are sitting or standing should be no darker than one third the brightness of the task.
4. Close surfaces—a desk top, for example—should not exceed three times the brightness of the task.
5. "A general harmony of brightness in the room is good, without too much contrast anywhere."

Practical use of these suggestions by the teacher can add much to the visual comfort of the learner.

Recent lighting practices. One of the newest school lighting practices is the use of motorized louvers that filter the daylight differently according to the hour and to the season. Schools equipped with these louvers are less dependent upon electrical illumination. In some experimental schoolrooms different colors of glass help diminish the brightness contrasts from outside. Progress has been made toward developing a plane that will glow by itself, although school experimentation in this area has been very limited. *Line source lighting,* represented by the fluorescent tube, and *plane source lighting,* represented by luminous ceilings made of glass or plastic or a metal honeycomb, are common in new schools.

One writer[21] suggests that lighting in a typical classroom can be economically and adequately provided through the use of six fixtures

---

[18]*Planning America's School Buildings,* p. 120.
[19]*Ibid.,* p. 120.
[20]McQuade, *op. cit.,* p. 156.
[21]*Ibid.,* pp. 162–163.

of 264 watts each. The plastic panels covering two of the thirty-inch fluorescent tubes in each fixture produce semidirect lighting. Excellent brightness patterns coupled with high efficiency are encouraging more frequent use of this device.

Temperature Control

Because of the close relationship of classroom temperature to individual student comfort and, hence, to willingness and desire to study, educators and architects have focused particular attention on the problems of heating and ventilation.[22]

The recent concern for total thermal control in the classroom has emphasized the possibility and desirability of air-conditioned school buildings for summer use. This is still a highly controversial subject. Identification of economical thermal systems that will accomplish the threefold task of heating, ventilating, and cooling has been the subject of continuing research.

One of the most promising systems is a forced air system. The air is mixed in the fan room, sent through ducts in the floor, delivered into the classroom through grills under the windows,[23] and exhausted through corridor ceiling ducts. Furnace-heated air may be pumped into the classroom during the winter, and refrigerated and humidified or dehumidified air may be introduced during the warm months; desired circulation of air can be maintained at all times. This system has the added advantage of operating quietly at normal speeds—a matter of great concern to the teacher. Although the necessary equipment occupies a relatively small space in the classroom, it takes considerable space in the central heating room.

When a central heating plant is employed, a decision must be made as to which medium—hot water, steam, or air—is best suited for transmitting heat. Because of the economy of operation, the possibility of fine temperature control, and long-range costs, hot water heating systems are currently favored over steam systems.

Classroom Furnishings

Classroom furniture also affects student learning. For this reason, the teacher must be concerned with the furnishings of his classroom. Frequently he is asked to assist in the planning and selection of furniture best suited to his area of specialization. Several general concepts have been developed to guide the selection and use of various types of secondary-school furniture.[24]

---

[22]*Ibid.*, pp. 175–190, presents a useful, pointed discussion of current school heating and plumbing problems.

[23]*Ibid.*, pp. 181–182.

[24]*Ibid.*, pp. 167–173, discusses the basic concerns in providing adequate furniture for a classroom.

The Student's Desk

Because the student's combination seat and desk is subject to the stresses of the teenager's body movements, it must be a particularly sturdy piece of furniture. If the desk is properly constructed, there will be (1) no pressure under the knees, (2) free space back of the inside angle of the knee, (3) room above the thighs, (4) an overlapping of the front end of the desk or table with the front end of the chair, (5) a low chair back that is open at the bottom and provides support for only the hollow of the back, and (6) a table or desk top that is higher than the student's elbow when his arm hangs straight.[25] Obviously these specifications can only be met when desks are varied to meet the body proportions of individual students.

Tablet armchairs that provide a writing surface extending across the full width of the chair are in common use. Such chairs tend to prevent the students from hunching to one side, a frequent difficulty when the tablet is limited to a particular side.

Desks surfaced with hardwood veneers are durable and can be kept in good condition without much difficulty. Writing surfaces should be soft enough to make writing easy, but they should be hard enough to prevent scratches and grooves, since they would spoil the appearance of the desk and hamper penmanship. Warm birch tones are desirable because they cut reflection and yet are light enough to enliven classroom decor.

Working Tables

In certain types of classrooms teachers as well as students prefer working tables geared to the average student and chairs of various heights. This arrangement permits desirable flexibility. Tables can be used separately to accommodate small groups of students with common instructional needs, or they can be combined into larger units of equal height to accommodate sizeable discussion groups or to provide large working areas. In classrooms where tables are to be moved, weight is, of course, an important concern. Individual seat-desk combinations with nonangled surfaces that, when pushed together, form sizeable working areas are also currently in use.

The Chalkboard and the Bulletin Board

Chalkboard and bulletin board space is essential to effective instruction in every classroom. The chalkboard should be placed so that glare is minimized and at a height that will permit easy use by students who are extremely short or tall. Portable small bulletin boards add flexibility to instruction and may be used to emphasize important points.

---

[25]*American School Buildings,* Twenty-Seventh Yearbook of the American Association of School Administrators (Washington, D.C.: National Education Association, 1949), p. 251.

Modern Writing Surfaces

Modern writing surfaces, though more expensive than standard painted hardboard or slate, avoid the poor lighting contrast of chalkboards and are easy to clean. Among these new types are porcelainized writing panels and panels of silicate glass. Clear acrylic plastic and milk-white opaque glass are also being used as vertical writing surfaces. Dark crayons must be used on the latter, and the glass may then be wiped clean with ordinary floor wax. Once cleaned, it may also double as a projection screen.[26]

Display Surfaces

A large number of materials are presently being used for display surfaces: fiber board, mounted felt, burlap, plastic, rough or finely grained cork, and soft woods free of resin. The finely grained cork is superior to the other materials because it holds a thumbtack easily, is relatively durable, and can be easily cleaned or sanded as desired. Displays may also be placed on walls of perforated metal or wood; golf tees can be inserted into the perforations to hold the displays in place. Foam rubber (1/4 inch) covered with fabric provides a useful display area and also absorbs sound. Some commercial firms now offer a complete vertical teaching wall consisting of panels of various sizes and materials, including bulletin boards, chalkboards, and projection screens. These panels are mounted on tracks fastened to the wall, thus insuring maximum flexibility. Specially constructed and surfaced mobile walls (partitions) may also serve as chalkboards or bulletin boards.

Classroom Storage

Storage is of concern in all classrooms, particularly those that are well equipped. Architectural and engineering ingenuity has been satisfactorily focused on meeting this problem. For example, ventilators constructed to fit under windows may now be bought with metal shelving designed to put unoccupied space to good use. Mounting large pieces of equipment (projection stands and display cabinets) on rollers for easy movement from one part of the room or the building to another has proved most helpful. Wall attachments and lightweight furniture provide desirable flexibility and thus help relieve storage problems. For instance, sliding chalkboards mounted on rollers attached to the wall, one above the other, combine easy storage with accessibility. The use of standard units has enabled stackable furniture to be developed, resulting in additional saving of valuable space.

Because equipment must be handled carefully to protect its usefulness, storage techniques should be simple. Moreover, needed items should be stored so that they are easily accessible. Essential

---

[26]McQuade, *op. cit.,* p. 170.

materials used in such subjects as music, shop, and art pose special storage problems that must be worked out by the individual teacher.

Variety of Needs in Different Subject Areas

The furniture needed in a classroom varies with the subject area. The furnishings in the dramatics classroom, for example, would be somewhat different from those in the mathematics or home-economics classroom.

Physical science classroom. The well-equipped physical science classroom often serves simultaneously as a laboratory and also provides reading areas and space for individual work. Other essential items of furniture and equipment include the teacher's desk and office area, a conference-table arrangement, divided demonstration tables, a work bench, a darkroom with double sink, hot and cold water, intake and exhaust fans, bookcases and magazine racks, plus the conventional chalkboards, tackboards, and steel panels.[27]

Social studies classroom. Ovard[28] suggests the use of nine basic areas within a social studies classroom (see Figure 1). The centrally located *pupil station area* would accommodate those activities in which students could participate while seated at their desks. The *primary teaching area* would be at the front of the room and would be equipped with a chalkboard; the teacher's desk; flag holders on each side of the room; maps, charts, and globes; audio-visual equipment; and teacher's storage area. In the *display area* there would be a bulletin board and a pegboard as well as a map display rail mounted above the tackboard or chalkboard. The *open display and exhibit area* would consist of a small table as well as a smaller *lockable display area.* A *creative project area,* normally a separate room, would facilitate making maps, diagrams, posters, and models. A small *group planning-consultation room* would be used for committee work and for the practice of group presentations and would also contain *storage facilities.*

Language arts classroom. The use of a *suite* for the effective teaching of language arts is receiving support from language specialists:

> Such a suite of rooms would include: (a) departmental offices (where teachers might retreat to be students for a while); (b) the instructional materials center; (c) a television unit for both closed- and open-circuit television viewing; (d) speaking and listening laboratories; (e) language laboratories; (f) special rooms for remedial instruction (which often best takes place with relatively small classes); (g) writing booths or rooms; (h) conference rooms for student and teacher-student discussions (glass paneling allows for appropriate supervision); (i) a relatively secluded area to which students might

---

[27]Leroy C. Olsen, "Planning High School Physical Science Facilities," *American School Board Journal,* 1962 (March), *144*: 31.

[28]Glen F. Ovard, "Social Studies Facilities for the Modern Secondary School," *American School Board Journal,* 1962 (April), *144*: 33–34.

Fig. 1. Floor plan for a social studies classroom.

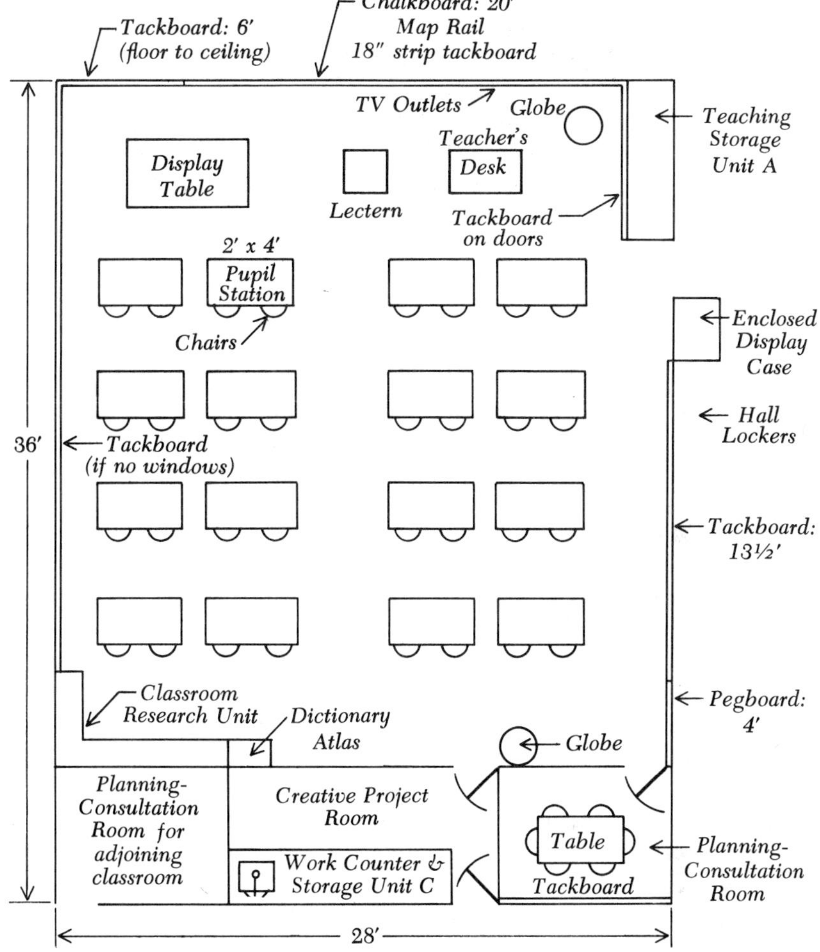

Classroom: 28' x 30'
Planning-Consultation: 6' x 8'
Creative-Project: 6' x 12'
Total Area: 924 sq. ft.

retreat to do some independent reading so important to literary growth and development; (j) at least one room into which a large number of students might be gathered for lectures associated with team-teaching; (k) provision for movable panels or partitions to provide an opportunity for the small classroom approach associated with team-teaching; and (l) provision for expansion and adaptation when more nearly perfect teaching machines and programed materials become available.[29]

[29]Stanley B. Kegler, "Planning the Language Arts Classroom," *American School Board Journal*, 1962 (Aug.), *145*: 28–29.

Library and Special Study Facilities

The library plays a vital role in the secondary school. If the library is situated and stocked in order to encourage maximum use by the faculty and students, its contribution to in-school and out-of-school learning may be pronounced. Unfortunately, however, poor location, unattractive arrangement of furniture and shelving, and an inadequate selection of volumes make many school libraries uninviting—and even places to avoid. The competent teacher is quick to recognize the relationship between effective instruction and adequate library facilities. Such a teacher will make continuing use of these facilities to promote his own learning as well as that of his students.

Expanded Function of the Library

Often charts, pictures, slides, models, and recordings as well as books are kept in the school library, accessible to all who need to use them. To reflect its expanded function, such a library is sometimes renamed the "Instructional-Materials Center."[30] In addition to being a center for books, the library thus becomes a curriculum laboratory in which teachers may study and prepare their own materials and a supply center for audio-visual aids and equipment. Because of these varied functions, it is essential that the library be centrally located.

Trump and Baynham[31] envision a centrally located library reading room with a capacity for seating 5 per cent of the student body. In order to accommodate other learning-related activities, a viewing room, a listening room, and ten small conference rooms would be adjacent to the reading room. Five soundproof booths in or near the library would make possible the use of tape recordings and sound movies. Teaching machines would be housed in a special room.

Individual Study Areas

Recent emphasis on the individualization of instruction has led school architects to plan study spaces for single students. Such facilities are used most often in connection with team teaching involving large-group instruction, small-group instruction, and individual study. Individual study is aided by the use of a small study cubicle, or *carrel,* in which the student has his own office.[32] Enclosed on three sides, the carrel can provide the type of secluded environment that promotes individual effort. Teacher aid is provided only as needed.

One architectural plan (see Figure 2) provides for "Q" (for

---

[30]A brief discussion of the instructional-materials center is contained in *Planning America's School Buildings*, p. 60.

[31]Trump and Baynham, *op. cit.*, p. 39, describe the use of the library in the total secondary-school setting.

[32]Specifications for individual study cubicles are described by Trump and Baynham, *op. cit.*, p. 39.

Fig. 2. This is one student's "Q-Space" for individual learning.

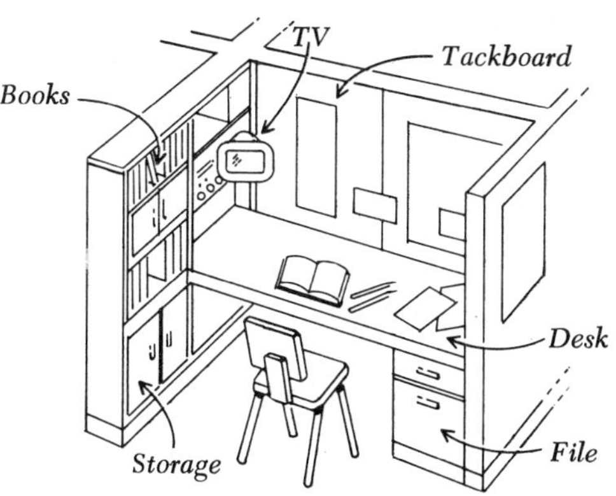

"quest") spaces accommodating sixty individual students.[33] All sixty students may meet at one time in an adjacent central room, or students may meet in groups of thirty for discussion purposes. Each unit of sixty carrels has a separate library area and a teacher's office in which small-group meetings may be held as desired. Within each cubicle are shelves for books, storage space for miscellaneous supplies, a file drawer, a small tackboard, a small television set, a desk, and a comfortable posture chair.

Many secondary schools are currently experimenting with similar but less expensively equipped individual study units. Typical carrels contain a comfortable, well-made chair without arms and a writing area two and one-half to three feet wide and two feet deep. A shelf running the full width of the booth is mounted above the writing area, and frequently a storage drawer with a lock is mounted below. The dividing partitions usually extend to a height of five feet on three sides of the carrel. Inexpensive but adequate illumination is provided by an individual desk lamp or a fluorescent light in the ceiling. When the student is confronted with a problem that requires help, he may signal with a small red flag placed on top of the partition or by pressing a button that lights up on the master panel at the teacher's desk.

LIMITATIONS OF OLD SCHOOL BUILDINGS

School plants that do not provide the best instructional facilities tend to short-change students academically. Such is the case, however, in hundreds of secondary schools across the nation where old structures, poor planning of new structures, or misplaced economy

[33]Charles W. Brubaker and Lawrence B. Perkins, "Sketch Book: Space for Individual Learning," *The School Executive*, 1959 (Feb.), 78: 46–47.

has restricted academic achievement. Some of the undesirable conditions of older or poorly equipped structures are listed below: [34]

Overcrowded classrooms

Classrooms not differentiated according to the nature of the instruction to be conducted in them

Poorly heated classrooms—extremes of temperature in the winter from underactive or overactive furnaces or exposure to the direct sunlight during the early fall and late spring

Lack of variation in student desk height

Lack of desk mobility—desks screwed to runners or to the floor

Poor interior and exterior illumination

Dull, uneven, or very small chalkboards as well as chalkboard glare

Failure to give consideration to brightness contrast

Excessively bright or excessively dull classroom colors

Scarred or grooved desk surfaces

Poor placement of student stations in relationship to the chalkboard, the bulletin board, or the teacher's desk

Inadequate storage facilities and shelving

Excessively small, coarse, misplaced, or missing bulletin boards

Inadequate electrical outlets for the use of audio-visual devices

No remodeling of any sort

The effect of these conditions on sound instruction is illustrated in the following narrative descriptions.

CENTRAL JUNIOR HIGH SCHOOL—A PAGE FROM THE PAST

Mr. McDowell, principal of Central Junior High School, took pride in the fact that he had not exerted pressure on his superintendent and school board for a new building. Agreeing with some of the school board members with whom he had talked, he felt that a substantial, three-story brick building simply could not be discarded.

Mr. McDowell was aware that when Central had been built forty-seven years before, it was considered the finest school building in the state. The building was first used as a four-year senior high school and was later made available for a junior high school when the new three-year senior high opened its doors. Because of its solid construction, the building simply did not lend itself to remodeling.

Although student desks were no longer screwed to the floor, the floors had not been resurfaced. Movement of school furniture was thus impaired. In spite of repeated attempts to overhaul the heating plant, which used steam radiators, it was almost impossible to maintain a constant, comfortable temperature during the cold months. Furthermore, classes located on the west side of the building were subjected to uncomfortable and uncontrollable afternoon warmth during the late spring and early autumn months. With in-

[34]This list may be expanded after thorough examination of several current well-prepared textbooks devoted to secondary-school housing problems.

creased enrollments, rooms designed to accommodate twenty-five to thirty students were now crowded with an average of thirty-five students and in some cases as many as forty. The limited provision for storage space made it necessary to place books and audio-visual equipment along the wall at the back of each room, thus aggravating the overcrowding. When the tape recorder or movie projector was used, the cord had to be draped across or looped around student desks from the machine to the one electrical outlet.

An attempt had been made to provide better interior lighting by increasing the wattage of the light bulbs but without adding additional fixtures. As a result the glare was very annoying to students in certain parts of the room. Student desks were of uniform height, regardless of the physical dimensions of students who occupied them, and although most of the desks had been resurfaced at least once, a majority of them were now pitted, grooved, and thoroughly initialed, making smooth writing impossible.

ROCKCREEK SENIOR HIGH SCHOOL—NEW BUT OLD

Two years after the fifteen hundred students at Rockcreek Senior High School moved into the new school building, the school board, the superintendent, the principal, and several teachers conducted a survey to determine the adequacy of the structure. Some of their findings were disheartening.

At the time the building was planned, air conditioning had been considered too expensive. Now, with the recent extension of the school year, certain seasons proved to be uncomfortably warm and hindered effective study. Unfortunately, the heating system that had been installed could not be converted to air conditioning.

Some of the errors were understandable in view of the fact that the planners had been forced into a crash program because the old school was so badly overcrowded. Only four months had been allowed for teachers to formulate their own ideas of what was necessary and desirable in their respective areas and communicate them to the architect. Those who did not take their tasks seriously had few suggestions to make. Unfortunately, the architect was not properly informed about the current needs and trends in subject-matter areas and relied heavily on teacher recommendations.

The physical education faculty, backed by sports-oriented townspeople and school patrons, had been very persistent in their demands for the best gymnasium in the four-county area. As a result the gymnasium was beautiful and equipped to accommodate large crowds but disproportionately expensive.

Except for adequate illumination and sturdy, movable desk-chair combinations, the classrooms looked very much like those that would have been built thirty years earlier. Storage space was very limited, the size of the rooms restricted the instructional activities, only two electrical outlets had been provided, little attention had been given to the possible use of teaching machines and closed-circuit television, and the physical facilities for counseling were limited to the office occupied by the vice-principal.

SPECIFIC SUGGESTIONS

Specific suggestions for planning and improving the secondary-school building should serve as effective reminders to educators who are cognizant of the close relationship between modern school housing and effective instruction.

Recommendations

1. Be sure that teachers, administrators, school patrons, and occasionally students are involved in planning new school buildings.
2. Make sure that the school building is considered a means rather than the end of educational effort.
3. School construction should be economically limited to what is educationally sound.
4. Arrange to remodel and rehabilitate old buildings if this can be done without short-changing the instructional program.[35]
5. Be sure that each area of the curriculum has up-to-date physical facilities to serve its unique instructional needs. Teachers should be aware of new methods in their teaching specialties and the implications of these methods for school plant construction.
6. Provide a curriculum workroom or workshop where teachers will be encouraged to produce their own aids and materials.
7. Establish a procedure whereby the school patrons and citizens at large may be consistently informed of the features and values of a modern school plant.
8. Determine whether your school is effectively equipped for the use of electronic teaching aids. If you find it financially impossible to equip your school with closed-circuit television, install the basic cables so that equipment may be added later.
9. Give attention to essential auxiliary facilities at the time your school building is being planned.
10. Be constantly aware of the necessity for re-evaluating the physical environment of students and its possible effect on learning.[36]
11. Reappraise how well the mental, physical, social, and emotional needs of differing students are being met by the physical facilities in your school.
12. Be sure that underprivileged children have the opportunity to enjoy, through the school, a physical environment that will serve to elevate and motivate.[37]

Cautions

1. Don't allow the pressure for quick completion of school plans to overshadow the need for a defensible educational program.

---

[35]A full chapter on "Rehabilitating Existing School Buildings" is presented in *Planning America's School Buildings*, Chapter 13.

[36]*Ibid.*, pp. 203–204, provides a checklist outline for evaluating an existing school building.

Strevell and Burke, *op. cit.*, Chapter 7, discuss in detail the procedures, techniques, and implications of evaluating the existing school plant.

[37]*Planning America's School Buildings*, Chapter 4, points out the need for providing physical beauty in the life of students through effective school plant design.

2. Don't sanction whimsical changes in the school plant; be sure that changes are educationally sound.

3. Don't forget that the attractiveness of the school plant is secondary to its instructional usefulness.

SECONDARY-SCHOOL HOUSING IN REVIEW

The close relationship between effective instruction and adequate school buildings has encouraged teachers to be intelligently critical of school housing. Teachers as well as administrators have sensed a responsibility for providing the physical environment in which students may make optimum progress.

Mental, physical, social, and emotional differences among students call for special building requirements. Specific teaching techniques also dictate to some extent the room size, equipment, and arrangement of furniture.

Flexibility in classroom use can be enhanced by extending the classroom, converting it to a different instructional use, expanding its physical dimensions, and rearranging the furniture. Moreover, the teacher must consider the optimum classroom illumination and thermal control.

Classroom furniture should be designed to facilitate learning. Sufficient chalkboard space, bulletin board space, and classroom storage space are also essential to effective instruction.

PROBLEMS FOR STUDY AND DISCUSSION

1. Discuss the following statement: Each classroom should be planned according to the functions to be performed there.
2. Indicate several reasons why the public is frequently unwilling to give adequate financial support to a school construction program.
3. Do you believe in having an elaborate gymnasium and auditorium in a new high school? Why?
4. Name the specific items of equipment and furniture that you would want to have in your classroom for ideal teaching. Now assume that the budget has suddenly been slashed by 50 per cent. Which items would you retain? Why?
5. Why is it important for students to find beauty in the school physical environment?
6. Identify recent teaching methods that should be considered in planning a new school.
7. How can a study carrel best be used?
8. Name the procedure (method) that you feel is used with greatest success in teaching your subject-matter major. Now identify the physical facilities that would contribute to its optimum success.

9. Name the physical facilities essential to each of the following: lecture, assignment, oral report, and individual project.

10. Describe the facilities and devices essential to programed instruction.

11. Describe a team teaching situation in which you might logically be involved. Now describe the kinds of rooms you would need to insure its instructional success.

12. Defend or reject the following statement: A scientifically determined combination of natural and artificial illumination is best for classroom lighting.

13. List several reasons why glare-free illumination is essential in the classroom.

14. Name the threefold task of providing total thermal control in a school.

15. What are the chief arguments in favor of air conditioning in school buildings?

16. Why are hot water heating systems currently favored over steam systems?

17. Describe the characteristics of an ideal student seat-desk combination.

18. Identify at least three vertical writing surfaces that serve as substitutes for the chalkboard.

19. What functions might be performed in a modern secondary-school "instructional-materials center" (library)?

20. Describe a carrel one might find in a school district forced to operate on a limited budget.

RECOMMENDED READINGS

American School Buildings, Twenty-Seventh Yearbook of the American Association of School Administrators. Washington, D.C.: National Education Association, 1949, Chapters 5, 6, 7, 13, 14, and 15.

Blackwell, H. Richard, "Development and Use of a Quantitative Method for Specification of Interior Illumination Levels on the Basis of Performance Data," *Illuminating Engineering,* 1959 (June), *54*: 317–353.

Chapman, Dave, *Design for ETV: Planning for Schools with Television.* New York: Educational Facilities Laboratories, Inc., 1960, pp. 16–80.

"Classrooms for the Gifted," *Educational Executives' Overview,* 1962 (May), *3*: 50–51.

Englehardt, N. L., N. L. Englehardt, Jr., and Stanton Leggett, *School Planning and Building Handbook.* New York: F. W. Dodge Corporation, 1956, Chapters 3, 4, and 7.

Kegler, Stanley B., "Planning the Language Arts Classroom," *American School Board Journal,* 1962 (August), *145*: 27–29+.

MacConnell, James D., *Planning for School Buildings.* Englewood Cliffs, N.J.: Prentice-Hall, Inc., 1957, Chapters 5, 7, and 8.

MacConnell, James D., and Glen F. Ovard, "On Planning Academic Classrooms," *American School Board Journal,* 1962 (February), *144,* 34–38.

McQuade, Walter (ed.), *Schoolhouse,* New York: Simon and Schuster, 1958, Chapters 6 and 9–19.

Nordberg, H. Orville, James M. Bradfield, and William C. Odell, *Secondary School Teaching*. New York: The Macmillan Company, 1962, pp. 191–196.

Olsen, Leroy C., "Planning High School Physical Science Facilities," *American School Board Journal*, 1962 (March), *144*: 28–31.

Ovard, Glen F., "It's Time to Plan Academic Classrooms," *American School Board Journal*, 1962 (January), *144*: 26–27.

Ovard, Glen F., "Social Studies Facilities for the Modern Secondary School," *American School Board Journal*, 1962 (April), *144*: 31–34+.

Peters, Jon S. (ed.), *Planning Tomorrow's Secondary Schools*. Stanford, California: Stanford University School Planning Laboratory, 1954, pp. 1–7, 10–32, and 42–56.

Planning America's School Buildings. Washington, D.C.: American Association of School Administrators, 1960, Chapters 3, 4, 5, 6, 8, 9, and 13.

Profiles of Significant Schools: Schools for Team Teaching. New York: Educational Facilities Laboratories, Inc., 1961, pp. 31–35.

Strevell, Wallace H., and Arvid J. Burke, *Administration of the School Building Program*. New York: McGraw-Hill Book Company, 1959, Chapters 7–10.

Trump, J. Lloyd, *New Directions to Quality Education: The Secondary School Tomorrow*. Washington, D.C.: Commission on the Experimental Study of the Utilization of the Staff in the Secondary School, 1960, pp. 3–15.

Trump, J. Lloyd, and Dorsey Baynham, *Focus on Change: Guide to Better Schools*. Chicago: Rand McNally and Company, 1961, pp. 1–130.

APPENDIX A

Additional Examples of Unit Plans and Daily Lesson Plans

The teaching units presented here were prepared and taught with varying degrees of success by teachers in the designated subject areas. They illustrate various methods of organization and individual styles of presentation. All of them, however, include the basic characteristics of teaching plans discussed in Chapters 3-8.

A TEACHING UNIT IN MATHEMATICS

This unit plan for Algebra I appears to be practical and useful for a teacher with some experience. Some of the material on activities, however, might have been more advantageously combined to eliminate repetition.

Algebra I: Equations and Problems

I. Basic Information

A. This is a three-week unit in Algebra I. There will be fifteen 55-minute class periods.

B. The class will be made up of sophomores, juniors, and seniors.

C. The ages will range from fourteen to twenty.

D. The class will have about 30 students, 18 boys and 12 girls.

E. This class will be in a high school of 400-500 students.

F. The text will be Algebra I, by Welchons, Krickenberger, and Pearson.

G. Just preceding this unit on "Equations and Problems," Chapter 2, is "Literal Numbers," Chapter 1. "Formulas," Chapter 3, is the unit that follows.[1]

H. Students have varied characteristics.

[1]It is obvious that this teacher is relying heavily on the use of the text, since unit titles conform to the chapter titles in the text. The wisdom of such a procedure may be open to serious question, particularly when the teacher has had several years of successful experience. Beginning teachers have a tendency to lean heavily on the text, a pattern that is also true of experienced teachers who have only limited subject-matter competence.

1. Larry Fullmer and Jean Simmons are slow and may need extra help.
2. Earl Jeppson is the principal's son. He is a bright student and well liked by his classmates, but he receives some abuse from the older students. It is important that he be treated as any other student.
3. Ken Nukaya is a Japanese student. He is well adjusted and liked.
4. Kent Dutson, Carl Holm, and Larry Fullmer sometimes show off and should be watched for discipline.
5. Sharol Garner, Betty Morrell, and Kent Beus are quiet and withdrawn. They are quite capable in math and begin to take part more if they are asked specific questions.
6. Carl Holm has put off taking algebra because he believes he dislikes mathematics. He has been promised a football scholarship from the state university and must have Algebra I. He now has the motivation to learn, but he must be given some special help.

I. The seating chart follows.[2] (See next page.)

II. Objectives

A. Concepts[3]

1. An <u>equation</u> is an expression of equality between two quantities.
   a. The part of the equation on the left of the equal sign is called the <u>left member</u>.
   b. The part of the equation on the right of the equal sign is called the <u>right member</u>.
   c. The members of an equation may be interchanged.
2. To solve an equation, find the value of the letter in the equation. <u>Example</u>: 3n = 15; n = 5 is the solution.
   a. 5 is the <u>root</u> of this equation.
   b. <u>n</u> is called the <u>unknown</u> of this equation.
3. The <u>addition rule</u> of an equation is: if the same number is added to both sides of an equation, the members will still be equal.

---

[2]The seating chart accurately indicates the location of students in the room, but it does not safeguard the anonymity of the father's occupation or the student's desired occupation, and the student's I.Q. is quite obvious. There must be assurance that confidential information does not become public property.

[3]Concepts (objectives) are generally well stated. Note that certain of the concepts involve the steps followed in solving problems and should not be confused with procedures employed in teaching the unit.

TEACHER

Earl Jeppson School principal Jr. 14x120x4 Accountant	Allene Cheney Teacher Jr. 16x110x2 Housewife	Karen Hastings Farmer Jr. 16x105x3 Secretary	Jean Simmons Farmer Sr. 17x90x4 Nurse	Larry Fullmer Farmer Soph. 15x90x4 Farmer
Farrel Hung Farmer Soph. 16x95x5 Farmer	Larry Robins Businessman Jr. 16x110x2 Businessman	Ronald Berrett Rancher Jr. 17x95x6 Cattleman	Harold Cramer Laborer Soph. 15x100x2 Contractor	Betty Morrell Salesman Soph. 15x125x4 Homemaking teacher
Bill Berrett Teacher Jr. 16x90x3 Farmer	Arlene Albertson Farmer Jr. 16x100x10 Secretary	Sharol Garner Butcher Soph. 16x105x3 Designer	Chuck Mueller Salesman Soph. 15x105x3 Baseball player	Kent Dutson Store owner Sr. 18x110x7 Penny's manager
Carl Holm State Representative Sr. 18x110x6 Business	Ken Nukaya Farmer Jr. 17x115x4 Artist	Tom Edwards Draftsman Jr. 16x110x3 Engineer	Ann Johnson Railroad foreman Jr. 16x105x2 Secretary	Dorothy Jensen Optometrist Soph. 15x100x4 Receptionist
Noel Hales Social worker Soph. 15x120x3 Architect	Martin Thorne Newspaper editor Soph. 15x115x2 Editor	Diane Lyman Laborer Jr. 16x100x4 Housewife	Ralph David Farmer Jr. 16x105x6 Engineer	Joe Henery Doctor Soph. 15x110x5 Dentist
Kent Beus Lawyer Jr. 16x110x2 Doctor	Jean Smith Farmer Jr. 16x100x3 Housewife	Marilyn Berret Teacher Sr. 17x100x3 Housewife	Larue Barrus Musician Soph. 14x115x3 Music teacher	George Simms Truck owner Soph. 15x105x3 Truck driver

4 Seniors, 14 Juniors, 12 Sophomores

Note: Seating block shows

Student's name
Father's occupation

School year
Age x I.Q. x Number of children in family
Desired occupation

4. The <u>subtraction rule</u> of an equation is: if the same number is subtracted from both members of an equation, the members will still be equal.
5. The <u>multiplication rule</u> of an equation is: if both members of an equation are multiplied by the same number, the members will still be equal.
6. The <u>division rule</u> of an equation is: if both members are divided by the same number, the members will still be equal.
7. To prove the solution of an equation, substitute the new solution for the unknown in the original equation. Then, after working the arithmetic, the left member will equal the right member.
8. Directions for solving equations are:
   a. If possible, simplify each member of the equation by combining like terms.
   b. If necessary, first use either the addition or subtraction rule to obtain an equation in which all terms containing the unknown are in one member and all other terms are in the other member.
   c. If step <u>b</u> has been used first, be sure to simplify each member.
   d. If the equation contains fractions, use the multiplication rule.
   e. If necessary, use the division rule.
   f. Prove the solution correct by substituting it for the unknown in the original equation.
9. It is important to know the meanings of signs used in equations:

+	plus	÷	divide	
-	minus	=	equal	
x	multiply	x	(or another letter)	the unknown

10. Directions for solving problems are:
    a. Read the problem and determine what number (or numbers) you are to find.
    b. Represent the unknown number (or numbers) algebraically.
       1) If you are to find only one number, let some letter equal it.
       2) If you are to find more than one number, let some letter equal one of them and then represent each of the other numbers in terms of this letter.
       3) When possible, make a drawing showing <u>a</u> and <u>b</u> above and the number relations of the problem.

c. From the condition of the problem, find two expressions or quantities that are equal. Then connect these two equal expressions with an equal sign, forming an equation.

d. Solve the equation for the unknown letter.

e. Prove the answer by seeing that it satisfies all the conditions of the problem.

B. Memorizations

1. Equation
2. Root of an equation
3. Addition rule
4. Subtraction rule
5. Multiplication rule
6. Division rule
7. Unknown of an equation

C. Skills

There are no skills in this unit.

D. Tastes

Students should gain a better understanding of algebraic concepts. They will realize more how equations and problems may be applied in the different fields in which they are interested, and they will desire to become competent in working these problems.

III. Activities

A. Recurring Activities[4]

1. Supervised study for 15 to 30 minutes on Monday, Wednesday, and Friday.
2. Homework will be assigned before the supervised study period.
3. Assign specific students to work problems at the blackboard for 20 to 30 minutes. Students not at the board will work the problems at their seats. All students will participate on Tuesday and Thursday.

B. Sequential Activities[5]

1. The teacher will review the definitions and terms used in equations.
2. The teacher will demonstrate new concepts on the board and initiate discussion by asking specific questions of individual students.

---

[4]It is useful to group recurring activities, thus eliminating the need for repetition.
[5]It is difficult to see that this section serves a useful purpose.

3. The teacher will work examples on the board. Some students will then be called to work some simple problems on the board.
    a. All of the students will participate.
    b. Those students not at the board will work the problems at their seats.
4. Assignments will be given.
5. 15 to 30 minutes of supervised study.

C. Daily Order of Activities[6]
1. Tuesday, October 5
    a. Discussion of the unit and objectives. (20 minutes)
    b. Find students' interests in different professions. (20 minutes)
    c. The teacher will work five or six problems that relate algebra to different fields. (15 minutes)
2. Wednesday, October 6
    a. Diagnostic tests. (25 minutes)
    b. Film: "Algebra and Your Profession." (30 minutes)
3. Thursday, October 7
    a. Discuss yesterday's film. Ask specific students questions concerning it. (10 minutes)
    b. Introduction of new concepts by the teacher. (20 minutes)
    c. Student questions. (10 minutes)
    d. Supervised study. (20 minutes)
4. Friday, October 8
    a. The teacher will use a chart to point out the different parts of an equation. Ask specific students to name the parts and define an equation in their own words. (20-25 minutes)
    b. Assignment that includes home study work.
    c. The teacher will briefly review problems on the board. (10 minutes)
    d. Supervised study. (20 minutes)
5. Monday, October 11
    a. Use a balance to show visually the rules of addition, subtraction, multiplication, and division of equations. (20 minutes)

---

[6]This enumeration of daily activities might well have been incorporated into the introductory, developmental, and concluding activities. Activities for days 1 and 2 are introductory, days 3 to 13 are developmental, and days 14 and 15 are concluding. It is true, however, that attention must be given to the number and sequence of activities on a particular day.

b. Assign these rules to be memorized.
   1. They will be written on the blackboard.
   2. They are on page 40 in the text.
c. Supervised study. (30 minutes)

6. Tuesday, October 12
   a. Blackboard work. (30 minutes)
   b. Review. (5 minutes)
   c. Quiz on the four rules to be memorized. (20 minutes)
7. Wednesday, October 13
   a. Tape recording: "The Role of Mathematics in Life," by Dr. John W. Hansen. (40 minutes)
   b. Class discussion. (15 minutes)
8. Thursday, October 14
   a. Four three-minute reports on "The Development of Algebra." (15 minutes)
      1) Kent Dutson
      2) Noel Hales
      3) Betty Morrell
      4) Larry Robins
   b. Blackboard work. (30 minutes)
   c. Assign 10 of the 20 problems on page 32.
   d. Study. (10 minutes)
9. Friday, October 15
   a. Quiz on the remaining 10 problems on page 32. (20 minutes)
   b. Class discussion. Bring into discussion: Jean Simmons, Larry Fullmer, Ron Berrett, Carl Holm, and Dorothy Jensen. (20 minutes)
   c. Assignment and supervised study. (15 minutes)
10. Monday, October 18
   a. Quiz. (15 minutes)
   b. Group blackboard game. (30 minutes)
   c. Discuss last Friday's quiz. (10 minutes)
11. Tuesday, October 19
   a. Opaque projector, visual problems display. (35 minutes)
   b. Class discussion of visual problems. (15 minutes)
12. Wednesday, October 20
   a. Finish showing any problems that were not shown Tuesday.
   b. One student will report on the recording by Dr. Hansen. (5 minutes)
   c. Teacher's summary of recording. (10 minutes)

      d. Hand out review study guide of unit.
      e. Supervised study for the remaining time.

   13. Thursday, October 21
      a. Have students volunteer to put problems on the board. (25 minutes)
      b. Discuss study guide. (15 minutes)
      c. Quiz. (15 minutes)

   14. Friday, October 22
      a. Review of unit concepts. (25 minutes)
      b. Film: "Mr. Equation." (30 minutes)

   15. Monday, October 25
      a. Test on unit. (40-55 minutes)
      b. Introductory problems to next unit for those students who finish early.

D. Introductory Activities (2 days)

   1. Pass around a sheet of paper listing the names of all the students. The students will write their first and second choice of professions under their names.
   2. The teacher will then work 5 or 6 problems on the board, using equations to show how problems related to different fields are worked algebraically.
      a. The teacher will choose these special interest problems in advance.
      b. The problems used will also make students apply what they have learned from previous units.
   3. There will be a teacher-student discussion. The teacher will explain the unit and how it relates to previous units.
   4. A diagnostic test will be given. It will contain problems from previous chapters as well as simple sample questions from this unit on equations. (25 minutes)
   5. A film entitled "Algebra and Your Profession" will be shown during the last half of the period This film is very interesting for students of high-school age, because it relates algebra to the professions the students are particularly interested in.
   6. The bulletin board for these two days will be prepared in advance by the teacher. It will show different people using mathematics in their fields of work.
   7. Student evaluation procedures for this unit are the same as for the previous unit. The teacher will very briefly recall these procedures for the students.
   8. Ask Noel Hales, Kent Dutson, Betty Morrell, and Larry Robins

to prepare three-minute reports on "The Development of Algebra." These reports will bring out the early use of equations.

a. The reports will be prepared under close teacher supervision.

b. The reports will be presented to the class on October 14.

c. Mrs. Herd, the school librarian, has consented to help these students do research.

d. The students will work together to avoid repetition. They will decide among themselves what period of development they will report on.

E. Developmental Activities[7] (11 days)

1. At the beginning of these developmental activities each student will be assigned to prepare a visual display of one of the problems from the unit. These problems will be shown on October 19 and 20.

   a. They will write their names and the problem they have chosen on a paper sent around the room. This paper will be placed on the bulletin board.

   b. Each student must take a problem that has not yet been chosen.

   c. Students may select problems from supplementary texts after first consulting with the teacher.

   d. Each problem will be put on a sheet of 8½" x 11" paper.

   e. The teacher will show some examples from previous classes to help the students form a concept of what is to be done.

   f. Each student will show his problem on the screen by using the opaque projector. He will then explain the problem to the class.

   g. Some of the better problems, chosen by the teacher, will be put on the bulletin board for the remaining four days of the unit.

2. The teacher will explain the parts of an equation to the class by using an equation chart.

   a. The chart is an equation drawn on 11" x 17" 8-ply paper. Plastic sheets that fold over the chart identify each part of the equation.

   b. The teacher will fold the sheets back and ask specific students to name the different parts. He will also ask

[7] No procedure has been used for relating activities to specific objectives—a necessity in organized planning.

students to explain in their own words what an equation is.

3. Using a balance, the teacher will explain the rules of addition, subtraction, multiplication, and division and show how they affect a balanced scale.
   a. The rules will be assigned for memorization.
   b. They are found on page 40 of the text.
4. Blackboard work: The teacher will call on students to come to the board and work assigned problems. One of the students will explain the procedure he used to arrive at the correct answer. The teacher will point out any noticeable errors.
5. Most of the period on October 13 will be spent listening to a recording of "The Role of Mathematics in Life," a very interesting talk given by Dr. John W. Hansen during freshman orientation at the state university. This talk is especially interesting to students in high-school algebra as well as college students. The teacher will furnish the recording.
6. A volunteer will be asked to make a five-minute summary and review of this recording.
7. Noel Hales, Betty Morrell, Kent Dutson, and Larry Robins will present their reports on "The Development of Algebra."
8. Problem game: Put some problems in a small box. Have each student draw one problem as he comes into the room. Each sheet will have a group number on it and the order in which that problem appears in the group.
   a. There will be six groups of five students each.
   b. The teacher will call for the first person in each group to come to the board, then the second person, etc.
   c. Each person will have three minutes to complete the problem.
   d. The group with the most correct problems will win.
   e. This game will be used as a review.
9. A review study guide will be duplicated and passed out to help students prepare for the unit exam.
10. Assignments will be called for regularly to check whether students are able to work the problems and to see if they understand the concepts.[8] Check for neatness. The entire problem must be shown.

[8]This activity and its related subactivities should be classified as *recurring activities*.

a. Assign reading material one day before discussion.
b. Assign problems related to fields that the students are interested in. Point out in which professions the concepts may be used. This will stimulate interest and a desire to learn.

11. In the class discussions bring out specific students so that everyone participates.
12. During supervised study help students that are slower and require individual attention.

F. Concluding Activities (2 days)

1. Review unit concepts. Ask specific students to answer questions.
2. A 30-minute film entitled "Mr. Equation" will be shown. This is a very good film for high-school students; it summarizes and clinches most of the concepts in this unit on equations.
3. A final unit test will be given.
   a. The teacher will ask Mr. Bliss, the chemistry teacher, to criticize this test.
   b. This test will completely review the unit and will contain some questions on the oral reports.
4. Introductory problems for the next unit will be given to those students who finish the test early.

IV. Materials and Resources[9]

A. Textbook: <u>Algebra I</u> by Welchons, Krickenberger, and Pearson

B. Supplementary texts
   1. <u>Algebra I</u> by Smith, Totten, and Douglas
   2. <u>Algebra Course I</u> by Fehr, Carnhahan, and Beberman

C. Balance scales

D. Films
   1. "Algebra and Your Profession" (30 minutes), available through the V.T.U. Audio-Visual Center and ordered for October 5 and 6. $2.50.
   2. "Mr. Equation" (30 minutes), from V.T.U., ordered for October 22. $2.00.

E. 35-mm. projector with sound equipment
   1. Screen
   2. Opaque projector
   3. Tape recorder

[9]The list of materials and resources is complete and well organized.

F. Tape: "The Role of Mathematics in Life" (40 minutes), by Dr. John W. Hansen; owned by the teacher.

G. Duplicated Quizzes
   1. Reviews
   2. Tests

H. Sheets of 36" x 48" colored paper for bulletin boards.

I. Encyclopedias and reference books located in the library.

J. An equation chart

V. Evaluation Procedures[10]

A. Evaluation plan: Students will be evaluated on the following basis:
   1. 20% for final unit exam
   2. 30% for assignments
   3. 20% for quizzes
   4. 10% for attendance
   5. 20% for attitude involving study habits, class participation, neatness, and behavior in class.

B. Quizzes and assignments will be given according to the daily outline. 15- to 20-minute quizzes will be given on:

Tuesday, October 12	Monday, October 18
Friday, October 15	Thursday, October 21

C. The final unit test will include a range of problems from the unit as well as 4 or 5 from the previous unit. Some questions will be about the oral reports.
   1. The test will take about 40 minutes.
   2. Students who finish early will be given introductory study questions for the next unit.

D. Encourage students to appraise themselves. They will write a short paragraph in class expressing their attitude toward the unit.

E. Teacher's self-evaluation: The teacher will write a brief evaluation of his lesson and teaching at the end of each lesson.
   1. Was the class atmosphere and discipline good?
   2. What progress did the slow learners make?
   3. Did the students' attitude toward algebra improve?

---

[10]Evaluation procedures are generally well organized. The very heavy emphasis on testing may be questioned, however.

FOREIGN-LANGUAGE TEACHING PLANS

A unit plan is a device primarily designed to help the instructor teach more effectively. If this purpose is not met by the unit plan, a more practical device should be sought. This is precisely what has happened in the case of the teacher whose plans are reproduced here.

The following plans for first-year high-school Spanish present an Overall Plan and the first group of related daily lesson plans for the course. Only the daily lesson plans for the first through the sixth day and the fifteenth through the seventeenth day are presented. Continuity of work from one day to another, however, is revealed in these few examples.

Spanish I: Overall Plan

I. Course Objectives[11]

A. Listening

1. Major objective--The student should be able to understand any moderately fast conversation using the vocabulary and grammar to which he has been exposed.
2. Time spent--First semester, 1½ periods out of 5; second semester, 3/4 period out of 5.
3. Activities
    a. Teacher reads; students mimic for correct pronunciation. Taught during all 36 weeks.
    b. Spanish records used during all 36 weeks.
    c. Teacher reads known material; students listen for understanding. Taught during all 36 weeks.
    d. Teacher tells story in Spanish. Taught weeks 9 through 36.
    e. Students in class give short talks. Taught during second semester.
    f. Visitors give talks in Spanish. Taught from weeks 27 through 36.
    g. Students listen to own voice over tape recorder. Taught from week 2 on.

---

[11]Note that the basic objectives of modern foreign-language instruction are recognized in seven headings of which "Listening" is the first. These areas are covered throughout the school year with varying degrees of emphasis. For each area the approximate time to be spent is indicated, general activities are briefly described, and the teacher expectations of student learning are listed as the major objective. This information can be most helpful, but it must be realistic in terms of a specific class.

B. Vocabulary

1. Major objective--The student should have a speaking vocabulary of 900 words and a reading vocabulary of about 1300 words, most of the additional reading words being cognates.
2. Time spent--First semester, ½ period out of 5; second semester, ½ period out of 5.
3. Activities
   a. 30 new words presented each week.
   b. 5-10 of the words are cognates.

C. Grammar

1. Major objective--The student should know the basic rules of grammar and should master the use of verbs in all tenses except the subjunctive, both in oral and written work.
2. Time spent--Total of one period each week throughout the year.
3. Taught during the complete year, with special emphasis on verbs and their tenses.

D. Speaking

1. Major objective--The student should be able to form grammatically correct sentences using a 900-word vocabulary. His speed in forming many sentences will be slow and deliberate, depending especially upon the difficulty of the verb tense he is using.
2. Time spent--First semester, 3/4 period out of 5; second semester, 1-3/4 periods out of 5.
3. Activities
   a. Students read or pronounce lesson orally, and teacher corrects all pronunciation. Taught during all 36 weeks.
   b. Teacher asks questions concerning lesson, and students answer with complete sentences. Taught from weeks 2 through 36.
   c. Students read previously practiced paragraph or words into tape recorder. Done about every 3 weeks.
   d. Students give short talks on easy subjects. Taught during second semester.
   e. Teacher converses with students. Taught during all 36 weeks.

E. Reading

1. Major objective--Although his 1300-word reading vocabulary won't be adequate, the student's knowledge of grammar should enable him to read simple Spanish stories with the help of a dictionary.

2. Time spent--First semester, ½ period out of 5; second semester, ¼ period out of 5.
3. Activities
   a. A short story is presented that includes all new vocabulary words and points of grammar and that concerns itself in some way, though in a very elementary form, with the cultural unit being studied. Taught from weeks 4 through 36.
   b. Student reads additional material written or prepared by teacher. Taught during the second semester.

F. Writing
1. Major objective--The student should be able to write anything that he is able to speak, using correct spelling and punctuation.
2. Time spent--First semester, ¼ period out of 5; second semester, ½ period out of 5.
3. Activities
   a. Students write answers to questions that they have practiced and that are delivered orally by the teacher. Taught from weeks 2 through 36.
   b. Students write answers to questions not previously practiced. Taught from weeks 8 through 36.
   c. Students write short essays on easy subjects. Taught during the second semester.
   d. Students write from teacher dictation. Taught from weeks 2 through 36.

G. Culture
1. Major objective--The student should have a very basic knowledge and understanding of all countries and cultures in which Spanish is spoken.
2. Time spent--½ period out of 5 throughout the year.
3. As much time as possible will be spent discussing culture in the Spanish-speaking countries. When possible, the discussion will be carried on in Spanish.
   a. Spain, 3 weeks.
   b. Mexico, 3 weeks.
   c. South America, 4 weeks.
   d. Other Spanish-speaking countries, 2 weeks.
   e. Special Spanish customs, 3 weeks.
   f. Spanish influence in the United States, 2 weeks.
   g. Fiestas, 2 weeks.
   h. Christmas, 1 week.

i. Balboa and DeSoto, 2 weeks.
j. Cortes and Pizarro, 2 weeks.
k. Bolivar and San Martin, 2 weeks.
l. Spanish history, 2 weeks.
m. Spanish music, 2 weeks.
n. Spanish art, 2 weeks.
o. Spanish and Latin American sports, 2 weeks.
p. Two weeks unassigned for special student interests.

II. Basic Information [12]

A. Nature of the Class

1. Out of 24 students, there are 11 boys and 13 girls.
2. The class is composed of sophomores, juniors, and a few seniors. (See seating chart on next page.)
3. The I.Q. range is from 90-140. (See seating chart.)
   a. Drusilla Smith has a low I.Q. but is a high achiever and with extra help should do all right.
   b. Oliver Owens is an underachiever and will need special stimulation.
   c. Barbara Monroe and Bob White are both very intelligent and industrious.
4. The age range is from fourteen to eighteen, most of the students are fifteen and sixteen. (See seating chart.)
5. All of the students are of a middle-class socioeconomic standing, with 5 from the upper-middle and 3 from the lower-middle class. (See seating chart.)
6. Students with special problems or experiences:
   a. Maria Gomez is from a Mexican family that speaks non-standard Spanish.
   b. Dennis Mitchell is very outspoken and exhibits rude behavior.
   c. Jane Blair is shy and has an inferiority complex.
   d. Amy and Lucy Pritchard-Jones are sisters and spent last summer touring Mexico and South America.

B. This course will be developed around groups of related daily lesson plans.[13] The first group is intended to cover the first three and one-half weeks of the school year; therefore, pronunciation and very basic grammar will be emphasized.

---

[12]Basic Information has been included as a part of the Overall Plan. This is entirely sound since it is to be assumed that the group will remain relatively stable from the beginning of the school year to the end.

[13]In teaching modern foreign languages, a series of related daily lesson plans is often used as a substitute for a unit plan. The first group of plans is presented here.

TEACHER

Kent Clark 3201, 21015	Amy Pritchard-Jones 2111, 31217	Bonnie Stevens 3301, 21116	Dennis Mitchell 4501, 21016
Deanne Woodruff 1621, 31117	Lewis Martin 3101, 21117	Jane Blair 3790, 11015	Lucy Pritchard-Jones 2511, 31015
Willa Glover 3601, 11015	Hazel Call 1521, 21015	Barry Wilson 3601, 21015	Barbara Monroe 1041, 31015
Marvin Melvin 3890, 21116	George St. Clair 2501, 21015	Oliver Owens 4711, 21015	Drusilla Smith 3090, 21218
Joy Stone 3590, 21015	Roy Jones 3611, 31116	Bob White 1631, 21117	Gretchen Brown 2211, 11117
Sumner Brooks 3601, 21116	Hildy Lyman 4390, 21116	Maria Gomez 3990, 21015	William Silverstine 3001, 31218

Seating Chart Code[14]

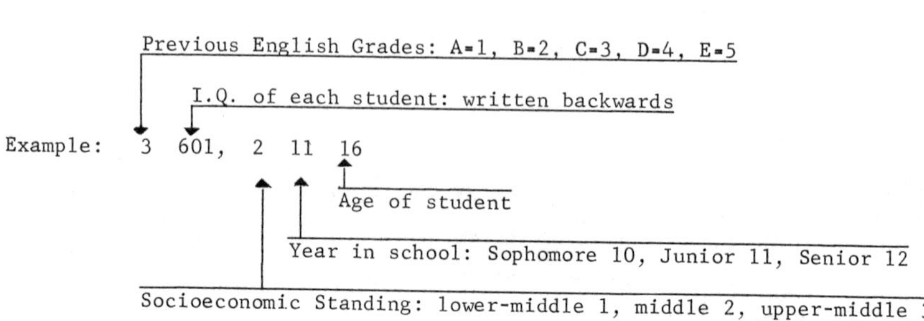

[14]Information included in the coded seating chart is easily understood, rather complete, and helpful.

DAILY LESSON PLAN[15]

DATE: First day

MAJOR OBJECTIVE: To become acquainted with the students and to explain the general nature of the course and the grading procedure.

TYPES OF LEARNING INVOLVED:

WHAT (SUBJECT OUTLINE)	HOW (ACTIVITIES AND AIDS)	TIME
1. Getting acquainted.	A. The teacher will introduce herself, telling where she went to school and where she is from. B. The students will each introduce themselves, telling their year in school, their special interests, and why they are taking Spanish.	30
2. The general nature of the course: a. The emphasis will be upon oral work, and each student will be encouraged to speak aloud in Spanish. b. The students will be required to learn about 30 new words each week. The words will be presented on Monday and a quiz will be given on Tuesday to encourage students to learn the words at once. c. Short quizzes will be given frequently and perhaps without warning. d. Students will always be given advance warning for larger tests. e. During the first two weeks almost all of the work will be oral, but the students will not be graded or tested on this oral work. (This is to encourage each student to become accustomed to participating orally without too much shyness or fear or pressure.) The students will be graded for their oral work later on, however.	A. Teacher explanation.	25

ASSIGNMENT:

[15]The daily lesson plan form has much to commend it. There is provision for indicating the major objective of the day, the types of learning involved, the specific goals sought, and the activities designed for achieving these objectives. The column arrangement lends itself nicely to a one-to-one relationship of objectives and activities. It is noteworthy that the first day is devoted to what might be termed "Introductory Activities" in a unit plan.

DAILY LESSON PLAN

DATE: Second day

MAJOR OBJECTIVE: To understand and to pronounce the Spanish greeting buenos días (good morning) plus señor (mister), señora (madame), and señorita (miss).

TYPES OF LEARNING INVOLVED: Skill, memorization[16]

WHAT (SUBJECT OUTLINE)	HOW (ACTIVITIES AND AIDS)	TIME
1. Pronunciation of buenos días.	A. Teacher will say the expression several times, reminding the students to listen carefully and to try to form the sounds silently. She will walk around the room, making sure that each student can see and hear her.	5
	B. Teacher will explain that the students are to reply aloud with the same expression, and the whole class will answer her. She will have to make the sounds separately and repeat them slowly.	10
	C. Teacher will then have the students repeat the expression row by row, making sure that each row repeats it accurately before she moves to the next.[17]	5
2. Pronunciation of señora.	A. Same process as A-C above.	10
3. Teacher: Buenos días, señores. Students: Buenos días, señora.	A. Whole class will respond. B. Row by row will respond. C. Student by student will respond. (The teacher will drill until she is satisfied with each response, but she will not drill slow students so long as to embarrass them.)	10
4. Pronunciation of señor and señorita.	A. Same as A-C at top of page.	10
5. Pupil 1: Buenos días, señor (señorita). Pupil 2: Buenos días, señor (señorita).	A. The first pupil in each row will turn around and speak to the second. The second will speak to the third, etc., forming a chain. B. The teacher will walk around and help individual students.	5

ASSIGNMENT: The teacher will warn the students not to practice much outside of class until they are more sure of themselves, because she does not want them to form bad speaking habits.[18]

---

[16]The types of learning are accurately indicated.

[17]Activities reflect a knowledge of proper procedures for developing skills and memorizing efficiently.

[18]The small space reserved for the assignment is used carefully.

DAILY LESSON PLAN

DATE: Third day

MAJOR OBJECTIVE: To have students clinch buenos días conversation, to help them feel at ease when conversing orally, and to have them understand and pronounce adiós, amigo.

TYPES OF LEARNING INVOLVED: Skill, some memorization

WHAT (SUBJECT OUTLINE)	HOW (ACTIVITIES AND AIDS)	TIME
1. Teacher: Buenos días, señoritas. Buenos días, señores. Students: Buenos días, señora.	A. Teacher-students response. B. Teacher-each row response. C. Teacher-individual response.	5 5 10
2. Pupil 1: Buenos días, señor (señorita). Pupil 2: Buenos días, señor (señorita).	A. The whole class will form a chain with student 2 repeating the same conversation to student 3, etc. B. The teacher will tell everyone to listen closely to see if each person is pronouncing it correctly.	10
3. Pronunciation of adiós, amigo.	A. Use steps 1-A-C of second day.	10
4. Pupil 1: Buenos días, señor (señorita). Pupil 2: Buenos días, señor (señorita). Pupil 1: Adiós, amigo. Pupil 2: Adiós, amigo.	A. Students will form a chain around the room. B. Teacher will stop those individuals who need help. (From here on, adiós, amigo will be included as part of the buenos días conversation.)	15

ASSIGNMENT:

DAILY LESSON PLAN

DATE: Fourth day

MAJOR OBJECTIVE: Spanish pronunciation is much more uniform than English, and each of the five vowels has only one pronunciation.

TYPES OF LEARNING INVOLVED: Conceptual,[19] skill, memorization

WHAT (SUBJECT OUTLINE)	HOW (ACTIVITIES AND AIDS)	TIME
1. Buenos días conversation.	A. Teacher-class response.	5
2. Although vowels in English can be pronounced in many different ways, Spanish vowels have only one sound:	A. Teacher will ask for English words with a in them in which the vowel is pronounced differently, like hat, father, day. Teacher will point out that this is typical of all English vowels.	10
a is pronounced like a in father. e is pronounced like e in cafe. i is pronounced like i in machine, and so is y. o is pronounced like o in obey. u is pronounced like oo in cool.	B. After the teacher explains the concept, she will have the students repeat the phonetic sounds after her: "a"--father (Continued through all five words and sounds.)	15
	C. Teacher-class response over the following words and sounds: "a"--casa, habla, cada "e"--mesa, clase, usted "i"--Felipe, sí, días "o"--no, todo, solo "u"--usted, uno, alumno	15
	D. Teacher-individual response over the words listed in C above.	10

ASSIGNMENT: Learn the English words presented today that represent the Spanish pronunciation of the five vowels.

[19]Where conceptual objectives are sought, they are so indicated.

DAILY LESSON PLAN

DATE: Fifth day

MAJOR OBJECTIVE: Word stress in Spanish is very uniform and always follows certain rules.

TYPES OF LEARNING INVOLVED: Conceptual, memorization

WHAT (SUBJECT OUTLINE)	HOW (ACTIVITIES AND AIDS)	TIME
1. Buenos días conversation.	A. Teacher-student response. B. Student-student response; the teacher will ask for volunteers to come to the front of the room and repeat the conversation. If no one volunteers, she will call on two students that she has observed do it well. (Barbara and Bob)	15
2. Review Spanish vowels presented yesterday.	A. Teacher will have the students repeat the sample Spanish words of the fourth day after her. B. Teacher-student repetition. C. Teacher-student double repetition.	10
3. Word stress follows these rules:		
a. Most words that end in a vowel and in n or s are stressed on the next to last syllable.	A. Teacher explanation of concept and teacher-student repetition: casa, casas, habla, todo, entran.	10
b. Most words that end in a consonant, except n or s, are stressed on the last syllable.	B. Teacher explanation of concept and teacher-student repetition: usted, hablar, papel.	10
c. Words that are not pronounced according to these rules have a written accent on the stressed syllable.	C. Teacher explanation of concept and teacher-student repetition: café, inglés, lección, también.	10

ASSIGNMENT: Be sure you know the rules of vowel pronunciation, and learn the rules of word stress. There will be a short quiz tomorrow over these two areas, asking students either to write these two sets of rules or to apply them.

DAILY LESSON PLAN

DATE: Sixth day

MAJOR OBJECTIVE: Spanish consonants are pronounced less strongly than those in English. Most of them are pronounced farther forward in the mouth with the tongue close to the upper teeth and gums.

TYPES OF LEARNING INVOLVED: Skill, conceptual

WHAT (SUBJECT OUTLINE)	HOW (ACTIVITIES AND AIDS)	TIME
1. Quiz: a. For each vowel, a, e, i, o, and u, write an English word that contains the same phonetic sound as the vowel in the Spanish pronunciation. b. According to rules learned yesterday, underline the syllable on which the stress should fall in each of the following: 1. es-pañ-ol 5. a-sı 2. Car-men 6. Ma-drid 3. so-lo 7. me-sa 4. Car-los 8. Fe-li-pe	A. Each student will receive a stenciled copy of the quiz.	15
2. See major objective. If the student will hold his lips tightly as if he were smiling, he can easily produce the quick, sharp sound that is required in Spanish.	A. Teacher-student repetition of <u>buenos días</u> conversation, making special effort to hold lips tight.	5
3. <u>B</u> and <u>v</u> are pronounced exactly alike. The sound is that of a very weakly pronounced "b" in English, and it is formed by touching the lips lightly with the tongue while breath passes between them.	A. Teacher writes <u>buenos</u> and <u>vida</u> on the board and pronounces them several times. B. Teacher-student repetition: <u>lavo</u>, <u>Cuba</u>, <u>escribo</u>, <u>habla</u>, <u>libro</u>, <u>bien</u>, <u>vida</u>, <u>buenos</u>.	10
4. <u>D</u> is pronounced somewhat like the English "th" in <u>this</u>. [20]	A. Teacher explanation. Teacher-student repetition: <u>cada</u>, <u>todo</u>, <u>usted</u>, <u>Madrid</u>. B. The four rows will each form a chair and practice the <u>buenos días</u> conversation, making a special effort to pronounce the consonants correctly. Teacher will help individual students.	10 15

ASSIGNMENT:

[20]From the first day through the sixth day a desirable and gradual movement from simple to more difficult skills and memorizations is discernible.

DAILY LESSON PLAN

DATE: Fifteenth day

MAJOR OBJECTIVE: The students will learn to count from 13 through 29 and begin to learn to tell time.

TYPES OF LEARNING INVOLVED: Memorization, skill

WHAT (SUBJECT OUTLINE)	HOW (ACTIVITIES AND AIDS)	TIME
1. Counting from 13-20.	A. Teacher will point to the symbols 13, 14, and 15 written on the board and repeat them several times. B. Teacher-student repetition. C. Teacher will present 16-20 in the same manner (steps A-B). D. Drill: a. Teacher-student repetition of 13-20. b. Teacher-student repetition of 1-20. c. Students counting together from 1-20.	20
2. Counting from 21-29.	A. Teacher will explain that in counting from 20-29, one says "twenty and one" (veinte y uno), "twenty and two" (veinte y dos), etc. a. Teacher counts from 20-29. b. Teacher-student repetition. c. Teacher-student repetition from 1-29.	15
3. Counting from 1-29.	A. The class will form a chain in which the next student will count one number higher up to 29. This chain will go around the room several times.	15
4. Telling time by the hours.	A. Teacher will set the clock face, ask the time in Spanish, and call on individual volunteers for the answer.	5

ASSIGNMENT:

DAILY LESSON PLAN

DATE: Sixteenth day

MAJOR OBJECTIVE: The students will learn more about telling time.

TYPES OF LEARNING INVOLVED: Memorization, skill

WHAT (SUBJECT OUTLINE)	HOW (ACTIVITIES AND AIDS)	TIME
1. Counting from 1-29.	A. Class will count together.	10
2. Reviewing telling time.	B. Teacher will set the clock face, call on individuals and then have class repetition	5
3. More about telling time. a. Vocabulary *y* means "and" *menos* means "less" *media* means "half" *cuarto* means "quarter"	A. Teacher explanation, pronunciation, and teacher-student repetition.	10
b. Up to the half hour one says "Son las ___ y ___," the first blank representing the hour and the second representing minutes.	B. Teacher sets clock at 2:10 and says "Son las dos y diez." a. Teacher-student repetition. C. Teacher sets clock two more times and repeats step B.	5
c. When it is the half hour, one says "Son las ___ y media," the blank representing the hour.	D. Teacher sets clock at 8:30 and says "Son las ocho y media." a. Teacher-student repetition. E. Teacher sets clock two more times and repeats step D.	5
d. After the half hour, one says the hour that is approaching minus the appropriate number of minutes.	F. Teacher sets clock at 2:40 and says "Son las tres menos veinte." a. Teacher-student repetition. G. Teacher sets clock two more times and repeats step F.	5
e. When it is a quarter to or a quarter after the hour, one uses the word *cuarto*.	H. Teacher sets clock at 6:15 and says "Son las seis y cuarto." a. Teacher-student repetition. I. Teacher sets clock two more times and repeats step H.	5
	J. Teacher sets clock at various times. a. One student responds. b. Teacher-student repetition.	10

ASSIGNMENT: Practice all the rules of telling time for an oral test tomorrow. This includes being able to count as well as to tell time.

DAILY LESSON PLAN

DATE: Seventeenth day

MAJOR OBJECTIVE: The students will be tested on oral proficiency in counting and telling time and will continue to improve their pronunciation through drill.

TYPES OF LEARNING INVOLVED: Memorization, skill

WHAT (SUBJECT OUTLINE)	HOW (ACTIVITIES AND AIDS)	TIME
1. Test.	A. Students will go to a prearranged room, one by one, where the tape recorder is set up. A piece of paper with instructions on it will be placed next to the recorder. B. The paper will read:[21] 1. State your name. 2. Count from 1-29. 3. Read the time on each of the four clocks. 	55
2. Drill on pronunciation of buenos días conversation, ¿Que tengo? plus vocabulary.	A. While individual students are taking the test, the teacher will drill the students on their pronunciation, helping each student when necessary.	(55)

ASSIGNMENT:

[21]This test is functional and should give an accurate indication of the student's skill. It provides a refreshing, needed variation from the paper-and-pencil test.

MATERIALS AND RESOURCES [22]

A. The following teaching aids will be used:

1. The blackboard and chalk
   a. For illustrating various grammar points.
   b. For learning to count.
   c. For learning to spell.
2. The tape recorder
   a. As a help in pronunciation.
   b. As a testing device.
3. Clock face
   a. For learning to tell time.
   b. As a testing device.
4. Flash cards with pictures
   a. For learning vocabulary words.
   b. For testing vocabulary.
5. Two bulletin boards on Spain (teacher-made) will be on display. They will show a map of Spain and various pictures of famous sights there. They will be used at first mainly to create atmosphere and for individual observation.
6. Spanish records
   a. During the first three weeks Spanish or Latin American music will be played to create atmosphere as students enter class at the beginning of the period.
   b. Later the records will be used to teach a unit about Spanish music.

B. The following written materials will be used by the teacher:

1. Foundation Course in Spanish, by Laurel Herbert Turk; published in 1957 by D. C. Heath and Company.
2. Modern Foreign Languages in High School, by Patricia O'Conner; published in 1960 by United States Office of Education.

EVALUATION PROCEDURES [23]

A. Although students have been told they won't be graded on oral work during the first two weeks, the teacher will, nevertheless, constantly evaluate their work.

---

[22]Materials and resources—which usually comprise one division of the unit plan—are listed with each group of daily lesson plans. This particular list covers the first seventeen days of the course.

[23]This section gives an overview of all evaluation procedures employed in the first group of daily lesson plans.

B. The teacher will frequently walk around the room and help individual students during chain-practice times.

C. The teacher will always drill students in pronunciation until she is satisfied with the sound, either in group or in individual responses.

D. Each student will be evaluated upon his industriousness and conscientiousness in perfecting his accent, as well as on his interest and cooperation.

E. On the sixth day a quiz will be given asking for pronunciation of Spanish vowels and word stress. (See sixth day for test.)

F. The teacher will give a written test on the eleventh day requiring students to write from dictation and flash cards. (See eleventh day for test.)

G. On the eleventh day students will be required to read words into the tape recorder, and the teacher will prepare a list of mistakes for each student. (See eleventh day for words.)

H. On the seventeenth day an oral test will be given to evaluate each student's proficiency in pronunciation, counting, and telling time. (See seventeenth day for test.)

I. On the seventeenth day the teacher will spend the period drilling individual students waiting to take the test. He will evaluate, criticize, and help each student during this time.

A TEACHING UNIT NEEDING REVISION

The handwritten numbers and letters that appear on this unit plan are coded criticisms based on the "Self-Scoring Instrument for Teaching Units" contained in Appendix B. Large numbers and letters indicate general criticism, and small numbers refer to specific criticisms.

Twelfth-Grade English: Learning and Using New Words

19-2 22-2

Unit Objective: The students are to study how to learn and use new words in order to be able to better express themselves in both writing and speaking as well as to be able to recognize more difficult words in context. 16-2

I. Basic Information

A. Age and Grade Level I-4

1. The course is set at the twelfth-grade level. 1-5
2. The students are seniors in high school. 2-5
3. The course is optional.

4. The ages of those enrolled will be from seventeen to nineteen.

B. Length of Time Allowed for This Unit

1. Approximately three weeks. 3-5
2. Provision is made on the overall plan to allow this unit to run an additional three days if necessary.

C. This unit is number 6 in a sequence of 21 units of variable length to be presented during the school year.

1. Preceding unit: "Basic Punctuation."
2. Following unit: "How to Say What You Mean." 4-5

D. Nature of the Class

1. The class is composed of a sampling at large from a high
6-0 school of approximately 400 students in a town of approximately 8000 people.
2. The school requires three years of English for graduation; therefore, students have the option of taking this class (third year) in their senior year or taking eleventh-grade English.
3. There are more girls than boys in the class. Total number of students is 27.
   a. Girls: 16. 9-5
   b. Boys: 11.
4. The majority of these students are from Catholic homes;
11-5 however, there is one Seventh Day Adventist and two Protestants in the class.
5. Three of the students have traveled extensively. The remainder have not been outside of the state.
6. The socioeconomic background of the members of the class is varied.
   a. Children of industrial workers: 8.
7-5 b. Children of locally employed (nonindustrial) people: 6.
   c. Children of local professional people: 3.
   d. Children of political officeholders: 2.
   e. Children of local farmers: 5.
   f. Children of locally employed farm laborers: 3. 5-5
7. The I.Q. range is from 95 to 135+.
8. The median of the I.Q. range is about 110.
9. One of the students has had polio and has one arm that is useless to him. (James)
10. Three of the boys and one girl are potential disciplinary problems.
   a. One boy is very intelligent and is a show-off. (Larry)

8-5

b. Two boys are not too bright and feel that the class is a "magic carpet" to better English. (Lee and Vincent)

c. The girl is of average intelligence but is an all-around problem. (Celia)

E. Seating Chart (See next page.)

II. Unit Objectives Stated as Concepts *II A-4*

A. All class members are to begin keeping Word Notebooks.

These are procedures, not objectives

List under introductory activities

1. The content of these notebooks is specific. *22-3*
   a. Each word is to be given in context.
   b. The standard pronunciation of each word as given in the dictionary is to be recorded.
   c. The part of speech of each word as given in the dictionary is to be listed. *16-0*
   d. An original example is to be given for each word and for each part of speech it may be. (This need not be a sentence.)
   e. Where applicable, the definition of each word is to be recorded in the notebook.
   f. The word must be used in an original sentence.
2. The notebooks are to be graded at the end of the unit.
   a. They will be graded on the following points:
      1) Completeness
      2) Neatness
      3) Spelling
      4) Punctuation
   b. No grade will be given to students who do not hand in a notebook.

well-stated concepts

B. Context can be a clue to the meaning of a word in four ways:
1. By definition *19-4*
2. By example
3. By comparison
4. By contrast

well-stated concept

C. The place to efficiently find the meanings of new words is the dictionary. *196-2* *20-5*
1. The dictionary gives the meaning, origin, and parts of speech of words. *21-4*
2. Frequently it gives a phrase or sentence that will help make the meaning of the word clear. Knowing the exact meaning makes a word easier to remember. *23-5*
3. Words that are exceptions to standard English usage are noted.

Bulletin Board — Blackboard — Bulletin Board

15-0 — Why are these three different? — 12-5

Kay 128 G	Kathryn	Lynell	Stewart	James 110 Polio B	Keith 119 B
Ruby 112 G	Deanne 109 G	Aliene 103 G	Carol 111 G	Celia 114 G	Carl 120 B
Zelda 113 G	Sarah 109 G	Larry 135+ B	Lee Ann 122 G	Marie 116 G	Lillian 107 G
Lee 98 B	Vincent 95 B	Louise 105 G	George 116 B	Don 111 B	Patty 110 G
Jim 110 B	June 119 G	Kit 130 B	Hal 112 B	Randy 114 B	Judith 109 G

Bulletin Board (left wall) — Windows (right wall) — Door

Why are some names underlined?

Teacher's Desk

Closet and Bookcase — Blackboards

Well-stated concepts

D. A study of the origins of words helps make their present meaning clear.
   1. Prefixes have special meanings.
   2. Word roots have special meanings. *24 – ?*
      a. The words we will be dealing with are of Latin and Greek origins.
      b. We will study Latin prefixes and roots.
      c. We will study Greek prefixes and roots.
      d. We will study the combining forms of Latin and Greek numbers from one to ten and others.
      e. Suffixes will not be dealt with in this unit.

E. Many languages have influenced the English language.
   1. Anglo-Saxon influence dates from 410 A.D.
   2. The Anglo-Saxons were influenced by the Celtic language.
   3. The first Latin influence was in geographical names.
   4. The second Latin influence was in religious terminology.
   5. The English language was further influenced when the Danes invaded England.

F. Our language is constantly changing.
   1. Words are lost from the language.
      a. Loss begins when words fall into disuse.
      b. After a word is no longer in common use, it becomes <u>archaic</u> or <u>obsolete</u>.
   2. Words change in meaning.
      a. Words may undergo a general change.
      b. Words may become restricted in meaning.
      c. Words may take on broader meaning.
   3. Words are constantly being added to the language.
      a. Words are derived from names.
      b. Words are derived from scientific processes and discoveries.
   4. The grammatical rules for using words change.
      a. At one time the double negative was accepted as correct.
      b. Now the double negative is considered incorrect.
   5. The pronunciation of words is constantly changing.

G. The study of prefixes and roots helps a person increase the number of words in his vocabulary.
   1. The Latin prefixes and roots we will study (listed under Memorizations) are to be memorized.
   2. The Greek roots and prefixes (also listed) are to be memorized.

well-stated concepts

3. Many Latin and Greek prefixes and roots have lost their original meaning through years of use in English.

H. Words have <u>synonyms</u>--words that are similar in meaning.

I. Words have <u>antonyms</u>--words that are opposite in meaning.

J. Description requires vivid, exact words.

1. Description points out the particular from the general.
2. Description must communicate.

K. It is best to use short, simple words. Avoid roundabout expressions and euphemisms--mild, vague, indirect expressions that are used in place of blunt, direct statements.

L. Avoid vague, abstract nouns. (Examples: <u>case</u>, <u>instance</u>, <u>degree</u>, <u>thing</u>, etc.)

M. Avoid wordy and stilted expressions. The repetition of a noun or the use of a pronoun is better than a forced synonym.

N. The passive voice should not be used extensively. The active voice is more effective than the passive voice.

O. The purpose of language is to communicate.

1. Words are used in communication.
2. We must know the meaning of words if we are to be able to communicate.
3. Good communication can be learned.

III. Unit Objectives Stated as Memorizations *II B-4*

All materials listed in this section are to be dittoed and handed out (or listed on the blackboard and copied) and are to be memorized in connection with the related developmental activities.

A. The following Latin prefixes are to be memorized as they are used in specific words. (The student is to find and memorize the words.)

<u>a</u>, <u>ab</u> = from
<u>ad</u> = to, toward
<u>ante</u> = before
<u>cum</u> (dom, col, com, con, cor, co) = together, with
<u>de</u> = from, down
<u>dis</u> (di, dif) = apart, away from; not
<u>e</u>, <u>ex</u> (ec, ef) = out of, from
<u>extra</u> = beyond
<u>in</u> (il, im, ir) = in, into; not
<u>inter</u> = between, among
<u>intra</u> = within, inside
<u>non</u> = not
<u>ob</u> (oc, of, op) = over, against
<u>per</u> = through, thoroughly
<u>post</u> = after
<u>pro</u> = for, before, in favor of
<u>re</u> = back, again *25-5*
<u>retro</u> = backward

se = withdrawal

sub (suc, suf, sug, sup, sur, sus) = under, below

super = above

trans = across, beyond

ultra = beyond, extremely

B. The following Latin roots are to be memorized as they are used in words. (Each student is to find and supply his own words.)

ag, act = do, act, drive

aud, audit = hear.

cad, cas = fall

caed, cais = cut, kill

cap, capt = take, hold

ced, cess = go, yield

curr, curs = run

da, dat = give

dic, dict = say

duc, duct = lead, draw

fac, fact = make, do

fer, lat = bear, carry

flect, flex = bend

flu, flux = flow

frang, fract = break

grad, gress = go, walk, step

jac, ject = throw

jung, junct = join

leg, lect = gather, read

loqu, locut = speak

mitt, miss = send, cast

mov, mot = move

pell, puls = drive, urge

pend, pens = hang, pay

pet, petit = ask, seek

pon, pos = place, put

port, portat = carry, bear

prehend, prehens = seize, grasp

rump, rupt = break

scribe, scrip = write

sec, sect = cut

sed, sess = sit, settle

spect, spec = watch, look at

sta, stat = stand

string, strict = draw tight

tang, tact = touch

ten, tent = hold, keep

torqu, tort = twist

trah, tract = draw

ven, vent = come

vert, vers = turn

vid, vis = see

vinc, vict = conquer

viv, viva = live

voc, vocat = call

volv, volut = roll, turn

C. The following Greek roots and prefixes are to be memorized as they are used in words. (Again, the student is to supply words that are meaningful to him.)

anthrop = man

anti = against

arch = chief, first

astr = star

auto = self

bi = life

chron = time

dem = people

epi = on, to

eu = well, good

graph = written

homo = same

krat, cracy = rule

logo = speech

micro = small

nom = law

onym = name

ortho = straight

<u>pan</u> = all

<u>path</u> = suffering

<u>peri</u> = around 25-5

<u>phil</u> = loving

<u>phob</u> = fear

<u>phon</u> = sound

<u>phos</u> = light

<u>poly</u> = many

<u>syn</u> = together

<u>techno</u> = art

<u>tele</u> = far

<u>therm</u> = heat

D. The following combining forms of Greek and Latin numbers are to be memorized. (Students are to supply their own words.)

Why was number 9 omitted?

Greek	Latin	
hemi	semi	½
mon, mono	uni	1
di	bi	2
tri	tri	3
tetra	quadra	4
penta	quinque	5
hexa	sexa	6
hepta	septem	7
octo	octo	8
deca, deci	deci	10
hecto	centi	100
kilo	milli	1000

25-5

IV. Tastes

The students are to develop the feeling that hard words can be understood and thereby become relatively easy words to use. They are to learn how to communicate with each other more effectively.

34-4

V. Skills

This unit does not require teaching any direct skills. 27-5

VI. Introductory, Developmental, and Concluding Activities 46-3

(This unit is to correspond with the arrival of the first issue of <u>Reader's Digest</u>, which was subscribed to about 4 weeks ago.)

A. Introductory Activities (2 days) 82-5 48-0

43-5 1. The students are to test themselves on the section "It Pays to Increase Your Word Power." Each student is to record

44-0 his score on the first page of the Word Notebook. 50-5

45-4 2. The twenty words from the above selection are to be recorded as prescribed in II A 1's subtopics. (Home assignment)

47-0 3. A more extensive test, patterned after the example of the <u>Reader's Digest</u> section, will then be given.

4. The teacher will correct and record this test for future evaluation.

B. Developmental Activities (15 days) 82-5

1. The teacher will present a short lecture on the idea that context can be a clue to the meaning of a word. (II B and subconcepts)
2. The students will read a selection from the text in class. The italicized words in the reading selection are listed IIB-5 and defined at the end of the selection. The students are to find the meaning of the words from the context and point out the method that gave them the meaning of the words. (The methods are given in II B 1-4.)
3. The teacher will lecture on the ideas of concepts II C and D and sample the students' comprehension by asking questions during the lecture.
4. The students will read the selection "History of English" in class and answer the questions at the end of the selection. This relates to concepts II D and E.
5. By use of a modified lecture and the blackboard, the 51-5 teacher will explain the idea that old words take on new meanings. (II F and subconcepts)
6. The students will do the exercise in the text dealing with 52-5 this section and will record words in their notebooks as 54-5 directed. They should record all new words and words whose meanings they are not sure of. Dictionaries will be needed for this exercise. (II C)
7. The students will be assigned a list of ten words--old 57-4 words with new meanings--that they are to define and hand in at the beginning of class the next day.
8. The teacher (outside of class) will correct and record 105-3 these lists as a basis for future evaluation. 75-5
9. The class will compile a list of words derived from names. 106-5 This is to be done orally with direction from the teacher. Kit will act as scribe and list the words on the board. (II F 3) 77-4
10. 107-5 The students are to record the words in their notebooks.
11. The teacher will move the discussion from words derived from names to new words derived from science. (II F 3)
12. The students will be assigned a list of ten words derived 109-5 from science that they are to define and hand in at the beginning of class the next day.
13. The teacher will prepare a display of Latin prefixes and 111-5 roots on the large bulletin board.

14. The class will be given a dittoed list of Latin prefixes
113-5 and root words.

15. The list will be discussed in class, and the students will
114-5 be asked to furnish words using the prefixes and roots.

Should related concepts be identified?

16. If sufficient time remains to be of value (20 minutes or
116-3 more) the class will be allowed to use the dictionaries and
117-4 look up words they could not supply in class.

17. During this time, the teacher will move about the class and survey what work is done and, if necessary, help certain students.

18. The students will be directed to complete the list of words
58-5 and will be warned of a test on the list to be given the next day. (II G)

19. A dittoed test will consist of sentences using words with a Latin prefix or root that is represented by a blank, such
59-0 as: "The planets in our solar system ___volve around the sun." (II B and G)

20. The tests will be exchanged, corrected, and discussed in
60-5 class. (Allow at least 1½ class periods.) 86-5

21. The students will be furnished with a list of Greek prefixes and roots and the list of numbers they are to learn.
61-5 (II G)

22. The class, under teacher direction, will list words using the Greek prefixes, roots, and numbers. These are to be recorded and, if necessary, finished at home. In class, June may act as scribe. The students are to be warned of a quiz the next day. 89-3

23. The same type of quiz as in activity 19 will be given. The same procedure as in activity 20 will be followed. (II B and G)

24. The teacher will lead the class in a discussion of the words listed and give a general review of what has been covered to date.

25. The class will engage in a "Word Game": The class is divided into two sides, each side having a moderator. The side that is first (in order of where they are standing) will give a Greek or Latin prefix, root, or number to the opposite side. The second side must then give a word using the part given and define the word. The moderator may select the person on his side who is to give the answer. The teacher will act as coordinator and judge in case of disputes in meaning and also as scorekeeper. Each side is awarded one point for each correct word and

definition. The teams will alternate giving parts and definitions.

26. The class will be given a lecture on synonyms and antonyms and will be assigned to look up synonyms and antonyms for a list of words. (II H and I)
27. The class will be given a dittoed word list giving one word, then five others; among the five will be a synonym and/or an antonym for the first. The students are to identify the synonyms and/or antonyms.
28. The papers will be graded and recorded by the teacher. If appropriate, a student may assist in the correction.
29. The teacher will go over the text material on the use of adjectives.
30. The students will be assigned to write a description (theme) of any subject of their choosing.
31. The concepts listed in II K, L, M, and N will be included in a lecture. During the lecture, the teacher will sample the students' understanding by frequent questions.
32. The teacher will correct the themes and record the grades.
33. An article in the current issue of <u>Reader's Digest</u> (previously selected by the teacher) is to be discussed in terms of its use of language to communicate. Examples of anything covered in the unit are to be pointed out. Here, the teacher may ask the students to find examples of specific things. This is to serve as a review for the test the next day. (2 days)

C. Concluding Activities (1 day)

1. The same test that was given in VI A 3 will be given with modifications to include the following:
    a. Recognizing words in context.
    b. Providing words of Latin and Greek origin.
    c. Finding synonyms and antonyms.
    d. Making descriptions more specific.
    e. Pointing out the use of the above four things to establish effective communication.
    f. A short written description of the classroom as it is on the day of the test.
2. The teacher will correct the test and discuss it with the students just after the beginning of the next unit. (To serve as part of the introductory activities on the unit "How to Say What You Mean.")
3. Call for the Word Notebooks to be handed in.

VII. Materials and Resources

A. The text, Chapter 13 IV A-3

B. The current issue of Reader's Digest 151-5

C. Class dictionaries (at school and at home)

D. The teacher-made bulletin board on Latin prefixes and roots

E. Dittoed sheet of Latin and Greek prefixes, roots, and numbers

F. Dittoed quizzes 155-5

G. Supplementary sources:

1. Students may use the library. 156-5

2. The teacher will use any available college texts. 157-1

3. The notes and accumulated references from the teacher's college course in vocabulary building. 160-5

VIII. Evaluation

A. The Word Notebooks will be graded on the items listed under II A 1 and 2. 162-5

B. The pretest VI A 3. 164-1

C. The word list from VI B 7. 166-?

D. The word list from VI B 12. 167-0

E. The test from VI B 19. 168-?

169-5 F. The test from VI B 23. Tests indicated in E and F are
170-4 together to be of equal value to the final examination
172-0 (in VI C 1).

174-1 G. The list required in VI B 27. The lists in C, D, and G
175-3 combined are to be of equal value with either E or F.
177-0 (i.e. C = 1/3 of E)

178-3 H. The theme in VI B 30. (Equal in value to E.)

179-4 I. The teacher will record a written evaluation of each day's lesson plan.

182-5 J. The teacher will make subjective judgments on:

185-? 1. Attendance

2. Class participation

3. Study habits

4. Classroom behavior

5. Individual effort in relation to estimated capacity

K. The examination in VI C 1. (Equal in value to E and F.)

187-4 190-4 196-3 202-3

188-4 195-5 198-2

APPENDIX B

Self-Scoring Instrument for Teaching Units

The device presented here is designed to help the teacher—the experienced teacher as well as the beginning teacher—evaluate his own unit plans by assigning a specific numerical score to each of 205 relevant questions, grouped according to the areas involved in unit planning. This device may also be used to evaluate units obtained from other sources—teaching colleagues, school districts, and commercial publishing houses. The use of this instrument is illustrated in the sample units needing revision in Chapter 7, pp. 159–168, and in Appendix A, pp. 537–548.

How to Score Your Unit[1]

1. Below is a graduated numerical scale descriptive of how well planning responsibilities have been discharged:

5 . . . Cared for unusually well
4 . . . Well cared for, only minor errors or omissions
3 . . . Cared for moderately well
2 . . . Given limited attention
1 . . . Given token attention
0 . . . Given no attention but recognized as being needed
NA . . . Question has no application to this particular unit

2. Place your numerical response in the blank to the left of each question.[2]

3. Score the unit according to the above graduated numerical scale. If the responsibility called for in a specific question has been discharged unusually well, assign it a score of 5. If the responsibility has been overlooked, assign the question a score of 0. If the question does not apply to the particular unit, write NA (not applicable) in the adjacent space.

4. A properly organized unit will warrant a response to each question.

[1]This scoring procedure was adapted from marking procedures used in the *Junior High School Evaluative Criteria* (Salt Lake City: Utah State Board of Education, 1960), p. 8.

[2]Another practical variation in the use of this instrument involves writing the specific numbers of questions and the accompanying scores directly on the unit being criticized. This procedure is employed to appraise the units in need of revision in Chapter 7 and in Appendix A.

Questions for Evaluation

I. Basic Information

A. Age and Grade Level

____ 1. Is the age level of the students expressed in terms of a range of ages?

____ 2. Is the grade level of the unit indicated?

B. Length of Time for Unit

____ 3. Is the proposed duration of the unit indicated accurately?

C. Relationship of Unit to Other Units in the Overall Plan

____ 4. Is the relationship of the teaching unit to the preceding and following units, as well as to other units in the overall plan, noted with sufficient clarity?

D. Nature of the Class

____ 5. Is the I.Q. range of the students indicated?

____ 6. Is the students' average achievement in the subject area involved indicated?

____ 7. Is the social and economic status of the students included?

____ 8. Are students with particular mental, physical, emotional, or social difficulties identified?

____ 9. Is the proportion of boys to girls in the class noted?

____ 10. Are students who may cause classroom control problems identified?

____ 11. Is attention given to the range of experiential backgrounds represented by the different students in the class?

E. Seating Chart

____ 12. Is there a seating chart giving the location of each desk in the room and its occupant?

____ 13. Are each student's level of achievement, I.Q., socioeconomic status, and special problems noted in coded form on the seating chart?

____ 14. Is the code arranged to protect the confidential nature of the information?

____ 15. Is the key to the code placed in a safe place where it can be referred to easily if necessary?

II. Objectives to Be Achieved

A. Objectives Stated as Concepts (Understandings) to Be Learned

____ 16. Are all conceptual objectives (understandings) to be achieved in the unit listed in this category?

____ 17. Are objectives that are frequently termed "mental skills" but that primarily involve concept formation classified as concepts?

____ 18. Is appropriate attention given to the conceptual aspect of learning skills or symbols (memorization)?

____ 19. Are concepts arranged in hierarchical order so that it is easy to see that the all-encompassing unit objective is composed of still smaller subobjectives?

____ 20. Are concepts stated in full-sentence form?

____ 21. Are concepts stated in the simplest form compatible with clarity and meaning?

____ 22. Have all procedural elements (methods) been eliminated from the statement of concepts?

____ 23. Are concepts above or below the range of possible achievement for the grade level and group involved?

____ 24. Have other sources (usually textbooks designed for student use) been consulted to determine whether desirable concepts have been omitted?

B. Objectives Stated as Memorizations (Associations or Symbols) to Be Learned

____ 25. Are all names, dates, terms, phrases, or passages that should be memorized noted?

____ 26. Are the concepts underlying the symbols to be memorized listed as concepts to be learned?

C. Objectives Stated as Skills (Involving Motor Functions Only) to Be Learned

____ 27. Do all the objectives listed as skills to be learned involve motor functions?

____ 28. Are the concepts related to the skills to be learned listed as concepts to be learned?

____ 29. Are skills broken down into the essential subskills?

____ 30. Are all skills and subskills stated meaningfully?

____ 31. Are all listed skills and subskills achievable in view of the physical and intellectual readiness of the class?

____ 32. Have textbooks been consulted to determine whether necessary skills have been omitted?

D. Objectives Stated as Tastes (Preferences) to Be Developed

____ 33. Is each major taste or preference to be developed during the teaching of the unit identified and classified properly?

____ 34. Is recognition given to the fact that positive tastes and preferences for a given subject or unit usually develop as the result of acquiring clear concepts of the content involved?

____ 35. When the subject is concerned directly with appreciation (music appreciation, art appreciation, etc.) are the preferences or tastes to be developed listed in this category?

E. Questions of General Concern Related to Objectives

____ 36. Is consideration given to the degree of student

participation in determining certain unit objectives before the objectives are stated?

____ 37. Are the stated objectives attainable in view of the capabilities of the group being taught?

____ 38. Is there a clearly understood relationship between objectives and activities?

____ 39. Are all objectives stated with appropriate simplicity and clarity?

____ 40. Are the objectives comprehensive enough to cover adequately all major objectives and supporting objectives that should be treated in the unit?

____ 41. Do all supporting objectives bear a clear relationship to major objectives?

III. Activities in Which Students Will Engage to Achieve Objectives

A. Introductory Activities

____ 42. Is recognition given at the outset of the unit to the general and special interests of the group to be taught?

____ 43. Do the introductory activities avoid the commonplace?

____ 44. Are steps taken to insure that students will understand the objectives of the unit in terms of their individual experiences?

____ 45. Do the introductory activities encourage the students to identify themselves with the major purposes of the unit?

____ 46. Will the students have a satisfactory comprehension of the scope and significance of the unit when the introductory activities are completed?

____ 47. Is attention given to physically preparing the classroom for the introduction of the unit?

____ 48. Is the relationship between the unit being developed and other units of the Overall Plan clearly established in the introductory statement?

____ 49. Are students permitted to share sufficiently in planning the various aspects of the unit?

____ 50. Is a pretest (diagnostic test) provided if one would be useful?

B. Developmental Activities

____ 51. Is the objective to which an activity relates clearly indicated in every case?

____ 52. Are the developmental activities appropriate for the maturity of the class?

____ 53. Is there an attempt to keep students aware of what has been achieved and what remains to be achieved?

____ 54. Are lengthy study periods provided where desirable.

____ 55. Is there appropriate use of group work?

____ 56. Is attention given to building social cooperation during the developmental phase of the unit?

____ 57. After examining the results of the pretest, does the teacher provide an appropriate study guide for the students?

____ 58. Are developmental activities planned in considerable detail and in writing?

____ 59. Is the number of activities to be covered during specific class periods indicated when this step is practical?

____ 60. Is an appropriate variety of procedures used in the developmental activities?

____ 61. Is the number of procedures used extensive enough to encourage efficient movement toward desired goals?

C. Concluding Activities

____ 62. Do the concluding activities include some procedure of extreme interest to students that will clinch many of the basic points of the unit?

____ 63. Is an exhibit of graphical representations or student-made items employed to conclude the unit where appropriate?

____ 64. Are papers, themes, or articles used as concluding activities where appropriate?

____ 65. Are practical problems used to help complete the unit where appropriate?

____ 66. Are students given practice in applying generalizations to new situations?

____ 67. Are students asked to make unit summaries when this would be a sound procedure?

____ 68. Does the teacher review basic concepts, emphasize the important relationships between the concepts, and cite applications during the culmination of the unit?

____ 69. During the final stage of the unit are students given the opportunity to relate details, search for larger meanings, establish closer relationships with other subjects, and integrate details into an expanded concept?

____ 70. Is there appropriate variety in the concluding activities?

____ 71. Does the plan include a procedure for summarizing the unit that is quite different from those employed in developing the unit?

____ 72. Is provision made early in the unit for planning concluding activities?

____ 73. Is a performance or exhibition used as a final activity where appropriate?

D. Questions of General Concern Related to Activities

____ 74. Are recurring activities (those that are repeated at certain intervals) grouped together with an indication of their frequency?

____ 75. Is it clear which activities are to be carried out by the teacher, which are to be the responsibility of the student, and which are joint responsibilities?

____ 76. Is there appropriate differentiation between the types of activities designed to teach concepts, preferences, and skills?

____ 77. Are activities arranged in proper sequence so that they provide a gradual unfolding of concepts?

____ 78. Does the unit provide a suitable amount of pupil activity?

____ 79. Are first-hand experiences employed where desirable?

____ 80. When films, resource speakers, and special demonstrations are to be presented in class, is the length of time accurately stated?

____ 81. Are activities unduly time consuming in proportion to their value?

____ 82. Is particular attention given to the timing of introductory, developmental, and concluding activities?

____ 83. Is there appropriate use of activities involving physical movements?

____ 84. Is an appropriate variety of methods employed?

____ 85. Are unusual activities placed where they are most psychologically and educationally valuable?

____ 86. Are activities described in terms of specific things to be done, rather than as general procedures?

____ 87. Is the teacher's ingenuity expressed in the types of activities chosen?

____ 88. Will students be able to distinguish between activities and objectives?

____ 89. Is the relationship between different activities clearly established?

____ 90. Will the relationship between activities and unit objectives be clear to the students?

____ 91. Are activities described in sufficient detail to provide a second teacher with a clear, well-rounded picture of what is to take place?

____ 92. Has the teacher avoided scheduling too many activities to be successfully completed within the allowed time?

____ 93. Are the activities practical in terms of the group and the circumstances in which the teaching must take place?

____ 94. Will the activities be educationally sound as well as interesting to the students?

____ 95. Is attention given to the preparation necessary to insure the success of the activity?

____ 96. Is there an appropriate balance between individual and group activities?

____ 97. Is there an appropriate balance between oral and written activities?

____ 98. Is there an appropriate balance between teacher-centered and pupil-centered activities?

____ 99. Is there provision for individual study supervised by the teacher?

____ 100. Are activities related appropriately to the here-and-now?

____ 101. Has the teacher avoided activities that, although of immediate interest to students, do not serve the basic purposes of the unit?

____ 102. Do the activities planned aim at the formation of clearer concepts?

____ 103. Are student activities sufficiently varied to maintain interest and to insure that individual differences are properly met?

____ 104. Is sufficient flexibility built into the unit to accommodate unforeseen accelerations or slowdowns?

E. Activities Related to the Achievement of Concepts

____ 105. To what extent do the activities follow the essential steps of (a) showing, (b) discussing, (c) memorizing, and (e) applying?

____ 106. To what extent do the activities provide meaningful and vivid experiences for the learner?

____ 107. Is sufficient attention given to procedures that promote an understanding of the concepts underlying new words and symbols?

____ 108. Are activities sufficiently related to everyday life to promote maximum insight into the meaning of concepts?

____ 109. Are the past experiences of pupils properly employed to add meaning to the concepts being taught?

____ 110. Are concepts presented in concrete form before students are required to make generalizations?

____ 111. Does the development of concepts within the unit move from the simple to the complex?

____ 112. Is one carefully planned activity used to teach more than one concept when practical?

____ 113. Are activities arranged in proper sequence to provide a gradual unfolding of concepts?

F. Activities Related to Memorization

____ 114. Are the concepts underlying each word, phrase, term, or passage taught before the drill aspect of memorization is undertaken?

____ 115. Is drill used sparingly or extensively, depending on the purpose to be served?

____ 116. Is there appropriate differentiation between the degrees of memorization required for various purposes?

____ 117. Are learning experiences grouped so that students are encouraged to form associations of symbols and concepts that are meaningful?

G. Activities Related to the Development of Skills

____ 118. Is there provision for learning the concept related to the skill or subskill before it is tried?

____ 119. Is emphasis placed upon practice under supervision?

____ 120. Are performance errors quickly identified and corrected by the instructor?

____ 121. Is practice continued under supervision until the desired level of proficiency is attained?

____ 122. Are practice periods effectively distributed?

____ 123. Is there appropriate use of activities involving physical movements?

H. Activities Related to the Development of Tastes and Preferences

____ 124. Is the environment of the class consistently pleasant and conducive to the enjoyment of learning?

____ 125. Do the activities stop when enjoyment is at its peak?

____ 126. Is the learning experience satisfying to the student?

____ 127. Are the conceptual aspects of an experience clearly formed, thus promoting satisfaction?

____ 128. Are psychologically sound steps followed in developing tastes and preferences?

____ 129. Do the activities used in developing tastes begin with the students' relatively limited appreciation of the course content?

IV. Materials and Resources

A. Teaching Aids

____ 130. Are the pictures, models, or charts used sufficiently accurate to prevent the development of false concepts?

____ 131. Are the unit teaching aids chosen for their educational rather than their entertainment value?

____ 132. Is the use of educational radio and television programs coupled with other learning activities to clinch an understanding of concepts?

____ 133. Are visual aids employed to help concept formation when it is impossible to provide first-hand experiences?

____ 134. Are visual materials used to clarify abstract relationships?

____ 135. Are models used in preference to pictures or verbal descriptions when the students' experiences make this desirable?

____ 136. Are students properly briefed on what to look for in the filmstrip, movie, or field trip?

____ 137. Are pupils stimulated to think about the relationships of ideas presented by the teaching aids?

____ 138. Is the best possible aid chosen to accomodate the type of learning and the group involved?

____ 139. Does the instructor have a first-hand knowledge of the content of records, filmstrips, or movies before they are used in class?

____ 140. Is the availability of aids determined before a definite choice is made?

____ 141. Does the teacher make his own visual aids to demonstrate unit objectives if appropriate aids are not otherwise available?

____ 142. Does the value of a given aid in terms of its assistance to learning justify the amount of time spent in preparation, procurement, and/or use?

____ 143. Are maps employed to develop proper concepts of location, direction, relative size, or topography?

____ 144. Is an overemphasis on aids avoided?

____ 145. Are all aids used properly as an aid to concept formation, not as ends in themselves?

____ 146. Are some of the following aids used to achieve unit objectives?

Television	Films	Relics
Models	Microscopic slides	Exhibits
Chalkboard	Cell overlays	Globes
Bulletin board	Charts	Specimens
Pictures	Maps	Collections

____ 147. Are some of the following projection devices used most advantageously?

Overhead projector
Opaque projector
Glass slides, filmslides, and microslides

Silent motion pictures
Sound filmslides
Sound motion pictures

____ 148. Is there provision for determining whether the right concepts emerge from the use of aids?

____ 149. Are visual aids used as a means for summarizing and clarifying relationships?

____ 150. Are objects, specimens, and models used to teach concepts in preference to first-hand experiences when such materials are just as effective in concept development and when use of first-hand experiences calls for a greater expenditure of time and effort?

B. Written Materials

____ 151. Is all the reading material suitable in consideration of the maturity, vocabulary, and previous experiences of the students?

____ 152. Are students informed about desirable supplementary sources of information relating to the unit?

____ 153. Do students have access to a variety of reading materials (including programed texts) when these materials will assist in learning desired concepts?

____ 154. Is the very best student text selected in terms of educational psychology, reading level of pupils, presentation, illustrations, and format?

____ 155. Is a wide range of nontextbook material provided where it is appropriate to the learning undertaken?

____ 156. Are encyclopedias and other reference books used effectively?

____ 157. Does the unit plan include complete and exact references to the textbook and other sources to be used?

____ 158. Are students encouraged to bring special items of information to class?

____ 159. Are workbooks used as aids to develop concepts, not as ends in themselves?

____ 160. Are hand-out materials prepared for distribution to students when they would be useful?

____ 161. Is a study guide prepared to assist students in acquiring significant points, answering basic questions, and studying most advantageously?

V. Evaluation Procedures

A. Tests and Examinations

____ 162. Is a diagnostic test used as an introductory activity where appropriate?

____ 163. Are quizzes given frequently when they would be useful?

_____ 164. Is there provision for reviewing tests with students?

_____ 165. Is a comprehensive test, covering the content of the entire unit, used as a culminating activity where appropriate?

_____ 166. Is there provision in the tests for measuring the progress of the brightest as well as the slowest student in the group?

_____ 167. Is a sample of the written unit test included as a part of the unit plan?

_____ 168. Are both subjective and objective tests used to advantage?

B. General Evaluation Procedures

_____ 169. Are various evaluation procedures used at intervals throughout the unit?

_____ 170. Are evaluation procedures sufficiently varied and extensive to provide a valid measure of pupil achievement?

_____ 171. Are evaluation procedures arranged to determine whether students possess true understanding of the material?

_____ 172. Are evaluation procedures for different phases of the unit weighted in proportion to the emphasis given to the objectives of the unit?

_____ 173. Do the evaluation procedures reflect the idea that the major purpose of evaluation is to assist in improving student behavior?

_____ 174. Are evaluation procedures organized so that they enable the teacher and students to determine whether stated goals have been reached?

_____ 175. Does the evaluation scheme help determine to what extent the student can apply what he is supposed to have learned?

_____ 176. Is there a procedure that enables the student to keep an accurate check on his progress at all times?

_____ 177. Is provision made for pupil evaluation of the teacher and the unit?

_____ 178. Is specific as well as general observation included among the evaluation procedures?

_____ 179. Where observation is employed as an evaluation procedure, is it so systematized that it provides maximum benefit for the student?

_____ 180. Is attention given to the capacities of individual students in the assignment of final grades?

_____ 181. Are themes and written work incorporated into the evaluation scheme where appropriate?

_____ 182. Is a notebook required where appropriate?

_____ 183. Are the pupils' study habits given proper consideration in the total evaluation procedure?

____ 184. Are the undirected activities of students properly appraised in the total evaluation of the unit?
____ 185. Where desirable and practical, are individual student conferences held?
____ 186. Is a rating scale employed as an evaluation device where appropriate?

VI. Questions of General Concern to the Teaching Unit

A. Form and Make-up

____ 187. Are the objectives, activities and other portions of the unit clear enough that another teacher could teach the unit?
____ 188. Does the write-up of the teaching unit avoid the danger of undesirable and unnecessary brevity?
____ 189. Is more detail included in the unit plan than is necessary?
____ 190. Is consistency in form maintained in the unit plan?
____ 191. Is there a strong interrelationship of parts within the unit?
____ 192. Is the title of the unit appropriate and descriptive?
____ 193. If the title of the unit is to be used by the students, is it motivational, attractive, and interesting?

B. English Usage

____ 194. Is the teaching unit correctly punctuated?
____ 195. Is an outline form employed in the various divisions of the unit so that relationships of major and minor parts are clearly indicated?
____ 196. Is the unit written in correct and appropriate English?
____ 197. Are the activities and procedures clearly stated?

C. Miscellaneous

____ 198. Is there provision for flexibility in the unit in terms of timing, individual differences, and possible activities?
____ 199. Is planning sufficiently flexible to accommodate worthy student interests that vary to some extent from the unit plan?
____ 200. Is duplication of content avoided?
____ 201. Are there opportunities for student self-expression at appropriate times throughout the unit?
____ 202. Is the relationship between (a) objectives, (b) activities, and (c) evaluation procedures clearly established in all cases?
____ 203. Is appropriate attention given to the cohesiveness and interrelationship of the unit activities?
____ 204. Is the unit organized logically or psychologically, as assumed most appropriate?
____ 205. Does the unit planning avoid the commonplace?

INDEX

5 6 7 8 9 10 11 12 13 14 15 16 17 18 19 20 21 22 23 24 25 SH 74 73 72 71 70 69